ENVIRONMENTAL DECISION-MAKING

ENVIRONMENTAL DECISION-MAKING

EXPLORING COMPLEXITY AND CONTEXT

Ronnie Harding

Carolyn M Hendriks

Mehreen Faruqi

THE FEDERATION PRESS
2009

Published in Sydney by:
    The Federation Press
    PO Box 45, Annandale, NSW, 2038
    71 John St, Leichhardt, NSW, 2040
    Ph (02) 9552 2200 Fax (02) 9552 1681
    E-mail: info@federationpress.com.au
    Website: www.federationpress.com.au

National Library of Australia
Cataloguing-in-Publication entry

        Environmental decision-making : exploring complexity and context.
            Ronnie Harding, Carolyn M Hendriks, Mehreen Faruqi.

        ISBN 978 186287 748 1 (pbk.)
        Includes index.
        Bibliography.

        Environmental policy.
        Natural resources – Management
        Environmental protection – Decision making.
333.7

Typeset by Pindar NZ, Auckland, New Zealand.
Printed by Ligare Pty Ltd, Riverwood, NSW.

Contents

Preface and Acknowledgments

The topic: environmental decision-making

Over the past 30 to 40 years the environment and sustainability have gained a place in the institutions of governments around the world, in international agreements and in the corporate policies and plans of businesses. Recently, issues such as human-induced climate change and water use have become priority public concerns with a central place at the decision-making table.

During this same period we have made great progress in our scientific understanding of natural environments and our impacts on them. The public has also been much more aware of, and involved in, decision-making on environmental issues. Yet despite this attention, in many areas environmental degradation is worsening and resources such as fresh water, food and clean energy supplies are stretched or not meeting human needs. Many problems now need global cooperation and agreement.

Why should we find ourselves in this position? Certainly the world's growing population and increasing per capita consumption in many parts of the world have put great pressure on natural systems to meet human needs and wants. But we have also made advances in efficiency of delivering for human needs through innovative science and technology. And, there has been much activity in institutionalising environmental decision-making processes. Nevertheless, in many instances, from local to global societies we have been unable to make the transition to a more sustainable future for current and succeeding generations. Too often decision-making on environmental and sustainability issues has failed to prevent further degradation and instead has fostered practices and institutions with unsustainable outcomes.

This book is about the context and complexity of these decision-making processes. Context includes the formal and informal structures and processes for environmental decision-making (EDM) and also public expectations. These in turn are influenced by layers of complexity which include values, political systems, the state of the environment, other 'competing issues' such as the global financial crisis, and so on.

Sustainability provides the overarching context for EDM and we explore this concept in Chapter 2. Chapter 1 'sets the scene', considering the evolution of environmental concern and approaches to EDM and the emergence and role of 'environmental professionals'. It defines key concepts and 'maps' the environmental decision-making cycle. Chapters 3 to 9 cover a range of important influences on EDM. These include: values and value systems; institutions; actors outside government; multiple knowledges; public participation; tools; uncertainty, risk and the precautionary principle. Chapter 10 briefly considers progress towards sustainability and changes required in EDM structures and processes to facilitate sustainability outcomes. These main themes are also explored through three case studies of contemporary Australian environmental controversies on issues as diverse as recycling policy, water management and infrastructure development. The focus of the book is predominantly on Australian issues and decision-making processes. While there are some examples from other countries and some discussion of the role of international organisations, the global dimension of environmental issues has not been our central focus in this book.

Who is this book for?

Environmental Decision-Making. Exploring Complexity and Context is designed for the diverse group of people who are studying to become, or are working as, 'environmental professionals'. These include both undergraduate and post-graduate students in environment and sustainability programs and from a wide range of related disciplinary backgrounds. The book's exploration of socio-political issues will make it particularly useful for students from the natural sciences and engineering/technology. The book is also relevant for students in the built environment areas, planning, health sciences, social sciences, economics, mining, business, agriculture and natural resource management, among others. It will also be of great use to those employed in government agencies, research organisations, the private sector and other non-government organisations, whose work interfaces with environmental professionals or has some influence on sustainability outcomes. We also anticipate that the book will be highly relevant to members of the public interested in understanding decision-making processes associated with environment issues.

Background for the book

Environmental Decision-Making. Exploring Complexity and Context is a new book. It is aimed at filling a role previously occupied by *Environmental Decision-Making: the roles of scientists, engineers and the public* (editor Ronnie Harding), that was published in 1998 by Federation Press. This earlier book was the product of a 'group effort' from within the Institute of Environmental Studies at the University of New South Wales, with advice from academics in a range of disciplines across that campus. The driver for that book came in the early to mid-1990s when science and engineering programs at universities around Australia began to embrace the importance of environmental issues and discussed solutions to these. However, that discussion typically failed to acknowledge the socio-political context of environmental issues and its influence on the uptake or otherwise of natural science, engineering and technology aimed at environmental solutions. While designed primarily for use by undergraduate engineering and natural science students, the book has been used by a much wider audience including students from Masters programs in the environment field and other disciplinary areas; by those working in the environment and sustainability areas; and interested 'others'. More than ten years on, this book is still in use and so has clearly filled an important gap in the environmental literature.

However, a decade is a long time in the world of environmental management and decision-making. Much has changed not only in human impacts on the environment but also in our understanding and management of these. For example, it is now 17 years since sustainability principles became part of our legislation and policy. We have had considerable opportunity therefore to learn from our successes and failures in decision-making in accord with sustainability principles. Appreciation of the importance of the socio-political context has increased as has the engagement of social scientists in environmental matters. This is demonstrated by the strong and growing academic literature on environmental themes from various social science disciplines such as sociology, political science and psychology, whose findings are working their way into day-do-day environmental management and decision-making. Linked to this, many from these fields are working in government, the private sector and non-government organisations (NGOs).

In *Environmental Decision-Making. Exploring Complexity and Context*, we have taken these changes into account, and particularly the recent learnings from the social sciences. We have also sought to provide a more sophisticated and nuanced approach in keeping with society's greater understanding of environmental matters compared to ten years ago. At the same time we have been conscious that this is a book for people from a wide range of disciplinary backgrounds and the language we use must be widely accessible and understandable. So while striving for greater depth we hope we have retained language that is 'inclusive'.

We felt that too much has changed since the publication of the 1998 book and an updated version as the 2nd edition would not provide the most useful book for these times. Accordingly, *Environmental Decision-Making. Exploring Complexity and Context* is a new book intended for an expanding group of people involved in, and affected, by contemporary environmental decision-making.

Acknowledgments

As noted above the 1998 book that provided the inspiration for this new book was a group effort from the Institute of Environmental Studies at UNSW. Two of the present authors (Ronnie Harding and Carolyn M Hendriks) were part of that group. We thanked the many people that contributed towards that earlier book in its Preface, and would like here to acknowledge the important role that earlier discussion has played in providing the 'springboard' for this new book.

One of the authors (Ronnie Harding) would like to acknowledge the support of the Rockefeller Foundation through provision of a one month residency at the Foundation's Study and Conference Center at Bellagio in Italy in late September 2006. This provided an ideal setting for researching and thinking through the issues that are central to this book.

We have each been inspired by our students. For Ronnie Harding, the students of many varied disciplinary backgrounds that entered the Master of Environmental Management program, developed by the Institute of Environmental Studies at UNSW from 2000, provided inspiration and evidence of the fast-growing interest in environmental and sustainability matters.

Carolyn M Hendriks would like to thank her students, particularly those undertaking the undergraduate course in Environmental Governance in 2007 at the University of Canberra.

Mehreen Faruqi would like to acknowledge her post-graduate students at the University of New South Wales, and her two children, who are the present and future custodians of the environment and provided her the motivation for this book.

We are also grateful to Clare Hallifax, Chris Holt and other staff at Federation Press for their assistance.

Finally, a very special thanks to our families and friends who have encouraged and supported the completion of this book.

Ronnie Harding
Carolyn M Hendriks
Mehreen Faruqi
June 2009

About the Authors

Dr Ronnie Harding is a Senior Visiting Fellow with the Institute of Environmental Studies at the University of New South Wales (UNSW). She started lecturing in the broad field of environmental decision-making at UNSW in 1974. She has a BA (U Syd) (Archaeology and Anthropology) and a BSc (Hons 1) and PhD (Zoology) from UNSW. In 1992 she became the founding Director of the Institute of Environmental Studies at UNSW and in that role developed, and ran from 2000, the University-wide Master of Environmental Management program. Her main areas of expertise include application of the principles of sustainability, and especially the precautionary principle, state of the environment and sustainability reporting, environmental education, and more broadly environmental decision-making. Ronnie retired from UNSW in late 2004. Since that time she has worked in a range of advisory positions involving natural resource management, urban water management, energy conservation and environmental education, for public, NGO and private sector organisations. Among these positions she chaired the NSW Council on Environmental Education from 1999–2007 and has been an Assistant Commissioner for the NSW Natural Resources Commission since 2004.

Dr Carolyn M Hendriks is based at the Crawford School of Economics and Government at the Australian National University. Over the past 15 years she has worked as a researcher in consulting and academic environments based in Australia and Europe, including Germany, The Netherlands, Switzerland and Austria. She has a PhD in Political Science (ANU) and a B Env Eng (Hons I) (UNSW). Her fields of research include deliberative democracy, democratic practice in public policy, and governance for sustainability, and she has published in various international journals including *Policy Sciences, Politics and Society, Public Administration*, and *Political Studies*. She has also practised as an environmental engineer, and has conducted research for the Institute for Sustainable Futures (UTS), management consulting firm Arthur D Little (Zurich), and Sydney-based engineering group CMPS&F. See <www.crawford.anu.edu.au/staff/chendriks.php>.

Dr Mehreen Faruqi is Manager Environment and Services at Mosman Council and Visiting Fellow at the University of New South Wales. Mehreen is a civil engineer with 20 years experience in sustainability and environmental management. She has worked as a lecturer and researcher at UNSW, as a consultant with multinational and local consulting firms and in local government. Her research interests and areas of expertise include integrated water-cycle management, catchment management, organisational change and capacity building, education for sustainability, sustainability planning and reporting and public participation in environmental decision-making. Mehreen has chaired and been a member of a number of committees and expert panels on sustainability, hazardous waste and stormwater management for industry, local and state government.

List of Acronyms

ABARE	Australian Bureau of Agricultural and Resource Economics
ABC	Australian Broadcasting Corporation
ABS	Australian Bureau of Statistics
ACF	Australian Conservation Foundation
ACT	Australian Capital Territory
ADt	Air Dried tonnes
AEF	Australian Environment Foundation
AHPWA	Anvil Hill Project Watch Association
AIGN	Australian Industry Greenhouse Network
ALARP	As Low As Reasonably Practical
ALP	Australian Labor Party
AMA	Australian Medical Association
ANZLIC	Australia New Zealand Land Information Council
ASEC	Australian State of the Environment Committee
BIEC	Beverage Industry Environment Council
BSE	Bovine Spongiform Encephalopathy
CAMBA	China-Australia Migratory Bird Agreement
CAP	Community Advisory Panel
CADS	Citizens Against Drinking Sewage
CBA	Cost-Benefit Analysis
CBD	Central Business District
CDL	Container Deposit Legislation
CEM	Community Environmental Monitoring
CEO	Chief Executive Officer
CFCs	Chlorofluorcarbons
CFMEU	Construction Forestry Mining Energy Union
CG	Collaborative Governance
CIS	Centre for Independent Studies
CLC	Community Liaison Committee
CMA	Catchment Management Authority
CO_2	Carbon Dioxide
CoA	Commonwealth of Australia
COAG	Council of Australia Governments
CoEs	Codes of Ethics
CPRC	Community Participation and Review Committee (for Orica)
CRC	Cooperative Research Centre
CSR	Corporate Sustainability Report
CSIR	Council for Scientific and Industrial Research (South Africa)
CSIRO	Commonwealth Scientific and Industrial Research Organisation
DDT	Dichloro-Diphenyl-Trichloroethane
DEAD	Decide-Educate-Announce-Defend
DECC	Department of Environment and Climate Change (NSW)
EDM	Environmental Decision-Making
EF	Ecological Footprint

EFA	Ecological Footprint Analysis
EIA	Environmental Impact Assessment
EIANZ	Environment Institute of Australia and New Zealand
EIMP	Environmental Impact Management Plan
EIS	Environmental Impact Statement
EM	Ecological Modernisation
EMAS	Eco-Management and Audit Scheme
EMS	Environmental Management System
EPA	Environmental Protection Agency (United States) (see US EPA)
EPBC Act	Environmental Protection and Biodiversity Conservation Act
EPHC	Environment Protection and Heritage Council
EPR	Extended Producer Responsibility
ESD	Ecologically Sustainable Development
FCCC	*Framework Convention on Climate Change*
FOI	Freedom of Information
GBR	Great Barrier Reef
GDP	Gross Domestic Product
GEO	Global Environment Outlook
GIS	Geographic Information System
GMOs	Genetically Modified Organisms
GNP	Gross National Product
GRI	Global Reporting Initiative
GTP	Groundwater Treatment Plant
HCB	Hexachlorobenzene
HEC	Hydro-Electric Commission
HPI	Happy Planet Index
IA	Integrated Assessment
IAM	Integrated Assessment Models/Modelling
IAP2	International Association for Public Participation
IGAE	Intergovernmental Agreement on the Environment
IIA	Integrated Impact Assessment
IIS	Integrated Impact Statement
IMC	Independent Monitoring Committee
IPA	Institute of Public Affairs
IPCC	Intergovernmental Panel on Climate Change
ISO	International Organization for Standardization
JAMBA	Japan-Australia Migratory Bird Agreement
LA21	*Local Agenda 21*
LCA	Life Cycle Assessment
LCI	Life Cycle Inventory
LULU	Locally Unwanted Land Use
MCA	Multi-Criteria Analysis
MCDA	Multi-Criteria Decision Analysis
MDB	Murray-Darling Basin
MDG	Millennium Development Goals
MEA	Multilateral Environmental Agreement (Chapter 4)
MEA	Millennium Ecosystem Assessment (Chapters 1 and 2)
MFA	Material Flux Analysis

MUSIC	Model for Urban Improvement Conceptualisation
NCC	Nature Conservation Council (NSW)
NEF	New Economics Foundation
NEPI	New Enviromental Policy Instrument
NGO	Non-Government Organisation
NHT	Natural Heritage Trust
NIMBY	Not-In-My-Backyard
NLP	National Landcare Program
NPC	National Packaging Covenant
NPI	National Pollutant Inventory
NRM	Natural Resource Management
NTN	National Toxics Network
NWC	National Water Commission
NWI	National Water Initiative
OECD	Organisation for Economic Co-operation and Development
PCB	Polychlorinated Biphenyl
PDCA	Plan-Do-Check-Act
PEP	Profile-Educate-Participate
PMAA	Pulp Mill Assessment Act
POPs	Persistent Organic Pollutants
POSS	Project Of State Significance
PRI	Principles for Responsible Investment
QBL	Quadruple Bottom Line
QRA	Quantitative Risk Assessment
RA	Risk Assessment
RFA	Regional Forest Agreement
RPDC	Resource Planning and Development Commission
SA/SNZ	Standards Australia/Standards New Zealand
SBS	Special Broadcasting Service
SDI	Sustainable Development Index
SE	South East
SEA	Strategic Environmental Assessment
SEQ	South East Queensland
SIA	Social Impact Assessment
SLAPP	Strategic Lawsuit Against Public Participation
SMH	Sydney Morning Herald
SoE	State of the Environment
SoER	State of the Environment Report/Reporting
SRG	Stakeholder Reference Group
SWAC	State Waste Advisory Committee
TBL	Triple Bottom Line
TCC	Toowoomba City Council
TCCI	Tasmanian Chamber of Commerce and Industry
TEK	Traditional Ecological Knowledge
TMgt	Transition Management
TNS	The Natural Step
TRS	Total Reduced Sulphides
TWS	The Wilderness Society

UK	United Kingdom
UN	United Nations
UNCED	United Nations Conference on Environment and Development
UNDP	United Nations Development Programme
UNEP	United Nations Environment Programme
UNESCO	United Nations Educational, Scientific and Cultural Organisation
US EPA	United States Environmental Protection Agency
WCED	World Commission on Environment and Development
WCS	World Conservation Strategy
WHO	World Health Organisation
WSSD	World Summit on Sustainable Development
WTP	Willingness To Pay
WWF	World Wide Fund for Nature

1

Environmental Decision-making in a Complex World

1.1 Introduction

Box 1.1: Coal mining in the Hunter Valley – New South Wales

The Hunter Valley is a major coal mining, coal export and coal-fired power generation area located about 120 kilometres north of Sydney. The Hunter area is also a long-established and high quality wine production area, a popular tourist destination, and a prime area for horse breeding and for cattle.

Around 30 to 40 years ago a proposal for a new coal mine in the valley would have been assessed in engineering terms and economic feasibility with some attention given to environmental impacts involving dust, noise and potential impacts on river systems.

In an assessment undertaken today all of these issues remain relevant, but consideration of environmental and social issues is subject to closer scrutiny. Not only have the issues covered broadened, but the potential range of actors participating formally in the decision-making process has also widened. This is well-illustrated by a 2006 proposal for an open-cut coal mine at Anvil Hill near Muswellbrook, 250 kilometres north of Sydney.

Assessments show that the mine will produce 10.5 million tonnes of coal a year for 18 years, with an 80:20 ratio of export to domestic use. The total value of the coal is around $9 billion with royalties to the New South Wales government of $33 million per annum. The mine is claimed to generate many jobs in construction, ongoing operations and indirectly as a result of the development.[1]

Strong opposition to the mine developed with claims that coal extraction will 'accelerate the onset of dangerous climate change' and damage 'the largest intact stand of remnant vegetation on the Central Hunter Valley floor'.[2] A court challenge was lodged in September 2006 by environmentalist, Peter Gray, on the grounds that climate change impacts from burning the mined coal had not been considered in the approvals process.[3] In an historic decision in late November 2006, Justice Pain of the New South Wales Land and Environment Court ruled that the Minister 'must consider the public interest – including climate change' (Farrelly 2006, p 1). This significant ruling did not prevent the development since the Minister for Planning had simply to demonstrate that climate change had been given due consideration.

Following preparation of an environmental assessment report by the proponent, public comment on this, and a report of an independent panel, the Minister in June 2007 approved the Anvil Hill project with 80 conditions, including a requirement that the company secure and conserve at least 2800 hectares of surrounding land (including land of high conservation significance) as an offset for the land damaged by mining.[4]

However, legal appeal against the mine's approval continued through an appeal to the Federal Court. In May 2007, the community group, Anvil Hill Project Watch Association (AHPWA), argued that the Federal Minister for the Environment should have declared the development a 'controlled action' requiring assessment under the federal environmental legislation, given its impacts of national significance involving climate change and biodiversity. In September 2007, Justice Margaret Stone of the Federal Court dismissed the appeal on the grounds that determining whether a development is a 'controlled action' or not, is a matter for the Federal Minister. The AHPWA then appealed to the Full Federal Court against Justice Stone's decision, but in February 2008 the Full Court dismissed the appeal.[5]

The coal mining development case outlined in Box 1.1 illustrates the layers of complexity associated with contemporary environmental dilemmas. It shows a case that 30–40 years ago would have been seen as a local issue, now argued, in part, on the global impacts of climate change and on Australia's moral responsibilities to the global community regarding climate change. The case also demonstrates the wide access of protesters to formal avenues of appeal through complex layers of legislation at State and federal levels. These represent some of the new complexities of contemporary Environmental Decision-Making (EDM). Today many of the issues under consideration are complex and involve a host of moral, social, legal and political dimensions, interrelated with various biophysical, technical and economic factors. Today EDM not only encompasses broad temporal and spatial scales, but also typically involves multiple actors with different values and competing interests and competing sources of knowledge, as well as significant risks and uncertainties. Such characteristics also feature in other areas of public policy such as health, but environmental issues tend to overwhelm decision-makers because of their scale, interdependencies and unknown consequences (Dovers 2005a). Moreover, many environmental issues are concerned with

---

1   <www.abc.net.au/news/newsitems/200706/s1945236.htm> (accessed 19 April 2009).

2   <www.anvilhill.org.au> (accessed 19 April 2009).

3   <www.hcec.org.au/node/62> (accessed 19 April 2009).

4   See footnote 1.

5   <www.blakedawson.com/Templates/Publications/x_article_content_page.aspx?id=51649> (accessed 19 April 2009).

'commons problems' which occur when shared natural resources such as water, air, forests and fisheries are susceptible to overuse and mismanagement (Dietz et al 2003; Hardin 1968). Environmental issues are also inherently complex because they provide goods and services (such as clean air and water, aesthetics, wilderness) that are difficult to quantify and include in dominant valuation systems, such as money.

Since environmental issues first emerged on political and social agendas in the 1960s, our knowledge of their causes and impacts has greatly improved. Today environmental management is informed by large bodies of research from both the physical and social sciences. Unfortunately additional insights and knowledge have not always translated into effective action (Lowe 2003). Indeed, for some environmental issues it seems that the more we learn, the more we recognise the complexities and uncertainties involved.

EDM has never been straightforward but we are beginning to recognise that the current period represents the most profound shift in human-environment relations the Earth has yet experienced (Flannery 2008; Steffen 2008). Recognising this, the term 'Anthropocene' has been coined (Crutzen 2002) for the geological epoch starting about 1800, to suggest that 'the Earth has now left its natural geological epoch' (the Holocene) and '[h]uman activities have become so pervasive and profound that they rival the great forces of Nature and are pushing the earth into planetary *terra incognita*' (Steffen et al 2007, p 614). Significantly, our institutions and decision-making processes have failed to deal with the inherent complexity and politics of environmental issues, and as a consequence progress in addressing our impacts on the environment has been painfully slow (Flannery 2008; Lindenmayer et al 2008a; Lowe 2009).

Given these inadequacies, there is an urgent need to better understand and improve EDM processes. The role of this book is to unpack EDM and reveal its complexities. More specifically we explore how decisions on environmental dilemmas are made and shaped by their socio-political context. For example, how do different value systems influence what environmental issues come onto the public agenda, and their management? What institutions and actors are involved in EDM processes and how? What tools are available to assist EDM and what are their limitations? How should we deal with uncertainty and risk? How do we incorporate relevant but very different forms of knowledge, into EDM and how do we manage the explosion of information now available?

We begin by clarifying several core terms used throughout the book.

1.2 Definitions

1.2.1 Environment

The term 'environment' has been elucidated by a variety of definitions and its meaning has changed as society has changed. The term stems from the word 'environ', which means to surround. In its narrowest sense, 'environment' refers to our natural surroundings which have traditionally being described in biophysical terms. However over time these 'surroundings' have been interpreted more broadly to encompass:

- ecosystems[6] and their interactive parts;

---

6   The term 'ecosystem' refers to an interacting functional system, such as a lake, grassland or a forest, comprising both living organisms and their non-living surroundings. It is a shortened form of 'ecological system'.

- natural resources;

- characteristics and qualities of human settlements (such as facilities, infrastructures and developments) that influence the balance, well-being and amenity of society;

- the social, economic and cultural dimensions that define and influence the health of all communities, areas and locations.

It is notable that this broader definition of the environment is prevalent in most relevant Australian policy and legislation. It is also anthropocentric, that is emphasising the utility of the environment for humans. In this book, we will use 'environment' in this broadest sense to encapsulate all those dimensions (biophysical, social, economic and political) which define our surroundings.

1.2.2 Environmental Decision-making (EDM)

In general terms environmental decisions are those choices or judgments that have a significant impact on the environment. They include much more than just decisions on environmental matters per se. For instance, decisions to construct a freeway or to amend an irrigation policy are not directly about the environment, but both may have considerable consequences for the environment.

We all make decisions that affect the environment. For example, on an individual level our lifestyle choices affect the amount of materials and water we consume, as well as the energy consumed by our choice of travel. While these kinds of individual decisions are significant for the environment, our primary focus in this book is on the *collective* decisions made by governments, businesses and non-government organisations (NGOs). More specifically, we are interested in the procedures and context of EDM and how these influence decision outcomes.

To explore these and other questions this book draws on a range of literature from different disciplines including political science, law, economics, philosophy, natural sciences, geography, engineering and sociology. Of particular importance to our discussions on EDM is the field of policy studies, which is concerned with how particular issues get onto the public and government agenda, and the processes and politics of policy-making (see Box 1.2).

Box 1.2: What do we mean by 'policy' and 'public policy'?

The term *policy* carries many meanings. It can refer to a document, a strategy such as a piece of legislation, a program, an agenda, a decision outcome, or an institution. In its broadest sense, policy is about connecting ends with means: 'we want to achieve a particular outcome, so we follow the course of action that we calculate will produce that outcome' (Fenna 2004, p 4). In the context of EDM, policy usually refers to a particular decision or program of a government, business or organisation. A policy might also refer to a directive, for example a 'policy to conserve water' or a set of values, for example, a corporation's sustainability policy stipulating its goals for environmentally sensitive business conduct.

In the realm of government, we typically speak of *public policy* which is classically defined as 'whatever governments choose to do or not to do' (Dye 1972, p 1). In other words, public policies express an intention, or a choice, made by government (Stewart and Ayres 2001, pp 20–21). But as we shall see throughout this book, today the governance of environmental issues extends well beyond the work of governments – many other actors, including businesses and NGOs, are also involved in defining and managing environmental problems. Thus contemporary public policy on the environment can best be described as: 'processes and decisions enabled, made and/or coordinated by government and other institutions operating in the public domain' (Dovers 2005a, p 18).

The process of developing and implementing (public) policies on the environment can be highly political and complex. Typically multiple actors from within and outside government interact to put issues on the agenda and influence decisions (Stewart and Ayres 2001, p 20). The political nature of policy-making makes it an inherently contested and messy process. It can also be highly irrational – where decisions do not accord well with the type of issue or problem at hand (see Colebatch 2006).

Although the policy process might be messy in practice, it is typically conceptualised as a cycle composed of various stages from identifying issues, analysing problems, assessing policy instruments, consulting and coordinating with different stakeholders, making a policy decision, and then finally implementing and evaluating that decision (Althaus et al 2007). The policy-making process rarely proceeds in the orderly way this cycle suggests, but these stages help policy-makers and those studying it make sense of their contribution to the process.

We draw on this cycle metaphor in our conceptualisation of the EDM process further below.

1.2.3 Sustainability

Closely related to the term 'environment' is the concept of 'sustainability', which is often used to denote the ultimate goal in development where social, environmental and economic needs are all achieved concurrently. More formally sustainability 'refers to the ability of human society to persist in the long term in a manner that satisfies human development demands but without threatening the integrity of the natural world' (Dovers 2005a, p 7). The path to 'sustainability', often referred to as 'sustainable development', is commonly defined as that development which allows the present generation to meet their needs without undermining the ability of future generations to meet theirs (WCED 1987). As we show in Chapter 2, there is a range of interpretations of these concepts and how they can be achieved. The key message to appreciate at this point of the book is that sustainability now forms the normative (or moral) framework in which EDM takes place.

To appreciate how contemporary EDM works, it is useful to consider sustainability and the state of the environment on a global and then national scale.

1.3 State of the world

An important influence on EDM is the 'state of the world', encompassing the condition of the world's environments, and broader sustainability issues. 'Ecological Footprint' (EF) analysis was developed in the early 1990s as a coarse tool to demonstrate how sustainably we are living as a global community (Wackernagel and Rees 1996). The EF measures the amount of biologically productive land and marine areas required to produce the resources a human population uses and to deal with the wastes produced, using current technology.[7]

---

7   Details of methodology for ecological footprinting can be found at the Global Footprinting Network website <www.footprintnetwork.org/en/index.php/GFN/> and in the *Living Planet Report 2008*, <wwf. org.au/publications/livingplanetreport2008/> (both accessed 6 April 2009).

Figure 1.1 Global Ecological Footprint (WWF 2008)

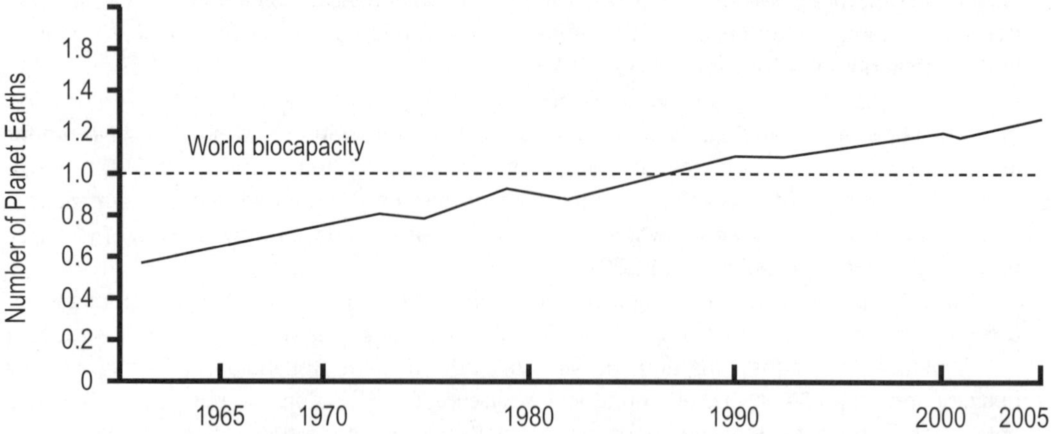

Hence, it provides a rough assessment as to whether we are living within the regenerative capacity ('biocapacity') of the planet or instead are eating into natural capital.[8] In financial terms this would equate to living off interest rather than reducing capital.

Humanity's ecological footprint has grown rapidly in recent years. Figure 1.1 shows that according to EF analysis we started to exceed the planet's regenerative capacity around 1988 and by 2005 the global EF exceeded this capacity by 30 per cent (WWF 2008). This means that we currently require about one and a third planet Earths to support the global population within Earth's regenerative capacity. Clearly, this equates to living unsustainably, since we are running down natural capital.

The trend shown in Figure 1.1 is towards further unsustainability. Unless we take urgent action this will intensify for at least the following reasons:

• World population is expected to grow from 6 billion in 1999 to 9 billion by 2042, with most of this growth in poorer countries.[9]

• The need for development in poorer countries which will require that they gain a greater share of access to use of the world's resources.

The vast inequity in such access is evident from Table 1.1 which shows per person EFs in a range of countries and also global averages. The sustainability challenge is: how can we meet the needs of those in poorer countries and for a growing world population, without increasing the global EF? To do this will require reducing EFs in richer countries in order to provide space for development in poorer countries and for inevitable population growth. This development will need to take place in a manner that does not further increase the global EF. This is an immense challenge, as the energy component of the global EF requires a global cut in greenhouse gas emissions of 50 per cent on 2000 emissions by 2050 and for Australia a 90 per cent cut (Garnaut 2008).[10]

---

8   Natural capital refers to natural resources both living and non-living (see Chapter 2 for further explanation).

9   US Census Bureau, International Data Base, World Population Information, <www.census.gov/ipc/www/ idb/worldpopinfo.html> (accessed 13 March 2008).

10   This is the cut required to achieve a 450 ppm concentration of greenhouse gases in the atmosphere. measured using carbon dioxide as the benchmark (CO_2-e). 450 ppm is widely regarded as a limit to avoid dangerous climate change.

Table 1.1 Ecological Footprint Inequity

Comparative figures for per person EF. Global and high, medium, low income countries averages and selected nations, 2005 figures (WWF 2008); 2003 figures (WWF 2006)

Country or region	Ecological Footprint (global hectares per person)	
	2005	2003
World	2.7	2.2
High-income countries	6.4	6.4
Middle-income countries	2.2	1.9
Low-income countries	1.0	0.8
United States	9.4	9.6
Australia	7.8	6.6
United Kingdom	5.3	5.6
China	2.1	1.6
India	0.9	0.8
Bangladesh	0.6	0.5

The *impact* of increasing EFs can be seen in numerous reports, which at regular intervals track changes in a range of environmental parameters. At global and regional levels, these include the *Living Planet* report produced annually by the World Wide Fund for Nature (eg WWF 2006, 2008), the annual *State of the World* reports from the Worldwatch Institute,[11] and the *Global Environment Outlook* (GEO) reports produced by the United Nations Environment Programme (UNEP 2007). These reports show continuing and escalating degradation of the Earth's environments – atmosphere, land, water and biodiversity – as a result of human activities, and suggest that this environmental degradation 'threatens all aspects of human well-being' and can increase human vulnerability (UNEP 2007, p 4).

The Millennium Ecosystem Assessment (MEA 2005a), involving 1360 experts from around the world, has provided many detailed reports into the extent and consequences of ecosystem change.[12] Initiated by the United Nations (UN) in 2001, the MEA aimed to provide a scientific basis for how societies might move towards more sustainable use of ecosystems and support of human well-being. The MEA found changes in the Earth's ecosystems over the past 50 years as a result of human activities to be greater than at any equivalent period of time previously, and to have caused irreversible loss in biodiversity, and exacerbation of poverty for people in some areas. The MEA predicted that these changes will be significantly worse in the first half of the 21st century unless major changes in policies and institutional arrangements are put in place. The MEA also concluded that the level of changes in ecosystems was increasing the likelihood of nonlinear changes, that is, abrupt alterations of a system, such as collapse in a fishery or disease emergence.

Many reports on the state of the environment are also produced at regular intervals in Australia at a range of levels (national, State, regional, local) (see 8.9). The 2006 State of the Environment Report for Australia showed that while Australia has put in place steps to halt broad-scale clearing of vegetation, and to protect fisheries and specific marine areas such as the Great Barrier Reef, much of the coastline is suffering environmental degradation as a

---

11   <www.worldwatch.org> (5 May 2009).

12   <www.millenniumassessment.org/en/index.aspx> (accessed 19 November 2008).

result of increasing population density, and parts of the country are badly affected by salinity and acidity of the land (and associated waterways) (Beeton et al 2006). But of most concern for Australia is water management, both urban and rural, particularly in the south-east and south-west of the continent. Severe and prolonged drought since 2002 has led to concerns that our major cities and population growth areas, Sydney, Melbourne, Perth and South-East Queensland, may run out of water, prompting development of desalination plants in Perth, Sydney and Melbourne and controversial recycling plans in South-East Queensland (Wahlquist 2008; and see Case Study C). Australia's major food basket, the Murray-Darling Basin,[13] is in crisis. Historic over-allocation and extraction of water for irrigation coupled with the current extended drought, and high temperatures in the summer of 2008–2009, have led in the first quarter of 2009 to the lowest inflows to the Murray River since records started in 1892 (Ker and Arup 2009). In turn low flows have resulted in 800 kilometres of algal blooms (Ker and Arup 2009), and severe impacts on high conservation value wetlands and river red gums (CSIRO 2008). Farms in the Basin, dependent on irrigation water, unavailable in the drought, are suffering badly, leading to discussions on whether the Murray-Darling Basin can continue to play such a dominant role in Australia's agricultural production (Garnaut 2008; Pincock 2008).

A further major concern for Australia is climate change. For the already stressed Murray-Darling Basin it seems that the recent extreme climatic conditions may be partly attributable to anthropogenic (human-induced) climate change and that 'such conditions are likely to become more common', particularly in the south of the Basin (CSIRO 2008, p 7) with the possibility of a 50 per cent loss in annual output from irrigated agriculture (Garnaut 2008). More generally, Australia is seen to be particularly vulnerable to climate change with impacts including: stresses on urban water supplies and agriculture; storm and flood damage to settlements; sea level rise affecting coastal infrastructure; possible destruction of the Great Barrier Reef; increase in bushfires; human health effects from heat stress and wider spread of insect borne diseases (such as Ross River fever); loss of many species (Garnaut 2008).

It seems that the effects of our environmental mismanagement are returning to haunt us at global, regional and local levels – the environment is biting back.[14] Yet, the signals of looming environmental problems have been present long before action has been taken (Harremoës et al 2002). And, with a few exceptions, when problems have been addressed successfully, progress has tended to be painfully slow. Moreover, any gains made have often been overtaken by the pressures of human activity, in broad terms driven by continued growth in population and consumption (Lowe 2009; MEA 2005b).

So despite the above catalogue of woes, this is not intended to be a book of doom and gloom about particular environmental issues. Rather, it aims to reveal the complexities of EDM and the influence of social, institutional and political factors. Once we appreciate this broader context we are able to better understand why our progress towards sustainability has been so slow and what may be required to proceed more rapidly.

While this is essentially a book about the socio-political context of EDM, we need to keep a watch on the state of the environment and its impacts on human well-being, since these are important influences on the extent to which the environment becomes a central consideration in decision-making. This influence has grown rapidly over the last 40 years.

---

13   The Murray-Darling Basin produces 40 per cent of Australia's gross value of agricultural production and is a major contributor to Australia's economy (CSIRO 2008).

14   See also Economy and Lieberthal (2007) on China. They quote reports that environmental degradation cost the Chinese economy the equivalent of 10 per cent of GDP annually, and more than 400,000 people die annually from air pollution (p 90).

1.4 Rising environmental awareness

A close awareness of, and association with, the environment is not new. Traditional peoples over a lengthy time period have depended on good experiential understanding gained from observation and experience, and a close spiritual relationship with their environment (see Box 3.3). Nevertheless, this has not prevented the collapse of some early societies as a result of environmental degradation. A prime example is the collapse of the Easter Island civilisation somewhere between the 10th and 17th centuries AD, mainly as a result of deforestation (Diamond 2005).

The Industrial Revolution, starting in Britain around the mid-18th century, accelerated environmental degradation through mining, manufacturing and more intense agriculture. Further impact on the environment came from a sharp increase in population growth and urbanisation, starting at this time. Industrialisation created pollution of the air and waterways and markedly changed landscapes, but the impacts were local and regional. By the late 1940s air pollution in the Los Angeles Basin was such that the first strong emission controls were enacted, and the London smog episode of December 1952 which was responsible for 4000 additional deaths, led to a Clean Air Act (Smil 1993), and was an important wake up call regarding the impacts of unregulated anthropogenic activities.

The period following World War II saw an explosion in the development of synthetic chemicals producing a wide range of plastics, pesticides, drugs and industrial and domestic process chemicals (such as solvents and detergents) (Crone 1986). Apart from drugs, these were essentially unregulated and through widespread use entered the world's ecosystems. Many spread widely from their point of use and/or built up in food chains; for example, persistent pesticides such as DDT were found in Arctic polar bears (Colborn et al 1996). Hence, local pollutants had become global pollutants. In the early 1960s, Rachel Carson, a United States marine biologist, drew attention to the impacts of synthetic pesticides, such as DDT, on birds and other wildlife. She had an engaging writing style and her book *Silent Spring* (Carson 1962) had a profound impact on alerting people to the dangers of persistent pesticides, and to the importance of ecology[15] for understanding the workings of nature and human impacts on natural systems. Carson's publications were also important in linking industrial activities to impacts on human and ecological health. The work of Carson and others on detrimental effects of synthetic chemicals in the environment led to the introduction of legislation in the United States in 1976 aimed at preventing harm from new chemicals to humans and the environment.[16] More broadly, *Silent Spring* and Carson's other work is credited with setting in train the environmental movement (Cadbury 1997; see also 3.9).

The latter years of the 1960s and into the early 1970s saw attention directed to the linked impacts of population growth and resource use on the environment and the notion of 'limits to growth' (Ehrlich 1968; Ehrlich and Ehrlich 1972; Meadows et al 1972; see also 2.4.2), with some sheeting blame beyond population growth and affluence to the inertia of the economic and political systems in dealing with environmental degradation and to links between profits and pollution (Commoner 1971). Strong counter-literature argued that these 'prophets of doom' over-exaggerated the impacts on the environment and underestimated the role that technology and regulation can play in overcoming limits and in preventing environmental degradation (eg Maddox 1972). Twenty years after Meadows et al (1972) published their influential book, *The Limits to Growth*, they responded to their critics showing how many

---

15   Ecology is a branch of science that studies the relationships of living organisms with one another and with their environment.

16   The *Toxic Substances Control Act*. See <www.epa.gov/lawsregs/laws/tsca.html> (accessed 10 April 2009).

of the original critics had misunderstood their work. The key message of *Limits* was that within the next 100 years, *if* current trends continued, the world's integrated human and natural systems would 'overshoot and collapse' as a result of population growth and consumption of resources. Meadows et al (1992) pointed out that their critics assumed that they were making *predictions* in *Limits*, when actually they were presenting scenarios – *if* certain trends continue, *then* certain consequences would follow (Meadows et al 1992). Interestingly, a recent comparison of the scenarios in *Limits*, using historical data from 1970–2000, shows that this period corresponds well with the business-as-usual scenario in *Limits*; that is, the scenario assuming current trends would continue. This is the scenario that *Limits* said would result in collapse of the global system in the mid-21st century (Turner 2008).

Pollution continued to be a key issue in people's developing awareness of the impacts of human activities on the environment and human health. Recognition that nations' boundaries did not limit the spread of pollution gained attention. Complaints by Scandinavian nations in the late 1960s that burning of fossil fuels in Britain's power plants was causing acidification[17] of lakes in their countries was important in putting transboundary pollution on the agenda, and international agreements to deal with transboundary issues became common. For example, in 1989 the *Basel Convention* was adopted, which aims to prevent cross-border movements of hazardous waste (particularly from developed to developing countries) and encourages the disposal of waste as close as possible to its source.[18] In 1995 the United Nations Environment Programme (UNEP) resolved to address a group of synthetic chemicals described as 'persistent organic pollutants' (POPs). POPs are characterised by their persistence in the environment (and associated ability for long-range transport), their ability to bioaccumulate[19] through food chains, and their potential to adversely affect human health and the environment. An international agreement, the *Stockholm Convention* on POPs, came into force in 2004 to address management of POPs, starting with 12 chemicals. These 12 included a number of pesticides such as DDT and also certain industrial chemicals.[20] Growing concern regarding the intrusion of harmful synthetic chemicals into all parts of our day-to-day existence in all corners of the world, and a growing catalogue of human and wildlife health issues which may be linked to such chemicals, has provided a contemporary focus on Rachel Carson's early warning (Cadbury 1997; Colborn et al 1996; Shabecoff and Shabecoff 2008), and the development of a flourishing organic food industry.

While pollution played a strong role in the emergence of environmental concern (and has continued to do so), the rapid alteration of natural systems through human habitation and agricultural and industrial activities raised awareness that human actions were causing extinctions of species thousands of times faster than the natural rate (Brenton 1994) and led to the *Convention on Biological Diversity* signed in 1992.[21]

---

17   'Acid rain' was recognised as the cause of this acidification. Acid rain develops when sulphur and nitrogen oxides, emitted from power plants and other industrial sources, react in the atmosphere with water and oxygen to form sulphuric and nitric acid. These substances can be carried over long distances before falling as rain: see <www.epa.gov/acidrain/what/index.html> (accessed 16 April 2009).

18   US Environmental Protection Agency <www.epa.gov/oia/toxics/pop.htm#timeline> (accessed 11 April 2009).

19   Bioaccumulation refers to the process in which chemicals are taken up by organisms from the environment or food and accumulated in living tissues. The low solubility of many POPs in water and high solubility in fatty tissue, is an important factor in their accumulation in living tissue. Biomagnification is a related term that refers to the build up of the concentration of a chemical in living tissue moving up a food chain.

20   UNEP <www.chem.unep.ch/pops/> (accessed 11 April 2009).

21   <www.cbd.int/convention/> (accessed 11 April 2009).

Recently, as indicated above, issues of 'limits' have resurfaced in relation to both supply (such as concern about water supply in many parts of the world, and critically in Australia), and impact, such as our ever-increasing ecological footprints. The latter has led to calls for greater efficiencies in production systems (Factor 10 Club 1995; Hargroves and Smith 2005; Hawken et al 1999) and to a move to sustainable consumption.[22]

The growing awareness and concern regarding environmental issues have been tracked through numerous public opinion surveys (see 3.9). For example, a Roy Morgan research survey conducted in May 2008 found that 35 per cent of Australians considered environmental issues to be the biggest problem facing the world (up from 14 per cent in 2006), ahead of economic issues (24 per cent in 2008[23]). In terms of issues facing Australia, 30 per cent of respondents considered environmental issues the biggest problem facing Australia (up from 8 per cent in 2006). Such surveys are useful for tracking the growth of environmental awareness, and reveal that since the early 1970s awareness has generally been increasing to such an extent that environment is now considered to be a mainstream concern (Papadakis 1996). Further evidence of the growing concern regarding the environment comes from trends in expenditure on environmental issues. Environment-related expenditure by the Australian Government has steadily increased from around $1.7 billion in 2001–2002 to $3.1 billion in 2005–2006,[24] while environmental expenditure for all levels of government in Australia in 2002–2003 was around $12 billion.[25]

Nevertheless, people's concern about the environment may wax and wane depending on a range of factors (Downs 1972) including what other issues are attracting attention at the time (for example: global financial crisis; drought; unemployment; terrorism and so on). Popular awareness of environmental issues is also influenced by the attention given to individuals and groups that hold contrary views on the environment. For example, the critics of *The Limits to Growth* in 1972. More recently Bjørn Lomborg (2001[26]) has received much media attention for his view that doomsday predictions from a range of prominent environmentalists and organisations such as Al Gore[27] and the Worldwatch Institute,[28] have provided an exaggerated picture of the severity of a range of environmental problems, including climate change, and that this has diverted money to environmental matters that would be better spent on other problems facing the world. Contestation over environmental issues can confuse the public as they try to sort out who to believe and what messages to send to decision-makers.

Of course the factors that determine the level of public awareness and concern over environmental issues, whether or not issues will get onto the public agenda, and how they will be treated through the EDM process, are complex. Typically numerous factors come together to open a window that puts an issue on the agenda (Kingdon, 2003). The key purpose of this book is to attempt to shed some light on that complexity.

In parallel to this rising social awareness of environmental issues, approaches to environmental management and EDM have changed over the past 40–50 years.

---

22   See UNEP <www.unep.org/themes/consumption/index.asp?page=home> (accessed 11 April 2009).

23   Though this was before the global financial crisis became a major issue in mid-2008.

24   <www/deh.gov.au/about/publications/budget/2005/ebo/index.html> (accessed 15 April 2009).

25   <www.environment.gov.au/soe/2006/publications/drs/indicator/411/index.html> (accessed 15 April 2009).

26   See also <www.lomborg.com> (accessed 17 April 2009).

27   See <www.algore.com/> (accessed 21 April 2009).

28   See <www.worldwatch.org> (accessed 21 April 2009).

1.5 Evolution of approaches to EDM

Governments at all levels, international organisations, business, and other non-government bodies, have each responded to the growing environmental awareness and concern by a gradual process of institutionalisation of environmental matters into their strategic planning and operations. By this we mean the development of formal processes for environmental planning, management and appraisal of performance. For example:

- development of a wide range of international agreements dealing with environmental matters (see 4.7);

- enactment of environmentally related legislation and courts of law for environmental disputes (see 4.4);

- establishment of bureaucracies for administering environmental matters and programs (see 4.4);

- development of formal mechanisms for public access and participation in decision-making (see 4.6.6 and Chapter 7).

These changes within government have been followed by changes within the business world and other NGOs that have also institutionalised environmental concerns. For example, organisations (both government and non-government) have adopted formal environmental or sustainability policies and standards for a wide range of environmental processes such as Environmental Management Systems (see Chapter 8).

In addition to this institutionalisation of environmental concern, there has also been an evolution in the approaches to environmental management and decision-making as illustrated in Table 1.2. In sum, our approaches have become more systems-based[29] (rather than reductionist and siloed) and integrated, more anticipatory of future impacts of activities, and more collaborative and inclusive of a wider range of actors and different sources and forms of knowledge. The move towards more collaborative approaches represents a shift from environmental management to environmental governance, where multiple actors are involved in developing and delivering programs for sustainability (Meadowcroft 2007; Stewart and Jones 2003).[30]

As part of this evolution, the way we approach environmental impacts and pollution control has taken account of a wider range of matters and broadened the spatial and temporal scales for consideration. Consider 'pollution control' at the bottom of Table 1.2. In the 1970s we took an end-of-pipe view of waste management. Waste was simply disposed of in landfill or incinerated. By the 1990s the emphasis was shifting to source control for waste. The waste management hierarchy of 'avoid-reduce-reuse-recycle-dispose safely' became the mantra. In other words disposal to landfill is the least desirable option and the aim now is to avoid this by moving up the hierarchy, towards waste minimisation and avoidance. We are now moving towards the concept of 'materials (or resource) management' rather than 'waste'. Greater emphasis is now being placed on encouraging producers to be responsible for their products from cradle to grave, for example by considering materials reuse and avoidance in the design and use of products (see Case Study A).

---

29 Meaning focused on the interdependence and connectedness between an assemblage of components as a complex whole (*Oxford English Dictionary Online*).

30 For a broad discussion on governance and sustainability, see Jordan (2008).

Table 1.2 Evolution of approaches to EDM

Approach to . . .	1970s	1990s	2010s
Decision-making (Chapters 2 and 7)	Linear decision-making, mainly informed by scientific and technical expertise	More open decision-making through bargaining and negotiating competing interests	Adaptive decision-making through collaborative learning
Mode of governing (Chapters 4, 5 and 7)	Hierarchical modes of governing – one way flow of information	Inform, and consult with key stakeholders	Broader engagement of community and co-production of policy through forming networks and unusual alliances
Planning (Chapters 2 and 9)	Short-term reactive	More proactive – anticipate impacts and take precautionary responses	Steering long-term change-accepting and dealing with complexity, ambiguity and uncertainty
Environmental Impact Assessment (Chapter 8)	Through policy Piecemeal Local impacts Short temporal scale	Through regulation Cumulative Regional impacts Longer temporal scale	Through regulation Cumulative and strategic Ecosystem to global (depending on the issue) Intergenerational
Form of Knowledge (Chapter 6)	Siloed and reductionist	Multidisciplinary but not integrated	Transdisciplinary[1]
Breadth of Knowledge (Chapter 6)	Knowledge *about* the environment Technical and scientific expertise (technocracy)	Knowledge *about* the environment Physical science meets social and economic knowledge	Knowledge *for* sustainability Emphasis on capacity building and bringing together multiple perspectives – different ways of knowing and doing
Application of Tools (Chapter 8)	Narrow range of biophysical, technical and economic tools and models Adapted for EDM	Wide range of tools to inform and assist environmental management and for decision support Developed for EDM	Continuing expansion of tools to serve broader roles – emphasis on integration in their use; broader recognition of their limits in use Developed for EDM
Pollution control (Chapters 2 and 4)	End of pipe	Source control	Systems thinking

1   Transdisciplinarity involves a very high degree of integration across the disciplines. See 6.3.4 for discussion of this concept.

As approaches to EDM have evolved, significant development has occurred in the way various professionals interface with environmental issues – giving rise to the emergence of environmental professionals.

1.6 Environmental professionals

The number of people working in an environmentally-related industry has grown rapidly over the past decade (see Annandale et al 2004), raising the question: who is an environmental professional?

In the 1970s and 1980s environmental professionals were primarily linked to engineering and science roles and separated into specific environment departments in organisations. Today environmental professionals are found in wide range of organisations, from traditional areas such as mining and industrial pollution control, through to newer placements in finance, banking and law. They also come from a much wider range of disciplinary backgrounds. The social science professionals have now joined the science and engineering/technical experts, and importantly some environmental professionals now also have training in transdisciplinary approaches (Wever et al 2008). As well, environmental professionals are increasingly becoming integrated throughout organisations rather than being located in separate environment departments. Today we also see much more fluidity of movement for environmental professionals amongst government, business and environmental NGOs.[31] In contrast, in the early days of environmental concern, it would have been unthinkable that a leader of an environment NGO could move to become a senior public servant.

Today there is ongoing debate over whether a distinct environment profession exists or whether the environment is increasingly becoming part of every profession. In 2003 a House of Representatives Inquiry into *Employment in the Environment Sector* wrestled with this issue at length, and in the end adopted a broad view of the environment industry seeing it not as a discrete profession, but rather as a process of greening of mainstream business and professional practices (CoA 2003a). The central argument here was that (CoA 2003a, p 17):

> [J]ust as information technologies are now a standard tool in the jobs of many workers, and occupational health and safety is a shared workplace responsibility, so environmental awareness and management must be integrated into the daily work practices of employers and employees.

This may well be the way of the future. It is predicted that in Australia green employment (also labelled as 'green jobs', 'green collar economy' or the 'environmental goods and service industry') will rise in the coming years particularly if serious steps are taken towards a low carbon economy (Diesendorf 2004). One recent report predicts that as many as 850,000 green collar jobs could be created by 2030, particularly in the areas of renewable energy, energy efficiency, sustainable water systems, biomaterials, green buildings and waste and recycling (ACF & ACTU 2008). In response to this potential growth, there have been strong calls to boost training and skills in environmental areas (Hatfield-Dodds et al 2008).

We turn now to introduce our conceptualisation of the EDM process and how it relates to the chapters in the book.

---

31 An early example is Phillip Toyne who was Director of the Australian Conservation Foundation from 1986–1992, and in 1994 became a senior public servant in the federal environment agency.

1.7 The EDM process in context and scope of the book

There may be considerable differences in the way environmental decisions are made depending on the issue at hand, and its broader legal, political, economic and social context. Nevertheless, a general structure of the EDM process can be identified, which draws on the notion of the policy cycle discussed above (see Box 1.2). Here we use the cycle as a heuristic device only; that is, it serves as a conceptual tool to help break open what is in practice a complex process with many overlapping components.

It is important to note the EDM cycle is not a closed system. It is situated in a sea of political, social and biophysical influences that shape each component of the EDM cycle. Throughout the book we focus on these socio-political issues, and broader contextual themes, discussing their influence on the procedures and outcomes of EDM. Figure 1.2 shows the key stages of the EDM cycle, and highlights the contextual themes we discuss in different chapters in the book.

One particularly significant feature of contemporary EDM is that it increasingly takes place within the framework of sustainability – the aspiration that society achieves its social, environmental and economic needs concurrently. In Chapter 2 we explore the meaning and evolution of sustainability and the related concept of sustainable development. Not surprisingly, there are many interpretations of these concepts and how they can be achieved. Numerous countries around the world, including Australia, have embraced the notion of sustainability by adopting a set of objectives and principles of sustainable development. These serve to guide government policies and legislation.

1.7.1 Identifying issues, setting the agenda, problem framing

In most cases, the EDM process begins when a person, group of people, or organisation (private or government), perceives and identifies a problem, a risk or a need. This is the point at which a solution to a perceived problem or issue is sought.

The way in which we each frame an issue or problem is greatly influenced by our personal value systems and beliefs. Individuals and groups place different values on the environment which ultimately stem from a range of value positions and world views. In Chapter 3 we draw specific attention to the role of values and value differences in EDM and explore how these might be best accommodated. Gaining insight into these different value frameworks can help develop an understanding of why people respond in different ways to certain activities or decisions. In order to ensure that the process of EDM is effective, one must appreciate and accommodate the spectrum of environmental values held by interested parties throughout this process.

In considering this stage of the cycle we also need to reflect on the influence that formal institutions, structures and processes have on EDM and its outcomes. Many of the possible routes and opportunities along the EDM cycle are defined and restricted by these factors. For example, the capacity for decisions to support sustainability are influenced by our federal structure, the terms of reference for government departments, the way in which government agencies are divided between ministerial portfolios, the representativeness of our elected officials, and our commitments to global treaties. In Chapter 4 we provide an overview of the formal institutional context in which much of EDM takes place, from the local through to the international level.

Figure 1.2 The EDM cycle and the socio-political and contextual themes explored in the book

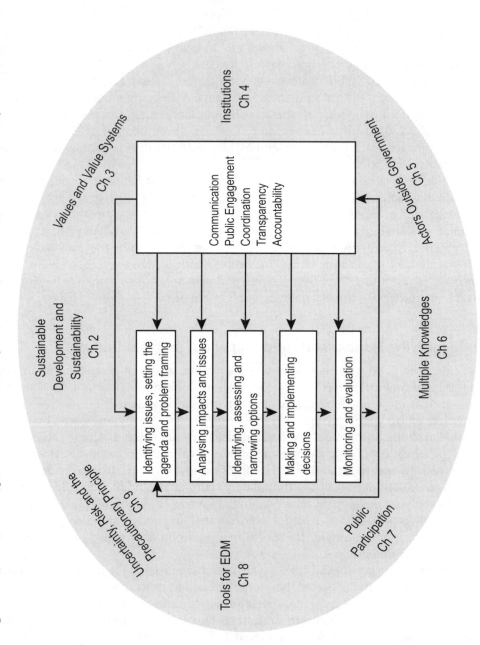

Adapted from Dovers 2005a.

The process of identifying a problem and the relevant boundaries of an issue or project requires information about the issue and may involve considering the perspectives of relevant groups that are affected by, or that seek to influence EDM outcomes, and those who may bring knowledge from a range of different sources. In Chapter 5 we explore the diversity of such actors including business, pressure groups, media, the broader public and global institutions, and consider the roles they play in EDM.

Ideally, EDM seeks to actively engage from the earliest stages all those 'publics' (including pressure groups and the broader community) who may be potentially affected by an issue or proposal, as well as those with particular insights or knowledge. In Chapter 7 we examine ways in which different kinds of publics might participate in EDM, and the benefits and costs of doing so.

Public participation is an important concept which is both a generic skill as well as a vital component of EDM. There are many levels at which the public can participate in environmental decisions and the level which is most appropriate will depend on the nature of the project. Failure to involve the public in the process can have enormous ramifications including increased costs, time-delays and poor public relations.

1.7.2 Analysing impacts and issues

Having now identified the problem, risk or need, it is necessary to analyse potential impacts. This means that decisions need to be made concerning which matters are relevant to the problem and need to be researched, what depth of research is necessary, and what associated data are considered relevant. To adequately analyse the impacts of environmental issues, data and information must be collected (Chapter 6). This is commonly the task of experts (for example, scientists, engineers, and social scientists) whose role is to describe, explain and predict the environmental interactions, the possible impacts and consequences of a proposal, and the possible solutions or mitigation strategies. There are two main sources of information or 'knowledge-bases' researchers may need to consult depending on the nature of the proposal – specialised expert knowledge and a range of extended knowledges, such as local and Indigenous perspectives. Chapter 6 discusses the role and significance of these different knowledges in contemporary EDM and also considers the challenges associated with their integration.

1.7.3 Identifying, assessing and narrowing options

Moving around the cycle, it is necessary to identify and assess the merits of possible options or solutions. In Chapter 8 we explore a range of tools developed to help make sense of environmental problems, and to develop possible courses of action. Such tools help identify and diagnose problems, assess their impacts and assist decision-makers to evaluate the consequences of alternatives, set priorities, allocate resources and implement decisions. For example, in Australia, the legally required process of identifying the potential environmental consequences for certain proposed activities or actions is known as Environmental Impact Assessment (EIA). EIA is an institutional response by governments to achieve environmental protection.

While such tools can help to process and analyse data into more meaningful information, their application also involves considerable subjectivity, including assumptions about how particular systems work, and judgments about what to include and exclude in the assessment. In Chapter 8, we explore these socio-political and value-laden aspects of tools, and consider their uses and strengths for informing and improving EDM.

1.7.4 Making and implementing decisions

This is the stage of the cycle where the research and collected data are called upon to aid in the assessment of a particular proposal and inform the decision-maker. In most situations, environmental professionals will play an important role at this stage as advisers to the decision-makers. For instance, decisions in local government are usually made by elected councillors based on the advice received from the experts researching the proposal. Finally, after any legal requirements have been fulfilled, public comment has been considered, and the broader social context including politically based factors taken into account, a final decision is made, and implementation can commence. When implementing environmental decisions there are a number of design questions to consider. For example, if a decision-maker seeks to implement an environmental audit program, they need to determine who will manage and deliver the program, how it will be resourced, how well it will work alongside existing programs, the underlying assumptions the program makes about its target group, and who is accountable for its success or otherwise (Althaus et al 2007).

An important consideration to be made at this stage of the EDM cycle (and indeed throughout) is the inherent complexity of environmental issues, and the risks and uncertainties they entail – themes we explore in Chapter 9. Over the past 30 years there have been a number of 'surprise' environmental events with unpredictable impacts. These include: depletion of the stratospheric ozone layer through the action of human-made chemicals (see 9.2.3); concern regarding lowered male fertility from certain pesticides and plastics which disrupt the endocrine system (Cadbury 1997); and widescale food and health crises such as that caused by mad-cow disease[32] (Jasanoff 1997). Unexpected events such as these have focused attention on the complexity of environmental issues, and associated with this, the high potential for uncertainty and ignorance regarding the possible environmental impacts of our activities. Consequently, much greater attention is being given to uncertainty in EDM and the adoption of the precautionary principle as a principle of sustainable development (Chapters 2 and 9) and environmental/ecological risk assessment as a part of Environmental Impact Assessment (Chapters 8 and 9) is evidence of this.

1.7.5 Monitoring and evaluation

Once decisions have been made and implemented, a process of monitoring and evaluation begins. This represents both the end and beginning of the EDM cycle, where the lessons and failings of previous decisions help shape future EDM processes. Tools are available for monitoring the progress of environmental decisions, for example, auditing and reporting on the state of the environment (see Chapter 8). However, in practice tracking the progress of an environmental decision is complicated by the uncertainty of sustainability issues (Chapter 9) and the typically long time lags involved between intervention and effect (Dovers 2005a). Moreover, as with most attempts to evaluate policy, measuring the success or otherwise of a decision or program can be a highly politicised process influenced by the focus and funding of the evaluation, its criteria and how results are interpreted (Bovens et al 2006). To avoid some of the problems associated with assessing the outcome of specific decisions, increasing emphasis is now placed on more adaptive approaches where the

---

32   More formally know as BSE or Bovine Spongiform Encephalopathy (see 9.1).

implementation of decisions is viewed as an experiment from which future projects can learn (Chapter 2).

In the final part of the book, we present three contemporary Australian environmental controversies to explore the main themes discussed in this book. These case studies on a) container deposit legislation, b) Gunns' pulp mill and c) Toowoomba's sewage recycling project cover a wide range of themes and help illustrate the complexities of EDM in practice.

From the outline of the chapters above, we can see that this book is not structured specifically around different stages of the EDM cycle. Instead the chapters focus on themes that speak to the socio-political context within which environmental decisions are situated. More specifically, we draw attention to the broad *conceptual landscapes* surrounding EDM, particularly in relation to recent debates on sustainability and sustainable development. We discuss how environmental issues and decisions are shaped by *beliefs* and competing *values*, as well as formal *institutions*. We also explore the role and involvement of different *participants* in environmental issues and decisions, and examine how EDM is *informed* and *supported*.

2

Sustainable Development and Sustainability

2.1 Introduction

Chapter 1 provided a broad outline of trends in the state of the world and of developments in our responses to this. We have moved from a reactive, 'end of pipe' and siloed approach to addressing environmental problems, to recognition that much deeper, more integrated and complex responses are required. Such responses move further back up the pipe to identify underlying causes of problems. This also helps us to appreciate the complex inter-relationships between environmental issues, the need to take an anticipatory and long-term view, and to recognise that environmental problems are embedded in social, political and economic contexts, and need to be addressed accordingly.

The contemporary approach to environmental management is shaped by the concepts of sustainable development and sustainability. These concepts now provide the framework through which we aim to achieve economic and social development whilst maintaining the long-term integrity of ecological systems. Hence this has become the framework for environmental decision-making (EDM).

Since the early 1990s, governments around the world have been seeking to institution-alise sustainability, yet we remain on a steep learning curve regarding implementation of sustainability, still unclear as to *exactly* what is required. What does seem clear is that sustainability requires new attitudes, approaches, skills and new ways of going about our business – learning and adapting.

This chapter explores sustainable development and sustainability – their conceptual development and nature; principles for their application; means for their implementation and necessary associated skills; and broad examples of implementation. Not least, we con-sider why they remain such difficult and contested concepts. But we will start by exploring the characteristics of sustainability problems.

2.2 The characteristics of sustainability problems

Addressing sustainability problems is fraught with difficulty. They display a number of characteristics of 'wicked problems' – a term introduced by Horst Rittel in the late 1960s to describe the nature of issues confronting the planning profession. Wicked problems involve complex interconnected systems linked by social processes, with little certainty as to where problems begin and end, leading to difficulty in knowing where and how constructive inter-ventions should be made and where the problem boundaries lie (Rittel and Webber 1973).

Most environmental issues display a number of 'wicked problem' characteristics (see Box 2.1). They are multi-layered in that there may be a range of possible causative factors, with complex interrelationships between them, and with some 'causes' actually symptoms of underlying problems. In addition, such problems sit in complex social contexts involving a diversity of views, values and vested interests (see Chapter 3) (Lach et al 2005). As we will argue further in this chapter sustainability problems demand an integrated approach where environmental, economic and social factors are taken into consideration (see 2.5).

Box 2.1: Anthropogenic climate change as a wicked problem

Anthropogenic climate change is a sustainability issue that displays a number of character-istics of wicked problems.

For example, what is the exact nature of the problem? Superficially, it is that human actions are causing a build-up of greenhouse gases in the atmosphere. While this is true, what are the underlying reasons for this? Is it simply a technological problem? Or is it the nature of our economic systems? What role do human aspirations and behaviours play? Each of these possible problems is linked to a set of solutions. Taking technology as the problem, possible solutions in the energy area include clean coal, nuclear power, renewable sources, efficiency gains through a range of means, and so on. Each of these in turn may bring another set of problems into the picture. Similar expanding sets of solutions can be provided for problems arising from the nature of our economic system or human aspirations and behaviour, as well as from further problem sources not identified here.

The scale of this issue makes for further complexities. It is a global issue that needs to be addressed at a range of scales from the global to the family unit. Is it the relations between developed and developing countries that are stalling agreements on emissions reduction? Or, is this problem underpinned by the internal politics of individual nations?

This brief discussion of a very small part of the problems involved in the global climate change issue gives a flavour of the nature of wicked problems, showing how even 'the formulation of a wicked problem *is* the problem' (Rittel and Webber 1973, p 161). It also shows how complex interrelated networks of potentially relevant factors quickly develop, and the boundaries of the issue expand in response.

Dovers (1997, 2003a, 2005a) elaborates further on the characteristics of sustainability problems by identifying a set of their attributes. He suggests these include (2005a, p 44):

- extended temporal and spatial scales;
- possible ecological limits and thresholds;
- cumulative impacts;
- irreversible impacts;
- complex connections between issues;
- typically high level of uncertainty and poor information;
- new moral dimensions;
- lack of agreement on appropriate research methods, policy instruments and management approaches;
- non-traded and non-valued assets as typical components;
- ill-defined property rights and responsibilities for assets;
- mixed public and private costs and benefits;
- need for community involvement;
- novelty of problems;
- need for integrative and interdisciplinary research to address the problems.

But are sustainability problems *really* different from a range of other complex problems facing society? Dovers (2005a) suggests that while other policy problems may share some of these attributes, in sustainability problems they typically occur in combination. A special feature of sustainability problems, by definition, is responsibility to future generations. As well, the environmental aspects of sustainability problems bring in attributes including ecological limits, irreversible impacts, poor information and high uncertainty. So, while other policy areas, such as health policy, may also be concerned with wicked problems, sustainability problems do have some distinguishing features.

It is clear that sustainable development and sustainability problems provide a special set of characteristics that are proving extremely challenging to address. Before we further explore their nature we need to discuss the terminology associated with these concepts.

2.3 Clarifying terms: sustainability and sustainable development

Sustainability and sustainable development are often used interchangeably, but is this appropriate? Or, do they have different meanings? While considering these questions it is worth keeping in mind that the common English meaning of 'sustainable' is 'maintainable' or 'capable of being maintained at a certain rate or level' (*Oxford English Dictionary Online*).

Some, particularly environmentalists, avoid the term 'sustainable development'. They are concerned that the word 'development' signifies growth and see continuing growth as problematic. Consequently, they see 'sustainable development' as an internally contradictory term (an oxymoron) (see Newman 2005). For this reason, the term 'sustainability' is often preferred by some. Others see no necessary contradiction in the term sustainable development, suggesting that development has meanings other than continuing growth in use of material and energy resources. It may, for example, involve technological or innovative development leading to greater efficiency in production processes. It may involve international agreements leading to greater equity between developed and developing nations. Or, it may refer to development of societal capacity at a range of governance levels. Holling (2001, p 399) sees 'sustainable development' as a 'logical partnership' between 'sustainability' and 'development', that refers to 'the goal of fostering adaptive[1] capabilities while simultaneously creating opportunities'.

In Australia, the term Ecologically Sustainable Development (ESD) is commonly used. In the discussion process on sustainable development set up by the Federal Government in the early 1990s (see 2.4.7; Diesendorf and Hamilton 1997a; Dovers 2003b; Downes 1996), the participating environmental groups lobbied strongly for use of this term. They were concerned that without this ecological focus the term 'sustainable development' would be seen as referring to *economically* sustainable development and the environment would have a minor role (Harris and Throsby 1998).

While some may use the term 'sustainability' simply to avoid use of 'development', others give different meanings to sustainability and sustainable development, suggesting that they are sequential stages in a process. Sustainability refers to the ultimate goal or destination while sustainable development is the framework and path through which sustainability is achieved. This is controversial and is discussed further in Section 2.10.

There has been a trend towards use of the term 'sustainability', but we will use the terms interchangeably in this book.

We turn now to examine briefly the conceptual development of 'sustainability'. This provides an avenue for understanding the intentions behind the concept. Why did it emerge? How did it develop over time? And, what were the key international and Australian processes that facilitated this development and adoption of the concept?

---

1   See 2.9.2.

2.4 Development and adoption of the concept of sustainability

The Brundtland report,[2] *Our Common Future* (WCED 1987), is generally regarded as the catalyst that put 'sustainable development' on the agendas of governments and businesses around the world. However, as discussed by Blutstein (2003), Gończ et al (2007) and Rogers et al (2008), the origins of the *concepts* of sustainable development and sustainability can be traced back to much earlier sources. The terms have been linked to the idea of 'sustainable yield' used in relation to biological resources such as forests, fisheries or game animals, but this is far more limited a concept than sustainable development (Dryzek 2005).

In what follows some of the key milestones in the development of these concepts are discussed, focusing on international developments from the early 1970s.

2.4.1 United Nations (UN) Conference on the Human Environment

The UN Conference on the Human Environment held in Stockholm in 1972 is a useful place to start our discussion on the conceptual development of sustainability. It put environmental issues onto the international agenda for the first time and initiated the establishment of the United Nations Environment Programme (UNEP) (Dresner 2008). The conference focused on the link between environmental problems and economic development, and Brenton (1994, p 37) notes that it 'was the first high-profile political attempt to draw the developing countries into international discussion of environmental issues'. This drew out a critical tension between developing (third world) and developed (first world) countries. Developing nations saw current environmental problems as mainly due to industrial pollution from the developed world. In contrast the main problems facing the developing world were poverty-related and the solution to this lay in economic development. Developing nations feared that this emphasis on industrial pollution may put a brake on their desperately needed economic development. It was this vexed nexus between economic development and the environment that was later addressed by the Brundtland report in the context of 'sustainable development'. For this reason the 1972 Stockholm conference has considerable relevance in the history of the sustainability debate.

This discussion linking environment and development occurred at the same time as a widespread and controversial debate on limits to growth emerged. These two strands came together to influence the development of the concept of sustainability.

2.4.2 Limits to Growth

The publication of *Limits to Growth* (Meadows et al 1972) was an important milestone in discussion on human and environmental futures. Its key message was that within the next 100 years, if current trends continued, the world's integrated human and natural systems would 'overshoot and collapse' as a result of population growth and consumption of resources. This book was a publication of the Club of Rome, an influential group of business people, statespeople, scientists and others, brought together by Aurelio Peccei, a leading Italian industrialist. While the ecologist and environmentalist Paul Ehrlich (Ehrlich and Ehrlich 1972) and others had earlier delivered similar messages, the prominence of the Club of Rome ensured that the *Limits to Growth* received much wider circulation and critical

---

2   Called after the Chair of the Commission, Gro Harlem Brundtland, then Prime Minister of Norway.

attention (see for example, Cole et al 1973). These messages of 'limits' were precursors to aspects of sustainability thinking.

As put by Mitcham (1995, p 315), the 'shift from emphasising what *should not* be done to stressing what *should* and can be done is constituted by the shift from a discussion of "limits to growth" to "sustainable development". This shift in the framework of the discussion was decidedly initiated by two other reports'. These reports were the World Conservation Strategy (1980) and the Brundtland report (WCED 1987).

2.4.3 The World Conservation Strategy

The World Conservation Strategy (WCS) was launched in 1980 by the IUCN (International Union for the Conservation of Nature), UNEP and WWF (then the World Wildlife Fund and now called the World Wide Fund for Nature).

The WCS was clearly focused on developing countries' need for economic development. However, it recognised 'limits' (Mitcham 1995) and stressed that development *requires* the conservation of the living resource base on which it ultimately depends. Equally, it argued that conservation will not occur unless at least minimal standards of development are met – basic needs such as food, shelter and clean water. The emphasis on *conservation* and *development* as interdependent, rather than mutually exclusive activities (as had generally been argued up until that time), was a significant turning point in the development of sustainability thinking. Indeed the term 'sustainable development' was used in the WCS and defined as 'the integration of conservation and development to ensure that modifications to the planet do indeed secure the survival and well being of all people' (IUCN et al 1980, s 1.12).

However, the WCS was not particularly politically influential, perhaps because its emphasis on environment and its foundation in environment organisations did not win support from development groups. As well, it did not suggest political and economic pathways required to bring about sustainable development (Dresner 2008).

2.4.4 The Brundtland report – 'Our Common Future'

The Brundtland report of 1987 (see 2.4) gained the political traction that the WCS lacked. Its definition of sustainable development remains the most widely quoted – '[h]umanity has the ability to make development sustainable – to ensure that it meets the needs of the present without compromising the ability of future generations to meet their own needs' (WCED 1987, p 8). This report built on the WCS in 're-emphasising the shift in terms of discussion from limits to sustainability' (Mitcham 1995, p 317).

Why did the Brundtland report gain such high political acceptance? As discussed below (see 2.6), the vagueness of its definition of sustainable development enabled its acceptance by widely differing groups and interests. Environmentalists could see their concerns being acknowledged to the extent that environmental limits were recognised, although many environmentalists were critical that it offered only weak environmental protection. Industry and development interests could accept the environmental limits because the report suggested these limits could be overcome and therefore did not put a brake on economic development (Dresner 2008). For example (WCED 1987, p 8):

'The concept of sustainable development does imply limits – not absolute limits but limitations imposed by the present state of technology and social organization on environmental resources and by the ability of the biosphere to absorb the effects of human activities.

But technology and social organization can both be managed to make way for a new era of economic growth.'

The significance of the Brundtland report is that it gained widespread political support for the concept of sustainable development and as a result became the blueprint for the important second UN Conference on Environment and Development (UNCED), the Earth Summit.

2.4.5 UNCED – Second United Nations Conference on Environment and Development – The Earth Summit

The Earth Summit, which was held in June 1992 in Rio de Janeiro, essentially institutionalised the Brundtland concept of sustainable development. It promoted worldwide cooperation for a number of important international agreements (including the *Framework Convention on Climate Change* and the *Convention on Biological Diversity*) and the development of a worldwide partnership in planning for environmental protection and social and economic development. It also framed the environment as a vital partner and an essential component of economic development, thus promulgating the key messages of the Brundtland report. Actions required to accomplish these objectives are contained in a number of documents, including the *Rio Declaration* (1992) which contained 27 principles to guide governments towards sustainable development and *Agenda 21* (UNCED 1992), which set out an action plan for the 21st century encompassing the goals for global sustainable development (see Dresner 2008; Thomas 2007). It is notable however, that tension between developing and developed countries that was evident at the first UN conference in Stockholm remained, and the wording in these documents was modified to ensure scope for development would not be sidelined by environmental concerns (Dresner 2008).

Nevertheless, in the 20 years between the Stockholm and Rio conferences, environmental issues assumed a central place in world political and economic debate (Bhaskar and Glyn 1995). Indeed Dresner (2008, p 48) sees the significance of the Earth Summit as 'the emergence of *global environment* as a major issue in international politics', and says that 'Rio was a major political event in a way in which Stockholm had not been'. The latter is clear from the fact that while two national leaders (Sweden and India) attended Stockholm, over one hundred were in Rio, which, at the time, was the largest ever gathering of Heads of Government.

The discussion above has provided insight into the development and meaning of the concept of sustainability from the First UN Conference on the Human Environment in 1972 to the Second UN Conference on Environment and Development in 1992. It has shown that concern about limits to growth, and tension between economic development and environmental protection, were strong driving forces. This meant that a way to jointly achieve economic development and environmental protection was required. It also shows that social aspects were of concern – achieving greater equity both between the world's peoples now and between these and future generations was required. This led to sustainability being emphasised as a concept concerned with integrating these goals.

2.4.6 Key developments since the Earth Summit

Since the Earth Summit international discussions on sustainability have continued, particularly through the work of the UN. In 1992 the UN established the Commission on Sustainable Development to monitor and promote implementation of the UNCED agreements (Osborn and Bigg 1998) and set in train five year reviews of this progress by the UN

General Assembly meeting in Special Session. The 10 year review was the 2002 UN World Summit on Sustainable Development (WSSD) held in Johannesburg. Its focus was on eradicating poverty through sustainable development, whereas the 1992 Earth Summit focused more on *environmental* sustainability (Rogers et al 2008). The WSSD's focus on poverty eradication built on the Millennium Development Goals (MDGs) set by the UN General Assembly at its Millennium Summit held in 2000.[3]

Linked to the potential for achievement of the MDGs, is the work of the UN-initiated Millennium Ecosystem Assessment (MEA). As already mentioned in Chapter 1 (also see Box 2.5), the MEA report in 2005[4] painted a bleak picture of loss of natural capital as a result of human actions and noted that 'the ability of the planet's ecosystems to sustain future generations can no longer be taken for granted'.[5] The report also noted that turning these trends around requires significant changes in policies, institutions and practices, and that these are not currently underway.

Despite the international progress made on fostering sustainability via these formal international agreements for action, progress has been slow. The very different situations of developing and developed countries adds to the complexity of implementing the necessary changes to move towards sustainability outcomes. This is well demonstrated by difficulties in getting agreement on reducing greenhouse gas emissions through the Kyoto Protocol (see 4.7) with the relative responsibilities of developed and developing countries an important issue (Dresner 2008).

In addition, since the 2002 Summit the international focus has to some extent shifted away from broad sustainability outcomes. Concern about anthropogenic climate change increased considerably following release of the Intergovernmental Panel on Climate Change's Fourth Assessment Report (IPCC 2007) and much of the international focus turned to this issue. However, in mid-2008 the international focus was influenced by the emergence of the global financial crisis. It is too early to predict the outcome of this on environmental and sustainability issues.

2.4.7 Developments in Australia

Australia was a fairly early player in addressing sustainability, with the Federal Government starting a comprehensive and multi-stakeholder discussion process in 1990 (see 2.3; Diesendorf and Hamilton 1997a; Dovers 2003b; Harris and Throsby 1998). This resulted in a *National Strategy for Ecologically Sustainable Development* (CoA 1992a) which was adopted by all levels of government (Thomas 2007) and 500 recommendations relating to a range of sectors (agriculture, industry and so on) and cross-sectoral issues (see CoA 1992b). However, there was no institutional means established to drive implementation and a lack of leadership from the Federal Government when Paul Keating replaced Bob Hawke as Prime Minister in late 1991 (Dovers 2003b).

Institutionalisation of sustainability principles in policies and legislation was further promoted by the signing of the Intergovernmental Agreement on the Environment (IGAE) (CoA 1992c) by all three levels of government (national, State and local) in 1992 (see 4.5.2). The IGAE included principles of sustainability (see 2.7). Consequently, from 1992 these principles have been incorporated into environmental and natural resource legislation and

---

3   See UN Millennium Development Goals website: <www.un.org/millenniumgoals/> (accessed 19 November 2008).

4   <www.millenniumassessment.org/en/index.aspx> (accessed 19 November 2008).

5   Quote from <www.millenniumassessment.org/en/About.aspx#1> (accessed 20 March 2009).

policy by all levels of government. There clearly was an increased awareness of sustainability and actions towards its application as a result of the ESD discussion process, the *National Strategy for ESD* and the IGAE, and many public and private sector organisations have developed environmental or sustainability policies and plans based on this Strategy and the IGAE principles (Thomas 2007).

Recently the federal House of Representatives Standing Committee on Environment and Heritage (CoA 2007a) carried out an Inquiry into a Sustainability Charter and recommended that the Parliament of Australia should establish a Sustainability Commission headed by a Sustainability Commissioner. The Commission should have a range of roles including: defining what sustainability means for Australia; creating an aspirational Sustainability Charter with objectives and milestones; evaluating progress towards meeting national sustainability goals and targets and reporting on this to both Houses of Federal Parliament; plus a range of inquiry and influencing roles. The Standing Committee also recommended that the Australian Government should take a leadership role in advancing sustainability through assessing existing and future policy against the proposed Sustainability Charter, and through the use of monetary and non-monetary incentives for governments, industry and the community in advancing sustainability outcomes. It is these actions that many hoped to see after the launch of the *National Strategy for ESD* in 1992. However, to date (late 2008) the recommendations of the Standing Committee have not been adopted.

2.5 Sustainability as an integrating concept

It is now generally accepted that sustainability requires integration of economic, social and environmental factors. Meeting environmental criteria in a society which fails to meet economic and social goals concerning justice and equity does not qualify as sustainability. This tripartite nature of sustainability has often been shown diagrammatically as in Figure 2.1.

This figure contrasts two interpretations of the nature of this tripartite relationship. In Figure 2.1(a) a weak form of sustainability is shown and represented by the area of overlap between the social, economic and ecological circles. It has been argued that this over-emphasises the social and economic factors at the expense of the environment. In contrast, the depiction in Figure 2.1(b) shows a stronger version of sustainability since it gives primacy to the ecological aspects and assumes that our social framework is constructed within the ecological reality and the economic factors are a sub-set within this social framework (Lowe cited in Harding 1996, p 182).

An earlier definition of the terms 'weak' and 'strong' sustainability came from Pearce (1993) in relation to maintenance of 'capital' as a key requirement for sustainability, and the substitutability of different forms of capital (see Box 2.2).

The term 'triple bottom line' was introduced by British consultant John Elkington in 1994 to link sustainability to language familiar to business. Sustainability meant linking the bottom line of profits or economic performance with the need to now also meet environmental and social bottom lines (Elkington 1998). More recently a fourth or quadruple bottom line has been added in response to a series of events that drew attention to failure by businesses to address the social bottom line. For example, protests against Shell for its treatment of local people affected by its oil operations in Nigeria, was one such event (Livesey 2001). Another was the Enron scandal in the United States (Bala 2008). The quadruple bottom line concerns corporate governance and creating an internal culture in business that encourages ethical behaviour (Bala 2008; Foran et al 2004). To give emphasis to social factors, the term

Figure 2.1 Diagrammatic representation of the tripartite nature of sustainability, contrasting a weak and strong sustainability interpretation

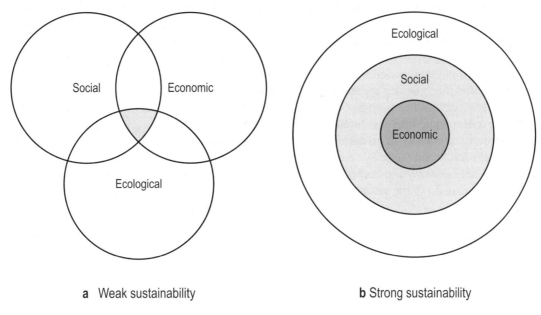

a Weak sustainability   **b** Strong sustainability

Source: Ian Lowe, cited in Harding (1996).

Corporate Social Responsibility (CSR) became shorthand for sustainability by businesses (Holliday et al 2002).

Accepting the need for integration of social, environmental and economic factors in addressing sustainability problems is one thing, but achieving it is proving challenging (see 2.2 above). As indicated in 2.1 above, sustainability requires new approaches and methods for addressing problems. For example, Robinson (2004, p 378) suggests that what is needed is a 'form of transdisciplinary[6] thinking that focuses on the connections among fields as much as on the contents of those fields; that involves the development of new concepts, methods and tools that are integrative and synthetic, not disciplinary and analytic; and that actively creates synergy, not just summation'.

Box 2.2: The 'constant capital' requirement for sustainability

An economic approach to exploring the nature of sustainability involves seeing sustainability as the maintenance of a constant level of 'capital' between generations. That is, we need to pass on to succeeding generations an equivalent stock of capital to that we have inherited.

This leads to the question – 'What type of capital?' Capital may include natural capital (natural resources both living and non-living); human capital (accumulated knowledge, skills and culture); and built capital (stock of infrastructure and machines made by humans).

A critical question is 'How substitutable are these forms of capital for one another?' That is, is it in keeping with sustainability, for natural capital to be lost but the income from this loss to be used to develop built or human capital? For example, depleting natural capital by clearing a forest, and using the income from sale of the wood and the land to build a factory (ie develop built capital).

---

6   See 6.3.4 for discussion of transdisciplinary knowledge.

There has been much discussion on this question and two contrasting positions have been identified (Neumayer 2003; Pearce 1993, pp 16–17).

The 'weak sustainability' position sees no special place for the environment. All forms of capital are substitutable for one another and the form in which we pass on capital does not matter. Hence we can deplete the environment and ecological assets so long as we offset this by passing on an increased capital stock of human or built capital.

The 'strong sustainability' position denies the equivalence of all forms of capital, maintaining that many ecological assets are essential to human survival. For example, ecological functions such as the cycling of elements, including nitrogen, phosphorus and carbon. In the context of the capital substitutability debate these constitute 'critical natural capital'.

Hence the strong sustainability position requires that as a minimum we protect critical natural capital and this may be set in a broader rule that the overall stock of natural capital should not be allowed to decline (Pearce 1993). These positions of strong and weak sustainability are linked to the value positions people hold as discussed in Chapter 3.

The discussion so far has focused on how the concept of sustainability has evolved, but as the next section demonstrates, considerable difficulties remain in its interpretation and application.

2.6 Multiple interpretations of sustainability

The concept of sustainability has been progressively included in policy and legislation around the world over the past 20 years. It has been much discussed and a search of the World Wide Web (the 'web') reveals a vast array of definitions of the term, yet we seem no closer to reaching agreement on its exact meaning, nor how it should be implemented. We will start with an example of the difficulty in implementing a broad definition of sustainability.

Taking the widely quoted definition of sustainable development from the Brundtland report that we should meet 'the needs of the present without compromising the ability of future generations to meet their own needs' (see 2.4.4) and thinking about applying this definition to carrying out a task, such as planning a new suburb and its infrastructure, quickly reveals the problems in interpreting what is required (see Box 2.3).

Box 2.3: Difficulty in applying the Brundtland definition of sustainable development

Imagine you are a planner given the task of applying the Brundtland definition of sustainable development to planning a new suburb and its infrastructure. Considering this definition is likely to provide you with more questions than answers.

For example, what exactly are the 'needs of the present' (rather than 'wants' or 'desires')? Whose needs should you consider? Those of the potential occupants of the suburb? Those from a wider group of society who will be impacted either directly or indirectly by the way in which you choose to meet the needs? If so, how do you decide the boundaries for this wider group? What means can you use to discern these needs? Within either of these groups are you likely to find agreement on their needs?

How can we know future generations' needs? Surely what these may be will depend on a range of factors including: technological change and its socio-cultural context into the future. Change in both of these areas has evolved rapidly and is likely to continue to do so.

Can we confidently predict what the environmental impacts of the new suburb and its infra-structure will be over the short and longer terms and how these will be judged in relation to sustainability? How may social factors influence the environmental impacts? And so on.

It is clear that the answers to the questions raised in Box 2.3, and many other relevant questions, rest not only on scientific knowledge, which is likely to be incomplete or even non-existent, and which to varying extents is socially constructed, but also on value judgments on matters such as quality of life. It is therefore not surprising that the concept of sustainability has produced so many interpretations and so much controversy.

The very open-ended nature of the Brundtland definition is both a strength and a weakness for EDM (Jamieson 1998; Robinson 2004). Weakness comes from the lack of precision in the definition, since those lacking precise guidelines may place the application of the concept in the too hard basket and opt for business as usual. Or, indeed, may use this ambiguity to deliberately avoid taking hard decisions to improve environmental and social performance. This weakness also provides for a more active response with interest groups steering the interpretation of sustainability in ways most favourable to their views. For example: 'environmentalists might try to build in a respect for intrinsic values in nature' and 'Third World advocates would stress the need for global redistribution' (Dryzek 2005, p 146).

However, the ambiguity of the term may also be a strength, since people and groups with very different value systems or with very different living conditions, are able to provide variable interpretations that meet their own situations. In this sense sustainability can play a powerful role as a 'boundary object' (Star and Griesemer 1989) where different institutions (governments, organisations, businesses) and individuals are able to work together constructively despite their varied values.

Despite this potential strength, it is important to avoid the weaknesses identified above. This is why the principles of sustainability, which we explore next, are so important, because they provide further guidance for implementation, while still leaving room for values-based interpretation.

2.7 Principles of sustainability

To provide clearer guidance on applying the concept of sustainability, principles have been developed by many international bodies, by nations, and by organisations. These principles provide a set of statements or propositions that act as a basis for conduct and as a guide to action (*Oxford English Dictionary Online*). They are aimed at achieving particular objectives and direct our efforts towards these.

There are now many sets of principles developed by different groups but the common elements shared by most include:

Equity – which is about fairness and has been further defined as follows (Falk et al 1993, pp 2–5):

Equity derives from a concept of social justice. It represents a belief that there are things which people should have, that there are basic needs that should be fulfilled, that burdens and rewards should not be spread too divergently across the community, and that policy should be directed with impartiality, fairness and justice towards these ends.

Equity is not *necessarily* the same as equality. While equity does suggest equality of opportunity among all individuals (Rawls 1972), it does not *necessarily* imply equality beyond that. In other words, equity is a value-laden concept and may be interpreted as meaning *adequate* standards (as suggested in the quote above) or *equal* standards.

In relation to sustainability it is important to consider equity over different time scales. We may consider equity between current and future generations (intergenerational equity) and also among people on Earth at any one time (intragenerational equity).

Intergenerational equity is about 'fairness' between generations. It sees the occupants of planet Earth at any time as having a responsibility to maintain or enhance the health, diversity and productivity of the environment for future generations. This means that we should not pass on the negative impacts of development produced by this or past generations, to future generations. This principle recognises that while we cannot pass on the same stock of non-renewable resources to future generations, we should deliver a planet that offers at least as many physical, ecological, social and economic opportunities as were available to previous generations (see Box 2.2).

Intragenerational equity is about fairness among the current generation. It recognises the highly disproportionate share of resources and opportunities among the peoples of the world at present, and calls for the eradication of poverty, and a fairer share of access to resources. As well, the burdens of environmental problems are disproportionately borne by the poorer and weaker members of society. Not all members of society have equal opportunity to influence decision-making. Knowledge, skills, power and access through the structures of decision-making are not equally shared. Hence intragenerational equity concerns both equity within and between nations and is linked to the concept of environmental justice (see Box 2.4).

Box 2.4: Environmental justice

Environmental justice emerged in the 1980s as a grassroots social movement[7] in the United States, to protest against the siting of toxic waste disposal and hazardous and polluting industries in areas primarily occupied by minority ethnic groups. The movement began with a strong racial dimension with coloured people claiming that they were affected by environmental hazards far more than whites, and gained its success through 'linking environment, labour and social justice into a master frame through which to communicate claims and clarify goals and grievances to others' (Agyeman et al 2003, p 7). Many studies have since shown that both minority and low income groups in the United States have typically borne a disproportionate share of negative environmental impacts (Hamilton 2006; Peterson et al 2007), and research shows a similar situation in the United Kingdom (ESRC 2001).

However, this 1980s United States concept of environmental justice is about more than unfair distribution of environmental impacts. It also involved recognition of the diversity and cultural identity of affected communities, and need to enable meaningful participation in the development, implementation and enforcement of environmental laws, regulations and policies (Schlosberg 2004).

---

7   A social movement refers to 'an association or set of associations organized around a common interest that seeks to influence collective outcomes without obtaining authoritative offices of government' (Dryzek et al 2003, p 2). Social movements include the women's movement, gay rights movement, and the environmental movement. Environmentalism describes the environmental movement. Note however, that it is hard to get agreement on a precise definition of 'social movement'.

This broader interpretation acknowledges that not all disproportionate exposure to negative environmental conditions is a deliberate action against minorities and the poor. Rather, that in the United States such groups typically lack the ability and access to power elites that enable wealthier and non-coloured groups to prevent location of hazardous facilities in their neighbourhoods and to ensure enforcement of environmental laws (Roberts 2007).

The environmental justice movement has had success in the United States (Agyeman et al 2003), with President Clinton establishing an office of environmental justice as part of the EPA (Jamieson 2007) and in 1994 signing an Executive Order that 'all communities and individuals, regardless of economic status or race are entitled to a safe and healthy environment' (Roberts 2007, p 289). However, implementing the order has proved difficult due to its vague nature and claims by industry that it will hinder provision of employment to the areas and groups claiming injustice (Roberts 2007).

The concept of environmental justice has expanded from exposure to local pollution to encompass a much wider range of injustices (Roberts 2007). For example, equity in per capita access to use of the world's environmental resources, encapsulated in the concepts of 'environmental space' and 'ecological footprint' (see Chapter 1). Also, 'ecological debt', referring to the historic over-appropriation of local and global resources by developed countries leaving damaged environments in developing countries, and global impacts such as depletion of the stratospheric ozone layer and the build up of greenhouse gases in the atmosphere (Blewitt 2008; Byrne et al 2002; ESRC 2001; McLaren 2003). To date the primary contributors to this global pollution have been developed countries, and while all nations share the impacts, the developing countries may be less equipped to cope. These examples also show that environmental justice now embraces injustices between nations and between generations. Further examples come from the appropriation of Indigenous people's knowledge about the natural environment and use by outsiders of their local flora or fauna for commercial purposes, referred to as 'biopiracy' (see 6.4.2.3).

Whilst the discussion above makes it clear that environmental justice holds an important place in moving towards sustainability, there are situations in which policies to address *environmental* sustainability matters may be regressive and may have greatest impact on the already disadvantaged members of societies. This is a controversial and complex issue (see Serret and Johnstone 2006) which is well illustrated by the present attempts to move to a carbon constrained economy.

Conservation of biological diversity and ecological integrity – are concepts concerned with the maintenance of the diversity of life on Earth and of the processes which link these life forms and the non-living components of Earth's systems into healthy functioning and productive ecosystems. We are dependent on these 'free processes of nature' for maintaining hydrological cycles and water quality; preventing land degradation; cycling essential elements such as nitrogen, phosphorus and carbon; breaking down pollutants into less harmful forms; and for the flow of energy through ecosystems. These processes underpin the production of our food, fibres and other components of nature that yield human well-being and are known as ecosystem services (see Box 2.5). They may be regarded as 'critical natural capital' (see Box 2.2).

Box 2.5: Ecosystem services

Ecosystem services are 'the benefits people obtain from ecosystems' (MEA 2005a, p v). The United Nation's Millennium Ecosystem Assessment (MEA) distinguishes four types of ecosystem services:

- *provisioning* – food, genetic resources, fresh water, timber, fibre, fuel;

- *regulating* – influencing climate, floods, erosion, disease, wastes, water purification, pollination;

- *cultural* – aesthetic, spiritual, recreational, educational;

- *supporting* – nutrient cycling, soil formation, photosynthesis.

These together provide for human well-being and indeed for human survival.

The MEA found rapid and escalating change to the world's ecosystems over the past 50 years (MEA 2005a). While these changes have provided for human well-being and economic development, this has come at the cost of degradation of many ecosystem services. The MEA found that 60 per cent of the 24 ecosystem services examined are being degraded or used unsustainably, and this degradation could intensify considerably over the next 50 years. Indeed, we are squandering our natural capital (see Box 2.2). As well, many of the impacts of degradation have led to increased poverty for the world's poor – an environmental injustice (see Box 2.4).

While the notion of nature providing services for human needs is not new, the term ecosystem services has received increasing attention recently (de Groot et al 2002; Irwin and Raganathan 2007), along with the concept of 'natural capital'. In both cases this reflects a growing recognition of the economic value of nature's services, the cost of loss of these services, and the need to appropriately value them. An independent report for the Australian Government noted the high economic value of ecosystem services to Australia. For example, the value of pollination to Australian agriculture is $1.2 billion per year (PMSEIC 2002). The cost to Australian agriculture from loss of ecosystem services was calculated at around $1.2 billion per year, and environmental repair at $2 to $6 billion per year (compared to an annual production value of $25 billion). The report also noted the very high costs of repair to damaged ecosystem services. For example, estimates of the repair bill for salinity and water logging resulting from removal of vegetation that regulated groundwater flow, range between $20 and $65 billion over 10 years depending on what aspects of salinity are included (PMSEIC 2002). The report concluded that *maintaining* natural systems is far cheaper than paying to repair damaged ecosystems or bearing the costs of lost ecosystem benefits.

One important reason for loss of ecosystem services is the lack of incentives for their protection by landholders. For example, there may be advantages for a landholder in converting native forested land into annual cropping, since the harvested crop enters the market and brings income (at least in the short term), while the native forest cover which protects soil from erosion, provides biodiversity, and clean water flow to rivers, brings no income for these services. There are a range of techniques that may be used to redress this lack of incentive to protect non-marketed ecosystem services (see Irwin and Ranganathan 2007). One such idea that is gaining currency internationally (Irwin and Ranganathan 2007; MEA 2005) and within Australia (Hatfield-Dodds 2006; Wentworth Group 2003; Young et al 2003), is to pay farmers to support ecosystem services beyond a defined publicly expected level of stewardship or duty of care.

The precautionary principle – aims to *anticipate* serious or irreversible environmental harm and hence reverses earlier modes of operation that waited for clear evidence of harm before taking preventive action.

There are many examples where it has not been appropriate to wait until damage is demonstrated since by then it is too late to ameliorate the problem. Classic examples are the impacts of asbestos fibres on human health; the build up of greenhouse gases in the atmosphere leading to climate change; the impact of certain chemicals on ecosystems.

We explore the precautionary principle in detail in Chapter 9.

Integration of environmental, economic and social aspects in decision-making – as discussed in Section 2.5, this principle says that these three pillars of sustainability must support one another. Policy decisions that provide desired economic outcomes at the expense of environmental degradation or increasing social inequity are not in line with sustainability. For example, allowing location of high impact industries in poorer parts of a city is likely to impose risks disproportionately on the poorer members of society. In relation to this principle, an economic approach to such a situation, involves internalisation of environmental costs into the value of assets and services. This means that those who generate pollution or other negative impacts through production of goods or providing a service should bear the cost of curtailing that pollution. Such pollution may impose costs, known as externalities, on people directly, or indirectly through environmental damage or harm to human health. This approach requires the challenging and controversial task of evaluating environmental or social assets (see Hargroves and Smith 2005; Rogers et al 2008).

However, environmental *protection* measures that lead to perverse social justice outcomes or increased poverty are also not sustainable. For example, attempts to reduce carbon dioxide emissions from transport typically focus on increasing fuel costs. This may disproportionately impact on the poor who, for reasons of cost, may live on the fringe of spread-out cities with poor public transport. This leaves little option but to use private transport for essential travel. Higher fuel costs also raise the prices of essential domestic goods such as food.

This principle is applicable on a wide range of scales, from local to global. At the global level it requires a strengthening of international cooperation. It also requires that we consider the impacts of policy decisions across these various spatial scales. What are the possible wider impacts on sustainability outcomes from a particular local or national decision? And what are the possible impacts of global policy decisions on national situations?

Public participation – recognising that environmental decisions typically involve social values and may entail risks. It is important therefore that those who live with the consequences of environmental decisions should have the opportunity to express their values and engage in discussion about the type of future they want (Robinson 2004). Those who bear the risks from environmental decisions should also be involved in making those decisions. This links closely with the intragenerational equity principle. It has been suggested that we should also be concerned with giving future generations a seat at the table in decision-making that involves important *inter*generational consequences. This could be done by appointing representatives of future generations (Weiss 1990).We explore the ideas and practices of public participation further in Chapter 7.

2.7.1 Other sets of sustainability principles

Six common elements of sustainability principles are highlighted above, but it is important to note that other principles have been proposed, reflecting the main interests of the proponents. Also, the key elements identified above may be packaged in different ways to encompass similar intents (see for example Diesendorf 1997; Dovers 2005a, pp 95–97).

For example, the WCED (1987, pp 363–367) at the close of its final meeting issued the Tokyo Declaration which included a set of principles to guide the policy actions of nations as they attempted to integrate sustainable development into their goals. These principles reflected a strong emphasis on the plight of developing nations and the poor of the world.

In contrast, the Natural Step principles developed in Sweden by an international group of scientists led by Dr Karl-Henrik Robèrt, one of Sweden's foremost cancer physicians and scientists, are based on scientific understanding (see Box 2.6).

Box 2.6: Natural Step sustainability principles

The Natural Step (TNS) sustainability principles are based on the premise that the accumulated impacts of industrial human society are damaging nature and altering life-supporting structures and functions in three ways. Accordingly three *system conditions* are identified as necessary if we are to maintain the Earth's essential structures and processes that sustain human well-being. A fourth necessary system condition recognises the role of social and economic factors that influence the human treatment of the environment, and the capacity of humans to meet their basic needs. The four system conditions are reworded as *principles of sustainability* as follows:

To become a sustainable society we must:

1. Eliminate our contribution to the progressive buildup of substances extracted from the Earth's crust (eg heavy metals which get into food chains and are toxic; fossil fuels, that when burnt release the greenhouse gas – carbon dioxide).

2. Eliminate our contribution to the progressive buildup of chemicals and compounds produced by society (eg DDT and PCBs[8] that are not produced in nature, are harmful to organisms and/or humans, and that may accumulate in food chains).

3. Eliminate our contribution to the progressive physical degradation and destruction of nature and natural processes (eg overfishing, removing important wildlife habitat for urban settlements or agriculture).

4. Eliminate our contribution to conditions that undermine people's capacity to meet their basic needs (eg unsafe working conditions, unfair trade arrangements).

These principles are set within a *framework* that enables organisations or communities to strategically plan their activities to meet sustainability outcomes. The TNS framework has been

---

8   Polychlorinated biphenyls (PCBs) are human-made chlorinated hydrocarbons that have been used in a range of industrial and commercial applications. They have a long life in the environment and can move long distances in air or water, entering food chains. They can cause cancer and a number of other health effects in humans (see US EPA website <www.epa.gov/epawaste/hazard/tsd/pcbs/pubs/about. htm> (accessed 2 May 2009). DDT is also a human-made substance used as a pesticide and similarly with properties of long life in the environment, build up in food chains, and detrimental effects on humans and other organisms.

used by major corporations around the world and a number of countries have TNS offices that promulgate use of the framework.

Source: The Natural Step website: <www.naturalstep.org>
(accessed 28 December 2008).

We have attempted to tease out the meanings of sustainability through exploring its conceptual development, its nature as an integrating concept, and some of the principles developed to guide its application. We turn now to explore briefly the implementation of sustainability.

2.8 Implementing sustainability

Putting sustainability principles into practice needs to occur at all levels from the international to the individual. This is neatly summed up by the common saying – 'think global, act local'.

However, there are differing views as to whether sustainability is best driven from the bottom up, involving individuals, communities and local government, or the top down, involving international agreements and organisations, and national and state governments (Brown 2008). It seems likely that we will be most effective in embracing sustainability, and seeing evidence for this through implementation, when the drivers come from both directions and bring with them all levels and sectors in between. As we have seen through the earlier discussion in this chapter, sustainability is a complex concept that requires an integrative approach. It also requires an adaptive management framework (see 2.9.4), resilience thinking (see 2.9.2), and educated communities that understand the issues and have the capacity and willingness to contribute to solutions (see 6.2). Such approaches will not occur unless all institutions, levels of governance and communities come together in defining problems, devising solutions and acting on them in a coordinated manner. Given this it is best to leave discussion of implementation by governments, governance organisations and various non-government organisations, communities and individuals to the chapters that introduce the relevant institutions and actors – namely, Chapter 4 on Institutions and Chapter 5 on Actors. In this chapter we will provide an hierarchical framework to show the guiding concepts, frameworks, tools and policies, strategies and actions that influence implementation of sustainability.

2.9 An implementation hierarchy

Interpretation and implementation of sustainability take place at a number of levels ranging from broad aspirational statements or visions of a sustainable society, to more explicit principles and objectives for achieving sustainability, through to specific actions on the ground. Figure 2.2 is an attempt to illustrate such a hierarchy. It draws on similar work by James and Lahti (2004) and Dovers (2005a).

Levels 1 to 3 cover a hierarchy of concepts, principles, frameworks and tools that tease out the meaning of, and means to move towards, sustainability. Level 4 brings the components of the upper levels together in a structured manner to address particular sustainability problems. That is, through policies, strategies and actions.

Figure 2.2 Hierarchy for interpreting and implementing sustainability approaches

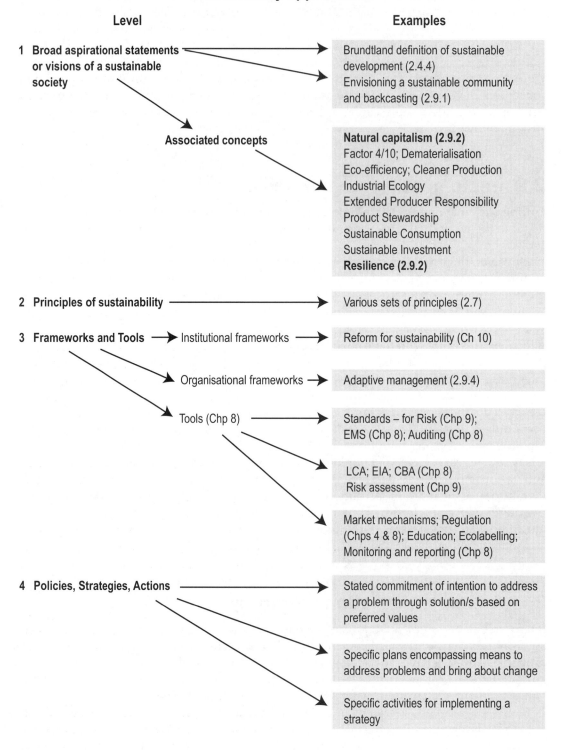

The figure provides a useful structure for the following discussion which attempts to briefly schematise the *types* of approaches for interpreting, informing and implementing sustainability approaches. However, with a matter as complex as sustainability, any such attempt to structure this information in a figure or table is unlikely to be clear-cut. Rather, messy boundaries between the levels are common. For example, 'frameworks' and 'tools' have been combined as level 3, in acknowledgment that some of the approaches included there such as the standards for risk management (see Chapter 9) and for Environmental Management Systems (EMS) (see Chapter 8) do provide both a framework that may be applied at an organisational level, as well as tools for assessment and understanding of environmental impacts. In what follows we will move down the hierarchy from the broad and aspirational to the more specific in levels 1 to 3, and then to the implementation through policies, strategies and actions in level 4, briefly discussing examples from each level and where appropriate making linkages to other chapters where more detailed discussion of an example occurs.

2.9.1 Broad aspirational statements/visions

Brundtland definition – starting at level 1, the Brundtland definition of sustainable development which provides a broad aspirational statement (see 2.4.4), aptly matches this level. So too does the exercise of developing visions of future sustainable outcomes.

Envisioning – this approach takes a statement (such as the Brundtland definition) or set of principles regarding sustainability, and based on these a vision of a preferred future sustainable state is developed. This envisioning exercise may apply at many levels, from a state or region, through to a city, community, organisation, sector (such as agriculture), issue (such as addressing anthropogenic climate change), or even an individual. It will typically provide much more detail than a simple statement or definition. For example, for an urban settlement a number of elements may be outlined, that when integrated will provide a sustainable urban system. Elements considered may include: How will energy (power) be provided? What will be the design of settlements? How will this relate to access to work, goods and services and recreation? And what transport provision and modes of transport will be used to assist this access? And so on. Once the characteristics of that future sustainable state are defined, backcasting can be used to design one, or a number, of paths for reaching it. Backcasting works back from the desired sustainable state and goals to the present to determine feasible paths for their achievement (Robinson 2003). That is, scenarios are developed showing alternative ways of reaching the vision. The scenarios include both scientific and socio-economic analysis necessary to understand the requirements and possible barriers to achieve the envisioned state, and can reveal trade-offs that may be required (Robinson 2003).

Envisioning sustainable futures has now been undertaken at many levels and for many sectors. We will use one illustrative example here, the Georgia Basin Futures Project, which envisions a sustainable future for a region located in western Canada (see Box 2.7).

Box 2.7: **Envisioning a sustainable region – Georgia Basin, Canada**
The Georgia Basin Futures Project (GBFP) was a major five year research project involving a range of partners. The project combined expert knowledge (see 6.3) and considered opinion of community members to develop and analyse the implications of scenarios of economic,

ecological and social transitions in the Basin over a 40 year period, that would result in lowered ecological impacts and enhanced human well-being (Robinson 2003).

Considerable focus was placed on development of a 'fun-to-use' modelling tool (GB-QUEST) that enabled people (including lay community members) to develop and explore feasibility and desirability of alternative sustainability scenarios of the future.[9] In contrast to typical backcasting exercises, the QUEST model runs forward through time and leaves the user to compare its outcomes with their desired future state for the region. They then change their inputs and examine trade-offs until reaching their preferred scenario path to the desired outcome. It also allows the desired future state to be modified depending on the consequences of the various paths identified and trade-offs involved. Indeed 'the desired future is a product of the process of trying to reach it' (Robinson 2003, p 849). This does not mean that the process starts without specific goals, but simply that they may be modified through the learning process of examining paths to the ends and their consequences. This is seen by some as highly desirable for addressing sustainability which is 'a product of a social learning process that is inherently open and unpredictable' (Robinson 2003, p 854).

The involvement of citizens in this form of backcasting has a deliberate purpose. Clearly it is a transparent, inclusive process that provides for strong learning about the issue, consequences of various paths and why trade-offs may be required. In turn, this helps to provide vital social acceptability of the changes required to reach the desired sustainability outcomes. Politicians need such support to act on the necessary changes (Robinson 2003).

2.9.2 Associated concepts supporting sustainability

There are a number of concepts that are not strictly either 'broad aspirational statements' or 'principles', but are worthy of inclusion as fairly high level concepts that support a move towards sustainability. We will consider two such concepts here – 'natural capitalism' and 'resilience'.

2.9.2.1 Natural capitalism

Natural capitalism describes a new form of industrial society that sees natural capital as the limiting factor to future economic development (see Box 2.2). Natural capitalism rests on four strategies (Hawken et al 1999):

1. Major increases in the efficiency with which resources are used, thus slowing resource depletion and reducing pollution and environmental degradation. For example, the concepts of *Factor 4* (von Weizsäcker et al 1997) and *Factor 10* (Factor 10 Club 1995) urged the need for much greater efficiency in resource use and decoupling economic growth from the flow of materials and energy. Factor 4 means a 75 per cent reduction in energy and materials intensity in production and Factor 10 a 90 per cent reduction. *Dematerialisation* (Riele et al 2001), *eco-efficiency* (DeSimone and Popoff 2000; Schaltegger

---

9   Such reliance on the modelling tool may be criticised on at least two grounds. It is difficult to get the balance right between a tool that encourages use by citizens because it is fun-to-use, and one that fairly represents the complexity of the issue. Secondly, through enabling participants to modify the goals or outcomes, the process allows them to prefer unsustainable outcomes (Robinson and Tansey 2006). However, these authors suggest that since social acceptability is a significant barrier to social change, the aim of the modelling is to elicit informed preferred scenarios.

et al 2003) and *cleaner production* (UNEP undated), are each associated with increasing efficiency in resource use.

2. Biomimicry. That is, mimicking biological systems in which there is no waste but rather the continuing reuse of materials within closed cycles, and often with the elimination of toxicity. For example, *industrial ecology* (Fiksel 2006).

3. A shift from an economy resting on *goods* to one that emphasises *services* and *flows* of economic services. That is, we may pay for a *service*, such as clean floor covering for an office, rather than *purchase* carpeting. This puts pressure on the provider to find efficient ways to maintain that service with least material wastage, which in turn encourages recycling.

4. Investment in natural capital so as to sustain and restore natural systems which are the basis of natural resources and ecosystem services (see Box 2.5).

A number of associated instruments are relevant to natural capitalism. As shown in Figure 2.2 these include:

Extended Producer Responsibility (EPR) which is a concept that extends the responsibility of a producer for a product to the post-consumer stage of its life cycle. The intention is to reduce the impact on the environment from waste products, by providing a strong incentive for producers to redesign their products such that less waste remains at the end of the product's life. Waste may be reduced because parts of products may be reused (eg computer parts or car parts) or readily recycled, and because there is less packaging waste (OECD undated).

Product stewardship which is concerned with reducing the environmental impacts of a product throughout its life cycle. Responsibility is shared across the life cycle and hence may involve designers, manufacturers, distributors, retailers and consumers (Beder 2006).

A new form of industrial society that takes a whole system approach to the way in which we provide for our needs is increasingly seen as necessary if we are to move towards a more sustainable world (Hargroves and Smith 2005). The four strategies of natural capitalism outlined above are an important basis for achieving this end.

However, there is little point in making gains in production efficiencies and impacts if growth in consumption overtakes these gains, as seems to have been the case since the 1992 Earth Summit (Ryan 2005). Growth in consumption may arise from population growth and from increased per capita consumption. As well, the so-called rebound effects have been identified as an unwelcome consequence of achieving efficiencies. For example, low-energy light bulbs provide an efficiency gain. However, the lower energy costs may lead people to think that the energy cost and use is so low that lights can be left on for lengthy periods. Rebound effects may also occur when consumers use money saved through efficiency gains to purchase additional consumer goods (Voet et al 2003). Indeed, there 'is increasing evidence of rebound effects, in which improvements in efficiency actually become a stimulus for increased consumption' (Ryan 2005, p 408).

Hence there has been growing interest in the concept of *sustainable consumption* and recognition that it is a complex phenomenon, with numerous interacting factors between production and consumption, or producers and consumers, that need to be addressed in an integrated manner (Ryan 2005).

Sustainable investment which is a related concept from the finance sector concerning investment in companies that, through a selective screening process, are deemed to display characteristics that comply with ethical investment or socially responsible investment, and these increasingly include elements important for sustainability. The investment in such funds has grown rapidly since about the mid 1990s (Hargroves and Smith 2005).

2.9.2.2 Resilience

Resilience is a concept that is relevant to all sorts of systems – ecological, business, agriculture, urban settlements, industries, and particularly the relationships between these. Resilience has become an extremely relevant concept for sustainability because it refers to 'the capacity of a system to absorb disturbance and still retain its basic function and structure' (Walker and Salt 2006, p xiii). For example, the capacity of farmed land to recover from prolonged drought and continue to provide ecosystem services that underpin the farming enterprise (Walker and Salt 2006). Resilience is not a new concept and has long been used in ecology. However, it has recently gained much attention in addressing the 'wicked problems' of sustainability involving systems with strong functional cross-links, such as linked economic-social-natural systems. As such it is clear that resilience thinking requires transdisciplinary[10] approaches.

We have seen above that efficiency in production systems, and more generally in meeting human needs, has been promulgated as an important contributor to achieving sustainability. However, it has been argued that efficiency *applied alone* is not a complete solution and may indeed work against sustainability (Walker and Salt 2006). How can this be?

Business as usual approaches to sustainability typically seek to optimise delivery of goods and services through maximising production of particular components of systems and controlling others. For example, production of timber or agricultural products may be maximised in an ecosystem. Optimisation involves attempting to maintain the system in an optimal steady-state and provide for maximum efficiency in production of the targeted products. In doing so, other attributes, such as ecosystem services, which are not so readily quantified or valued, are not promoted (Walker and Salt 2006).

However, sustainability should not be represented as a steady-state equilibrium of our intertwined natural, industrial, societal, economic and political systems (Irwin and Ranganathan 2007). Rather, such systems are best seen as 'dynamic, open systems that operate far from equilibrium, exhibiting nonlinear and sometimes chaotic behaviour' (Fiksel 2006, p 16). Technological, geopolitical, and climate change, and at the time of writing (late 2008) a global financial crisis, will each disturb these cycles.[11] Change, both slow and sudden, is the norm, and extreme events rather than average conditions are often the key influence in system change. Attempts to distort this real situation, by marginalising some system components for efficiency and optimisation, increase the vulnerability of the system to change and reduce resilience (Walker and Salt 2006). Mistakes of optimising production on the basis of average or best conditions have been damaging in Australia in relation to grazing on marginal lands in the semi-arid zones of New South Wales and South Australia where drought later led to major land degradation and economic losses (Bolton 1981; Davison 2005).

It follows that the 'bottom line for sustainability is that any proposal for sustainable development that does not explicitly acknowledge a system's resilience is simply not going to keep delivering the goods (or services). The key to sustainability lies in enhancing the resilience of social-ecological systems, not optimising isolated components of the system' (Walker and Salt 2006, p 9; see also Brinsmead and Hooker 2005). This means focussing on

---

10   See 6.3.4.

11   Indeed the financial crisis is a good example of a system in which optimisimg particular outcomes and ignoring a wide range of relevant factors led to high vulnerability and low resilience.

the ability of social and ecological systems to adapt to, and benefit from, change (Irwin and Ranganathan 2007).

Resilience needs to be considered in association with the concepts of *adaptability* and *thresholds*. *Thresholds* are key crossing points in systems. If a system crosses over a threshold it will have a different structure, changed relationships between its components and will behave differently and often in an unexpected and unwelcome manner. Resilience describes the distance of a system from thresholds. The closer the system is to a threshold (low resilience) the less change is required to move it over the threshold and into a new state. That is, reduced resilience means higher vulnerability to disturbance (Resilience Alliance undated). *Adaptability* refers to the capacity of actors in a system to manage its resilience. This may involve moving the system state away from a threshold. Summing up, sustainability 'is all about knowing if and where thresholds exist and having the capacity to manage the system in relation to these thresholds' (Walker and Salt 2006, p 63).

What promotes adaptability or adaptive capacity? Diversity is generally important in influencing resilience whether we are concerned with ecological or social systems or linked ecological-social systems (see Box 2.8). For ecosystems, biodiversity and landscape diversity are important. For social systems, breadth of knowledge, stored experiences, and learning networks and institutions provide capacity for flexible problem-solving and for adaptive capacity (Resilience Alliance, undated).

Box 2.8: Diversity and resilience – coral reefs

Coral reefs have been very resilient ecosystems. Generally found in areas of high impact from tropical hurricanes, in their healthy state they have bounced back from such disturbances. However, the Caribbean coral reefs have been in sharp decline with an 80 per cent loss in hard corals over the past 30 years. These reefs have suffered many pressures associated with human activities, including sewage discharge, sediment runoff from urban development and agriculture, chemical pollution from agriculture, discharges from ships, oil spills, damage from anchors, overfishing. Recently, outbreaks of disease and coral bleaching linked to climate change have added to this list.

The Great Barrier Reef (GBR) of Australia has also suffered many of these pressures from human activities, except it has been exposed to less fishing intensity. However, to date it has not experienced the massive reef decline seen in the Caribbean. A suggested reason for this is that the GBR has a much higher species diversity. The Caribbean reefs went through species decline around 2 million years ago and have around 28 per cent of fish diversity and 14 per cent of coral diversity compared to the GBR.

Biodiversity enhances resilience through having a greater number of organisms carrying out similar functions in an ecosystem and potentially having different responses to disturbances. This increases the likelihood of essential functions continuing following disturbance, and may account for the different responses between these two reef systems to anthropogenic pressures.

Addressing issues such as the demise of the Caribbean coral reef requires lessening pressures and building resilience. This requires improving water quality and building diversity in fish species. The means for achieving this involve cross-linked social, economic and political systems. They in turn require adaptability to successfully achieve these changes.

Source of case study: Walker and Salt 2006.

2.9.3 Principles of sustainability

In terms of interpreting and addressing sustainability issues, these principles sit below the broad statements of sustainability, drilling down to provide more detailed interpretation and guidance for implementation. Section 2.7 discusses these principles and notes that there are numerous sets of such principles, but with recurring common themes.

2.9.4 Frameworks and tools for sustainability

2.9.4.1 Frameworks

Frameworks provide structures, processes and contexts. These provide a means to bring together in a structured manner, the associated concepts for sustainability and the principles shown in levels 1 and 2 of Figure 2.2. Such a structured approach assists implementation of sustainability.

We distinguish two types of frameworks here. Of course, these frameworks do not exist in isolation but rather come together in an integrated manner.

Institutional frameworks, including the structures and formal processes of govern-ance, can have a strong influence in facilitating or acting as a barrier to sustainability. As we have seen, sustainability is, by definition, an integrating concept and one that requires transdisciplinary approaches. Yet most of our institutional arrangements promote a siloed approach to addressing problems. Our institutions also favour short-termism, governed by the length of political cycles. In addition, governance arrangements tend not to provide an institutionalised 'voice for sustainability'. An example of such a voice is the Sustainability Commissioner proposed (but not as yet accepted by government) by the Australian House of Representatives Standing Committee on Environment and Heritage (CoA 2007a) in their Inquiry into a Sustainability Charter (see 2.4.7). Institutions are discussed in Chapter 4 and institutional barriers to sustainability are further discussed in Chapter 10.

Organisational frameworks – the concept of *adaptive management* provides a vital organisational framework for sustainability. CS Holling in the early 1970s drew attention to uncertainty and surprise events in ecological and social systems and consequently the need to take a flexible, adaptive approach to managing natural resource systems (Allison and Hobbs 2006). This is termed adaptive management – a process of 'learning by doing' using a quasi-experimental approach to increase understanding of complex interrelated ecological-social systems. Lee (1999) has described this as 'implementing policies as experi-ments'. Adaptive management can be used to maintain or increase resilience in a system and hence is a very important management framework for sustainability. Given the complexity of interlinked ecological and social systems, *adaptive co-management* has developed to link a range of participants who bring different forms of knowledge (see Chapter 6) about eco-logical and governance systems to the learning process and who may share governance and collaborative problem-solving over a number of levels, in a natural resource management structure (Berkes 2007).

The second organisational framework example involves the various international and national standards that provide frameworks for processes that are important in an envir-onmental management context and that can, if used appropriately by organisations, also facilitate sustainability. These include standards for Environmental Management Systems (EMS) and auditing (see Chapter 8), and for risk management (see Chapters 8 and 9). Box 2.9 provides an example of a new form of standard specifically designed for organisations making decisions on Natural Resource Management (NRM).

Shared value systems or 'ways of seeing the world' (see Chapter 3) can also provide frameworks for interpreting sustainability. For example, 'ecological modernisation' provides an example of a value-based framework, resting on the belief that transformation of production processes towards dematerialisation and decoupling of economic growth and resource use is the most appropriate means for achieving sustainability. It sees this happening through political commitment providing the institutional and economic context for business to recognise the advantage of, and to adopt, new production processes that will save money (see 3.6.1; Carter 2007). Values will also influence the way in which the institutional and organisational frameworks listed here are used (see Chapters 3, 8 and 9).

Box 2.9: New South Wales Standard for Natural Resource Management (NRM)

The New South Wales Standard for Quality Natural Resource Management (the Standard) was designed to give confidence to the public, government, other interested parties, and those natural resource managers using it, that investment in NRM is targeting priority natural resource issues effectively. The Standard establishes quality processes for seven interdependent components relevant to NRM decision-making. These are:

- Collection and use of knowledge – is best available knowledge used to inform decisions in a structured and transparent manner?

- Determination of scale – is management of NRM issues taking place at the optimal spatial, temporal and institutional scales to maximise effective contribution to meeting goals?

- Opportunities for collaboration – is collaboration with other parties explored and pursued wherever possible to maximise gains, share or minimise costs and deliver multiple benefits?

- Community engagement – are strategies in place for meaningful participation of the community in the planning, implementation and review of NRM strategies and achievement of identified targets and goals?

- Risk management – is consideration and management of all identifiable risks and impacts taking place to achieve efficiency and effectiveness and avoid, minimise or control adverse impacts?

- Monitoring and evaluation – is regular monitoring, measuring, evaluation and reporting of organisational and project performance taking place and are results being used to guide improved practice?

- Information management – is management of information taking place in a manner that meets needs of users and satisfies formal accountability and transparency requirements?

The Standard supports adaptive management through application at all phases of the decision-making cycle: planning, implementation, audit and response. It can be integrated with other formal standards such as for EMS or audit (see Chapter 8).

While the Standard is mandatory for use by the New South Wales Catchment Management Authorities (CMAs) in setting their strategic priorities for investment in NRM through their Catchment Action Plans (CAPs) and implementing, monitoring outcomes, and reviewing these plans, it is also useful for any organisation, at any scale involved in NRM. The CMAs are regularly audited against the Standard to give assurance that their investments are making progress towards the State-wide targets for NRM in New South Wales.

Source: New South Wales Natural Resources Commission website <www.nrc.nsw.gov.au> (accessed 16 March 2009).

2.9.4.2 Tools

There is also a wide range of tools that can assist progress to sustainability. They drill down from the principles and other higher levels in Figure 2.2 to provide more precise means of meeting eco-efficiency, informing sustainable consumption, and so on. Many are used within the frameworks outlined above and some may also be described as frameworks (eg EMSs). Briefly, they include tools:

- that help us predict and avoid or minimise environmental impacts from developments (EIA);

- for assessing and comparing impacts over the life cycle of a product or process enabling choices to be made to meet a need with least impact (LCA);

- for comparing the costs and benefits of projects (CBA);

- that use market mechanisms to encourage lower impact activities and to internalise environmental costs (eg emission trading schemes for carbon dioxide pollution);

- that encourage environmentally-friendly choices by consumers – such as ecolabelling;

- that build knowledge, skills and commitment by people towards sustainability – that is education programs;

- for informing us about the state of the environment and human activities that lead to changes in that state – that is, monitoring and reporting on environmental and sustainability performance at various levels from organisations, local communities, regions, states to nations;

- for informing on our individual pressures on the environment such as through ecological footprinting.

Most of these tools are discussed in Chapter 8. We turn now to discuss briefly level 4 of Figure 2.2 that is concerned with bringing together the range of interpretations of sustainability, and guidance and tools for its application, into policies and strategies for implementation and associated actions. In other words, we turn from the conceptualising, information-gathering and designing to the planning and doing.

2.9.5 Policies, strategies and actions

The term *policy* is loosely used and numerous definitions around common themes exist (Althaus et al 2007; Dovers 2005a). For the purposes of this book, policy will be taken to mean a stated commitment of an intention to address a problem (Dovers 2005a). The solution to this problem ('the policy') will be based on preferred values and include a commitment to money or services for its implementation.

Strategies provide a means to implement policies. One or more strategies may be defined to carry out a policy. The factors needed to facilitate change and those that might hinder it are considered. *Actions* describe specific elements within a strategy – specific things that need to be done to bring desired outcomes of a strategy to fruition. To work towards sustainability, the policy and strategy design, and each action component within a strategy should be informed and guided by the various levels of principles, concepts, frameworks and tools as illustrated in Figure 2.2, and sequentially ordered to work to best effect. To illustrate the relationships consider an example involving waste management.

A State or national government may develop a policy aimed at reducing waste or waste may be treated as part of a broader emphasis on sustainability. For sustainability we should aim not only to deal with waste responsibly, but also to *eliminate* waste by focusing on dematerialisation, sustainable consumption, and having closed loop cycles such that waste becomes a resource (see Case Study A). The New South Wales Government has developed the *NSW Waste Avoidance and Resource Recovery Strategy* 2007 that identifies four key waste challenges and targets, including preventing and avoiding waste, increasing the use of renewable and recovered materials and reducing the toxicity of products and materials. These elements of the strategy need to be addressed across the life cycle of goods and materials, from extraction to manufacturing, distribution, consumption and recovery for reuse, recycling or disposal. The New South Wales Department of Environment and Climate Change (DECC) has developed a number of programs and actions to implement this strategy. These include:

- sustainability compacts with sector leaders to change their own practices as well as their supply chains;

- use of government contracts to support recycled content products;

- support for waste and sustainability educators to promote positive environmental actions in the community;

- identifying particular wastes of concern in New South Wales and devising the best approaches to address these, including EPR schemes (DECC 2007a, 2007b).

In relation to wastes, strategies may also be developed to focus on particular items or materials, such as tyres, computer hardware or glass.

Policies are generally thought of as coming from governments (public policy), but may also be developed by corporations, professional associations and a wide range of other non-government organisations (Thomas 2007) (see also Chapters 1 and 4). Strategies may address problems over varying spatial and governance ranges and will vary in kind according to this scope. However, at the level of a local municipality, the scope of influence and authority is considerably less than at a national scale. Hence there are a number of the higher level concepts and means that would be beyond the level of influence of the local authority. For example, EPR schemes applied to, say, computers and tyres would need to be regulated at a higher (State or national) level, though specific actions for their implementation, such as collection schemes, may be supported at a local level.

This section on the 'implementation hierarchy' has taken us through a range of concepts, principles, frameworks and tools that assist governments and organisations at all levels to develop policies, strategies and actions for implementing sustainability. However, we have not discussed overall progress to sustainability. Progress to sustainability is deeply influenced by a range of matters to be discussed later in this book. For this reason it makes sense to leave discussion on progress and challenges to implementation, and also the challenges of measuring progress to sustainability, to Chapter 10. We conclude this chapter by exploring some recent approaches to implementing sustainability that can accommodate its contested interpretations.

2.10 Sustainability – dynamic goalposts?

The purpose of this chapter has been to explore the concept of sustainability, which has undoubtedly been the most important context for EDM since the early 1990s. We have unpacked the concept and its development, examining various definitions, its underpinning principles, and related approaches, frameworks and tools associated with its implementation. Despite better understanding of the nature and intent of sustainability through this examination, we are left with the conclusion that sustainability remains a contested concept that is difficult to apply. We will conclude this chapter by exploring the core of that contestation – whether sustainability should be regarded as a journey or a destination – and introducing big picture integrative approaches to address sustainability that acknowledge this ongoing contestation.

There has been much discussion as to whether sustainability is a journey or a destination. Submissions to the Australian House of Representatives Standing Committee on Environment and Heritage Inquiry into a Sustainability Charter (CoA 2007a) were split in their views on this matter. Those suggesting that sustainability should be regarded as a journey stressed that a journey facilitates a process of continual improvement and flexibility. Some taking the view that sustainability is a destination, pointed out that it is not possible for a particular resource to be partially sustainable as the term 'journey' implies. Yet others, saw sustainable development as the journey and sustainability as the destination (see also discussion in 2.3), while a variant of this view using just the term 'sustainability' saw it as both a journey and a destination.

Given the very large uncertainties regarding exactly what might constitute 'sustainability' either in terms of biophysical or socio-economic factors, the complex interrelationships between these factors, their dynamic nature, and also recognising very different values positions, it is clear that in one sense sustainability will remain a journey as we seek greater clarification and consensus. Indeed for many, sustainability, like democracy, liberty or justice, is a contested concept supported by people as necessary and good, but with much continuing debate about *exactly* what constitutes the concept (Dresner 2008). We do not abandon democracy, liberty or justice as worthwhile endeavours, but rather we muddle through, and so we should with sustainability, often having to make do with clumsy solutions to what have been defined as 'wicked problems' (Verweij and Thompson 2006).

Others emphasise that since complex ecological and social systems are dynamic, the journey is about adaptation, and we need to have the capacity to continually adapt to change (Holling 2001; Newman 2005). As discussed in 2.9.2.2, resilience is becoming a central concept in discussion on sustainability and achieving resilient systems very much depends on adaptive capacity.

However, it may also be argued that unless we have a destination in mind – either targets set for biophysical and socio-economic parameters and/or a vision of a sustainable future city, region, corporation or nation – we will not only lack a yardstick for measuring progress, but also lack a sense of obligation to achieve the target within a specified time-frame.

Targets can also release creativity to achieve goals through new means (Yencken and Wilkinson 2000).

A useful example of the value of targets is the current debate on anthropogenic climate change resulting from the build-up of greenhouse gases in the atmosphere. We can see this as one of many issues which are highly relevant to sustainability. There has been continuing international negotiation on targets for emission reductions by particular dates to achieve specified atmospheric concentrations of CO_2-e.[12] These are aimed at providing a destination towards a more sustainable position with regard to anthropogenic climate change (ie 'avoiding dangerous climate change'). At the same time it is recognised that these may be temporary targets. We have already seen the reduction percentages required by 2050 (compared to 1990 emissions) increase over the last couple of years as the scientific information coming from the Intergovernmental Panel on Climate Change (IPCC 2007) has become better substantiated. However, in the absence of targets such as those suggested with respect to CO_2-e emissions, it is unlikely we would acknowledge the extent of the challenge we face, but rather, continue in a business as usual manner. The targets promote action but can be adjusted as information improves and/or as our value positions change. Hence an approach as described here combines targets (destination) and a journey (through adaptively managing the targets and/or our actions, as information and/or our values change).

But, what might be required for such a 'directed journey'? As discussed in Chapter 1, and further in Chapter 10, many indicators suggest that we are not progressing towards a more sustainable planet at present, and it is evident from issues such as water management in South-East Australia (Murray-Darling Basin), and anthropogenic climate change globally, that our institutions and processes of governance at many levels are not coping with these current challenges. There is recognition that we need to reflect on the inadequacies of our current arrangements and develop 'fresh approaches and forms of governance capable of engaging with complex challenges of this kind' (Shove and Walker 2007, p 769). One such fresh approach is the idea of 'reflexive governance' which involves steering society towards sustainability in such a way that recognises the dynamic political and social world we live in (Voß et al 2006). Reflexive governance requires that actors and their institutions 'reflect on how their frames, structures and patterns of action contribute to persistent problems' and that they consider ways to fundamentally transform existing practices and systems (Hendriks and Grin 2007, p 334).

A practical example of reflexive governance is 'transition management' which has developed, particularly in the Netherlands, as a policy framework for reforming large socio-technological systems, such as those associated with agriculture, energy and health (Loorbach and Rotmans, 2006). The aim of transition management is to steer long-term (25–50 year) change processes towards sustainability – conceptualised here as a dynamic destination that is constantly renegotiated in society (Rotmans et al 2001).[13] Under the transition management framework government works in partnership with different actors to envision multiple sustainable futures, and innovate and experiment with these through

---

12   CO_2-e is a measure that compares different greenhouse gases in relation to their potential to cause global warming, using carbon dioxide as the reference measure. In terms of atmospheric concentrations it provides a single figure which accounts for all types of greenhouse gases.

13   Transitions are described as non-linear change processes spanning one to two generations that involve multiple forces and actors (Rotmans et al 2001). The typical (very Dutch) examples of transitions include the shift from wind to steam powered ships, or the shift in water management strategies from engineering control to 'giving water room' in spatial planning (Rotmans et al 2000; van Brugge et al 2005).

concrete projects (Kemp and Loorbach 2006). Actors are encouraged to be reflexive and scrutinise the very systems, institutions and paradigms within which they operate.

Numerous criticisms have been made regarding the feasibility of transition management, particularly its political and democratic implications (Hendriks 2008; Meadowcroft 2005; Shove and Walker 2007). It is clear that much work remains to be done, but transition management does embrace many of the concepts, principles, frameworks and tools and the challenges, that we have seen are important for sustainability. These include acknowledging complexity, uncertainty and cross-connections among social and ecological systems, the importance of participation to incorporate differing values and knowledge, and the need for long-term planning that incorporates resilience thinking and adaptive management. We briefly revisit these matters in Chapter 10.

3

Values and Value Systems

People who hold different sets of values may choose different actions when faced with the same evidence. Therefore, societal perceptions, attitudes and values must be considered along with knowledge of environmental systems.

(Kim 1994, p 60)

3.1 Introduction

The world would be a boring place if people were all the same! Fortunately that is far from the case. People differ considerably in the way they perceive their surroundings. Starting with a simple example, consider possible responses of a group of people provided with a picture of a kangaroo and each asked for their quick reaction as to what it means to them. As shown in Figure 3.1, the responses are likely to be very varied.

Figure 3.1 Differing perceptions of the importance of the Red Kangaroo

The range of views is likely to be even wider for more complex examples such as how we perceive environmental and sustainability issues. For example, it is very clear that there is a wide range of views on the nature of our current energy-climate change problem and perhaps an even wider range of views on the possible solutions.

The purpose of this chapter is to explore *why* we hold such varying views when confronted with the same information. What is the role of value differences in underpinning such varying views and what are the bases of these differing values? How do value differences impact on environmental decision-making (EDM), and how can we accommodate potential value conflicts in EDM?

Chapters 1 and 2 introduced the complex nature of environmental and sustainability issues, with an important part of that complexity resulting from the way in which such issues are derived from, and embedded in, a socio-political context. In this chapter we explore an integral part of that socio-political fabric – that dealing with value systems of individuals, groups and society more broadly. Discussion in earlier chapters has already shown that people, groups and different cultures, vary in their perceptions of environmental issues and the ways in which humans and the environment should relate. The strong and weak interpretations of the principles of sustainability discussed in Chapter 2 is one such example.

Tensions between different values and consequent different interpretations of information may occur at all stages of the decision-making cycle, as described in Chapter 1, including: issue identification; the methods and type of knowledge we use to inform understanding of the issue (Chapter 6); who is involved in scoping of policy responses (Chapter 5); the processes and instruments used to address issues (Chapter 8); implementation of public consultation programs (Chapter 7); dealing with uncertainty and negotiation of acceptable levels of risk (Chapter 9). More broadly, values influence the identification of particular groups as relevant stakeholders in an issue, and the roles of various actors in decision-making (Chapters 5 and 7). Values also influence the type of institutions we develop to run our society and the way in which they relate to one another (Chapter 4). Values also weave their way through the range of themes we take up in subsequent chapters.

However, this chapter is *not* concerned with moral judgments over which value positions are right or wrong. Rather, it is concerned with exploring the roots of these various value positions as a means for better understanding environmental and sustainability issues. This in turn should help us discern how to most effectively operate in EDM to achieve desired goals. Failure to acknowledge the values of different participants in decision-making processes will exacerbate the likelihood of conflict and work against the possibility of achieving creative solutions.

We will also briefly consider changes in value positions over time. It is important to gain some understanding of where we have come from in order to be well positioned to consider where the trends might go in the future and the possible consequences of this for environmental management.

But first we need to consider what we mean by 'values', and what other terms and concepts are relevant to this discussion?

3.2 What are 'values' and 'interests'?

'Values' has many meanings in the English language. A number of these have to do with measurement – some linked to monetary worth, others to different parameters. However, the 'values' we are particularly interested in here are well described by Berlin (1997, p 127) as 'what we think good and bad, important and trivial, right and wrong, noble and contemptible'.

Many factors influence the values we each hold. They include the society we live in and its history and various cultures. Our families, religion, friends, gender, education, profession, media, economic status, and so on, all influence our values. Values also may vary culturally (eg between nations and between some groups within nations), spatially (between cities and rural areas and between different regions in a nation) and over time (eg between generations, but also our individual values vary over time as we move through and accumulate different life experiences).

While values are an important basis for the views we hold on environmental issues, so too are 'interests'. 'Interests' are concerned with having some personal or group advantage or detriment associated with a decision (*Oxford English Dictionary Online*; Stone 2002). There are different forms of interests, that is, advantage may relate to financial, strategic, material or instrumental matters (see also Chapter 5). For example, as individuals we may have interests which relate to financial advantage, such as maintenance of a licence that allows us to access a certain quantity of water from a river. Or, interest in a government decision to change local zoning that enables us to profit from subdividing our land. At a corporate level, resource extraction companies may lobby to maintain their rights to access resources such as mining of uranium or logging of forests. These examples are essentially vested interests since some right or power is vested in an individual or group enabling them to maintain their position of dominance, typically (but not only) in relation to a financial situation.

We may also see organisations representing the interests of others (and themselves!). For example, governments represent the 'national (or State) interests' in policy-making. Businesses represent the interests of shareholders, and so on (Blowers 1997).

While values and interests are not the same (Stewart 2009), the line of demarcation is blurred in many cases, and values also underpin interests. We would probably all agree that the above examples demonstrate 'interests', while also accepting that values may inform those interests. Consider an environmental advocacy organisation that successfully lobbies for setting aside an area of native bushland as a national park. Clearly, this represents a strong commitment to their environmental values, but such success is also related to their interests as an environmental lobby group. In this case the interest is a strategic one that involves having their position adopted.[1] The blurred demarcation between values and interests is well illustrated through recent experiences around the world in siting wind power farms (see Box 3.1).

But values and interests may also clash and no doubt each one of us has experienced such clashes personally. Consider for example the group of environmentalists portrayed in the television program 'Chant of the Scrub Turkey'[2] who had bought their properties in the Maleny region of the Sunshine Coast of Queensland because of the opportunity provided there to be relatively self-sufficient through growing their own food in a fine natural bush setting. However, an invasion of native Brush Turkeys wreaked havoc in their gardens and homes (ABC 2006a). Their *values* regarding the rights of native fauna to occupy the area, clashed with their *interests* of maintaining their vegetable gardens and homes.

Box 3.1: Values, interests and wind power

Strong public support for wind *power* to provide electricity is evident in all countries using this source. However, this support does not necessarily translate into approval of wind *farms* at the local level. This apparent anomaly has long been explained by the NIMBY syndrome (Not In My BackYard). In other words local people wanting to maximise their individual *interests* (NIMBY), overcome shared community *values* regarding the desirability of a clean green source of renewable energy. Research in a number of countries has now shown the explanation to be far more complex than NIMBYism (Devine-Wright 2004; Jobert et al 2007; Warren et al 2005; Wolsink 2000, 2007).

A number of factors have been identified that might contribute to NIMBY-type opposition to siting of wind farms. These include noise, light and shadow flicker from moving turbines and bird and bat kills (Wolsink 2000, 2007). However, of most significance is the visual impact of turbines on the landscape and in particular the *type* of landscape.

For example, turbines sited in industrial areas, along roads, out to sea, and in some farming or grazing areas, may be acceptable (even welcomed!), while siting in natural and especially noted scenic areas (eg along the Great Ocean Road in Victoria) is regarded as highly unacceptable (Wawryk 2004; Wolsink 2007). This factor surpasses all other influencing factors, including the general support for wind *power*, and aspects of wind *farm* design such as the number, size and design of turbines (Wolsink 2007).

---

1   Though there may indirectly be financial advantage for the environmental organisation in that the advocacy success may encourage supporters to continue their financial support.

2   Usually called the 'Brush Turkey'. A medium sized bird (around 70 cm long) found along the east coast of Australia from Cape York to south of Sydney. The birds rake leaf litter to gather food and the males build large mounds of leaf litter for incubation of eggs, <www.austmus.gov.au/factsheets/brush_turkey.htm> (accessed 29 March 2009).

However, studies have not shown that local opposition based on these factors is best explained by selfish NIMBY motives.[3] First, such opposition may be shared by those who are not locals. Secondly, an important reason for local opposition seems to rest on matters of fairness in decision-making and equity in relation to others. This suggests that local involvement in decisions on siting is vital and needs to be linked with open and collaborative processes (see 3.11.2) that allow local people to express local values in processes that are seen as 'fair' (Wolsink 2007). 'Fair' processes influence people's views of the legitimacy of outcomes and their willingness to accept outcomes (Agterbosch et al 2009; Gross 2007). In contrast, processes and their outcomes perceived as 'unfair' may divide local communities, as demonstrated by cases from Victoria (Saulwick 2004) and New South Wales (Gross 2007). In these cases non-inclusive decision-making processes were followed, and some landholders received payment for having wind turbines on their land while neighbours were not offered this opportunity, but had to put up with any detrimental effects. This created winners and losers and split the communities. 'Ownership', achieved for those landowners siting turbines on their land, clearly favoured a positive view of the local wind farm.

The local acceptance of, or opposition to, wind farms provides an example of the blurred line between values and interests. The supposed *interest*-based (NIMBY) opposition to local siting is now seen to be rare and instead local opposition is most likely to revolve around broader *values* of support for renewable energy, and *value*-based concern of the need for processes that favor inclusion, openness, collaborative decision-making, and fairness, in both these processes and their outcomes. However, even these distinctions are not clear cut. For example, it could be argued that favouring non-fossil fuel energy sources is in fact in our interest with regard to climate change.

We will return to further discussion of values later in the chapter but we turn now to explore why people view environmental issues differently.

3.3 Why do people view environmental issues differently?

In this section we will outline the many influences that contribute to the values we bring to EDM.

To start with, the extent to which we will be influenced by external factors is governed by our personality – that combination of genetic heritage, gender and range of experiences that make each of us unique. External factors include the values (see 3.2), ethics, paradigms, discourses, and ideologies that form part of the broad societal sea of influences within which we exist. Closer to home our socio-economic situation is important and there is also a range of cultural influences including from our family, education, religion, history, and the social groups we mix with. We are also bombarded with a mass of tangible information. For example, reports on the state of the environment, information and opinion pieces through the media on day-to-day happenings and trends. At the present time, wars, terrorism, energy prices, extreme weather events and the global financial crisis, are critical items in the news that may influence our thinking on specific environmental issues

---

3   Similarly, a study in California regarding siting of offshore oil drilling concluded NIMBYism was not the explanation for protests by local people. In fact proximity to the oil drilling either had no effect on attitude or increased support for drilling (Michaud et al 2008).

or more broadly. These all come together, as shown in Figure 3.2, acting like a set of filters or spectacles through which we interpret information regarding an environmental issue, to arrive at an 'ultimate value position', or in relation to broader matters, a 'world view'.[4] Our value positions will be further influenced in some cases by vested interests (see 3.2) and professional obligations which have some specific relevance to the issue in question. Note that Figure 3.2 also shows a response loop, indicating that our response to an environmental issue is similarly affected by this range of influences.

We move now to discuss some of these influences, including ethics (see 3.4), paradigms (see 3.5), discourses (see 3.6) and ideologies (see 3.8). In addition, over the past 30 years scholars have developed schemas by analysing and grouping factors that differentiate individuals and groups in terms of their environmental value positions and world views

Figure 3.2 Factors influencing value positions of individuals

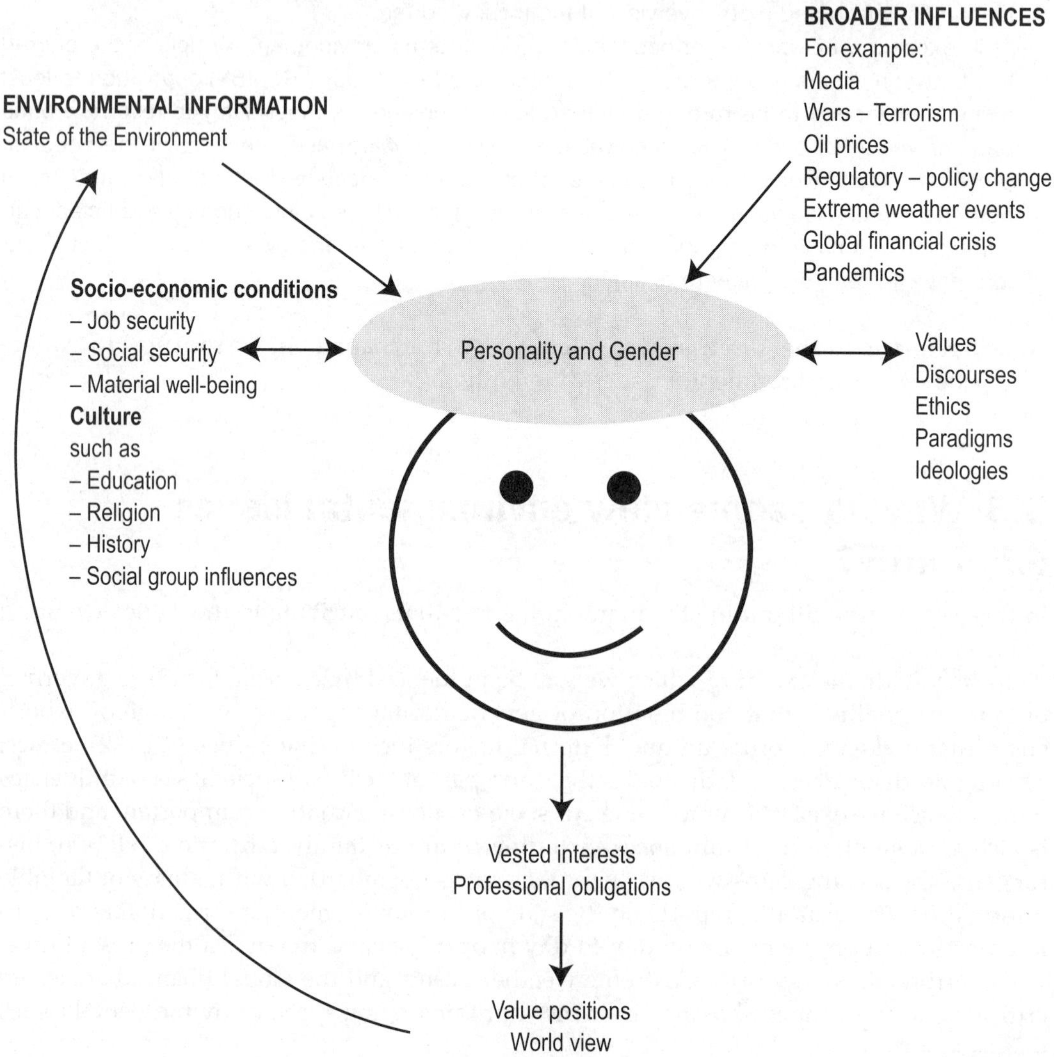

BROADER INFLUENCES
For example:
Media
Wars – Terrorism
Oil prices
Regulatory – policy change
Extreme weather events
Global financial crisis
Pandemics

ENVIRONMENTAL INFORMATION
State of the Environment

Socio-economic conditions
– Job security
– Social security
– Material well-being
Culture
such as
– Education
– Religion
– History
– Social group influences

Personality and Gender

Values
Discourses
Ethics
Paradigms
Ideologies

Vested interests
Professional obligations

Value positions
World view

---

4   By world view we mean essentially how we see the world, including modes of governance, social, economic and political relations, and relationships with nature.

(see 3.5 and 3.7). Such analysis helps us to understand others' values and views and thus facilitates our interaction with individuals and groups who see the world through value-based lenses which differ from our own. The discussion below is based on Western societies. For discussion on values of other groups in relation to the environment see Knudtson and Suzuki (1992), Marshall (1992), Nash (1990), Rolston (1987).

3.4 Ethics

Ethics are an important factor in influencing the positions people take on environmental issues. For some people consideration of environmental issues goes beyond scientific and ecological matters and is concerned more with our ethical relationships with nature.

Ethics is a branch of philosophy concerned with moral principles by which human actions and proposals may be viewed as 'good' or 'bad', 'right' or 'wrong'. Ethics are applied in a range of different professions or situations. The code of ethics governing medical practitioners was the first form of applied ethics to be developed and is perhaps the best known of the professional ethics, with clear rules and remaining extremely influential.

Environmental ethics on the other hand is not clearly linked to a single profession. It is also far less clearly defined and lacks a 'rationally ordered set of rules that can automatically be applied with great precision' (Hargrove 1989, p 8). Broadly we may think of environmental ethics as being concerned with how humans should morally interact with, and relate to, nature. But what might this mean? Are humans a part of nature or are they superior to, and in control of, nature? What values should we place on nature? How should we implement those values in our interaction with nature? Is all of nature of equal value?

Let's consider a couple of examples where such questions are evident. In parts of Australia kangaroo numbers have become artificially inflated due to human actions, such as providing secure watering points. Should we cull these kangaroos in order to protect local populations of the species, or follow an ethic which protects the life of individual kangaroos? As a second example, should we allow developments that will provide needed employment to go ahead even though we know it will be at the cost of lost biodiversity? See for example Case Study B.

Various kinds of values are identified with regard to human-nature relationships. A typical distinction is that made between:

Instrumental value – where something has a value because it provides some tangible use or outcome. For example, we might value a forest as a provider of timber or as an environmental service, such as a source of pollen for bee foraging. So the forest is valued as the means to produce timber, or to produce food for bees; and

Intrinsic value – where something has value of itself, independently of anyone finding it useful. For example, a forest has value not because humans want to use its timber or even because they want to enjoy walking through it, looking at it, or simply knowing it exists. Rather it has value just of itself (Carter 2007).

These definitions of different types of values come from philosophy, and may be linked with strong ethical positions.

Economists also have something to say about values in the context of natural resources. Broadly, economists distinguish *user values* from *intrinsic values*, with the latter referred to by economists as *existence values* (Pearce et al 1989). Pearce et al (1989) describe *user values* (essentially the same as the philosophers' instrumental values) as derived from use of nature which may take several forms, some direct use (as in hunting or birdwatching), others indirect and concerned with *potential* benefit (such as protecting nature for some future use).

These various descriptions of values have been used by scholars to construct schemas of value positions and/or ethical positions with regard to nature, and the environment more broadly (see Table 3.1). A major distinction has been made between anthropocentrism and ecocentrism. Anthropocentrics are mainly concerned with human interests and see humans as the source of all value, while ecocentrics extend moral concern to non-human organisms and see humans as subject to the principles governing ecological systems (Carter 2007; Elliot 1995).

Considering the types of values outlined above, anthropocentrics would see nature as having instrumental value while for ecocentrics the intrinsic value of nature is a strong ethic. This is well shown in Table 3.2 (compare the ethics of the anthropocentrics-technocentrics and the 'deep ecologists'). However, while the 'anthropocentric-ecocentric dualism is a key conceptual distinction in environmental philosophy . . . this simple twofold typology fails to capture the rich complexity and variation within environmental philosophy' (Carter 2007, p 17). The latter is well demonstrated by Table 3.2 and also through the following example.

Consider the definition of intrinsic value from philosophy. This may be applied either at the ecosystem level or at an individual organism level. At the individual organism level animal liberationists argue for the rights of individual animals. The Australian Peter Singer

Table 3.1: Counter paradigms of human interaction with the environment

	Alternative Environmental Paradigm	Dominant Paradigm[1]
Core values	– Non-material (self-actualisation) – Natural environment intrinsically valued – Harmony with nature	– Material (economic growth) – Natural environment valued as a resource – Domination over nature
Economy	– Public interest – Safety – Egalitarian	– Market forces – Risks and reward – Differentials
Polity	– Participative structures: (citizen/worker involvement) – Non-hierarchical – Liberation	– Authoritative structures: (experts influential) – Hierarchical – Law and order
Society	– Decentralised – Small-scale – Flexible	– Centralised – Large-scale – Ordered
Nature	– Earth's resources limited – Nature benign – Nature delicately balanced	– Ample reserves – Nature hostile/neutral – Environment controllable
Knowledge	– Limits to science – Rationality of ends – Integration of fact/value, thought/feeling	– Confidence in science and technology – Rationality of means – Separation of fact/value, thought/feeling

1   'Dominant paradigm' here refers not necessarily to the paradigm held by most people in society but rather that held by those who dominate major societal decisions.

Modified after Cotgrove 1982.

(1975) has led the worldwide animal liberation movement by arguing that sentience, or the capacity for sensation or feeling, should be the criterion for determining which animals have such rights. However, as Dryzek (2005) points out animal liberation does not necessarily sit easily in the ecocentric position, since its emphasis on the *individual* animal may often conflict with broader ecological concerns at the *ecosystem* level. For example, an animal liberation position may be concerned with the welfare of *individual* introduced predators in Australia such as foxes and feral cats which prey on native wildlife. In contrast, an ecocentric position may be primarily concerned with maintaining whole ecosystems and their populations of native wildlife, and hence support eradication of introduced predators.

This discussion gives us some idea of why defining an environmental ethic is so difficult. Not only is there a wide spread of values regarding human-nature relations, but increasingly a range of other philosophical matters may be seen as important in environmental ethics (see Hay 2002, pp 35–36), including human-human relations, such as those encompassed in environmental justice (see 2.7). The result is that environmental ethics could embrace a range of positions including those from the technocentric/anthropocentric positions shown in Table 3.2. No wonder Sylvan and Bennett (1994, p 9) note that among philosophers there is disagreement about 'what constitutes an environmental ethic, about how to achieve such an ethic, and to what degree such a thing is desirable'.

Some see an environmental ethic[5] as a means to assist political processes in protecting the environment (Hargrove 1989, p 207, citing Leopold 1949). Aldo Leopold was a famous United States environmentalist working during the first half of the 20th century. He argued that citizen support is necessary to enable political action favouring environmental protection, and that such citizen support would only come about when people were educated to hold and support an environmental ethic.

Leopold's view remains credible today with many arguing that the development of an environmental ethic that values nature quite apart from any economic value it may have for individuals or groups is a necessary pre-requisite for serious political commitment to environmental protection and sustainability.

Others argue that only by bringing nature into dominant value systems, such as capitalism, will environmental goods and services be appropriately valued (Pearce et al 1989). For example, economists argue that it is necessary to put a monetary value (a cost) on carbon dioxide emissions to ensure that these emissions are taken to account in decisions made by individuals, companies and government (Garnaut 2008).

Further debate has been concerned with whether the strong distinction between instrumental and intrinsic value and between anthropocentrism and ecocentrism is useful, or rather, whether it provides a barrier to accommodating the wide range of cultural views in attempts to protect nature (Eckersley 2005).

So, 'environmental ethics' rests on values and provides a set (or sets) of moral principles for people to follow in their relationship with the environment. But there are other descriptors relating to the way in which humans value and relate to nature, and more broadly to the environment. One such term is 'paradigm'.

3.5 Paradigms

The British sociologist Stephen Cotgrove (1982, p 26) says that paradigms 'provide maps of what the world is believed to be like. They constitute guidelines for . . . identifying and

---

5   Meaning here an ethic which favours protection of nature.

solving problems. Above all, paradigms provide the framework of meaning within which "facts" and experiences acquire significance and can be interpreted'.

Table 3.1 (see page 58) contrasts aspects of two alternative paradigms with respect to human interaction with the environment and environmental management. These two paradigms will conceive and define problems and solutions differently. For example, the alternative environmental paradigm may emphasise uncertainty of prediction of environmental impacts of a proposed development and may downplay the importance of economic growth. In contrast, the dominant paradigm may focus on the need for economic development and human progress, playing down the possibility of detrimental impacts and placing faith in the efficacy of science and technology to solve any environmental problems that may arise. The different conclusions deriving from the two paradigms rest not only on the interpretation of the facts regarding the impacts of the development, but also on their different views of the relationship of humans and the environment and how development should proceed. The alternative environmental paradigm broadly matches the value position of ecocentrics; and the dominant paradigm is similar to anthropocentrics.

Not only does exploration of paradigms related to human-environment interactions help us to understand the differing views on environmental management in society, but it also helps us to understand the role that paradigm shifts may play in moving towards a more ecocentric society (see Box 3.2).

Box 3.2: Ecological revolutions and paradigms

Well-known environmental philosopher and historian, Carolyn Merchant (1989), explored the ecological and social history of New England in the United States through the concept of what she calls 'ecological revolutions'. She identifies two such revolutions. First, the 'colonial ecological revolution', when the coming of European settlers and their animals and plants caused the collapse of the Indigenous Indian ecological systems and society. Secondly, the 'capitalist ecological revolution' around 1860, when a growing market economy led to importation of natural resources and exportation of finished products and resulted in air and water pollution and depletion of resources.

Merchant (1989, p 2) suggests that each of these revolutions altered not only the local ecology and human society, but also human consciousness since the ways in which 'humans socially constructed and interpreted the natural environment were reorganized'.

She sees ecological revolutions as occurring when 'tensions and contradictions' form between a society's mode of production and its ecology. As a result 'new forms of consciousness, ideas, images, and worldviews' are supported (p 3). One of the frameworks she uses to explain these 'revolutions' is Thomas Kuhn's explanation of revolutions in the field of science. Kuhn in his 1962 book *The Structure of Scientific Revolutions*, explained major periods of rapid change in scientific thinking, such as those associated with Newton in the 17th century, Darwin's evolutionary theory in the 19th century and Einstein's relativity theory in the 20th century, through the concept of 'paradigm shifts'.

Kuhn saw scientific paradigms providing the framework or lens through which scientists approach and solve problems, or as put by Pepper (1996, p 262) 'an outline map of a discipline'. The paradigm provides the accepted theories and methods of analysis for scientists to carry out their work. However, when anomalies arise, such as results which do not match the conventional wisdom or theories, the paradigm may be challenged. As a result, following a long period of stability there may be a sudden change in the conventional wisdom – a paradigm shift or 'scientific revolution'.

While Merchant saw the 'ecological revolutions' in New England accompanied by a paradigm shift in societal values associated with human-nature relationships, Kuhn's explanation of scientific revolutions fails to recognise the potential influence of society on the directions of science (Merchant 1989; Pepper 1996).

Merchant finished her 1989 book with a chapter in which she situated New England in the late 20th century as part of a possible Global Ecological Revolution which would lead to adoption of an ecocentric ethic based on 'a network of mutual obligations rather than natural rights, and on values that are based on the ecosystem rather than on human interests' (p 263). In other words adoption of many aspects of the 'alternative environmental paradigm'.

As we discuss later in this chapter, various crises relating to climate change, water shortages and questions over food shortages, are causing discussion in many developed and developing societies regarding the need to appropriately value 'natural capital' (see Box 2.2), but we seem still a long way from a paradigm shift to a global ecocentric ethic.

Of further relevance to forming our views on environmental issues are the ways in which environmental issues are recognised. That is, the way in which problems may be constructed and in turn how this influences the types of solutions that may be sought. In other words, how are values expressed in EDM and why is that important? One approach is to explore the competing narratives (stories) about the environment.

3.6 Discourses and storylines

Some scholars use the notion of 'discourse' to make sense of the wide range of perspectives on environmental issues.[6] For example, Dryzek (2005, p 9) argues that:

> A discourse is a shared way of apprehending the world. Embedded in language, it enables those who subscribe to it to interpret bits of information and put them together into coherent stories or accounts. Discourses construct meanings and relationships, helping to define common sense and legitimate knowledge. Each discourse rests on assumptions, judgments and contentions that provide the basic terms for analysis, debates, agreements, and disagreements. If such shared terms did not exist, it would be hard to imagine problem-solving in this area at all, as we would have continually to return to first principles.

Taking a simple example, in the 1950s in Australia the dominant public discourse (or set of ideas) about mangroves lining the foreshores of many estuaries was that they were ugly plants that collected smelly mud among their roots and with their pneumatophores (breathing roots) protruding upwards provided an unwelcome swampy barrier between humans and the waterway. Central to this dominant discourse was the notion that mangroves need to be cleared. Today the discourse on mangroves in Australia is more positive and encourages their protection. Mangroves are seen to stabilise the shoreline, provide sheltered nurseries for young sea life, and as an important part of the ecology of an area. The common discourse regarding mangroves in Australia is very different today from the 1950s and has

---

6   The use of 'discourse' here needs further clarification. To be clear, the term is being used in its Foucauldian sense to describe a shared set of constructs and ideas. This is not to be confused with the Habermasian use of discourse or 'discursive' which refers to a social communicative process in which actors expose and discuss different viewpoints, ideas, stories and arguments (see Howes 2005, pp 30–34).

brought with it significant changes in the way we treat these ecosystems through individual actions, policy and regulation.

Similarly, Hajer (1993) provides an example of how language matters in discussing the issue of acid rain[7] in Europe. He points out that a large group of dead trees may be interpreted in many ways. They could be seen as the result of a natural phenomenon such as drought, cold or wind, or they may be seen as the result of pollution, as for example from acid rain. He suggests that (p 44), the acid rain discourse 'labels the dead trees as victims of pollution, and thus dead trees become a political problem'. Discourses may be condensed into metaphors that provide a shorthand for discussion. For example, in Hajer's study the metaphor of 'acid rain' helped frame the idea that rain is unnatural and dangerous, and that dead trees can be seen as an 'indicator, a sign, a piece of evidence, of a broader crisis in industrial society' (Hajer 2005a, p 299).

But what is the relevance of discourses in the political context of determining policy and EDM? Discourses and their associated storylines are significant for EDM because they influence how we perceive and interpret (construct) environmental problems, and thus shape our political views on how we believe they ought to be solved (Dryzek 2005). As Hajer (2005a, p 299, emphasis in original) explains 'large groups of dead trees are, of course, not a social construct; the point is how one *makes sense* of dead trees. In this respect there are many possible (political) realities'.

Shared storylines can also be important in bonding people together in the context of particular 'practices' to form 'discourse coalitions'. Such a coalition of actors can be an important influence in policy development and EDM when the discourse begins to dominate the way a particular social unit (such as a firm or a government agency) sees the world. For example, the civil rights movement in the United States may be seen as a discourse coalition that led to recognition of the social and political rights of African-Americans. The women's movement influenced the discourse relating to gender and family and this is turn has influenced policy. The discourse of environmentalism has had a clear influence as evidenced by the vast array of environmental policies developed over the past 40 years, within nations and internationally (Dryzek et al 2003).

If the discourse then becomes embedded in institutions and the practices of organisations, Hajer (2005a) describes this as 'discourse institutionalisation'. Such institutionalisation may involve the discourse forming the common way of reasoning or governing organisational practices. Either way it is likely to set the boundaries for decision-making. Hajer (2005a) further notes that discourse institutionalisation is self-promoting. For example, those working in bureaucracies within a particular discourse will socialise those joining the bureaucracy to operate within the same discourse.

Planning for wind power in the north west of England provides an example of the importance of discourse coalitions in EDM. Mander (2008) identified two strong discourse coalitions that developed during planning for wind energy use – the 'wind supporters' who supported development of both onshore and offshore schemes, and 'landscape protectors' who opposed further installation of wind schemes in the upland sites but who saw a role for offshore installations. She found that the distinct narratives of the two coalitions 'can be brought together into an "offshore story line" that coalesces members of both coalitions into an "offshore coalition", whilst allowing them to maintain their different world views' (p 597). This finding supports Hajer's view that 'the politics of discourse is best seen as a

---

7   Acid rain is rain that has become more acidic (with a pH below about 5) than 'normal' as a result of contact with gases in the atmosphere such as sulphur dioxide, nitrogen oxides and carbon dioxide, released as pollutants from human activities.

continuous process' (2005a, p 305), that is discourse coalitions can be fluid, and also that members of a discourse coalition may not necessarily share deep values. With regard to local authorities seeking to site controversial renewable technologies such as wind power, this English case shows both the important role of discourse coalitions in framing the debate, and the need for decision-making authorities to seek 'space for solutions with overlapping story lines' (Mander 2008, p 599).

An Australian study dating from the late 1990s and concerning climate change and energy use, identified two discourse coalitions – a resource-based coalition and a greenhouse action coalition. It showed that actors within each of these groups may have very different interests and beliefs but could follow similar storylines regarding the nature of the climate change issue and possible solutions. This was particularly true of the greenhouse action coalition which included international groups such as the Intergovernmental Panel on Climate Change (IPCC), various Australian Commonwealth, State and local government agencies, environment lobby groups and some research organisations such as CSIRO (Bulkeley 2000).

The discourse of industrialism[8] has long dominated Western thinking but from the 1960s environmental discourses have gradually challenged industrialism (Dryzek 2005). Dryzek (2005, p 22) argues however that environmentalism is not a unified counter discourse to industrialism, but rather comprises a variety of discourses 'sometimes complementing one another, but often competing'. This variety of environmental positions is certainly evident from Table 3.2, but the range of discourses goes much further than shown in that table. For example: ecofeminism, social ecology, bioregionalism, and Earth First![9] each provide discourse coalitions (Carter 2007).[10] However, while most of these discourses seem to have had little influence on governments, one discourse that has had such influence in some countries is 'ecological modernisation'. It is a particularly ambiguous discourse because it weaves a narrative that speaks to both ecocentric and anthropocentric values. As we will now show this ambiguity is the source of its power in decision-making circles of both business and government.

3.6.1 An example of a discourse: ecological modernisation

Ecological modernisation (EM) emerged in the 1980s in northern Europe and has since gained traction in many developed countries (including Australia). It is a reformist[11] rather than a radical discourse. It recognises environmental problems caused by industrial capitalism but rejects the radical environmentalist call for major reconstruction of the market economy and the liberal democratic state (Carter 2007).

---

8   Industrialism is characterised by an 'overarching commitment to growth in the quantity of goods and services produced and to the material wellbeing that growth brings', with scant regard to the environment other than as a provider of raw materials and energy (Dryzek 2005, p 13).

9   Earth First! is a deep ecology group committed to civil disobedience and 'ecotage' – illegal actions such as spiking trees to be logged, and destruction of logging machinery.

10 It is beyond the scope of this book to explore these and the many other environmental positions that may be identified. For discussion of a range of these positions see Carter 2007; Dryzek 2005; Hay 2002; Jamison 2001; Pepper 1996. Nor have the range of non-Western perspectives been included; that would require another book!

11 Reformist suggests gradual or subtle rather than radical change. It does not involve throwing out current systems and replacing them by entirely new institutions, policies and modes of management, based on a different set of values.

As with sustainable development EM seeks to reconcile economic and environmental goals, but EM is more focused in outlining means for this reconciliation than is the discourse of sustainable development (Dryzek 2005).

The discourse of EM focuses on transforming the production processes of industrialisation through dematerialisation and decoupling economic growth and resource use. It sees this happening through political commitment providing the institutional and economic context for business to recognise the advantage of, and adopt, new production processes that will save money (Carter 2007; Dryzek 2005). Indeed, Blowers (1997, p 847) suggests that EM 'regards the environmental challenge not as a crisis but as an opportunity'.

In the EM discourse, EM provides a number of advantages for business. The storylines include (Dryzek 2005, pp 167–8):

- 'Pollution prevention pays' as pollution is a sign of waste.

- Not addressing environmental problems can simply lead to larger costs in the future. Best is to prevent such problems in the first place. For example, this might mean moving to cleaner production processes.

- A clean and attractive environment makes for a happier and healthier workforce.

- Money can be made by selling green goods and services

- Business needs political commitment to: take a long term view; take an holistic approach; place greater value on scarce nature; and apply the precautionary principle.

This means that the role of government changes under EM. It involves partnerships between government, industry, scientists and moderate green groups, and steering towards improved environmental outcomes, rather than centralised regulation to achieve such outcomes (Carter 2007).

Ecological modernisation has been criticised on a number of fronts. First, despite the suggestion above that it is more focused than the discourse of sustainable development, Christoff (1996) has identified a continuum from weak to strong interpretations of EM. The weaker version emphasises technical solutions to environmental problems, a style of policy-making that gives privilege to economic, scientific and political elites, and an emphasis on developed nations at the expense of poor nations. Strong EM in contrast, takes a much broader approach seeing these technical solutions set in changed institutional and social settings which are more open to community participation and transparent in communication with the community. The strong version also addresses relations between the North and the South (ie, developed and developing nations) with regard to environmental issues and their social consequences. Hence, the strong version takes account of many of the criticisms of EM.

But criticism of EM also represents a clash of underpinning values. Those from an ecocentric value position may see EM as threatening 'to deflect their critiques of industrial society' (Dryzek 2005, p 179). For less radical environmentalists, EM may be welcomed as providing an entry point to influence governments, but at the same time there is the threat of cooption. That is, by entering into discussion within the framework of EM, environmentalists may not have an avenue to express their position, and may be seen as supporting storylines they do not share (see 5.4.1 and 7.7).

3.7 Value positions and world views

The discussion above has explored how values, ethics, paradigms and discourses may strongly influence the views we hold on environmental issues and human-environment relationships. But as we saw in 3.3 and Figure 3.2, there are a range of other factors that also influence our overall value positions and world view.

We return to our discussion of value positions by examining a spectrum of such positions related to human-environment relationships. Table 3.2 is a schema aimed at illustrating the spread of values across society in relation to four factors: attitudes to resources; type of economy; management strategies; and ethics, and how these combine to identify four value positions. This is just one schema of a number that aim to classify such a spectrum of environment-related value positions in society and attach labels to these.

Given the discussion on discourses in 3.6 it is worth noting that the value positions in Table 3.2 can be described through discourses and the discussion below goes some way to producing storylines for the four value positions.[12]

Table 3.2 shows a major division between technocentrics/anthropocentrics and ecocentrics and these two major categories are further divided, to produce four labelled value positions. In essence the further to the right in the Table, the greener the values.

Considering the four value positions in Table 3.2, at one end of the spectrum are the Cornucopians (the horn of plenty from Greek mythology) who see the world as composed of discrete, separate parts which we can manipulate to serve human needs. They believe in the substitutability of different forms of capital (see Box 2.2) and assume that human ingenuity will overcome environmental issues, whether these arise from resource scarcity or waste disposal issues, a view often referred to as a technocentric position or a technological fix outlook. Cornucopians' primary social objective is to maximise economic growth. They acknowledge that some environmental problems should be dealt with through environmental taxes and regulations, but consider that the mechanisms of the free market in combination with constantly developing science and technology can ensure conditions and opportunities for continued growth. They also see humans as separate from nature and recognise the natural environment only in terms of its value to humans – instrumental value (see 3.4). The Cornucopians hold a similar value position to the dominant paradigm in Table 3.1.

Moving towards a slightly greener set of values is the value position described by Pearce (1993) and O'Riordan (1981) as 'accommodating'. The underlying ethic here is also human-centred and separatist from nature. However, there is some emphasis on resource conservation through making society's use of resources more efficient over time and thus achieving some decoupling of economic growth and environmental impact. Accommodators have faith in technology but they also recognise that not all technological change is benign and that it will not solve all our problems (Pearce 1993).

Moving into the ecocentric territory, there is belief that neither free nor adjusted markets can deal with environmental problems and that more direct regulation and planning is required, as well as reduction in the scale of economic activity (ie, throughput of materials and energy, which ecocentrics believe cannot occur through decoupling alone). The deep ecologists at the far end of the spectrum see the need for strong regulations to achieve a much reduced scale of economic activity and strong environmental preservation. However, for some deep ecologists these outcomes may be primarily achieved through a spiritual

---

12   Dryzek (2005) has identified and discussed four environmental discourses which we may equate to four
     different value positions.

revolution leading to voluntary behaviour change (Pearce 1993). As we saw earlier (3.4) ecocentrics see human-nature relations very differently to anthropocentrics and extend ethical concern to non-human organisms.

For convenience anthropocentrics and technocentrics are grouped in Table 3.2. We have already discussed some of the differentiating characteristics of anthropocentrics and eco-centrics (see 3.4), but it remains to identify any differences between anthropocentrism and technocentrism.

Technocentrics and anthropocentrics share the same values with respect to the relationship between humans and the environment. As shown in Table 3.2 the shared values derive from a number of factors, and it is the differing emphasis given to particular factors that has provided the two names. As the name suggests, the major emphasis for technocentrics is strong faith in technology, classical science and the ability of humans to apply this science and technology to solving environmental problems (Pepper 1996). While sharing these values with technocentrics, the term anthropocentrism comes from its strong human-centered focus, whereby: 'human values are the source of all value' (Pepper 1996, p 19).

It is important to note that these labelled groups of values (ie the value positions) do not necessarily represent specific types of individuals. The schema is clearly a simplification of reality. As individuals we are not so neatly categorised and a wide range of influences come together to determine the positions we hold.

3.8 Ideologies – putting environmental concerns into politics

Schemas, such as that shown in Table 3.2 have often been titled as a 'spectrum of environmental ideologies' (eg O'Riordan 1981; Pearce 1993) suggesting that technocentrism, anthropocentrism and/or perhaps their underpinning value positions are ideologies. However, as we will see below that is probably not appropriate in terms of the specific meaning of an 'ideology'. There remains debate about whether there is in fact an environmental ideology, or rather simply a number of value positions or world views. We need to start by exploring the definition of 'ideology'.

Ideologies may be thought of as coherent sets of ideas that 'can link values to programs of action, and bind their adherents into unified groups' (Doyle and Kellow 1995, p 38). As such they can be a rallying point influencing and reinforcing the value positions people hold on issues relating to the environment. Importantly the coherent set of ideas is regarded as justifying actions.

Examples of political ideologies are conservatism, liberalism, feminism, socialism and nationalism (Dobson and Eckersley 2006b).[13] We recognise such ideologies as playing an important role in influencing political decisions. The environmental variant of such political ideologies is claimed to be ecologism (Carter 2007; Dobson 2000) though there has been debate as to whether it should be regarded as an ideology in its own right (Carter 2007; Dobson 2000; Dobson and Eckersley 2006b). To be recognised as an 'ideology', there is general agreement that three criteria must be met (Carter 2007, p 11):

(1) a common set of concepts and values providing a critique of the existing social and political systems;

---

13   For a good overview of these political ideologies see Dobson and Eckersley (2006a).

Table 3.2 The spectrum of environmental value positions

| | TECHNOCENTRIC/ANTHROPOCENTRIC | | ECOCENTRIC | |
	Cornucopian	Accommodating	Communalist	Deep Ecology
Green labels	Resource exploitative, Growth-oriented position	Resource conservationist and managerial position	Resource preservationist position	Extreme preservationist position
Type of economy	Anti-green economy, ie unfettered free markets	Green economy, ie green markets guided by economic incentive instruments (eg pollution charges etc)	Deep green economy, ie steady-state economy regulated by macro-environmental standards and supplemented by economic incentive instruments	Very deep green economy, heavily regulated to minimise resource-take
Management Strategies	Primary economic policy objective, maximize economic growth – Gross National Product (GNP)	Modified economic growth (adjusted green accounting to measure GNP)	Zero economic growth; zero population growth	Reduced scale of economy and population
	Assumption that unfettered free markets in conjunction with technical progress will ensure infinite substitution possibilities capable of mitigating all scarcity/limits constraints (environmental sources and sinks)	Decoupling of economic growth and environmental impact important but infinite substitution rejected. Sustainability rules: constant capital rule*	Decoupling plus no increase in scale of economic activity. Systems perspective – health of whole ecosystems very important	Scale reduction imperative
Ethics	Support for traditional ethical reasoning: rights and interests of contemporary individual humans; instrumental value (ie of recognised value to humans) in nature	Extension of ethical reasoning: 'caring for others' motive – intragenerational and inter-generational equity; instrumental value in nature	Further extension of ethical reasoning: interests of the collective take precedence over those of the individual; primary value of ecosystems and secondary value of component functions and services	Acceptance of bioethics (ie moral rights/interests conferred on all non-human species and even the abiotic parts of the environment); intrinsic value in nature (ie valuable in its own right regardless of human experience)

*See Box 2.2

Source: Based on diagram and ideas of Pearce et al (1993, p 18). Reproduced with permission of Earthscan Ltd <www.earthscan.co.uk>.

(2) a political prescription based on an alternative outline of how a society ought to look;

(3) a programme for political action with strategies for getting from the existing society to the alternative outline.

Hence, judged by these criteria, ideologies are closely linked to political motivation and this is a critical distinguishing feature. In this regard they may be distinguished from the concept of a 'paradigm' which also refers to a group sharing 'a scheme of ideas' but does not necessarily involve political motivation. Indeed paradigms may simply be concepts and methods shared within a discipline and providing rules for the conduct of the discipline. Similarly, ethics, discourses or values positions should not be regarded as ideologies.

Dobson (2000) claims that 'ecologism' conforms to these three criteria. In terms of the first criterion, ecologism critiques the impact of current industrial societies on the environment with particular emphasis on two core concepts. First it requires a re-thinking of the ethical relations between humans and nature, away from a strong anthropocentric (instrumental) view of nature. Secondly, it accepts the idea of 'limits to growth' (Carter 2007). Regarding the second criterion, ecologism prescribes an alternative sustainable society involving ecological responsibility, social justice, grassroots democracy, and non-violence. This certainly provides an alternative view of how our society should be. Ecologism also suggests strategies for change to achieve this alternative society, which satisfies the third criterion, although these are not well-defined (Carter 2007).

If these three points outline the broad nature of ecologism, and considering Table 3.2, we can see that ecologism must sit towards the ecocentric, or radical end of addressing environmental problems. But has ecologism really been recognised as an ideology by the public or does it remain confined to texts on political ideologies? We hear much about Green Parties in politics but not about 'ecologism', yet the ideology of Green Parties is presumably ecologism. Is it rather, that environmental concerns have been adopted by mainstream ideologies such as liberalism, conservatism and socialism? (see Carter 2007; Dobson and Eckersley 2006b).

The answers to these questions remain under debate (Carter 2007; Dobson and Eckersley 2006b), but it does seem that there has been a move away from a deep ecology position towards a more accommodating position (see Table 3.2) in defining the characteristics of ecologism. Deep ecology has failed to gain traction in the political arena, its prescriptions have been too radical for most people and its platform has often lacked coherence. Given this, and as sustainability has become the mainstream rhetoric 'the centre of gravity in environmental politics has undoubtedly shifted from a *radical* rejection of industrialism and a *narrow* concern with ecological issues, to a *reformist* acceptance of capitalism and liberal democracy based on a *broader* (and, in many respects, more radical) social justice agenda' (Carter 2007, p 356). Whether this is too reformist to meet criteria 1 and 2 above and hence classify as an ideology is debatable. However, Carter (2007, p 356) suggests that adoption of a strong version of sustainability (see 2.2) 'would certainly result in a form of capitalism so radically different as to be virtually unrecognisable'. As such it should satisfy the criteria for defining an ideology.

'Environmentalism' is a much better known term than ecologism, but is it an ideology? We have yet to define environmentalism (see 3.9.1) but of relevance to this discussion, environmentalism is a broad term simply covering concern for the environment, and with regard to Table 3.2 could be seen to span from the accommodating value position through to the deep ecologists. Given that scope it does not tightly bind a set of social actors as does ecologism, and cannot provide a single clearly defined alternative society. Dobson (2000, p 1) clearly distinguishes *ecologism* and *environmentalism* and does not regard environmentalism as an ideology. Rather he sees it as reformist and in that sense not sufficiently providing an alternative political prescription to present society (criterion 2 above). Certainly the accommodator value position in Table 3.2 is reformist. Linked to this point, Dobson (2000) also suggests that environmentalism is sufficiently non-specific to be accommodated within certain other political ideologies such as conservatism, liberalism or socialism.

3.9 Changing value positions over time

The discussion in this chapter has focused primarily on modern Western societies, but it is worth noting that Indigenous peoples around the world have typically held very different views on human-nature relationships than have modern Western societies (see Box 3.3). The exception among Western peoples is perhaps those holding deep ecology value positions.

Box 3.3: Indigenous perspectives on the environment

Indigenous peoples all over the world, including the Australian Aborigines have a unique relationship with the environment which significantly differs from traditional Western perspectives. Knudtson and Suzuki (1992, p 13) explain that 'traditional Native knowledge about the natural world tends to view all – or at least vast regions – of nature, often including earth itself, as inherently holy rather than profane, savage, wild or wasteland. The landscape itself, or certain regions of it, is seen as sacred and quivering with life'.

Whilst there are thousands of Indigenous cultures each with their own belief system, there are a set of mutual values which these groups hold in relation to the natural world. An Indigenous perspective of the environment tends to emphasise (Knudtson and Suzuki 1992, p 14):

- a deep reverence for nature;

- the need for 'reciprocity' where humans express gratitude and make sacrifices in return for the benefits they receive from nature;

- time as a circular phenomenon;

- nature is for human survival as opposed to material advantage;

- a human obligation to maintain balance and health of the natural world;

- that events and processes of the universe are linked and intertwined, often through a spiritual context;

- a strong sense of kinship and empathy with other forms of life.

See Chapter 6 for discussion of Indigenous knowledge.

Among modern Western societies, environmental value positions have changed over time at both the personal level and more broadly for society as a whole, towards greater recognition of, and care for, the environment. This has been particularly evident since about the mid-1960s. Clearly there is a range of positions in society at any one time, but we can track the changing value positions of society at large through changes in: policies and regulations relating to the environment; the type of institutions we develop; the place of environmental matters in our educational institutions; and so on. There are also a number of surveys that help us to understand trends in individual value positions, including the regular Australian Bureau of Statistics (ABS) survey – *Environmental Issues: People's Views and Practices*, which started in 1994 and has been conducted annually since 1998,[14] and the New South Wales Department of Environment and Climate Change's (DECC) *Who Cares About the Environment* series produced every three years.[15] Table 3.3 gives a very general picture of changes in community expectations towards business, governments, environmental groups and individuals, as a reflection of changing value positions. It suggests that expectations have expanded over time. That is, in 2000 communities still expected businesses to obey the law and pay for pollution, but they *also* expected them to go beyond compliance.

Table 3.3 General changes in community expectations regarding environmental management

Community expectations towards	1960	1980	2000
Business	To obey the law	To pay for pollution	To move beyond compliance. Take leadership and initiative, encourage government to act
Government	To regulate and provide safe reliable services and infrastructure	To penalise polluters	To work internationally, nationally and locally to steer change towards sustainability
Environmental groups	To protest	To influence policy	To work with government, industry and community towards sustainability. Solution focus in lobbying
Individuals	To obey the law	To support governments' policies for environmental controls	To develop understanding of sustainability issues and participate in decision-making. To take voluntary action to lessen personal ecological footprint

We have explored reasons for change in value positions, but not the nature of that change. Is it typically by a gradual evolution or a more sudden shift? Much has been written about the evolution of modern environmentalism and we will start with this.

---

14   These ABS surveys can be found at <www.abs.gov.au/ausstats/abs@.nsf/mf/4602.0> (accessed 3 February 2009). Although they are annual, different environment-related themes may be addressed from year to year.

15   The *Who Cares* surveys can be found at: <www.environment.nsw.gov.au/community/whocares.htm> (accessed 3 February 2009).

3.9.1 The evolution of 'modern environmentalism'

'Environmentalism' has a dual meaning according to the *Oxford English Dictionary Online*. On one hand it refers to the idea that environmental factors, both physical and cultural, have paramount influence on the development of humans and other animals both individually and socially. On the other hand it refers to concern with the preservation of environment and the politics and policies associated with this. Hence we can identify a two-way process between humans and the environment and this is evident in Figure 3.2. This involves, on the one hand, environmental influences and information about the environment flowing to humans and Figure 3.2 suggests this is one of many factors influencing our value positions regarding the environment. On the other hand these value positions then influence the way humans treat the environment (the feedback loop in Figure 3.2). It is the latter meaning of environmentalism that is of most concern to us in this section, but the two types of environmentalism just described are not independent of one another – each influences the other.

The term 'modern environmentalism' is often used to distinguish a process of social evolution which has occurred over about the past 45 years involving the development of widespread concern regarding environmental degradation and vast changes in attitudes about what constitutes appropriate environmental management and human relationships with nature.[16] This does not mean there has been an absence of concern over environmental quality and management in the past, but rather that this became a widespread rather than elite concern. Many see the development of modern environmentalism as constituting an important social revolution, equivalent in importance to other major revolutions in history, such as the Renaissance and the Industrial Revolution (eg Smil 1989).

As discussed in Chapter 1, increasing evidence of environmental degradation and associated impacts on human health has been an important factor in putting the environment on the discussion agenda around the world. Different value positions have emerged in relation to perceiving the underlying causes of the problems and the types of solutions required. These include the differing value positions in Table 3.2. These have changed over time as a result of the complex array of influences shown in Figure 3.2. Governments and policy-makers have responded to the evidence for the changing public mood as seen through polls and the election of Green Party members to parliaments, by institutionalisation of environmental concern through setting up a range of formal structures and processes for environmental protection – ministries, agencies, policies, regulations, legislation, decision-making processes (see Chapter 4). This continuing process has meant the evolution (or perhaps revolution) in environmentalism. Environment lobby groups (see 5.4.1) have emerged and become part of the formal processes of decision-making. As their role has developed in this setting, the use of direct action[17] has lessened, but not vanished entirely (consider the protests against Japanese whaling), and the lobby groups themselves have become far more formal structures run on business principles.

Of course success in influencing governments will be greatly facilitated by having wide public commitment to the value position being promulgated. There is a vast literature on the factors that enable value positions to have political influence. For example, Dryzek et al

---

16   The conceptual development of sustainability discussed in 2.4 provides one example of the evolution of thinking on human-environment relationships.

17   Direct action refers to protest actions taken outside the institutionalised framework for EDM. For example, physical protests at development sites or the protests by ships against Japanese whaling in the southern ocean.

(2003) explore the characteristics of nation-states that enable social movements,[18] such as the environment movement, to influence core government imperatives, such that a new type of government approach results. As an example they show how the social movement of the organised working class against a capitalist-dominated liberal State produced the welfare state. In the case of a social movement such as environmentalism the result would be a green state. Dryzek et al (2003) compare the place of environmentalism in four nation-states to test their assertion that if a social movement cannot make a strong connection to a core government imperative, it will at best receive marginal gains and is likely to be coopted (see Chapters 5 and 7). They argue that this has been the fate of environmentalism and that ecological modernisation may achieve what environmentalism has failed to achieve – the development of a new government imperative: environmental conservation, and a green state. Nevertheless, those from a deep green value position would no doubt see this as incrementalism[19] within a continuing shallow-dry green state.[20] Beder (1992) has argued that a paradigm shift of the type described by Merchant in Box 3.2 would be necessary to move society from a 'shallow' to a 'deep green' value position.

An important question is what is required for such a paradigm shift to occur? Many suggest that for radical change the belief systems of policy elites have to be disrupted by external factors (see Carter 2007). One such external factor Carter suggests (p 197) is the appearance of a 'new problem' such as climate change, for which 'the dominant interests in the policy community have no immediate solution'. So far responses to climate change have not involved radical shifts in value positions, but increasing recognition of the urgency of addressing the issue and inadequacies of current arrangements in the face of the current global financial crisis may change that.

Jamison (2001, p 180) suggests that perhaps 'the most important effect that environmentalism has had over the past thirty years is to help people worldwide to rediscover their relationship with the earth'. If this is so, it may provide the seed for a paradigm shift in regard to human-nature relationships.

While overall societal concern for the environment has certainly evolved dramatically, there remain considerable differences in value positions between individuals and groups within societies.

3.10 Exploring the influence of value positions in EDM

As we have seen values influence the way we view environmental issues and how we respond to them. They influence all stages of EDM. The history of environmental debate

---

18 The term 'social movement' refers to 'an association or set of associations organized around a common interest that seeks to influence collective outcomes without obtaining authoritative offices of government' (Dryzek et al 2003, p 2). However, the term is hard to define *precisely* and definitions have varied over time. The environment movement, gay rights movement, women's movement, are each widely regarded as social movements.

19 The practice of introducing change gradually or incrementally (*Oxford English Dictionary Online*).

20 The terms dry, shallow and deep green were used by O'Riordan (1991a) to describe a spectrum of environmental value positions in place of the technocentric – ecocentric spectrum shown in Table 3.2. O'Riordan wanted to make the point that by the early 1990s society had become much 'greener', everyone is 'somewhat green'.

also shows us that these value positions are often both strongly held and incompatible. To participate effectively in EDM it is important to understand the basis for differing views put forward in discussions. To what extent do the views reflect strongly held value positions? What do these value positions primarily concern? To what extent do views rest mainly on interests? Often debate seems to be about the so-called 'facts' of the issue, but as we have seen 'facts' are socially constructed and influenced by values. The debate on the use of nuclear energy for power supplies provides a good example. Those in favour and against nuclear power emphasise different aspects in determining the facts of potential environmental and social impacts. The emphasis is typically influenced by their value position. The discussion in this chapter is aimed at helping you to explore and understand the role played by values when examining an environmental issue.

In terms of the primary concern of a particular value position, it is useful to distinguish value positions relating to 'ends' from those relating to 'means'. By 'ends' we mean outcomes. For example, cessation of forest clearfelling, an end to whaling, a major move from private car use to public transport, might be ends in line with ecocentric value positions. Values about 'means' are concerned with the way in which we achieve desired ends, and this involves many aspects of how our societies operate, including the types of institutions we use for making and implementing decisions (see Chapter 4) and the type of instruments we use to bring about behaviour change (see Chapter 8). For example, how do we govern behaviour that impacts on the environment – through the firm hand of strong regulation and punishment, or the softer hand of education, economic incentives and gentle disincentives? Who takes part in decision-making on environmental issues and in what way? Is it an open process involving a strong focus on meaningful public participation in EDM, or is it a closed process favouring professional expertise? Is it a top-down or bottom-up process? (see Chapter 7). Consider also provision of energy. There are clearly strong differences in views relating to the use of different energy sources such as fossil fuels, renewables and nuclear fuels. But beyond this, there may also be strong values regarding the means of producing energy. For example, what sort of energy economy should we have? One based on centralised, high capital, exclusive[21] technology such as required by nuclear energy? Or, one based on decentralised renewables? That is, much energy collected or generated locally through say household solar collectors for water heating and photovoltaics for power generation (see Lovins 1977). Box 3.4 provides a useful example of conflict over 'means'.

Box 3.4: Value conflict in seeking 'acceptance' of nuclear power

Consider the option of nuclear power as a source of energy. The principal reasons for most people's opposition to nuclear power are commonly assumed to be: (i) the problem of disposal of waste radioactive material, which will remain active for perhaps 1000 years, (ii) the risk of a Chernobyl-type accident, and (iii) siting of the plant. However, considering just the waste problem, even if this problem could be overcome, many people holding strong environmental value positions may still be opposed to nuclear power. For instance, nuclear power is a large-scale, centralised form of power supply, as opposed to the small-scale and decentralised ideals of those who hold strong environmental value positions such as the 'alternative environmental paradigm' in Table 3.1 or the 'ecocentrics' in Table 3.2. Nuclear power is associated with a well-defined and policed hierarchy of responsibility in operation and management as opposed to providing democracy in decision-making. It is an energy option that does not empower the

---

21   Meaning in this case that ordinary people are excluded from operating the technology. In contrast many
      renewable technologies can be managed day-to-day by non-expert people.

community, but makes them vulnerable to the decisions and interpretations of scientific and technological experts. Hence the values-based objections to nuclear power for those holding strong environmental value positions go far beyond concern for safe disposal of radioactive waste. Even if this environmental threat could be eliminated, values-based conflict would still remain. The same holds true for the other two grounds for opposition listed above.

However, while characterising value positions in this way is an aid to understanding the role and influence of people's value positions in EDM, it does not resolve values conflict. How do we deal with value conflict in EDM? Is value conflict necessarily a bad thing?

3.11 Dealing with competing values

Conflict arising from competing values is common in environmental and sustainability decision-making. This is to be expected given the range of value positions in societies. Such conflict has typically been seen as a problem.

For example, the proponent of a development (whether from the private or public sector) who encounters violent protest when in the late stages of planning, will certainly see such conflict as a problem. Considerable financial and personnel costs will probably have occurred to reach this stage if the development is a complex one. It would have been much better to have had a clear understanding of the range of value positions and perspectives on the development at the concept stage (see also 7.4.3). This would have provided space and time to explore these other perspectives and possibly modify the concept as a result. At worst, it would have given the opportunity to negotiate with potential protesters for an agreed solution. Such negotiation has a much greater chance of success at the early stages of planning when a number of options may be possible and positions may not be so entrenched. Case Study C is a good example of such a situation.

Outright values conflict can also be destabilising to government policy processes (Stewart 2009). Governments may ignore such conflict hoping it will go away, but as Dovers (2005a) points out this is typically counterproductive as value conflicts tend to re-emerge. It is necessary therefore to address values conflict through decision-making processes (Lee 1999). Typically, this has been done through governments trying to manage and accommodate value conflict using various methods as discussed in 3.11.1. But a number of innovative approaches have been developed that show value conflict can be beneficial if navigated properly, not only avoiding negative and destabilising situations, but also contributing positively to creative compromise and change. We discuss some of these innovations in 3.11.2.

3.11.1 Avoiding or managing value conflicts

A first step in managing value conflicts by governments is typically to seek a compromise position. However, this may reveal much about embedded values that show that compromise will not be possible. For example, it may demonstrate that policies aimed at satisfying one value position may undermine satisfaction of other value positions (Thacher and Rein 2004). Many examples of this are evident from the discussion in 3.10 above. For example, satisfying a position which values centralising of services, such as energy provision, conflicts directly with the position that values a decentralised approach to energy provision.

Such incompatibility between values may make compromise impossible. If compromise is not possible, how else may value conflict be accommodated?

Accommodation of incompatible values is typically seen as occurring through governments balancing competing goals or making trade-offs between competing value positions. However, this is just one of many ways governments may treat competing values. For example (Stewart 2006; Thacher and Rein 2004):

Firewalls describe a situation where multiple institutions are formed, each committed to different values. This serves to provide champions for each of the values and segregation of main responsibility for each in separate agencies. An example of this in the environment context is the segregation of environment departments from economic development departments. Stewart (2006, p 187) suggests that this allows production or economic-related departments to continue with little interference from environment departments and with coordination between the two occurring at low management levels, if at all.

Cycling occurs when conflicting values are recognised and addressed sequentially. The attention given to each of particular competing values by public institutions alternates between the opposite positions 'subordinating one-half of a dilemma and then the other' (Thacher and Rein 2004, p 465). The natural resource management (NRM) field in Australia provides an example of this. There has been long debate over the value of centralised versus decentralised delivery of NRM activities. The Natural Heritage Trust (NHT) introduced by the Howard Coalition Government in 1997, distributed significant funding for environmental repair and conservation. In the first five years of the program 40–60 per cent of funds bypassed State and local governments and the focus was on regional community-based delivery (Crowley 2001). This community emphasis followed the example of the previous Federal Labor Government's National Landcare Program. The value position expressed through the NHT program emphasised decentralised planning and expenditure on environmental repair and conservation. The NHT concluded in June 2008 and the incoming Rudd Labor Government replaced it with the Caring for Our Country program which has considerably broadened the range of players who will be funded for on-ground work (Australian Government 2008), thus potentially reducing the prominence given to community delivery. Stewart (2006) sees this type of organisational change, often involving shifts between more or less devolved structures, occurring when a significant number of actors become dissatisfied with the outcomes of the policy in place. In this regard there has been ongoing discussion regarding the efficiency of the NHT process (see Crowley 2001).

Incrementalism refers to taking small policy steps rather radical or strategic leaps. Some scholars argue that many policy decisions proceed incrementally (Lindblom 1959). Incrementalism may be useful in situations where radical change may arouse value conflicts and produce situations which are difficult for governments to manage. In the environmental field responses to challenges such as climate change have typically been incremental, despite increasing reports suggesting that radical responses are required (eg Stern 2006). By taking smaller steps, decision-makers can try to avoid opposition from those espousing radical change values, since at least a move in the desired direction is evident, but also avoid opposition from those whose values oppose radical change.

Decision delay can provide a way for governments to manage value conflict, at least in the short term. One way of doing this is to appoint an inquiry to advise on the issue or to ask for advice from an independent authority such as that sought from the Australian Chief Scientist in the Gunns pulp mill case (see Case Study B). In many cases this is simply a political tactic to take the heat out of an issue until an important event, such as an election, is over (see also 7.4.3). In such cases the terms of reference for the inquiry or the independent expert may be set narrowly so that they do not provide the need to address value differences. Consequently, the conflict is unlikely to go away with the outcomes of the inquiry.

While each of these means may provide useful stopgap measures for governments in managing value conflict, they are unlikely to lead to constructive outcomes in the longer term.

3.11.2 Bringing values to the fore

There has been considerable discussion on the failure of contemporary liberal democratic institutions to satisfactorily accommodate the range of values expressed in EDM (Smith 2003). Much work has followed in developing means to bring such values to the fore through deliberative processes.

'Deliberation' is a particular kind of communication that is characterised by informational, argumentative, reflective and social dimensions (Dryzek 2000a). Ideally, participants are *informed* about an issue with all its complexities, uncertainties and trade-offs. Deliberators *reason* and *argue* together, and question underlying concepts, frames, and values. They also *reflect* on their own preferences and the arguments of others and are encouraged to provide reasons in terms that others may appreciate and accept (Benhabib 1996). As they interact in a *social* environment, deliberators ideally become aware of their shared membership in a broader group (Dryzek 2000a). In this social context people can discover similarities and differences, and find opportunities for reaching common ground (Benhabib 1996; Gutmann and Thompson 1996). We will discuss here two examples that use processes for dialogue that lead to deeper understanding of the issue by participants, respect for others' views and values, and appreciation that decisions have been reached by a rigorous and fair process. Typically the latter leads to greater acceptance of a decision. Further deliberative methods are discussed in Chapter 7.

3.11.2.1 Collaborative learning

'Collaborative learning' is one such process that was developed by Steven Daniels and Gregg Walker in the United States for addressing complex land management issues on public lands (such as management of recreation areas within public forest lands) taking account of multiple conflicting interests and values and with a whole of ecosystem focus (Daniels and Walker 1996). Collaborative learning enables conflicting parties to enter into a learning process about one another's values and perspectives with regard to the ecosystem issue at hand. This involves participants identifying the range of values about the issue and through deliberation developing visions for how the landscape should look in the future and 'the role of people in achieving this vision' (Cheng and Fiero 2005, p 169). This learning process enables participants to widen their understanding of a situation 'by learning to see it as a complex system of issues' (Daniels and Walker 1996, p 97) and discern where there may be shared interests and areas of disagreement, and possibly new ways of framing the problem. The challenge for this social learning is 'not to resolve or eliminate conflict; rather it is to learn about complex issues in an inherently conflictual environment' (Daniels and Walker 1996, p 74). Essentially this is a process of negotiation through careful constructive dialogue. Collaborative learning draws on systems thinking and learning and alternative dispute resolution (mediation and negotiation). It uses techniques to help conflicting parties to better understand others' perspectives and the legitimacy of these. It uses guidelines to promote productive dialogue and does not aim for a 'solution to a problem' but rather to 'develop improvements over the status quo situation'. Results are measured as progress rather than against a defined goal (Daniels and Walker 1996). Success of the collaborative learning process, as judged by participant satisfaction, has been reported by Daniels and Walker (1996) and Cheng and Fiero (2005) for developing management plans for public forest areas in the United States.

Means for accommodating a range of value positions and interests through collaborative dialogue, aimed not only at developing plans or policies, but also in their implementation, have gained increasing interest over the last 10 years and include 'collaborative governance' (CG) (Ansell and Gash 2008; Connick and Innes 2003; Leach et al 2002) and 'co-management' (Armitage et al 2007a, 2007b; Plummer and Fitzgibbon 2004).

3.11.2.2 Collaborative governance and co-management

Collaborative governance (CG) involves public agencies and non-government actors in collective decision-making. The process is 'formal, consensus-oriented and deliberative', and 'aims to make or implement public policy or manage public programs or assets' (Ansell and Gash 2008, p 544). It has emerged to deal with inadequacies in top-down traditional bureaucratic forms of governance that have frequently failed to resolve long-standing natural resource management conflicts and that are typically inflexible, slow to respond to changing circumstances, and slow to anticipate needed changes (Connick and Innes 2003). As with collaborative learning, discussed above, the key attribute of CG is not simply to reach an agreement, but rather to develop understanding and long-term relationships between previously opposing actors. Such understanding may allow long term adversaries to move off a collision course and let policy development move in new directions (Connick and Innes 2003, p 186).

Analysis of a large number of cases of CG across a range of policy sectors has identified important factors for the process to be successful. These include the following (Ansell and Gash 2008; Connick and Innes 2003):

Face-to-face dialogue is at the core of CG and is vital in building trust, shared understanding, mutual respect and commitment to the process. Commitment to the process involves mutual recognition of interdependence[22] of participants, openness to seeking mutual gains, and shared ownership of the process. The latter comes with risks for participants who may fear being left as joint owners of a decision-making process and its outcomes with others who have very different value positions. Will they be seen as coopted? Hence trust in fellow participants to respect your views and interests is vital. This is one reason why building trust in the early stages of dialogue is critical, but building trust may also be time consuming, particularly where antagonism has previously been rife between parties. To have any chance of moving through to consensus, participants need to identify common values, must develop a shared understanding of the nature of the problem or issue under discussion, and a clear view of what the group may hope to achieve. Consensus should not be sought until discussion has brought out interests, issues and values and 'significant effort has been made to find creative responses to difference' (Connick and Innes 2003, p 180). Finally, CG is best seen as cyclical and iterative in the sense that participants need to be prepared to modify deliberative processes if necessary and learn by doing.

---

22   Meaning here that participants see that achievement of their desired outcomes is dependent on the cooperation of other stakeholders in the CG process. Participants fear they will lose out in decision-making if they are not at the table (Ansell and Gash 2008).

Connick and Innes (2003) examined three major water management issues in California that had experienced long-term conflicts, including the CALFED Bay-Delta Program (see Box 3.5). They suggest that the agreements reached in each of the three cases they studied would have been impossible without the collaborative dialogue and that none of the agreements represented the 'lowest common denominator results that some fear from consensus building' (Connick and Innes 2003, p 187).

Box 3.5: Collaborative water policy-making – the CALFED Bay-Delta Program

The CALFED Bay-Delta Program was a collaborative policy-making and water management process aimed at developing a plan for restoring the Sacramento-San Joaquin Delta ecosystem, from which much of the California's water is supplied. Concern for endangered species, habitat restoration, flood protection, water supply and water quality were issues to address. The group also needed to develop new operations and management strategies to achieve the plan.

The program involved 18 state and federal agencies with responsibility for managing water supply and protecting the related natural resources. There had been long-term conflict among a number of these agencies. It also included actors from non-government interest groups, Native American tribes, and local and regional urban water agencies.

The CALFED process appears to have been extremely successful and has been described as bringing 'to an end 100 years of water wars' (Connick and Innes 2003, p 183). Its results included:

- many examples of progress with previously antagonistic parties moving towards agreement on issues;

- an agreed design for a commission involving non-government actors, representatives of state and federal agencies and Native American tribes, to bring a coordinated approach to overseeing future water management. This was established under legislation in 2002 and provided a stark contrast with the previous uncoordinated and conflictual approach among several agencies;

- development and joint advocacy of schemes to raise billions of dollars for environmental restoration and improvements in water quality, use efficiency and supply facilities;

- development of an 'environmental water account' that provided water for fisheries protection in an efficient manner, such that new regulatory measures could be avoided and more water would be available for urban and agricultural uses;

- influence on change in water policy development across the entire State of California, towards more collaborative dialogue processes.

Source: Connick and Innes (2003).

A number of important advantages for the management of complex natural resource issues are claimed for the CG process (Connick and Innes 2003). Continuing incorporation of actors' value positions and knowledge makes for a process that is well-equipped to deal with the ecological and social complexity of such issues. In turn the collaborative dialogue builds ongoing networks and 'distributed intelligence' that provide flexibility to respond to unanticipated changes. In other words they enable adaptive management (see 2.9.4). As is evident from Box 3.5, a number of innovative solutions emerged in the CALFED case from the process of disparate actors trying to solve policy problems in a consensual manner (Connick and Innes 2003).

Analysis of numerous cases shows that CG has many potential advantages over traditional siloed bureaucratic wrangling and adversarial policy-making. However, it is also important to acknowledge and explore the context within which a CG program is to take place. Factors such as the power relationships between participants, incentives and/or disincentives for participation, previous history of cooperation or conflict between participants, the design of the collaborative process, and the existence or otherwise of facilitatory leadership, are each important influences on the success of the process (see Chapter 7). So while studies show many very positive outcomes from collaborative governance programs, there are also cases where the factors outlined above have not been met and programs can founder (Ansell and Gash 2008). Ansell and Gash (2008) found 'time, trust and interdependence' to be the key factors influencing the likelihood of success. For example, considering 'time', relationships and consensus cannot be built overnight, consequently CG exercises need to be given time to mature before their effectiveness is judged (Leach et al 2002). For this reason, CG may not be a useful process where decisions need to be made quickly (Ansell and Gash 2008).

Co-management shares with CG recognition of the importance of broad-based participation when devising management systems that can respond to change and uncertainty inherent in complex interlinked social and ecological systems. It shares many of the suggested advantages of such involvement outlined for CG. However, it is distinguished in that an essential component concerns the distribution of rights and responsibilities regarding a particular resource, with this sharing typically between government and local users (Plummer and FitzGibbon 2004), although this can take a number of forms representing a continuum in level of power sharing (Armitage et al 2007a). Co-management may be codified in law and that is seen in cases involving Indigenous land or resource rights in Australia, the United States, Canada and New Zealand (Armitage et al 2007a). An emerging field combining the attributes of co-management and adaptive management (see 2.9.4) is 'adaptive co-management' (Armitage et al 2007b).

Collaborative learning, governance and co-management provide encouraging examples of how through inclusive deliberative processes conflict can be turned into productive dialogue and consensus may be reached in situations that were previously stalled and hostile.

3.12 Conclusions

Value differences play an important role in EDM. For some they provide an impediment to efficient decision-making, but others see them as a rich source of information, different ways of seeing an issue and possible solutions to it. This latter view is gaining prominence as decision-makers realise that values cannot be ignored. If value differences are not accommodated in decision-making, they are likely to re-emerge leading to conflict which can be unproductive for all concerned and destabilising to government policy processes.

To accommodate value differences we must first understand their basis. Why, when confronted with the same information, do people differ in their interpretations of environmental issues, in the ways they consider appropriate for addressing those issues, and in possible solutions?

The factors that contribute to our views on issues are complex, coming from within – our personalities, and from without – a wide range of external factors. External factors include the state of our environment, the economy, information from the media, through education and from our cultural history, as well as less tangible influences from family, friends, religion and society more broadly. This complex array of influences, coupled with any interests (financial or otherwise) that we may bring to an issue, produce our value positions on issues. Notably the broader societal influences include values, ethics, paradigms, discourses and ideologies that are important in governing the way we interpret other external influences. These are not static, but evolve over time in line with a changing mix of the influences outlined above.

Understanding the value positions people may hold is the first step in seeking means to accommodate conflicting values. Traditional approaches by governments have attempted to manage conflicting values through a range of methods including balancing competing goals, making trade-offs between competing value positions, siloing conflicting values in different agencies of government, and delaying decisions. But at best these are stopgap measures. Recent approaches seek not to bury value differences, but rather to bring them to the fore through deliberative and collaborative processes that give people the chance to explore one another's views in informational, argumentative and reflective social settings, that enable similarities and differences to come to the fore and common ground to be found. Such processes in themselves help to dampen ongoing conflict since participants are more likely to accept decisions they can see have been reached through rigorous and fair processes. Most importantly, such collaborative processes foster the type of governance that is flexible, adaptive and more broadly informed than traditional top-down bureaucratic forms of government. In turn, this makes for a society that is well-suited to address the challenges associated with the 'wicked problems' of sustainability (Connick and Innes 2003).

4

Institutions

4.1 Introduction

Environmental decisions are ultimately political decisions, and these are profoundly influenced by their surrounding institutional context. For example, the way legislation and policies are made, the kind of elections we hold, and the nature of our legal system all shape the way decision processes proceed and affect resulting environmental outcomes. Moreover, the government of the day also determines the allocation of ministerial responsibilities and their relative power, and influences where the environment sits in relation to other portfolios. Political processes also directly or indirectly determine the terms of reference for decision-making; that is, what is deemed relevant and what is not, and which institutions and organisations are involved.

To be an effective participant in environmental decision-making (EDM) processes (in either a professional or private capacity) it is necessary not only to appreciate this broader institutional and procedural context, but to keep pace with changing circumstances and to understand how they might influence your role and decision outcomes. Such knowledge is crucial for anyone interested in working out how best to influence environmental decisions and effectively negotiate the maze of bureaucratic, legal and parliamentary institutions (Duffy 1996).

One way to conceptualise the institutional context of environmental decisions is to think of it as a kind of scaffolding that shapes how and where decisions are made. In this chapter we explore some of the main features of this scaffolding, including the formal political structures in Australia involved in EDM. We begin our exploration by clarifying the meaning of the term 'institutions' as used in this chapter. Next, we consider the role and influence of some of Australia's key political institutions such as federalism, parliaments, political parties, the bureaucracy and the courts in EDM. We also briefly step into the global realm and survey some of the key international institutions that influence EDM in Australia. To conclude, we consider how our existing political institutions might be improved to facilitate better progress towards sustainability.

Given the breadth of issues, our purpose here is to introduce readers to the formal political context of environmental governance, and to consider its influence on environmental decisions more broadly. Readers wishing to learn more about particular institutions or topics are encouraged to pursue the references provided.

4.2 What do we mean by 'institutions'?

The term institution is notoriously slippery. It is commonly used in a narrow sense to refer to organisations of the nation-state, society and the international system (March and Olsen 1989). Under this definition, institutions display formal organisational characteristics, such as memberships, rules and operating procedures (Howlett and Ramesh 2003). Such rule-based structures relevant to EDM include: systems of government and law such as parliament, political parties, elections, the public sector and the courts. One particularly significant formal institution in Australia is federalism, where political authority and responsibility is divided between different levels of government.

In addition to this formal definition, the term institution also has a much broader meaning (Bell 2002). Consider, for example, one of the *Oxford English Dictionary*'s definitions of an institution: "[a]n established law, custom, usage, practice, organization, or other element in the political or social life of a people".[1] In relation to the environment, these kinds of broader institutions might include:

- financial structures such as the economy and market forces, which can encourage and discourage particular activities and behaviours;

- social norms, routines and practices that affect resource usage (for example, notions of comfort, cleanliness and convenience (Shove 2003));

---

1   From *Oxford English Dictionary Online* <http://dictionary.oed.com/> (accessed 13 March 2009).

- urban structures and design, which can influence waste and waste management, as well as transport decisions and energy consumption;

- paradigms particularly in relation to the use and dominance of scientific knowledge (see Chapters 3 and 6);

- religious and cultural institutions, that can affect the priorities and values of individuals, communities and societies.

These broader institutional forces are considered throughout the book particularly in Chapters 2 and 3. Our primary focus in this chapter is on the key formal political institutions in Australia and their meaning for EDM.

4.3 Key political institutions in Australia

Australia is a liberal democracy to the extent that its political institutions ascribe to two core goals. First, a degree of liberty is guaranteed by checks and balances to ensure that citizens are protected from the abuses of power by the state. Secondly, political authority is based on popular consent and is determined through regular competitive elections (representative democracy) (Heywood 1997). In other words, decision-makers are accountable (that is, answerable) to their citizens (typically via an elected assembly) for their decisions and actions. Political accountability in Australia's system has been influenced by the British Westminster model of 'responsible government' where the political executive (cabinet) are members of parliament, and hence held to account through regular elections (Weller and Jaensch 1980). There are three broad arms of responsible government (Althaus et al 2007, p 13):

- The **legislature**, also known as the parliament, which is composed of elected representatives and has the authority to enact legislation (make laws).

- The **political executive** (or the administration), which is responsible for administering and enforcing laws and policies. In practice the political executive is the cabinet, which is composed of those ministers (members of parliament) who are responsible for core government portfolios (Fenna 2004, p 197).

- The **judiciary**, or the judges and the courts, which has the authority to apply and interpret the law and to resolve legal disputes.

In Westminster systems such as in Australia and Great Britain, the legislature (parliament) and the executive (the government acting through cabinet) are closely linked. Cabinet members are selected from the parliament, and because they represent the major party in the parliament, it is often said that government effectively controls the parliament (at least in numbers) (Parkin and Summers 2002). This system of government contrasts with the American model where the functions of the legislature (Congress) and the executive (administration) are intentionally separated. Where the United States and Australia share much in common is their federal structure – an institution which we now explore.

4.4 Federalism and the environment

Australia once consisted of six self-governing colonies with independent systems of law, rules and administration. It was not until 1901 that an overarching national government was formed in a process known as 'Federation'. The formal document which defined the structures and conventions of this new nation is *The Constitution of the Commonwealth of Australia* (known simply as 'the Constitution'). Formally, the Constitution is an articulation of the 'most fundamental rules' of a nation (Lovell et al 1998, p 57). It lays downs the duties, powers and functions of a government and defines the relationships between the state and its citizens (Heywood 1997).

One of the driving forces behind the charting of the Australian Constitution in the early 1900s was the desire to have a unified *national* voice in the international arena. There were also efficiencies to be gained by coordinating the activities of independent states, for example forming one defence force. The Australian constitutional designers selected a federal system because it offered a structure whereby political authority could be divided territorially. In other words, different levels of government could be formed, and could be responsible for administering particular portfolios (Lovell et al 1998, pp 61–63). At the same time there was a strong desire to retain government at the colonial (which became the State) level. So at the national level, new structures were created and powers at this level were specified in the Constitution. The newly formed States retained their autonomy and regional power (Janesch 1997).

4.4.1 Division of powers

At the time of Federation in Australia, the Commonwealth Government was given only a few very specific but significant powers which were set out in s 51 of the Constitution. Today these powers include control over issues such as defence, external or foreign affairs, currency, telecommunications, provision of social services, family law and immigration. Not surprisingly, at the time of Federation in 1901 the environment was not considered significant enough to list under the Commonwealth's powers.

Those powers not listed in s 51 of the Constitution (termed *residual* powers) remain with the States. Thus the States have power over land use and resource management, agriculture, employment, industrial matters, criminal law, as well as providing essential services such as water, power, transport, housing, hospitals and education (Thompson 1997a). State governments have a large number of responsibilities and functions particularly in establishing infrastructure and fostering development. This means that many of their activities involve consideration of environmental issues.

To finance the extensive range of services that they provide, the States are reliant on funds from the Commonwealth. Today, the Commonwealth raises approximately 80 per cent of all government revenue (generated mostly through income tax) but it is only responsible for about 50 per cent of spending (Fenna 2004, p 173). This is referred to as the 'vertical fiscal imbalance'; the States have the responsibility for providing most public services, but the Commonwealth has the bulk of the funds. Traditionally, States have supplemented their constrained budgets by raising revenues through natural resource royalties, stamp duties, motor vehicle licences and traffic fines, property taxes, payroll taxes, their own business enterprises and gambling taxes (Fenna 2004, Ch 7). At times this has meant that States have been more interested in facilitating large scale infrastructure development projects and encouraging resource extraction than in protecting the environment (Walker 1994).

Whilst some of the powers listed in s 51 are exclusive, most are *concurrent* powers on which both the Federal and State governments can legislate. The environment is a case in point as we will show below in relation to the Commonwealth *Environment Protection and Biodiversity Conservation Act 1999*. However, when a legislative conflict arises between Commonwealth and State parliaments, the national legislation prevails (Fenna 2004, p 169). The Constitution makes no provisions for local governments which were created by State governments through local government Acts (Fenna 2004). This third tier of government was established to meet specific needs which are most appropriately delivered at the community level. Typically State governments delegate a number of duties to local government such as: provision of public works and services; management of recreation facilities; town planning and land-use decisions and authority to license and approve various local and commercial activities (Singleton et al 2006).

Each tier of government plays a role in environmental management. Although there are some specific divisions of responsibility, generally the boundaries are unclear. As discussed below, this has created difficulties and conflict and in recent years there have been numerous attempts to better specify relative responsibilities.

4.4.2 Environmental responsibilities of the Commonwealth

Although the Constitution does not give the Commonwealth any *specific* powers on the environment, it has nevertheless acquired extensive environmental powers. This has come about through various interventions, particularly its judicial interpretation of s 51 of the Constitution. In cases through the 1980s the High Court deemed the legality of linking the Commonwealth's actions on the environment to a specified power or powers under s 51, a number of which have been shown to possess significant capacity to regulate environmentally damaging State activities. These include (Bates 2002; Saunders 1996):

- *Corporations power* – for issues involving foreign and most Australian corporations. For example, it was employed in the *Franklin Dam* case (in conjunction with other powers) to prevent the Tasmanian Hydro-Electric Commission (HEC) (deemed to be a 'corporation') from constructing a dam in the Franklin wilderness area (see Box 4.1).

- *External affairs power* – for issues involving international treaty obligations, such as the *World Heritage Convention* and the 1992 United Nations *Framework Convention on Climate Change*.

- *Overseas trade and commerce power* – for issues relating to imports and exports. For example, this power has been used to control and prevent sand mining and wood chipping activities and management of kangaroo culling where kangaroo products are for export.

- *Races power* – relating to the people of any race for whom it is deemed necessary to make special laws. This may be used to protect Aboriginal artefacts and sacred sites.

- *Finance and taxation power* – used in environmental matters where the government may wish to create financial incentives or disincentives for particular activities, such as an Emissions Trading Scheme to reduce carbon emissions.

Box 4.1: The Franklin Dam battle

In the late 1960s pressures on the largely untouched wilderness areas in South-West Tasmania, one of the world's three largest remaining temperate wilderness areas, began to mount. The pressure on the wilderness came primarily through threats to the river systems by Tasmania's Hydro-Electric Commission (HEC) – a powerful and politically independent institution that, unlike government departments, was not responsible to any minister. For well over 50 years HEC, along with the major political parties, maintained that hydro-industrialisation was Tasmania's principal and preferred means of sustaining and securing the State's future economic wealth.

However, during the late 1960s and 1970s a series of HEC proposals received serious public scrutiny, namely the flooding of Lake Pedder and the proposal to dam parts of the Franklin River in Tasmania's South-West. The issue of damming the Franklin was particularly controversial; it split the Tasmanian public and became an iconic national environmental issue. In the absence of a meaningful and transparent public participation program, came an explosion of demonstrations, blockades and confrontations supported by thousands of people all over Australia. Today, the Franklin Dam controversy stands as the single largest conservation issue in Australia's history. The period between the flooding of Lake Pedder and the Franklin proposal saw the emergence and maturation of a widespread conservation movement in Australia (see Lohrey 2002).

In the early 1980s the Franklin dam controversy featured in federal election campaigns. Much pressure was focussed on the then Prime Minister Fraser (Liberal) to intervene in the Tasmanian Government's plan to construct the dam. Fraser refused to intercede in the debate but did declare the South-West, including the Franklin River, part of Australia's national heritage. The area was later formally declared a World Heritage site. Pressure on the Federal Government also came from the Labor opposition leader (Bob Hawke) who had stated that, if elected, Labor would terminate the construction of the dam. In 1982 environmental action climaxed. Conservationists successfully blockaded the Franklin construction site where over 1200 demonstrators were arrested. Prime Minister Fraser was forced to respond to the unprecedented public outcry and offered the HEC $500 million for an alternative coal-fired power station (Tighe 1992). The offer was refused.

In 1983 the Hawke Labor opposition won a landslide federal election. The Hawke Government was swift in its action to cease construction of the Franklin Dam and challenged the Tasmanian State Government's authority to construct a dam in a World Heritage area (Tighe 1992). It sought to prevent HEC (deemed to be a 'corporation') from constructing a dam in the Franklin wilderness area by employing the corporations power under s 51 of the Constitution. It also argued under its external affairs powers (for issues involving international treaty obligations) that the dam would significantly damage the wilderness significance of Tasmania's South-West World Heritage area.

In response to the Hawke Government's intentions to block construction of the Franklin Dam, the Tasmanian Government took the matter to the High Court, challenging the constitutional right of the Federal Government to intervene (The Blockaders 1983). The Franklin Dam controversy formally came to a close in 1983. The High Court's historic decision declared that the Commonwealth's power to stop the Gordon-Below-Franklin Dam was valid. In 1984, Tasmania was financially compensated ($276.5 million) for the loss of the Franklin scheme by the Federal Government.

The Franklin case represents a landmark decision for environmental management in Australia's federal system. It effectively found that the Commonwealth could use its various constitutional powers to override State land use decisions (Fenna 2004, p 173). The political test, however, is whether the Commonwealth is able to win enough national political support for intervention (Summers 2006).

Another method by which the Commonwealth Government can influence environmental matters is through s 96 of the Constitution, concerning tied grants to the States (also known as Specific Purpose Payments SPPs). As the name suggests, the terms and conditions on which the money is provided to the States are specified by the Commonwealth (Fenna 2004). For example, Queensland may receive a financial grant from the Commonwealth to initiate programs or policies for an environmental purpose (such as soil conservation) if they supply matching funding, or agree to meet certain policy objectives (such as reducing land clearing).

During the 1990s the Commonwealth began to actively facilitate more integrated and ultimately national approaches to environmental management. To this end it established a series of national environmental strategies and programs such as Australia's coastal policy (Living on the Coast), Oceans Policy, the National Forest Policy, the National Greenhouse Strategy, the National Strategy for Ecologically Sustainable Development (see Chapter 2), the National Strategy for the Conservation of Australia's Biological Diversity, and many others (see Bates 2003). In the late 1990s and into the 2000s, the Commonwealth Government also embarked on a series of large funding programs including:

- **the Natural Heritage Trust (NHT)**: a funding partnership arrangement aimed at 'stimulat[ing] significant investment in the conservation, sustainable use and repair of Australia's environmental, agricultural and natural resources into the twenty-first century' (Crowley 2001, p 255). The NHT emphasised community, regional and State government involvement in biodiversity, natural resource management and sustainable agriculture programs (Crowley 2001). The estimated total funding allocated to the program between 1996–1997 and 2007–2008 was around $3 billion (Stewart and Hendriks 2008).

- **The National Water Initiative (NWI)**: a $2 billion program to improve water management in rural and urban Australia, introduced by the Howard (Coalition) Government in 2004. Part of the NWI was a plan to introduce water trading (Stewart and Hendriks 2008). In 2006 the NWI was accelerated in view of the intensification of the drought and limited progress (see Box 4.3).

The Commonwealth Government has also enacted several pieces of legislation on environmental matters, though on the whole its approach has been piecemeal (for a good overview, see Thomas 2007, Ch 4). In 1999 a senate committee examining environmental reforms concluded that a significant proportion of Australia's national legislation on the environment had been driven by responses to one-off international and national concerns (SECIT and ALC 1999). The report recommended that the Commonwealth's role in environmental management should be better defined and a more holistic and integrated approach was needed. A similar recommendation was made by the international body, the Organisation for Economic Co-operation and Development (OECD), in its 2007 report card on Australia's environmental performance (OECD 2007a).

One significant attempt to create a more cohesive national environmental response was the *Environment Protection and Biodiversity Conservation Act* (EPBC Act), which was passed in 1999. The key objectives of this legislation are to promote the sustainable use of natural resources at the national level and to ensure that actions affecting 'matters of national environmental significance' were subject to permission and control (McGrath 2005). The Act also seeks to protect biological diversity on a national scale. Issues of national significance under the Act are considered of key importance to the Commonwealth and include (Thomas 2007, p 78): world heritage properties; Ramsar listed wetlands; nationally endangered or vulnerable species or communities; migratory species; nuclear activities and the management and protection of marine and coastal environments. The EPBC Act also develops bilateral agreements with State and Territory governments, and further clarifies roles (Thomas 2007). Opinion remains divided on the effectiveness of the EPBC Act (see Gumley 2005; MacIntosh 2006; MacIntosh and Wilkinson 2005; McGrath 2005; Scanlon and Dyson 2001). The most problematic aspects of the Act appear to have been in its implementation; it has lacked resources and neglected biodiversity protection by not maintaining up-to-date registers of threatened species (see Chapple 2001; Gumley 2005).

Today the Commonwealth Government has a number of avenues through which it can influence and shape EDM in Australia. Rather than intervening via the courts, its role is increasingly one of initiating and coordinating policies with the States (and with local government) (Bates 2003). Much of the work of the relevant Commonwealth environmental departments is to fund, coordinate, administer and evaluate programs rather than to implement them on the ground (Bates 2003). The effectiveness of this shift towards more 'cooperative federalism' on EDM depends on the extent to which the Commonwealth and States are willing to overcome intergovernmental conflict and work effectively together – an idea easier in theory than practice. We return to the challenge of intergovernmental relations below in 4.5.

4.4.3 Environmental responsibilities of State governments (and Territories)

Since the environment is a residual power, it is the State governments who play a major role in EDM in Australia. This phenomenon also has historical roots, since it was the States who first responded institutionally to rising environmental concerns in the 1960s. However, not all Australian States responded in the same manner, giving way to what Christoff (2003) refers to as State *leaders* and *laggards*. In the 1970s a group of States (namely New South Wales, Victoria and Western Australia) led the way by establishing agencies charged with protecting the environment. In the remaining jurisdictions environmental matters were delegated to existing public health, infrastructure and agriculture authorities. It was not until the early 1990s that these laggard States (including Queensland, South Australia and Tasmania) consolidated their environmental activities into autonomous environmental departments (Christoff 2003).

Today all Australian States and Territories have established a number of environmental protection and conservation institutions (for an overview, see Thomas 2007, Ch 5).[2] In their earlier days, State (and Territory) environmental agencies focused predominantly on environmental protection and pollution control, particularly in urban environments. Their role has expanded considerably to include activities such as biodiversity conservation, planning and land use and environmental education. Despite the increased environmental responsibilities of State governments, they have been criticised for failing to tackle rural problems, biodiversity, energy use, transport and non-point source pollution (Christoff

---

2   As these agencies change titles and responsibilities periodically, readers are encouraged to visit their particular State government websites for up-to-date information on environmental agencies.

2003). However, a more optimistic assessment is suggested by the recent initiatives of some States and Territory governments, where sustainability principles are being incorporated into relevant institutions (see Box 4.2).

Box 4.2: Example of State-based initiatives to drive sustainability

All States in Australia are required to include the principles of sustainability in their legislation and policy relating to the environment (see Chapter 2). To date attempts to turn this goal into action on the ground have been patchy. There have been some States, however, that have taken bold steps to drive sustainability outcomes, as the following examples demonstrate.

In September 2003, the Western Australian Government became the first Australian State or Territory to release a comprehensive sustainability strategy (WA Government 2003a). The strategy aims at an integrated whole of government approach. It is based on a framework for thinking and decision-making about sustainability. The framework comprises:

- an underpinning set of 11 principles;

- six visions (see 2.9.1 for envisioning) covering governance, global contributions, natural resources, settlements, community and business;

- sustainability goals and priorities to deliver the visions.

The strategy emphasises the importance of partnerships and while its focus is primarily directed at government actions, business and community contributions are also covered. It provides a major contribution to furthering sustainability by a State, but as so often happens, a change in Premier in 2006 has seen the loss of much momentum in its implementation.

Victoria appointed a Commissioner for Environmental Sustainability in late 2003 under an Act of Parliament that sets the role as providing an independent voice to advocate, audit and report on environmental sustainability, including preparing the state-wide State of the Environment Report.[3] Victoria also developed a Sustainability Framework in 2005 to give direction to government, business and the community in putting environmental considerations into our life and work. The framework sets objectives and interim targets. In 2006 this was followed by a Sustainability Action Statement, identifying specific actions and providing investment for these and in December 2007 a two-year report showing progress against the framework's objectives was released.[4] The framework and action statement are complemented by a focus on education and behaviour change outlined in a 'Learning to Live Sustainably Strategy'.

The Australian Capital Territory (ACT) Government in September 2007 appointed a Commissioner for Sustainability and the Environment, expanding the Office of the Commissioner for the Environment (established in 1993) to include sustainability. This Office is responsible for producing State of the Environment reports for the ACT and has an independent role in investigating complaints from the community regarding the management of the ACT's environment by the ACT Government or its agencies. It may also initiate investigations where actions of the ACT Government or its agencies have a substantial adverse impact on the ACT's environment.[5]

---

3   From <www.ces.vic.gov.au/CES/wcmn301.nsf/childdocs/-2159FBE93013A83ACA256F250028BECC?open> (accessed 21 December 2008).

4   From <www.dse.vic.gov.au/ourenvironment-ourfuture> (accessed 21 December 2008).

5   From <www.environmentcommissioner.act.gov.au> (accessed 21 December 2008).

Promising features of these initiatives in Victoria and the ACT are not only the focus on sustainability (rather than just environment), but also the level of independence accorded the Commissioners and the emphasis on monitoring and auditing progress relevant to sustainability outcomes.

4.4.4 Environmental responsibilities of local government

Local government plays an active and influential role in environmental decisions in Australia (Wild River 2003), despite the fact that it has limited formal political power. According to Crowley (2004, p 402) local governments now have a wide and diverse environmental agenda including 'local conservation, coastal management, integrated catchment management, flora and fauna protection, waste minimisation and management, energy management, environmental impact assessment, urban and rural regeneration, traffic calming and environmental education'.

The role of local government in environmental management has changed over time and also varies between States (for an overview, see Thomas 2007, Ch 5). The trend across Australia is that local government is taking on an increasing number of environmental responsibilities, many of which have been devolved from State governments (Adams and Hine 1999). Local government is also closer to the people and therefore under pressure to respond to changing community values. In this sense local government sits in an unusual position; it faces global problems, such as climate change, but it needs to address these on a local scale. While there is a certainly a ring to the popular phrase 'think globally, act locally', putting this into practice can be difficult for local authorities when they lack resources and decision-making power to promote effective change.

It is important to recognise that local government in Australia has next to no autonomy; formally and financially its administration is under the control of the States. This means that State governments can override local government decisions (especially when developers or citizens dispute the local council decisions). States can also reorganise jurisdictional boundaries and merge councils as the State governments of Victoria and Queensland have done (Fenna 2004). Research has also found that many Australian local governments are not being adequately resourced to cope with their additional environmental responsibilities (Wild River 2003). Only around 40 per cent of council revenue is generated by rates (land taxes) in Australia (Singleton et al 2006). For most of the remaining funds, councils are reliant on States for funding. In some States, such as in New South Wales and Queensland, local governments can fund environmental activities by charging environmental levies.[6]

Many believe that local government is the key level for achieving community involvement in, and understanding of, sustainability principles (see Brown 1997, 2005a; Buckingham-Hatfield and Percy 1999). Local government is in a unique position to demonstrate integration between the social, economic and environmental spheres of management required to move towards sustainability, since it is at this level of government where the pressures of human impact on environmental conditions are most visible and immediate. This view was acknowledged internationally in 1992 by the United Nations Conference on Environment and Development (the Rio Earth Summit) in one of its key documents – *Local Agenda 21* (LA21). LA21 was envisaged as an international global strategy for managing

---

6   See for example, the initiatives of Ashfield Council <www.ashfield.nsw.gov.au/page/environment_levy. html> (accessed 20 February 2009) and Mackay Regional Council <www.mackay.qld.gov.au/environment/ natural_environment_levy> (accessed 20 February 2009).

sustainability at the local level; it focuses on policy integration, long-term planning and community involvement (Linder 1994; Thomas 2007).

In Australia, LA21 has been taken up by well over a hundred local councils. However, many local authorities remain lost when it comes to developing and implementing their own local LA21s (Adams and Hine 1999, p 189). Some practical international models have emerged, including the implementation suggestions developed by the International Council for Local Environmental Initiatives.[7] One of the essential features of any LA21 program is a commitment to local participatory processes for developing short and long-term actions for sustainability (Adams and Hine 1999) – a theme we explore further in Chapter 7.

4.4.5 Implications of federalism for environmental management

Australia's federal system of government, with its division of powers, makes for complex and confusing environmental management arrangements. In the first instance, federalism can generate significant inefficiencies and duplications. In Australia instead of one parliament and one public service there are nine, comprising the Commonwealth Government, the six State governments, and the Northern Territory and the Australian Capital Territory. In addition there are some 700 local government bodies throughout Australia (ALGA 2008). In this sense Australia may seem to be over-governed, though opinion polls suggest that Australians support the idea of multiple layers of government (Brown 2008a).

Secondly, federalism can create inconsistencies between jurisdictions, which can frustrate and confuse citizens and businesses. For instance, companies operating across the country have to gear their activities to deal with different environmental standards, which may lead to inefficiencies. As well, States may compete to attract industry, and hence revenue and employment, by offering low price access to resources such as energy or water. A clear example of this has been the cut-price energy war between certain States to attract high energy users such as aluminium smelting corporations. Competition between States, particularly for economic development, can also produce perverse incentives in schemes to attract industry, such as lowering environmental standards.

Thirdly, federalism is notorious for causing policy paralysis, especially where there is a lack of national consensus, poor leadership and significant uncertainty. This situation arose during the early to mid-2000s when Australia's policy response to climate change remained divided and uncertain. Frustrated at the lack of leadership by the Commonwealth (Howard) Government, the Australian States decided to establish their own national body for investigating a unified carbon trading system for Australia, the National Emissions Trading System. This move was supported by industry leaders who were keen to see a nationally consistent response to renewable energy and emissions trading (ABRCC 2006; BCA 2007).

Probably the most significant disadvantage of federalism for the environment is that it creates division of powers along political boundaries which may be meaningless in ecological terms (Kellow 1996). For example, some State and local government boundaries cut right across significant ecological systems, such as water catchment areas. In many cases, such boundaries have led to delayed responses in addressing wide-scale environmental problems, particularly in the assignment of environmental responsibility (Doyle and Kellow 1995). For example, consider the ongoing struggle to coordinate the management of the Murray-Darling Basin (MDB) system, which sits across four States and one Territory (see Box 4.3).

---

7   See <www.iclei.org> (accessed 20 April 2009).

Box 4.3: Murray-Darling Basin – geographical borders versus political borders

A classic case which highlights the problems associated with the inconsistencies between jurisdictional and natural boundaries is that of water management in the Murray-Darling Basin (MDB). Water under the Australian Constitution is a State resource. Over the past 150 years each State has evolved its own management systems by establishing departments, regulatory bodies and legislation.

The MDB is a river system located in South-East Australia that incorporates over 1 million square kilometres. Its water resources are required for a number of competing interests such as agriculture, hydro-electricity, urban water supply, as well as the ecological needs of the rivers' ecosystems. The Basin includes parts of South Australia, Victoria, New South Wales, Queensland and the Australian Capital Territory. Thus together with the Commonwealth, the management of the MDB involves six jurisdictions (Connell and Colebatch 2006).

Since the early 1900s water allocation in the MDB for drought and irrigation purposes has been an ongoing source of intergovernmental conflict. Downstream states, such as South Australia, receive reduced flows as a result of large water diversions upstream. More recently, serious water quality issues have arisen including: algal blooms from high levels of phosphorus and nitrogen and high salt concentrations due to dryland and irrigation salinity. As a consequence of resource exploitation and poor management practices upstream, South Australia often has to engage in some hard bargaining with the other involved States to adopt reforms (Doyle and Kellow 1995).

The Murray-Darling Basin Council and its executive arm, the Murray-Darling Basin Commission, were established at the federal level to coordinate State governments and community endeavours to manage the Basin and particularly those aimed at water allocation and water quality. Despite the existence of these bodies, the Basin is not entirely protected from interstate conflicts. This seems to be an inherent historical feature of the Basin's management (see Connell 2007). The ongoing contest centres on competing demands for irrigation, especially from upstream States such as Queensland and New South Wales but also Victoria, and the need for adequate urban water supply for South Australia. The rivers and lakes in the system also need a certain amount of water for their ecological functioning (so-called 'environmental flows').

Since the mid-2000s there have been a number of attempts by Federal and State governments to reach agreement. For example, in 2004 a $2 billion National Water Initiative was announced by COAG under the leadership of the Howard (Coalition) Government. Originally proposed as a 10-year program, the NWI included plans to introduce a water trading system to be administered by a new independent statutory authority, the National Water Commission (Stewart and Hendriks 2008). Then in 2007 the Commonwealth (Howard) Government announced a National Plan for Water Security, part of which included an investment of $9 billion over 10 years to water management in the MDB (CoA 2007b). Such initiatives represent the political response to the worsening biophysical conditions of the Basin, in severe drought from 2001–2005, which followed a less severe but extensive drought in the 1990s (Stewart and Hendriks 2008).

Despite federal initiatives and significant injection of funds, intergovernmental differences continue to plague the management of the MDB, with some jurisdictions reluctant to put the national interest before the rights of their own State. The strong opposition to a national MDB approach has come particularly from Victoria which has been reluctant to lose water security rights and any gains it has made from investments into well-managed irrigation schemes. Water trading proposals have also been strongly resisted by South Australia which argues that water licences have been over-allocated particularly in upstream states. South Australia demands that more fresh water be returned to the River Murray to restore its ecological health. In March 2009 the Premier of South Australia (Mike Rann) announced that the state was pursuing a constitutional challenge to protect South Australia's water rights, and to help save the integrity of two significant ecosystems in South Australia, the Lower Lakes and Coorong (Rann 2009).

Though federalism poses many drawbacks for EDM, it does offer some advantages. For example, multiple layers of government can foster more open decision-making, since there are multiple access points for citizens and affected groups to influence decisions. In a federal system, multiple levels of government enable closer links to the people; much more so than in the case of one central government (Cook 2004). Federalism can aid productive competition (Fenna 2004). It can also enable issues to be considered at the State (or local) level which can be important when populations are fractured by geographical differences and distances. Thus if you are a resident in Perth concerned about future water supplies, you do not need to rely on public servants on the other side of the continent in Canberra to develop and implement local policies (Lovell et al 1998, p 62).

Further, federalism can also promote more effective policy-making by encouraging individual States to experiment with different policy approaches. Other States or the Commonwealth Government may copy those that are successful. For example, since the early 1970s South Australia has taken a different path to other States in managing waste generated from beverage containers (for example, bottles, cans and so on). More specifically the South Australian Government introduced a deposit refund system where deposits are placed on containers to encourage their return. Although initially introduced to combat litter problems, the deposit system has also proven to be an effective recycling policy instrument. In 2003 the South Australian Government expanded the system to include a range of other container types (SA EPA 2003). Other States such as New South Wales, Queensland and Western Australia have been watching the South Australian experience closely but are holding off until a decision for a national deposit system is made (see Case Study A).

Although the Commonwealth Government has a number of powers to influence environmental decisions (as discussed above), it may not always intervene unless pressured to do so. When it does intervene, there is often strong resistance from State governments who fear that increased federal involvement scares investors away from State development projects. Clearly, the States want sovereignty over development decisions, but it is the Commonwealth's role to ensure that decision outcomes are in the national interest.

This situation has led to great uncertainty as to whether the Federal Government or State governments will take the primary role in numerous environmental decisions. Industry lobbies want greater certainty on which to base their investment plans, while community and environment groups have often pitched their lobbying to take political advantage of the confused environmental responsibility. Much conflict has resulted: the prime example being the Franklin Dam battle (see Box 4.1). Australia's intergovernmental battles were vividly displayed on the international stage in 1988 when the Commonwealth Government argued the case for World Heritage listing for the wet tropical forests of North Queensland at UNESCO (United Nations Educational, Scientific and Cultural Organisation), while the Queensland Government argued against such recognition (Toyne 1994).

4.5 Fostering cooperative federalism for environmental management

> It needs to be stressed that the missing element in any attempt to establish a national approach to environment management is the will to do it, not the power to do it.

> (Toyne 1994, p 185)

Though Australia's form of federalism has traditionally been one of conflict and negotiation, there has been an increased effort by all governments to create more effective intergovernmental relations particularly on environmental issues. At various times successive Commonwealth governments have established a number of integrative structures and agreements aimed at encouraging more holistic management approaches, coordination and standardisation of environmental management across the States and Territories. We considered some of these national policy initiatives and strategies in our discussion on the Commonwealth above. Here our focus is on some of the other institutional mechanisms that have been employed in Australia to facilitate intergovernmental cooperation on the environment.

4.5.1 Ministerial councils

Ministerial councils provide one means of formalising consultative processes and cooperative agreements between the Commonwealth and the States. They comprise Commonwealth and State ministers, supported by standing committees of officials (nominated by the ministers) which provide advice to the council, and various specialist sub-committees (Bates 2006). The number of ministerial councils has fluctuated over time, but they 'tend to multiply in response to arising issues' (Fenna 2004, p 181). At the time of writing there were approximately 40 ministerial councils, many of which related to environmental issues (COAG 2007). The two most significant ministerial councils directly related to the environment include the Environment Protection and Heritage Council (EPHC) and the Natural Resource Management Ministerial Council.

Ministerial councils can be important in driving the kind of coordinated action that sustainability demands especially in bringing together different levels of government (Dovers 2001). They also have the potential to foster broad long-term policy solutions for the environment, provided they are not constrained by political factors (Bates 2006). Here the willingness of States to engage in cooperative solutions is significant because they retain considerable independence, and they may not be prepared to invest the time and effort involved in forging an agreement and reaching common standards. In order to achieve reliable outcomes it is often necessary for the Commonwealth and each State to pass uniform legislation (Toyne 1994).

4.5.2 Intergovernmental Agreement on the Environment (IGAE)

Another important institutional mechanism for fostering cooperative federalism is to establish formal agreements between relevant jurisdictions. The most significant of these for the environment is the Intergovernmental Agreement on the Environment (IGAE), which was signed by the Commonwealth, the States, the Territories and local government in 1992. The IGAE attempts to spell out environmental policy and management responsibilities of each level of government, and allows the Commonwealth to become involved in issues where it has demonstrated responsibilities and interests. The IGAE is also aimed at providing better and more standardised environmental management across Australia (see 2.4.7).

While the IGAE provides a start to more cooperative federalism, it certainly does not provide solutions to all the identified issues. In his review of the IGAE, Philip Toyne (1994) is highly critical, claiming that the scope of the IGAE is too narrow, its processes too slow to meet demand, and that it reverses the trend towards greater Commonwealth involvement in environmental management, restoring the States' control over environmental issues. The argument here is that IGAE essentially constrains and streamlines the Commonwealth's involvement in environmental issues, and in doing so hands considerable decision-making power over to the States (Lane 1999). The risk for the environment is that in their race to promote economic development States may promote ecologically questionable forms of industrial development or resource extraction (Thomas 2007, pp 418–422).

4.5.3 The Council of Australian Governments (COAG)

Another significant intergovernmental institution is the Council of Australian Governments (COAG) which was formed in 1992 to foster more cooperative federalism. COAG is essentially the platform or meeting place where the Prime Minister interacts with the State and Territory leaders. Formally it consists of 10 members including: the Prime Minister, State Premiers as well as Chief Ministers from the Northern Territory and the Australian Capital Territory, plus the President of the Australian Local Government Association (Fenna 2004, p 182).

COAG promises significant potential for the kind of intergovernmental cooperation that environmental issues demand. To date, however, the practice of COAG has been relatively weak in terms of fostering collaborative governance (Fenna 2004). Part of its failure is that it is under the direct power and administration of the Prime Minister; the Prime Minister calls the meeting, sets the agenda and chairs the discussion. Furthermore, COAG is vulnerable to the influence of particular political parties at the Commonwealth and State level. In circumstances where the Commonwealth Government is under the leadership of a political party that differs from most of the States (as was the case in 2006–2007 towards at the end of the fourth Howard Government), COAG can become a political battleground for ideas.

4.5.4 Intergovernmental agencies and regional initiatives

Cooperation between governments has also been facilitated through various intergovernmental agencies as well as regional initiatives. Agencies such as the former Murray-Darling Basin Commission have been explicitly established in legislation to foster cooperation between various levels of government.

In addition to formal statutory bodies, regional organisations have been established or appointed by governments to address sustainability issues on a spatial level of governance – typically located between the State and local government levels. The regional approach supports the view that sustainability outcomes are more likely to be achieved through close involvement of people at an appropriate spatial level, in identifying problems, allocating resources and building capacity to develop solutions (Campbell 2006). The presence of regional organisations does not remove a top-down role for this may be important in providing funding and setting national or State-wide priorities. Importantly, the regional approach provides the opportunity for EDM to be aligned with ecological boundaries. That is, with boundaries that are functionally relevant in terms of the workings of natural systems, rather than with politically derived boundaries that commonly define State and local government areas (see Box 4.3). Regional forms of governance have also been embraced as an opportunity to improve the way communities engage in Natural Resource Management (NRM) issues (Lane 2006).

Governing through regional programs or institutions is certainly not a new phenomenon in Australia (Dore et al 2003), though they have become increasingly popular for resolving NRM issues. There is no one standard form of regional organisation, as they vary considerably with the kind of region, and the community and stakeholders involved. Some of the key varieties include (Dore et al 2003):

- Development boards (State government with or without local governments);

- Regional NRM organisations (see Robins and Dovers 2007), such as various catchment management bodies across Australia that are responsible for land, water and biodiversity initiatives (Ewing 2003);

- Regional coalition or regional organisation of councils (ROCs) of local governments;[8]

- Specific regional sustainable development groups such as the Lake Eyre Basin Coordinating Group, Keeping it Great! (Great Barrier Reef), and Team West (Greater Western Sydney).

While regional-based institutions might make good sense for ecosystems and communities, their success is not always guaranteed. Many regional programs lack the necessary administrative and political capacity to tackle the sustainability issues they confront. This is particularly the case in remote areas where leadership and management skills may be lacking. More problematic is that many regional initiatives lack decision-making power, and so program leaders constantly need to negotiate with multiple jurisdictions, many of which can have competing objectives. This can raise concerns about the accountability and legitimacy of regional initiatives, particularly when relationships between different levels of governance are ambiguous (Wallington et al 2008). Short-termism can also be a problem as regional programs are mostly funded (and assessed) for limited time periods. This can work against the implementation of long-term solutions, as well as the need to develop trust between multiple stakeholders and institutions (see Dore et al 2003). Effective regional governance requires (among many things) programs that are well-integrated into, and supported by, existing governance structures, environmental managers who are equipped with skills to work and network across multiple organisations, and programs that are adequately resourced (Lane 2006).

4.6 Institutions of responsible government in Australia

As mentioned at the beginning of this chapter, Australian governments are based on the idea of responsible government which entails three formal roles (Janesch 1997):

1. to create laws (legislate);

---

8   See <www.alga.asn.au/links/regionalOrgs.php#a1> (15 April 2009).

2. to implement these laws (administrate); and

3. to ensure that the laws are appropriately interpreted and applied (judicial function).

To perform these roles the nine systems of government in Australia (one Commonwealth, two Territories and six States) each have a parliament (or legislative assembly), a public service and public sector, and a legal system. While there are differences between the nine jurisdictions, there are a number of common components. In this section we take a closer look at these components focussing particularly on their role in EDM. For example, what is the role of the parliaments and cabinets in producing and amending environmental policies? To what extent have political parties accommodated environmental concerns? How does the election system influence the representation of environmental concerns in parliament? Where do the courts fit in?

4.6.1 The Legislature (Parliament)

Parliament is the core of government. It is an assembly of representatives elected by the public with three main functions (Singleton et al 1996):

1. to discuss, amend and pass legislation;

2. to supply money for the conduct of government; and

3. to question and investigate the actions of government and the needs of the community.

Typically in Australia, each government has two houses of parliament, an upper and a lower house (known as bicameralism). These are called, respectively, the Senate and House of Representatives in the Commonwealth Parliament, and the Legislative Assembly (or House of Assembly in Tasmania and South Australia) and the Legislative Council in the States. The exceptions are Queensland, the Northern Territory and the Australian Capital Territory, which each lack an upper house.

In Australia, the lower house represents the people and functions as the 'house of government, policy and legislation'. The upper house acts as a 'house of review' for the actions of the lower house, and successful passage of a Bill through parliament requires that it be accepted by both houses.[9] Consequently, the balance of power in each house is of extreme importance. Since the government is represented by that party or coalition with the majority of seats in the lower house, if the same party holds a majority in both houses, then the government is able to pass legislation quite easily. However, if the opposition is in the majority in the upper house then the government is likely to face difficulty in its legislative agenda. A third scenario may occur in which there is no clear party (or coalition) majority in the upper house. Under these conditions, independents or minor party representatives may hold the balance of power and are in a particularly powerful position.

One of the functions of parliament is to scrutinise the actions of government. It achieves this through a series of activities on the floor of the house such as question time and debates, as well as through various committees appointed by parliament (Singleton et al 2006). Governments might also present a ministerial statement or policy paper to the parliament. For example, they might release a discussion document (known as a Green Paper) which outlines their broad thinking on a particular issue, and possible courses of action. After

---

9   A Bill is a proposed (or draft) piece of legislation introduced into either house of parliament.

consultation and further consideration, the government may then release a White Paper, which represents the government's formal policy statement on the issue.

4.6.2 Political parties

Political parties are formed by groups of people that have common ideals and aspirations, and through their organisations they select people to run in elections (Woodward 2006). Instead of elections being contests between hundreds of candidates with a wide variety of different platforms, the existence of political parties transforms these into choices between a small number of policies (Lovell et al 1998). Since approximately 1910 Australia's party system has been dominated by two major parties broadly representing the interests of Labor (workers) and anti-Labor (Janesch 1997).[10] Though operating under various names, today these two parties are the Australian Labor Party (ALP) and the Liberal Party (which typical operates in a coalition with the Country/National Party).[11]

At general elections, parties compete against each other and the party with the majority of seats in the lower house forms the government, its leader becomes the Prime Minister (or State Premier) and its senior politicians become members of cabinet. The opposition is formed by the party which has the next greatest number of elected candidates (Singleton et al 2006).

The environment, once of no or little consequence in the platforms of the major parties, has become an important election issue over the past 25 years. There have been many drivers for the uptake of environmental values by major political parties. Most significant has been the pressure from environment groups, and the rising awareness of environmental issues in the electorate. Voters want their political representative to act responsibly on environmental issues. Although neither the ALP nor the Coalition (Liberal/National) have received wholehearted support from environmentalists, closer alliance has generally occurred with the ALP (see Jensen-Lee 2001). However, since the mid-1990s the differences between the major parties on environmental issues appear to have been diminishing, especially in relation to controversial issues such as logging of native forests.

Another driver greening political parties has been the mounting pressure from the business sector and governments worldwide to implement sustainability principles. There have also been dramatic biophysical indicators of the urgency for action, such as the severe water shortages across South-Eastern Australia during the drought of the mid-2000s. As we discussed in Chapter 1 in some senses the environment appears to be 'biting back'.

While the major parties in Australia are trying to green their political manifestos, some voters remain dissatisfied with their environmental policies and performance. This has led to the emergence of a number of minor groups and independents running on green tickets such as the Australian Greens (and their State equivalents), the Liberals for Forests[12] and the Conservatives for Climate and Environment.[13] Despite the growth of support for green parties and independents since the early 1990s, this has not always been matched by electoral success (Stock 2006). The reasons for this can be found in the electoral systems of Australia as explained below.

---

10   For an overview of different political parties in Australia, see Parkin et al (2006).

11   Though the modern Liberal Party of Australia was formed in 1944, its roots go back to various parties of the former Australian colonies. Since 1909 the Liberal Party has operated under three different names: Liberal Party, National Party and United Australia Party (Janesch 1997).

12   See <www.liberalsfor.forests.org.au>.

13   See <www.cfce.org.au>.

4.6.3 The electoral system

> An electoral system is a structure that helps decide which kind of values and policies should assume the main stage of a nation's political life. An electoral or voting system can often be responsible for silencing certain voices in a democratic society, while promoting others.
>
> (Doyle and Kellow 1995, p 130)

Elections are the mechanism through which citizens determine their decision-makers (representatives in parliament). Regular voting is also the means through with decision-makers are held to account (see Figure 4.1 further below). In Australia elections take place approximately every three to four years, depending on the jurisdiction (see Janesch 1997). On the one hand, frequent elections help to promote accountable government as representatives have to convince their electorate regularly that they are worthy of election or re-election. Yet on the other hand, frequent elections can foster short-term thinking where politicians concentrate their efforts on policy initiatives that best serve their re-election interests. This often results in a neglect of the kind of strategic and long-term planning that sustainability issues demand (see Chapter 10).

The type of voting system through which the government is elected can greatly influence representation in our political institutions (see Box 4.4). Some systems strongly favour major parties, others give greater scope for minor parties and independents to be represented. In parliaments where different voting systems are used in the lower and upper house, the constellation of political party membership tends to differ in each house. As mentioned above in situations where the government has the majority in the lower house and the opposition party the majority in the senate, independents and minority parties such as independents and the Greens can wield considerable power.

Box 4.4: Preferential and proportional voting systems

A commonly used electoral approach in Australia is a preferential voting system. It applies to the lower houses of parliament (House of Representatives) at the Commonwealth level and for all States and Territories except Tasmania and the Australian Capital Territory. In a preferential system, voters rank *all* candidates in order of preference (Costar 2006). To be elected, a candidate has to achieve an absolute majority (at least 50 per cent plus one vote) of the valid votes cast, either on first preferences or after distribution of preferences. If no candidate has an absolute majority, the preferences are distributed, starting with the candidate with the lowest number of first preference votes. The process continues until a candidate reaches an absolute majority. Preferential systems tend to disadvantage minor parties and independents, though it does give them the possibility to negotiate preference deals with the major parties (Doyle and Kellow 1995).

In contrast, proportional electoral systems give minor parties and independents their best chance of election because they allow seats to be fairly allocated according to the proportion of votes cast (Costar 2006). In other words, if a party received 30 per cent of the votes, then they are awarded 30 per cent of the seats. Proportional representation involves the election of numerous candidates, rather than a single candidate, in each electorate (Janesch 1997). It has been the main avenue for green representation in parliaments in Australia. Variations of this system are used for the upper houses at Commonwealth level and in several States and Territories (Painter 1997). The 'Hare-Clark' system of proportional representation used in Tasmania has been a major reason for the success of the green independents in gaining a significant number of seats in the House of Assembly (Doyle and Kellow 1995).

In sum, Australian electoral systems tend to favour the election of major parties over special interest minor parties and independents. In this sense the environment can only gain a representative voice in our parliaments if it is accommodated by the major parties (Labor, Liberal and the National Party). As mentioned above this has certainly been the case since the mid-1990s, when voters began to demand action on environmental issues. However, since public support for the environment has tended to wax and wane over the years (Jensen-Lee 2001), there is always the risk that major political parties loosen their commitments to sustainability.

4.6.4 Ministers and Cabinet

Cabinet is the committee of senior politicians responsible for directing the government policies. It is the centre of power, the repository of legitimate political authority and the top political prize in the Australian system of government.

(Page 1997, p 124)

Australia's system of responsible government is based on the Westminster tradition where all members of cabinet (the executive) are elected members of parliament (that is, from the legislature). Thus in all Australian governments the minister responsible for the environment is also an elected member of parliament. This means that ideally they are directly accountable to the parliament (and hence to the people) for their actions (see Figure 4.1).

The majority party (or coalition) chooses the ministry from its elected parliamentarians (in the upper or lower house) and ministers administer the activities of government through their associated departments or agencies. The ministers collectively form cabinet, although some Prime Ministers have adopted a two-tier ministry with only the senior ministers in cabinet. As well, within cabinet, ministers will vary in their seniority and influence.

Cabinet is where the major decisions of government are made, and importantly for environmental concerns it is here that the activities of many disparate public sector agencies are integrated and that 'ministers pushing for environmental protection confront those pushing for development' (Doyle and Kellow 1995, p 157). Where the minister or ministers representing environmental interests stand in the cabinet hierarchy, and how environmental issues are allocated among government departments and hence among ministers, are crucial influences on the outcomes for the environment. Typically, ministers for conservation and environment are not as senior as those responsible for industry, commerce and resource development.

The extent to which cabinet must resolve conflicts between environmental and resource use interests is influenced by the way in which environmental responsibilities are split between government agencies and ministers. For example, forestry conservation might be managed by the national parks agency, land use development by a planning authority, water by a water infrastructure body, rural issues by an agricultural department and energy by a resources and minerals agency. Separating contentious issues into different institutions is a classic strategy (referred to as firewalls) employed by government to deal with conflicting values (Thacher and Rein 2004, pp 469–470) (see also Chapter 3). While institutional firewalls might help to contain value conflicts, in environmental policy they invariably generate policy tensions as agencies place demands on the system that may pull in different directions (Doyle and Kellow 1995, p 189). Such tensions tend to surface in cabinet, or at the policy coal face where implementers face the challenge of making sustainability policy work (Stewart 2006, p 187).

An alternative to separating environmental issues into multiple portfolios is to bring them all under one 'mega-agency'. According to Doyle and Kellow (1995, pp 150–151) this 'politicis[es] the administrative process dealing with natural resources' because it effectively places environmental conflict under the one roof rather than allowing for it to be fractured across agencies where it might only surface occasionally at the cabinet level. Environmentalists may be nervous of this approach, fearing that in a single agency (say for land management) environmental interests may be swamped by more powerful resource development interests and would no longer have the backstop of a named institution, in the form of a conservation agency, to promote their cause. In practice large environmental super agencies do not necessarily appear to overcome the problems of institutional firewalls. Consider, for example, the experience of a number of recently created mega-agencies in

Figure 4.1: The (ideal) Westminster chain of accountability

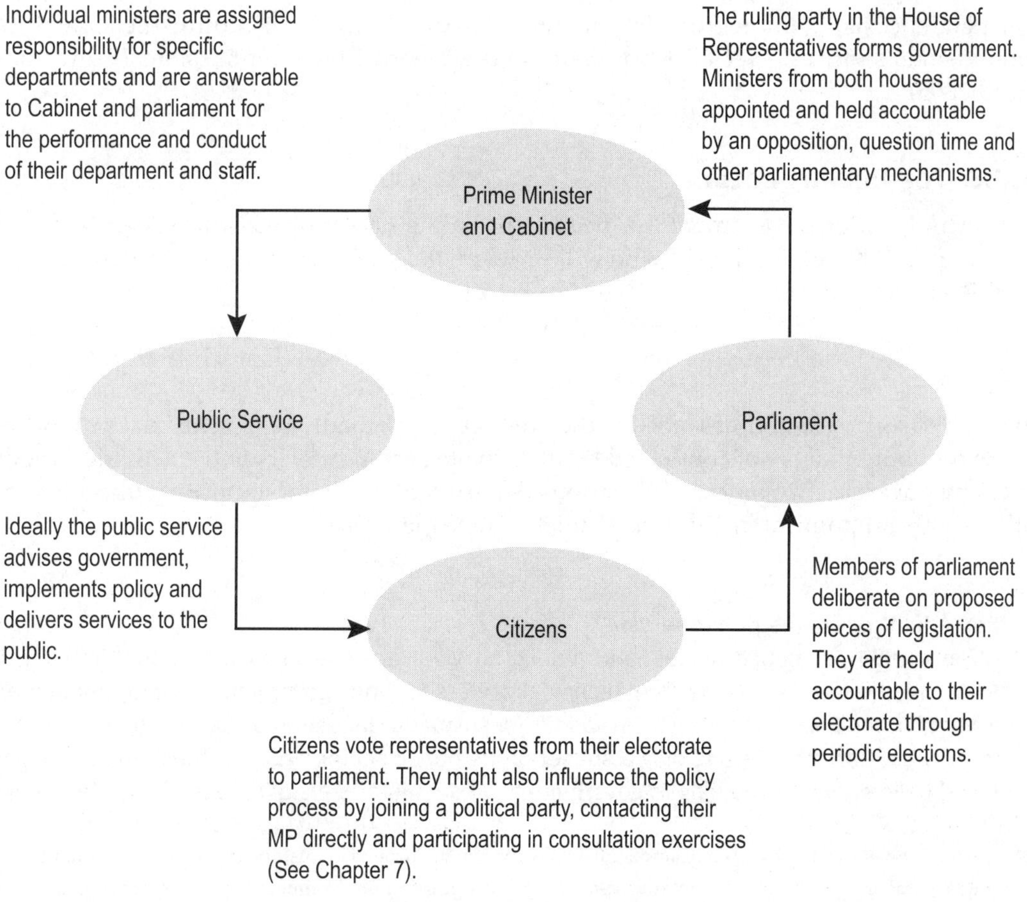

Individual ministers are assigned responsibility for specific departments and are answerable to Cabinet and parliament for the performance and conduct of their department and staff.

The ruling party in the House of Representatives forms government. Ministers from both houses are appointed and held accountable by an opposition, question time and other parliamentary mechanisms.

Prime Minister and Cabinet

Public Service

Parliament

Ideally the public service advises government, implements policy and delivers services to the public.

Citizens

Members of parliament deliberate on proposed pieces of legislation. They are held accountable to their electorate through periodic elections.

Citizens vote representatives from their electorate to parliament. They might also influence the policy process by joining a political party, contacting their MP directly and participating in consultation exercises (See Chapter 7).

Adapted from Ward 1995, p 15.

Victoria, Western Australia and New South Wales where attempts have been made to integrate environmental protection and resource management agencies. Though the rationale for these organisational restructures has been to facilitate communication between related agencies, there is no guarantee that such integration will take place. Moreover, large public sector organisations can be inefficient and difficult to manage.

There has been considerable experimentation with varying arrangements of responsibility across government agencies and between ministers, and these continue. The perfect solution to balancing inter-agency and cabinet resolution of competing interests has yet to be found. It is clear though that moves towards sustainability require economic and social development to be complementary to ecological goals. It seems that this is more likely to be achieved if these goals are integrated at the earliest stages of planning, which might best be done via interdepartmental arrangements, where relevant agencies (and external non-governmental organisations) work together to set common goals. Alternatively the independence and integrity of agencies working on environmental issues could be protected by an independent institution, or commissioner who has the mandate, power and resources to promote sustainability. For example, in Canada the Government of Ontario in the early 1990s established a Commissioner of the Environment to ensure checks and balances on its ministries responsible for environmental protection (see Webb 2005). Some jurisdictions in Australia have begun to experiment with Environmental or Sustainability Commissioners (see Box 4.2).[14] However, to date these initiatives lack the kind of resources and political independence of other integrity institutions in Australia such as an auditors-general office, ombudsman's offices, specialist complaint and anticorruption commissions (Brown and Head 2005).

4.6.5 The public sector

> Any form of government . . . needs to establish a set of institutions and an organisation of employees who will provide the machinery necessary to put its decisions into effect.
>
> (Janesch 1997, p 173)

The public sector (sometimes labelled the bureaucracy) broadly represents that proportion of the economy that is not conducted by the private sector. It refers to the activities undertaken by government agencies and various departments of State, statutory authorities and other legal and political institutions (Aulich and Nutley 2001).

Box 4.5: What is the public service?

Often the terms 'public sector' and 'public service' are used synonymously. However, in Australia, the term 'public service' technically refers to those government employees who are covered by the Public Service Acts in various jurisdictions (Janesch 1997).[15] In other words, the term public service refers to only a subset of the public sector – namely the group of employees (public servants) working in government to administer legislation passed by parliament.

---

14 As mentioned in Chapter 2, an example of such a voice is the proposed Sustainability Commissioner by the Australian House of Representatives Standing Committee on Environment and Heritage (2007) in their 'Inquiry into a Sustainability Charter'.

15 For more on the Public Service Acts in Australia, see Coventry (2001).

Thus there are numerous government employees that are not formally in the 'public service' because they are governed by Acts other than the Public Service Acts including police, teachers and employees of local government and statutory authorities.

The primary role of employees in the public service is to develop regulations, details and procedures to apply legislation (Janesch 1997). A second important role for the public service is to provide expert advice to government and parliament including development of policy options. Given the ever-increasing range of activities in which governments are involved, the need for expert advice has grown. This has resulted in a diverse number of roles that public servants can play in the public service, such as leading large public infrastructure programs, designing and managing policy initiatives, funding programs run by external parties, coordinating and consulting with networks of actors, regulating and ensuring compliance, educating and informing the community, researching, monitoring and collecting data.

Under the Westminster tradition, public servants are expected to be neutral, anonymous, and able to perform for any government in power (Fenna 2004). Ideally they provide their advice to the minister without becoming entangled in the politics of the issue, or without any fear of losing their job (Thompson 1997b). But in practice the public service can be highly politicised, and public servants can be silenced if their opinions or views do not match those of the government (Brown 2008b) (see also Box 5.12).

Within the public service and the public sector more broadly there is a bank of wisdom and experience gained from discussion and development, and trial and error with policies. This can generate considerable policy learning about what tools and policy instruments work best when and where, how problems are socially constructed, and the politics and arguments surrounding particular issues. Such policy learning is a crucial component of adaptive approaches to resolving sustainability issues where problems are typically urgent and complex, management solutions are evolving and experience is limited (Dovers 1997; Dovers 2005a). However, policy learning can be difficult when public sector institutions and personnel are constantly changing and in reform mode. While change is a key characteristic of modern organisations, it can create discontinuities for programs aimed at long-term environmental change. Consider, for example, the significant loss of corporate and institutional memory in environmental policy in Victoria following the Kennett (Coalition) Government's dismantling of the Victorian public service between 1992 and 1997. During this period the Victorian Department of Conservation and Environment cut over 40 per cent of staff, 'undermining its capacities for consensus formation, strategic development, policy implementation and the integration of ecological values in broader government policy and actions' (Christoff 1998, p 10).

It is not just that the institutional landscape continues to change, but that the charter or terms of reference of different agencies can work against meeting new challenges for environmental management and sustainability (Papadakis 1996). For example, the terms of reference of some government agencies may be inappropriate and too restrictive to cope with the changing needs or values of society, so that decisions are still governed by outdated organisational structures and inadequate frameworks. Over the years this has been at the root of numerous environmental disputes. For example, during the 1980s the Sydney Water Board (now Sydney Water) was focused so narrowly on pursuing engineering solutions for ocean disposal of sewage waste that it neglected to act on emerging evidence of rising toxicity levels near its ocean outfalls. Only after media exposés and public protests did the Board review its emission standards and institutional structures to better align with community and legislative requirements (Beder 1989).

A number of government bodies in Australia have had their charters brought up-to-date with current community expectations regarding environmental management. This has come in a number of forms from the more formal incorporation of sustainability principles into relevant legislation and policies (see Chapter 2 and Box 4.2), through to more informal processes such as greening the offices and operations of the public sector (CoA 2003b).

An important trend in the public sector that deserves mention is the rise of market-oriented and managerial reforms. Since the 1980s there has been a push to streamline the public sector through the deregulation, outsourcing, privatisation and corporatisation of government institutions and services (Dovers and Gullett 1999; Thompson 1997b). In the environmental area this has resulted in relevant government agencies being heavily reliant on external contractors for expertise, and limited investment in strategic policy development (Christoff 1998). Organisational models from the private sector have also been applied to make the public sector more cost-effective and in some cases even profitable. This has been particularly the case in the utilities sector, such as for water, telecommunications and electricity services.

Alongside these reforms, has been the push in the public sector for evidence-based policy-making (Davies et al 2000). The idea here is that policy-making should be based on sound evidence that a particular policy problem exists, or that particular tools or instruments are working (or not). This trend towards evidence-based policy-making has had consequences for environmental policy – particularly because data is often absent, ambiguous, or produced and interpreted variously (see Chapters 6, 8 and 9). Many programs for environmental management are now funded on the basis that managers can demonstrate 'evidence' of a problem or the effectiveness of the solution. However, an in-depth study of Western Australia's Salinity Investment Framework found that in practice evidenced-based priority setting is a highly political process in which competing understandings of evidence, and knowledge more broadly, come into play (Black 2008).

A more recent phenomenon in the public sector is the attempt to seek expertise and perspectives from outside government. This is particularly the case in environmental issues where complexity and controversy abound. Traditionally external input has come in the form of individual experts such as the Commonwealth's Chief Scientist (see Case Study B), or panel of experts such as an advisory committee or board (see 7.6.1). However, increasingly governments also seek inputs into environmental decisions and strategies from affected parties (often labelled 'stakeholders' – see Box 5.1), and ordinary citizens (Fung and Wright 2003; Gastil and Levine 2005). This is part of a broader trend towards more networked forms of governing where multiple actors are brought together to work with the government to develop and implement policy (Hendriks and Grin 2007; Kjær 2004).

4.6.6 The Judiciary (the courts)

Australian law has two sources: legislation and case law. Legislation refers to the creation of laws (statutes) by an elected parliament – federal, state or territory-based. Case law (sometimes referred to as the 'common law') emanates from the process of judges deciding particular cases, and it is a distinguishing feature of English (and therefore Australian) law that much of it flows from, and relies on, decisions set by previous cases (precedents). So, under common or case law, legal decisions are based on the principles and precedents of former cases (Cook et al 2009, p 59).

Statutory legislation can be enacted by any parliamentary government, including the Commonwealth, State and Territory legislatures. Where there is any possibility of conflict between legislation enacted by different legislatures, the Commonwealth version is superior, and a court has the power to strike down a statute as invalid if it decides the act is contrary to a provision in the Constitution.

The organisations responsible for administering and adjudicating the law are courts and tribunals. The senior Australian court is the High Court, which determines all matters relating to the interpretation of the Constitution and other significant issues of national importance. Much of the day-to-day case load of the High Court has been taken over by the Federal Court which was established in 1976. Each State has a Supreme Court, which deals with the most serious criminal and civil cases within its jurisdiction, and various inferior courts. In more recent time, specialist courts have evolved, such as the federally-based Family Court, or the NSW Land and Environment Court, which as their titles suggest, focus on those cases where adversarial conflicts require particular experience and expertise for their ready solution.

The High Court in particular has played a significant role in environmental controversies because of its central role in judging disputes between states and the Commonwealth, as well as being the final Court of Appeal in Australia. As discussed above (4.4.2), the Commonwealth has very limited formal power over environmental issues under the Constitution. However, its powers have expanded considerably through the judicial interpretation of the High Court (see Box 4.1).

Notwithstanding the significance of the High Court, much of the legal system's influence on environmental issues in Australia has been through the common law. This is primarily because common law is essentially concerned with protecting 'private property rights and economic interests of the owners of land and other natural resources' (Bates 2002, p 20). One of the key challenges in environmental law is to balance these property rights (which essentially allow unrestricted rights to natural resources) with environmental values (Bates 2002).

There are numerous courts in Australia that play a role in EDM including specialised courts dealing with environmental issues, such as the Land and Environment Court in New South Wales (and similar in the other States) (see Cook et al 2009). Ideally courts provide a forum where different parties can be heard and their arguments considered by an independent and politically neutral judge. In other words, they can play an active role in protecting public interest by weighing up arguments and evidence in conflicts (Bates 2002). However, there are some good reasons why courts may not always be the most appropriate institutions for dealing with environmental disputes. First, courts are by design adversarial; their procedures set out to produce a winner and a loser. According to some commentators the emphasis on victory is often at the expense of weighing up the evidence (see Stewart 1993). Secondly, there is a tendency for lawyers to use science as a weapon, for example, by bolstering their own arguments or discrediting witnesses (Bates 2002, p 115). Thirdly, the legal system assumes not only that there is someone or a party available with the resources to pursue litigation, but that they have the legal right ('standing') to take action in the courts. As we will explore further in Chapter 7, 'standing' is a legal concept that refers to the right to take action in court. Standing may be conferred through legislation relating to particular situations, or through demonstration that you have a legitimate interest in a particular matter (Bates 2002). Conventionally, a legitimate interest or stake concerned protecting private interests, such as property or economic values (see Lynch and Galligan 1996). However, in many environmental issues, people might wish to pursue legal action in order to protect the environment rather than personal property. In some instances environmental groups have been able to gain standing by demonstrating that they have a special interest in the issue (see Box 7.5).

Some legal firms take on public interest cases with reduced fees or pro-bono (free). There are also legal aid centres, such as the Environmental Defender's Office in all Australian States and Territories that provide resources, advice and grants for specific cases.[16] The role of the law is explored further in Chapter 7 in the context of public participation.

4.7 Global institutions relevant to environmental management in Australia

So far we have been concerned primarily with the relevant policy and political institutions in Australia that play a role in domestic environmental decisions. We turn our attention now to the international realm, and briefly consider some of the significant global institutions that also shape environmental outcomes in Australia.

The transboundary nature of environmental issues means that they cross political borders, and require nation-states to work together to resolve issues. This phenomenon is especially evident in Europe where countries share land and river borders. In Australia we may feel geographically isolated, but this does not mean we are not immune to the effects of global environmental problems. Consider, for example, the impacts in Australia of the depletion of the ozone layer, global climate change, and over-fishing.

Without a doubt the most significant international organisation on the environment is the United Nations (UN), which was formally established in 1945 (previously the League of Nations). The UN has played a key role in forging worldwide responses to environmental problems. In its early days, the UN created a few environmentally related multilateral agreements, for example on wildlife conservation and maritime pollution (Carter 2007). However, since the 1970s the UN has taken a more active and coordinated response to global environmental issues by convening international conferences for world leaders, and funding environmental programs and initiatives. As we saw in Chapter 2, the UN conference of 1972 in Stockholm was a milestone event in putting sustainability on the agendas of governments around the world. Since then significant global treaties and conventions on the environment have been agreed upon, for example the *Rio Declaration*, *Agenda 21* and various international agreements (particularly those on climate change and biodiversity).

An important function of the UN has been the establishment of Multilateral Environmental Agreements (MEAs), which oblige signatory countries to action (see Box 4.6). There are now over 200 MEAs covering a range of issues including whaling, the transport of hazardous materials, desertification, biodiversity, stratospheric ozone layer depletion and climate change (Carter 2007, p 242). Some of these have been more successful at achieving international cooperation than others. For example, the Montreal protocol aimed at protecting the ozone layer (by regulating the production and consumption of CFCs and halons), has had far more support and policy success than other treaties. Success is heavily dependent on the complexity of the issue at hand; for example, compared to the global challenges of climate change the task of protecting the ozone layer was relatively straightforward – substitutes for ozone depleting substances (such as chlorofluorocarbons (CFCs) used as propellants in spray cans, among a range of uses) were available and financial losses were relatively minor.

---

16   See <www.edo.org.au>.

Box 4.6: Multilateral Environmental Agreements – what is the difference between signing and ratifying a UN treaty?

Most UN multilateral treaties involve a two-step process: first, a country needs to *sign* the treaty (the so-called 'simple signature'), and second, the treaty needs to be *ratified* before the country is bound by it. Thus signing a treaty represents only a preliminary step towards approving a treaty and it does not impose any obligations on the country under the treaty. In other words, a (simple) signature merely requires a country to refrain from any activities that would endanger the object and purpose of the treaty. Only when a country ratifies a treaty does it formally accept or approve the treaty and agrees to be bound by it. It also means that the state must comply with certain international legal requirements.

Source: <http://untreaty.un.org/english/treatyhandbook/glossary.htm#grat>
(accessed 17 March 2009).

It is important to note that international environmental cooperation in the form of agreements can be institutionally fragile. As DeSombre (2005, p 2) explains:

> No state can ever be required to join an environmental agreement or to undertake a particular regulation. The international system is anarchic in that there is no overarching authority (in this case, world government) that can dictate to individual states, actors within those states, what they must do. And although there are international courts and tribunals, no state can ever be forced to appear before them, or to accept punishment from them.

This does not mean that states do not take international agreements seriously. Indeed comparative research suggests that most states recognise the need to work cooperatively on global environmental problems (DeSombre 2005). Yet the influence of international agreements on domestic environmental policies is variable, with compliance and effectiveness being difficult to measure. Certainly in Australia some conventions have had some effect on national responses, such as the management and movement of toxic wastes and hazardous chemicals (for example, the *Basel Convention*), and the protection of migratory birds (for example, JAMBA and CAMBA).[17]

Many other international bodies also exert their influence (sometimes indirectly) on EDM in Australia. For example, the OECD provides useful reporting and benchmarking on environment performance (eg OECD 2007a), and thus an international impetus for the Commonwealth and State governments to take action. Similarly, the regulations of the World Trade Organisation have had an impact on how some environmental standards are designed and implemented in Australia (McDonald 2007; Robertson and Kellow 2001). The World Bank, which funds many international development projects, runs programs on environment and trade issues, and has an extensive Environmental Impact Assessment program (Thomas 2007). There are also numerous international non-government organisations (NGOs) that play a role in fostering sustainability at the international level. These include groups such as Greenpeace, the World Wide Fund for Nature (WWF), the International Institute for Sustainable Development, the Global Reporting Initiative (GRI), the World

---

17 For more on Australia's international cooperation on hazardous wastes, see <www.environment.gov.au/settlements/chemicals/hazardous-waste/conventions.html> (accessed 15 April 2009); and on migratory birds, see <www.environment.gov.au/biodiversity/migratory/waterbirds/index.html> (accessed 15 April 2009).

Resources Institute, the Rocky Mountain Institute, and many others. We take a closer look at the role of NGOs in Chapter 5.

4.8 Conclusion

> Virtually every discussion of sustainability concludes that our existing institutional arrangements are part of the problem and that significant reform is required.
>
> (Dovers 2001, p 7)

Institutional arrangements play a significant role in EDM. As we have seen, Australia's Constitution and federal structure, its political system, courts, cabinets and public sector all have the capacity to shape how we respond to sustainability challenges, and the effectiveness of these measures. The fact that elections typically occur in Australia on a three-to-four year cycle also has repercussions for the kind of proactive and long-term planning that sustainability issues demand.

On the one hand institutions provide mechanisms for different actors to bring environmental matters onto the public agenda, and offer structures through which decisions are made and legitimised. Yet on the other hand, institutions can deeply constrain our capacity to achieve sustainable outcomes, for example by preferring particular problem frames over others, and creating administrative or political barriers to more integrative and adaptive solutions.

How well then are Australian institutions performing in helping society respond to the challenges of sustainability? Not very well according to most assessments (eg Dovers 2001, 2008; Dovers and Wild River 2003; OECD 2007a; Papadakis 1996; Ross and Dovers 2008). Some of the enduring institutional problems facing environmental management in Australia relate to inappropriate administrative and political boundaries (many associated with federalism), reactionary and short-term thinking, inadequate community involvement, lack of independence, and ultimately a lack of political will to support long-term transitions to sustainability (see Dovers 2001). There is no shortage of suggestions for how to improve the capacity of our institutions to foster sustainability. Commentators have argued that sustainable development demands that our institutions need to be more adaptive in the sense that they be more experimental and flexible in their approaches, while also purposefully oriented towards sustainability (Dovers 2003a) (see Chapter 2). Our institutions should also be more inclusive of affected actors (Eckersley 2003), less adversarial and more collaborative and interactive (Ison et al 2007), and foster cultural and behavioural change (Papadakis 1996; Shove 2003) as well as social learning (Blackmore 2007). We consider some of these suggestions further in Chapter 10.

While institutional change is important, we should also be aware that it can only promote environmental outcomes so far (see Papadakis 1996, p 199). The comparative work of Dryzek et al (2003) shows how the incorporation of green values into political institutions (through green parties and environmental agencies) has not been as successful for the environment in some northern European countries, such as Norway, as anticipated. This study suggests that change for sustainability cannot be achieved through institutional reforms alone, but it also requires the counter activities of non-government actors (Dryzek et al 2003). In the next chapter we take a closer look at the roles that some of these groups and organisations play in EDM.

5

Actors Outside Government

5.1 Introduction

As we have seen from previous chapters, environmental decisions are complex. Typically they involve a host of groups and individuals with competing vested interests and value positions. These participants take on different roles depending on the issue. For example, environmental groups may lobby decision-makers for greener outcomes, corporations may seek special concessions for development or production, experts may inject specialist insights into an environmental controversy, and the media may campaign to put an issue on the agenda. These are just some of the diverse players that seek to influence how environmental matters are framed, discussed and acted upon. There are also a host of individuals and organisations that are brought into decisions because they are affected by environmental controversies, procedures or outcomes. For example, communities living near a proposed development, or a specific group adversely impacted by a new environmental regulation, or a bank that finances a controversial environmental project (see Case Study B).

In this chapter we refer to all these different entities as 'actors'. In the context of environmental issues, an actor is an individual, association or organisation that participates in, or is affected by, the environmental decision-making (EDM) cycle (see Figure 1.1) from problem definition through to implementation and evaluation. It is important to note that we are referring to much more than conventional decision-makers, such as politicians, heads of government departments, public managers, developers or corporations. The term 'actors' also encapsulates a broader set of entities than the term 'stakeholder' – which is typically reserved for organised groups and associations seeking political influence (see Box 5.1).

Box 5.1: Who is a 'stakeholder'?

In this chapter we prefer to use the term 'actor' rather than 'stakeholder' – a term which has its origins in organisational management. In EDM, stakeholders are typically organised groups or organisations that have a particular interest in a given issue, and are able to muster some political force. For example, consider the various stakeholders associated with a proposed marina development. This could include a planning authority (typically the local council), developers, those funding the project, engineers, fishing and boating groups, the tourism industry, local environmental groups, and concerned residents.

In most environmental decisions there are many entities that are not considered stakeholders even though they may potentially have a stake in the issue in the sense that they might be affected by the outcomes. For example, in the marina example above, affected communities might include citizens in the area, future generations and the environment itself (especially vulnerable fish and sea grass species). Clearly the term 'stakeholder' is open to considerable interpretation in a given context. This is largely because 'stake' can carry multiple meanings depending on whether one is concerned with issues of power, legitimacy or urgency (Mitchell et al 1997).

Our goal in this chapter is to explore the diversity of actors involved in and affected by environmental decisions and the various roles they play. Whereas in Chapter 4 we explored the role of government and its institutions, here our focus is on the range of actors from outside government engaged in environmental decisions. In particular we take a look at business, pressure groups, think tanks, funding bodies, the media, individuals and experts. Towards the end of the chapter we explore the rise and role of professionals in environmental decisions, and consider some of the ethical dilemmas they may face.

5.2 The roles and influences of actors in EDM

[I]t is difficult to avoid the role of groups in the policy process. Business and trade associations, unions, residents' associations, consumer groups, professional associations, welfare lobbies, rights organisations, environmental groups, ethnic councils, women's groups – there is no area of public policy where collective actors do not seek to influence the decision-making process.

(Fenna 2004, p 151)

Actors outside government have a number of ways to influence environmental decisions. In broad terms they can seek to influence the decision-makers directly, for example through advocacy activities such as lobbying and providing advice, or by offering funds and donations. Direct signals can also be sent to governments through their voting preferences, and to corporations through the products that consumers choose to purchase. Alternatively actors might decide it is more strategic to try and influence decision-makers indirectly by stimulating public debate (Fenna 2004, p 152), for example, through protesting, education or advertising.

Yet not all actors try to influence decision-makers through direct or indirect means. Some prefer to collaborate and work with decision-makers as active participants of governance programs. As discussed in Chapters 1 and 3, this shift towards environmental governance occurs when different actors work collaboratively with governments and other decision-making bodies to resolve and address pressing environmental issues (Stewart and Jones 2003). In other words non-government actors are increasingly engaged as partners to work together with decision-makers to assist in monitoring and governing environmental matters. For example, actors may be closely involved in the policy process by developing programs and implementing them. Groups might also work together, for example, to form networks and coalitions in which they exchange knowledge and resources. Other actors might be brought in to monitor or evaluate a decision or series of programs.

Despite this trend toward more cooperative forms of governance most actors remain differentiated in terms of their influence on outcomes. Some groups are particularly advantaged by existing political and institutional frameworks. They might, for example, have access to useful resources (such as money, knowledge, organisational capacity and administration) and this may provide them with considerable access to those in power. Over the medium to longer-term privileged groups are often as much concerned with fighting to preserve those aspects of the system that facilitate their interests in decision-making, or against those that hinder these, as they are with fighting for specific shorter-term causes. The most influential actors in environmental matters tend to be well-organised groups that are able to effectively pressure and lobby decision-makers. That said, individuals too can influence environmental decisions, for example, as activists, consumers, shareholders or as champions of a particular cause.

What is the best way to make sense of the diversity of actors (outside of government) involved in, and affected by, environmental decisions? In the following sections we explore different categories of actors based broadly on their sector or interests. This list is not exhaustive. Instead it seeks to demonstrate the diversity of actors and their roles and influence in EDM.

5.3 Business

In broad terms business actors are private entities seeking to make a profit from their goods and services. The business sector is full of diverse actors which vary in size, business activities, and environmental performance. Business actors range from local shops, industries, companies, firms, and corporations. What they hold in common is that their world is the highly competitive marketplace, which in many cases today is the global market.

Private business actors are often framed as the bad guys when it comes to environmental matters. Indeed some of the roots of the environmental movement are embedded in a reaction to polluting industries (eg Carson 1962). But the poor reputation of business on environmental matters is not only their association with industrial pollution and disasters. Business actors represent privileged and thus powerful players in most decision-making processes (Beder 2002; Doyle and McEachern 2008; Lindblom 1977; Pearse 2007). Typically they are well resourced and possess capital, labour, influential networks and knowledge. The economic might of business is probably their most powerful political weapon. In the face of environmental degradation business can provide strong counter-arguments in terms of their economic contributions, including their export value, and the employment and tax revenue they provide (see Case Study B). Moreover, some sectors of business have gone to great lengths to resist government regulation on environmental matters, and fought hard for voluntary or self-regulated approaches (eg Pearse 2007) (see also Case Study A).

However, business is increasingly recognised as a necessary partner and potential leader in the transition to sustainability (Lovins et al 2000). Even in the early stages of the sustainability debate (see Chapter 2), business was invited to make a significant contribution to the 1992 Earth Summit (Schmidheiny et al 1992). Since then the general approach has been to encourage the corporate sector to appreciate that environmental reforms can make good business sense. As we will explore further in Chapter 8, a large number of tools have been developed to improve the accountability, transparency and innovation of businesses when it comes to environmental matters.

There have also been many external and internal drivers encouraging businesses to take up the sustainability challenge. In particular, legislation and government policy have been significant drivers for change (see Chapter 4). Indeed some comparative studies single out government and its regulatory framework as one of the most influential factors shaping corporate environmental performance (Gunningham et al 2003).

International organisations and networks of many types have also significantly promoted sustainability in the business sector, including those institutions that fund and insure business activities (Clarke 2007). Such global initiatives include:

- the World Business Council for Sustainable Development, which has played a key role in promulgating business engagement with sustainability;[1]

- the Global Reporting Initiative (GRI), which provides guidelines for reporting on Corporate Sustainability Reporting (see 8.10 and 10.2) and a fast growing number of corporations now publicly report using GRI guidelines;[2]

- the Carbon Disclosure Project, which encourages major corporations to disclose information on their greenhouse gas emissions;[3]

- the Equator Principles, which provide a set of principles relevant to sustainability for major banks to voluntarily adopt;[4]

- the Dow Jones Sustainability Index, and a number of other such indices, which rank corporations on their sustainability performance and publish the results;[5]

- the Principles for Responsible Investment (PRI) (developed in partnership between global investors and two UN agencies) which provide a range of ways to incorporate environmental, social and corporate governance issues into mainstream investment decision-making.[6] By mid-2008 the signatories to the PRI managed US$14 trillion of investments (PRI 2008).

---

1   See <www.wbcsd.org>.
2   See <www.globalreporting.org>.
3   See <www.cdproject.net>.
4   See <www.equator-principles.com>.
5   See <www.sustainability-index.com>.
6   See <www.unpri.org>.

There are also drivers for corporate sustainability from environment and other non-government organisations (NGOs), which run public advocacy campaigns attacking brands, and promoting ethical conduct (see Steger 2006). In some cases these efforts provide strong pressures for corporations to meet community, shareholder and consumer expectations, and to develop a reputation as a company with strong ethical and sustainability standards and as an employer of choice (Benn et al 2006).

There are also critical internal drivers for achieving rapid change, such as the management style of the corporation (Gunningham et al 2003), and the leadership by the CEO, by board members and by a range of other employees (Brown, V 2008; Dunphy et al 2007). With respect to leadership a key example is Ray Anderson, CEO of Interface, who from the mid-1990s drove a rapid turnaround towards sustainability in that company's performance (see Doppelt 2003; Hargroves and Smith 2005; Holliday et al 2002). We discuss leadership issues further in 10.4.

While there have been multiple drivers to promote sustainability in the business sector, responses have been mixed. Some businesses have been very slow to take up the sustainability challenge, while others have demonstrated considerable progress (see 10.2). Evidence for this progress comes from increasing uptake of various frameworks, principles and tools for achieving sustainability (see Chapters 2 and 8), the number of groups promoting these, and the use of transparent processes for reporting progress to sustainability.

Other roles that business plays in the EDM that we have yet to discuss are lobbying and advocacy. We consider these below in our broader discussion of pressure groups.

5.4 Pressure groups

Pressure groups or lobby groups are political organisations that seek to influence decision-making by pushing a particular interest such as business conditions, employment rights, environmental outcomes or professional standards. Pressure groups differ from political parties in that they are not seeking election into government (Warhurst 2006). Instead their goal is to ensure that the specific interests of their sector or members are taken into account in relevant decisions. It is this role which makes pressure groups important players in our political systems; their activities shape the way issues are framed, discussed, and decided upon (Richardson 1993).

How do pressure groups seek to influence EDM? Typically pressure does not come in the form of direct threats or coercion but rather through persuasion and advocacy (Matthews 1997). In other words, the core mission of most pressure groups is to convince relevant decision-makers of their particular position or idea. They will adopt strategies for doing so based on the accessibility of relevant decision-making structures. The participation of pressure groups in the policy process in Australia is relatively unstructured when compared to some Western European countries. For example, in Austria and Sweden it is common for large pressure groups representing business, labour and social interests to be integrated into the policy process through structured consultation arrangements (referred to as corporatism) (see Fenna 2004, p 160).

There have been periods in Australia, for example during the 1980s and early 1990s, when various governments have flirted with more consensual forms of interest group involvement, for example, by establishing formal consultative structures aimed at policy development. This was particularly the case for environmental policy during the Hawke Government (see Downes 1996) (see 7.3). Though few of these consultative structures survived beyond the mid-1990s, governments in Australia continue to rely heavily on pressure groups in an advisory capacity. For some issues, governments have established formal advisory committees that are composed of different representative groups (see 7.6.1). The more common picture, however, is a kind of stakeholder style of policy-making, where government agencies seek one-off feedback from well-organised pressure groups on particular issues or proposals (Laffin 1997, p 53).

Notwithstanding these more formal avenues to influence decisions, most pressure groups in Australia concentrate their efforts on lobbying. Lobbyists are generally employees of pressure groups, but they can also be consultants or intermediaries that work on behalf of the group (Warhurst 2006). For most groups lobbying involves the dual orientation of pushing ideas both within and outside government. For example, lobbyists might meet individually with ministers and staffers, attend and speak at hearings, network with like-minded groups, and circulate relevant information. At the same time many pressure groups also work outside government trying to mobilise public opinion via media campaigns and other promotional activities (Warhurst 2006).

Much of the lobbying within government is directed at the department and cabinet level, rather than at the parliament, or courts (Matthews 1997; Matthews and Warhurst 1993). Given the relative strength of cabinet in the Australian political system (see Chapter 4), most legislative Bills are government-sponsored and ministers and their departments typically have a prominent role in drafting policy (Matthews and Warhurst 1993). In this drafting process, ministerial bureaucrats often consult with representatives from pressure groups for advice and as a means to secure their cooperation. Indeed some pressure groups may write policy papers or statements and have these adopted by government (see Pearse 2007). Other pressure groups might direct their lobbying efforts towards the international arena.

The success or otherwise of a pressure group depends not only on the match between its strategy and the opportunities offered by the political system, and on the relative influence of any opposing pressure groups, but importantly also on the nature of the pressure group itself. According to Jaensch (1997, p 350):

> [A] group which has resources, a large membership, is united internally in the formulation of its aims and in regard to methods of action, which has developed organisational skills and has professional expertise and a clear knowledge of the machinery of government, has a head-start to success.

Frequently, consultation between government and pressure groups will take place through umbrella organisations or peak bodies, which are established to represent the interests of similar pressure groups (see Box 5.2 below). This has the advantage of pooling resources, but the danger is that in creating a unified voice, alternative views are suppressed.

Box 5.2: Nature Conservation Council (NCC) – an example of a peak environmental body
The NCC of New South Wales is a non-profit environmental organisation that represents approximately 120 community environment groups across the State. Since it was established in 1955, the NCC has grown into a highly professional and productive pressure group with three core goals:

1. to coordinate and drive various campaigns;

2. to represent member groups in providing advice to government and communities (for example, to prepare submissions for policy proposals); and

3. to educate the community.

The NCC also offers a range of administrative and support services to its members, such as preparing media releases, training, guest speakers and office services.

Source: NCC 2008.

Different pressure groups also have varying degrees of influence, depending on characteristics such as whether the group is viewed by policy-makers to be representative, informed and responsible and if it is hence regularly consulted (insider group) or whether it is kept at arm's length (outsider group) (Matthews 1993). Many insider groups have been institutionalised within the Australian political system, as successive governments become dependent on particular groups for information, to assist in policy development and to act as a sounding board for developing new policies. Insider groups with the most influence are those with strong socio-economic leverage and access to resources, such as business and producer groups (Matthews 1993, pp 233–234). For example, since the early 1990s the fossil fuel lobby has had considerable influence on Australia's policy response to climate change, as Box 5.3 outlines.

Box 5.3: The ongoing influence of the fossil fuel lobby on Australian climate change policy

Since the mid-1990s when policy debates on reducing greenhouse gas emissions began, the fossil fuel industry has wielded considerable influence. In June 1994, under the Keating (Labor) Government, the National ESD and Greenhouse Roundtable was established to allow business, environmental and community groups and government to discuss the enhanced greenhouse effect and related sustainability issues. The fossil fuel lobby was particularly well represented at the roundtable as they occupied 10 seats, while the renewable energy sector was provided with only one seat (SEICA, cited in Henderson and O'Loughlin 1996).

The influence of the fossil fuel lobby over government policy was further demonstrated at the *Framework Convention on Climate Change* (FCCC) meeting in July 1996, when the newly elected Howard (Coalition) Government opposed legally binding targets for greenhouse gas emissions. The rationale here was that Australia was a special case country with an economy unusually dependent on energy-intensive exports, and with correspondingly large greenhouse gas emissions per capita (Dey and Lenzen 1996). The concern was that if Australia was committed to binding emission targets, then it would incur severe economic costs. This perspective rested heavily on controversial economic modelling conducted by ABARE (the Australian Bureau of Agricultural and Resource Economics) (McDonald 2005), whose greenhouse policy research was being generously funded by many of the country's largest carbon emitters (Pearse 2007). Indeed, ABARE's research steering committee was disproportionately represented by fossil fuel interests since membership was exclusively reserved for those who could afford $50,000 per annum for a seat at the table.

At the meeting of the parties to the FCCC in Kyoto in December 1997, Australia maintained its opposition against legally binding greenhouse emission targets, stating that it should be granted special allowances for emissions, due to being an energy exporter to Asia (Woodford and Millet 1997). This occurred despite considerable community outrage at home and the disapproval of national leaders from around the world. At this meeting the then Environment Minister, Robert Hill, managed to secure an emissions target for Australia of an 8 per cent *increase* over the 1990 level, while other nations on average were required to *decrease* their emissions by approximately 5.2 per cent (McDonald 2005, p 227). Hill also managed to push through a special clause (often referred to as the 'Australia clause') that included land clearing in emissions calculations. This effectively increased Australia's baseline because 1990 was a year of very high land clearing emissions. Despite Minister Hill's efforts, Cabinet support for the Kyoto Protocol declined considerably between 1997 and 2002 (McDonald 2005; Pearse 2007). Then on World Environment Day, 5 June 2002, Prime Minister Howard announced that Australia would *not* be ratifying the Kyoto Protocol.

Thus in the end despite the fact that Australia had negotiated significant changes to the Kyoto Protocol, it refused to ratify it. There are different ways to make sense of this decision, but most analyses draw attention to the considerable influence of the fossil fuel lobby (eg Christoff 2005; Hamilton 2007; McDonald 2005; Papadakis 2002). According to a Liberal Party insider, Guy Pearse (2007), the Howard Government's response to climate change was grossly shaped by the lobbying efforts of the Australian Industry Greenhouse Network (AIGN) which represents the nation's largest carbon polluting industries including coal, petroleum, aluminium, cement and electricity generation. Pearse's (2007) study reveals how the AIGN has financed and promoted successive research on greenhouse policy, and shows their intricate involvement in pivotal policy decisions. More revealing, Pearse (2007) demonstrates how the boundaries between government and industry became increasingly blurred on greenhouse issues, as personnel moved freely between the AIGN and relevant government departments.

The lobbying efforts of the fossil fuel sector continued after the election of the Rudd (Labor) Government towards the end of 2007 (see Pearse 2008). Initially the new government acted quickly on climate change issues; it ratified the Kyoto Protocol in December 2007 and promoted its commissioned Review on Climate Change (Garnaut 2008). However, when more concrete policy actions began to surface in 2008, the ongoing influence of the fossil fuel lobby was visible. For example, the Rudd government has preferred to invest large funds in clean coal technologies rather than in renewables (Rodgers 2008), and its proposed Carbon Pollution Reduction Scheme (CoA 2008) has been criticised for over compensating large carbon emitters rather than stimulating innovation and reform (Denniss 2009; MacGill and Betz 2008). The true power of the fossil fuel lobby was exposed in late 2008 when the Rudd Government announced its modest carbon emissions target of between 5 to 15 per cent. Its own policy adviser, Professor Ross Garnaut, publicly condemned the government's plan, arguing that there had been 'unprecedented lobbying from vested interests . . . unprecedented in Australian policy-making, the extent of it . . . There's no doubt that the rate of return in lobbying has been very high' (*The Australian* 2008).

This example demonstrates the significant and ongoing influence that the fossil fuel lobby has had on the Commonwealth Government under various political leaderships.

Some governments have sought to rectify the dominance of economic interests, especially in formal advisory bodies, by providing funds to weaker or outsider groups, such as those working on environmental, women's or Indigenous issues. However, accepting government funding can be problematic for some pressure groups because it can limit their independence, and make them vulnerable to the policy preferences of the government in power

(Hamilton and Maddison 2007).[7] Moreover, funding does not necessarily translate into political access and influence.

It is also important to note that since the early 1990s there has been considerable fluidity between personnel in pressure groups, government, and business (see Box 5.3). Consider the career path of Peter Garrett – once rock singer, environmental campaigner and President of the Australian Conservation Foundation (ACF) – who became a Member of the Federal Parliament (MP) in 2004, and in 2007 was appointed as Minister for the Environment, Heritage and Arts in the newly elected Rudd (Labor) Government. Another example is the Australian Paul Gilding, who after directing Greenpeace International for several years returned to Australia where he set up a consultancy, Ecos Corp, which advises major firms in Australia and abroad on sustainability issues.

Below we take a closer look at some of the key pressure groups involved in EDM. Having considered the role of business actors above, our focus from here is mostly on environmental groups, with some brief consideration of other relevant groups.

5.4.1 Environmental pressure groups

Environmental pressure groups, also known as environmental NGOs, environmental advocacy groups and green activists, are typically independent non-profit organisations that seek improved environmental outcomes. Since the early 1970s there has been a proliferation of environmental groups in Australia, though up-to-date data on the exact number is difficult to source.[8]

One of the key political tasks of environmental groups is to inject a voice for nature, and the environment more broadly, into decision-making processes. This has been particularly important for Australian environmental groups which have their roots in the conservation movement, rather than in pollution prevention and waste management as was the case in Western Europe (Tranter 2004). Today the agenda for most environmental groups in Australia is much broader than just protecting nature; their campaigns also address the social and economic aspects of sustainability. For example, some environmental groups are now concentrating on social justice issues by trying to ensure that marginalised populations are not exposed to the worst environmental conditions (eg ACF et al undated).

How do environmental pressure groups inject their green values into decision-making processes? The answer to this question depends on whether the group operates predominantly as a *lobby* group or as a *protest* organisation (adapted from Carter 2007). Environmental *lobby* groups in Australia are diverse. Some are large, operate nationally and cover a broad spectrum of issues (such as the ACF and The Wilderness Society (TWS)), while others are focussed at the State or local level with specific interests (such as the such as the National Parks Association of New South Wales, or the Bellingen Environment Centre[9]). Today many environmental lobby groups are highly professionalised organisations with directors, policy officers, public relations staff, scientists and governing bodies. The tasks of environmental lobby groups are similar to those of other conventional pressure groups; they seek to mobilise public concern, lobby decision-makers, provide information and auditing

---

7   For example, when the Howard Government was in power some commentators argued that marginalised interests were systematically excluded from much of the policy process (see Hamilton and Maddison 2007; Sawer 2001).

8   See the *Australian Directory of Associations*, or *The Green Pages* <www.thegreenpages.com.au>.

9   See <www.ecobello.org.au/groups/bello-enviro-centre.html> (accessed 15 April 2009).

services, advise governments and business, produce counter-expertise and knowledge or form partnerships and alliances with government and business.

In contrast, environmental *protest* organisations focus their activities on more disruptive forms of political engagement such as activism, protests, direct action and even confrontational tactics. Greenpeace began with such a mission, but its role in Australia and internationally is expanding into a host of more conventional pressure tactics (Beder 2002; Carter 2007). One radical protest organisation is the international anti-whaling group, the Sea Shepherd Conservation Society, which uses direct action tactics on the high seas to protect marine wildlife.[10] Many environmental protest groups are engaging in alternative forms of activism via the internet. Some have developed websites and weblogs, and contact their members directly via email about protest events and campaigns (see Pickerell 2003). Research from the United Kingdom suggests that environmental activists have been quick to embrace internet technology because it supports and facilitates the cultural norms of environmentalism, for example, of being participatory and local (Horton 2004).

Box 5.4: Using the internet for environmental campaigns – GetUp! Action for Australia

GetUp! is an Australian based activist organisation that actively uses the internet for its campaigns. The environment represents just one of a number of its campaign issues, which according to the GetUp! website, are broadly 'focused around shared progressive values such as social justice, economic fairness and environmental sustainability'. Get Up! was one of the first activist groups in Australia to use email and the internet to distribute information about campaigns. Some of its environmental campaigns have included action on climate change, public transport, and a call to close the Tamar Valley pulp mill (see Case Study B).

Source: <www.getup.org.au> (accessed 10 February 2009).

While environmental groups have diversified particularly in terms of their size and focus, some convergence also appears to have taken place when it comes to their internal governance and the forms of pressure they exert. There is a tendency for environmental groups to shift from participatory and organic organisational structures towards more centralisation and institutionalisation (see 3.9.1). The tactics of environmental groups are also changing. There appears to be less emphasis on radical direct action and more on publicity, lobbying and expert testimony (Carter 2007). Consider the Total Environment Centre in Sydney which was originally amongst the most radical green groups in Australia. Today it takes a more cooperative approach by working closely with business to facilitate change in the corporate sector (TEC 2009).

In response to the increased institutionalisation of environmental groups there has been a resurgence of grassroots environmentalism in some parts of the world, most notably the United States and the United Kingdom during the late 1980s and 1990s. This has come in the form of radical social movements, such as Earthfirst! which engages in various forms of direct action, sometimes illegally. Grassroots environmentalism has also been revitalised through the growth of local community-based environmental groups that form often in response to Locally Unwanted Land Uses (LULUs) such as controversial roads, incinerators or wind farms. Local community-based environmental groups are often labelled (derogatively) as NIMBY groups (Not-In-My-Backyard) because their members are opposed to a particular proposed development in their local area (see Box 5.5 and also Box 3.1).

---

10 See <www.seashepherd.org> (accessed 20 April 2009).

Box 5.5: What is NIMBY?

The term NIMBY emerged in the 1980s to describe the negative responses of communities to particular kinds of proposed infrastructure or development near their homes such as freeways, landfills, prisons, power stations and airports. Today the term NIMBY tends to carry negative connotations, denoting an emotional response to a proposed development by the community based on narrow, selfish and parochial interests (Kraft and Clary 1991). NIMBY is also used to describe communities that are content to have the development or technology sited elsewhere, just not in their neighbourhood (Blowers 1997).

There are, however, a number of criticisms of the use of the expression 'NIMBY politics' to describe local environmental protests. In some cases local opposition may be less about parochial issues, such as concern over falling property values, but rather an opposition to broader national and international trends that concern the community, such as global climate change (Rootes 1999). Thus to describe a protest against a particular local project as NIMBYism, can be to disregard some of the larger issues at the heart of the campaign to block a project (Michauda et al 2008), as illustrated in relation to wind farms in Box 3.1.

Membership numbers of environmental groups in Australia have been growing steadily over the years. Consider the ACF whose membership increased from 3513 in 1970 to 15,605 in 1996 (ACF 1997) to 21,000 in 2007 (ACF 2007).[11] These trends, however, may not necessarily be indicative of the future; if community interest in environmental issues decreases as it has done in the past (see Downs 1972), it is plausible that membership of environmental groups could decline.

It is also important to keep in mind that membership figures can be misleading. Not all environmental groups have formal members who pay regular membership fees, but rather have supporters who make ad-hoc donations (see Box 5.6).

Box 5.6: The funding base of environmental groups – memberships, supporter and sponsors

Environmental groups operate under different kinds of funding bases, and thus maintain different kinds of relationships with those that fund them. For example, some environmental groups have members that pay a regular membership fee. In turn members might receive different services such as political representation, advice and information. They might also have a say in the direction and activities of the organisation, though the involvement of members varies considerably between groups. Having a strong membership base is politically advantageous; a group claiming to represent X number of people or Y number of organisations has more political clout than a group with few or no members. The political weight of such claims, however, is coming under increasing scrutiny, with some research suggesting that many groups do not accurately represent the views of their members (Skocpol 1999; Strolovitch 2006). A common scenario, particularly for environmental groups is that members are relatively inactive in the organisation and participate only on a 'cheque-book' basis. That is, they pay their annual member fee and that is it.

Other environmental groups have supporters rather than members. The distinction here is that supporters make a payment (often in the form of a donation) but this does not give them any formal governance or organisational rights (Carter 2007). For example, by the end of 2007

---

11   These figures only refer to financial members, and do not include supporters who contribute one-off donations.

Greenpeace International had 2.8 million supporters worldwide, and Greenpeace Australia Pacific had approximately 100,000 supporters (Greenpeace 2007). Despite these impressive numbers, supporters of Greenpeace have limited say in the governance of the organisation or where it focuses its campaigning efforts (Warhurst 2006). Instead Greenpeace operates as a highly centralised and hierarchical management system. The board of Greenpeace International consists of four members and a chairperson. It has 41 offices worldwide with representatives from the boards of these offices meeting once a year to determine key strategic directions and funding (Greenpeace International 2009).

Pressure groups struggling for funds may seek to supplement their incomes through sponsorship. Often this comes in the form of bequests or government support, but increasingly from the corporate sector. According to the free-market think tank, the Institute of Public Affairs (IPA) (see 5.5), more noise should be made about corporate sponsorship of environmental groups. The IPA argues that 'corporations have increasingly sought to protect their reputations from attacks by the likes of Friends of the Earth and Greenpeace by getting an environmental NGO "on board" to sign off on its projects and defend them in public debate' (D'Cruz 2003). An alternative interpretation is that environmental groups are trying to influence corporate actors by engaging and working *with* them. Further below we discuss some of the potential dangers facing pressure groups when they accept funds from external parties, such as government or corporations.

Environmental groups also vary considerably in terms of their ideology and willingness to work cooperatively with government and business. There is now a spectrum of groups from the more radical and critical of the status quo at one end, to those who work closely with the corporate and government sector at the other end. Moreover, Australia now has environmental groups that can be positioned across the entire political spectrum, from groups adhering to left or more social democratic ideals through to other groups that support right-of-centre political ideals (for example, social conservatism and free markets) such as the Lavoisier Group[12] and the Australian Environment Foundation (see Box 5.7). Thus, today most of us can arguably find a specific green group that matches our particular set of environmental values (see Chapter 3).

Box 5.7: An example of a counter 'environmental' group

The Australian Environment Foundation (AEF) was established in 2005 as an organisation to counter the political influence of conservation and radical green groups. The AEF describes itself as 'a different kind of environment group, caring for both Australia and Australians'. Some of the AEF campaigns have included criticising the science of the Intergovernmental Panel on Climate Change (IPCC), questioning the notion of human induced climate change, putting nuclear energy on the agenda, and removing bans on genetically modified organisms (GMOs).

Source: <www.aefweb.info> (accessed 15 February 2009).

The increased differentiation amongst environmental groups has meant that the onerous task of environmental advocacy is now spread amongst many groups, enabling different organisations to specialise on particular issues. Yet diversification has also created considerable

---

12   The Lavoiser Group campaigns against government intervention on climate change, see <www.lavoisier. com.au>.

competition amongst environmental groups for members, funding and political influence. The increased differentiation of green groups can also come at a cost for the environment itself; issues that are not as publicly salient can be neglected. Groups are more likely to attract members if they are working on 'green' conservation type issues such as the protection of forests and endangered animals. This has often been at the expense of the attracting funding for so called 'brown issues', such as waste management, transport and urban planning.

Some argue, however, that environmental groups have failed to connect to the public's views on the environment altogether. Pakulski and Tranter (2004) contend that in Australia the public have been mostly concerned with ecological risks such as the health and lifestyle implications of environmental impacts, yet environmental groups have been more focused on the effect of human activities on nature such as logging of forests and habitat destruction. According to Pakulski and Tranter (2004, p 225) this disconnect is also reflected in the 'bifurcation of environmental coverage in the media'. They argue that green campaigns have focused on two fronts: health and well-being issues that appealed to a broader set of the public, while on the other hand smaller campaigns have been run on green conservation issues aimed predominantly at a small, well-educated, urban population.

Environmental groups, like many other NGOs, are concerned about cooption or capture by government. This risk increases when they become reliant on government for funding and grants, for representation on committees, and when there are close formalised links with government officials. Since a key purpose of pressure groups and the environment movement more broadly, is to be 'an important source of political change in Western democracies' (Papadakis 1996, p 206), the potential for curtailing these roles through too close a relationship with government is indeed a valid concern. How environmental groups operate in relation to government depends in large part on the openness of institutions towards pressure groups. For example, whether group input is actively sought in policy development and implementation, or whether environmental groups are excluded by limiting their access to formal policy deliberations and/or by restricting their funding. This has happened to some radical arms of the environmental movement at some point in most Western countries (see Dryzek et al 2003).

In some cases cooption can be a more subtle process, where the agenda or framing of the problem limits the capacity for different groups to contribute their perspective. Merely by participating in debates and discussions for which the terms of reference have been set by government, many environmental groups are to an extent being captured by the dominant paradigm (see Chapter 3). This is often because the structure for discussion, and issues considered relevant for inclusion, follow the ideology of government and the bureaucracy and typically endorse the status quo. Since the way discussion is structured will be an important determinant of outcomes, change is not likely to be facilitated, and indeed some environmental groups may find they are not even able to raise issues of concern to them. Hence, their key role in providing a critique of the status quo may be undermined. This is an important reason why some pressure groups choose to exert influence by staying outside government processes and often resort to direct action to make their point (see 7.7).

Apart from cooption, environmental groups face a number of other dilemmas when it comes to engaging in formal decision-making processes, such as:

1. **How should environmental groups secure funding?** Many green groups (along with other NGOs from civil society) lack adequate resources to participate in the growing number of emerging environmental issues. In some cases groups might choose to supplement their income with government funds, but as discussed above this can

reduce their freedom to critique government policy, and also make them vulnerable to changes in the political landscape such a change in government. Other groups might seek to generate funds from public donations. The dilemma here is that the effort of fundraising can detract from time spent on promoting political change.

2. **How can environmental groups remain relevant in a greening society?** As environmental values become more popular and institutionalised (see Chapter 3), green groups have in a sense lost their monopoly on speaking for the environment (Pakulski and Tranter 2004). Their central task is now less about raising community awareness about the environment, and more about deepening society's understanding of key issues, and translating this into real action. The ongoing challenge here for environmental groups is to influence core economic decisions (in finance, trade, energy and agriculture) which tend to be dominated by corporate and producer interests. Moreover, the political tactics of green groups needs to shift from taking a predominantly defensive stance to one where proposals for long-term reform are injected into the debates (Carter 2007).

3. **To what degree should environmental groups centralise their resources and efforts?** On certain political issues green groups seek to provide a united voice for the environmental movement. This might be necessary when decisions become more centralised (for example, they shift from the State to the Commonwealth level) or when the environmental groups want to demonstrate large public support on an issue. Yet there are circumstances when presenting a united green voice can be problematic for the environmental movement (Doyle 2000). For example, groups could lose their members or supporters if they start working too closely with other groups that represent different interests or political values. Centralising resources and efforts can also be divisive for the environmental movement particularly when more radical green groups protest against a decision to work closely with industry and government. This is what happened in early 2008 when the World Wide Fund for Nature (WWF) joined an alliance with the Australian Coal Association, the Construction Forestry Mining and Energy Union and the Climate Institute to promote clean coal. Radical environmental groups such as Friends of the Earth were quick to publicly criticise WWF arguing that the alliance damaged its credibility (Hammer 2008). Other groups such as the ACF and Greenpeace were also unimpressed; arguing that government funds should not further subsidise the coal industry (Breusch 2008). WWF defended their decision to join the alliance arguing they are intent on 'finding solutions and working with others to find solutions' (Hammer 2008).

4. **How professionalised and institutionalised should green groups become?** The increasing complexity of government functions, its spread over three levels in Australia, and continuing institutionalisation of environmental concerns makes the task for environmental groups ever more complex and expensive (see 3.9.1). For success, such groups need to match these changes in government by developing their internal professional skills (including scientific, technical, economic and legal), as well as embracing sophisticated public relations and marketing techniques. It is not surprising that we have witnessed a convergence in mode of operation between the major environment organisations and their private sector business counterparts, and that there is considerable movement of personnel between them as mentioned above in 5.4 (see also 3.9.1).

5. **How closely should environmental groups work with other groups and business?**
    If groups get too close to the corporate sector they can damage their public credibility
    which in turn can harm their membership base and ultimately their political influence.
    However, in some cases unusual and productive alliances have been formed. For example,
    in the late 1980s two pressure groups that had long been enemies on environmental
    matters – the ACF and the National Farmers' Federation – began a fruitful alliance
    that has delivered a series of reforms on salinity, land care and water efficiency (Henry
    2006).

5.4.2 Other pressure groups

A host of other pressure groups also actively work on environmental issues. These include
some of Australia's most powerful producer or industry groups such as (see Marsh 2002):

*   the National Farmers' Federation – the national peak body representing farmers;

*   the Australian Council of Trade Unions – the national peak body representing workers
    from approximately 46 affiliated unions;

*   the Business Council of Australia – an association of the CEOs of 100 of Australia's
    leading corporations;

*   the Australian Industries Group – an industry lobby group representing various sectors
    including manufacturing, engineering, construction, defence, transport and infrastruc-
    ture services;

*   Minerals Council of Australia – the key group representing Australia's exploration,
    mining and minerals processing industry;

*   Environment Business Australia – representing businesses active in the environment
    area.

These business and industry groups typically operate as peak bodies that represent a
number of member-based organisations. Like all pressure groups, they become active in
environmental matters when a particular issue, regulation or policy affects their constituents. For example, various industry bodies have been trying to assess the implications of
climate change on their particular sector, especially the introduction of the proposed Carbon
Pollution Reduction Scheme (CoA 2008). To assist their members, industry groups might
commission research, conduct seminars, and lobby governments to ensure their perspectives are taken into consideration.

In addition to peak bodies, some industry sectors form specific organisations to lobby
on a particular environmental issue. A classic example here is the now defunct Beverage
Industry Environment Council (BIEC), which was established to represent the views of
the beverage and packaging industry on environmental issues, particularly on packaging
and recycling policies (see Case Study A). Alternatively, industry pressure groups might
establish a specific department that deals with environmental matters. One of the most
diversified groups in this respect is the Minerals Council of Australia (MCA), which has an
Environmental and Social Policy Committee, as well as an Education Team committed to
working on sustainability related issues. More specifically, the MCA has developed numerous environmental resources for schools, such as the primary school program *Envirosmart*

which has case studies of environmental practices at mine sites around Australia.[13] This example illustrates the subtle means through which some pressure groups seek to influence public debate and decision-makers.

Environmental issues have also attracted the interest of social advocacy groups, which typically represent the interests of marginalised and lower socio-economic individuals and groups in our society. For example, the Australian Council of Social Service, which is a national umbrella organisation representing around 60 subgroups, has been particularly active on ensuring that climate change policies take into account issues of equity and access (ACF et al undated). Other welfare and social justice organisations provide regular commentary on environmental policies such as the Brotherhood of St Laurence, the Australian Catholic Social Justice Council, the Salvation Army and the St Vincent De Paul Society of Australia.

Another important pressure group in Australian environmental debates is CHOICE (formerly the Australian Consumers' Association). CHOICE is an independent national association that represents the voice of consumers in Australia. It actively campaigns on sustainability issues such as corporate social responsibility, appropriate ecolabelling of products and climate change. Apart from its lobbying work, CHOICE provides resources to its members on products, with many assessments taking into consideration environmental factors such as water and energy efficiency.

Another significant set of pressure groups on environmental issues are experts and professional bodies, which we consider further below in 5.9.

5.5 Think tanks

Think tanks are research institutes that inject ideas and stimulate debate on public policy issues. In Anglo-American societies think tanks were traditionally understood as independent bodies that conducted applied research for the policy process. Their chief task was to provide a thinking space where objective rational arguments on public policy matters could be nutted out (Stone 2007). Today the meaning of the term 'think tank' carries a variety of connotations. For some, think tanks are essentially ideas factories, whose role is to sponsor and conduct policy research, and encourage intellectual discussion on the issue (Goodman 2005). Others argue that while think tanks might produce research, one of their key roles lies in processing and mediating knowledge ('t Hart and Vromen 2008). For example, they might seek to edit or validate information, or they might bring a particular issue into the public spotlight, or try to inject their perspectives into different fields of influence. In this latter respect, the work of think tanks overlaps considerably with that of pressure groups.

Today in Australia there are four main types of think tanks ('t Hart and Vromen 2008):

1. **Think tanks based in academia and endowment-based/independent** (such as the Lowy Institute which is an example of the latter and works on foreign policy and regional issues);

2. **Think tanks within government** (such as Australian Bureau of Agricultural and Resource Economics (ABARE), and the Productivity Commission);

3. **Think tanks operating on research contract**s (such as the Social Policy Research Centre);

---

13   See <www.minerals.org.au/primary/primary/primary_resources/envirosmart> (accessed 20 April 2009).

4. **Think tanks aimed at policy advocacy** (typically driven by an ideological agenda) (such as the Australia Institute, Institute of Public Affairs and the Centre for Independent Studies).

Policy advocacy think tanks (type 4 above) have attracted the most attention in recent years; these are the institutes that engage most vigorously in the battle of ideas by conducting and using research to promote particular values or ideological principles (Warhurst 2006). The most well-known Australian advocacy think tanks are located at different ends of the political spectrum. The most influential are the conservative (or right of centre) groups such as the Institute of Public Affairs (IPA) based in Melbourne and the Centre for Independent Studies (CIS) in Sydney. Both organisations are committed to free market and pro-business principles, and have strong connections with the corporate sector and the Australian Liberal Party (Glover 2006; Marsh and Stone 2004).

On the left are the so called 'progressive' advocacy think tanks, such as the Australia Institute, which was formed in 1994 to inject more community, environmental and ethical perspectives into decision-making processes. The Climate Institute, established in 2005, is another progressive think tank working on climate change issues. There are also think tanks associated with the Labor Party (ALP), namely the Australian Fabian Society, and the Evatt Foundation, however these are not well-resourced or particularly involved in research (Hart and Vromen 2008).

The funding base of think tanks varies considerably (see Marsh and Stone 2004). The conservative institutes do very well through donations from corporations and individuals, and sometimes government funding (for example, during the Howard Government the CIS received funds for particular research projects ('t Hart and Vromen 2008)). Philanthropic organisations and bequests form the bulk funding source for progressive think tanks in Australia.

Think tanks have become a formidable force in environmental debates worldwide, particularly the more conservative groups. According to a recent international study, conservative think tanks (particularly in the United States) are playing a crucial role in fuelling environmental scepticism, and in doing so they are effectively working as an elite counter-movement to environmentalism (Jacques et al 2008). There is evidence that this is beginning to occur in Australia. For example, the conservative IPA has a specific environment division that regularly produces commentaries and reports criticising environmental groups, and arguing for market-based solutions for environmental matters.[14]

5.6 Non-government funding bodies

Funding bodies are also significant actors in EDM because they hold the purse strings. While government agencies fund a considerable amount of research and policy advocacy work on the environment, what interests us here are the various non-government entities that allocate funds to individuals and community groups (sometimes even larger NGOs and think tanks) for environmental projects. The work of such entities is often referred to as philanthropy, which is broadly defined as the 'planned and structured giving of money, time, information, goods and services, voice and influence to improve the wellbeing of humanity and the community' (PA 2008). Many philanthropic bodies are foundations or trusts that provide grants for public benefits and charity. These can include family foundations, private

---

14   See <www.ipa.org.au/sectors/food-environment/controller/sectors> (accessed 20 April 2009).

foundations, corporate foundations and community foundations (PA 2008). One of the most active funding bodies on the environment is the American group, the Pew Charitable Trusts. In 1998 the Pew Environmental group established the Pew Centre on Global Climate Change, and more recently it has funded campaigns to stimulate policies in the United States on fuel efficiency and climate change more broadly.[15]

For many foundations that sponsor environment and sustainability projects, these themes are viewed as part of a broader set of social change issues. This is certainly the case for some of Australia's prominent philanthropy bodies such as the Myer Foundation, and the Ian Potter Foundation. Some foundations have taken a particular interest in environmental themes, particularly since the rising concern over climate change. Consider the Australian Poola Foundation, which in 2005 provided a $10 million endowment over five years to establish the Climate Institute ('t Hart and Vromen 2008).

5.7 Media

[T]he media, though they have their own particular preoccupations (namely, simplifying and selling news), are a significant agency for the agenda-setters . . . [T]he media draw on a variety of sources: the expertise of scientists and the arguments of intellectuals as well as information provided by established parties, by governments and by social movements. Information from the media is crucial in framing and forming public opinion.

(Papadakis 1996, p 164)

The term media refers to 'those agencies and their products which serve to deliver information, opinion and entertainment to the people' (Lovell et al 1998, p 355). Today 'media' is often used as a short hand for 'mass media', which is the modern system of producing and distributing information and news for large audiences (Newman 2006, p 30). The most obvious media outlets include television (TV), radio and newspapers, as well as magazines, books, pamphlets, and films. But contemporary mass communication also encompasses a host of new media such as the internet, virtual reality communications, social networking spaces (for example, Facebook) and citizen journalism (for example, blogging).

In Australia, the media largely consist of privately-owned organisations which derive revenue from advertising (Ward 2006). There are of course exceptions here; consider the fully or partly government funded media organisations, such as the Australian Broadcasting Corporation (ABC) and the Special Broadcasting Service (SBS), as well as community media, and some internet-based media.

The high concentration of commercial media in Australia means that a few organisations control what news and information is distributed and how. One of the most powerful commercial media entities is News Corporation (a giant global company owned by Rupert Murdoch) which runs approximately two-thirds of Australia's newspapers (Ward 2006). Commercially operated media have a dual function: on the one hand they operate as advertising businesses and on the other hand they are providers of information and entertainment to the public. The media pitch information at a particular audience in order to maximise advertising revenue. Thus depending on the nature of the targeted audience a different emphasis may be placed on which news is reported, and how.

---

15   See <www.pewglobalwarming.org> (accessed 20 April 2009).

The media play a number of important roles in EDM. Ideally they act as a communication conduit between decision-makers and the public by putting issues onto the public agenda, delivering news and current affairs and encouraging public debate. In this sense the media play a crucial part in maintaining a healthily democratic society. But herein lies a potential danger of the media because they have significant power in shaping public opinion and debate (Ward 2006). Behind the power of the media in public debates there is an intricate network of relationships between media owners, managers, advertisers, sponsors, governments, reporters and audiences (Smith 1997).

There is ongoing debate on the exact extent to which the media can influence the government and the political system and if they are capable of reshaping social norms and values. On one level media organisations have the potential to wield considerable political power, largely because politicians are concerned about the media's influence on the electorate. According to Tiffen (2004, p 209) '[w]hile academics debate the power of the media, politicians act as if there were no doubt'. Thus when the media (and its reporters) have a vested interest in a particular political decision, they can use their political power to restrict, limit or alter certain news items to portray their particular point of view. Some media programs, such as investigative journalism, not only put issues onto the agenda, but they can stimulate government action (Singleton et al 2006).

On another level the media's power over how they portray issues and news is constrained by audience demand. In order to attract viewers and readers, media organisations have to be responsive to the tastes and wants of the public (Tiffen 2004). One consequence of this consumer-driven approach is that some media organisations tend to present news stories as infotainment, where the emphasis is on entertaining or sensationalist content (Singleton et al 2006, p 442), rather than on exposing broader or long-term issues (see ABC Radio 2008).

How the media engage in different elements of environmental issues affects what the public considers salient and what is not. There is a tendency for the media to focus on the conflictual or polemic aspects of environmental matters, rather than on their scientific aspects or other complexities (Rydin 2003, pp 10–12). For instance, when the language of environmental coverage is analysed, studies reveal how the media dramatise issues by constructing oppositions, and using conflict metaphors (eg Rydin and Pennington 2001). There is also the tendency for the media to focus on the more sensationalised or event-centred stories such as beached whales, protests and pollution disasters, such as oil spills (Beder 2004). According to Doyle and McEachern (2008) this has led to media stereotyping of the environmental movement; greenies are often portrayed as abnormal deviants with special interests rather than as ordinary citizens concerned about public goods.

In the race to sensationalise the events and stories of environmental problems, the media (and their audiences) often do not engage in relevant background information or the underlying social and structural causes of issues (Allan et al 2000; Beder 2004, p 216). This is particularly problematic in environmental debates where contestation, uncertainty and complexities abound (see Chapter 9). Biased reporting is also exacerbated by the particular communication strategies used by competing groups who are trying to get their particular story into the media. The resulting picture can be an imbalanced view of what constitutes our most pressing environmental problems, and this has consequences for how we manage and resource these problems. This ultimately influences the allocation of funding and the nature and types of institutions which are established. Moreover it can affect the nature of the debate itself: it can polarise debates or fuel ignorance. This is exactly what occurred when the issue of genetically modified organisms (GMOs) was first reported in the Australian press in the late 1990s (following the British trend). At the time there was a tendency to frame the complex socio-technical debates surrounding GMOs into one of two narratives, namely 'GMO will increase food production' or 'GMO will result in Frankenstein foods' (see Pockley 1999; White 1998).

Not only do journalists and media companies use the media to deliver messages to the public. The media are also a forum for governments, companies and pressure groups to sell ideas to the public and more importantly to decision-makers. In other words the media are used as a public relations stage; actors carefully package media releases and run controlled press conferences to promote their message. According to one large empirical study in the United Kingdom, much of this promotional activity is focussed on elites rather than the general public (Davis 2003, p 673):

> Corporate and political elites, while needing to communicate with larger publics, also spend a significant amount of time targeting rival elites at all levels: within their own organizations, in rival organizations and in organizations in related influential sectors. Together these points suggest a scenario in which elites are simultaneously the main sources, main targets and some of the most influenced recipients of news.

Environmental and community groups also engage in this media game (see Case Study C). At times some groups have been particularly successful at using the media to get their concerns into mainstream public debate and potentially onto the political agenda (Papadakis 1996, p 141). Often environmental groups need to use direct forms of action such as confrontational protest to attract media attention (Hutchins and Lester 2006; Rydin 2003).

The media can also be an active promoter of environmental improvements. For some audiences environmental reporting adds legitimacy and credibility to the media source. According to the sociologist, Manuel Castells (2004, p 187), environmental themes are areas where the media can 'assume the role of the voice of the people, thus increasing their own legitimacy, and making journalists feel good about it'. Consider, for example, how some Australian newspapers (such as the *Sydney Morning Herald* and *The Age*) regularly have front page environmental stories, often written by their designated environmental reporter. We also see the rise of environmental lifestyle programs on some television networks, such as Channel 10's *Cool Aid: The National Carbon Test*, and the ABC's, *Carbon Cops*. Some high profile media players have also actively sought to be viewed as environment leaders. For example, in 2007 the Chief Executive and Chairman of News Corporation, Rupert Murdoch, announced that he would ensure that by 2010 his global media organisation was carbon neutral and that he would 'weave this issue into our content . . . to inspire people to change their behaviour' (Nason 2007, cited in van Vuuren and Lester 2008, p 75).

5.8 Individuals

In addition to organised groups, individuals can also make a significant contribution to EDM. For example, they might engage as a voter, as a consumer interested in green purchasing, as a lobbyist, as a member of an environmental group, as a community member of an advisory group to government or the private sector, as a commentator on a policy proposal or document, or as a participant in an environmental project.

Some individuals have no difficulty gaining political and public attention due to their controversial position or celebrity status. These kinds of actors have been prevalent in the climate change debate. Consider, for example, the role of high profile figures in promoting global public awareness and action on climate change, such as former United States Vice-President Al Gore with the release of his film *An Inconvenient Truth* in 2006, and the film star (and Republican Californian Governor from 2003) Arnold Schwarzenegger. Closer to home is the popular science writer (and 2007 Australian of the Year) Tim Flannery, whose books including *The Future Eaters* and *The Weather Makers*, have taken complex environmental issues and made them accessible to the public.

Other individuals such as the Danish economist, Bjørn Lomborg have become popular after injecting controversial positions into environmental debates. In 2001, Lomborg released a book on global warming claiming (among other things) that the 'real' state of the world was not as dire as environmentalists claim (Lomborg 2001). His book was a best seller and sparked outrage within the environmental movement worldwide. There is no doubt that Lomborg's controversial claims earned him considerable publicity and influence. According to Lomborg's personal website, he was named by *Time* in 2004 as 'One of the world's 100 most influential people'.[16]

But individuals do not necessarily need to be popular or controversial to make a difference to environmental decisions. Indeed the efforts of individuals are becoming increasingly significant (see Box 5.8), as more traditional forms of political participation such as political party memberships decline. European studies have found that people participate in politics as 'everyday makers'; that is, they engage in political issues when they can and how they can (Bang 2003). This might be via a school board, or at a local sporting club or in the workplace.

Box 5.8: Avenues of green influence for individuals

A citizen with an environmental agenda can seek to influence decision-makers through a number of means including:

- Voting in elections for the greenest candidate or party.

- Lobbying politicians – for example, either by personally asking a Member of Parliament for assistance in some matter or through a coordinated lobby or action group.

- Using the media – for example, by writing a letter to a newspaper, making a contribution to an online forum, or through a protest stunt.

- Joining a political party – either a major political party and attempting to green the party from within; or through attempting to influence policies of the major parties in return for green support; or by joining a minor party with a green agenda.

- Taking part in largely impromptu group activity – attending a demonstration, a rally, a stopwork meeting, or participating in an online blog or campaign.

- Acting in company with others in a matter which is of common but short-term concern to them – for example, making up a deputation of local residents to see the mayor about a zoning matter or approaching a minister on a question such as greenhouse gas emissions.

- Forming or belonging to an association which has a particular and relatively abiding focus of interest – for example, NGOs such as the ACF have become deeply involved in politics,

---

16   From <www.lomborg.com> (accessed 10 December 2008).

particularly on government advisory and review committees dealing with environmental issues.

Source: adapted from Singleton et al (1996, p 157).

Individuals can also play their part in fostering the social aspects of sustainability. For example, helping others develop knowledge and skills for sustainable behaviour, or building capacity for social change. Consider the work of the Victorian Women's Trust (2007) led by Mary Crooks, which has played an important role in connecting with citizens in Victoria, building their understanding of water issues and empowering them to become super-efficient water users.

Another important role for individuals in EDM is to act as change agents within organisations or communities (Brown, V 2008; Doppelt 2003). Their role in bringing together groups to advocate change is vital politically. In democratic systems governments require evidence that a majority of the voting population want, or at least will accept, changes to policies and regulations.

Individuals also play an important role in helping societies realise sustainability. Domestically we all have impact through the use of water, power, fuel for transport, consumption of goods and services and so on. Choices in each of these can, in sum, have a profound effect on our overall ecological footprint. But choices rest on knowledge, skills to put that knowledge into practice and the attitudes we hold. Like businesses (see 5.3), individuals come in many shades of commitment to making changes, influenced by their values (see Chapter 3), understanding of the issues, and influence from peer groups. This is confirmed by the regular social studies on 'Who Cares about the Environment' in New South Wales which find that people have become better informed over the past 12 years and are changing their behaviour regarding environmental impacts (DEC 2006b). Of course, some people are better placed to make changes towards sustainability – they can afford to buy new energy saving appliances such as washing machines and refrigerators, or to install solar energy for their household hot water or electricity, or to retrofit their house to recycle waste water. Governments can help by providing incentives for such changes, and there are many examples of such support from the States across Australia.

As individuals we can wear many hats when it comes to environmental matters and sometimes this creates tensions. The most prevalent tension in EDM is that between 'the citizen' and 'the consumer'. If we think as citizens then theoretically we are more likely to be interested in civic virtues and behave with the collective good in mind (Sagoff 2008). In contrast, as consumers, economists predict that when making decisions we act as utility maximisers where our preferences are aimed at maximising our individual welfare or utility (Berglund and Matti 2006). We all experience some ambivalent attachment to the roles of a citizen and consumer, and this can result in conflicting preferences, as Sagoff (2008, p 48) describes:

I, too, have divided preferences or conflicting "preference maps" . . . I speed along the highway; yet I want the police to enforce laws against speeding. I used to buy mixers in returnable bottles – but who can bother to return them? I buy only disposables now, but to soothe my conscience, I urge my state senator to outlaw one-way containers. I love my car; I hate the bus. Yet I vote for candidates who promise to tax gasoline to pay for public transportation . . . The political causes I support seem to have little or no basis in my interests as a consumer, because I take different points of view when I vote and when I shop.

The tension between the citizen-consumer has significant implications for environmental decisions. Many environmental policies are based on the assumption that individual environmental behaviour (for example, energy usage) is motivated predominantly by the market and therefore they aim to provide consumer incentives such as increased energy prices to reduce demand. Yet in many instances people change their environmental behaviour for more altruistic and community-based reasons. In some cases perverse environmental outcomes can result when policies do not acknowledge potential differences between consumer and citizen preferences (Berglund and Matti 2006; Hobson 2002). For example, cost subsidies for insulation may entice consumers to make their housing structures more energy efficient, but subsidies alone do little to address the underlying motivations, routines and habits influencing how people actually use energy within their homes (Chappels and Shove, 2005).

5.9 Experts, professionals and professional bodies

Some individuals are more influential in the EDM process than others. This is especially the case for those experts and professionals whose work relates directly to EDM. An expert is someone who has specialist knowledge and/or formal training in a particular field. It is however, important to recognise that the term 'expert' is relational; a person who is considered an expert in one field, is likely to be a novice in another. The role of expert knowledge is a theme we explore in detail in Chapter 6.

Experts engage in EDM in various capacities, for example:

- as a professional providing advice and knowledge on issues relevant to a particular discipline (see Box 5.9). For example, a chemist might be required to determine the chemical composition of the pollution emitted from a stack, or a traffic engineer might be asked to design a major motorway, or a doctor might be required to give evidence in court on the health impacts of a large pollution source. Professional input is not necessarily limited to technical input alone; it often involves developing and formulating environmental policy, or community consultation programs (see Chapter 7);

- as an individual holding a strong value position on an issue (see 5.8);

- as a concerned citizen;

- as a member or representative of a pressure group (see 5.4).

In many cases experts may take on a number of roles simultaneously, and it is often in these situations that professional dilemmas can occur. With each role played in the decision-making process experts adopt new rights, privileges, duties and responsibilities.

Box 5.9: What is a profession?

'A profession consists of a group of people organised to serve a body of specialised knowledge in the interests of society . . . At the centre of a profession is a set of skills, proficiencies, techniques and competencies involving a line of work . . . Each professional maintains standards of excellence, oversees work performance, and trains new members. Each shares a professional vocabulary, usually not understood by the lay person. Each provides a means of professional communication . . . and each has its professional Code of Ethics which specifies the moral considerations of professional life as well as penalties and sanctions for violating them.'

Source: Appelbaum and Lawton (1990, p 4).

Members of a profession are educated by the community to be their representatives in regard to that body of knowledge. Because of their special knowledge, status and autonomy, society vests power in the profession as a group for a particular area of expertise. In return, the profession has a responsibility to protect society's interests, often formally recognised and defined in a code of ethics (see 5.10.1). There is a large degree of trust in this partnership. A profession must interpret and perceive society's interests as best it can. Thus, taking on a professional role involves meeting a number of specific societal expectations and responsibilities (Appelbaum and Lawton 1990). This is particularly the case for members of professions associated with EDM where expectations are high and there is increasing public pressure to be more open and transparent.

Some experts and professionals are particularly influential in EDM. They might, for example, be successful at promoting an innovative idea because of their persuasive manner or their access to decision-makers. It may also be that their idea is proposed at the right moment in the political cycle (see Box 5.10). Such experts have been labelled *policy entrepreneurs* because they are actively engaged in promoting their ideas and solutions. As Kingdon explains, policy entrepreneurs (2003, p 205):

[W]rite papers, give testimony, hold hearings, try to get press coverage, and meet endlessly with important and not-so important people. They float their ideas as trial balloons, get reactions, revise their proposals in the light of reactions and then float them again. They aim to soften up the mass public, specialized publics and the policy community itself. The process takes years of effort.

Box 5.10: The land and water policy entrepreneurs – the Wentworth Group of Concerned Scientists

The Wentworth Group of Concerned Scientists came together in 2002 at a time when Australia was in prolonged drought and populist ideas such as turning coastal rivers inland to drought proof Australia were being promoted by influential media figures. Such ideas posed grave risks to the long-term ecological health of Australian landscapes. At a week's notice a small group of prominent scientists and a conservation-minded businessman met at the Wentworth Hotel in Sydney to discuss their views with three key journalists. The group of 11 outlined a five-point plan for how better to address the ecological issues facing Australia and committed to presenting a detailed plan to the Prime Minister within two weeks. The debate exploded through the media and the blueprint produced by the then-named Wentworth Group of Concerned Scientists garnered interest from both major political parties (WGCS 2002). Other solutions-oriented papers on landscape conservation in New South Wales and national water policy followed and had considerable influence on government environmental policy in Australia.

As a group of policy entrepreneurs, the Wentworth Group operates on three fronts. First, it lobbies decision-makers and engages in public debates to drive innovative thinking and action in the management of Australia's land, water and marine resources. Secondly, it works with business, community and political leaders to help develop and implement solutions. Thirdly, it mentors young natural scientists and resource economists to develop their skills and understanding in public policy. The unique power of the Wentworth Group is that is represents a collective voice of prominent thinkers speaking out on environmental matters, rather than just an individual expert. This combined with savvy political knowledge and financial independence has enabled the group to play an influential role in national debates on water reform and land conservation.

Source: <www.wentworthgroup.org> (accessed 17 February 2009).

Another way in which experts and professionals are involved in EDM is via their representative bodies. For example, many professional engineers are affiliated with Engineers Australia, chartered accountants are accredited with the Institute of Chartered Accountants in Australia, and doctors are represented by the Australian Medical Association (AMA). These and many other professional bodies serve their respective professions by offering training and resources, as well as providing political representation. Many professionals are beginning to recognise the relevance of their work for the environment and vice versa (see Box 5.11).

Box 5.11: AMA and climate change

The Australian Medical Association (AMA) is the professional body that represents more than 27,000 doctors in Australia. Historically the AMA has been a formidable political voice, particularly on heath policy issues (see Grey 2006). Since the early 2000s, the AMA has been an active campaigner on climate change. It has raised concerns about the potential health risks that global warming poses for Australians, including: temperature extremes; increased frequency of natural disasters (fire and flood); impacts on food and water supplies; food and water-borne diseases; vector-borne and rodent-borne diseases; population displacement and mental health of affected people.

To foster its campaign on the health effects of climate change, the AMA has worked on a number of fronts. In 2004, it formally released a Position Statement on Climate Change. In 2005 it commissioned research (together with the ACF) on the health impacts of climate change for Australia. In the lead up to the 2007 federal election, the AMA actively pushed for government action on climate change.

Source: <www.ama.com.au/web.nsf/topic/media-releases>
(accessed 18 February 2009).

Professional institutions also fulfil an important role in controlling occupations by defining standards, codes of practice and ethical conduct (Johnston et al 1999). In Australia, the peak body representing environmental practitioners is the Environment Institute of Australia and New Zealand (EIANZ). Its mission is to 'lead all Environmental practitioners, support their profession, set standards for best available practices and enable practitioners to promote and achieve a sustainable Australia and New Zealand'.[17] Among its many activities, EIANZ provides members with newsletters and networking events, organises training and regular conferences, and edits the professional journal, *Australasian Journal of Environmental Management*.

---

17   From <www.eianz.org> (accessed 5 February 2009).

5.10 Ethical dilemmas for environmental professionals

There are many factors which influence the extent to which a professional contributes to the EDM process. In many cases professionals feel that by speaking up on the environment they may be threatening their career prospects, violating their professional codes or they may even be jeopardising the safety of their families. For instance, what would you do if you become aware of deliberate actions or negligence on the part of your colleagues or employer that appear to pose a threat to public interest? In this section we highlight some of the professional dilemmas that may arise when you are involved in environmental matters and draw attention to the codes, policies and structures which may be of assistance.

Some issues may directly challenge the boundary between your personal and professional responsibilities, whilst others may be quite removed from your private interests yet challenge your moral position. One of the greatest challenges for professionals involved in EDM occurs when professional goals such as reputation, career development, stability and income, conflict with ethical beliefs. For example, you may not consider yourself an active environmentalist, but you become aware that one of your clients is illegally dumping waste into a local river. Do you speak up and blow the whistle, threatening client relationships and future work opportunities or do you remain silent? The dilemmas of whistle blowing are also prevalent in public sector organisations (see Brown 2008b), where government employees might witness corruption, or experience intellectual suppression (see Box 5.12).

Box 5.12: CSIRO climate scientists silenced by the system

In 2006, Professor Graeme Pearman spoke out publicly about how the government was trying to limit the public release of his research work on the severity of climate change for Australia. At the time Professor Pearman was a distinguished atmospheric scientist, who had been based at the government funded research organisation CSIRO for over 30 years. In 2004, Pearman was involved in a joint research project with a group of scientists and industry leaders (known as the Australian Climate Group). Their project sought to assess the environmental, economic, and social impacts of climate change for Australia. When the time came to publicly release the research report in mid-2004, Pearman was instructed by CSIRO management to 'confine his public remarks to the climate science and refrain from commenting on the policy issues' (Lowe 2004, p 63). Later Pearman was also explicitly asked not to say anything publicly that disagreed with the Federal (then under Howard) Government's policy on climate change (ABC 2006b).

As was revealed in an ABC *Four Corners* program, Pearman was just one of many employees under instruction from CSIRO management not to release particular kinds of detail to the public on the effects of climate change (ABC 2006b). For example, some controversial topics, such as environmental refugees, were off limits. In the end Pearman was made redundant, and he along with many other climate scientists left the climate division of CSIRO.

This attempt by the Federal Government to effectively gag CSIRO scientists raises questions about the relationship between scientists and the policy process. Pearman's own view is that while policy is the domain of bureaucrats and politicians, scientists should be able to openly inject their research findings into the decision-making process to inform policy development and public debate (ABC 2006b).

Many ethical dilemmas facing professionals are related to the traditional structures and approaches of the professions themselves. For example, a traditional approach within many engineering and science professions is the assumption that science and technology hold the solution to environmental problems. Often, little consideration is given to the ethical, social or even political issues behind the problem. The focus in many cases is on determining 'can it be done?' rather than standing back and considering 'ought it be done?'

In addition to the dilemma of speaking up with unwelcome results, professionals and practitioners may be reluctant to be involved in the decision-making process because of the uncertainty and complexity inherent in environmental issues (see Chapters 6 and 9). Many may choose to remain silent on environmental matters, fearing their credibility will be at stake if they make claims which cannot be supported by 'hard' evidence. How does a professional respond to situations of uncertainty? Is remaining silent safer than revealing the uncertainties and the possible effects of a particular course of action?

Professionals who speak out as advocates for public causes (sometime called 'whistle blowers') also face possible legal ramifications. Prevalent in the United States is a phenomenon known as SLAPP (Strategic Lawsuit Against Public Participation) where people and non-government organisations are sued for speaking out (Pring and Canan 1996). The essence of a SLAPP is that it seeks to discourage public criticism of a particular activity or development.[18] SLAPP-like situations are beginning to emerge in Australia. Consider the Gunns 20 case, where a group of 20 individuals and organisations were sued for over $7.8 million dollars by the large timber enterprise Gunns Limited (see Case Study B). The lawsuit referred to 10 separate protest actions against the company over a four year period (Darby 2006). The initial list of 20 included The Wilderness Society (TWS), federal Senator Bob Brown, and many individual activists who would be financially crippled by the damage claims. The case was condemned by national and international lawyers who argue that Gunns was silencing voices on public issues (Darby 2006). In the end the case was unsuccessful for Gunns; after four years of legal battles a final settlement was reached in the Victorian Supreme Court in 2009 whereby Gunns was required to pay TWS $350,000 in costs and discontinue its legal action, and the TWS was required to pay Gunns $25,000 for protest damages (EDO 2009).

The lack of professionals and activists speaking out about environmental issues can incorrectly indicate that there is unanimous scientific agreement in support of the status quo. For example, silence from experts can suggest that the Environmental Impact Assessment (EIA) is accurate and appropriate, and/or the decision of a determining authority is appropriate. In other words, minimal public debate is often interpreted as 'all experts agree' (Martin 1992). Some have suggested that the public would have more respect for professionals such as scientists if there was a greater balance of their input on both sides of a controversy rather than its preponderance on the proponent's side (Beder 1990a). On the other hand, Cullen (1998, p 57) reminds us that when scientists battle their particular positions via 'advocacy science' the risk is that '[l]ay persons tend to see such assertions not as inputs to a scientific dialogue but as the outputs of a flawed scientific discourse that cannot find agreement' (see also Susskind and Cruikshank 1987).

So far in this section we have highlighted some of the ethical issues relating to the environment which may confront professionals. What codes and guidelines are in place to assist professionals facing such dilemmas? Are there potential difficulties in the application of such codes and guidelines? Are there alternative sources of ethical guidance?

---

18 SLAPPs are formally defined as lawsuits involving (Pring and Canan 1996, pp 8–9) 'communications made to influence a governmental action or outcome' with the following components: '(a) a civil complaint or counterclaim (b) filed against nongovernment individuals or organizations (NGOs) on (c) a substantive issue of some public interest or social significance'.

5.10.1 Code of ethics for environmental professionals

Codes of ethics (CoEs) encourage professionals to behave in certain ways and serve as a public expression of a group's commitment to some moral standard. They can be defined as a 'set of governing principles or values which in turn are used to judge the appropriateness of a particular conduct or behaviour' (Laplante 1993, p 1). A code of ethics is more than a minimum standard of conduct; it requires that relevant professionals engage with the codes and develop a personal position which they can defend. A code is also a means to protect the professional from shady practices, giving members weapons against clients who want them to do something which the profession may consider inappropriate or unprofessional. As Lichtenberg explains (1996, p 15), '[a] code of ethics can give people a reason – perhaps a decisive reason – to act in one way rather than another'.

The extent of prescription varies among the CoEs of various professional groups. Some CoEs are merely statements of ideals where compliance is voluntary, while others are mandatory. It is important to recognise that most CoEs are not legally binding and can only provide guidance for reasons to act. If, however, there is non-compliance with a particular code, sanctions are usually imposed. These may range from fines or penalties, censure or reprimands, to expulsion from the professional organisation or even expulsion from the profession itself (Lichtenberg 1996).

Box 5.13 An example of a code of ethics for environmental practitioners

Since 1989 the Environment Institute of Australia and New Zealand (EIANZ) has had Code of Ethics and Professional Conduct that governs the professional activities of its members. Among many things the EIANZ code stipulates that members conduct their professional activities in accordance with the principles of sustainable development (see Chapter 2), and adhere to best practices for environmental protection. The EIANZ code also forbids its members to engage in professional activities that involve dishonesty, fraud, deceit, misrepresentation or bias.

Source: <http://eianz.org> (accessed 5 February 2009).

One of the principal reasons that difficulties arise when CoEs are applied to particular situations is that they require interpretation and understanding. This process will inevitably differ between professionals. Keep in mind that CoEs are not intended as a substitute for individual conscience, nor can they be expected to be a stand-alone guarantee of ethical conduct. Some of the potential difficulties of applying CoEs include:

- **CoEs rely heavily on personal interpretation**: Due to their all encompassing and general nature, many CoEs tend to provide little guidance on specific situations or ethical dilemmas.

- **It is difficult to determine how best to serve society's interests**: How can a practising professional determine the 'best' interests of society and moreover, which interests are most representative of the public interest?

- **CoEs have limited moral power relative to the power of an employer**: There are a number of professional factors, such as a promotion or dismissal, which may override your ethical conscience and obligations.

- **CoEs provide little guidance on the level of involvement a professional should take in public debates on environmental issues**: Where is the boundary between commitment to the profession and obligations to serving society? Ideally these activities should be one and the same but often this is not the case. Society's interests are wide, varied and changing.

As discussed above, CoEs require interpretation. In some cases, CoEs will be accompanied by a brief explanatory statement but essentially interpretation is difficult due to imprecise wording. In order to assist interpretation of your particular professional code in relation to environmental matters, it may be useful to consult a number of other sources of guidance. For example, you might refer to specific environmental policy statements prepared by your professional institution, or relevant environmental legislation and government policies. Alternatively, you might look into your own employer's or organisation's environmental policy. It is also important is to listen to your own personal values (see Chapter 3), and to communicate any dilemmas with relevant networks and peers.

5.11 Conclusions

In this chapter we have explored the diversity and multiplicity of actors engaged in, or affected by, environmental decisions. In any given environmental problem or conflict a host of different entities will emerge and seek to influence the decision-making process and its outcomes. This has long been the game of environmental issues where different groups mobilise to defend or promote their values and interests. While many contemporary environmental problems are of this ilk, the emergence of more collaborative ways of governing the environment is changing what kinds of actors engage in decision-making and how. Three particular trends are worth mentioning. First, there is increasing diversity of values amongst actors. As we saw in Chapter 3, a spectrum of environmental values exists in contemporary Australia from deep to shallow green. What we have seen above is that most shades of green can be found within, and amongst different actors.

Secondly, the boundaries between different kinds of actors and the roles they play are increasingly blurry. For example, there is considerable cross-fertilisation across different actors as they network in professional associations and move between organisations. Moreover, as individuals we wear many hats and our environmental preferences can often change depending on the role we take on.

Thirdly, though the boundaries may be increasingly undifferentiated there are some real and material differences between different sets of actors. For example, some actors are more professionalised, institutionalised, and politically oriented than others. Different groups and individuals also have different capacities to participate in EDM. Some have greater technical knowledge, or administrative or institutional capacity, and hence they may have greater opportunities or authority to access decision-making processes. Given all these variations, it is inevitable that in any given environmental decision some actors will have more power than others.

The political strength of a particular actor depends not only on resources and organisational capacity but on the nature of the issue and its public salience. The various actors who emerge and participate in EDM are also constrained and conditioned by the broader context within which they operate. In the next chapter we explore an important part of this context – the role and influence of knowledge for EDM.

6

Multiple Knowledges

6.1 Introduction

Decision-making in any area requires the provision of information and knowledge as a starting point. For example, a fairly simple decision may involve how you will get from point A to point B in a city by public transport. *Information* on what public transport options are available is well documented and will come from route maps and timetables. This may be supported by *knowledge* on the reliability of the various options, including your own experiences and the views of others. In most cases this is a relatively straightforward exercise of collecting and assessing material, and making a clear-cut decision.

In contrast, decision-making on environmental and sustainability issues will typically be neither simple nor clear-cut. This is a consequence of the complex and controversial nature of these issues lying as they do at the intersection between ecosystems and human social systems. There are typically considerable uncertainties regarding our knowledge of both the natural and social science systems[1] involved. To address such issues 'multiple knowledges', that is, knowledge of different types and from different sources, are likely to be important. Moreover, decisions on what type of knowledge is required are likely to be both iterative and controversial.

In analysing environmental issues it is important to consider the different and influential roles played by knowledge throughout the environmental decision-making (EDM) cycle. For any given environmental issue it is crucial to ask: How has the environmental knowledge been produced that has led to the recognition of the environmental problem? What do different knowledges tell us about the issue and how are they brought together to address it? What are the power relationships between the different knowledges during decision-making on the issue and how are these expressed?

The purpose of this chapter is to explore these multiple knowledges and the roles they play, or might play, in EDM.

Our exploration begins by unpacking the terms 'knowledge' and 'multiple knowledges'. Specialised expert knowledge dominated the early days of institutionalised EDM, but increasingly greater recognition is being given to a range of extended knowledges, such as local and Indigenous perspectives. Next we consider the contributions and limitations of these various knowledges. Particular attention will be given to the limitations of traditional scientific approaches in dealing with the complex situations that characterise sustainability. We explore new approaches embracing characteristics suited to addressing sustainability, including the challenges of integrating different types of knowledge. We conclude by considering the need for, and challenges associated with, knowledge management.

6.2 What do we mean by knowledge, data, information and opinion?

Knowledge is simply 'what we know', as a society and as individuals. Knowledge is not static but accumulates over time with continual additions and modifications as a result of research, observations and experience and includes both theory and practice.

A tighter definition sees knowledge as 'justifiable belief' where justification is provided by the norms of the knowledge in question. So, scientific knowledge is judged as justified by the accepted standards and peer review of the particular branch of science. Local knowledge is justified 'according to claims of connection with a particular place' (van Kerkhoff and Lebel 2006, p 447).

But knowledge comes in many forms. We briefly consider some of these below and others in more detail in following sections of this chapter. As well we need to distinguish here between 'knowledge', 'information', 'data' and 'opinion'.

Formal and informal knowledge

We may distinguish *formal* and *informal* knowledge. Formal knowledge is that which at a particular time is accepted by a disciplinary, professional, religious, or some other grouping, and is passed on through written texts, or orally, such as with the traditional stories

---

1 We will use *natural* science to refer to the sciences associated with nature such as biology, geology, physics, chemistry, and *social* science for study of the social life of humans and individuals such as social anthropology, economics, political science, sociology, psychology.

of Indigenous peoples. The major education institutions (universities, schools, technical colleges) are a central means of passing on formal knowledge. Informal knowledge lacks the recognition accorded to formal knowledge and is typically based on observation and experience and passed on through word of mouth, such as from parents to children (or vice versa), from workplace mentors, or through written documents such as news sheets. The development and growth of the internet as a means of information exchange is now blurring this distinction between formal and informal knowledge. For example, Wikipedia[2] is taking on the role of a formal dictionary or encyclopedia.

For the most part formal knowledge on the environment has focused on providing insights into the state or condition of the natural environment and the effect of human activities. This is labelled by environmental educators as knowledge *about* the environment. Over the last decade or so environmental educators have distinguished, and stressed the importance of, two other forms of knowledge and related environmental education – education *in* and *for* the environment (Tilbury and Cooke 2005).

Education *in* the environment provides learners with direct experience of the environment. It involves experiential learning, that is, learning from experience gained from observing the environment. For example Streamwatch[3] is a long-running program in the Sydney catchment involving school and community groups monitoring water quality and macroinvertebrates[4] (see also Box 6.5). By observing and linking activities in the catchment with changes in water quality, participants can learn much about the impact of human activities on the environment. Typically such learning will rest on earlier knowledge *about* the environment. Education *in* the environment is typically also aimed at fostering values towards environmental protection.

Education *for* the environment aims to equip learners to play a role in social change towards environmental protection and more particularly to lifestyles that will foster sustainability. It involves learners in critical reflection and aims to build capacity to participate in decision-making, and skills for taking positive action, *for* the environment.

Explicit and tacit knowledge

A distinction can also be made between *explicit* and *tacit* knowledge. Explicit knowledge is knowledge that is captured and stored in some medium (written, audio, video and so on) and hence is accessible for use (though it may be held in confidence by an organisation and so not available in the public domain). Tacit knowledge is personal knowledge gained by experience. It is carried in the minds of people and is therefore context sensitive and difficult to access, particularly since people may be unaware that the tacit knowledge they possess may be of value to others. There has been much recent interest in tacit knowledge at the organisational level (see Box 6.1), though Box 6.1 should not be taken to suggest that interest in tacit knowledge is just confined to private sector corporations. For example, there has been much interest in capturing tacit knowledge within a range of other areas, such as in Australian catchment management, involving farmers and public sector agencies (see Campbell 2006; LWA 2006).

---

2   See <http://en.wikipedia.org/wiki/Main_Page> (accessed 25 August 2008).

3   See <www.streamwatch.org.au/cms/about_streamwatch/> (accessed 20 March 2008).

4   Macroinvertebrates are animals without backbones that are large enough to be seen with the naked eye. They may be insects, small crustaceans such as crayfish or worms. In river systems or lakes they are frequently used as a surrogate indicator for the health of the waterbody.

Box 6.1: Tacit knowledge in organisations

Organisations have typically relied on formal *explicit knowledge* in environmental management. For example, formalised technical procedures, impact studies, work manuals and audits. Indeed Boiral (2002, p 296) suggests that organisations rely on these formal structures and processes to 'establish their legitimacy in the minds of the government and public'.

However, there has been increasing interest in the role of *tacit knowledge* in fostering organisational learning to support reduction of the environmental impact of operations, manufacturing and products. Using case studies Boiral (2002) has shown the role of tacit knowledge in identifying pollution sources, managing emergency situations and developing preventive solutions. For example, those working in operations roles in processing plants are best placed to notice changes that may lead to a pollution episode or to a major incident. They are also repositories of lessons from past events – which approaches to a problem worked and which did not and why? What do we need to remember about past practices that may cause future problems? For example, Boiral cites the example of retired workers in a Canadian factory brought back to find the location of previous burial sites for wastes, untouched for many years, so that proposed drilling operations could be sure to avoid these sites.

Information and data

Other terms we may associate with knowledge are *information* and *data*. Information is not the same as knowledge. It involves the communication of some fact or occurrence related to a particular event or subject (*Oxford English Dictionary Online*). We process information to contribute to our stock of knowledge. This means that we each bring our value positions, interests, presently held knowledge and the context in which the information is received to this processing of information (Brown 2008; Campbell 2006; Harris 2007; Spangenberg 2005). So the same information will contribute in different ways to various individuals' knowledge. As discussed further below, such understanding of how knowledge is acquired has importance for the way individuals learn. However, the terms knowledge and information are often used interchangeably. The distinction made here is likely to be followed by those who acknowledge and stress that all knowledge is socially constructed, or as Brown (2008, p 29) puts it 'knowledge is not the inert information stored in libraries and textbooks, but a dynamic interaction between people, time and place'.

Similarly, 'knowledge' has a broader meaning than 'data'. Data refers to a set of factual information, typically organised to provide a basis for analysis and often for quantitative analysis. So data are used to develop information.

Opinion

Another term often encountered in discussions on environmental knowledge is 'opinion'. In addressing environmental issues we are faced with an exponentially growing body of information from a wide range of sources. The complexity of environmental issues typically results in dispute about 'the facts'. And, as we saw in Chapter 3, strong value differences are common. Those commenting on environmental issues cannot be specialist experts in all the relevant areas of information and must also deal with uncertainty and various value positions. Often they are generalists, capable of accessing and bringing together disparate, but necessarily relevant, information to address environmental issues. Hence, such commentary on a particular issue may often be best described as informed opinion. That is, the commentator has formed a judgment and reached a conclusion to the best of their ability. They will of course bring their own values to this judgment and we have seen the emergence of opinion leaders on issues coming from a range of different value positions. For example, in relation to climate change, opinion leaders have emerged from the green groups, business leaders, political parties, universities, think tanks and many other groups (see Chapter 5). In this chapter however we will be primarily concerned with knowledge and to a lesser extent with information, and not with opinion.

6.3 Expert knowledge

An expert is someone who is regarded as an authority for their particular knowledge, or skills gained through experience (*Oxford English Dictionary Online*). Typically experts specialise in a particular discipline or field, with their expertise recognised formally. For example, a person with scientific or technical knowledge gained through tertiary study and perhaps also accredited by a professional body such as Engineers Australia, would be regarded as holding expert and specialised knowledge. However, an expert may also be someone whose expertise derives from a special skill. For example, a birdwatcher who over lengthy experience knows intimate details of the habits and calls of a wide range of birds.

Expert knowledge is primarily derived from verifiable investigations and experiments based on peer accepted methodologies. It is not static but 'seeks to move forward on the basis of broad principles, theories, laws and hypotheses, namely statements of interpretation that apply to a broad array of circumstances, and which are subject to continuous scrutiny through experiment, observation, falsification, verification and replication' (O'Riordan 2000, p 19). Such knowledge generation is institutionalised and exclusive, defining scientific, professional and intellectual elites (Brush 1996; Petts and Brooks 2006). This method of knowledge generation applies to both the natural and social sciences (Brown 2008), though the social science disciplines vary considerably in the extent to which they have adopted the rationalist mode of inquiry of the natural sciences.

Expert knowledge from the natural sciences and technology professions, such as engineering, has long played the dominant role and has been the most trusted form of knowledge for EDM based on its supposed objectivity. While the influence of the social sciences in EDM has been much slower to develop, their importance has gained greater recognition. People play a central role in causing environmental problems and in being part of their solution. Understanding these roles and how they interface with natural science and technology applied to environmental issues is vital, and relies on the specialist expert knowledge from the social sciences. For example, what influences human behaviours and preferences, and the way people organise and operate collectively? Beyond this, the social sciences are important in explaining the social context within which knowledge is generated and interpreted and the values that we bring to EDM. These matters have received attention in most of the earlier chapters and are also discussed in the chapters to follow. For this reason, and because of their dominance in EDM, our focus in this chapter is mainly on the natural sciences.

6.3.1 The natural sciences and technological studies

Natural science aims to explore and understand the structure and processes of the universe. But within this broad aim it covers a very wide range of activities and methods which make it difficult to universally characterise this science (Chalmers 1982; Irwin 1995; Martin 1979). Many natural science disciplines are relevant to environmental management as are many different scales of inquiry. These may range from cell biology and biochemistry to help understanding of the breakdown of contaminants in soil, through to the contribution of atmospheric physics in modelling the role of clouds in global climate change. 'Basic science' is motivated by curiosity about the workings of nature and its governing principles. 'Applied science' is aimed at applying information from basic science to address specific problems. The mode of inquiry ranges from reductionist approaches which examine isolated parts of nature in great detail and often from singular disciplinary perspectives, to ecological studies which take an holistic and systems view of nature. Both approaches are vital for understanding how the natural world works, but often reductionist approaches have been dominant and their importance has rested on the notion that we will best understand the bigger picture by studying the components in depth and then putting them together. However, this fails to acknowledge that the whole may not be the same as the sum of the parts (Suzuki 1995).

Natural science and technological studies – different roles?

The role of technologists such as engineers in providing information and knowledge for EDM differs from that of natural scientists. While scientists want to understand the working of natural systems and principles underpinning this, engineers focus on solving problems to meet human needs. For example, while scientists investigate the biology of microorganisms, engineers use this information to provide a means for human settlements to dispose of their sewage safely. Despite this distinction between scientists and engineers, the differences between the two fields are becoming blurred and this is especially true in environmental management where many professionals in environmental engineering and in applied science may undertake similar roles.

Developing information

The natural sciences provide information to the EDM process for: the identification of an issue or problem; collection of data to inform and analyse the issue; design, use and evaluation of tools to assist such analysis (see Chapter 8); and interpretation and use of the data. The social sciences provide information on the role of humans, communities and socio-political institutions in influencing each of these steps.

How objective is natural science?

Expert knowledge from the natural sciences has been the most trusted form of knowledge for EDM based on its supposed objectivity.[5] But is this claim of objectivity entirely warranted? Science, after all, is embedded and constructed within a social context as are the scientists that practise it. It is not possible to totally separate either the processes of science, or the choice of questions addressed by science, from this context (Albury 1983; van Kerkhoff and Lebel 2006). Nevertheless, while we might expect that science is not value-free, this is not necessarily widely recognised (O'Riordan 2000), so it is important to consider the scope for, and sources of, subjectivity.

The wide range of activities and scales of inquiry that comprise natural science, bring with them varying scope for subjectivity deriving from decisions that must be made on, for example, drawing boundaries for a study (spatial, temporal and matters of relevance). For a large complex ecological study, there are more choices to be made and potentially greater scope for subjectivity to enter the study, than for, say, a relatively simple biochemical study

---

5   Objectivity refers to the representation of information without being influenced by personal feelings or opinions. In contrast subjectivity refers to viewing things through the lens of one's own thoughts, views or concerns (*Oxford English Dictionary Online*).

involving an experiment bounded by a test tube and involving few variables that are also well-defined. So, in terms of the *processes* of science, the scope for subjectivity is very variable due to the nature of the natural sciences that might be involved and the type of questions they are being asked to answer.

But, since 'scientific advisory processes are deeply intertwined with political processes' (Bäckstrand 2003, p 28), the type of questions addressed by science is also subject to influence. Governments in democracies rely on science to support major environmental and resource use decisions (Albury 1983). So, the type of science that is carried out is strongly influenced not only by current paradigms (see Chapter 3) and peer review, but also funding and government priorities (Ravetz 1999; van Kerkhoff and Lebel 2006). For example, governments may determine terms of reference for scientific advice that set convenient boundaries, ruling out areas that may find reason for a proposal not to go ahead (see Case Study B).

6.3.2 The limitations of 'normal' science for EDM

The term 'normal' science derives from the work of Thomas Kuhn (1962) who saw scientists carrying out their work within the paradigms (see Chapter 3) of their particular scientific community; for example, cell biology, wave mechanics, atmospheric physics.[6] Such paradigms provide the theoretical assumptions, laws and methods for their application, as followed by members of each scientific community. According to Kuhn (1962) when a particular paradigm no longer matches behaviour of the 'real world' as revealed through experimentation, a 'crisis' emerges as members of that scientific community abandon the paradigm. The crisis is resolved when a new paradigm develops and increasingly attracts 'converts' from the old paradigm. Kuhn saw science progressing through such 'scientific revolutions' (Chalmers 1982).

Normal science has increasingly been seen as not meeting the needs of current environmental issues such as complex land management, climate change, and more broadly, sustainability challenges. These are issues that have been described as 'wicked problems' (Rittel and Webber 1973; also see 2.2). They are complex and multifaceted with interconnected ecological-social systems associated with a high level of uncertainty, and they may emerge and impact over a lengthy time span. Many of these issues are global in scale (Funtowicz and Ravetz 1991).

There are a number of characteristics of normal science which make it ill-equipped to deal with issues of these types. We will explore these characteristics and their consequences under three headings.

Much normal scientific investigation is not holistic
While the reductionist approach of much normal science is an important contributor to understanding components of complex environmental issues, it is not sufficient on its own to deal with complex environmental issues that require exploration of the interconnectedness of the parts of the system, including between science and society. Of the natural sciences, ecology is the discipline most suited to a more holistic approach. Yet even ecology does not necessarily deal with important interactions between people and the natural environment, including the need to accommodate values – hence the emergence of human ecology and ecological economics (Boyden and Dovers 1997; Diesendorf and Hamilton 1997b; Hamilton 1997).

---

6   Although our emphasis in this chapter is on the natural sciences, Kuhn's 'scientific revolutions' are equally relevant to the social sciences (see *Stanford Encyclopedia of Philosophy* 2004).

Normal science is not equipped to deal with high levels of uncertainty

Uncertainty arises from many sources in investigations of natural systems (see Chapter 9). The sources are magnified by bringing together natural systems with complex social systems, and magnified even further when considering these systems into the future. This is well demonstrated by anthropogenic climate change (see Box 6.2). However, normal scientific methodology 'is difficult to apply as situations become more variable, less controllable and less predictable as complexity increases' (Allison and Hobbs 2006, p 6). As shown in Box 6.2, such uncertainty opens the door for political manipulation of issues (Funtowicz and Ravetz 1991).

Box 6.2: Anthropogenic climate change – uncertainty and political manipulation of expert scientific advice

Expert scientific advice on anthropogenic climate change has relied on large scale modelling exercises of the atmosphere and carbon cycle. These models in turn rely on evidence from basic science of the behaviour of the various components of the models and theories on their interrelationships. Here uncertainty and probably also ignorance (see Chapter 9) is present. Thousands of scientists from around the world have been involved in interpreting the results from these models and in peer review, under the auspices of the Intergovernmental Panel on Climate Change (IPCC). The sequence of reports from the IPCC show increasing confidence in the modelling results with the 2007 Fourth Report saying that evidence that the Earth's climate systems are warming is 'now unequivocal' and that there is 'very strong' evidence that since the mid 20th century that has been mainly due to anthropogenic greenhouse gas emissions (IPCC 2007). Nevertheless, the conservative qualifications (eg 'very strong') about the reliability of the results have provided an opening for climate change sceptics in the scientific community to deny the IPCC conclusions (see Hamilton 2007; Pearse 2007). These sceptics are a relatively small group whose views are well-promoted by certain think tanks and associated public relations groups (Pearse 2007). Such public dispute between expert scientists confuses the public, decision-makers and political debates, where there is strong reliance on expertise for 'objective information'. This can also lead to a loss of credibility for the legitimating function of expert science in political decision-making (Bäckstrand 2003; Pollack 2003).

Normal science is not always compatible with questions posed by policy makers and regulators

There are a number of reasons why natural scientists may be in this position.[7]

First, in addition to the situations of high uncertainty inherent in highly complex issues such as anthropogenic climate change, there are other situations in which scientific information may not be readily available to provide answers to questions posed by decision-makers. In some cases the information is lacking but possible to achieve through research over a reasonable timeframe. Resolving this depends on the priority given to acquiring the answers and the availability of researchers capable of doing the job. In other cases the questions posed may require a long-term research program. This is particularly the case for impacts of human activities which have delayed effects on ecosystems, or for particular pollutants for which there is a lengthy time lag between exposure and effect, as for example may be

---

7   A number of the matters discussed here also apply to social scientists, but our focus here is on the natural sciences.

the case with carcinogens. In these cases the normal science timeframe and the political timeframe are not compatible and scientists are left with the dilemma of providing answers based on limited and inadequate information, or remaining silent. Peer group pressure has typically encouraged scientists to remain silent until they have sufficient evidence to comment with a reasonable level of confidence. However, such silence has also led to public criticism of natural scientists for not providing warning of possibly harmful issues at an early stage. There are numerous examples of this phenomenon including stratospheric ozone layer depletion (the hole in the ozone layer), asbestos and human health, mad cow disease and radiation (Harremoës et al 2002).[8]

Secondly, governments seeking advice on environmental matters typically want straightforward and definite answers to questions such as: Does the scientific evidence suggest this pesticide should be banned? Is this food safe for human consumption? In contrast, natural science communications generally include reservations, qualifications and probability estimates that confuse lay readers and also provide an opening for those who have an interest in continuing with an activity that scientists suggest is harmful. For example, in the health area, cigarette companies used the initial qualified evidence of harm from smoking to make their case for continuation of cigarette sales and advertising. Indeed, Hamilton (2007) describes the role of public relations companies and lobbyists in the United States in undermining mainstream science advice on harm from smoking by promoting counter views from a minority of scientists, as sound science. He shows how this approach was then adopted in relation to climate change science and the same tactics taken up in Australia.

But there is another reason that questions such as 'is this food safe for human consumption' pose problems for scientists. Scientists may be able to give probability estimates of the type of harm to human health from a particular food source, but 'safe' is a normative term based on people's willingness to accept particular risks (see Chapter 9). So safety questions depend on people's values. The scientist is not well placed to answer these questions, yet they are often the type of response required by policy-makers and regulators.

These limitations in normal science for addressing environmental and sustainability issues have led to much discussion over some years on the need for a 'new science' with a paradigm better suited to such issues (Funtowicz and Ravetz 1991; Ravetz 1999; Weale 2001b).

6.3.3 Towards a 'new science' for complex environmental issues

Funtowicz and Ravetz (1991) proposed a new term, 'post-normal' science, to deal with situations where 'facts are uncertain, values in dispute, stakes high, and decisions urgent' (1991, p 138). They stressed that this 'new' science would complement 'normal' science. Post-normal science does not pretend to be either value-free or ethically neutral. It has a primary focus on coping with uncertainty (Funtowicz and Ravetz 1991) and on natural and human *systems* examined at different hierarchical scales, recognising that the sum of lower levels in the hierarchy does not necessarily equate to a higher level, but rather that new properties may emerge at higher levels of complexity (Allison and Hobbs 2006).

Post-normal science needs to provide policy advice on future states of complex natural systems and human societies and the interactions between the two. Anthropogenic climate change is one example. Use of gene technology to produce new crop varieties is another. Such situations involve uncertainty and probably also ignorance (see Chapter 9) regarding outcomes, and the challenge becomes coping with uncertainty rather than removing it

---

8   The precautionary principle (see Chapters 2 and 9) provides a basis for scientists to recommend preventive action on potentially harmful effects before reasonably certain scientific evidence is available.

(Funtowicz and Ravetz 1991). Such issues also produce conflicting values within and between societies, and the challenge is to make these explicit in decision-making.

The role of post-normal science can be characterised by comparing three types of problem-solving strategies across two attributes – 'system uncertainty' and 'decision stakes' (Figure 6.1). The types of input and problem-solving strategies that are appropriate depend on the level of uncertainty and the potential consequences of decisions ('decision stakes'). Along the system uncertainty axis three levels of uncertainty are shown – technical, methodological and epistemological – corresponding to 'inexactness, unreliability and "bordering on ignorance", respectively' (Funtowicz and Ravetz 1991, p 143).

Considering first the *system uncertainty axis*: uncertainty at the *technical* level is managed by standard techniques established for different disciplinary or professional fields, when parameters are clear and the methodology used is unquestioned (*applied science*) (Funtowicz and Ravetz 1991). If decision stakes are also low the decisions can be left to applied scientists.

Methodological uncertainty occurs when more complex situations are involved and the potentially relevant parameters may not be well-defined. The appropriateness of the

Figure 6.1 Science and environmental problem-solving strategies

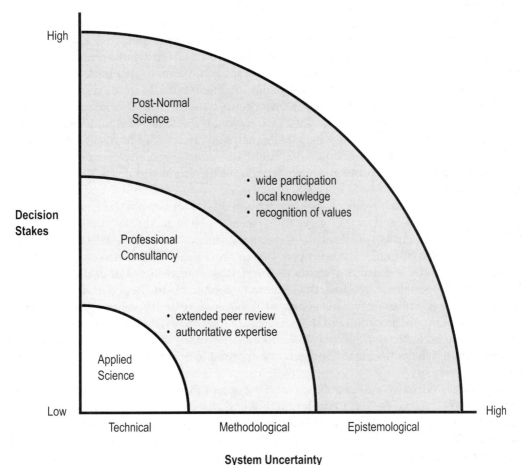

Source: Modified from Funtowicz and Ravetz (1991); O'Riordan (1991b).

scientific *methods* used to provide advice may not be clear and inputs from a wider range of professional experts are sought to help better define the key issues, boundaries of concern and most appropriate methodologies (*professional consultancy*) (Funtowicz and Ravetz 1991; O'Riordan 1991b). For example, consider a situation involving the potential for impacts from a contaminated site on wildlife in nearby bushland. A wildlife ecologist charged with advising on this will probably need the help of a range of other scientists who have knowledge on the behaviour and movement of the toxic substances through soil and water (hydrologists, geologists, chemists, biochemists) and zoologists and toxicologists who can advise on impacts of the substances on various wildlife species. If decision stakes are low to medium the advice to decision-makers will rest on both the non-controversial information from standard scientific methodologies (*applied science*), and also potentially controversial advice drawing on *professional judgment* covering aspects where complexity and uncertainty rule out clear-cut answers to questions. Notably the bringing together of different disciplinary perspectives is challenging, firstly in deciding what disciplinary inputs are relevant and then in integrating these perspectives. This is addressed below in 6.3.4.

At the *epistemological* level of uncertainty, the type of knowledge considered relevant is open to question (eg what areas of natural science and social science are relevant and what role should lay knowledge play?), and the potential that ignorance regarding key parameters may vitiate any advice given, is acknowledged.

Turning to the *decision stakes axis* we can compare at the low end of the scale a decision such as whether to allow discharge of small quantities of stormwater from a non-industrial catchment into a large and well-studied bay, with, at the high end of the scale, decisions on major activities that are likely to influence anthropogenic climate change. What is at stake varies not only in spatial scale (local compared to global) but also in the number of potentially affected parties. Hence, as with the uncertainty axis, there needs to be an extension of participants in determination of advice as we move up the scale. This wider participation not only contributes values and views, but potentially also wider forms of knowledge. It may be regarded as providing 'direction, quality assurance, and also the means for a consensual solution of policy problems in spite of their inherent uncertainties' (Funtowicz and Ravetz 1991, p 145).

Coping with uncertainty, incorporating extended facts (eg from a wider set of expertise and local knowledge), and factoring in values (see Chapter 3) and broad public participation (see Chapter 7) is central to post-normal science[9] (Funtowicz and Ravetz 1991). As suggested by Figure 6.1, post-normal science is necessary to provide advice to decision-makers when systems uncertainty and decision stakes are high. It also suggests that if decision stakes are high, even if uncertainties are low, the issue may need to be addressed at higher than the technical level of uncertainty. This is primarily because very different perceptions of risk and/or acceptance of environmental outcomes are likely to exist among the community as a result of the high decision stakes (see Chapter 9). Similarly, if decision stakes are low but uncertainty high a post-normal approach is suggested to bring in extended knowledges to address uncertainty.

The discussion above makes it clear that if we accept that post-normal science is important for addressing the complex environmental and sustainability issues we now face, we need to consider the challenges involved in embracing these extended knowledges. This involves identifying and describing informal kinds of knowledge and considering how they might be integrated with more formal knowledge types. Before we do so, it is important to note that embracing post-normal science does not negate the value of inputs from applied

---

9   O'Riordan (1991b) has used the term 'vernacular science' to refer to this 'new science'.

science and professional consultancy to EDM. 'Professional consultancy' in Figure 6.1 refers to the idea of expert knowledge from various disciplines. Below we consider some of the particular challenges with the idea of integrating the knowledge from expert disciplines.

6.3.4 Integrating the disciplines of expert knowledge

The challenges from sustainability and the emergence of large scale environmental issues such as climate change have driven much attention to how best to achieve integrated approaches not only across the formal expert disciplines but much more broadly (see 6.3.3).

But what do we mean by 'disciplines' and what terms are used to describe various levels of integration across the disciplines?

Disciplines are branches of expert knowledge each with their own paradigms involving methods of addressing issues. Chemistry, physics, mathematics, history and economics are each disciplines. Disciplines are the prime structures for production of expert specialist knowledge (Maasen et al 2006). However, disciplines themselves have undergone increasing specialisation. As the amount of information produced by any one discipline has exploded in recent years, it has become impossible for researchers to remain specialists across their entire disciplinary field and they have been forced into even narrower areas of specialisation (Brown 2008). Hence disciplines themselves have become fractured and *intra*disciplinary integration is also required (Grafton and Robin 2005a).

Multidisciplinarity involves a number of disciplinary experts each focusing on a specific issue but carrying out their analyses separately using the methods of their discipline. Each offers a different disciplinary perspective on an issue (Meeth 1978). The product will be additive without any synthesis (Dovers 2005b; Max-Neef 2005).

Interdisciplinarity brings disciplines together but in a manner that is integrative rather than additive. Integration is achieved through the various disciplines addressing a common purpose. To do so the individual disciplines cannot stay entirely within their disciplinary comfort zones and there needs to be questioning about appropriate theory and methods to address the issue in question (Dovers 2005b). Some characterise interdisciplinarity as coordination over two hierarchical levels. For example, chemistry, biology and sociology at one level of disciplinarity are coordinated and their approaches purpose-driven to address a problem in agriculture which occupies a higher hierarchical level (Jantsch 1972; Max-Neef 2005). For example, the impact of salinity on the viability of rural townships. Interdisciplinarity may take place over various numbers and scope of disciplines depending on the problem to be addressed (Dovers 2005b). For example between two or more science disciplines, which may lead to the formation of a new discipline (Maasen et al 2006), such as biochemistry (from chemistry and biology), or, between a range of science and social science or humanities disciplines[10] (such as human ecology or environmental politics). The problems of integration are likely to become more difficult across major disciplinary divides, such as between the natural sciences and the humanities (Grafton and Robin 2005b; Meyer 2007). This is because the assumptions and methodological differences are likely to be greater. For example: 'deeply quantitative researchers find it difficult to accept that "rigour without numbers" (ie qualitative analysis) is possible' (Dovers 2005b, p10).

---

10 Humanities here refers to disciplines such as the study of literature, philosophy and art. Humanities are distinguished from the social sciences such as sociology and psychology.

Transdisciplinarity goes beyond interdisciplinarity in integrating knowledges. However, the distinction between the two remains somewhat blurred. Transdisciplinarity can be regarded as the highest level of integration and 'beyond the disciplines' (Meeth 1978). But exactly what this means is controversial. 'Ecological economics' is claimed by some to be a new transdisciplinary field aimed at addressing 'relationships between ecosystems and economic systems in the broadest sense' (Costanza et al 1991, p 3). Costanza et al (1991) see this occurring by focussing on the issue to be addressed, evaluating existing tools' abilities to carry out the work, and designing new tools if the current ones are deemed unsuitable. However, others have questioned the extent of interdisciplinarity in ecological economics, suggesting instead that it is dominated by traditional economics (Dovers 2005b).

Other groups take a far broader approach to defining transdisciplinarity. Some characterise transdisciplinarity as coordination between a number of interdisciplinary assessments embracing multiple goals and within a broad framework of overall purpose and values (think about sustainability as an overall system goal and acknowledge the many values perspectives on sustainability) (Jantsch 1972; Max-Neef 2005). Perhaps the dominant view of transdisciplinarity goes beyond integration between the disciplines and also includes integration of knowledge from a range of societal stakeholders from government agencies, NGOs and the private sector (Maasen et al 2006; Meyer 2007; Pohl 2005; Pregernig 2006) to produce knowledge that is 'not only scientifically sound but also socially acceptable' (Maasen et al 2006, p 394). Pregernig (2006) identifies four key elements of transdisciplinarity: (i) *interdisciplinarity*, (ii) *participation of non-expert stakeholders*, (iii) *problem orientation* (problems are real world problems not simply basic science) and (iv) *solution orientation* (the main purpose of transdisciplinary research is not to produce new cutting edge knowledge but rather to provide practical solutions). It is important to emphasise that transdisciplinarity does not replace disciplinary research, but rather they are complementary.

The difficulties in bringing together disciplines for interdisciplinarity are mentioned above, but it is not hard to appreciate that even further challenges lie in the path to transdisciplinary approaches. These can be identified at three levels. First the *cognitive level* where different disciplines have very different concepts, methods, theories and tools for analysis. Second, the *organisational level*, since the range of disciplinary experts that need to be brought together as teams will typically come from different organisations that have their own ways of operating so that new routines and norms need to be developed to accommodate all groups. Third the *procedural level* to ensure the complex tasks between organisations and individual researchers are efficiently coordinated (Maasen et al 2006).

There clearly remain a number of challenges in developing successful transdisciplinary projects to address complex and urgent environmental and sustainability issues and the Swiss Academies of Arts and Sciences has proposed principles and tools for carrying out transdisciplinary research (Pohl and Hirsch Hadorn 2007). But we need to consider the transaction costs in achieving inter- or transdisciplinary approaches when deciding on the appropriate level of integration across disciplines to apply to a particular issue (Grafton and Robin 2005b).

6.3.5 Beyond integration? – towards sustainability science

'Sustainability science' emerged in the early 21st century as a new paradigm of science to address sustainability issues. It shares elements of post-normal science and the methods espoused for transdisciplinarity (Martens 2006), and seems to have developed from the expert science arena and to be strongly linked with mainstream scientific institutions.[11] Yet it 'is not a "science" by any usual definition – that is, it is not yet a set of principles by which knowledge of sustainability may be systematically built' (Rapport 2007, p 77). Rather, it has been described as 'a vital area in which science, practice, and visions of North and South meet one another, with contributions from the whole spectrum of the natural sciences, economics, and social sciences' (Martens 2006, p 38).

Sustainability science focuses on the interactions between nature and society and on addressing sustainability problems (Clark 2007; Clark and Dickson 2003, Kates et al 2001). Within this broad canvas a number of essential elements of sustainability science have been identified. These include:

- an integrative approach across disciplines and styles of knowledge;

- integration across wide spatial scales from the local to the global;

- addressing temporal scales at the problem level, such as the long-term expression of impacts associated with anthropogenic climate change;

- addressing temporal scales at the solution level through scenario development and backcasting (see 2.9.1);

- ability to deal with complex systems with multiple interacting stresses, dynamics, actors and networks;

- participation by scientists, stakeholders, advocates, active citizens, and users of knowledge to co-produce knowledge (Clark and Dickson 2003; Kasemir et al 2003a);

- an innovative approach to methodologies and learning through doing (Kates et al 2001; Martens 2006).

Sustainability science remains a work in progress (Kajikawa 2008) and there is recognition that effort is required to foster worldwide discussion of important questions for sustainability science to address, and methodologies for use (Kates et al 2001), as well as capacity building over a wide geographic scale and range of participants to promote 'the social learning that will be necessary to navigate the transition to sustainability' (Kates et al 2001, p 642).

Post-normal science and sustainability science share many characteristics. Perhaps the main distinction is that the primary focus in post-normal science is on dealing with extreme system *uncertainty* and the policy context of technological risk (see Chapter 9), while the primary focus in sustainability science is on dealing with extreme systems *complexity* and the issue of sustainability (Ravetz 2006).

We have seen above that post-normal science involves embracing not only expert disciplinary knowledge and the integration of these disciplines, but also a wide range of extended knowledges which bring values and different perspectives. Sustainability science similarly, seems to be grounded in expert specialist science, but with a wider array of knowledge inputs.

---

11   While the origins of sustainability science go back to around the mid-1980s, its institutionalisation by mainstream science perhaps occurred with publication of an important articulation of the concept by a number of leading scientists in the prestigious *Science* journal in 2001 (Kates et al 2001), its recognition as a field of research in its own right by the National Academy of Sciences of the United States in 2006 (Clark 2007), and the launch of a journal devoted to *Sustainability Science* in 2006 (Komiyama and Takeuchi 2006).

We turn to explore these extended knowledges and the concerns and issues involved in their integration for decision-making.

6.4 Extended knowledges

While expert specialised knowledge is typically formal and institutionalised and has been the most dominant form of knowledge, there are a number of other knowledge types. These include local, traditional, Indigenous, experiential, lay and individual knowledge. Many are best described as informal but with much variance in their degree of informality. Some, such as aspects of Indigenous ecological knowledge, may have oral traditional knowledge formally integrated into a particular cultural setting. Notably some of these groupings overlap (see Box 6.3), and there is considerable variation in definitions in the literature (see Fischer 2000) but the exploration of each of these knowledge types is worthwhile to draw attention to their potential roles in EDM and contribution to post-normal and sustainability science.

6.4.1 Local knowledge

The name suggests that local knowledge is knowledge associated with a specific place. Of course specialised expert knowledge may focus on a locality. However, the term 'local knowledge' is used to refer to the knowledge of local community members regarding local matters and acting as residents rather than in their professional or other work-related roles (Brown 2008). It is informal knowledge that is typically 'experiential'; that is, knowledge derived from experience or observation (see Box 6.3). More recently, local knowledge has also been used to refer to traditional and Indigenous knowledge (Fischer 2000). However, it seems useful to distinguish between these groups (see Box 6.3).

Local knowledge, in the sense defined here, may be passed on through oral or written communications. In traditional communities of herders, farmers or fishermen, oral communication is typically the vehicle, while in local community groups in developed countries both oral and written communication is used. However, increasingly, local knowledge is recorded through publications and through the internet, either described in specialist papers or shared by local groups themselves.

Box 6.3: Traditional, Indigenous and local knowledge – is there a difference?

Terminology regarding these knowledges in the literature is very messy. While acknowledging the potential for overlap we will make the following distinctions in this book.

Indigenous ecological knowledge is also often described as 'traditional ecological knowledge' (TEK). However, TEK while sharing many of the characteristics of Indigenous ecological knowledge, has a broader meaning, encompassing also the knowledge of farmers, herders and fishermen, gained through lengthy experience and adaptation of traditional methods in a local context, as against more modern scientific methods, but who are not Indigenous peoples in the way this term is defined in 6.4.2. Hence Indigenous knowledge may be seen as a subset of traditional knowledge.

Both traditional and Indigenous knowledge are also described as local knowledge but are best regarded as sub-sets of local knowledge (as illustrated below). This is because local knowledge is also used to refer to communities who bring knowledge from experience in a shared locality, but who belong to neither Indigenous nor traditional communities. That is, they may include modern rural and urban-based communities with a shorter experience of a locality, and who may work outside their locality, but who nevertheless may bring valuable local experiential knowledge to EDM. Box 6.4 provides an example of local knowledge of upland sheep farmers in Cumbria in Britain that may also be seen as traditional knowledge.

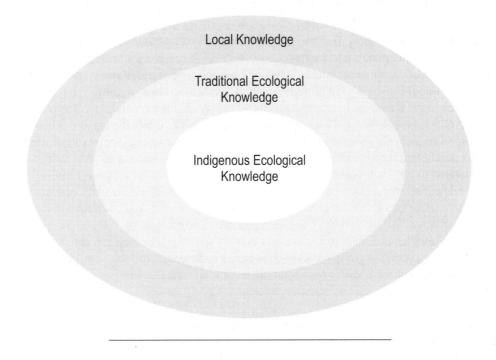

Box 6.4: Local knowledge, radioactive fallout and sheep farming

In 1986 the nuclear reactor at Chernobyl in the Soviet Union exploded releasing radioactive materials that were deposited over a wide area including parts of Britain. British academic Brian Wynne (Wynne 1989, 1996a) studied the clash of knowledges that took place in Cumbria in the northwest of England between scientists and the local sheep farmers following fallout of radioactive caesium in this area.

Of potential concern was that the radiocaesium could enter the food chain. However, British Government authorities were initially optimistic that there was no need for a ban on sheep products from this area. The basis for this optimism was expert scientific advice that suggested that the radiocaesium would be rapidly locked onto clay particles in the soil and hence would not enter the food chain. This optimism was supported by falling measurements of radiocaesium in a lowland agricultural area in southern England in the weeks following the Chernobyl fallout. But in the upland areas, such as Cumbria, radiocaesium levels in sheep were rising. Consequently the government, some seven weeks after the Chernobyl explosion, placed a ban on movement and slaughter of sheep over many upland areas in northwest England, including Cumbria (Bell and Shaw 2005). Despite government assurances that the ban would be short it was repeatedly extended and 20 years after the Chernobyl explosion some farms are still subject to the ban.

The scientists' assumption that radiocaesium in the upland soils of Cumbria would behave in the same way as in the lowland soils of southern England was flawed (Bell and Shaw 2005).

Instead the low clay content and other characteristics of the upland soils meant that radiocaesium remained mobile in the soil and readily taken up by vegetation consumed by sheep. Bell and Shaw (2005, p 777) suggest that 'with a more holistic approach the confident cheerful predictions of the future significance of the Chernobyl deposition for the UK would not have been made. The lesson is that a full understanding of the biogeochemistry of contaminants can only be developed by a strong ecological approach to pollution problems'.

The inaccuracy of the scientific predictions regarding the fate of radioactive caesium in the upland areas of Cumbria, and the certainty with which predictions were made, reduced the sheep farming community's confidence in the expert scientific knowledge. The subsequent advice from scientific experts to authorities on treatment of the problem failed to include the local knowledge of the sheep farmers, built up over generations, regarding the special characteristics of hill sheep farming and associated management practicalities. The sheep farmers felt that their specialist local knowledge was downgraded and saw the experts as both ignorant (of specific local conditions and farming practices) and arrogant. The result of the failure to incorporate this local knowledge was that official advice on means to deal with the problem continued to be inappropriate to the local conditions (Irwin 1995; Wynne 1996a).

The high level of analysis and discussion of this case study over a lengthy period has made it widely known. As a result public confidence in expert science and corresponding government authority advice on such issues has been damaged. The case illustrates well the importance of the incorporation of extended knowledges in such situations. However to achieve this, respect and trust between the groups holding the various knowledges is important, as is finding effective means to share knowledge across different knowledge cultures.

Local knowledge has been recognised in relation to a wide range of environmental issues that include, but extend beyond, the natural resource management (NRM) matters that dominate Indigenous and traditional ecological knowledge. For example, the relevance of local knowledge has been demonstrated in pollution and related health matters (Brown 2005b; Fischer 2000; Irwin 1995).

Local communities may also play a significant role in the production of natural science information through routinely collecting data about a range of natural resource parameters. The integration of some of these data into expert knowledge systems is well institutionalised (see Box 6.5).

Box 6.5: Community environmental monitoring

In Australia, collection of rainfall data across the continent has long depended on local volunteers, and in 2004 some 6000 volunteer stations were operated by local people (Australian Bureau of Meteorology 2004).

Birds Australia, a conservation non-government organisation (NGO) operating since 1901, has bird experts on its staff, but calls on thousands of local volunteers to assist in monitoring bird species numbers and locations. Since 1998 Birds Australia has coordinated over 7000 people who carry out field observations that have produced over 420,000 bird surveys comprising over 7.1 million bird records. From these records the *Atlas of Australian Birds* is produced. The *Atlas* is an ongoing project that allows us to track changes in the distribution of bird species across the continent. In turn this provides information for government bodies reporting on the state of the environment (see Chapter 8),[12] and for monitoring the effects of land use change (Birds Australia undated).

It is estimated there are 300,000 people across Australia involved as volunteers in community environmental monitoring (CEM) programs such as Streamwatch, Frogwatch, Saltwatch and Reef Watch (Alexandra 2007). The dispersed networks of volunteers across the vast Australian continent provides the potential to gather ecological data over spatial and timescales not possible solely by expert government funded scientists (Alexandra 2007). Such information is vital if we are to know the impacts we are having on the continent and the effectiveness or otherwise of our ecosystem management actions. An added benefit is that CEM can also serve an important community education role through guided observation in the environment and engagement with environmental issues (see 6.2).

One potential danger with CEM is that it concentrates knowledge production where human settlements are (ie where people live), but this is not always where the most dire ecological problems lie. CEM could plausibly skew our knowledge base and be dangerous in this respect if used as a means to fund solutions to NRM problems.

However, further controversy regarding the role of CEM is demonstrated by a Royal Zoological Society of New South Wales forum that examined the integration of community knowledge into expert research programs aimed at addressing conservation problems. A number of researchers questioned the worth of community generated data citing poor data quality through bias and lack of rigour. Some felt expert science was being marginalised in the push to community involvement. Others stressed the potential value of CEM and benefits of community involvement more broadly and provided 'key factors for successful partnerships' (see Lunney et al 2002).

Dismissal of local knowledge by specialist experts as lacking in rigour and as unreliable is common in a wide range of situations (see Boxes 6.4 and 6.5; Brown 2008; Petts and Brooks 2006; van Kerkhoff and Lebel 2006). Such downgrading of the worth of local knowledge exacerbates the difficulty in bringing together specialist expert and local knowledges since '[e]ach of the groups contributing to integrated decision-making . . . has their own set of priorities, sources of evidence and ways of testing it, all adding up to distinctive ways of constructing knowledge' (Brown 2005b, p 134).

This latter point is one of the strong reasons for the claim of superiority of expert scientific knowledge over local knowledge. The separation from local culture is seen as necessary for 'objectivity', which provides 'facts' as against value-based opinions. However, as discussed above, it is now generally recognised that expert scientific and technical knowledge also involves bias and value judgments.

6.4.2 Indigenous knowledge

A particular kind of local and traditional knowledge is Indigenous knowledge.

Also referred to as Native, Aboriginal or First Peoples, Indigenous peoples have a strong sense of self-identification linked to their very close relationship with 'place'. They are generally regarded as descendants of the original human inhabitants of an area that may have later been taken over by outsiders (Knudtson and Suzuki 1992). Indigenous peoples include

---

12   The status of bird populations is often used as a surrogate for the health of the landscape and its constituent fauna and flora, and assists in decisions on land use change and planning.

the Australian Aborigines, the First Peoples of North America, and many groups from South America, parts of Asia, far northern Europe, and the deserts of North Africa.

Indigenous people have developed intimate connections with their environment often over thousands of years and many generations. Their livelihood and indeed existence has relied on the development of detailed knowledge of all aspects of their environment – the plants, animals, weather systems and seasons – and of the effects of their use on the environment. This knowledge has come from observation, experience, trial-and-error. It represents unique local knowledge and is woven into the culture and fabric of their society to provide guidance for how to relate to the environment (Grenier 1998; Hunn 1993; Smallacombe et al 2007; Usher 2000; Viergever 1999). However, to varying extents, Indigenous peoples are living in contemporary worlds and this means that amongst them there is great diversity in maintenance of their Indigenous knowledge and on how they should relate to nature (see for example Wynberg 2004).

Indigenous ecological knowledge is important for EDM in a number of ways. It can provide valuable input for research and management regarding NRM (see Box 6.6 as one example). Taking a specific example, it provides a vital contribution to Environmental Impact Assessment (EIA) (see Chapter 8) in situations where proposed development may directly affect Indigenous cultures. For example, uranium mining in a remote Australian region occupied by Aboriginal people (see Craig et al 1996). It may also be an important contributor in EIAs involving NRM that do not involve *direct* impact on Indigenous people (Craig et al 1996; Usher 2000). In addition, we saw above (6.4.1) the importance of gaining knowledge from a wide range of values and views for EDM, and Indigenous people provide a special and important perspective. Beyond this there are moral and, increasingly, policy or legal reasons, for including Indigenous knowledge in EDM.

6.4.2.1 Comparing Indigenous ecological knowledge and expert natural science

Indigenous ecological knowledge differs from expert natural scientific knowledge in the ways in which it is generated, recorded and transmitted (Johnson 1992). Indigenous knowledge about the natural world has typically been regarded as inferior to expert natural science since it is seen as anecdotal, intuitive and informal, lacking rigorous method, and at best only of local relevance (Smallacombe et al 2007). Recall that in general, expert science explores nature from a 'removed position' with nature as secular rather than sacred, and as an 'object', 'resource' or 'commodity' to be studied and explained using the rational scientific method described above. Table 6.1 provides a generalised comparison between these knowledge systems.

A number of key international documents and organisations have acknowledged the value of the knowledge of Indigenous peoples in sustainably managing complex ecological systems, and called for the use of Indigenous knowledge of ecosystems in decision-making (*Convention on Biological Diversity* 1992; MEA 2005c; The World Bank undated; UNCED 1992; WCED 1987).

While, on one hand, Indigenous peoples see this as affirming the 'validity and relevance of their knowledge, experience, and competence' and reversing 'a long history in which those attributes were ignored or discounted' (Usher 2000, p 191), on the other hand they have concerns about the way their knowledge is being (mis)used.

Table 6.1 Contrasting Expert Natural Science and Indigenous Ecological Knowledge

Natural Science	Indigenous Ecological Knowledge
Gained through rational scientific method – planned observation, experimentation, modelling, reproducibility and verification	Gained through casual observation, experience, trial-and-error
Knowledge gained by researchers at an objective distance from nature	Knowledge gained by observers and participants connected to and situated within nature
Data generated by specialist experts (exclusive) – secular	Data generated by users of nature (inclusive) – social and spiritual links
Reductionist and ecological approaches	Holistic approach
Analytical and abstract reasoning	Intuitive thinking
Frequently quantitative	Usually qualitative
Based on general laws of nature, theories and testing of these	Based on cumulative collective experience
Attempts to be universal	Culture-specific
Wider focus and local focus to provide *general* concepts, hypotheses, theories, and laws	Local focus to provide *unique* knowledge
Spatial information through maps, models and digitised in Geographic Information Systems (GIS)	Spatial information in the minds and performances of people, and their art, crafts and stories
Knowledge typically accumulated episodically in shorter time frames	Knowledge accumulated gradually over generations
Communicated globally in written form – peer-reviewed books, articles, internet	Communicated locally in oral or visual form through stories, songs, dance, performance and art
Access – specialist and expert based	Access – locally and socially based
For a wider audience – meaning lost through specialist language, but can be communicated through lay language	For a wider audience – meaning lost as a consequence of localised spiritual links to knowledge

Modified from Brodnig and Mayer-Schönberger 2000; Brush 1996; Johnson 1992.

6.4.2.2 Issues in integrating Indigenous ecological knowledge into EDM

The many differences between Indigenous ecological knowledge and expert natural science outlined above show that integration involves bringing together two very different knowledge systems situated in an uneven power relationship. In most governance systems for environmental issues, Indigenous knowledge occupies a subordinate position that means (Johnson 1992, p 16):

> All too often, it is the Aboriginal researcher who is taught the scientific method and forced to adapt his or her cultural reality to that model. Western scientists need the same exposure to the knowledge system of the Aboriginal group they are working with. Only when both groups develop an appreciation of, and sensitivity to, the strengths and limitations of their respective knowledge systems can integration begin to occur.

Regarding the power imbalance between these contrasting knowledges, key concerns include the risk that the Indigenous knowledge and its presenters may not be treated with respect (CoA 2004), and that codifying the knowledge in writing as part of a formal process (such as EIA) and using the knowledge in a situation that is separated from the cultural context in which it operates, is inappropriate and may result in misinterpretation and even misuse (Usher 2000).[13]

A further major concern is the risk that the knowledge will be appropriated and possibly used to benefit other, non-Indigenous, people (see Box 6.6).

Box 6.6: Indigenous knowledge and intellectual property rights – the *Hoodia* case from southern Africa

An issue of major concern for Indigenous peoples around the world is that recognition of their understanding of their natural environments, and particularly the biodiversity, has brought with it appropriation of this knowledge for commercial purposes involving pharmaceuticals, agriculture, horticulture and cosmetics.

One example is the *Hoodia* case from southern Africa.

The San are Indigenous inhabitants of the Kalahari Desert in southern Africa. They have long used a species of the cactus *Hoodia* as a drink substitute and to suppress their appetite during lengthy hunting trips in the desert, when food and water are scarce.

The first colonial recording of this use of the *Hoodia* species seems to have been by the botanist Francis Masson in 1796. The South African government research organisation, the Council for Scientific and Industrial Research (CSIR), was prompted by such colonial records to investigate, from 1963, the properties of *Hoodia* and other edible plants from the region. By 1995 the CSIR had identified the active structure in *Hoodia* that acted as an appetite suppressant and filed for a patent. In 1998 they signed a licence agreement with a small British company, Phytopharm to give Phytopharm an exclusive worldwide licence to manufacture and sell products from *Hoodia*. Phytopharm further developed the drug potential of the active structure in *Hoodia*, gained international patents and entered into sub-licences first with the pharmaceutical giant Pfizer and then with Unilever. The growing obesity epidemic promised a bright commercial future for an appetite suppressing drug (Wynberg 2004).

The CSIR in 1998 published a Bioprospecting Policy that committed it to share any benefits of bioprospecting with holders of associated traditional knowledge, and in 1999 signed a Memorandum of Understanding with traditional healers from South Africa and started to document the use of traditional knowledge associated with biodiversity. Despite these moves the San people were apparently not consulted about this research and patenting of *Hoodia* active ingredients until 2001, nor was there acknowledgment of the contribution of their knowledge (Wynberg 2004, p 859). In 2001, criticism by South African and international NGOs led to widespread media coverage of the San case, and raised an awareness about the links between traditional knowledge, patents and the need for sharing the benefits from the use of this knowledge. As a result the CSIR started negotiations on a Memorandum of Understanding with the San people that led in 2003 to an agreement to establish a San Hoodia Benefit-Sharing Trust. The Trust will receive royalties and payments from CSIR to distribute to the San people (Dutfield 2004; Wynberg 2004). This notion of benefit-sharing was institutionalised in South Africa in 2004 when the government brought in a Biodiversity Act that required development of a benefit-sharing agreement with holders of traditional knowledge when that knowledge is

---

13   Such misinterpretation and misuse is not a problem exclusive to Indigenous knowledge but common also with the presentation of expert specialised knowledge in the law courts (see Lunney 1992) and the media.

used for bioprospecting.[14] This benefit-sharing agreement has been described as an 'historic breakthrough' and 'one of the first of its kind in the world' (Wynberg 2004, p 865).

6.4.2.3 Protecting Indigenous ecological knowledge from 'biopiracy'

The *Hoodia* case and other examples have led to much discussion worldwide on how Indigenous peoples can be protected from appropriation of their traditional ecological knowledge, also graphically named as 'biopiracy'. The issue is challenging on many fronts. As shown by the *Hoodia* case, Western and international patent laws allowed CSIR to gain a patent in relation to *Hoodia* because they developed a *process* to extract and isolate an active substance from the plant. This satisfied common requirements for achieving a patent – that it was 'novel', involved an inventive step, and was capable of industrial application (Dutfield 2004). In contrast Indigenous communities cannot patent a useful property of a plant known to them through their traditional knowledge, because under patent law this is not seen as 'novel' (Wynberg 2004). Hence Indigenous ecological knowledge needs to have wider means of protection.

There have been increasing efforts to institutionalise the protection of Indigenous knowledge, particularly in the area of biodiversity and genetic resources. At the international level the *Convention on Biological Diversity* (1992) and more recent conferences of the parties to the Convention have played an important role in encouraging national policy and legislative responses, as have other international conventions (see Craig and Davis 2005 and for details of Australian experiences and challenges, see Craig and Davis 2005; Smallacombe et al 2007).

Despite these developments there remain many challenges in protecting the rights of Indigenous people with regard to their traditional ecological knowledge, largely emanating from the overarching difficulty of bringing Indigenous rights into Western socio-political and legal systems without undermining the very essence of Indigenous knowledge and culture (Craig and Davis 2005; Usher 2000; Williams 1998; Wynberg 2004). A further example of this difficulty comes from attempts to prevent loss of Indigenous knowledge.

6.4.2.4 Loss of Indigenous knowledge

The growing appreciation of the value of Indigenous knowledge has come at a time when many Indigenous knowledge systems are disappearing. The passing of traditional elders and integration of Indigenous people into wider societies, means that these orally-based knowledge systems lose their means of transmission (Johnson 1992). In turn this has led to endeavours to preserve Indigenous knowledge, typically through documentation and storage outside the social and biophysical environments where it was produced. At best this can preserve a partial and static museum piece. It fails to acknowledge the all-important cultural context of Indigenous knowledge, and that it is not static but is the product of innovative social systems that have, over time, continued to adapt that knowledge to new challenges (Smallacombe et al 2007; Viergever 1999) such that traditional ecological knowledge is best regarded as 'the products of generations of intelligent reflection tested in the rigorous laboratory of survival' (Hunn 1993, p 13). For Indigenous peoples the means to *conserve* (rather

---

14 Bioprospecting refers to the search for biological, genetic and chemical contents of living organisms in the natural environment that may have potential use for human purposes, and particularly for commercialisation.

than *preserve*) their knowledge requires land rights and self-determination, that is, continuation of the social systems that have produced the knowledge and its continuing evolution (Craig and Davis 2005; Smallacombe et al 2007; Viergever 1999).

6.4.3 Lay knowledge

The relevance of lay knowledge has particularly come into prominence with recognition that expert scientific knowledge is limited in dealing with so-called 'wicked problems' and needs to be complemented by input from ordinary people displaying common sense that takes account of their everyday life and the social and community contexts in which they operate (see 6.3.3) (Petts and Brooks 2006). Such inputs also serve to 'challenge the quality of existing knowledge and the claims made about its robustness' (Petts and Brooks 2006, p 1047).

Lay knowledge is similar to local knowledge in being community-based, but is not necessarily linked to a specific locality. Rather, it is also relevant in broader issues such as our development and use of genetically modified organisms (Einsiedel et al 2001; and see Box 7.3), whether or not a society chooses to use nuclear power for electricity generation, and the way a society responds to the threat of anthropogenic climate change. Each of these issues is as much about societal values and views about risk as about natural science, and decision-making must take this into account. But exactly what role lay publics should play in such decision-making has been controversial. A common (negative) view that has been described as the 'deficit model', sees the public as lacking the scientific understanding to contribute meaningfully in scientific debates (Bäckstrand 2003; Eden 1998; Petts and Brooks 2006; see also C.4.2). Recently, Einsiedel (2007, p 5) noted that this has been replaced by a view of publics as 'active, knowledgeable, playing multiple roles, receiving as well as shaping science'. But she suggests both these views are extreme and that a more nuanced view is emerging, that recognises a wide range of interest and understanding among the publics. 'Civic science' and 'citizen science' are common labels for the 'changing relationship between science, expert knowledge and citizens in democratic societies', whereby 'citizens and the public have a stake in the science-politics interface, which can no longer be viewed as an exclusive domain for scientific experts and policy-makers only' (Bäckstrand 2003, p 24). This is a key part of the post-normal science called for by Funtowicz and Ravetz (1991), O'Riordan (1991b) and others.

Civic science has been described as the efforts of scientists to reach out to the public and to increase public understanding of science (see Clark and Illman 2001), while citizen science has been described as both 'a science which assists the needs and concerns of citizens' (Irwin 1995, p xi), and as citizens in the role of non-expert scientists, engaging in the production of scientific knowledge. Community Environmental Monitoring (CEM) discussed in Box 6.5 above is one example of the latter (Clark and Illman 2001). However, these terms have also been used in relation to fostering public participation in science and technology decisions and more generally their use has been overlapping and inconsistent (Bäckstrand 2003; Clark and Illman 2001). While participation of the lay public *in debate* on complex environmental issues has been generally accepted as useful, though possibly difficult to get right (see Chapter 7), involving citizens in the *production of scientific knowledge* has been far more controversial (Bäckstrand 2003) as seen above with regard to CEM (Lunney et al 2002).

As discussed in Chapter 7 there are now many examples of the use of lay knowledge in decision-making on a range of environmental issues and there has been considerable attention to developing means to bring expert and lay knowledge together in dialogue, such as consensus conferences and citizens juries (Miller 2001). An interesting development in bringing lay and expert knowledge, and different areas of specialist knowledge, together via the internet, is 'crowdsourcing' (see Box 6.7).

Box 6.7: Crowdsourcing

Crowdsourcing provides perhaps the ultimate example of participatory innovation and knowledge generation. It opens up addressing a problem (typically technical or scientific) to a wide group of people, generally through an open invitation via the internet (Alsever, undated; Boutin 2006; Travis 2008). Crowdsourcing has been used to address a variety of challenges including:

- improving solar lighting for poor African people (Walsh 2008);

- cleaning up oil spills in Arctic and sub-Arctic waters;

- solving problems in drug synthesis and development (Travis 2008);

- art designs for T-shirts (Boutin 2006).

Crowdsourcing is very much a child of the internet. It depends on the internet for its operation and it has emerged from other internet-related developments. Its antecedents can be seen in open source (Howe 2008) and Web 2.0:

- Open source is a term applied to software development where the source code of programs is provided freely and people can use it to modify, improve, develop new programs and share results with the community. This has resulted in enormous innovation often involving thousands of voluntary contributors from around the world. The internet, including Google, now strongly depends on open source software (Hope 2008; Weber 2004). The concept of open source has now been taken up in other areas such as biotechnology, to encourage innovation to assist the poor in developing countries (Hope 2008).

- Web 2.0 is a somewhat slippery term, but refers to a set of changed characteristics relating to the operation of the internet. These include participation and harnessing collective intelligence (eg Wikipedia and crowdsourcing); an emphasis on services rather than just selling software as a package (eg Google); treatment of users as co-developers of software (O'Reilly 2005).

Crowdsourcing shares these wide participatory characteristics aimed at encouraging innovation, but does not necessarily result in free products. Much crowdsourcing takes place through InnoCentive[15] a web-based company that connects 135,000 solvers worldwide with clients from the private and public sectors, seeking solutions to technical and natural science challenges. InnoCentive has had a 35 per cent success rate in providing solutions for some 600 challenges posted on the internet since 2001. Solvers may receive prize money for their work but curiosity and pride seem to provide equal motivation to prize money (Travis 2008). Crowdsourcing has enabled companies to solve intractable problems that could not be solved by company staff and 'can be better, faster, cheaper than traditional in house research efforts' (Travis 2008, p 1750). Many major corporations now use crowdsourcing to help solve

---

15   See <www.innocentive.com> (accessed 21 January 2009).

problems and typically they will provide a monetary reward in exchange for the intellectual property rights over the solution provided (Howe 2008).

Interestingly, research on the success of crowdsourcing in delivering solutions has shown that 'the more diverse the pool of solvers, the greater the odds of a solution' and 'the further a challenge was from a person's field of interest, the more likely they were to solve it' (Travis 2008, p 1752, citing Lakhami). This further supports the role of multi-, inter- and transdisciplinarity in addressing complex environmental issues (see 6.3.4).

There is no doubt that crowdsourcing, open source and Web 2.0 are revolutionising the way knowledge is developed and shared, and must be an important consideration in knowledge management (see 6.5). Paradoxically, they may both assist and further complicate knowledge management.

Local, traditional, Indigenous and lay knowledge each contribute to the widened participatory inputs required by post-normal and sustainability sciences to address sustainability issues (see 6.3.3 and 6.3.5).

6.5 Knowledge management

We continue to witness exponential growth in the amount of information available for EDM. Paradigm shifts are one reason for growth and change in knowledge. However, an increasing pace of knowledge development has also come from a range of economic and other societal drivers. The result has been an explosion of information and knowledge in recent years, leading in the 1990s to development of the terms 'knowledge society' and 'knowledge management' to indicate the central economic role knowledge now plays in many societies and the need for systems to manage the vast and growing store of knowledge now available.

This growth comes not only from accumulation of information in the conventional sources of specialised expert knowledge, where we have seen increasing specialisation into sub-disciplines (see 6.3.4), but also from inclusion of a wider range of sources, including local, traditional, Indigenous and lay knowledges. Such diversity further increases the challenges of integrating the various knowledges in decision-making, referred to throughout Section 6.4.

However, not only is there substantial growth in the amount of information available, but also the means through which we access information are increasing in type and complexity. The internet in particular has transformed the way we access knowledge and our ability to search for information. It has also brought many more actors into the knowledge game (see Box 6.7), and increasing difficulty in determining how to judge the worth of information provided. The consequence of these trends is that despite the advantages of the internet in enabling searches for information, the wide range of information relevant to EDM and sustainability ensures that the difficulty in keeping abreast of relevant information remains. As well, much relevant experiential and tacit knowledge (see 6.2) is informal knowledge that is not necessarily recorded and must be sourced through other methods. As a result of these trends, coupled with business focus on the knowledge economy, growing attention has been paid to the need for knowledge management, involving knowledge systems and knowledge brokers (Campbell 2006).

Knowledge management aims to achieve organisational objectives through making the best use of knowledge. It involves the development of *processes* (both technological and social) for acquiring, creating, organising, sharing, applying, using and transferring knowledge. A 'plan-implement-check-review' cycle (see Figure 8.1) is applied to ensure learning and continuous improvement in these knowledge management processes (LWA 2006; New York State undated; SA 2005).

Hence there are three main components in knowledge management (New York State, undated):

- **People** – who create, share and use knowledge, and who collectively comprise the organisational culture that nurtures and stimulates knowledge sharing.

- **Processes** – the methods to acquire, create, organise, share and transfer knowledge.

- **Technology** – the mechanisms that store and provide access to data, information and knowledge created by people in various locations.[16]

Knowledge management is generally defined in terms of an organisation, and the Australian Standard for knowledge management (SA 2005) is focused at that level. But knowledge management may also be relevant at other levels, for example, a regional association of bodies, such as catchment management authorities in an Australian State, or a 'community of practice'. A community of practice refers to 'a network of people who share a common interest in a specific area of knowledge or competence and are willing to work and learn together over a period of time to develop and share that knowledge' (LWA 2006, p 28). They are often communities of expert specialists but need not be confined to these.

Knowledge management requires a systematic approach to integrate the people, processes and technology described above. The concept of a *knowledge system* recognises the range of both explicit and tacit knowledge (see 6.2 and Box 6.8) from both public and private sectors, at a range of scales – individual, organisational, sectoral, local, regional, national and global – and the need to bring these together as an overall knowledge system. Typically this bringing together will include technical aspects of information and communications technologies. Focus needs to be concentrated on the boundaries between the *types* of knowledge (eg expert natural science and local knowledge) and the boundaries between the knowledge *sectors* (eg research, policy, management, evaluation). In the context of NRM, Campbell (2006 p 11) particularly emphasises the importance of the interface between natural science knowledge and the strategic knowledge associated with administration, governance and policy, noting the frustration often felt by scientists that major public policy decisions are 'at best imperfectly informed by the best available science'.

Box 6.8: Building tacit knowledge into a knowledge system

Tacit knowledge (see 6.2) and the specialist knowledge of environmental experts are complementary. Bringing these knowledges together in an organisational knowledge management system requires means to bring workers together to share and interpret experiences and expertise.

An important part of this exercise is to codify, and hence retain, the personal experience of workers, in essence converting it to explicit knowledge. This can be challenging. People may be unaware that the tacit knowledge they possess may be of value to others, and transfer of this knowledge typically requires extensive personal contact and trust (New York State undated).

---

16   There are now many web-based tools for finding and sharing information relevant to environmental management. For an example from NRM see the NRM toolbar developed by Land & Water Australia, <www.nrmtoolbar.net.au> (accessed 21 March 2009).

So this is a major task, particularly in organisations with a high staff turnover, but these are the organisations most in need of retaining tacit knowledge.

The challenge of incorporating tacit knowledge into knowledge management systems should not be underestimated. It may require deep change in corporate culture to recognise the worth of tacit knowledge and to put in place means to encourage its acquisition and internalisation in a knowledge management system. Such means will need to encourage and reward workers for developing and sharing their tacit knowledge. Nevertheless, there may be strong rewards for the corporation since tacit knowledge, unlike explicit knowledge, is very difficult for other firms to copy and so can provide strong competitive advantage (Lubit 2001).

The complexity of knowledge systems has led to the emergence of *knowledge brokering* defined as 'processes used by intermediaries (knowledge brokers) in mediating between sources of knowledge (usually science and research) and users of knowledge' (Campbell 2006, p 15). Knowledge brokers need to be multi-skilled. They first need to assist users in determining exactly what information they need. They then find the most relevant sources of information to meet this need and ensure that it is put into an accessible and useful form for the users. This may involve facilitating exchange and understanding between very different knowledge types, such as expert natural science and Indigenous knowledge. But knowledge brokering can also serve a wider purpose of influencing research and technology to better assist users (Campbell 2006; van Kerkhoff and Lebel 2006).

Within Australia, Campbell (2006, p 15) suggests that servicing the knowledge needs of catchment management and other regional NRM bodies is 'one of the biggest challenges in NRM today'. Box 6.9 shows the challenges faced.

Box 6.9: Challenges for knowledge management for NRM in Australia

Andrew Campbell (2006), then Executive Director of Land & Water Australia, has explored the extent of the challenges faced in developing a knowledge system for the agricultural sector of NRM in Australia.

He identified around 80 organisations at the federal level responsible for delivering aspects of NRM natural science. If NGOs such as the Farmers' Federation and community-based organisations such as the Australian Conservation Foundation (ACF), Greening Australia and WWF are added in, the figure would be more than 100 nationally. Taking this down to State level across the eight States and Territories and to intergovernmental organisations such as ANZLIC,[17] the number expands to several hundred groups managing formal scientific NRM knowledge. If universities and technical colleges are added, the number doubles. This estimate covers simply the public money spent on generation and management of formal scientific knowledge for agriculture-related NRM. But Campbell estimates that there are also around 80 private consulting firms involved in knowledge supply to this sector.

The above discussion covers just the formal scientific knowledge supply and management. However, there is also the informal generation and exchange of tacit, local and Indigenous knowledge by farm businesses, catchment and landcare bodies and other community groups. Including these, Campbell (2006) added around 80,000 farm businesses, 57 catchment management bodies, several thousand landcare and other community groups, hundreds of

---

17   Australia New Zealand Land Information Council. ANZLIC's role is to facilitate easy and cost effective access to the wealth of spatial data and services provided by a wide range of organisations in the public and private sectors, <www.anzlic.org.au/> (accessed 28 March 2009).

Indigenous communities, 722 local governments, hundreds of State government agencies and many industry and sectoral (such as water) bodies. In sum, Campbell identified several hundred organisations in Australia who need to access NRM knowledge to carry out their roles, and several thousand organisations, groups and individuals who both contribute to, and use, such knowledge. The task of sharing knowledge among these numerous groups is significant and making that sharing meaningful extends the challenge.

Yet Campbell (2006) found that while there are a number of areas of excellence in NRM knowledge management systems in Australia, there are also significant gaps. He found the system as a whole to:

- lack overall purpose;

- be weak in generating practical, profitable and adaptable solutions for implementation over a range of scales;

- be poor in providing for monitoring and evaluation needs;

- have poor communication of knowledge between sectors and between knowledge domains (such as local, Indigenous and expert natural science).

In sum, he concluded that (p 24) 'we have a system that seems better designed for forgetting, overlooking and ignoring than for remembering, learning and understanding'.

Box 6.9 lays out the challenge of knowledge management in one sector – agriculture. But environmental professionals and organisations working in other environment and sustainability fields face similar challenges. Informally, environmental professionals need to work hard to stay up to date in their area of professional responsibility. Some environmental professionals work within a narrow disciplinary area (such as a hydro-geologist providing advice on sub-surface water flow for a pollutant movement study). But others work in a broader environmental management context which requires an integrative approach. Keeping up to date for these professionals is likely to be more difficult given that a number of specialised areas may be relevant (eg someone working to develop policy for sustainable consumption may need to cover a wide range of disciplinary information from life cycle assessment through to incentives for behaviour change). Environmental professionals may use training, seminars, conferences and networking to keep up to date. Professional organisations may play an important role in each of these means.

But there is also a trend towards more formal knowledge management in both public and private sector organisations in the environment and sustainability fields. This is particularly important where there is high staff turnover or public sector departmental restructuring, and when tacit knowledge is involved (see Boxes 6.1 and 6.8).

6.6 Conclusions

We suggested in Chapter 2 that sustainability now forms the framework for EDM. This brings with it a number of challenges in relation to knowledge for EDM. For example, are our present knowledge systems suitable to inform decision-making for sustainability? If not, what is required?

We have suggested in this chapter that the wicked problems typical of sustainability, require the incorporation of new forms of knowledge that can deal with system complexity, high uncertainty and contested values. In turn, this has led to recognition of the need to complement information from disciplinary expert science with integration across a wide range of other relevant disciplines, and with knowledge from a wider range of sources – local, traditional, Indigenous and lay – that is, extended knowledges. 'Post-normal science' and 'sustainability science' have been proposed as having characteristics to address these needs. However, integrating these knowledges brings many challenges that are still works in progress (eg what to do when different knowledges conflict) and also exposes power relationships (eg when certain knowledges carry more legitimacy than others). Expert natural science remains the dominant form of knowledge at least in the formal institutional processes of governments, but has lost some public trust since it is seen as often overly narrow, poor in acknowledging uncertainty, faulty in its claims to objectivity, and dismissive of the values and concerns of the public (Irwin 2001). Information, from the wider sources (local, lay and so on) continues to be seen by some, as inferior to expert science – lacking in rigour and objectivity. Nevertheless, appreciation of the benefits of incorporation of these extended knowledges continues to grow. However, these dominant-inferior power relationships are particularly concerning when they lead to misuse (eg misinterpretation through using Indigenous knowledge outside its cultural context) or appropriation of Indigenous or traditional knowledge. Progress has been made in addressing appropriation but many challenges remain.

Integration of knowledges requires collaborative forms of knowledge production and this in turn requires the establishment of collaborative spaces, which leads us to Chapter 7 on public participation.

7

Public Participation

7.1 Introduction

All environmental decisions have some effect on particular groups and the broader public. The purpose of public participation (sometimes referred to as community consultation or engagement) is to ensure that those affected by environmental decisions have the opportunity to contribute to, and ideally influence, the decision-making process. Many environmental decisions are processed by government agencies, or in the private sector, rather than via the formalities of parliamentary decision-making (see Chapter 4). For this reason supplementary democratic institutions are needed to incorporate the views (interests and values) of those potentially affected by decisions. In this sense, public participation provides decision-makers with more detailed insights into what the community thinks about a particular issue, plan or proposal. This not only facilitates discussion on some of the underlying values and beliefs at the heart of the issue (see Chapter 3), but it enables decision-makers to access valuable ideas and knowledge from the community (see Chapter 6). Public participation also expands the judgment of environmental uncertainties, complexities and risks into the public realm (see Chapters 6 and 9). More pragmatically, public participation can facilitate community ownership and implementation of a particular policy, project or proposal.

Achieving all these benefits from public participation is no easy undertaking. It involves not only identifying the relevant constituents potentially affected by an environmental decision, but also designing and convening a timely process that ensures meaningful engagement. All this demands skills, resources, and time as well as community trust. Effective participation also requires a commitment on the part of decision-makers (whether elected representatives or company directors) to listen to the community, and to act on their input. At the same time public participation can also be a highly politicised process. It can exacerbate existing conflicts, polarise communities and stall projects.

For all these reasons and more, public participation is probably the most feared and poorly executed phase of the environmental decision-making (EDM) process. In the wrong form, or poorly facilitated, participation can produce more harm than good. The consequences of not including public input, or of a mistimed or badly managed participatory process can cost the proponent of a development or policy initiative substantial time delays, resources and loss of public confidence. As we learned in Chapter 6, too often expert and scientific forms of knowledge are privileged in environmental controversies, at the exclusion of local, experiential and Indigenous perspectives. Omitting these latter perspectives from EDM can skew the way a particular problem is framed, investigated and addressed.

Today most EDM processes involve some form of participation. However, participatory processes vary considerably in terms of who they involve, and how. For example, some processes focus on involving experts or high profile figures, while others might target affected stakeholder groups, or elicit input from the broader public. Depending on the nature of the process, different kinds of actors (see Chapter 5) will have more access than others. Typically it is the more organised and well-resourced groups that engage in public participation processes (Carson and Martin 2002).

There are also multiple roles that actors can play in public participation. For example, you may be involved in organising or administering a public participation process for industry or government. Alternatively you might participate in a consultative exercise as a representative of a community group or the business sector, or as a concerned resident or consumer. In whatever capacity you may be involved, it is important to understand the rationale behind public participation, and how to make it meaningful and effective.

In this chapter we explore the concept of public participation and consider its history and rising importance in the context of environmental decisions. We discuss the spectrum of participatory methods from information provision through to empowerment, and explore some of the designs that target the involvement of stakeholders, experts and lay citizens. We also briefly examine public participation in relation to the legal system. In the final section we discuss some common pitfalls encountered when seeking to engage the public, and offer some suggestions for how to make participation more appropriate and effective.

7.2 Sorting out some terms

The field of public participation is full of terms with slippery meanings. Before we proceed, it is useful to unpack what we mean by first, 'participation' and secondly, 'the public'.

The term 'participation' can be ambiguous. For some, it is a process of educating the community through the provision of information. For others participation refers to a deeper process in which the public and relevant groups engage interactively with an issue to influence decisions. Participation is also a term that can be applied to informal activities where actors seek to push their agenda, for example, through protests, campaigns, blogs and boycotts. In its fundamental sense, participation refers to involvement or active engagement in something. Ideally, public participation is a dialogical process where communication occurs between participants and decision-makers. In the context of environmental decisions, participation is typically undertaken in a structured process, where different individuals and groups are invited by government, a corporation or a non-government organisation (NGO) to engage in discussion, and sometimes decision-making. The nature of the participation varies depending on how much control and power is handed over to the participants (Arnstein 1969). We explore the range of forms of participation later in the chapter (see 7.6).

What is meant by 'the public' in public participation? In this book we take a broad interpretation of the term 'public'. It includes a range of actors who contribute to, or are potentially affected by environmental decisions including policy-makers, experts, pressure groups, businesses, interested individuals, and everyday citizens (see Chapter 5). As mentioned above, different participatory processes tend to target particular kinds of actors. In other words, the relevant 'public' for a participatory program will be defined or constituted by the nature of the procedure, its goals and political context (Barnes et al 2003). Targeting certain 'publics' means that most participatory exercises invariably exclude some actors. For example, an advisory panel might focus on expert involvement at the exclusion of community members. Ideally an effective participatory program offers a variety of processes to ensure that multiple 'publics' have the opportunity to contribute (eg Carson et al 2002).

The term 'stakeholder' also deserves some attention here, since it is used widely in discussions on public involvement in environmental issues. A stakeholder broadly refers to anyone who holds a stake or interest in something. The term originated in the corporate sector, referring to various external parties affected by a company decision (Mitchell et al 1997). Today the term 'stakeholder' commonly refers to any group or individual that has a special interest or concern in an organisation, proposal or project. Usually (but not always) the term is reserved in environmental decisions for identifiable groups or organisations that have expressed an interest in the issue or proposal. They might also be entities that have useful knowledge or perspectives, or the power and resources to block or promote proposals (see Bingham et al 2005; Glicken 2000; Mitchell et al 1997). Unorganised or informal communities such as everyday citizens are not usually labelled as stakeholders (see Box 5.1).

7.3 The evolution of public participation in Australia

Public participation has not always been a key component of the EDM process. In most Western nations, decisions on the environment were once considered the reserved realm of experts and government officials. Participation of this kind (also referred to as 'technocracy' (Fischer 1990)) tends to be restricted to a select few individuals with specialist or expert knowledge. However, as we saw in Chapter 1 this mode of decision-making was challenged considerably in the 1960s and 1970s by the environmental movement, which staged public protests and campaigns to block undesirable proposals. One institutional response to the rise of modern environmentalism has been to provide more structured avenues through which affected publics can provide input.

As with many other western nations, Australia has witnessed considerable evolution of public participation over the past 40 years, particularly in the realm of EDM.

In the early 1970s and 1980s, opportunities for participation focussed on legal and administrative procedures. For example, avenues were created to require public input into planning and development proposals, typically via comment-by-written-submission or public hearings. A series of legal opportunities were also created providing people with the opportunity to comment on environmental issues (see 7.8).

In the 1990s more emphasis was placed on stakeholder involvement in government advisory bodies, particularly pressure groups representing business and environmental interests (McEachern 1993). One notable experience was the Hawke Government's consultation process in 1990–1991 which engaged business and environmental groups to develop a strategy for implementing Ecologically Sustainable Development (ESD) in Australia (Downes 1996) (see 2.4.7). The notion of stakeholders expanded towards the late 1990s beyond organised pressure groups to include shareholders, users, clients and customers. This shift coincided with the uptake of corporate and managerial ideals in the public sector (see 4.6.5), where terms such as 'citizens' and 'the public' were at times substituted with 'users' and 'clients' (Alford 2002).

In the late 1990s and during the 2000s public participation in environmental issues expanded to include the informed and considered views of everyday citizens. Different innovative participatory projects were conducted using alternative recruitment methods (such as random selection) and new forms of electronic media, such as email, blogs and on-line discussion forums (eg Carson and Hartz-Karp 2005; WA Government 2003c).[1] A particular emphasis of this new wave of participatory experiments was to extend debates beyond the 'usual suspects'. Since the mid-1990s there has also been an increase in partnership-based projects where decision-makers and relevant actors work together to co-produce strategies to address common problems (see 3.11.2) (Reddel and Woolcock 2003;

Figure 7.1 From DEAD to PEP

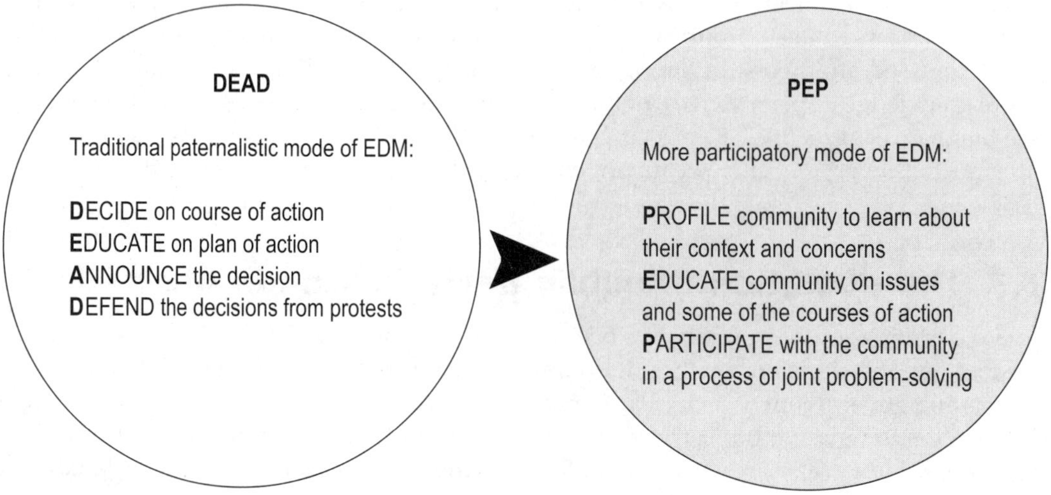

DEAD

Traditional paternalistic mode of EDM:

DECIDE on course of action
EDUCATE on plan of action
ANNOUNCE the decision
DEFEND the decisions from protests

PEP

More participatory mode of EDM:

PROFILE community to learn about their context and concerns
EDUCATE community on issues and some of the courses of action
PARTICIPATE with the community in a process of joint problem-solving

Adapted from WA Government 2006, p 5.

---

1 For more on e-engagement, see WA Government (2006). For details on e-governance more broadly, see the Victorian Government's e-democracy website, <www.egov.vic.gov.au> (accessed 20 April 2009).

Wallington et al 2008). As discussed in Chapter 1, this shift in the environmental sector has been described as a move towards 'environmental governance' (Stewart and Jones 2003).

The evolution of public participation in Australia is not unique; similar experiences have been recorded in the United Kingdom, the United States and in most of Western Europe (Barnes et al 2007; Gastil and Keith 2005; Renn et al 1995). In most Western liberal democracies, public participation is now recognised – at least in theory – as a significant component of EDM, and indeed all public policy-making (Althaus et al 2007). In principle governments are moving away from an era of top down decision-making (Decide-Educate-Announce-Defend (DEAD)) to one where affected parties are involved and engaged (Profile- Educate-Participate (PEP)) (see Figure 7.1).

7.4 Why support public participation in EDM?

How can this shift towards increasing opportunities for public participation in EDM be explained? Below we consider some of the key reasons why decision-makers and other actors support the idea of public involvement in EDM.

7.4.1 Moral reasons

One of the most significant drivers for participation in EDM is a commitment to the democratic ideal that people should have the opportunity to have a say in decisions that affect them. When communities are excluded from contributing to decision-making processes, they are left frustrated and angry, and question the fairness and authority of the imposed decision (Renn et al 1995). In other words they may not accept the legitimacy of the decision (Parkinson 2006). This can create significant problems for decision-makers, particularly during implementation where the project or proposal might require cooperation from the community, such as paying a road toll or using a recycling program.

There are of course many other moral reasons why decision-makers support public participation. For example, active citizen involvement in public policy (especially over the long-term) can promote more equitable outcomes and address systemic inequalities in communities (Schneider and Ingram 1997). Participation is also said to promote more transparent decision-making, and thereby improve trust in public institutions and citizenship more broadly (Putnam 1993).

The moral value of public participation has also been actively promoted by international bodies such as the UN and OECD, who argue that communities should have the opportunity to participate in decisions that affect them (OECD 2000, 2001, 2007b). A number of significant international initiatives on public participation in EDM have emerged including the UN's *Local Agenda 21* (see 4.4.4), and the *Aarhus Convention on Public Participation* (Hartley and Wood 2005).[2]

7.4.2 Epistemic reasons

Another important driver of public participation in EDM is the desire to capture a broader set of knowledges. As we saw in Chapter 6, knowledge on environmental issues extends well-beyond the realm of science and technical expertise; it can also include local, experiential and Indigenous knowledge. Public participation is a useful means for bringing these

---

2   See <www.unece.org/env/pp/> (accessed 20 April 2009).

multiple areas of knowledge into a decision-making process (Kasemir et al 2003b), and facilitating the move towards 'post-normal science' (Weale 2001b; Wynne 1996b) (see Chapter 6). Participation also promises governments and other organisations better problem-solving capacity. When different actors work together on problems they have the opportunity to share knowledge and resources, which can improve the efficiency of public programs and services (Kickert et al 1997; Kooiman 1993). Participatory and collaborative approaches also present decision-makers with an alternative approach to dealing with the complexities and uncertainties of modern policy issues (Koppenjan and Klijn 2004).

7.4.3 Administrative and managerial reasons

There is also a host of administrative and managerial reasons why public participation is appealing to decision-makers. At minimum, participation may be a necessary administrative requirement, for example, to fulfil certain legal or company requirements, such as an Environmental Impact Statement (see Chapter 8). Alternatively, a participatory process might be conducted to help prevent or resolve a conflict. For example, since the 1970s consultation exercises have been used by governments as a means to prevent protest politics and restore trust in political institutions. A related motive here is to use participation to help share the responsibility for policy outcomes (including successes and failures) (Head 2007).

Another administrative driver of participation is the idea that when public concerns are taken on board at an early stage, decision-making and implementation are more effective. For example, in planning a large infrastructure project the early involvement of local residents to discuss the costs, benefits and alternatives may identify and give opportunity to alleviate tensions that might arise if the plan had reached a highly developed stage without such input. In some cases participation can also foster the community's acceptance and even ownership of controversial developments (see Box 7.1).

Box 7.1: The benefits of open and transparent public participation

Siting a permanent nuclear waste disposal site is politically controversial worldwide. In most countries, including Australia, the process typically ends in gridlock where local communities are at loggerheads with industry. In the end many politicians delay decisions in the hope that conflicts will dissipate. But they rarely do (see Holland 2002a, 2002b).

Sweden has taken a participatory approach to determining suitable nuclear waste disposal sites that is based on 'the principle of complete openness among politicians, agencies, industry, public and local municipality' (Dawson and Darst 2006, p 615). A centrepiece of this approach is extensive, up-front public participation involving a long period of discussion and negotiation. Through this open and transparent process, trust between the community, industry and government is built and reinforced. In some localities communities have actively helped to shape and negotiate the economic and social benefits from the project. Research suggests that in comparison with other countries, the Swedish approach generates much higher levels of social acceptance for nuclear waste facilities (Dawson and Darst 2006; Lidskog and Sundqvist 2004, 2005).

Public participation is increasingly advocated as a means to improve the managerial efficiency and service delivery of government agencies. For example, seeking user feedback on public services (such as recycling), or engaging community members in the redesign, evaluation or even delivery of particular services (Bovaird 2007). The rationale here is that governments (and their contractors) will be able to deliver better services to the community, if users and clients are involved in the design and delivery of public services. These arguments have shaped a number of community participation programs on the generation and delivery of renewable energy in the United Kingdom. In this context, participation may come in various forms, for example, through the initiation of an energy project, its administration, financing, construction, governance or ownership (Walker 2008). In some schemes the community is encouraged to become involved in micro-generation of energy, for example, through the household production of solar or wind power (Sauter and Watson 2007). These so called 'bottom up' forms of energy development have been particularly successful in promoting renewables in Germany and Denmark (Reiche and Bechberger 2004; Wüstenhagen et al 2007), the United Kingdom (Walker 2008), and more recently in Japan (Maruyama et al 2007). In-depth empirical studies also suggest that community-based investment schemes can serve to improve the social acceptance of siting energy technologies, such as wind farms (Maruyama et al 2007; Sauter and Watson 2007; and see Box 3.1).

More ambitious managers and administrators might utilise public participation to catalyse change, or to shift the nature of the debate. For example, they might turn to more deliberative processes in order to expand discussion on a controversial policy issue beyond symbols and narrow interests (eg Carson et al 2002; Einsiedel et al 2001; Niemeyer 2004).[3] Public administrators might also seek to overcome some of the limitations of existing methods of community involvement (such as opinion polls and pressure group politics), by experimenting with new participatory processes (Hendriks 2002; Reddel and Woolcock 2003). It may also be the case that participation might be used paradoxically not to deepen democracy, but as an administrative device to avoid it. For example, a participatory process might be used to postpone or avoid making a difficult decision, or to promote an idea or organisation (Seargeant and Stelle 1998; Taplin 1992).

The managerial push for more public engagement in decision-making has also come from some actors within the private sector interested in improving shareholder and client cooperation, or improving relations with neighbouring communities. Many companies now refer to public participation in their corporate policies, and consult with their stakeholders (and sometimes the broader public) through advisory boards and various community outreach activities (Dunphy et al 2007). For example, some international corporations, such as the resource company BHP Billiton, and the healthcare company, Novo Nordisk, openly publicise who their key stakeholders are, and the various ways they engage with them.[4]

7.4.4 Ecological reasons

Public participation has also been promoted as a means to achieve better environmental outcomes (Baber and Barlett 2005; Vigar and Healey 2002). The argument here is that participation (and democracy more broadly) can assist sustainability because it enables collective judgments about what we ought to do in the face of multiple values and sets of interests

---

3   By 'deliberative' here we mean an interactive form of communication in which participants provide reasons for their positions, listen to the arguments of others, and are open to changing their position in view of the better argument (Dryzek 2000b; also see 3.11.2).

4   For BHP, see <www.bhpbilliton.com/bbContentRepository/docs/ourStakeholders2008.pdf> (accessed 20 April 2009).
    For Novo Nordisk, see <www.novonordisk.com/sustainability/stakeholder_engagement/stakeholder_engagement.asp> (accessed 20 April 2009).

(Dryzek 1990) (see 3.11.2). Advocates of this position argue that public participation, particularly when it is highly deliberative can help the public and their decision-makers make informed collective choices in the face of uncertainty and contested knowledge (Fischer 2000; Smith 2001; Weale 2001a). Experiences with highly deliberative and inclusive forms of public participation suggest that participants' preferences shift towards more ecological outcomes (Niemeyer 2004). This happens not only because participants have greater access to information, but because they are encouraged to challenge, question and critically engage with various perspectives put before them (see Fung 2006; Niemeyer 2004). According to Carson et al (2002) participants favour more ecological outcomes when they have either direct experience with the issue or policy under consideration, or if they can collectively discuss its pros and cons. Their study suggests that simply providing the public with information (without the opportunity for dialogue and questioning) on complex environmental issues is not enough; it tends to lead to policy confusion. They argue that space needs to be provided where the public can collectively consider the arguments in favour and against all proposals (Carson et al 2002).

It is important to acknowledge that open and participatory decision-making does not necessarily always lead to greener outcomes (eg Zwart 2003). The public may decide that they do not want to bear the financial or aesthetic costs of a proposal, regardless of its benefits to the environment. Consider, for example, the opposition that many wind farm proposals face from communities worldwide. Despite strong ecological arguments in favour of renewable energy, some communities are not prepared to accept the visual and aesthetic changes that wind farms might impose on their local landscapes (Wüstenhagen et al 2007) (see Box 3.1). However, some argue that opposition to wind farms stems from procedural rather than substantial reasons; that is, communities are being excluded from planning and decision procedures (Hindmarsh and Matthews 2008). Emerging research suggests that when the public is meaningfully engaged in the design and implementation of wind farms, it is more accepting of the technology (Gross 2007; Wolsink 2007).

7.4.5 Advocacy reasons

Most of the reasons considered so far are drivers where public participation occurs in an *invited space*; that is, where a decision-maker creates a space where citizens and relevant groups are invited to offer their considered perspectives on a particular issue (Carson 2008). For example, a government department might convene a participatory process in relation to a new water management scheme (eg Nancarrow and Syme 2001). Less common are *insisted spaces* where a participatory process is instigated by an advocacy group, such as an environmental organisation, 'to build community capacity, to evaluate projects and programs, and to influence governments and their own institutional decision-making' (Hendriks and Carson 2008, p 298). Insisted spaces can also be used to promote a particular cause or to foster public debate on a controversial issue (Carson 2008). This was exactly the motivation for the NGO, CHOICE (formerly the Australian Consumers' Association), when it instigated a consensus conference (see Box 7.3) on genetically modified foods in 1999 (see Hendriks 2005b). CHOICE was looking for a way to improve dialogue between the biotechnologists, opponents and the public (Renouf 1999).

We turn now to discuss what is involved in designing a public participation program.

7.5 Designing public participation

A consultation strategy is driven largely by the nature of the problem at hand. Deciding when to consult (or whether to consult at all) is as much political judgement as a procedural issue.

(Althaus et al 2007, pp 99–100)

There are a number of tasks involved in running a public participation exercise. The scope and boundaries of the project need to be determined, participants selected, facilitators engaged, information prepared, venues organised, meetings convened and so on. In many cases these tasks can be outsourced to a consultant specialising in participatory design. Though this is increasingly the case (see Hendriks and Carson 2008), it is important for those commissioning, and those participating in, participatory exercises to be aware of various design issues.

In the first instance, we need to ask: *is it necessary and appropriate to engage the public on the issue at hand?* Not all issues or projects demand public participation. There are some instances when the community is happy to delegate responsibility to relevant decision-makers, for example, when an urgent decision is needed (such as an emergency oil spill), or when the issue involves highly sensitive or discriminatory material. In other cases, participation might be inappropriate because a decision has been made already, or the *terms of reference* for participation may be so limited that there is no room for the public to have their ideas incorporated. This can occur, for example, when the public is given specific scenarios and asked to decide which one is preferable, or when important options are not placed on the table such as the choice to do nothing at all. Another reason not to convene a participatory project is when it is known in advance that community input will not be incorporated, for example, if the commissioning organisation has no power over the final decision (WA Government 2006).

If public participation is deemed necessary and desirable, then the purpose, scope and nature of the process need to be determined. Some important design questions here include:[5]

- What is the impetus and purpose of the participation exercise?

- What level of engagement is appropriate, and when?

- Who is going to participate and how?

- What promises can be made to the participants, and what will be done with their input?

- Does the project have the necessary resources, time and skills?

There are also many risks that need to be managed as part of any participatory project (WA Government 2006). These risks might be associated with the participatory procedure itself, such as low participation or response rates, poor representativeness, ineffective facilitation, or budget problems. Risks might also relate to political or social factors, such as the withdrawal of support and commitment from decision-makers or participants, conflict and

---

5   For more questions to consider when designing participatory projects, see Cooper et al (2006), Gastil and Levine (2005) and WA Government (2003b).

hostility, or strategic influences from external organisations, such as the media. It may also be difficult for the decision-making process to accommodate the broad range of community views, especially if they are conflicting. Designers need to be mindful of the range of factors that may influence the success or otherwise of their participatory project. We return to some of these risk factors later in the chapter (see 7.9).

Whether you are designing, participating in, or observing a participatory project, it is important to appreciate the variety of ways the public might be involved in EDM.

7.6 Participatory methods

Over the past two decades, a plethora of participatory methods has emerged, many from the field of environmental policy (eg Gastil and Levine 2005; Kasemir et al 2003b; Renn et al 1995). Accompanying these developments have been several attempts to categorise different participatory designs, for example on the basis of their aims, scope or types of participants (Cooper et al 2006; Fung 2003; Hendriks et al 2007). For our purposes, it is useful to consider a spectrum of different forms of participation (as shown in Table 7.1) from informing, data gathering, consulting, partnering through to empowering (adapted from IAP2 2007a).

As one moves along the spectrum in Table 7.1 from left to right, participants have increasing control over the agenda, outcome and ultimately the decision. At the left end of the spectrum, communication is one-way and participation minimal. Informing involves sending messages out to the public, whereas gathering information is essentially about collecting specific data from a target group. In either case there is little interaction between the participants and decision-makers, and thus the participatory experience is extremely limited. In many cases, processes located at this end of the spectrum can distort community participation into a public relations vehicle for government or industry (Arnstein 1969).

As we move further to the right of Table 7.1, there is an increased level of interaction between decision-makers and the public. For example, consultation may involve public meetings arranged by government or industry to present a proposal and receive feedback through a question-and-comment time at the end of the session. At this level there may be limited opportunity for meaningful participation as communication may occur after key decisions have already ('unofficially') been made. One-sided consultation often signifies attempts by government or industry to justify or market a particular decision or activity rather than a genuine interest or willingness to collect and consider community feedback.

Moving along the spectrum we find more interactive forms of participation where ideally the public engage in various dimensions of an issue, and provide feedback to decision-makers. Dialogue and exchange are intensified in programs where the public works closely with governments or organisations in partnerships, for example via an advisory committee or collaborative arrangement (see 3.11.2). Here the communication is two-way; the public can speak and be heard and government or industry can explain their ideas and be listened to.

Towards the end of the spectrum are procedures that empower the public by delegating more control over the process, and in some cases responsibility for decision-making. Some procedures at this end of the spectrum, such as citizens' juries and consensus conferences are highly deliberative – in the sense that they provide sufficient and credible information for discussion, choice and decisions, and there is space to weigh options and develop common understandings (IAP2 2005).

Table 7.1 Varieties of public participation

Inform	Gather information	Consult	Partner	Empower
Goal	*Goals*	*Goals*	*Goals*	*Goals*
To inform the public by providing balanced and objective information to assist them in understanding the problem, alternatives, opportunities and/or solutions.	To obtain data on public preferences and opinion, and on their behaviour.	To explore public feedback on analysis, alternatives and/or decisions, and to provide feedback on how public input might influence the decision.	To partner the public in each aspect of decision-making (including the development of alternatives and the identification of the preferred solution), and to incorporate their advice and recommendations into the decisions to the maximum extent possible.	To leave the final decision-making in the hands of the public, and implement their decision.
Examples	*Examples*	*Examples*	*Examples*	*Examples*
Fact sheets Websites Open days Information kits/ campaigns Press releases	Call for written submissions Opinion polls Phone, web or email input Surveys Market research	Public meetings Focus groups Parliamentary committees Workshops On-line discussions	Advisory committees Collaborative planning Consensus-building	Citizens' forums (such as citizens' juries, and consensus conferences) 21st Century town meetings Referenda

Source: Adapted from IAP2 (2007a) and WA Government (2003b).

Other procedures at this end of the spectrum might hand over considerable power to the citizens but they are not particularly deliberative. For example, in a referendum issues are put to popular vote with citizens expressing their feedback to a proposal by voting either 'yes' or 'no'. Thus apart from informal public discussion, referenda provide limited structured opportunity for participants to engage in reasoned debate, or to provide more nuanced feedback (Parkinson 2001). Moreover, very few contemporary issues, particularly those related to sustainability, lend themselves well to yes/no framing (Franklin 1992).

It is not the aim of this chapter to detail all these specific methods of public participation.[6] Instead we focus our discussion on processes that target the involvement of particular kinds of actors such as experts, stakeholders and citizens. In doing so we touch on a number of controversial issues associated with the question of who participates in public participation and how. The selection of participants in any participatory process not only determines who is included and excluded from discussion but it also affects the way the procedure works, its legitimacy, and ultimately its political impact (see Hendriks et al 2007). Our brief consideration of different processes below serves to illustrate the strengths and weaknesses of engaging particular kinds of actors in public participation.

7.6.1 Involving experts and stakeholders

A common approach to public participation in environmental matters is to establish a committee composed of experts or representatives of pressure groups or a combination of both. This form of participation is premised on the idea that the participatory process needs to consider particular kinds of knowledge or perspectives. In other words participants are typically invited ('hand picked') by the commissioning body because they have specialist knowledge on the issue or because their organisation has been identified as an important stakeholder.

Since not all experts and pressure groups can be included in every participatory exercise, decisions need to be made as to who to include and exclude. Here careful consideration should be given to the rationale for participant selection, particularly with respect to representation, value positions and even individual personalities. When it comes to expert involvement the rationale for selection is typically based on the notion that *better* decisions will result if they include those most knowledgeable on the issue. It is important that designers reflect on why particular experts might be included over others, and how excluded perspectives might be incorporated.

A slightly different rationale underpins stakeholder (or pressure group) engagement. It rests more on the idea that decisions will be viewed as more *legitimate* if they include representatives of affected groups. Legitimacy is a central factor in the political success of any participatory project; if key stakeholder groups and the broader community support the process and its outcomes, then it is more likely that decision-makers will commit to implementing any recommendations (Parkinson 2003). Generating legitimacy is no easy task and the design challenge is determining which groups to include. Ideally, selection is not based on the squeaky wheel principle (where the loudest voices get to participate), but instead strives to include a diversity of perspectives. It is important to reach difficult to

---

6   For a good overview of a range of participatory methods, see Gastil and Levine (2005); Renn et al (1995) and Kasemir et al (2003a). Many excellent practical guides are now produced by government departments and international agencies on how to design and organise different kinds of participatory exercises (eg Carson and Gelber 2001; OECD 2000; WA Government 2003b; 2005).

access groups who may be marginalised for different reasons, such as their ethnicity, gender, disability, age, geography and even work commitments.

When there are multiple pressure groups representing the same sector, peak bodies or umbrella groups are often used (see Box 5.2). The danger here is that participation becomes dominated by a network of elite representatives who are disconnected from the constituents that they claim to represent (Skocpol 1999). According to Doyle, this is what happened to the Australian environmental movement during the 1987 federal election campaign. Doyle (2000, pp 171–172) describes how:

> [A] professional elite generated within two formal organisations [the Australian Conservation Foundation and The Wilderness Society] unilaterally acted as representatives for the environment movement. This changed the membership – along with the ideology – of the environment movement in Australia. The organised environment movement became more narrow in its base and less ideologically diverse.

Below we look briefly at a prominent model for engaging experts and stakeholders: the advisory committee.

Advisory committees

Advisory committees are a common form of public participation established by governments as well as business groups and NGOs to provide advice on environmental issues. Ideally an advisory committee is a form of partnering (see Table 7.1), where participants work closely with the commissioning body on a particular issue, debating, modifying and proposing ideas (Althaus et al 2007). For government-initiated advisory committees the deliberations are typically based on a set of pre-determined issues. The establishment of advisory committees may either be a legislative requirement (as for example under the *National Parks and Wildlife Act 1974* in New South Wales which requires community advisory committees for each region of the State) or initiated voluntarily simply because an organisation sees advantage in external input. For example, a number of local councils have established advisory panels to ensure that community feedback can be considered in their decision-making processes (see Box 7.2).

Box 7.2: Sustainability Advisory Group

In 2007, the Mosman Municipal Council in Sydney established a Sustainability Advisory Group to advise the council on various environmental issues and on the implementation of sustainability principles in its business and operational practices. The Advisory Group is composed of elected representatives and staff from the council, as well as six experts and six community members. The experts were invited individually by the council, whereas the community members were selected from a pool of individuals that responded to the council's call for expressions of interest from the public.

The advisory group meets four times a year, and its meetings are open for interested local residents to attend as observers.

Source: <www.mosman.nsw.gov.au/environment/management/sustainability> (accessed 25 March 2009).

Governments may receive advice from a number of specialist committees on any one issue, and these could be contradictory. This is often because different advisory committees are established under different terms of reference or with a specific focus, for instance energy, health or the environment. In other cases, the terms of reference may be so narrowly focussed that effective communication between related committees is inhibited. For example, when the Office of the Gene Technology Regulator was first established by the Commonweath Government in 2000, three advisory committees were formed: one to advise on scientific and technical matters, another to advise on ethical issues and a third to advise on community issues. By separating the advisory groups in this way, issues raised by community members on ethical and scientific matters were essentially kept at a distance from the more expert dominated ethics and scientific committees. A statutory review in 2005 found there had been considerable overlap between the ethics and community advisory committees and it recommended that these be merged. This advice was eventually acted upon and in 2008 a joint ethics and community advisory committee was formed.[7]

The type of advice that an advisory committee develops depends not only on its terms of reference, but also on the representativeness of its members and the personalities of the individuals concerned. Some advisory committees are relatively open in terms of membership. Others may be required by legislation to include representatives of specific government agencies or stakeholder groups. For representation from government agencies or clearly defined pressure groups, nominations of a representative will generally be sought from these groups. Where stakeholders include the public, applications for membership of the committee may be invited by advertisement (as in the example in Box 7.2). Some advisory committees with stipulated membership risk becoming unworkable particularly if they are too large, or if conflicting views amongst different representatives restrict dialogue.

Advisory committees are also established by corporations and NGOs for external advice and to build legitimacy. This has been particularly the case in the industrial sector where community advisory panels (CAPs) have been established by corporations to repair public trust (eg Lynn et al 2000). For example, in Australia a CAP was established to assist the company Orica manage its large stockpile of the hazardous hexachlorobenzene (HCB) at Botany Bay in Sydney. The panel, known as the HCB Community Participation and Review Committee (CPRC) was established in the mid-1990s after years of community distrust in the Botany region towards industry. The role of the committee, which is composed of representatives from Orica, local government and local residents, is 'to receive, and distribute information, consult the local community, participate in relevant process, and review and advise the NSW Orica on relevant proposals, including monitoring implementation of the [HCB] management plan' (Rae and Brown 2009, p 1587).[8]

One particular criticism of advisory committees is that they may be formed by the proponents of controversial developments as a public relations exercise to win the support of neighbourhood and community groups (Arnstein 1969). More so in the past than the present, proponents commonly established committees as a means to 'educate' the community, labelling it 'public participation' even when there was no effective input to discussions from the community members. Also, community advisory committees can become buffers between the organisation, whether a government agency or private corporation, and the

---

7   From <www.ogtr.gov.au/internet/ogtr/publishing.nsf/Content/committees-index-1> (accessed 20 December 2008).

8   For various interpretations of the successes and failures of the CPRC, see the special issue of *Journal of Environmental Management*, 2009, Volume 90, Issue 4.

community. The committee may be seen as simply paying lip service to the general public, pacifying their desire to have a representative body to voice public concerns.

7.6.2 Citizen engagement in complex environmental issues

We turn now to consider two different participatory procedures that target the involvement of ordinary members of the public: citizens' forums and 21st century town meetings.

Citizens' forums

Citizens' forums seek to bring the informed perspectives of the lay public into policy discussions, often for complex, controversial, or ethical issues. In contrast to expert and stakeholder forms of engagement, participants in citizens' forums have no particular expertise or specialist knowledge in the issue (Hendriks 2002). The citizens are also typically unaffiliated, at least in any substantial way, with any of the key pressure groups associated with the debate. There are many varieties of citizens' forums including citizens' juries, consensus conferences, and citizens' assemblies (see Gastil and Levine 2005; Khan 1999; Renn et al 1995). Notwithstanding some procedural differences, most citizens' forums share three common features, as shown in Figure 7.2.

Figure 7.2 General features of citizens' forums

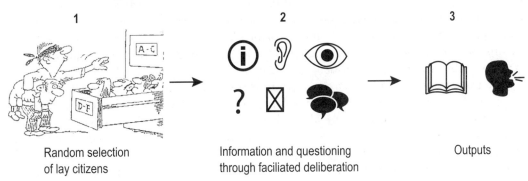

Random selection of lay citizens

Information and questioning through faciliated deliberation

Outputs

- **Feature 1**: Participants in citizens' forums are typically selected through random sampling. In other words, participants are selected on the basis of chance, rather than on the basis of what they know, or whom they represent.[9] Whereas random selection in politics might seem a novel concept today, it was a core democratic principle in ancient Athens and in the Italian republics of the Middle Ages (Carson and Martin 1999). Contemporary advocates of random selection in politics are motivated by a desire 'to incorporate greater political equality and better citizen deliberation in the process . . . [and] to make the decisions more responsive to the needs of constituents and more able to serve the public good' (Mansbridge 2000, p 106). Random selection also serves deliberation well because it is more likely to select participants with relatively open preferences than a process which draws on partisan actors such as pressure group representatives and even some experts (Hendriks et al 2007).

---

9 Typically *stratified* random sampling is used to ensure that the sample proportionally reflects particular characteristics of the total population. Strata are typically based on key demographic and socio-economic features such as sex, age, locality, education and occupation. All those within each strata or grouping have an equal chance of being selected.

- **Feature 2**: Citizens' forums encourage participants to learn about the issue, and question data, models and underlying assumptions. Information is disseminated through briefing materials, field trips, and presentations from experts, government officials, group representatives and activists. With the assistance of an independent facilitator, the citizens deliberate on the information put to them, question the presenters, and develop a series of policy recommendations. Facilitators must be impartial and, ideally, professionally trained with good pedagogic skills. It is also important that they, like the lay citizens, are not experts in the issue under deliberation.

- **Feature 3**: In the final stage of a citizens' forum, citizens typically present their findings to decision-makers (often in the form of a report that they have prepared) which then feeds into the policy process either directly (for example, tabled in parliament) or indirectly through wide public dissemination.

It is important to note that though Table 7.1 lists citizens' forums as procedures that empower and delegate control to participants, in practice this level of political delegation is rare. This is because the degree of citizen control is not determined by the procedure alone; political will is also a key factor. Unfortunately there are a number of examples where citizens' juries and consensus conferences have had only limited influence on decisions (Goodin and Dryzek 2006; Hendriks 2002; Kashefi and Mort 2004). That said, output from citizens' forums can provide a number of useful sources of advice for decision-makers, for example: feedback and suggestions on services; a measure of public opinion; an indication of citizens' concerns, preferences and priorities; or an appreciation of values and moral positions from an everyday perspective. In addition, citizens' forums can also stimulate broader public debate on the issue.

The most popular kind of citizens' forum is the citizens' jury, which was developed in the early 1970s by Ned Crosby from the Jefferson Center (Crosby 1995; Crosby et al 1986). The citizens' jury procedure typically brings together a panel of approximately 20 randomly selected citizens for several days to deliberate on a particular policy issue (Crosby 1999; Crosby and Nethercut 2005). Despite what the name suggests, citizens' juries are not legalistic procedures aimed at determining a unanimous policy verdict. Instead like most citizens' forums they produce a qualitative output from the citizens that records points of commonality and dissent. Citizens' juries have made a particular mark in Anglo-American countries such as the United Kingdom, United States and Australia, but the model has also been applied in India and Spain (see Crosby and Nethercut 2005; Font 2003; Parkinson 2004; Pimbert and Wakeford 2002).

Another related citizens' forum model is the consensus conference, which was developed by the Danish Board of Technology in the late 1980s as a means to include lay members of the public in debates on contentious science and technology issues.[10] Since the model was first piloted in 1987, hundreds of consensus conferences have been conducted worldwide with the most popular issue to date being genetically modified foods (eg Einsiedel et al 2001) (see Box 7.3). The consensus conference model is very similar to a citizens' jury, although the process is more time intensive with citizens typically engaged for three different weekends over a period of approximately three months (see Hendriks 2005b). An

---

10   The Danish consensus conference model described here is based on the consensus development conference, an expert-based model developed in the United States in 1977 for assessing medical technologies (see Jørgensen 1995). The Danes radically amended the American model by placing lay citizens at the centre of the deliberations.

important feature of consensus conferences is an external advisory committee. Apart from maintaining procedural integrity, an external advisory body adds legitimacy to the process (Grundahl 1995; Joss 2000).

Box 7.3: Australia's first consensus conference[11]

Australia's first consensus conference was held on 10–12 March 1999 at Old Parliament House, Canberra on the topic of gene technology in the food chain (Renouf 1999). The consensus conference was aimed at promoting public discussion on the future of genetically modified foods in Australia by exposing 14 randomly selected lay citizens to the various commercial, health and safety, environmental, ethical and trade perspectives on the issue.

The conference was initiated by the Australian Consumers' Association (now CHOICE) and sponsored by a range of organisations including government departments and Australia's largest national scientific body (CSIRO). To ensure process independence the conference was convened by the Australian Museum and overseen by a steering committee of 17 people. Independently facilitated, the process involved 13 experts including representatives from the CSIRO, the Gene-Ethics Network, the Organics Federation of Australia, the Australian Food and Grocery Council, corporations, scientists, farmers, religious and ethical groups, nutritionists, public health officials and consumer groups. The process was scheduled so that the citizens' report could feed into the Federal Government's decision-making process on gene technology and food regulation. The outcome of the conference included a citizens' report containing recommendations, most of which were directed at government.

The consensus conference process was covered extensively by the media including a radio documentary by the Australian Broadcasting Corporation (ABC). The project was also evaluated by independent consultants, whose positive appraisal of the process has contributed to the ongoing application of citizens' forums in Australia (see Carson and Hartz-Karp 2005).

Sources: Carson and Gelber (2001, p 41), Einsiedl et al (2001) and Renouf (1999).

21st century town meetings

One of the limitations with citizens' forums is that they only include a relatively small number of citizens. One process that addresses this scale problem is the 21st century town meeting, a procedure developed by the American not-for-profit organisation, America*Speaks*.[12] In a town meeting hundreds or thousands of people can participate in one or more venues. With the help of technology, such as networked computers and polling key pads, participants are able to work in small groups of around 10 and yet be collectively linked up to a central database. With the help of a trained facilitator each table engages in in-depth discussion on a set issue, and then types their ideas and preferences into a computer on their table. Feedback from each table is centralised, themed and sent back to the entire group. At various stages participants are asked to vote on different issues using keypads on their table. The effect of this networked group work is that it combines 'small-scale and large-scale dialogues' (Lukensmeyer et al 2005, p 159).

All town meetings strive to ensure that participants are demographically diverse. Unlike the citizens' forums described above, participants in a town meeting are selected through active recruitment. For example, outreach strategies are undertaken to target specific

---

11　For more details on this consensus conference, see <www.abc.net.au/science/slab/consconf/splash.htm> (accessed 15 April 2009).

12　See <www.americaspeaks.org>(accessed 15 April 2009).

demographic groups, with specific invitations going to those from hard to access sectors of the community, such as the youth or those from lower socio-economic groups (Lukensmeyer et al 2005, p 159).

Most town meetings to date have been convened by America*Speaks* together with a sponsor organisation such as a government agency, a private organisation or an advocacy group (Lukensmeyer et al 2005, p 159). By the end of 2008, America*Speaks* had convened well over 60 town meetings on issues such as the redevelopment of the World Trade Centre site (see Hajer 2005b); the rebuilding of post-Katrina New Orleans; health care reform; and childhood obesity. Given their large size and costs, town meetings are typically conducted on large public policy issues. More recently meetings have been conducted on environmental issues such as climate change and disaster management. In Australia urban planning issues have been popular topics for participatory projects inspired by the town meeting model (see Box 7.4).

Box 7.4: Using 21st century town meeting to assist urban planning

In 2003, the Western Australian Minister for Planning and Infrastructure convened 'Dialogue with the City' to elicit community input on how to accommodate the growth of the Perth metropolitan area (see WA Government 2003c). More specifically, the process was aimed at trying to create the world's most liveable city. According to the coordinator of the process Janette Hartz-Karp, the dialogue was designed 'to engage the whole community; thus, it included a survey of 8 thousand residents, an interactive Web site, a one-hour television broadcast, a series of full-page stories about planning issues in the major newspaper, art and essay competitions in schools on the future of the city, and additional listening sessions for those who are frequently not heard – youth, Indigenous people and those from a non-English-speaking background' (Carson and Hartz-Karp 2005, p 133).

As part of the 'Dialogue with the City' project, 1100 participants were engaged in a 21st century town meeting. Approximately one-third of the participants were invited stakeholder representatives, one-third were individuals who responded to advertisements, and the final third were respondents to an invitation that was mailed out to a random sample of the population (Carson and Hartz-Karp 2005). At the actual town meeting participants were engaged in innovative ways. For example, the participants were divided into small groups of 10 to play a planning game in which they faced a series of challenges confronting the region, such as how to accommodate rising population numbers (America *Speaks* 2008).

The discussion of different procedures above reveals that public participation can take many forms. The most appropriate method will largely depend on what the commissioning body (whether government, industry or an NGO) aims to achieve by including the public in the decision-making process. The level of participation will also depend on a range of factors including the level of public interest, political will, budget, time frame, social or environmental factors or the possible degree of controversy expected for a proposal (Thomas 1998). What tends to happen is that hybrid designs are created for the issue at hand, or a combination of processes are used at different stages of a project to ensure that all affected publics have an opportunity to participate (see Carson and Hartz-Karp 2005).

Clearly public participation today is much more than putting forward a written submission. There are a host of participatory designs available to engage affected publics in ways that suit the issue, and terms of reference. Indeed there is a thriving industry of consultants who now offer a range of goods and services to assist decision-makers engage with their constituents (Hendriks and Carson 2008). For example, consultants might: help governments and businesses design participatory strategies; facilitate community forums; evaluate processes; or sell software to help analyse community input. While decision-makers appear quite willing to contract out their pubic participation activities, it does mean that the skills for effective community engagement are increasingly brought in from outside the decision-making process. The danger here is that public participation is something packaged and purchased, rather than endogenous to decision procedures (Hendriks and Carson 2008).

7.7 Why participate and how?

While there are several reasons why governments, advocacy groups or proponents might seek public input (see 7.4), it is important to consider why members of the public (or representative groups) might want to participate. After all, participation is time consuming; it involves considerable preparatory work as well as attending regular meetings, forums and protests. Typically this is all done on a voluntary basis. What motivates groups and individuals to engage in a participatory process for EDM? Some possible reasons include (see also Hendriks 2006):

- to inject their perspectives and interests;

- to ensure that local and public interests are taken into account;

- to change or protect the status quo;

- to express their frustration and anger;

- to promote good public relations and demonstrate social responsibility;

- to protect the local environment, amenities and property values;

- to accept an invitation to participate, for example, out of a sense of public duty;

- to obtain secure funding, for example, if it is conditional on participation.

Many formal participatory processes are premised on the notion that the public will be more than willing to participate once invited. But there are certainly times when groups and individuals decide *not* to participate in a formal participatory process. In other words they choose to *self-exclude*. For example, they might lack the necessary finances, staff or time to participate. This is especially relevant when participatory processes proceed over long time periods. Some groups may also feel they are drowning in multiple participatory processes and exclude themselves to prevent overload.

Self-exclusion may also occur when a group or individual fears that the process may damage their strategic interests. A particular concern here is that a group or individual will be *coopted*. For example, their specific agenda might be ignored or marginalised by other interests and yet their name will be among those participating in providing recommendations. Cooption is a common concern for environmental groups, as discussed in 5.4.1. For example, in the consultation process associated with developing Australia's ESD framework (see 2.3), The Wilderness Society declined to participate because it argued that the consultative process was 'antithetical to an activist-oriented movement' (Economou 1993, p 408, cited in Downes 1996). Similarly Greenpeace pulled out because it did not agree with a number of decisions taken by the Commonwealth Government on controversial environmental matters (Downes 1996).

Some groups might also choose not to engage in a participatory project because they do not feel comfortable with the procedure, its terms of reference or the selected participants. For example, they might not be accustomed to the formal setting of the participatory process or its style of communication. These are subtle forms of internal exclusion, where groups may be invited to the table but not given the opportunity to express their views in terms and ways with which they are comfortable (Young 2000).

Ultimately the decision whether or not to engage in a participatory process is the prerogative of the individual or group. Decisions on the most appropriate strategy will be governed both by the personality of the individual and a range of factors concerning the particular features of the issue. However, process designers and decision-makers can seek to minimise any potential barriers to participation, for example by providing translators, child care, or travel allowances. In some processes, participants are even paid a small amount in honour of their services (see Hendriks 2005b). The process must also be designed with realistic time-frames in mind and have realistic expectations of participants.

In certain cases opposition from some sectors may come down to a conflict between competing and incommensurable value systems or world views (see Chapter 3). That is, regardless of the program of public participation administered and the opportunities for involvement it may be the actual proposal itself which is considered unacceptable. However, even in highly controversial cases public participation can be useful. After all by engaging in a scoping exercise with the public at an early stage in developing the proposal, the extent and nature of public concern will be revealed. This will help the proponent to decide if they should abandon the project, find an acceptable alteration, or press ahead with an enhanced public participation program involving those supporting the project.

Thus far we have considered various structured forms of public participation and the reasons why individuals or groups might choose to engage or not. As we have learned, since the 1970s and 1980s there are now a host of formal opportunities to contribute to environmental decisions but this does not necessarily guarantee that all views are heard, and taken on board. As a result individuals (or groups) may seek alternative avenues to influence decision-makers, for example, by lobbying or launching a public campaign (see Chapter 5). Alternatively like-minded individuals might seek to enhance their effectiveness by forming loose networks or groups to exchange information and ideas, provide mutual support and engage in rallies and protests. Or, members of the public might join a protest movement, boycott particular products or organisations, sign a petition, or write a blog or email their elected representatives (see Box 5.8).

7.8 Public participation and the law

There are also a number of legal avenues available to the public to influence environmental decisions. As mentioned earlier, public participation may be provided for in legislation, for example, in relation to Environmental Impact Assessment (EIA) (see Chapter 8). There may also be public reviews of the legislation itself (see Case Study A). However, public participation in legal matters on environmental issues is not a given right. Environmental legislation usually states who has *standing* to instigate legal proceedings against a particular decision or action (see 4.6.6). Standing is a legal term which describes whether a person is allowed to bring an action in court (EDO 1992). There are different types of standing. First, there is the standing permitted in legislation. Secondly, if there is no mention of standing in the relevant legislation then the court will look to the common law to determine if a person or group has standing to be heard in court. This is where an issue is decided by a judge who follows the decisions made in similar legal cases (see 4.6.6). Under the common law, a person has standing to sue only if they have a 'special interest' in the proposal or development which is over and above a general public interest (see Box 7.5). This may be a commercial interest, or it may be an interest by virtue of profession.

Box 7.5: Standing – an example of the 'special interest' principle

In the case of *Australian Conservation Foundation (ACF) and Harewood v Minister for Resources* (1989) 19 ALD 70 the ACF was granted standing to bring court proceedings challenging a government licence to export woodchips from the National Estate in the South East Forests of New South Wales. The ACF alleged that the licence was not in compliance with the *Australian Heritage Commission Act 1975* (Cth). The factors suggesting granting of standing to the ACF were that it was a major national conservation organisation, which received substantial government funding, and that there was a community expectation that the ACF would put forward alternative arguments to commercial exploitation of the forests. While the ACF was not entitled to standing to challenge any decision affecting the environment it was deemed to have a 'special interest' in protecting the environment. This meant that the ACF was able to take legal action against the minister.

Source: EDO (1992), Ramsay and Rowe (1995).

Related to the issue of public participation in the law is the community's right to access environmental information – otherwise known as their 'right-to-know'. Not only are people requesting more opportunities to participate in EDM processes, they are also asking for more information about environmental issues and risks. Thus the right-to-know on the environment refers to the 'right to be informed about the environmental compatibility of products, manufacturing processes, industrial installation and their effect on the environment' (Douglas-Scott 1996, p 115). Ideally, as consumers, workers or everyday citizens we have the right to request information from governments and industries on hazardous chemicals emitted from their products, workplaces, facilities and so on.

Several countries have provided for community-right-to-know under legislation, which specifically requires the disclosure of information regarding pollution and chemical hazards (see Beder 2006). In many countries this comes in the form of Freedom of Information (FOI) legislation, which enables the public to access information collected, and produced by, public authorities (Beder 2006). Though it is up to individuals to request specific information, FOI legislation places the onus on government to prove why certain information should *not* be publicly released. The principle behind FOI is that it improves the transparency and accountability of government processes and assists citizens and pressure groups to participate more effectively in the democratic process. Yet for environmental matters, FOI is not always suitable since it is restricted to information that the government has, and it is typically piecemeal and poorly integrated (Beder 2006).

A more proactive means of disseminating information on the environment to the public is for governments to establish registries or inventories on relevant data, such as the emissions of hazardous chemicals (see Box 7.6).

Box 7.6: The National Pollutant Inventory[13]

The Australian National Pollutant Inventory (NPI) is a joint State and Commonwealth program that requires some industries and government facilities to report their emissions to a public database. The inventory was launched nationally in 2000, after eight years of consultation, intergovernmental negotiations and implementation trials (Howes 2001).

While the NPI provides the public with access to data on the emissions of certain chemicals, critics have drawn attention to several shortcomings. In the first instance, data is largely based on estimates provided by the polluters themselves (Beder 2006). Second, the inventory lacks the necessary resources to ensure enforcement, and thus industry compliance in the initial stages was low (Gunningham and Cornwall 1994). Third, the scope of the NPI is relatively narrow compared with similar inventories elsewhere (Howes 2001); for example, it includes only a fraction of chemicals emitted and does not provide data on the use, storage, or disposal of hazardous chemicals (Beder 2006). Fourth, surveys indicate that there is a poor level of public awareness of the NPI, and this fact could encourage 'recalcitrant firms to undermine the inventory' (Howes 2001, p 550).

7.9 Participatory pitfalls: why can it go wrong?

> Public consultation, inappropriately pursued, will not enhance policy coherence or policy legitimacy.
>
> (Holland 2002a, p 77)

Realising effective and meaningful public engagement in environmental issues remains a constant challenge. There are many procedural, administrative and political reasons why participatory projects fail. When procedures are poorly designed or inadequately resourced for their purpose, they will struggle to succeed. For example, the process may be incongruent with the terms of reference or set up unreasonable expectations for the participants. Alternatively, the process might be poorly timed within the decision-making cycle (see Figure 1.1), rendering the participatory process tokenistic. The structure of the procedure might also be ill-suited to the issue at hand; too much structure can stifle creativity and the exploration of ideas, while not enough structure can result in the domination of the loudest and most articulate participants. Here an independent facilitator can play a crucial role in ensuring that all participants are involved in the discussion.

Beyond procedural matters, many participatory processes fail because of the broader political context within which the process is situated. One significant challenge is that many projects operate in an environment hostile to the democratic ideals underpinning public participation, such as inclusiveness, diversity and fairness. In most decision contexts, there will be existing ideas about who should participate in debates on the issue and how, and these may be incongruous with participatory ideals (Hendriks 2005a). For example, it is not uncommon for decision-makers and public servants to question the value of public engagement for effective EDM. They might worry, for example that public participation programs are lengthy, costly, unrepresentative and generally inefficient.[14] Some actors also query the capacity of citizens and particular groups to contribute to the issue (see Carson

---

13   See <www.npi.gov.au> (accessed 20 April 2009).

14   For an overview of these arguments, see Irvin and Stansbury (2004).

2000; Hendriks 2006). This is especially true of experts who raise concerns that the general public may misunderstand the complexity of environmental problems, or that their feedback is invalid since it is based on direct experience and anecdotal evidence rather than scientific explanation (Petts and Brooks 2006).

Another serious challenge to effective public participation is where the process lacks the necessary commitment (in terms of political will and resources) from the commissioning body (whether a government department or corporation). In many cases public input represents just one of many sources of advice to decision-makers; the degree to which they can act decisively on public feedback alone is constrained by political and financial pressures. For example, decision-makers need to weigh up multiple sources of advice and also consider their commitments to other organisations, institutions, international treaties and contractual arrangements (Holland 2002a). At the same time there are also long-term consequences of failing to implement the outcomes of participatory projects. The public can lose faith and trust in decision-makers and their institutions, and more significantly in the value of public participation itself.

Political forces outside the participatory process can also hinder its success. For example, some stakeholders and experts associated with the policy issue may resist participation because it poses a threat to the status quo. This was what occurred in the case of the CDL citizens' jury (see Case Study A) where industry groups chose to withdraw their support for the process because they feared losing the status quo policy arrangements, which they wanted to protect. In other cases groups external to the process (such as the media or excluded parties) might question the legitimacy of a process (and its outcomes). They might call into question the terms of reference of the process, the participants (and their representativeness) and the outcomes (Hendriks 2006; Wallington et al 2008).

7.10 Ensuring participation is appropriate and effective

Regardless of which level of participation is undertaken, it is essential that the program for public participation be *flexible*, as the desirable level of public involvement throughout the decision-making process may vary. From the point of view of decision-makers or proponents the obvious question is: when is it necessary to enhance public participation and move to a program which facilitates greater levels of community involvement? As argued in Chapter 6, a move toward greater participation is desirable when issues are complex (there may be several possible solutions or high levels of uncertainty), controversial or is likely to become so, or if there is a strong public reaction (Wynne 1996b). Since most contemporary environmental issues fall into one or more of these categories, offering more deliberative and empowering forms of public participation has become an essential component of EDM (see 3.11.2). At the same time care should be taken not to *over* consult the community, especially when previous experiences with participation have been tokenistic. With public participation becoming increasingly popular for private and public organisations, many groups and communities suffer from participatory fatigue, where they lack the energy and resources (particularly time) to contribute effectively to each process (WA Government 2006).

This chapter has avoided prescribing the designs and specific techniques available for public participation programs as they will vary between projects and need to be context specific. Different variables such as community interest, finance or resources, cultural context, size and scale of proposed project and so on will all influence the needs and objectives of participation programs. In addition to the design questions considered in 7.9, successful and effective public participation requires adhering to some core principles as outlined in Box 7.7.

Box 7.7: Core values for public participation

The International Association for Public Participation (IAP2) recommends using the following values when developing and implementing participatory projects (IAP2 2007b):

1. Public participation is based on the belief that those who are affected by a decision have a right to be involved in the decision-making process.

2. Public participation includes the promise that the public's contribution will influence the decision.

3. Public participation promotes sustainable decisions by recognising and communicating the needs and interests of all participants, including decision-makers.

4. Public participation seeks out and facilitates the involvement of those potentially affected by or interested in a decision.

5. Public participation seeks input from participants in designing how they participate.

6. Public participation provides participants with the information they need to participate in a meaningful way.

7. Public participation communicates to participants how their input affected the decision.

In addition to the core values listed in Box 7.7, consideration must also be given to the cultural context in which public participation takes place.

7.11 The cultural context of participation

Different cultures both within Australia and abroad have different expectations about what participation involves and what it should produce. It is important to acknowledge cultural issues when conducting public participation for to do otherwise may offend the community and create mistrust. It may also be necessary to involve translators to overcome language barriers, respect religious tradition or consult with community elders. For example, in parts of some Asian countries, a seniority system exists which requires that leaders of the community are respected and consulted on various issues. To gain the cooperation of the community, it is essential to obtain the support of community leaders. Without this support, implementation of the project may not be successful. This traditional form of community consultation is still expected in many areas.

While cultural considerations are clearly important for Australian professionals working outside Australia, they are equally important within Australia given our diverse and multicultural population. Thus participatory projects must pay particular attention to the special requirements of affected ethnic, minority and disadvantaged groups. Any potential for gender or age biases which might influence participation also requires careful scrutiny.

Participation with Indigenous peoples deserves particular mention. Designers need to be sensitive to the historical context influencing why Indigenous communities might be wary of government or industry intervention (WA Government 2005). The process also needs to respect different cultural norms, relationships, spiritual commitments and community arrangements. Considerable flexibility may also be needed to accommodate any variations to the timing and nature of a particular process. As one useful guide on Indigenous engagement explains (WA Government 2005, p 27):

> Aboriginal communities can be very busy, even in places that might seem isolated and remote to a visitor. As well as all the day-to-day community business, some communities, particularly in the winter months, can be in an almost constant state of meeting overload, with a continuous and seemingly never ending procession of government and other people wanting to engage the time and concentration of members. In addition, there may be occasions such as when a community member has died or when other important cultural business is taking place that the whole community is shut down for external business. In such instances, community business takes precedence, regardless of what meetings have been previously arranged, or the importance of the matters to be discussed.

For many practitioners consulting with Indigenous communities can be challenging work, not least because they are often in remote locations. However, they can also be the most rewarding projects. As Box 7.8 below shows, partnership-based projects with Indigenous communities can be an empowering experience for all involved.

Box 7.8: Engaging with Indigenous Australians through partnerships

A unique partnership between an Indigenous community and the Commonwealth and State Governments was trialled between 2001 and 2007 in Murdi Paaki located in the far west of New South Wales. The partnership was aimed at exploring new ways to deliver public services such as health and education to the community.

As a starting point the project team had to build trust in the community, which was very cynical of government intervention and attempts at consultation. The Murdi Paaki communities were asked how they would like to work together with government, and a strong preference for a consultative and coordinated approach was expressed. The key message to government was 'stop talking, start listening and work with us to deliver' (Jarvie 2008, p 6). The communities were also keen to develop their own priorities and to establish working parties with community representatives. Once established, the working parties developed Community Action Plans, which set out the priorities and expectations for each community. Resources and training were also invested in the community working parties to help their members build governance and leadership skills. For example, mentors and community facilitators were engaged to help transfer technical and professional skills, and regular workshops were convened.

To help improve government coordination and its interface with communities, a cross-jurisdictional team was set up with representatives from various Commonwealth and State departments. This served to minimise the policy fragmentation typically imposed on Indigenous communities, where multiple government departments run different and sometimes competing programs.

In the end the Murdi Paaki partnership generated a range of community projects, many of which have 'achieved very tangible benefits in education, health, law, justice and economic development' (Jarvie 2008, p 8). The communities themselves have also 'acknowledged the positive impact that the trial has made to their lives and their communities' (Jarvie 2008, p 5).

There appear to have been several elements to the success of the Murdi Paaki trial including (Jarvie 2008, pp 10–11):

- high-level and long-term commitment;

- building productive relationships;

- government really listening;

- the right people on the ground (and everywhere else);

- learning through doing (one size does not fit all);

- the power of ideas;

- accepting that progress would be slow and steady (and sometimes not so steady).

Source: Jarvie 2008.

The concept of 'culture' also extends into the business and industry world. The embedded culture of an organisation or industry may affect the way in which you design and approach public participation programs. For example, when consulting industrial organisations for their input into a project it is necessary to appreciate their value positions, the structure and lines of responsibility in the organisation, the corporate culture more broadly, and also particular issues which are unique to that community.

7.12 Conclusion

Participation is an important but often feared part of the EDM process. It opens administrators, businesses and decision-makers up to public scrutiny and judgment. But on the other hand it offers them insights into community views, innovative ideas and local knowledge. Participation also helps to legitimise decisions and aids their implementation. A large array of participatory processes now exist, providing novel ways to engage a range of different actors, including the broader public. Such public involvement can range from mere provision of information through to programs where communities work in partnership with decision-makers, and in some case are delegated the power to make decisions.

Our message here is that participation in context is what matters. Designing any public participation process must take into account the broader political and social context within which it is operates. Without adequate consideration of these contextual factors, attempts to meaningfully engage the public in environmental decisions are vulnerable to failure.

8

Tools for Environmental Decision-making

8.1 Introduction

In Chapter 6 we explored the wide range of information and knowledge available for environmental decision-making (EDM), the challenges in managing this knowledge and in bringing different forms of knowledge together to address environmental issues. Other chapters have shown the complexities of making decisions on contemporary sustainability problems that do not have clear-cut, straightforward solutions. This chapter examines the growing range of tools developed to help make sense of this complex decision-making landscape and to facilitate actions for addressing these problems.

Box 8.1: What is a 'tool'?

A 'tool' can be defined as: a device or instrument used to perform a particular function or job.

If we think of common tools, such as a hammer or a screwdriver, it is easy to recognise that they are designed to carry out a particular function. You cannot for example, effectively drive a nail into wood with a screwdriver, nor a screw with a hammer. Similarly, environmental decision-making tools are each designed for specific purposes. Extending this analogy, just as building projects may require the use of many tools, so too do complex environmental decisions.

Tools have been developed for a variety of purposes. They enable the collection, process-ing and analysis of *data* into more meaningful *information* to help identify and diagnose problems, assess their impacts and assist decision-makers to evaluate the consequences of alternatives, set priorities, allocate resources and implement decisions. For example, Ecological Footprint Analysis (EFA) (Wackernagel and Rees 1996) introduced in Chapter 1, is a tool that has shown our global consumption of material and resources is exceed-ing the regenerative capacity of our natural capital, and has helped us identify the urgent challenge of dramatically reducing Ecological Footprints (EF). A number of other tools can be used to inform us on the best way to meet this challenge of doing better with less. Life Cycle Assessment (LCA) is one such tool specifically developed for assessing impacts of a product or service throughout its life cycle to help us reduce material and resource inputs and waste outputs.

Then there are tools that are specifically designed to change the behaviour of individuals and organisations to achieve sustainability goals and targets. These include environmental education programs, taxes, subsidies and regulation.

The range of tools used for EDM has increased rapidly in recent years and is now extens-ive. Environmental professionals (see Chapters 1 and 5) use these tools and instruments to inform decision-making, while other participants in EDM may be interpreting and appraising information that is produced from these tools for making decisions. It is therefore essential for those involved in EDM to understand why and how these tools are used.

Of course, tools do not operate in a vacuum and are not purely technical or analytical devices – judgments, assumptions and choices made in the use of tools allow for subjectivity in what may appear to be a rigorous, rational and value-free process. Tools may also be used to *manipulate* data to achieve preconceived outcomes or support results that closely reflect an ideological or political viewpoint (Ness et al 2007). This is common in opinion polls or surveys where questions and responses can be manipulated to achieve desired outcomes (see 8.5 for Willingness to Pay surveys). The selection and use of tools is strongly influenced by the social and political setting within which decisions are made and depends on many factors including the bias, values, culture and capacity constraints of the individuals and organisations choosing and using the tools. For example, a decision-maker's choices are bounded by the 'trade-off between the desire to make the "correct" decision and the invest-ment of time and effort required to achieve this ideal' (Lockwood 2005, p 9).

These socio-political and value-laden aspects are often hidden inside a tool's 'blackbox'. In this chapter we intend to open up this blackbox to examine the uses and strengths of dif-ferent tools for informing and improving EDM and highlight their abuses and limitations. We will also examine the effectiveness of EDM tools in helping us satisfy sustainability principles and achieve integrated sustainability outcomes across all three Triple Bottom Line (TBL) dimensions (see Chapter 2). Much has been written on procedural and technical aspects of tools, hence we will *not* provide an in-depth explanation of these, but will refer you to literature which covers these areas.

We begin by establishing categories for examining numerous tools. This will allow us to introduce a wide range of tools, provide a broad understanding of their aims, interrelationships, complementarities, and role within EDM. This will be followed by discussion of individual tools. We conclude by considering some of the socio-political factors that influence decision-makers and tool users in the selection and application of tools.

8.2 Categories of EDM tools

There are many ways of representing and categorising tools (see Merkhofer 1998; Ness et al 2007; Petts 1999). For the purposes of this chapter it is useful to distinguish two broad types of tools depending on their role in the EDM process. First there are *behavioural* tools that seek to change the way a particular organisation, population or set of individuals behaves. These are the classic instruments of public policy where government may use authority to *regulate* to prevent pollution, or provide *incentives* such as rebates to encourage uptake of solar power, or *advocate* a particular behaviour such as recycling by educating the broader community, or seek to *build capacity* in the community through training and resources (Althaus et al 2007; Schneider and Ingram 1990).

Table 8.1 lists the various approaches and associated behavioural tools governments and organisations might use to induce behavioural change. A number of these approaches and tools are often used together to help deliver policy outcomes. For example, potable water conservation programs in New South Wales have included regulation and fines to enforce compliance with mandatory water restrictions, grants to local councils and community groups to develop and implement water conservation measures, rebates for installing rainwater tanks and community education campaigns to raise awareness about droughts, demand management, and water reuse.[1]

Although 'command and control' type behavioural tools, such as regulation, are most widely used, a new generation of policy tools – 'new' environmental policy instruments (NEPIs) has emerged and grown rapidly since the late 1980s. Examples of NEPIs include eco-taxes and other market-based instruments (MBIs) such as emissions charges and tradeable permits (Carter 2007), ecolabelling and voluntary agreements (Jordan et al 2003). Australia's experimentation with NEPIs has been driven by many different reasons including microeconomic reform and attention to property rights (Papadakis and Grant 2003). The most recent example of a NEPI in Australia is the Federal Labor Government's Emissions Trading Scheme being considered for adoption in 2009. Other examples include the Federal Government's Greenhouse Challenge,[2] the New South Wales Government's Extended Producer Responsibility (EPR) scheme[3] and the South Australian Government's Container Deposit refunds[4] (see Case Study A). In Australia, NEPIs are currently used as complementary tools alongside regulation. Their future role in achieving environmental protection will be determined by their success in achieving behaviour change (Papadakis and Grant 2003).

---

1   <www.waterforlife.nsw.gov.au> (accessed 7 March 2009).

2   <www.enviroment.gov.eau/settlements/challenge> (accessed 3 May 2009).

3   <www.environment.nsw.gov.au/war/EPRPriority2007.htm> (accessed 3 May 2009).

4   <www.epa.sa.gov.au/cdl.html> (accessed 3 May 2009).

Making a choice between different behavioural tools to achieve certain outcomes is based on many underlying assumptions about the effects these tools may have on target populations (Table 8.1). For example, incentive based policy tools assume that individuals are utility maximising rational actors[5] who respond to positive or negative incentives, have the opportunity to make choices and have adequate information to select an alternative which is in their own best interest. But we know that these conditions are not always present in environmental decisions. Moreover, in some areas of environmental policy people's behaviour might be more swayed by appealing to altruistic rather than instrumental goals (Schneider and Ingram 1990).

Table 8.1 Behavioural tools and their underlying assumptions

Approach Used	Example Tools	Underlying Assumptions
Authority	Regulation, Legislation	Target populations usually obey authority and are responsive to leader-follower relationships
Incentive/ Disincentive	MBIs such as Fines, Sanctions, Subsidies, Grants, Charges, Taxes	Individuals respond to positive incentives and most choose higher-value alternative
Capacity Building	Information, Education, Training	Lack of skills, resources, information result in barriers to decision-making
Symbolic	Pronouncements, Ecolabelling, Voluntary Action	People are motivated from within and make decisions about whether or not to undertake policy related actions based on their values and beliefs
Learning	Collaborative networks, Participatory approaches (see Chapter 7)	Agencies and target audiences do not know what needs to be done and can learn this to improve policy

Based on Schneider and Ingram 1990.

Since EDM is a political process where decisions are shaped by competing interests, the selection of particular behavioural tools to achieve policy outcomes is vulnerable to preferential choices influenced by these interests (Carter 2007). These vulnerabilities have significant implications for the resulting outcomes. The history of Container Deposit Legislation (CDL) demonstrates these socio-political influences on the choice of litter control tools (see Case Study A). For example, industry lobbied the New South Wales Government to reject CDL (an incentive tool) and funded the 'Do the Right Thing' litter campaign (an education tool) as a replacement. This thinking persists in New South Wales despite evidence from South Australia and internationally, where CDL is in place, and works well as both a litter control and recycling instrument.

The second category of tools is *analytical* tools used to inform and assist the process of EDM. Analytical tools are typically employed to gather and process data to evaluate and analyse particular activities, products, processes or policies. For example, Environmental Impact Assessment (EIA) may be carried out so that a proposal for a new road in your local area considers alternative strategies to the proposal and gives due consideration to environmental and social factors.

---

5   Assumes that, when making choices, individuals act to maximise their welfare/utility through satisfaction of individual preferences (Chee 2004; Sagoff 1998).

Table 8.2 presents a number of analytical tools clustered together based on their primary role.

Table 8.2 Analytical tools

Primary Role	Example Tools
Impact assessment	Environmental Impact Assessment (EIA), Strategic Environmental Assessment (SEA), Social Impact Assessment (SIA), Health Impact Assessment (HIA)
Risk management	Environmental, ecological and human health risk assessment
Environmental management of organisational impacts	Environmental Management System (EMS), Auditing
Options evaluation	Cost-Benefit Analysis (CBA), Multi-Criteria Decision Analysis (MCDA), Multi-Criteria Analysis (MCA)
Computer aided decision support	Modelling, Geographic Information Systems (GIS)
Material accounting	Life Cycle Assessment (LCA), Material Flux Analysis (MFA), Ecological Footprint Analysis (EFA)
Monitoring, evaluation and reporting	Environmental monitoring, Auditing, State of the Environment Reporting (SoER), Corporate Sustainability Reporting (CSR)

Although, each tool listed in Table 8.2 has been developed to perform a particular job, many have applications beyond just their primary role. For example, in addition to their primary functions, LCA, risk -management (see Chapter 9) and CBA each provide a *framework* for options evaluation. Table 8.3 further illustrates the primary and secondary roles of analytical tools across the EDM process.

Table 8.3 Coverage of tools across the EDM process

Decision-making Stage	Analytical Tools						
	SEA EIA	Risk	EMS	CBA MCDA/ MCA	LCA MFA	GIS Modelling	SoER CSR Auditing
Identifying issues and framing the problem	◆	◆	◆		◆	◆	◆
Analysing impacts	◆	◆	◆		◆	◆	
Identifying, assessing and narrowing options	◆	◆		◆	◆	Δ	
Decision implementation	Δ	◆	◆				
Monitoring and reporting	Δ	Δ	◆			Δ	◆

◆ Primary role Δ Secondary role
(Note: Behavioural tools are used mainly during the decision implementation stage)

The selection and use of tools is not a straightforward process of picking and mixing tools to address various problems. In reality, it is more complicated and requires an understanding of the application of each tool within the various stages of the decision-making cycle (see Chapter 1) and their inter-relationships and uses as complementary aids to decision-making.

A variety of tools, both analytical and behavioural, can be integrated such that outputs from the application of one tool can provide inputs for another (Petts 1999) and tools are often used in combination to improve decision-making. Environmental Impact Assessment (EIA) is a tool to evaluate impacts of particular projects. Many tools can be used to assist the analysis and effectiveness of an EIA. For example: GIS for data collection; modelling to predict the impacts of alternative strategies; risk management to assess and manage the ecological and human risk aspects of the proposed development (see Chapter 9); CBA to compare the overall benefits and costs of the proposal, learning tools like participation to involve the public in EDM and monitoring and auditing to evaluate the efficacy of measures implemented to mitigate impacts. However, not all tools are compatible and integration of tools should be used with caution (English et al 1999; Scrase and Sheate 2002).

Whereas behavioural policy tools are usually recognised as having a strong socio-political orientation, the technical nature of analytical tools makes us especially inclined to accept these as objective and apolitical means of achieving ends. This cloak of objectivity pervades EDM. In Chapter 6 we argued that scientific expert knowledge has remained dominant over other forms of knowledge because of its claims of objectivity, even though it is not value-free and is prone to the biases of experts and other interpreters. For this reason and also because analytical tools are prolifically used to inform every stage of the decision-making process (Table 8.3), we will devote most of this chapter to discussing the role and application of analytical tools and their limitations.

Of the large variety of analytical tools available, in the following section we will investigate only some of the key tools that are well-established and institutionalised. We also explore some of their newer applications and consider some emerging tools. Our selection of tools is such that we consider a tool from each of the groups represented in Table 8.2 (note: risk management is discussed in detail in Chapter 9) and across the various decision-making stages (Table 8.3).

We will start our discussion with two familiar and oft-used environmental decision-making tools – Environmental Impact Assessment (EIA) and Environmental Management Systems (EMS). Both these tools are based on systematic processes to assess and address environmental impacts, but are applied at very different decision-making scales. The focus of an EMS is on managing an organisation's operations and environmental impacts, while EIA is a public process through which the likely environmental effects of a proposal are taken into account by the consenting authority in the decision-making process (Sheate 1996).

8.3 Environmental Impact Assessment

Environmental Impact Assessment (EIA) is a tool designed to help assess the environmental impact of a proposed development, such as an infrastructure project, or a new policy or program. In practice EIA is a procedure that seeks to bring environmental factors into consideration alongside traditional considerations such as the economic costs and benefits of a development proposal. The environmental information obtained through EIA can assist decision-makers to determine whether a project should proceed, and if so, what conditions should be imposed on the development such that harmful impacts might be mitigated or avoided.

We usually think of EIA as a formal legislation-based process associated with assessing impacts of specific projects – building a freeway, a dam, or clearing a forest. However, as suggested above, EIA is relevant to a wide range of activities which include the development of 'new policies, plans or programs', administrative arrangements and legislation. In fact, indirectly, these activities may have far more powerful and widespread impacts on the environment than single projects such as a freeway or dam. Strategic Environmental Assessment (SEA), which covers these broader matters, has developed from EIA and, because of its focus on broader and longer-term planning, is considered a more effective tool for achieving sustainable development (Thomas 2005, also see Box 8.3).

Smyth (1990, p 4) has commented that EIA is said to be 'the single most important method of project evaluation we have'. However, EIA does not guarantee prevention of environmental impacts, but rather, it is a systematic process to ensure that decision-makers take into account possible risks and predicted environmental consequences of development proposals.

EIA deserves particular attention in this chapter since it is a tool specifically developed for EDM, and is well-established and widely used.

8.3.1 EIA process and its participants

Each jurisdiction has its own specific procedures and processes for EIA. For example the *Environmental Planning and Assessment Act 1979* (NSW) (and later amendments) lays out the EIA procedures for the State of New South Wales.

However, most EIA procedures have similar basic steps and common elements (Box 8.2). These steps are not undertaken as a linear process, rather there are many interlinkages and iterations. For example, the detailed evaluation of impacts during the EIA report preparation may lead to a review of scoping if impacts not considered before become apparent.

EIA is generally considered a technocratic, rational process which relies heavily on expert scientific input (Connelly and Richardson 2005; Jay et al 2007). However, as noted in Box 8.2, decisions made at each step are likely to reflect the interests and values of the participants in the process. The main actors and institutions involved are the proponent of the activity who is responsible for undertaking the assessment, the government agency responsible for administering the EIA process, the decision-making authority (usually an elected representative and/or government agency) that evaluates the EIA report and the public who are invited to comment on the findings of the EIA. There are also a number of expert consultants engaged by the proponent to undertake the various aspects of the EIA process. The fact that EIA reports are conducted or commissioned by the proponent is contentious as it means that the consultants working on the EIA report are 'either directly or indirectly, employed by a party whose interests may differ in significant ways from the public interest' (Beder 1990, p 45). Past experience has also shown that there are various ways in which proponents formulate EIA reports so that their proposal is seen in a more favourable light. Some have used the document to highlight the advantages and trivialise the disadvantages associated with the proposal. With the use of careful language, a proponent may try to brush over any adverse environmental effects, and any uncertainty surrounding the effects of the project is rarely acknowledged in detail (Beder 1995).

Box 8.2: Procedural steps in an EIA process

Consideration of alternatives – The identification and comparison of a number of alternatives (including not taking action) that can satisfy the aims of the proposed action is an important factor in determining the best option (Wood 2003). In some jurisdictions, this step is under-taken as part of *scoping* (Thomas 2005).

Screening – This step is about determining whether an EIA is to be undertaken and what level of assessment is needed. Different jurisdictions have particular criteria for triggering the need for an EIA based on the 'potential *significance* of environmental impacts' of the proposed activity (Thomas 2005, p 156).

Scoping – The purpose of scoping is to identify the issues and impacts that are relevant to the proposal and consider the depth of analysis required for the EIA (Thomas 2005).

Both screening and scoping increase the efficiency of the EIA process by early determination of the level of assessment required and by focussing attention and resources on significant issues (Wood 2003). However, *what's in, what's out and what's important* relies on subjective choices of the participants involved in these steps of EIA. Screening is generally conducted by the proponent and the relevant government agencies, while scoping usually involves public consultation (Thomas 2005; Wood 2003).

EIA report preparation – This involves the documentation and reporting of the information gathered during the EIA process and includes a description of the proposed activity, predicted environmental effects, alternatives to the activity, and mitigation measures to be adopted. This report can take many forms depending on the significance of anticipated impacts determined during the screening stage of the process. The Environmental Impact Statement (EIS) is prob-ably the best-known EIA report and represents the highest level of assessment.

Report review – Public review of EIA reports verifies the quality and adequacy of the assess-ment for the purposes of decision-making (Sadler 1996 cited in Wood 2003, p 198). This is the one step in the EIA process where formal public consultation takes place. In Australia, draft EIA reports are placed on exhibition usually for a period of a few weeks and public com-ments are published as part of the review process (Wood 2003).

Decision-making – Although decisions are required at each stage, the key decision in the EIA process comes after review of the EIA report when the decision-maker (for example, a minister or public authority such as local government) chooses whether or not to authorise the proposed activity and place conditions on the approval. Although decision-makers take account of the information in the EIA report, other perspectives, such as political considerations, may hold greater sway in the final analysis (Jay et al 2007). For example, the Western Australian Government approved the extension of an iron ore mine despite the EIA concluding that it was likely to result in the destruction of rare flora (Weir 2003 cited in Pope et al 2004, p 603).

Post-decision monitoring and auditing – Monitoring and auditing, sometimes referred to as EIA follow-up, are conducted by the proponent and the environmental authorities to assess outcomes against predictions, generally to ensure that terms and conditions of approval are met (Wood 2003) and, importantly, this information can be used to inform and improve future practice of EIA (Morrison-Saunders et al 2001).

Public participation (see Chapter 7) should be an integral component of the EIA process because this provides an avenue for informing the public, access to different types of knowledge (see Chapter 6), and identification of many values, views and concerns (see

Chapter 3). This also highlights areas of conflict, fosters trust and respect between the parties involved and enhances decision-making and the quality of decisions (see Thomas 2005; Wood 2003).

However, the level and effectiveness of participation in EIA are uneven. Typically, the public is consulted quite late in the process, *after* publication of the EIA report and just *prior* to the final decision (Wood 1995, 2003). Forms of participation are usually one-off public exhibits, public meetings and mechanisms for providing written submissions on the findings of the EIA to the proponent or decision-maker. These are neither particularly interactive nor deliberative forms of engagement (see Chapter 7).

If the public is to play an effective role during the EIA process, participation must commence in the early screening and scoping stages of the process (Thomas 2005). Moreover, the participatory mechanisms and information provided to the public must be designed to meet their needs. For example, the EIA documentation (for example, the EIS) must be clear, readable, well-presented and with limited technical information (Harvey 1998).

8.3.2 Discussion of EIA

EIA provides an opportunity for the whole process of development to be open to scrutiny for the benefit of all actors in the EDM process – the proponent, the government (or decision-making authority) and the public – resulting in more carefully thought out projects (Gilpin 1995). According to Jay et al (2007) EIA has made a significant contribution to development processes through not only modifying designs, but also institutional learning and stakeholder and community involvement. Similarly, Wood (2003, p 315) argues that the EIA process brings numerous *direct* benefits such as 'the increased use of modification and mitigation of projects, the use of more stringent conditions upon permissions and the refusal of potentially environmentally damaging proposals which might previously have been approved', as well as important *indirect* benefits such as changing the behaviour of the participants in the EIA process. Examples of the latter include increased public participation, increased coordination between environmental protection authorities and improved environmental awareness amongst proponents (Wood 2003).

Despite these benefits and EIA's theoretical capacity to prevent environmental damage from development, the practice of EIA has been criticised on many occasions for failing to deliver satisfactory environmental outcomes. We will now turn to these.

EIA is often criticised for being used as a tool to justify predetermined decisions. This criticism is commonly made when the public review of an EIA report does not influence the outcome of a proposed development. An example of this is the $1.9 billion desalination plant in Kurnell, New South Wales. There was much opposition to the development of the desalination plant and associated infrastructure based on inadequate environmental assessment of environmental issues such as impacts of high energy consumption, effects on groundwater hydrology of the Kurnell Peninsula, impacts of highly saline effluent on the ocean environment and the effects on the roosting site of the Grey-headed Flying Fox (EDO 2006). Although the New South Wales Government later signed a contract to establish a wind farm to power the desalination plant, critics maintained that green power would be wasted by supplying large amounts of energy to a project which was not necessary (Tadros and Robins 2008). There was also concern that adequate consideration had not been given to more sustainable water management alternatives, such as recycling (EDO 2006). Much of the criticism of the environmental assessment was also linked to new environmental planning legislation which allowed environmental assessment of the desalination plant to be based on concept designs, thus limiting detailed assessment of impacts. The construction of the plant went ahead despite widespread community opposition and concerns about the environmental assessment report and process. This gave rise to community suspicions about the process being a mere formality to justify a foregone conclusion. In a private members statement to the New South Wales Parliament, a local resident stated: 'This makes a sham of the public consultation process and the government has demonstrated that it is determined to ride roughshod over the residents' (Kerr 2007, p 652). The use of EIA as a legitimation device for predetermined decisions reflects a failure to integrate EIA into the planning and political processes.

Another failing of EIA is that it can neglect cumulative impacts as specific projects are assessed on a case-by-case basis. The impacts of individual activities may be small, but if many such activities are put together, the cumulative impact and the interrelation of various impacts could be significant (Beder 2006). This issue is highlighted by Glasson et al (1994, p 301) who argue that 'small individual mineral extraction operations may not need an EIA, but the total impact of several of these projects may well be "significant"'.

EIAs are often project specific and although alternative approaches are considered these are limited by the late stage at which EIA takes place in a project development cycle (Wood 2003). In many cases, a project will already be planned quite specifically by the time an EIA is prepared. For example, EIA for building a new road to alleviate traffic problems may be triggered only after this decision has been made. This limits the alternatives to the investigation of a number of different road routes only and does not allow consideration of alternatives such as other transport strategies, for example cycling or public transport, to address the problem.

EIA scope and boundary is often site specific and based on the local effects of a development. For example, the EIS and subsequent approval of Anvil Hill coal mine in the Hunter Valley of New South Wales has been the subject of several legal proceedings for failing to consider the indirect impacts of greenhouse gas emissions from the electricity generated by burning the coal mined from this development. In response to one of these appeals, the Land and Environment Court of New South Wales made a landmark ruling that the decision to accept the EIS was 'flawed and invalid' and the link between mining coal and greenhouse emissions should have been considered in evaluating the project (Davies 2006; also see Box 1.1).

EIA procedures are often undertaken in limited and inadequate time frames. This is a particular concern in cases where the results of biological studies are central to the assessment process. Short time frames for assessment do not allow collection of adequate *time-series data*[6] and consequently natural fluctuations in populations of animals and plants in the area may not be recognised. Without an understanding of natural cycles, it is not possible to know whether changes which may occur after a development are related to the development or are a part of a natural cycle of change.

This narrow spatial and temporal focus of EIA on individual, isolated projects which only allow consideration of limited alternatives rather than broader strategic options that consider far-reaching and cumulative consequences has raised questions about the effectiveness of EIA as a tool for achieving sustainable development. In response to these limitations, Strategic Environmental Assessment (SEA) has evolved to deliver a more comprehensive approach to environment assessment and planning (see Box 8.3).

---

6   Time-series data are data gathered for a particular area over time so that natural fluctuations in populations
     of animals and plants and other environmental parameters may be revealed.

Box 8.3: Strategic Environmental Assessment (SEA)

SEA is an extension of EIA and emerged to address project EIA weaknesses such as 'it starts too late, ends too soon and is too site specific' (Shepherd and Ortolano 1996, p 322). SEA is used to assess the impacts of 'policies, plans and programs' at various levels of governance – local, regional, national. It is a tiered approach to decision-making, with the expectation that if socio-economic and environmental impacts are considered at the top of the decision-making hierarchy, there should be fewer problems at the lower decision-making levels (Fischer 2003). This high-level strategic approach to impact assessment allows up-front consideration of cumulative and synergistic effects over longer temporal and broader spatial scales. SEA provides for integrated and consistent decision-making and a mechanism for trickling down sustainability principles from policies through to individual projects (Therivel et al 1992 in Wood 2003, p 332).

A case study (Sheate et al 2001) from the city of Erlangen in Germany demonstrates the benefits of SEA when developing a local land use plan for the city. The land-use planning was integrated with the city's landscape plan for a 10–15 years horizon. To ensure that all economic, ecological, social and cultural concerns were identified and addressed, the city council engaged a variety of actors when conducting the SEA. The following points demonstrate the effectiveness of SEA as a tool for achieving a high-quality plan (Sheate et al 2001):

- SEA strengthened the integration of the environment into decision-making.

- With respect to tiered decision-making, information transfer from the land use plan level down to the building plan level was evident.

- A high degree of integration and coordination was achieved since there were many channels of communication (horizontal and vertical, formal and informal).

SEA has been around since the mid-1980s and although different approaches to the application of SEA have led to some confusion about its exact nature, it is clear that SEA can improve the consideration of sustainability aspects in policies, plans and programs (Fischer and Seaton 2002).

Although there are in-built checks and balances to ensure that information contained in an EIA report is accurate and comprehensive (Kinnaird 1990), this does not necessarily guarantee validity and accuracy of information. For instance, there are often limitations and errors in scientific data provided for EISs. Common problems include the capability of investigators, the scientific methodologies applied, the timeframe chosen and limited consulting budgets.

Post-decision monitoring and auditing is one of the weakest areas of EIA systems all over the world. This also applies to Australia where the provisions for follow-up are discretionary and not mandatory (Wood 2003).

As tools for sustainable development both EIA and SEA are criticised for tending to focus on biophysical aspects of the environment. Both these tools emerged as an attempt to bring environmental consideration into decision-making to counterbalance the emphasis on economic issues. However, assessments are increasingly integrating the three pillars (environmental, social and economic) of sustainability (Morrison-Saunders and Therivel 2006). Such Integrated Assessments (IA) – also referred to as Integrated Environmental Assessments (IEA) or Sustainability Appraisals – may use other theme-specific assessments such as Social Impact Assessment (SIA) and Health Impact Assessment (HIA) in parallel with EIA or SEA to extend their coverage of sustainability issues (Vanclay 2004 in Hacking and Guthrie 2008, p 77). On the one hand, IAs improve efficiency, coherence and allow better identification of synergistic effects and linkages between triple bottom line (TBL) issues to help deliver sustainable outcomes. On the other hand, integration can marginalise biophysical environmental concerns and allow trade-offs between TBL issues to be hidden (Morrison-Saunders and Therivel 2006). To overcome this compartmentalisation of the three pillars of sustainability and successfully apply IA tools to inform decision-making for real world problems that intersect many disciplines (Schneider 1997) requires a more holistic view of sustainability (see Chapter 2) and transdisciplinary thinking (see Chapter 6).

8.4   Environmental Management Systems

An Environmental Management System (EMS) is a tool which provides a broad range of organisations including industries, companies and governments with a framework for proactively and *continually* improving their environmental performance. It follows a set of step-by-step procedures to *systematically* identify, assess and manage the impact of organi-sational activities, products and services through the development and implementation of environmental policy and management programs.

Although organisations can develop their own informal EMS based on the continuous improvement cycle of Plan-Do-Check-Act (PDCA) (Figure 8.1), formal voluntary *process standards* for EMS have been developed and provide a common set of rules and guidelines which have been approved by a recognised body (Starkey 1998).

The two main voluntary standards for EMSs today are the International Organization for Standardization's (ISO) ISO 14001 which has worldwide applicability and the European Union's Eco-Management and Audit Scheme (EMAS).

The global uptake of the international standard for EMS, ISO 14001 by a broad range of public and private sector organisations increased from 257 to 129,199 between 1996 and 2006.[7] Several factors influenced this strong growth in the use of EMSs. Rising public awareness and concern about environmental degradation and natural resource depletion, compliance with environmental laws and regulations, risks and costs associated with poor environmental management and issues related to the globalisation of business and trade led to a growing focus on corporate sustainability and social responsibility (Chapter 5). There is increasing pressure on industry and business to improve their performance in the areas of social and ecological responsibility while at the same time enhancing economic viability, profitability and market competitiveness.

We will briefly consider the nature and components of the most widely used EMS stand-ard – ISO 14001 before exploring the benefits and criticisms of EMSs.

8.4.1 The ISO 14001 standard

The ISO 14001 standard specifies the minimum requirements for an EMS against which an organisation may be audited and certified by an independent external third party

---

7   <www.iso.org/iso/survey2006.pdf> (accessed 3 May 2009); <www.iso.org/iso/pressrelease. htm?refid=Ref1021> (accessed 3 May 2009); <www.iso.org/iso/en/iso9000–14000/pdf/survey2005.pdf> (accessed 3 May 2009).

(Hortensius and Barthel 1997). This international standard was launched in 1996 and has been adopted by Australia and New Zealand (Thomas 2005).

The five main cyclical stages involved in preparing an ISO14001 compliant EMS and maintaining continuous improvement are represented in Figure 8.1. Guidelines for ISO 14001 recommend that an Initial Environmental Review should be undertaken before commencing the EMS process. An initial environmental review helps to ensure that organisation-specific issues and pressures are identified by establishing the internal and external context of the organisation through identification of the impacts and significance of environmental aspects, as well as legal, regulatory and existing management practices and procedures.

The EMS can be integrated with other management requirements (SA/SNZ 2004) and systems of an organisation that may include Occupational Health and Safety (OHS) Systems, Quality Management Systems and Risk Management Systems. In fact, the ISO 14001 standard for EMS has evolved from the ISO 9000 series of standards for quality management. Both these *process standards* follow the PDCA cycle (Figure 8.1) to meet the requirements of the standards. These similarities assist organisations with existing quality systems to adopt EMSs and even integrate these systems to improve efficiency and effectiveness.

ISO 14001 is the first of the ISO 14000 family of *voluntary* international standards which provide a suite of management tools to address environmental aspects and impacts of an

Figure 8.1 Plan-Do-Check-Act (PDCA) and ISO14001 EMS model

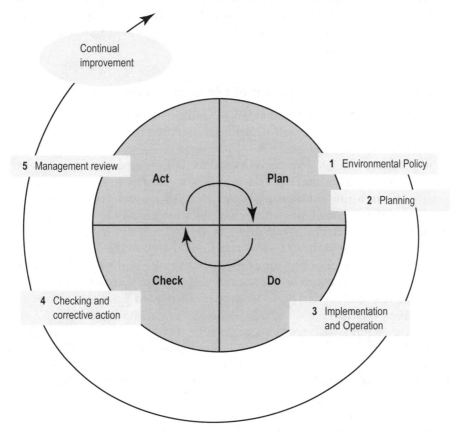

Adapted from Hortensius and Barthel 1997.

organisation's processes, products and services. These include LCA (ISO 14040 and 14041), and environmental auditing (ISO 14010, 14011 and 14012). While these standards are designed to be mutually supportive and inform an EMS, they can also be used independently (see 8.6 for discussion on LCA).

Environmental auditing has particular importance for an EMS. Broadly, it is a tool that helps systematic documentation and evaluation of an organisation's environmental performance against preset criteria. For example, industrial sites can be audited to confirm compliance with air and water emissions standards, occupational health and safety regulation and accident and emergency procedures. An EMS audit, specifically, provides a standard procedure for determining if an organisation's EMS conforms to ISO 14001 (or EMAS) specification by providing information to the management on proper implementation and maintenance (Hillary 1998). External accredited independent consultants can audit and verify an organisation's conformity with the ISO 14001 standard and provide certification. An organisation may choose to conduct internal audits to evaluate the adequacy of their EMS, without seeking external verification and certification. However, the benefits of certification include enhanced public image, increased confidence by investors, improved access to funds and improved organisational culture (Taylor et al 2001).

ISO 14001 is a *generic process* to achieve self-set environmental objectives and targets through incremental improvements. Unlike stringent government regulation, the voluntary, self-regulatory and flexible nature of EMSs allows organisations to respond to their specific needs in relation to their 'operations, characteristics, location and level of risk' (Rondinelli and Vastag 1996 cited in Morrow and Rondinelli 2002, p 163). The popularity of EMSs may be attributed to this flexible one-size-fits-all aspect, but as we will discuss below this has also been its greatest criticism.

8.4.2 Do EMSs achieve improvement in environmental performance?

The implementation of an EMS is intended to result in improved environmental performance, but does this happen in practice? Before responding to this question, let us consider the benefits and criticisms of EMSs.

At a minimum level, an EMS can act as a catalyst for the consideration of environmental issues in corporate decision-making and provides assistance to organisations that wish to improve their environmental performance (Nawrocka and Parker 2009). The adoption of EMSs facilitates risk management and pollution control and can save companies money by improving efficiency, reducing costs of materials, fines and penalties enabling 'the CEO to sleep better at night' (Morrow and Rondenelli 2002, p 164). It can also be used as a tool for helping organisations move away from mere end-of-pipe pollution control and regulatory compliance toward at-source pollution prevention and systems-based approaches (see 1.5) such as life cycle assessment, extended producer responsibility and cleaner production (see Chapters 1 and 2; Section 8.7) to achieve performance which goes beyond compliance but is still economically viable. Fuji Xerox Ltd[8] is one company that has used an EMS and these approaches for improving its environmental performance and profitability.

However, despite the reported benefits, EMSs based on the ISO 14001 standard have been criticised for failing to guarantee improvements in environmental performance and sustainability. Organisations can satisfy the standard and demonstrate commitment to continuous environmental management by achieving minimum compliance levels while

8   <www.fujixerox.com.au/about/media/articles/300> (accessed 2 December 2008).

having a terrible environmental record (Netherwood 1998). Dunphy et al (2007) support this point of view by arguing that organisations can falsely assume that implementation of an EMS produces sustainability outcomes, when in reality self-set performance targets with incremental performance improvements may not be enough to lead to significant improvements nor sustainability.

Audits of ISO 14001 EMSs and resulting certifications can be motivated by the organisation's desire to legitimise its operations and behaviour by improving public image, satisfying stakeholders about its environmental performance and hence increasing competitiveness rather than a concern with *actually* improving environmental performance (Taylor et al 2001).

Other criticisms of EMSs have included their use as an internal management tool only (Kao-Cushing 2000), hence neglecting consideration of indirect impacts which lie beyond the boundaries of the organisation. There is also a tendency for organisations to narrowly focus on only legal compliance and the biophysical aspects and impacts of their operations and products or services (Thompson 2002) rather than considering TBL. However, this view seems to be slowly changing as companies are recognising that environmental issues in business coincide with economic and public arenas, and that impacts beyond their boundaries need to be addressed by including consideration of supply chain and end of life impacts (Van der Vorst et al 1999).

Although the ISO 14001 EMS standard does not require public disclosure of environmental information and performance (Nawrocka and Parker 2009), it is clear that reporting, such as corporate sustainability reporting (CSR) discussed later in this chapter, is an important part of adaptive management (2.9.4), and a means to close the loop and provide feedback to the policy, objectives and targets set in the EMS.

Results of a recent study exploring whether EMSs improve environmental performance concluded that performance varies and depends on factors such as 'the management style and goals of the particular company, its operating environment, culture and stakeholders' (Nawrocka and Parker 2009, p 606). Further, the extent to which an EMS will help improve environmental outcomes, and beyond that facilitate a paradigm shift towards achieving sustainability (Netherwood 1998) also depends on the organisation's understanding of long-term TBL benefits, stakeholder engagement, and allocation of appropriate resources for on-going implementation, auditing and continual improvement of an EMS.

8.5 Cost-Benefit Analysis

Cost-Benefit Analysis (CBA), also referred to as Benefit-Cost Analysis, is essentially a tool for organising information on monetary costs (disadvantages) and benefits (advantages) of an activity and its various alternatives to select the best and most economically efficient option (Beder 2006; Dale and English 1998; Scrase and Sheate 2002). CBA is used extensively by governments, international banks, aid agencies and private corporations to evaluate and prioritise policies, projects and investment decisions (Beder 2006). For example, the World Bank routinely uses CBA to help prioritise various interventions with environmental consequences, for example, studies that estimate the health benefits of air pollution controls in developing nations (WBI 2002). CBA is also used as part of the EIA process to compare alternatives.

Sant (1992, p 63) and Common (1995, p 167) outline five steps to be followed when conducting a CBA:

1. The project must be clearly defined. Separate CBAs will be necessary if a choice of projects is being considered.

2. All the impacts and effects (that is, the costs and benefits) need to be identified. This includes private and social costs and benefits, present and future costs and benefits, and local, regional and national costs and benefits. These impacts need to be considered over the full lifetime of the project. For example, in the case of a nuclear power plant producing electricity, the end of the project is not when the plant stops producing electricity, but when the nuclear wastes associated with it no longer have the potential to cause damage through radiation.

3. The identified impacts have to be given a monetary value. In the case of costs and benefits of goods that are not traded in the market, various shadow pricing techniques are used (see Box 8.5).

4. An appropriate discount rate must be chosen so that future costs and benefits can be evaluated at current prices or *present values*[9] (see 8.5.2).

5. The final step involves aggregating all the costs and benefits over time, subtracting the total value of all the costs from the total value of all the benefits to calculate the net present value (NPV).

Sant (1992, p 63) points out that: 'Whilst the first and the final steps are relatively straightforward, the three interim steps are very difficult and require a considerable number of subjective decisions to be made'. Some of these difficulties arise from problems associated with valuation of natural resources and the distributional impacts of how costs and benefits are calculated (see 8.5.1 and 8.5.2).

While CBA will not *always* be the optimal decision-making tool, it can be particularly powerful in the right circumstances and should be used 'as a decision tool, not a single-minded decision rule' (Farrow and Toman 1998, p 16). Common (1995, p 178) emphasises that CBA is not a mechanical procedure for reaching a decision but can best be regarded as a way to facilitate judgment. He notes that with the computational power now readily available (see 8.7 and 8.8) comparison can be made between the results using different sets of input data. The differences between these sets would derive, for example, from different assumptions about external costs arising from environmental damage. This 'sensitivity analysis' reveals whether a decision on the project will be sensitive to variations in these costs or not. If it is not sensitive then dispute over environmental valuation is unnecessary. Sensitivity analysis helps to reveal those areas of the problem where judgment is required.

8.5.1 Valuation

CBA requires monetary values to be assigned to non-market natural capital in order to aggregate and weigh up all costs and benefits of a proposed activity. However, the determination of monetary values of natural resources and ecosystem services (see Chapter 2), which include non-market goods such as biodiversity, clean air, clean water and wilderness areas (Munda 1996), can be particularly difficult. For example, imagine the difficulty of conducting a CBA on a proposed policy to set aside an area as a national park. The benefits include use for recreation and biodiversity conservation. The costs include management

---

9 Future benefits and costs are converted to today's prices (present value) using a process known as *discounting* and the interest rate used for discounting benefits and costs is known as the *discount rate*.

and maintenance, land purchase, and loss of use of land for agriculture, mining or other purposes.

While some of these costs/benefits such as purchase price of the land or estimated maintenance of the park can be assigned monetary values as these goods are bought and sold on the market, others involving conservation of biodiversity are not readily quantifiable in monetary terms. These include the intrinsic values (see Chapter 3) associated with aesthetics or human well-being. For example: How do we price environmental areas to reflect cultural or spiritual significance? How do we value individual species that comprise global biodiversity? Furthermore, who should be responsible for valuing such components of the environments? – economists, environmentalists, local community members? Does the placement of an economic value on such things as cultural and spiritual worth undermine these values? Responses to these questions will depend on your value position (see Chapter 3). Despite these challenges of valuing environmental goods and services, various techniques have been developed to ascribe monetary shadow prices to such non-marketed items (see Box 8.4).

Box 8.4: Approaches for the economic valuation of non-marketed goods

Contingent valuation – This method is universally applicable and determines a monetary value by directly surveying affected parties about their maximum 'willingness to pay' (WTP) or minimum 'willingness to accept' (WTA) changes in environmental quality (Hanley 1992). Using this method, a survey in Queensland reported that about 65 per cent of the respondents were willing to pay about $22 per quarter for an increase, from 10 per cent to 12 per cent, in electricity generation from renewable energy sources (Ivanova 2005).

Travel cost method – This method assumes that the costs involved in visiting an area are indicative of the value which people place on this area (Sant 1992). If an area attracts people from great distances, such as the Great Barrier Reef which receives thousands of international tourists each year, the value is greater than a rarely-visited local park.

Hedonic pricing – This method works by establishing a relationship between a particular good and the value of its attributes (Hanley 1992). For example, air quality may be an attribute for residential properties in different locations and may result in property value variations. Using appropriate statistical techniques, the hedonic approach attempts to identify a relationship between property value differential and air quality and infers how much people are willing to pay to improve the quality (Pearce and Turner 1990).

Arguably, economic valuation techniques are useful because they provide monetary values when such values are not readily available for decision-making (Klauer 2000 cited in Venkatachalam 2007, p 553). Proponents of CBA also argue that economic valuations 'objectively reflect values of populations', even though subjective value judgments are involved at many stages (Beder 2006, p 132). For example, contingent valuation suffers from biased responses due to the nature of information provided to survey respondents, the hypothetical nature of the exercise and the possibility of strategic behaviour by the respondents (Hanley 1992). Respondents may overstate WTP to encourage the conservation of an area, or understate it to minimise the possibility of a user charge (Chee 2004).

Valuation techniques in CBA are rooted in neoclassical economic theory[10] and assume that as rational utility maximisers, individuals are willing to make trade-offs between market and non-market goods as long as suitable compensation, which maximises individual or social utility, is offered (Spash 2000). This assumption fails to recognise individual choices based on ethical and ecological reasons (Chee 2004; Spash 1997, 2000). Some believe that aspects of the environment are beyond price and have no adequate substitutes. They may argue that natural capital and non-human species have an independent value beyond any monetary value humans can assign to them (Beder 2006; Kotchen and Reiling 2000).

These difficulties can lead to biased valuations and often underestimation of environmental damage due to the omission of impacts which are difficult to value.

8.5.2 Distributional equity issues: Who benefits? Who pays?

Criticisms of CBA include its inability to satisfy *inter*generational and *intra*generational equity principles of sustainability. The issues of distributional equity are linked to foundations of CBA which assume a uniform distribution of net social benefit of a project across society. It does not consider *upon whom* the costs and benefits fall. We will now discuss the main influences on these distributional impacts of CBA.

Discounting is a key feature in CBA as it is used to convert future costs and benefits of alternatives to net present value in order to compare and rank alternatives. The choice of discount rate used in CBA and the time horizons selected for the analysis have a strong influence on the distribution of costs and benefits between generations (see Box 8.5).

Box 8.5: Choice of discount rate and time horizon

Generally, the higher the discount rate, the lower the value of future benefits (Sant 1992). A *high discount rate* (for example 10 per cent) implies that $1 today is worth far more than $1 in the future. In this way, projects such as mining, which reap the main benefits over a relatively short period of time will be favoured if a relatively high discount rate is used. Conversely, projects which have benefits which occur over a long time scale, such as forest conservation, are favoured when a *low discount rate* (for example, 2 per cent) is used since the value of the return from the project is worth a similar amount in the future as it is today (Beder 1996; Sant 1992).

The issue of time horizons is especially pertinent for environmental problems such as climate change, biodiversity loss and storage of radioactive wastes as their consequences occur over long time periods. Undertaking short-term discounting, such as less than 25 years, which is standard CBA practice, does not accurately reflect this context. Therefore, projects selected on this basis will inevitably impose risks on future generations.

In order to overcome these problems, there is growing consensus on moving away from a single fixed rate of discount and towards the adoption of a time declining discount rate over at least a 100-year time horizon (Turner 2007).

The valuation techniques used in CBA can produce situations where environmental burdens are greater on the poor and those who already bear the burden of other social inequities (also see discussion of environmental justice in Chapter 2). For example, siting a polluting

---

10   Neo-classical economics is concerned with efficient allocation of scarce resources to satisfy the wants and
    desires of individuals (Common 1997 in Chee 2004, p 551; Tisdell 1991).

industry in an already polluted area will be cheaper than siting it in a low-pollution area because the cost of pollution will be lower if measured in terms of the decline in property values (hedonic pricing and WTP) (Beder 2006). In addition, in standard CBA practice, no allowance is made for the importance of irreversibility of decisions which may result in welfare loss from forgone benefits and reduction of future options (Beder 1996; Chee 2004). One approach to overcome distributional impacts is to attach differential weights to costs and benefits that accrue to particular societal groups (Chee 2004).

Although advocates of CBA consider this tool to be a systematic procedure for comparing alternatives and an important aid to decision-making, the limitations discussed above do raise questions about its effectiveness for facilitating sustainable outcomes. This has given rise to the development and use of other options analysis tools which extend CBA and are better able to deal with contemporary, complex issues which move beyond mere monetary aggregation of individual choices made in a market context to real-world political economy in which plural and contested values have to be reconciled (Turner 2006). Multi-Criteria Decision Analysis (MCDA), sometimes also called Multi-Criteria Analysis (MCA) is one such tool. Although MCDA and CBA use similar structured frameworks for comparison of alternatives, there are operational differences which strengthen MCDA's capacity for improving EDM to deliver sustainable outcomes (Joubert et al 1997). For example, when using MCDA for deciding between options, several project selection criteria against which alternatives are ranked and/or weighted can be included and multiple actors can participate in decision-making. This allows for the inclusion of criteria other than mere monetary dimensions, and addresses *intra*generational equity through involvement of diverse actors.

MCDAs have also been used to enhance other EDM tools. For example, in the Netherlands, MCDA is used to increase transparency and public participation during the comparison of alternatives and the scoping stage (see 8.3) in the EIA process. These aspects of MCDA are aligned with the consensus seeking approach in Dutch EDM, where public participation is institutionalised (Janssen 2001, p 101).

8.6 Life Cycle Assessment

Life Cycle Assessment (LCA) is a methodology designed to quantitatively compile, analyse and assess material and energy flows, and environmental impacts of a product, process, service or activity over its entire life cycle (Ekvall and Finnveden 2001; Tillman et al 1994; Van der Vorst et al 1999). This requires accounting for all inputs and outputs such as raw materials, energy, water, emissions and wastes from cradle (extraction of raw materials) to grave (final disposal) and all stages in between including transport, processing, manufacturing, distribution, use and maintenance. The cradle-to-grave approach is the most important and unique aspect of this tool since it can include upstream and downstream effects throughout the supply chain.

LCA can help address the urgent problem of high material and resource use in developed economies by supplying and analysing data for informing dematerialisation strategies such as EPR, eco-efficiency, cleaner production, design for environment and the service economy (see Chapters 1 and 2 and Case Study A). In particular, LCA can advance sustainable production and consumption:

- by identifying environmental burdens associated with specific activities as well as comparing the impacts of different options (Tillman 2000), hence creating products and services that have a lower environmental burden but provide the same level of service (Mont 2002);

- through the identification of opportunities for reducing inputs and outputs in an efficient manner by targeting the most significant areas of material and resource use and environmental impacts.

LCA has wide applicability and can be used by various decision-makers in the process of EDM. For example, individual consumers can compare LCA studies conducted on products which perform similar functions (biodiesel vs petroleum fuel, paper bags vs plastic bags, disposable vs reusable nappies – see Box 8.6) to inform their choices. Similarly, organisations can use product and service comparisons to inform procurement policies and procedures; governments can use LCA to compare the impacts of various environmental management alternatives, such as options for waste management, to guide their policy and regulatory decisions; and LCA can help manufacturers to reduce the environmental burden of their products and processes while improving resource efficiency and meeting policy and regulatory obligations.

Information from LCA can also be used to facilitate comparison of alternatives in EIA. LCA is particularly useful in accounting for indirect impacts of projects (see 8.3.2) which are traditionally not considered in EIA (Tukker 2000).

Although LCA is the oldest (LCA originated in the 1960s motivated by the *Limits To Growth* report[11] (Van der Vorst et al 1999)) and most popular Material Accounting Tool in use, a variety of other approaches have been developed and are used to account for the flow of materials in our economies. EFA is one such material accounting tool which was introduced in Chapter 1. Others include Material Flux Analysis (MFA), Ecological Space (ES) and the Sustainable Process Index (SPI) (Daniels and Moore 2002).

LCA methodology

LCA methodology was standardised by the International Organization for Standardization (ISO) in 1997. Based on the standard (ISO 14040:2006) an LCA should consist of the following four phases (ISO 2006):

1. Goal and scope definition – includes the identification of the purpose of the study and its audience; the definition of product system, boundaries, procedures, impact categories as well as the assumptions and limitations.

2. Inventory analysis (also known as Life Cycle Inventory – LCI) – involves data collection and the compilation and quantification of all inputs and outputs.

3. Impact assessment – requires interpretation and evaluation of the results of LCI. Weighting of specific environmental impacts is undertaken to assess their effects.

4. Interpretation – findings from inventory analysis and impact assessment are considered to reach conclusions and make recommendations to decision-makers, in line with the goals and scope of the study.

---

11 Published in 1972 by the Club of Rome, the key message of this report was that within the next 100 years, the world's systems would enter an 'overshoot and collapse' mode as a result of population growth and consumption of resources (see Chapter 2).

Limitations of LCA

LCA is a powerful tool because of its unique capacity to address life cycle impacts of products, services and processes and its wide applicability by individuals, governments and industry to shape policies and decisions. However, like all other EDM tools, it has several limitations that can affect its use, reliability and legitimacy.

Issues of subjectivity

The process of conducting an LCA relies heavily on assumptions and value judgments which can introduce a bias towards a particular outcome. This has led to ambiguous and conflicting results produced from LCAs comparing the same product (see Box 8.6 on the LCA of different nappy types) or activity (see Ekvall 1999 for LCAs of paper recycling). Subjectivity can be introduced during LCA as analysts are confronted by questions that require judgment. For example: Where should the system boundaries be?

Ideally, all inputs and outputs required for the function of the product or process under consideration should be followed for the whole production and consumption cycle. However, while setting boundaries for large and complex systems, practical aspects of time and cost constraints and data availability have to be considered. This may lead to reduced system boundaries and increased reliance on assumptions (Tillman et al 1994). Questions that analysts may have to consider include:

- What assumptions should be made about consumer behaviour? Should it be assumed that a recyclable product will actually be recycled?

- Which environmental impacts are more significant than others and which should be included or ignored? What criteria should be used to determine significance? How should completely different sets of environmental impacts be compared?

Box 8.6: The great nappy debate – reusable (cloth) vs disposable

There has been a long-running controversy over which type of nappy is the better choice for the environment. Environmental groups criticise the use of disposable nappies highlighting the solid waste burden they impose (in Australia, one billion disposable nappies are thrown away every year (Langdon 2007) and make their way to landfills). Supporters of disposable nappies argue that cloth nappies require the use of large quantities of energy and water during their use. Many studies have used LCA as a tool to compare the environmental impacts of both types of nappies. The results of these studies often provide contradictory conclusions and no clear guidance to the consumer. A closer look at these LCAs highlights some of the subjectivity-based limitations of this tool.

Studies conducted in 1991 (Lifset 1991) by Proctor and Gamble and the American Paper Institute Diaper Manufacturing Group (both with an interest in disposables) and the National Association of Diaper Services (NADS) (with an interest in cloth nappies) revealed an obvious bias towards the nappy of interest. This bias was encountered because of assumptions made during the LCA about the various factors chosen for the analysis. For example, the NADS LCA leaves out the impact of detergents used in washing reusable nappies and the Proctor and Gamble LCA almost doubles the impacts of reusable nappies by assuming that in a day nearly twice as many cloth nappies are used as disposables (CHOICE 1993).

In 2005, to overcome biases introduced into LCA studies conducted by organisations with vested interests, the United Kingdom Environmental Agency commissioned consultants to provide an 'independent and objective' LCA of nappy use in the United Kingdom. The study compared three types of nappy systems, namely, disposable nappies, home laundered flat cloth nappies and commercially laundered prefolded cloth nappies delivered to the home. The study concluded that 'there was no significant difference between any of the environmental impacts – that is overall no system clearly had a better or worse environmental performance, although the life cycle stages that are the main source of these impacts are different for each system' (Aumônier and Collins 2005, p 9). An update of this study (Aumônier et al 2008) also revealed the sensitivity of the LCA to assumptions made about consumers' laundry habits. For example, if nappies were washed in fuller loads or line dried outdoors the global warming impact was 16 per cent less than the baseline scenario which assumed average washer and drier use. In contrast, if all reusable nappies were tumble-dried, global warming impacts were 43 per cent higher than the baseline scenario.

This report was welcomed by the manufacturers of disposable nappies, for example Kimberley-Clark (makers of Huggies) who saw it as confirming the findings of the LCAs conducted in 1991 (Huggies Nappies 2008). Some environment groups, however, saw the report as flawed, based on poor quality data and a wasted opportunity for putting this debate to rest (Warmer Bulletin 2005).

Although the debate on reusable vs disposable nappies continues, the LCA conducted by the United Kingdom Environmental Agency reveals the importance of explicitly stating assumptions when conducting such analyses. In the case of the great nappy debate, revealing the impacts of laundry choices provides clearer guidance to the consumer in the United Kingdom.

(Note: British results should be read with caution by Australian readers since assumptions made about consumer habits and significance of impacts are context dependent and can vary for different localities. For example, water use maybe particularly crucial in some parts of Australia, whereas landfill space and pollution from leachate[12] may be of concern in other regions.)

Issues of data quality and reliability

LCAs are very data intensive and like other quantitative analytical tools, such as models and GIS (see 8.8), produce results that are only as accurate as the data on which they are based. Although practitioners are well aware of the need to maintain data quality, this is not a widespread practice (Vigon and Jensen 1995). Data gaps, unreliable, inaccurate, insufficient or unrepresentative data can provide misleading results (Björklund 2002).

When conducting LCAs, generalisations are often made about the industrial practices, consumer habits, environmental context and environmental impacts of similar products and services between different geographical localities or sites. In some instances, data collected in one location may be representative for another location (Boguski et al 1996), but generally, such practice neglects the importance of spatial variations between regions and can significantly affect the outcomes of LCA. For example, material extraction, transport, energy use and emissions during manufacturing processing can vary by orders of magnitude from factory to factory and using averages can produce substantial inaccuracies (Greene and Ryan 1996). However, the cost and time involved in collecting and maintaining site-specific data may lead to the choice of representative data being used.

Similarly, it is important to include both short and long-term temporal variations. Temporal changes include conditions such as legislation, regulation and technology as well

---

12   Polluted liquid generated from the degradation of waste in a landfill (Marañón et al 2006).

as environmental conditions such as levels of pollution and rainfall patterns which may change over time.

The uncertainties associated with the limitations discussed above raise questions about the reliability of LCA as a tool for EDM. However, LCA allows clear identification of assumptions and transparent reporting of subjective choices (ISO 2006). Decision-makers can consider this information when drawing conclusions from LCA studies.

8.7 Modelling

Advances in computer science and information technology since the 1980s have led to the increased use of computer-based decision support systems (Box 2002; Zhu et al 1998) such as modelling and Geographic Information Systems (GIS) (see 8.8), to improve understanding of environmental problems.

Models are used to organise and use raw data to build simplified pictures of parts of the real world (Braat and van Lierop 1987) and hence are a vehicle of problem explanation and a device for communicating the relevant science to decision-makers and the general public (Parker et al 2002). Models are also used for designing, assessing and comparing environmental management options (see Box 8.7).

Box 8.7: MUSIC model – stormwater management

The Model for Urban Stormwater Improvement Conceptualisation (MUSIC) was developed by the Cooperative Research Centre for Catchment Hydrology to help catchment managers plan and evaluate conceptual designs of alternative stormwater management scenarios aimed at protecting aquatic ecosystems from the impacts or urbanisation. Specifically, it allows managers to determine the quality of run-off emanating from catchments, design an integrated stormwater management plan, and predict and evaluate the performance of specific treatment measures and systems.

MUSIC is a user-friendly Decision Support System designed to simulate the performance of a variety of structural stormwater systems and measures (constructed wetlands, rainwater tanks, gross pollutant traps, bioretention systems, vegetated swales, and so on) at a range of temporal and spatial scales. Using maps and plans, it allows complex stormwater management scenarios to be quickly and efficiently created and the results to be viewed through a range of graphical and tabular formats, such as time-series graphs of water flows and pollutant concentrations. Recent developments in the MUSIC model include the addition of a life cycle costing module. This allows life cycle cost (acquisition, maintenance, renewal and adaptation, and decommissioning) predictions as another model output which helps reduce the uncertainties associated with costs of alternative scenarios.

MUSIC has widespread applicability in Australia and is used by a number of water management agencies and consultants. For example, Melbourne Water is using MUSIC to plan and assess land development proposals, and to design stormwater treatment strategies for new and existing drainage schemes. This has resulted in significant savings on capital works, whilst still satisfying water quality criteria.

Sources: eWater CRC 2007; Fletcher and Taylor 2007; Wong et al 2002.

Models used in environmental decision-making can range from those dealing with specific biological systems and processes (for example, nutrient cycling) to broad Integrated Assessment Models (IAM) (see also 8.3 for Integrated Assessment) that are constructed to explain the behaviour of complex and interconnected physical, biological and social systems (Schneider 1997). An example of the latter is integrated catchment models that are constructed to help integrate contributions from many disciplines including agronomy, climatology, economics, hydrology and social science to take into account the multidimensional nature of catchment management issues (Jakeman and Letcher 2003). IAM uses many types of models together, such as conceptual and numeric models, for an improved understanding of a range of environmental problems spanning across spatial and temporal scales (Parker et al 2002).

The Intergovernmental Panel on Climate Change (IPCC)[13] has used integrated modelling tools to construct many future global climate change scenarios to examine the impact of various policy actions on the reduction of carbon emissions over a 100-year period. However, with such large scale and complex issues it becomes increasingly difficult to simplify environmental problems or processes to mathematical inputs and outputs. In such situations, reliance on values and assumptions to address data deficiencies and uncertainties increases (see Chapter 3; Kellow 2007). For example, some of the uncertainties in climate change scenario modelling arise from assumptions about future demographic change, economic growth and technological change. Based on the values and biases of the modellers and/or decision-makers, the selected assumptions can range from very optimistic to very pessimistic and both pessimistic and optimistic scenarios need to be considered when assessing uncertainties about future greenhouse gas predictions (Grübler et al 2004 cited in AGO 2006).

Outputs from modelling can also be limited by time constraints and data limitations. In such cases, the modeller may be left with no choice but to use data that may only be a snapshot in time. Making predictions about alternative scenarios based on such data sets may not be compatible with reality. This can often be the case with EIA, where the short timeframes do not allow for longer-term data collection.

Although the usefulness of models lies in their offer of a simplified and comprehensible version of reality, this is also their greatest drawback (Braat and van Lierop 1987). As indicated above, the influence of bias, values and assumptions during modelling means that models are only one version of the modellers' representation of reality.

Obscuring these human dimensions in the use of models can 'diminish the openness of a decision making process' (Schneider 1997, p 230). Confidence in the application of models and their outcomes can be increased by explicitly and *fully* disclosing the assumptions made and values represented during the development of models as this transparency allows for criticism and contestation of selected data, methods and values used during the modelling process (Kellow 2008; Parker et al 2002).

8.8 Geographic Information Systems

Geographic Information Systems (GIS) are tools that use spatial digital data (topographic features such as location of water bodies, stormwater pipes, streets) from a variety of sources such as satellites, aerial photos, hand-held Global Positioning Systems to visually display geographical characteristics of the real world. More specifically, GIS is a system for

---

13   <www.ipcc.ch>.

capturing, storing, checking, integrating, analysing and displaying spatial data about the earth (Dale and McLauglin 1988). GIS is used for transforming raw data into sophisticated visual images (two dimensional and three dimensional) which can have more meaning to decision-makers and the public. You may be familiar with Google Earth and Google Streetview which use GIS systems to create images.

GIS is a powerful analytical tool because it is capable of layering a number of data series (biophysical, economic, demographic, social, and so on) so that the user can identify links between different data sets. For example, during the process of an EIA, a map of the proposed development can be overlaid on a map of vulnerable ecosystems and/or a map of water bodies to determine the extent of impact the development may have on these. A range of alternatives, to minimise impacts, can then be examined in a flexible and efficient manner (Lovett 2000). Models can also be incorporated into GIS, or vice versa, to visualise scenarios. Floodplain management planning uses both these tools to assess and visually represent the extent of inundation caused by floods of different frequencies. This can help decision-makers and the affected community to plan for disaster management.

In Australia, GIS has been used in managing and evaluating environmental issues such as ecosystems management and land degradation. Australian governments, in partnership with community groups, address land degradation through many initiatives including the National Landcare Program (NLP). In order to evaluate the effectiveness of the NLP, LANDCARE GIS was developed to identify and analyse the spatial relationships between the NLP, land resource condition and land use practices (East and Wood 1998). Local governments also use GIS for informing land use and infrastructure planning decisions and their State of the Environment Reporting (SoER).

Similar to modelling, GIS is a data-hungry tool and there are a number of concerns regarding this aspect of GIS. Often not all required data is up-to-date, available or accessible and there may be no guarantees about the quality and accuracy of data. Using out-of-date data or overlaying data with different levels of currency will result in misleading outputs for decisions that require real-time information (Nix and Hill 2001). Since acquiring and maintaining spatial data is expensive, organisations may share data for cost efficiency, although there may be some barriers to data sharing. For example, some government organisations may not share data because of security reasons, or the data sets and variables used within these may be incompatible. Other issues with data sharing include political and institutional culture, liability, confidentiality, ownership, copyright and pricing (Carver et al 2001; Lovett 2000; Nedovic-Budic and Pinto 2000). These limitations must be considered while using GIS as a tool for EDM.

Box 8.8: GIS and public participation

The dependence of GIS and modelling on specialist expert knowledge and technology has raised questions about the accessibility of these tools to the various actors such as community groups and the general public. In some cases certain actors may lack required technical knowledge and hence their ability to provide meaningful input to decision-making involving GIS is limited (Lovett 2000). The application of Decision Support Tools is expanding to address these issues through public involvement and inclusion of lay and local knowledge (Forrester and Cinderby 2005; Korfmacher 2001; Siebenhüner and Barth 2005) (see also Chapters 6 and 7).

In one case study in South Africa (Forrester and Cinderby 2005), GIS was used to integrate expert information with local knowledge to make a stronger case for better water supply.

Specifically, maps were produced by combining data on water quality produced by a hydrological surveyor, with information from the local community about their water access points and typical household water use. Integrating multiple knowledges enhanced the understanding of all actors and provided a more informed picture of the problem to the decision-makers. For example, community information suggested there were far more bore holes than were identified by the surveyor and the data on water quality were useful to the community as many contaminants were identified in local water resources. This process also allowed the local community to be engaged on a more equal footing with technologically advanced agencies.

8.9 State of the Environment Reporting

State of the Environment Reporting (SoER) provides credible information about the changes in the state of the environment and their implications for the government, public, industry and others in a position to effect change (DEHAA, Government of South Australia 1999).

The most common SoER framework, Pressure – State – Response, is based on monitoring and measuring cause and effect relationships between the pressures we place on the environment through our activities, the resulting condition or state of the environment and our responses to address pressures to improve the state. Many institutions and agencies report on the environment at local, regional, State, national and global levels although most of the SoERs are conducted by governments. At a global level, the Global Environment Outlook (GEO) publishes the United Nations Environment Programme's (UNEP) major assessment of the state of the world's environment and provides guidance for regional and international policy setting and planning for sustainable development (IISD 2007). In Australia, a national and several State SoERs are prepared at regular intervals. In New South Wales local councils are required by legislation[14] to prepare comprehensive SoERs every four years and these reports must address the eight environmental sectors of land, air, water, biodiversity, waste, noise and Indigenous and non-Indigenous heritage. Many contemporary reports also include some discussion on progress towards sustainability (NSROC 2008). Obviously, the smaller scale SoERs provide quite specific descriptions of local environments, whilst broader scale SoERs tend to provide a more generalised overview of the whole area.

Although SoERs can be a powerful tool for tracking progress of environmental policies and programs, and communicating vital environmental information to the public and decision-makers to take actions for achieving sustainability targets, the effectiveness of this tool in achieving these goals is often limited. Some reasons for these limitations are discussed below:

* Long-term monitoring through the use of appropriate indicators (see Box 8.9) and the availability of scientifically credible data is essential for accurately reporting changes in the environment. The South East Queensland (SEQ) Waterways' Ecosystems Health Monitoring Program[15] is a good example of a regional monitoring program that uses consistent, standardised methods to provide a comprehensive picture of the health of SEQ's aquatic environment. However, such practice is rare and problems of access to

14 The NSW Department of Local Government is exploring changes to current planning and reporting legislation in order to improve the integration of planning mechanisms. These changes aim to improve local government's capacity for strategic planning through the development of an integrated planning and reporting framework (DLG 2006).

15 <www.ehmp.org> (accessed 28 February 2009).

data and inconsistency of standards and data collection methods still exist (ASEC 2001 cited in Harding and Traynor 2003, p 205). The summary of the Australian 2006 SoE report (Australian Government DEH 2006, p 3) identified that 'the lack of accurate, nationally consistent environmental data' limited the delivery of a comprehensive picture of the state of Australia's environment (see also 10.2). Inaccurate and incomplete data can lead to inappropriate and ineffective responses to address environmental problems.

Upgrading data monitoring and evaluation systems through a national environmental accounting framework would help guide future policy and investment decisions and address data gaps that have 'plagued the State of the Environment reporting process' (WGCS 2008, p 2). Beeton et al (2006, p 3) also emphasises the importance of a 'national environmental reporting system that is coordinated in its timing, reporting and has improved data management, sharing and aggregation protocols across all jurisdictions'.

- Theoretically, successive SoERs are a tool to inform adaptive management and long-term sustainability (Beeton et al 2006). They allow the detection of trends in the environment, and monitor the effectiveness of environmental strategies, policies and legislation to inform future long-term planning and decision-making which leads to strategic outcomes. Practically, this notion of integrating findings of the SoERs with planning decisions has been difficult (Griffiths 2000). For example, some challenges for local government include constraints such as the breadth and complexity of their functions and services, linking SoERs with other key planning documents and alignment of planning cycles.

The process of preparing SoERs requires gathering, harmonising, aggregating, and interpreting data and knowledge from a variety of disciplines and sources to provide a broad-based assessment that takes account of the complex connections between ecological, socio-economic and policy issues. These are significant challenges with respect to the time and money allocated to the process (Lyytimäki 2004; Pintér et al 2000).

- Values-based decisions on questions of what should be measured (do we measure only what we treasure?), what is included and excluded from the report, how we interpret data and reconcile contradictory scientific results also has implications for the quality and scope of SoER and its usefulness in tracking progress (Harding and Traynor 2003; Lyytimäki 2004; Pintér et al 2000).

- An important consideration with regards to the legitimacy and validity of SoER is who conducts the reporting, for example, a government agency or an independent body. In Australia, most reporting is conducted by government agencies, however this is potentially problematic as the selection, interpretation and presentation of data in an SoER can reflect the bias and predisposition of the reporters to present a particular perspective or message. Commentators of SoER have argued that 'in regard to acceptance, objectivity and scientific credibility' it is crucial that the process be conducted by an independent guiding body (Harding and Traynor 2003, p 216).

- The effectiveness of SoER as a communication tool has also been questioned (Kuiper 2001), especially as a single report is intended to meet the needs of diverse audiences such as policy-makers, planners and the public. This poses the challenges of determining the level of detail (or simplification) presented in the report and the types of indicators (see Box 8.9) selected to communicate this information.

Box 8.9: Indicators and Indices[16]

Environmental indicators help track changes in the environment by selecting key measures – which may be physical, chemical, biological or socio-economic – that provide useful information about the whole system.

ANZECC State of the Environment Reporting Task Force
2000, p 4.

Indicators are (typically quantitative) measures that generally reduce a large amount of complex data to a simple form. The Index of Stream Condition, for example, is a measure for representing the environmental condition of rivers. It integrates data on the condition of river hydrology, water quality, streambank vegetation, bed and bank condition, instream habitat and aquatic life into one index (Victorian DSE 2009). This allows communication of information to the public and policy-makers in a manner that is meaningful and can aid decision-making. The danger in selecting oversimplified indicators is that they may compromise scientific accuracy and be misleading. Ideally, indicators should have a strong scientific basis while resonating with the public and policy-makers (Macgillivray and Zadek 1995).

Various types of indicators are used for different purposes. For SoER, environmental indicators are used for measuring the pressure, state and response categories. For example, in the case of climate change, pressure indicators may include greenhouse gas emissions such as carbon dioxide and methane, state indicators include carbon dioxide levels in the atmosphere and atmospheric temperatures, and response indicators may be policies, such as emissions trading schemes, aimed at reducing greenhouse gas emissions. Indicators provide comparisons of a current situation with some reference value, such as comparing urban air quality to set national standards.

The emphasis on reporting on sustainable development as an integrated concept has given rise to the development of sustainable development indices (SDI) which attempt to aggregate various aspects of sustainability and provide a more nuanced approach on development than economic only aggregates such as Gross Domestic Product (GDP). Examples of these indices include the Human Development Index of the United Nations Development Programme; the Environmental Sustainability Index and the Genuine Progress Index calculated at the national or sub-national level. There is also political interest in developing green GDPs and national accounts that include the cost of pollution and natural resource depletion. However, concern from policy-makers and statisticians about the conceptual and technical challenges associated with SDIs has held back their implementation (Pintér et al 2005).

8.10 Corporate Sustainability Reporting

[T]he practice of measuring, disclosing, and being accountable to internal and external stakeholders for organizational performance towards the goal of sustainable development. 'Sustainability reporting' is a broad term considered synonymous with others used to describe reporting on economic, environmental, and social impacts (eg, triple bottom line, corporate responsibility reporting, etc). A sustainability report should provide a balanced and reasonable representation

---

16   An index is a composite measure that integrates a number of indicators. Indices is the plural of index.

of the sustainability performance of a reporting organization – including both positive and negative contributions.

GRI[17] 2006, p 3.

Corporate Sustainability Reporting (CSR) is used by a range of organisations – corporations, governments, non-government organisations (NGOs), as a mechanism to voluntarily disclose their sustainability performance information. While SoER focuses on measuring changes in the environment at various geographic scales, CSR is specifically concerned with presenting information about an organisation's sustainability performance. The reasons driving organisations to publish CSRs are similar to those leading them to adopt EMSs (see 8.4), namely, competitive advantage, public relations, pressure from internal and external stakeholders (employees, shareholders, customers and advocacy groups) legal compliance, economic advantage, ethical considerations and environmental duty (KPMG 2005; Wheeler and Elkington 2001).

CSR and EMS can be used as mutually supportive EDM tools. Although organisations that adopt an EMS based on ISO 14001 do not require public reporting of their environmental performance, CSR is an effective tool for doing so in the interest of corporate social responsibility, accountability and transparency. CSR can also complement the checking and corrective action stage of the EMS cycle (see Figure 8.1) by providing evaluation of environmental strategies, policies and programs. Similarly, an EMS provides a framework for measuring and recording data on environmental impacts and performance that can thus inform CSR.

Increasing scrutiny of corporations by stakeholders and encouragement by governments and industry organisations has led to CSR becoming a fast-growing area of reporting. Globally, not only has the number of companies producing CSRs increased, but the nature of reporting has also evolved from reports covering only environmental issues to integrated reports linking TBL outcomes supported by indicators of sustainability (Wilson et al 2002). In Australia, stand alone corporate environmental reporting emerged in 1996, and in 2005 23 per cent of the top one hundred companies in Australia had published CSRs. Despite this growth, reporting rates of Australian companies lag behind overseas companies (KPMG 2005).

Many organisations around the world are now starting to report on the TBL aspects of sustainability as opposed to reporting on just the environment, however a number of studies suggest that the coverage of social and economic issues is far more superficial in comparison to environmental issues (Kolk 2004; KPMG 2005) and 'the nature of the information reported was overwhelmingly positive, with negative information being couched in positive terms' (CAER 2005, p 1). External assurance, through third-party auditing and verification can be a way of reducing bias and increasing credibility, but the degree to which this will be achieved depends on the scope and extent of external verification. A survey of CSR (SustainAbility and UNEP 2002) reported that external assurances are mainly conducted by accountants and consultants, although a small number of companies are using NGOs to provide verification, for example Matsushita Electric Group's 2002 CSR was verified by The Natural Step[18] (TNS) (see also Chapter 2 for TNS sustainability principles).

---

17   The Global Reporting Initiative (GRI) is an independent global institution which develops and disseminates guidelines and indicators for sustainability reports. Also see 10.2.

18   The Natural Step is an international not-for-profit organisation dedicated to education, advisory work and research in sustainable development <www.naturalstep.org/> (accessed 7 March 2009).

8.11 Socio-political context of tools

In the preceding sections we have seen that the selection and use of tools in EDM is strongly influenced by ideology, bias, interests, values and politics. Environmental professionals, government agencies and other users of tools need to transparently acknowledge that these factors are an inherent part of selecting and applying the tools discussed in this chapter. Failure to do so can lead to conflict amongst the many actors involved and jeopardise collaborative processes that support robust decisions. We will conclude this chapter with a closer look at some of these themes.

8.11.1 Rationality in environmental decision-making

Environmental decision-making is a dynamic process which occurs within the political arena and is responsive to changing social constructs, electoral pressures, patterns of governance, the knowledge of actors involved and the institutional and organisational constraints within which they work. However, the logical and sequential step-by-step models used by the various tools to inform decisions often do not acknowledge these contextual factors. Many decision-makers purport to have reached their decisions through intelligent, rational choice informed by complete, objective and value-free science that indicates the most efficient means of achieving policy goals (Howlett and Ramesh 2003). The desire to appear 'rational' obfuscates the reality where rationality is 'bounded'[19] (March and Simon 1958; Simon 1979) and decision-making is value-laden, contested, and often uses incomplete data sets and inconclusive science. Kørnøv and Thissen (2000) provide the following reasons which limit or bound rationality.

Cognitive and resource limitations
Tool users and decision-makers, like all of us, have limited capacities and work within cognitive and resource constraints. More often than not, they do not have complete information and cannot know all alternatives and consequences of their decisions. For example, the outputs from modelling are limited by the choice of models, the quality and amount of data available and the expertise and knowledge of those interpreting the outputs. Furthermore, limited knowledge about environmental and social processes means that, often, decisions have to be made in the face of uncertainty (see Chapter 9).

Behavioural variations and biases
As discussed in Chapter 3, our view of the world is influenced by perceptions, norms, values and interests. These factors also influence our individual judgment and choices during a decision-making process. Similarly, organisational and institutional culture, biases and preferences also limit the type of tools that are accessible for decision-making. An organisation heavily reliant on science and engineering may have a preference for expert-driven quantitative and statistical tools (for example, CBA, numerical modelling) which hide subjective judgments as opposed to more participatory tools such as MCDA which allow transparent inclusion of subjective value inputs from actors (Chee 2004; Joubert et al 1997).

---

19 In the mid-1950s the theory of 'bounded rationality' was proposed as an alternative to 'perfect rationality' and 'utility maximisation'. This theory can be considered a closer approximation to the realities of problem-solving where decision-makers have to contend with and are 'bounded' by uncertainties, imperfect knowledge and limited resources (Chee 2004; Simon 1979).

Multi-actor decision-making

Rational views of decision-making assume that a single group or entity, such as an agency or government is capable of controlling decisions. As discussed in Chapters 4 and 5, in practice, EDM is essentially a process of negotiation between many individuals, organisations and institutions and 'views and preferences diverge and change just like the alliances between participants in the process' (Kørnøv and Thissen 2000, p 194).

The extent to which various actors can influence the use of tools or have access to them is largely dependent on the extent to which they are empowered to participate in decision-making (see Chapter 7).

8.11.2 Ideology and values

The many interpretations of sustainability from weak to strong (Chapter 2), are based on our value positions (for example, technocentric or anthropocentric) and ideologies (for example ecologism) as discussed in Chapter 3. These same influences also have implications for how we select and use tools to inform environmental decisions.

CBA can be considered an instrument of weak sustainability as it requires reduction of all values to monetary terms and allows substitutability between manufactured and natural capital (Rennings and Wiggering 1997). MCDA potentially represents stronger sustainability where 'there is no solution optimising all the criteria at the same time and therefore the decision-maker has to find compromise solutions' (Funtowicz et al 1999, p 16).

Soderbaum (2000) positions tools such as CBA, MCDA, EIA within categories based on whether they are ideologically 'closed' or 'open' and the allowance they make for inclusion of multi-dimensionality. He argues that CBA is ideologically closed as it is biased towards one particular market ideology, is technocratic and reduces all valuations to a single *monetary number*. In contrast MCDA and EIA are ideologically open as they can accommodate different ideologies and value inputs, encourage public participation and allow for comparison of alternatives without converting all dimensions into monetary units. These differences help explain why certain tools may be selected over others based on their compatibility with the user's value position. In Soderbaum's (2000, p 83) opinion, CBA is incompatible with democracy and 'should not be used at all as part of societal decision-making'. Despite the many limitations of CBA (see 8.2), its use in EDM is prolific because *numbers* can carry unwarranted authority when used to legitimate political decisions (Barbour 1980 cited in Beder 2006, p 138).

8.11.3 Assumptions and choices

As highlighted in the discussion above, we make decisions with limited data and many assumptions. This is particularly true for modelling as we try to simulate complex natural systems using data that may only be a snapshot in time and make predictions about alternative scenarios based on data sets which may not be compatible with reality. Another example is the assumptions made about the ability of behavioural tools to achieve certain outcomes (see Table 8.1).

Even when there is adequate data available, the criteria used for data selection and truncation are value-laden (Funtowicz et al 1999). Often, decision-makers do not try to obtain all the information relevant to the identification of problems and their solutions, 'rather they select the information they need on the basis of their goals and resources. In other words, they look for half-knowledge that can be safely organized into politics' (Liberatore 1995 p 62).

Climate change sceptics have, for many years, chosen to base policy decisions on data selected through half-knowledge presented as scientific facts (see Bodnar et al 2004 for a critique of *The Skeptical Environmentalist* (Lomborg 2001), such that decision outcomes represent their values. Of course climate sceptics say the same is true of climate change believers!

8.11.4 Disciplinary limitations

Many tools have emerged from specialist expert disciplines; for example CBA from economics, and modelling from mathematics. The mono-discipline focus of some tools limits their capacity to operate effectively in the interdisciplinary and complex context of sustainability problems. This has encouraged the extension and evolution of tools to overcome these limitations. For example, EIA, which originated from a scientific and quantitative basis but has evolved to incorporate qualitative information and value judgments when assessing the significance of various environmental impacts (Van der Vorst et al 1999). Integrated Assessment (IA) and Integrated Assessment Modelling (IAM) have emerged as extensions of EIA and modelling, respectively, to encompass the interconnected and synergistic aspects of environmental management decisions.

The various tools used to inform the different stages of an EDM process (Table 8.3) can be integrated in a 'consecutive, encompassing or overlapping manner' to complement each other (Baumann and Cowell 1999 cited in Scrase and Sheate 2002, p 285). For example, results from the use of one tool may be integrated into the other to facilitate information flow and enhance decision outcomes. This does, however, pose challenges for disciplinary specialists and tool users, especially when considering integration of quantitative information from natural sciences with qualitative information from humanities (see Chapter 6).

As we move from end-of-pipe, technocratic decision-making approaches towards systems-thinking and collaborative practice to address the emerging challenges of achieving sustainability (see Chapter 1), the range of EDM tools is also evolving and expanding to accommodate this change. Despite the many limitations associated with the use of EDM tools, their usefulness for organising, analysing, interpreting and evaluating data and information cannot be underestimated. However, an understanding and awareness of the uses and abuses of tools is essential for considered decision-making.

9

Uncertainty, Risk and the Precautionary Principle

9.1 Introduction

Uncertainty, which may be both scientifically and socio-politically based, is an inherent feature of environmental management and arises at many points through the environmental decision-making (EDM) process. Many examples are evident in the previous chapters, and particularly Chapters 6 and 8.

As emphasised throughout this book, EDM is complex. By definition, the environment comprises many components, numerous processes and complex interconnections and feedback mechanisms. As noted earlier, we use the term ecosystem to describe these components and processes within a defined area. The complexity of ecosystems exceeds that of technological systems and our *scientific* understanding is limited because we cannot be sure we have identified all the components of ecosystems, let alone that we understand more than a small part of the processes and interactions between them.

However, uncertainty over the workings of the natural world is further complicated by adding influences from human activities. Social and political processes are equally as complex as those in the natural world and we cannot be sure how the interaction between humans and the environment will unfold in the future. Will our society remain anthropocentric with emphasis on consumption of goods and a high throughput of materials and energy? Or will we move to a society which emphasises a low throughput of materials and energy and in which stewardship of the Earth and its natural systems is of primary importance? What will be the future environmental outcomes of the political choices we face today concerning technology and its management? There is much uncertainty surrounding these *socio-political* questions.

Whilst uncertainty has often been an unconsidered factor in EDM, this is changing. Increasing emphasis on risk and uncertainty at many levels of decision-making, and in an ever-widening sphere of activities, has followed recognition of the high environmental, monetary and social costs of failing to anticipate damage arising from human use of the environment and from modern industrial methods. The BSE[1] food crisis in Britain, effects of pollutants such as endocrine disruptors,[2] and recognition of the impacts likely to result from anthropogenic climate change, have each taken us by surprise. They are prime examples of issues that have fostered greater attention to acknowledging the potential for uncertainty and ignorance regarding the outcomes of our activities, and for adopting an anticipatory approach such as required by the precautionary principle (see 9.10), when considering impacts of human technology and activities.

Associated with this developing anticipatory approach has been a trend to integrate the treatment of risk and uncertainty into formal decision-making processes. Examples include the requirement for risk assessment as part of environmental impact assessment (EIA) in some circumstances (see Chapter 8 and 9.6.2), the incorporation of the precautionary principle into legislation concerning EDM (see 9.10), and the requirement that the catchment management authorities in New South Wales consider risk when investing in natural resource management (see Box 2.9).

---

1   BSE (Bovine Spongiform Encephalopathy) or Mad-Cow Disease is a fatal disease in cattle affecting the central nervous system. It attracted wide concern in Britain in the 1990s when it appeared that humans had contracted fatal degenerative brain disease from eating infected beef products.

2   Endocrine disruptors are chemicals in the environment (both natural and synthetic) that can affect the hormonal systems of wildlife and humans, and particularly the reproductive systems. See the European Commission Endocrine Disruptor website: <http://ec.europa.eu/environment/endocrine/index_en.htm> (accessed 25 February 2009).

In this chapter we examine the nature and origins of uncertainty and its treatment in EDM. By definition (see 9.2.1 and 9.3), risk is the most quantifiable and measurable type of uncertainty. We explore some of the formal ways of dealing with risk, shedding light on the subjectivity involved in these approaches. Given the increasing importance of risk management in EDM we discuss, in some detail, the formal process for risk management as outlined in the Australian Standard (SA/SNZ 2004b, 2006).

Environmental professionals continually confront uncertainty in various aspects of their work. In this role it is important not only to manage and minimise risk, but to communicate these risks to the public and decision-makers, and where appropriate to involve the broader community in risk management. In this regard it is important to acknowledge that members of the public, and their formal decision-makers, may perceive risks differently and we explore the reasons for this and ways of handling differing perceptions in decision-making.

The final part of this chapter is devoted to the precautionary principle – a key principle of sustainability (see Chapter 2) that provides guidance on how we should make decisions when confronted with *scientific* uncertainty.

9.2 Types of uncertainty

Uncertainty is a complex concept that is not well understood. Rather like peeling the layers of an onion, as we delve more deeply into the uncertainty surrounding an environmental management issue, we reveal *different forms* of uncertainty. The outcome is that whilst we can *reduce* uncertainty of *one kind* by application of more science to the problem, we cannot totally remove uncertainty (Burgman 2005). For example, considering anthropogenic climate change, we now know considerably more about the global atmospheric systems governing climate than we did say 20 years ago. However, in gaining this understanding we have also revealed new complexities that were previously unrecognised.

Brian Wynne (1992) has identified four kinds of uncertainty (risk, uncertainty, ignorance and indeterminacy) which we explore below.

9.2.1 Risk

Risk refers to situations in which the behaviour of the system in question is 'basically well known, and chances of different outcomes can be defined and quantified by structured analysis of mechanisms and probabilities' (Wynne 1992, p 114).

This is a good description of technical risk associated with machinery failure in an industrial complex. Uncertainty (in the popular sense) is present to the extent that we cannot be sure when machine failure will occur or how environmental factors will influence outcomes. For example, depending on the weather conditions, pollution released after equipment failure may be blown towards or away from sensitive environments or human settlements. In addition, other types of uncertainty may be present simultaneously as we will see below.

9.2.2 Uncertainty

Uncertainty is the condition when we 'know the important system parameters but not the probability distributions' – that is, we 'Don't know the odds' (Wynne 1992, p 114).

Anthropogenic climate change is a good example. The science concerning the role of greenhouse gases (eg carbon dioxide) in retaining heat within the Earth's atmosphere is well established. The wide range of parameters that make up the Earth's climate are also known (eg clouds, global air circulation, heat absorption by water, land and so on). There has been considerable progress in understanding the relationships between these parameters and likely outcomes across the globe, and increasing confidence that anthropogenic greenhouse gas emissions are causing climate change (IPCC 2007). However, uncertainty regarding precise relationships and impacts is still present as is ignorance.

9.2.3 Ignorance

Ignorance is when we 'Don't know what we don't know' (Wynne 1992, p 114).

An example of ignorance is the development of chlorofluorocarbons (CFCs) as propellants in spray cans and as refrigerants. These compounds were considered highly suitable for these purposes because they were seen as very stable and apparently not harmful to humans or ecosystems. Scientists did not predict that CFCs would enter into a chain reaction with ozone molecules in the stratosphere[3] destroying this vital filter for ultraviolet radiation (see US EPA undated). We were *ignorant* regarding this possibility. Similarly, we were ignorant initially regarding BSE and endocrine disruptors mentioned above (Stirling 2007).

The typical response when ignorance is revealed in EDM is to focus on improving the science, but Wynne (1992, p 115) suggests that of equal importance is examining the social commitments that rest on that scientific understanding since 'it is here that ignorance and its corresponding risks are created'. For example, in the case of stratospheric ozone layer depletion though action of CFCs and other ozone depleting substances, social commitments were demonstrated when businesses manufacturing or relying on use of CFCs became redundant and substitutes had to be found. Hence the ignorance became a business risk with associated social consequences. Further risk was associated with the higher levels of ultraviolet radiation reaching the earth's surface and the potential for increased incidence of skin cancers in people unless they reduced their exposure to the sun.

Others go further than Wynne and suggest that 'the knowledge-based worldview that has governed so much of Western culture for half a millennium is both flawed and dangerous' (Vitek and Jackson 2008, p 15), and should be replaced by an 'ignorance-based worldview' that recognises that 'no matter how much human beings discover about the natural world or ourselves . . . knowledge will always be dwarfed by what we do not . . know' (Vitek and Jackson 2008, p 9). Indeed, obtaining more knowledge reveals further layers of ignorance. This view does not suggest we should not seek knowledge, but rather that we need to keep the possibility of ignorance at the forefront of EDM. In this regard an ignorance-based world view can be seen as adopting a precautionary approach (Marocco 2008; and see 9.10).

9.2.4 Indeterminacy

Indeterminacies can arise from not knowing whether the type of scientific knowledge and the questions posed by scientists are appropriate and sufficient for the circumstances in question. For example, science 'can define a risk, or uncertainties, only by artificially "freezing" a surrounding context which may or may not be this way in real-life situations. The resulting knowledge is therefore *conditional* knowledge' depending on whether these assumptions turn out to be correct (Wynne 1992, p 116).

Indeterminacies can also arise from poor understanding of how scientific and technical knowledge of systems and activities relates to, and will be affected by, its social and political

---

3   The region of the atmosphere around 20–40 km above the Earth's surface.

context. For example, will quality control be maintained in operations and maintenance procedures associated with risky technologies, such as nuclear power? Will such control be equal in many different countries and cultures around the world in which these technologies may operate? Our assumptions regarding the risk associated with such situations is *conditional* on these factors remaining the same. Yet we cannot be sure we can establish all potentially influencing factors so the context is indeterminate.

9.2.5 Can 'uncertainty' be easily classified?

Wynne's (1992) classification of uncertainty is but one of a number of models that have been proposed. For example, in Chapter 6 (see 6.3.3), the role of science in informing decision-making under different types of uncertainty, described as technical, methodological and epistemological uncertainty, was discussed. The terms risk, uncertainty and indeterminacy, loosely relate to situations in which uncertainty derives respectively from technical, methodological and epistemological questions (O'Riordan and Rayner 1991). It would detract from the key purpose of this chapter to discuss further models here (for these see Burgman 2005; Dovers and Handmer 1995; Klinke et al 2006; Smithson 1989, 1991) but a few comments on Wynne's classification are relevant.

It would be a mistake to see Wynne's four types of 'uncertainty' simply as points along a continuum of increasing uncertainty, with risk at one end and indeterminacy at the other. Whilst this may provide a valid illustration of the relationship between risk and uncertainty, it is important to note that both risk and uncertainty are set within a context of ignorance and indeterminacy. Even matters that we think we understand may well provide surprises – remember CFCs! Also, for Wynne (1992, p 116), social analysis of scientific knowledge suggests that indeterminacy may be present 'even when "uncertainty" is small'.

In addition, the term 'risk' is used far more broadly than in the sense described by Wynne (see 9.2.1). Recently there has been much attention given to 'ecological risk assessment' and as shown below (see Box 9.2) this does not involve the level of system understanding suggested by Wynne's (1992) definition of risk. Beyond these technical and ecological views of risk, some risk assessments emphasise the sociological context (Burgman 2005) and indeed some sociologists suggest that risk is such a strong feature in modern lives that the current era may be best described as a 'risk society' (Beck 1992) as discussed below (see 9.4).

9.3 What is risk?

Risks to people and the environment are part of life on planet Earth. Some such risks derive from natural hazards – for example, lightning, bushfires, earthquakes and hurricanes. Whilst we cannot *prevent* risks from natural events, human actions and decisions may greatly influence their consequences. For example, siting a nuclear facility in an area of high earthquake potential, locating a tailings dam in an area prone to torrential rain and flooding, using routine building methods and materials in a cyclone-prone area, and siting residences in areas prone to bushfires, are all high risk choices. In some cases human activity may also increase the scale and frequency of natural hazards. For example, models indicate that anthropogenic climate change will generate severe storms leading to flash flooding in coastal urban centres of northern New South Wales and southern Queensland (AG DEH AGO 2006), and higher temperatures and drought conditions in some areas that will increase bushfire occurrence and intensity (Hennessy et al 2005). Risks may also directly result from human constructions and activities. For example, dam failure, hazardous industries, discharge of pollutants and travelling in motor cars.

Risk is a term we use loosely in day-to-day conversation but it has a more technical meaning:

- *Risk* refers to a combination of the probability, or frequency, of occurrence of a defined *hazard* and the magnitude of the consequences of the occurrence. In other words:

    — how often is a particular potentially harmful event going to occur?

    — what are the consequences of this occurrence?

- *Hazard* refers to 'a source of potential harm' (SA/SNZ 2004b, p 3). This may involve a situation that could occur during the lifetime of a product, system or plant that has the potential for human injury, damage to property, damage to the environment or economic loss.

For example, the existence of pipes carrying a toxic gas in a chemical plant is a hazard. The combination of the likelihood of pipe failure leading to leakage of the toxic gas and the consequences of this leak, is the risk. Consequence may depend on a range of factors – does the leak occur in the middle of the day when many people are in the vicinity and will be exposed, or does it occur in the middle of the night when the surrounding streets are deserted? Do prevailing winds carry the toxic release to sensitive downwind environments, or across far less sensitive environments?

9.4 The risk society?

Risk has gained increasing prominence in EDM, at least in Western nations, over the past 20 years. This has led some sociologists to argue that we now live in what is best charac-terised as a 'risk society' (Beck 1992, 1994; Giddens 1999). Ulrich Beck coined this term to describe the change from a modern industrial society concerned primarily with the distri-bution of wealth, that is, the distribution of 'goods', to one primarily concerned with the distribution of dangers (risk), that is the distribution of 'bads' – the 'risk society' (Beck 1992, 1994; Lash and Wynne 1992). Wealth distribution remains an issue, but the exponential growth in technology and production which have characterised modern society, has also brought many unforeseen risks such that these 'unknown and unintended consequences come to be a dominant force in history and society' (Beck 1992, p 22). The type of risks Beck is referring to are those associated with anthropogenic climate change, nuclear technol-ogy, biological warfare, genetic modification, development of new chemical substances, nanotechnology,[4] terrorism, global financial collapse, and so on. These are manufactured risks (Giddens 1999).

Risks associated with earlier industrial society included explosions in factories, collapse of bridges, failure of dams, and local pollution. Their impacts were typically fairly clearly bounded and immediately obvious, causal factors generally discernible, and remedies pos-sible through a defined set of institutions and regulations.

In contrast, characteristics of the 'new' risks include (Beck 1992):

---

4   Nano refers to 10^{-9}, so nanotechnology is about technology at the atomic and molecular levels, opening up new developments by manipulation at this level of matter.

- potential for widespread effects (often global);

- irreversible harm is common;

- particularly subject to social definition and construction, because initially they may be invisible and exist through knowledge only (eg long-term effects of exposure to particular chemicals or radiation);

- while some people may be more affected than others in terms of the distribution of these risks, not only the socially disadvantaged are likely to be exposed, but also the rich and powerful;

- may produce international inequalities (consider rising sea level associated with climate change on small island nations);

- affect not only human and ecological health but also have strong social, economic and political consequences.

For Beck (1994, p 5) the risk society is one 'in which the social, political, economic and individual risks increasingly tend to escape the institutions for monitoring and protection in industrial society'. Hence, dealing with such risks is likely to require reorganisation of institutions, roles of actors, power and authority (Beck 1992). Beck's risk society remains unresolved in a management sense – it affects all of us individually and as societies – but we have yet to put in place means of managing this risk society.

9.5 Dealing with risk in environmental decision-making

As our awareness of the impact of human activities on the environment has increased we have sought means to develop a process for rigorous consideration of risks to the environment and humans and a means for using the outcomes of this process to inform EDM. This process is known as 'risk management' and it may be divided into a number of phases as shown in Figure 9.1. As indicated earlier, due to the increasing importance of risk management in EDM, we provide a step-by-step outline of the process here, following the Australian/New Zealand Risk Management Standard 4360:2004 (SA/SNZ 2004b, 2006). The terminology used in Sections 9.5.1 to 9.5.5 below to describe these phases in risk management follows that of the Standard.

However, it is important to note that there is much variation in terminology. This is true not only between different areas of interest (eg financial risk, toxicological risk, environmental risk) but also between countries within the same area of interest, in this latter case particularly between use of the terms risk analysis and risk assessment. Note from Figure 9.1 that current usage in Australia defines risk assessment as the 'overall process of risk identification, risk analysis and risk evaluation' (SA/SNZ 2004b, p 4) and we follow this definition in this chapter. Examination of recent usage of these terms by the Society for Risk Analysis (USA) (SRA USA undated), the National Research Council (US) (NRC US 2008), SA/SNZ (2004b, 2006) and Burgman (2005), shows the terminology to be very messy.

Figure 9.1 The risk management cycle

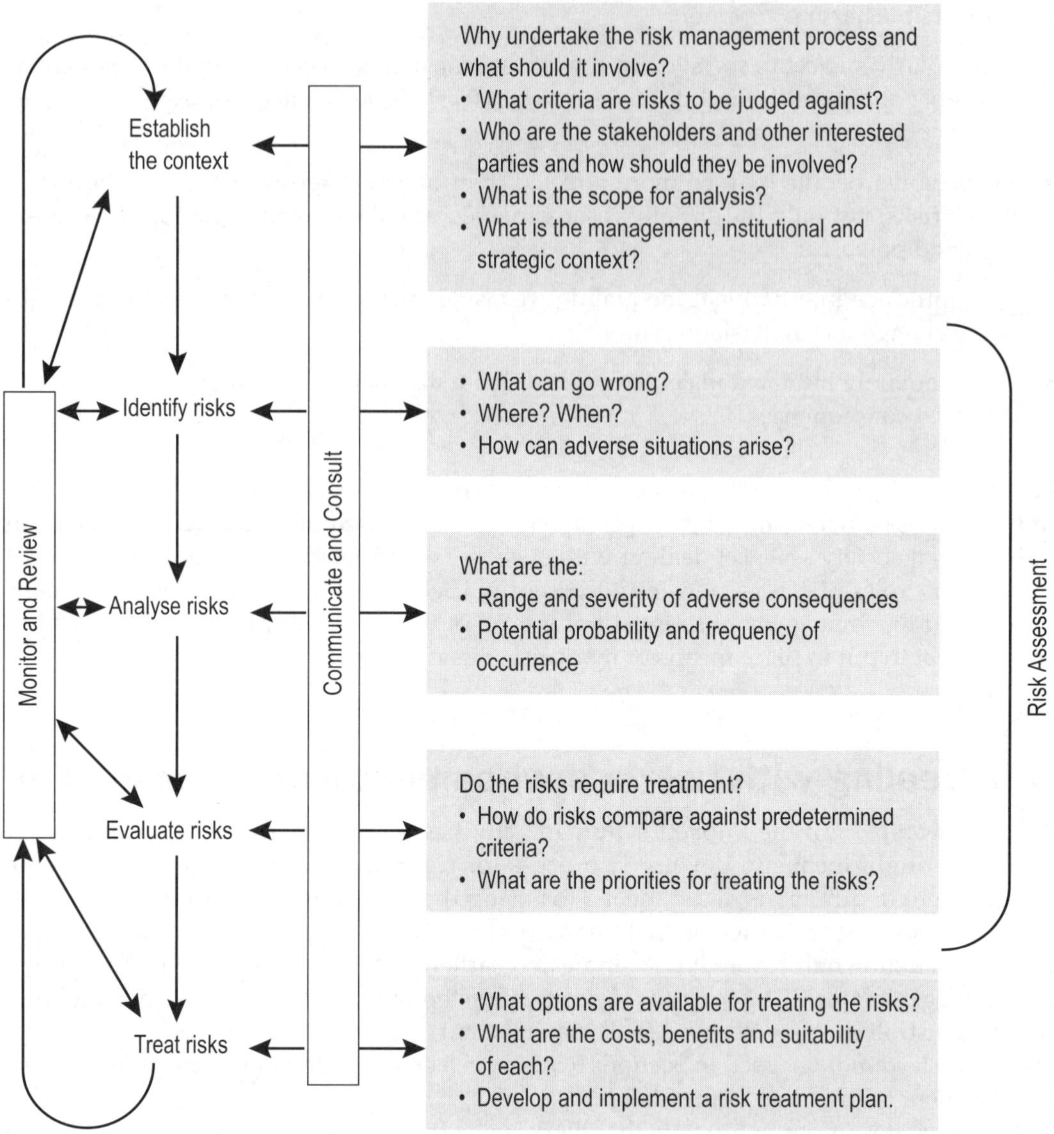

Why undertake the risk management process and what should it involve?
- What criteria are risks to be judged against?
- Who are the stakeholders and other interested parties and how should they be involved?
- What is the scope for analysis?
- What is the management, institutional and strategic context?

Establish the context

- What can go wrong?
- Where? When?
- How can adverse situations arise?

Identify risks

What are the:
- Range and severity of adverse consequences
- Potential probability and frequency of occurrence

Analyse risks

Do the risks require treatment?
- How do risks compare against predetermined criteria?
- What are the priorities for treating the risks?

Evaluate risks

- What options are available for treating the risks?
- What are the costs, benefits and suitability of each?
- Develop and implement a risk treatment plan.

Treat risks

Monitor and Review

Communicate and Consult

Risk Assessment

Based on SA/SNZ 2004b, 2006.

9.5.1 Establishing the risk context

The initial step in any risk management process is to understand the socio-political context of the risk. This is a particularly important exercise since it sets up the framework for the entire risk management process, including identifying stakeholders and others who may bear the risk or be interested, and/or whose contributions may be essential to meeting the desired outcomes of the risk management process. Careful consideration needs to be given to the best methods for communicating and engaging with these actors, and engagement should take place from the earliest stage of planning. It is important to cast the net broadly in identifying relevant parties (Burgman 2005; SA/SNZ 2006).

There are a number of contexts that need to be considered in relation to the planned activity, policy or process, starting with the external and internal contexts. Here the focus is on the regulatory, social, political and financial aspects and, internally, the organisational structure, capabilities and culture. The risk management context is also examined. That is, aspects relating to the activity under consideration – what are its major impacts and benefits? What are the objectives for the risk management study? For example, these may be to gain community acceptance for an activity and regulatory approval, as well as identifying actions to reduce detrimental impacts on the environment. Importantly, the criteria against which the risk will be evaluated (see 9.5.4) are determined, as is the way in which the process of identifying risks should be structured (SA/SNZ 2006). A recent report in the United States stressed the importance of this first stage in ensuring that the outcomes of the risk management process are most relevant for those who will manage the risk (NRC US 2008).

Following these considerations the system to be analysed is defined and the plan for risk analysis is documented.

9.5.2 Identifying risks

The second phase in the risk management process is to *identify* the risks that need to be managed. Risk identification is not simple, and ideally requires a good knowledge of the workings of the processes being examined together with an ability to think imaginatively and laterally. The human element must also be included since this is often a contributing cause to disasters.

Identifying the *sources* of risk, that is, the hazards (such as storage of a toxic chemical) and related incidents (such as leakage of the chemical from the storage tank) is the first task. The environment surrounding the incident site needs to be carefully examined to determine all possible significant impacts from such incidents. These may be biological (ecosystems and their contained flora and fauna), physical (groundwater, soil, atmosphere) and social (cultural heritage, demographics) (SA/SNZ 2006). However, the relationship between the source and the impact may be complex. For example, a single source of risk can have many impacts and a number of sources of risk may contribute to the same impact.

Hazards may be broadly grouped as acute or chronic:

- **Acute** refers to the immediacy and intensity of the effect, not its seriousness. An explosion followed by a fire is an immediate and intense event but depending on the circumstances its effects may not be very serious.

- **Chronic** implies a low level hazard whose impact may be continued over some time and whose readily observable effect may be delayed.

Hazard identification needs to employ an appropriate framework and tools in order to systematically link causes and effects. Matters that must be considered include:

- the nature of the activity (for example, chemical plant, dam and so on);

- its surrounding environment (ecosystem components);

- the effectiveness of the safeguards and management systems put in place to minimise chance of failure of equipment and processes;

- where to draw the boundaries of the system to be examined, that is, what should be included in the analysis and what can be left out.

Both past experience and use of imaginative 'what if' scenarios (to help identify possible problems or combinations of events not previously experienced) are required in hazard identification. For example, despite very detailed analyses on hazards associated with nuclear power plants, hazard identification failed to include the possibility of fire resulting from a technician using a candle to seek out an electrical fault! Yet a fire arising from this cause led to a major hazard event at the Browns Ferry nuclear plant in Alabama in the United States in 1975 (Cutter 1993). This illustrates Burgman's view (2005, p 142) that hazard identification is an area of environmental risk management that requires improvement, since 'there is a wide range of methods for hazard assessment that are rarely used'.

While this section has emphasised risks *to the environment* as a result of the activities of an organisation, the environment may also impose risks *on an organisation*. For example, drought will impact on agriculture businesses and pollution in waterbodies may impact on fish and tourism businesses (SA/SNZ 2006).

A most important early stage of hazard and risk identification is setting the boundaries for consideration. This can profoundly influence the outcome of the exercise and hence should involve appropriate experts (see Chapter 6) and a wide range of actors and affected parties in an early scoping exercise. Some relevant issues in setting boundaries include (ADB 1990):

- Should routine releases of a pollutant from an activity be considered or accidental releases, or both?

- Where should the demographic boundaries be set? Should they include just those people occupationally exposed to a hazard or should potential exposure of the general public be considered? Should potential impacts on future generations be considered?

- Is there a need to identify potentially vulnerable groups such as children, the elderly, the chronically ill?

- Where should geographic boundaries be set? These may extend way beyond the immediate boundaries of a project or facility, in relation to supply of raw materials, use of products, and disposal of wastes. In addition some pollutants or other impacts may pose particular hazards in sensitive or especially important localities such as nature conservation areas.

- Which phases of the project should be included? For example, construction, operation and disestablishment of a facility.

- What is the time span of concern? For some impacts of a proposal there may be a considerable delay between an action and its effect.

- What human health effects should be measured? Just mortality rates, or should chronic low level effects, effects transferred across generations through genetic damage, and so on, also be considered?

- What ecosystem parameters should be measured? Due to the complexity of ecosystems this is perhaps the most open-ended of issues to be considered in establishing boundaries of concern (see Box 9.2).

Decisions on each of these boundary matters will be subjective. Further sources of subjectivity in risk identification are discussed in 9.8. However, it is worth noting here that given the scope for subjectivity and inherent uncertainty associated with identifying risks, one way to enhance the quality and comprehensiveness of the hazard/risk identification is to use a team composed of appropriate technical expertise and experience, together with people with an understanding of local conditions and management structures and processes. Local, lay, and traditional or Indigenous knowledge (see Chapter 6) may make an important contribution. As we have seen in Chapter 6 such knowledge can bring an alternative perspective which may span a long period of time and thus may make an important contribution where time-series data from scientific sources are lacking. It is also important to ensure that those who will bear the risks are included (Burgman 2005). These same points regarding participants in hazard/risk identification, are also relevant to the next phase – analysing risk.

9.5.3 Analysing risk

Following risk identification an estimate is made of the *level* of risk. Taking account of existing measures to control the risk, this involves an analysis of (SA/SNZ 2006):

* The probability/frequency (likelihood) of occurrence of a defined risk (that is, the final environmental impact, not the likelihood of the initial hazard and incident (see 9.5.2)). There may, however, be a series of incidents which lead to the final impact and these need to be included in the calculations of the likelihood of the final impact.

* The magnitude of the consequences, which may be impacts on the environment (including humans) or on the business or organisation.

The likelihood and the consequences are combined to determine the level of risk. Risk analysis may produce quantitative and/or qualitative[5] results. Both past experience (historical records) and future predictions (modelling of the systems concerned) are used. Qualitative analysis may be used as a first step in indicating *which* risks are minor and acceptable and which are more serious and deserve detailed quantitative analysis (see Figure 9.2). However, in environmental risk analysis, the complexity of ecosystems and typically high levels of uncertainty mean that risk analysis is often qualitative. The risk remaining when the risk levels have been determined and existing controls are taken into account is termed the 'residual risk'. Its level is of course dependent on the effectiveness of the controls, and determining this is part of risk analysis (SA/SNZ 2006).

9.5.4 Evaluating risk

The purpose of risk evaluation is to provide a structured means for comparing risks associated with the activities in question, against other risks to which the public and the environment are exposed, and against predetermined criteria for desired environmental and social outcomes,[6] so as to arrive at a 'decision on the level of risk that is considered acceptable' (SA/SNZ 2006, p 42). Risk analysis provides necessary information for these comparisons,

---

5   Qualitative analysis uses words to describe the magnitude of the likelihood and/or consequences. These
    are scaled as shown in Figure 9.2. Quantitative analysis expresses likelihood and consequence results
    numerically (SA/SNZ 2004b).

6   Determined in the context establishment phase (see 9.5.1).

and the principles of sustainability (see Chapter 2), including the precautionary principle (see 9.10), provide an important part of the framework for risk evaluation.

Risks are typically classified into three categories as shown in Figure 9.2 (SA/SNZ 2006, p 42):

- Acceptable and do not need further consideration.

- Too high for acceptance and require treatment to reduce the risk to an acceptable level. These may also be tolerable, since they may be tolerated while treatment occurs, or under specific circumstances (see Box 9.1[7]).

- Unacceptable in any circumstances and at any level (also called 'intolerable').

As these categories suggest 'acceptable' and 'tolerable' are not the same. A risk may be unacceptable but still tolerable. That is, we tolerate a risk because of the benefits it brings us (eg high-risk employment, such as underground mining; a dangerous recreation activity, and so on), but unlike an acceptable risk, there is a need to continue to review the risk and reduce its level (SA/SNZ 2006). Using these three categories priorities may be set for making decisions about risk. Decisions range from (i) abandoning a planned or existing activity, either because the risks are too high and cannot (or cannot economically) be sufficiently reduced, or the risks are 'intolerable'; (ii) deciding if risk treatment is required; and (iii) prioritising (ranking) risks for treatment (see Box 9.1).

Risk evaluation is concerned with the significance and acceptability of risk probabilities and consequences, not only in relation to the risk generators but also those likely to be affected. It is primarily concerned with social rather than scientific assessment (though it draws on scientific information coming from the risk analysis) and involves consideration of social, political, financial, legal and cultural factors. The perceptions of different risks held by members of the public (see 9.7), and also their value positions, are important considerations in risk evaluation. Hence, appropriate and effective public participation involving all affected groups and individuals is critical (see Chapter 7). For this to occur, technical information regarding the risks under comparison and the treatment options must be in a form that is readily understood by the lay public. Data gaps, the confidence to be placed in data and the uncertainties should be given prominence in the information provided. It is also important that various options are *compared* as this can have an important influence on people's perceptions of the risks involved (ADB 1990). As well as communicating risk to the community, environmental professionals need also to distribute information and ideas amongst themselves. Too often, decisions are restricted to specific disciplines in isolation from the broader context. It is vital that multidisciplinary approaches are adopted so that ideas are shared and all possible outcomes or strategies are considered. However, remember that including a range of people in risk decisions involves two-way processes, not simply information delivery from risk professionals to the community. Good risk communication is vital and environmental professionals will play a key role in this process through provision of information (see 9.9).

---

7   Categories 1 and 2 here equate to the low and moderate classifications of risk discussed in Box 9.1.

Figure 9.2 Combining the results of risk analysis to evaluate risks

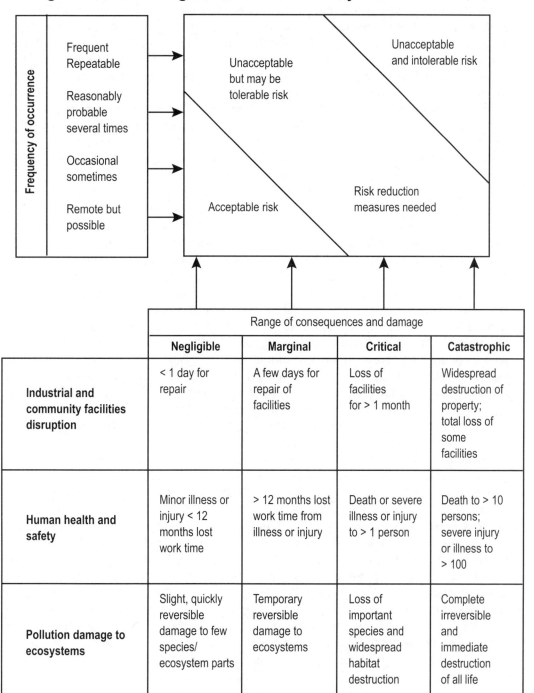

	Range of consequences and damage			
	Negligible	**Marginal**	**Critical**	**Catastrophic**
Industrial and community facilities disruption	< 1 day for repair	A few days for repair of facilities	Loss of facilities for > 1 month	Widespread destruction of property; total loss of some facilities
Human health and safety	Minor illness or injury < 12 months lost work time	> 12 months lost work time from illness or injury	Death or severe illness or injury to > 1 person	Death to > 10 persons; severe injury or illness to > 100
Pollution damage to ecosystems	Slight, quickly reversible damage to few species/ ecosystem parts	Temporary reversible damage to ecosystems	Loss of important species and widespread habitat destruction	Complete irreversible and immediate destruction of all life

This figure provides an example of qualitative estimates of the frequency of occurrence (likelihood) of a risk, and consequences, and the result of bringing these together through risk evaluation to provide classifications of risk as: acceptable and unacceptable, tolerable and intolerable (see text in 9.5.3 and 9.5.4 for further explanation).

Modified from ADB 1990; SA/SNZ 2006.

Box 9.1: Risk ranking

An ecological risk assessment carried out to examine the impacts of lobster fishing in Western Australia provides an example of the process by which risks are classified as 'acceptable', 'unacceptable but may be tolerable using risk reduction methods', and 'intolerable'. Such a process can also rank risks in relation to priority for treatment to reduce the risk.

The Western Rock Lobster is Australia's largest and most valuable single species fishery, worth $A250-$A350 million a year in export revenue. An average of 11,000 tonnes of lobster is harvested each year by around 500 boats, along the continental shelf of Western Australia from Shark Bay to Cape Leeuwin. It was the first fishery in the world to be certified as sustainable and well managed by an independent, third-party – the Marine Stewardship Council[8] (WRLDA undated). The certification enables the producers to attach an ecolabel (see 2.9.5) that should provide market advantage with green consumers.

The fishing vessels are licensed to fish professionally for rock lobster using traps (called pots), and the number of pots each licensee can use is strictly governed to ensure the harvest is sustainable. Management of the fishery began in 1963 and population trend data collected since that time are vital for scientific management of the fishery, enabling scientists to predict populations four years ahead. In turn this enables the industry and government to jointly develop management controls to ensure the fishery is sustainable (WRLDA undated).

The certification process required an ecological risk assessment (see Box 9.2). This process included risk ranking using expert judgment. Activities associated with lobster fishing were each examined separately to identify their ecological consequences. Activities included the physical impacts on bottom dwelling organisms, collection of bait, the fishing process, physical impact on corals, movement of biological materials (such as enhancing lobster stock, discarding wastes, use of bait), interactions with birds, air and water quality, and by-catch (including sea lions, eels, turtles, manta rays, dolphins). Diagrams were constructed by an expert group to show the functional relationships between these human activities, the fishery and the broader ecosystem. These formed the focus for brainstorming sessions and a workshop that included participants who brought expertise and perspectives from the industry, from conservation groups, and from scientific organisations. The group identified 33 hazards, four of which were ranked as being of moderate risk, and 29 as low risk, based on likelihood and consequence analysis (Burgman 2005). Risks classified as low are considered broadly acceptable and can be managed by current procedures. Those classed as moderate are acceptable as long as risk reduction measures are in place and continue to be applied to reduce risks to 'as low as reasonably practical' (ALARP) (Fletcher et al 2005). The risks classed as moderate included: mortality of sea lion pups in lobster pots; direct damage to coral by pots; leatherback turtles becoming entangled in fishing ropes; dumping of domestic waste at islands in the fishery (Burgman 2005). Burgman (2005, p 164) suggests that the rock lobster case is a good example of risk ranking but not without faults. For example, the 'risk assessment could have been made more honest and complete by using a more broadly-based group of participants,[9] providing a more detailed report of uncertainty, and anchoring values for unacceptable risks to something tangible or external to the group of experts'.

---

8   See <www.msc.org/> for the Marine Stewardship Council.

9   Burgman (2005) also notes that the expert group contained no social scientists, Indigenous representatives, seasonal island residents, marine engineers or toxicologists.

9.5.5 Treating risk

Risk evaluation determines which risks require treatment and the treatment priorities (ranking). Risk treatment identifies options for treatment. These may include control measures, alternative technologies, separation of target organisms from exposure and substitution of products (see SA/SNZ 2006, for a range of control measures). These matters all have to be weighed up within the socio-political context and a cost-benefit framework (see Chapter 8) to arrive at an appropriate treatment of risk to meet the desired outcomes identified in the risk evaluation process.

Finally, a risk treatment plan has to be developed and then implemented. Organisations and people generally need to understand their roles in the treatment and so an important part of risk treatment is to inform affected parties of the risks involved and treatment strategies adopted. Of course, it should be evident from discussion in earlier chapters (see especially Chapter 7) that communication and engagement are two-way processes and will not be restricted to this final phase, but as shown in Figure 9.1 take place right through the risk management cycle. We have already seen the importance of involving a range of stakeholders and interested parties in the context establishment phase, but as information is gathered through successive stages, there will be a need for continuing exchange of information and views with these groups and possibly also additional actors.

Just as communication and engagement run throughout the risk management process, as shown in Figure 9.1, so do monitoring and review. Monitoring how the risk treatment plan is being implemented is vital to assess whether the plan is effective in meeting desired outcomes regarding the nature and levels of any residual risks, and if not, what changes are required. This may be seen as a process of continuous improvement and an important example of adaptive management (see 2.9.4). It also demonstrates that the risk management process is better termed the 'risk management cycle', which sits within the overall EDM cycle (see Chapter 1). However, learning and improvement of the process also takes place at each of the steps within the cycle as shown in Figure 9.1.

9.6 The uses of risk assessment

> Risk assessment is just as important as a kind of social grease as it is an instrument of technical analysis. It may provide a focus for people who disagree to define what it is that they agree about and where they differ substantively and ethically.

> (Burgman 2005, p 61)

As shown in Figure 9.1 risk assessment = risk identification + risk analysis + risk evaluation, and hence combines a number of phases of the Australian/New Zealand Standard for Risk Management (AS/NZ 4360:2004).

Risk assessment (RA) is used in many fields of human endeavour, which differ considerably in their assumptions, methods, models, use of experts, and level and nature of interaction with stakeholders and the broader community. For example, comparing the approaches used by engineers, ecologists, ecotoxicologists, public health practitioners and economists reveals many differences in approach (Burgman 2005).

Engineering tends to use Quantitative Risk Assessment (QRA) and rely heavily on specialised experts who are viewed as 'unbiased interpreters of facts' (Burgman 2005, p 45). Previously, emphasis was on the hazards or *sources* of the risk and on technical matters such as failure of machinery and industrial plants based on historical data. Consequences dealt primarily with acute effects involving human injury and death and property damage. While that is still important, growing concern about environmental degradation from human activities led to a broader scope with increasing attention to a wider range of potential *consequences* of engineering-related hazardous events. The consequences considered now tend to include damage to flora and fauna and ecosystems in addition to humans and property, and there has also been increasing emphasis on *chronic* hazards. Moving consequence assessments out into the broader environment brings in enormous complexity and uncertainty and special characteristics that have to be dealt with in the RA process (see Box 9.2). As a result, the terms 'environmental' and 'ecological' risk assessment have been introduced and Standards Australia/Standards New Zealand has prepared a Handbook for Environmental Risk Management (SA/SNZ 2006), to address the special needs required by this broader approach.

Box 9.2: Environmental and ecological risk assessment

Environmental risk assessment is becoming increasingly important in planning and management by governments and corporations and is spreading over a widening range of issues.

Environmental risk assessment 'arises from the relationship between humans and human activity and the environment' (SA/SNZ 2006, p 4). Hence, environmental risks can be both risks *to* the environment (including human health and social and cultural welfare), and also risk to an organisation from an issue related to the environment that impacts on an organisation (SA/SNZ 2006), for example, loss of reputation and revenue from failure to comply with environmental legislation or community expectations.

Ecological risk assessment is a subset of environmental risk assessment that deals with risks 'associated with past, present, and future human activities on flora, fauna and ecosystems' (SA/SNZ 2006, p 4). The complexity of ecosystems, involving many organisms and multiple interactions between these and their inorganic surroundings, results in high levels of uncertainty that make ecological risk assessment an extremely difficult task. The long time spans that typify cause and effect relationships in ecosystems add further complexity. Given this complexity, the best we can do at present is to use techniques which greatly simplify the real world.

Such techniques include (ADB 1990, p 64):

- Data on chemicals whose effects are known on at least some species may be used to infer the effects of similar, but untested chemicals (ADB 1990).

- Use of conceptual models to 'represent how we think the world works' (Burgman 2005, p 127) in order to help understand the structure and processes in the system under examination.

- Use of computer simulations to answer 'what if' questions about a system and to predict future events (Burgman 2005).

These are but a few examples of many techniques that are each simplifications of real world situations, and, given the assumptions on which such techniques are based, results derived from them must be regarded as both subjective and uncertain (see 8.7). Subjectivity is involved when decisions are taken as to which species to use as indicator species, which components to include in models and so on (see 9.6.1 and 9.6.2).

Economists were early adopters of RA and Burgman (2005) notes that this profession also has to deal with high levels of uncertainty (consider the current, 2009, financial crisis) and also unquantifiable values and views on risk aversion.

RA has now become an important part of overall environmental planning and management and is incorporated into a wide range of government and corporate activities to inform decision-making. It can be used at a range of levels, from the strategic (see 2.9.5) to the operational levels. Sections 9.6.1 to 9.6.4 provide examples of some of the uses of RA.

9.6.1 Setting standards

Quantitative risk assessment (QRA) may be used to set standards for environmental management. For example, standards may be set to protect human health from environmental pollutants, such as ozone (O_3), a key component in photochemical smog, produced in urban areas mainly from the action of sunlight on car exhaust emissions (see also 10.2). Medical authorities examine the risks to human health from a range of ambient air ozone levels and make recommendations to government on a level that should not be exceeded in particular situations. Government, in turn, will consider the precursors to ozone formation in car exhaust emissions and may set in place standards aimed at reducing these emissions. For example, the Australian Design Rules for motor car design set such a standard.[10]

Standards may also be set in relation to risks to ecosystems. For example the potential damage of algal blooms associated with release of phosphorus and nitrogen compounds to waterways constitutes an *ecosystem risk*. To address this risk, water quality standards may be developed and linked with regulation on releases of nitrogen and phosphorus from sewage treatment plants.

9.6.2 Predicting impacts

Risk assessment may be used to predict impacts for Environmental Impact Assessment (EIA) (see 8.3). For example, in New South Wales since the mid-1980s RA has been a formal part of development approval procedures involving projects defined as being of a potentially hazardous nature.

However, RA is also used voluntarily for developments that do not fit within the definition of 'hazardous'. Indeed RA would seem an essential contributor to EIA, and partnership between EIA and RA seems certain to increase since calls 'for more scientific rigor and analysis of uncertainty push EIA toward risk assessment practices, while calls for legal and policy reviews and for more stakeholder and public participation push risk assessment toward EIA practices' (Suter 2006, p 21). Similarly, Thomas and Elliott (2005, p 38) suggest that considerations of risk may be incorporated into all stages of planning for a proposal since 'risk assessment and analysis are at the heart of environmental management generally, and EIA' and provide 'a framework for deciding which are the important (ie significant) impacts, and therefore which will be included in the study, and which will be included in management plans'.

---

10   See <www.infrastructure.gov.au/roads/environment/impact/index.aspx> for information on Australian Design Rules for Motor Vehicles (accessed 1 April 2009).

9.6.3 Strategic planning

Risk assessment is also used at a broader level to compare risks in order to set long-term strategic priorities for environmental management. RA for strategic planning purposes can take place at a number of levels within government and business.

A government department might compare environmental risks in order to decide on priorities for use of scarce resources available for environmental management. For example, should more attention be given to identification and remediation of contaminated sites or to prevention of eutrophication of river systems caused by agricultural run-off and discharge from sewerage systems? Use of RA in this way is called 'comparative risk assessment'. It involves public participation to identify issues and quantify concerns (Beer and Ziolkowski 1996).   Government may also use RA for Strategic Environmental Assessment (see 8.3) and hence to help in planning the siting of a number of industries within a region.

Corporations use RA to help assess possible future financial liabilities arising from their activities and products. These may include *processes* which lead to pollution, land degradation or accidents (such as explosions), or *products* which harm human or environmental health (eg hazardous chemicals). Assessments may be used to assist in designing ways to minimise identified risks or even to set a new direction or new priorities for the corporation's activities. Corporations are increasingly required to estimate these potential liabilities in their annual accounts.

9.6.4 Refining organisational Environmental Management Systems

Corporations and other organisations may use RA to refine their Environmental Management System (EMS) (see 8.4) and policies. As new scientific information becomes available regarding the potential environmental impacts posed by an organisation's activities, comparative RA across these activities can help identify the most efficacious and cost-effective changes in management arrangements to prevent environmental harm.

In considering possible risk treatment measures, organisations not only need to take account of scientific and technical solutions for lessening risks, but equally important may be work on improving management systems so that the safety devices in place perform to expectation and the chance of accidents from human error is minimised. An EMS can provide the framework for putting a risk management process into an organisation (SA/SNZ 2006).

9.7 Risk perception and defining 'acceptable' risk

The task of decision-makers in defining 'acceptable' risk, as part of the risk evaluation process (see 9.5.4), is complicated because people may not only hold different views about the acceptability of a *particular risk*, but also perceive '*different risks differently*'. Hence *risk perception* is a critical element of risk evaluation and treatment which is ignored at the decision-maker's peril!

9.7.1 Risk perception

> [R]isk perception involves people's beliefs, attitudes, judgements and feelings, as well as the wider social or cultural values and dispositions that people adopt, towards hazards and their benefits.

> (Royal Society 1992, p 89)

Some of us ride motor bikes, swim in a big surf with strong undertow, fly gliders or rock climb. Others may consider all these too risky but are happy to continue with their occupation as a coal miner or as a scientific researcher working on highly infectious diseases, or even just to sit in front of the television smoking cigarettes. Clearly people perceive risks differently and differ in their willingness to accept particular risks!

Peter Sandman, a risk communication researcher and consultant, points out that in the United States there is only a weak correlation between the potential harm from a hazard, and how upset people get about it. In other words 'the risks that kill people and the risks that upset people are completely different' (Sandman 2007, p 59). He suggests that this poor correlation indicates that people's concerns do not match the statistics. He also says that a similar disparity is seen in comparing people's concerns regarding ecosystems and the demonstrated risks to ecosystems. The problem with this poor correlation is that governments' political response is generally to introduce regulations and spend money addressing the matters that *concern* people, with the result that money may be directed away from far more needy (that is, more at risk) environmental issues. For example, in the United States people's concern about contaminated sites led, in the 1990s, to a large proportion of the EPA's budget going to clean up such sites, despite the technical experts maintaining that indoor air pollution was a more serious threat to human health (but was not perceived as such by the public) (Slovic 1999).

Does this disparity between technical measures of risks and people's perceptions of risk nullify the now common view, outlined above, of the importance of inclusion of public participation in risk management? Many have suggested the disparity rests on public ignorance of the science regarding an issue (see discussion in Bickerstaff 2004). This has led some to 'contend that public perceptions do not rest upon a firm scientific understanding of risk issues a priori, and that therefore to use them as a guide to policy would, at best, introduce noise into the system and at worst result in systematic bias' (Bickerstaff 2004, p 837). More recently however, the view has shifted to seeing the disparity founded on a range of important contextual and value-based influences rather than simply 'error or ignorance' (Bickerstaff 2004, p 836), and to recognising the inescapable fact that the public defines risk more broadly than the technical assessor[11] and that this must be taken into account in risk management (Sandman 2007; see also Jaeger et al 2001; Slovic 1999 and Box 9.3). However, while appreciating the benefits of this breadth of inputs, we should not underestimate the difficulties of bringing together the different inputs from scientific risk estimates and public perceptions into decision-making on risk (Bickerstaff 2004).

Box 9.3: Nuclear fuels reprocessing – risk perception

Brian Wynne, a United Kingdom sociologist, is a well-known researcher on risk and uncertainty. He analysed the United Kingdom inquiry into a proposal for a nuclear fuels reprocessing plant

---

11   Nevertheless, we should note that those carrying out technical assessments are not value free either (Burgman 2005, p 370; Peters and Slovic 1996).

at Windscale (now Sellafield). He noted considerable differences in the frameworks within which the experts and the public assessed the risk associated with the development. In particular, he found that the experts made certain assumptions about the social and institutional processes associated with risk management (eg that they are trustworthy, impartial and open-minded) and reduced the risk analysis primarily to technical matters. In contrast, the groups objecting to the proposal granted less credibility to, and placed far less trust in, the risk management institutions and processes. For this group, risk analysis could not be reduced solely to technical matters; rather the importance of the associated social factors in risk management was stressed.

Source: Royal Society 1992, p 117.

There has been considerable scholarly investigation of the factors that contribute to public perceptions of risk. We will briefly summarise the dimensions and conclusions of this research.

During the 1980s, *perceived* risk came to be seen as equally important as *objective* risk analysis, in risk management. Early work drew attention to the way individuals view different forms of hazards in terms of specific characteristics these hazards may share (see Box 9.4). Further work suggested that these hazard characteristics are correlated under two principal factors labelled as 'dread' and 'unknown'. 'Dread' hazards involve perceptions of risks that are uncontrollable, potentially catastrophic, involuntary and dangerous to future generations. 'Unknown' hazards involve characteristics relating to immediate or delayed effects, familiarity, known or unknown, observable or not observable. It was concluded that an individual's perception and acceptability of a risk is related to the position of a hazard mapped with respect to these two principal factors, and the 'dread' factor is the most significant in influencing acceptability of a technology or activity (Bickerstaff 2004; Furby et al 1995; Peters and Slovic 1996).

Box 9.4: Attributes of hazards which influence risk perception and acceptance
Not dreaded – dread hazard
Some risks seem to attract a high level of concern and publicity and are regarded as 'dreaded' hazards. Escape of radiation from nuclear power and weapons, biological warfare and terrorism would all qualify as dread risks.

Knowable – unknowable
People are more concerned by the unknown but likely low risk issue than by the lower uncertainty but demonstrated higher risk issue. For example there is likely to be greater risk perceived in relation to high temperature incineration of hazardous wastes or genetic engineering, for which risks are suspected but unclear, than say coal mining, for which the risk has been clearly demonstrated.

Risk assumed voluntarily – risk borne involuntarily
We are far more likely to accept risks or to perceive a lower level of risk if we are free to choose whether or not we are exposed to the risk. Voluntary risks may include hang-gliding, riding a motor bike, smoking cigarettes – situations in which we are free to choose involvement or non-involvement in the activity. Risks borne involuntarily are those imposed on us by another party whether that be government action or societal choice. These may include

siting of a waste incinerator in our neighbourhood, fluoridation of the municipal water supply, or passive smoking.

Natural – industrial
Sandman (1992) cites an example from New Jersey in the United States where some houses in north New Jersey have radon in their basements deriving from natural sources, sufficient to increase the rate of lung cancer by 1 to 3 per cent. It is apparently difficult to get the owners to spend a small amount of money on a charcoal canister to test the radon levels. In contrast houses in New Jersey which have been built on slag containing radium waste from luminescent watch face manufacture have been the target of a Superfund[12] project to remove the contaminated soil. This has occurred as a result of mass demonstration even though the radiation deriving from the slag is roughly equal to that from the natural sources in granite which are contaminating the basements described above. People apparently realise this but are not prepared to have the industrial risk added to the natural risk.

Familiar – exotic
Things with which we become familiar and live with day-to-day tend not to be seen as risky: the unflued gas heater in a classroom, the sprayed-on concrete ceiling containing asbestos, the solvent fumes in a factory. However, once attention is drawn to the risk by officers arriving in special protective clothing and/or with special measuring equipment, or plans for a clean up are announced, the perception of risk is likely to increase.

No alternatives – many alternatives
If no economically practical alternatives are available for particular technologies people are generally more willing to accept risks than if practical alternatives are available. We may be willing to spray our food crops with pesticides which pose some risk to humans if it is the only practical way to ensure the crop can be harvested. We have been fairly successful in reaching agreement to phase out CFCs as a propellant in spray cans in those cases where alternatives were available. However, we have not been prepared (yet), to terminate use of fossil fuels as an energy source.

Catastrophic – incremental
We are more concerned when a large number of people are killed in a sudden catastrophic event such as a plane crash or bridge collapse than when an equally large number are killed incrementally over a longer time period, such as by cigarette smoking or in car accidents. Diseases associated with smoking kill more than 19,000 people a year in Australia;[13] this number of fatalities would be regarded as totally unacceptable if they occurred in one event.

Source: Bickerstaff 2004; Covello and Sandman 2001;
Furby et al 1995; Lowrance 1976.

However, while these characteristics of hazards (illustrated in Box 9.4) may play some role in risk perception, they alone do not provide sufficient explanation for how and why we perceive risks the way we do, and further work has shown that a range of other factors are important (Slovic 1993). For example, individuals' world views (see 3.3) are also an important influence for risk perception (Bickerstaff 2004; Peters and Slovic 1996). With regard to

---

12   Superfund is a federal government program in the United States to clean up uncontrolled hazardous wastes sites. See <www.epa.gov/superfund/> (accessed 14 March 2009).

13   Heart Foundation Australia <www.heartfoundation.org.au/SiteCollectionDocuments/Cigarette%20 Smoking.pdf> (accessed 11 March 2009).

the influence of world views, Buss et al (1986) (cited in Royal Society 1992, p 111) found that those who emphasise the importance of economic growth and a high-technology society (the technocentrics) tend to place more importance on the benefits of technology than on the associated risks, and to endorse rationality in decision-making using quantitative techniques and primarily relying on advice from experts. In contrast, ecocentrics emphasise the importance of the environmental impacts associated with a high growth society, the social impacts of such growth and the equity issues in terms of costs and benefits related to risks. They also favour an important role for public participation in decision-making on risk issues (see also Chapter 3).

Other social, political and cultural factors now shown to influence risk perception include: influences of a locality and people's experiences in, and/or attachments to, a locality; gender, ethnicity, power and socio-economic advantage and agency (that is, the ability of individuals to influence conditions that affect them),[14] and, trust in the institutions that manage risk activities (both government and industry). The effectiveness of communication regarding risk has been shown to be strongly linked with the trust that people place in the communicator (Bickerstaff 2004; and see 9.9). To ensure that risk assessment takes into consideration these broader socio-political factors, a host of participatory techniques have been developed in which people assess risks collectively, through a process of informed deliberation (Joss and Bellucci 2002; also see 7.6.2).

The conclusion from these studies is that risk perception is 'multi-dimensional and influenced by complex social, political and cultural processes. Groups within society will therefore understand multiple risks in multiple ways' and 'there is no universal set of predictive rules of risk perception that can be applied to "the public" *en masse*' (Bickerstaff 2004, p 836, emphasis in original). Nevertheless, studies on risk perception can play an important role in helping to understand public concerns regarding issues such as acceptance of recycled water (see Marks et al 2008 and Case Study C).

9.7.2 'Acceptable' risk

It is clear from this discussion that even if risk *experts* could agree on a ranking of risks and a demarcation of 'acceptable' from 'unacceptable' risk (see 9.5.4 and Figure 9.2) society does not necessarily view 'equal risks equally'. As well as differing *perceptions* of risks and associated benefits, the 'fairness' associated with risks and benefits is an important element in risk acceptance. Who bears the risk? Who obtains most of the benefit? How fair is this share of risk and benefit? Another important influence on 'acceptability' is *trust* in the processes and institutional arrangements for management of risk (see 9.8, 9.9 and Box 9.5).

Hence what is an acceptable risk to one individual or group or to one society may be quite unacceptable to another individual or group or to another society. It follows that risk assessment requires negotiation between the affected actors to define an 'acceptable' level of risk for each 'risk situation'.

---

14   A number of these factors are linked with the concept of environmental justice as discussed in Box 2.4.

9.8 Subjectivity, objectivity and risk identification and analysis

Risk analysis, and especially quantitative risk analysis, is often portrayed as providing a rigorous and objective analysis of the relative risks facing humans and the environment and through this assisting in minimising those risks in a cost-efficient way. There is however growing recognition that risk analysis is far from objective and that subjectivity is present from the first stage of hazard/risk *identification* through to the much more obvious subjectivity inherent in risk *evaluation* (Burgman 2005, p 374; Slovic 1999). It is worth illustrating this point by outlining some of the areas of uncertainty in hazard and risk identification that require assumptions or choices to be made, which in turn makes for subjectivity.

First, quality and comprehensiveness of hazard/risk identification (see 9.5.2) is dependent on the skills, knowledge and imagination of those involved in the task – different teams are unlikely to reach exactly the same conclusions. Secondly, information about the range of possible hazard types is likely to be far from complete. Uncertainty may derive from (ADB 1990):

- Lack of understanding of important cause and effect relationships, lack of scientific theory to explain these (for example, effects of chemicals on humans and other organisms, concentration of chemicals in food chains).

- Models that do not correspond to reality because they are simplifications and/or because we lack understanding of processes (eg models of the flow of chemicals through an ecosystem and the impacts of those chemicals on ecosystem components) (see also Chapter 8).

- Poor quality of available data because of sampling or measurement inadequacies, lack of replication, lack of time-series data.[15]

- Data gaps, such as no measurements on baseline[16] environmental conditions at a project site.

- Toxicological data that have been extrapolated from animals to humans and from high dose short-term experiments to low dose longer term situations.

- Necessary assumptions on which estimates are based and the sensitivity of the resulting estimates to changes in assumptions.

- Novelty of the project in terms of technology, chemicals, or siting – lack of experience or historical data (for example, Genetically Modified Organisms (GMOs) in the food chain; use of nanotechnology).

Hazard and risk identification provides the basic information for risk analysis (see Figure 9.1). The inevitable subjectivity, illustrated above, in information provided from hazard/risk identification does not mean that risk analysis fails to provide a useful input for EDM and management. Rather, it is generally agreed that risk analysis is invaluable in providing a

---

15   Time-series data are data gathered for a particular area over time so that natural fluctuations in populations of animals and plants and other environmental parameters may be revealed.

16   Baseline information is information about environmental conditions in a defined area of land or water, at a specific time, from which changes and trends in the various parameters can be assessed.

structured process for thinking through causes and effects, in assisting identification of priorities and in designing solutions to minimise risks to humans and the environment.

Nevertheless, it is important that uncertainty, assumptions and hence subjectivity are clearly acknowledged in reporting on risk assessments. Those weighing up costs and benefits in making the final decision need to know how much confidence to have in the estimates. The limitations of the methods used and the data available should be shown. Assumptions that have been made, the reasons for them and the sensitivity of the analysis to these assumptions should also be clear (that is, how different are the results using other plausible assumptions). As well, any factors considered, but regarded as negligible or irrelevant and hence deliberately left out of the analysis, should be shown (SA/SNZ 2006).

Why is transparency important?

- the confidence that can be placed in the analysis is an important consideration in decision-making;
- different analysts may have very different views on the assumptions made;
- people hold very different views on how uncertainty (regarding data and assumptions) should be treated in decision-making.

These three points expose potential sources of disagreement over the risk analysis. Failure to acknowledge them is likely to lead to unproductive dispute over the apparent facts – a key factor in many environmental battles. Acknowledgment allows the debate to start at a more productive level – How should the inadequacies of information be treated? What process can we use to reach a fair decision?

Also, trust in the analysts and decision-makers is likely to be higher if the process is seen as transparent. Otherwise, people may be led to wonder – what are they trying to hide? Trust is likely to be enhanced also by having a representative range of potentially affected actors and experts provide input to decisions on the assumptions made in risk identification and analysis.

9.9 Risk communication and trust

Risk communication is 'an interactive process involving the exchange of information and opinion between individuals, groups and institutions' (Burgman 2005, p 410). It is important through all phases of the risk management process and essential for establishing acceptable levels of risk (Gough and Hooper 2003; SA/SNZ 2004b, 2006). It requires a two-way process of communication, rather than a one-way process of experts educating the public about risks.

Risk communication developed in the mid-1980s to address the disparity between expert assessments of risk and public perceptions of risk. Risk professionals felt that if they could educate people to accept their expert assessments of risk, using better explanation of risk data and better understanding of risk perception to do so, then tensions would be reduced and money could be spent by governments on addressing the most relevant risks, rather than responding to people's perceptions (Covello and Sandman 2001; Gough and Hooper 2003; Jaeger et al 2001; Slovic 1993; and see 9.7.1).

However, by the late-1980s people's perceptions of risks came to be seen as not based simply on ignorance, but rather to be the product of valid concerns emerging from a complex soup of scientific, institutional, political, psychological and socio-cultural factors (Slovic 1993; and see 9.7.1). This meant that risk professionals needed to consider not only their expert technical assessments in determining risk, but also people's perceptions. In turn this required greater dialogue between risk professionals and affected actors to provide mutual understanding (Covello and Sandman 2001). As well, risk communication was seen to serve further purposes, including informing the risk assessment process by capturing a wide range of public knowledge regarding hazards and risks (see 9.5.2), and avoiding conflicts that may prevent government and industry achieve organisational goals (Covello and Sandman 2001; Gough and Hooper 2003).

It is important to consider what might constitute effective risk communication. In the case of risk perceptions blocking achievement of organisational goals, the organisation concerned might regard effective risk communication as removing this block. Peter Sandman has been a successful consultant in this field and has coined the term 'outrage' to explain the difference between public perception of risks and statistical estimates. He suggests that the experts focus on the technical side of risk and statistical estimates and ignore the outrage, while the public focus on the outrage (Covello and Sandman 2001; Sandman 2007). Outrage can be positive or negative. That is, there are some risks that the public see as more risky than expert technical assessments, and hence the communications challenge is to reduce the (positive) outrage, and some risks that the public see as less risky than expert assessments (eg cigarette smoking), and here the task is to increase the outrage, that is, to increase the public perception of this as a high risk activity (Covello and Sandman 2001). Sandman has worked with many organisations to address such situations.[17] For example, considering some of the factors that may influence risk perception (see Box 9.4), he suggests that making a risk 'more familiar, and more voluntary does indeed make the risk smaller ... Similarly, because personal control is important, efforts to share power, such as establishing and assisting community advisory committees, or supporting third party research, audits, inspections, and monitoring, can be powerful means for making a risk more acceptable' (Covello and Sandman 2001, p 172; see Box 9.5).

Box 9.5: Facilitating risk acceptance – Orica's groundwater treatment plant at Botany, New South Wales

Orica is a large chemicals, mining and consumer products company that occupies a contaminated site in the Sydney suburb of Botany, close to Botany Bay. Contamination of the soil which has entered the groundwater under the site is a legacy of pre-Orica occupation. However, Orica is required by the Department of Environment and Climate Change (DECC) to clean up the groundwater and to establish and engage with a Community Liaison Committee (CLC) in the remediation process.

In 2004 the contaminated groundwater altered course and was moving towards Botany Bay. DECC responded by requiring Orica to build a Groundwater Treatment Plant (GTP) to treat the contaminated water, hence stopping contaminants entering the Bay. An Environmental Impact Statement (see Chapter 8) was prepared and included the recommendation that an Independent Monitoring Committee (IMC) be established to provide expert technical advice to the CLC regarding the operation of the GTP. Members of the CLC were particularly concerned that dioxins may be released from the GTP during operation.

While Orica staff, and/or consultants to the company, would routinely have carried out monitoring of emissions, it was clear that the community's acceptance of the risk of dioxin

---

17   See Peter Sandman's website <www.psandman.com>.

emissions would be more likely if they were to receive independent advice linked to the possibility to shut down the GTP if emissions exceeded set levels. The CLC was able to select the independent experts for the IMC, who covered not only monitoring of emissions, but also advice on groundwater behaviour, human health risk assessment, dioxins and process engineering. The process of obtaining independent advice was in the hands of the CLC but with funding provided by Orica. This was important in reducing community concerns and hence gaining community acceptance of the GTP.

Source: Ronnie Harding.[18]

However, risk communication has not always been effective and a number of obstacles have been identified. Of particular importance is lack of trust between the public, industry and risk management professionals (Slovic 1999), since the receptivity of the public to information is strongly influenced by the trust they have in, and level of involvement with, the communicator (Bickerstaff 2004). In terms of communicating information to the public, lack of trust can arise in a number of ways including (Bickerstaff 2004; Covello and Sandman 2001; Earle and Siegrist 2008; Hunt et al 1999; Johnson 1999; Slovic 1999):

- disagreements among experts;

- low transparency in construction of risk information provided by organisations (see 9.8);

- irrelevance of information to local situations;

- insensitivity to communication needs and concerns of public participants;

- a reputation for mismanagement in organisations providing information;

- a history of distortion or exaggeration by risk information providers;

- lack of a shared world view (see 9.7.1).

Beyond provision of information, risk communication also involves the *process* by which communication and decision-making takes place. As discussed in Chapter 7, the process by which decisions are made must not only *be* fair to all, but be *seen to be* fair and fairness contributes to trust of those managing the process.

How uncertainty is treated in risk communication is also an important contributor to trust in a risk professional or organisation. Members of the public are more likely to trust an expert if areas of uncertainty are clearly revealed and are in accessible language. Such openness builds credibility. In contrast, if uncertainty is not acknowledged members of the public are likely to wonder what information the risk communicator is hiding.

There are now many sources of advice on how to overcome such obstacles and carry out an effective risk communication program (see for example, Covello and Sandman 2001; Gough and Hooper 2003; SA/SNZ 2006; see also Chapter 7). Notwithstanding these suggestions, we still have a long way to go in understanding all the variables and possible multidimensionality of risk communication (Johnson 1999). Importantly, trust is typically gained slowly but can be lost very quickly (Slovic 1999).

---

18 Ronnie Harding was the Independent Chair of the CLC at the time of the establishment of the IMC.

9.10 The precautionary principle

We have seen that there may be considerable uncertainty regarding likely outcomes in risk situations involving impacts on the complex ecosystems which make up the natural environment. How do we deal with these situations in decision-making?

Typically, past practice has been to wait for clear evidence that environmental harm has, or will, result from an activity *before* we cease the activity or put in place actions to protect the environment. Indeed, we have often used lack of proof of harmful effects as a reason for not taking protective measures. However, there are now many examples of where this lack of precautionary action has resulted in damage to the environment which has often been serious and in some cases irreversible (see Box 9.6). For example, species have become extinct, soil has been degraded and contaminated, and the health of humans and other species has been damaged. Many cases of lack of timely precautionary action have now been analysed, and important conclusions derived to produce a set of late lessons that are worthy of careful examination to ensure similar mistakes are not made in the future (see Harremoës et al 2002).

The precautionary principle has emerged as one of the principles of sustainability (see Chapter 2) to provide guidance in situations of scientific uncertainty. This principle requires that we take *precautionary* action to protect the environment in advance of conclusive scientific evidence that some new or continuing human activity may cause harm. More formally it is defined as follows (CoA 1992c, p 13):

Where there are threats of serious or irreversible environmental damage, lack of full scientific certainty should not be used as a reason for postponing measures to prevent environmental degradation. In the application of the precautionary principle, public and private decisions should be guided by:

(i)   careful evaluation to avoid, wherever practicable, serious or irreversible damage to the environment; and

(ii)   an assessment of the risk-weighted consequences of various options.

Box 9.6: Examples of situations requiring application of the precautionary principle

Asbestos

It is now well accepted that asbestos causes the potentially fatal diseases of mesothelioma,[19] lung cancer and asbestosis.[20] The time between exposure and effect is delayed in some cases by up to 30 years or more, making cause and effect links difficult to prove conclusively. There were however, clear signs from the 1930s of the harmful effects of asbestos and a North American insurance company back in 1917 had the commercial wisdom not to insure asbestos workers. Nevertheless, it took until the early 1980s before asbestos was banned for most uses in Australia. Authorities waited for strong epidemiological evidence before responding, rather than taking precautionary action following the much earlier, suspicious but not conclusive, evidence available as early as the 1930s. A consequence of the lack of precautionary

---

19   Mesothelioma is a cancer caused by exposure to asbestos and typically develops in the tissue covering the outer surface of the lungs. Australia has the highest rate of mesothelioma in the world and there appears to be a link with blue asbestos (which was mined at Wittenoom in Western Australia).

20   Asbestosis is a fibrosis or scarring of the lung tissue caused by inhalation of asbestos fibres. This leads to reduced lung function and hence reduced exchange of oxygen between the air and blood vessels in the lungs.

action is that many people have died from asbestos-related disease, there have been large claims against corporations involved with asbestos mining and manufacture, and Australia has the highest rate of mesothelioma in the world (Deville and Harding 1997).

Pesticides

Within Australia numerous groups have lobbied for many years against the widespread use of a range of pesticides in agriculture and property protection, on the grounds that these were harming the health of humans and other species. Until relatively recently, the onus was on the complainants to demonstrate direct cause and effect links. Of course this is very difficult when dealing with organisms which are part of a complex web of relationships within an ecosystem and which are exposed to many substances. It is especially difficult when the effects may be delayed, as for example with human carcinogens where there may be 30 years or more between exposure to the carcinogenic substance and manifestation of the cancerous effect. Today we need to feel confident that there will be no harmful long-term effects before allowing use of such substances, rather than the other way around. As a result, a number of pesticides in use for many years, for activities such as termite protection in buildings, have been banned for this use (Deville and Harding 1997).

Acid rain

For many years Scandinavian countries maintained that sulphur dioxide emission from British power plants and industry was the cause of acidification of Scandinavian lakes. The British used lack of direct cause and effect evidence as a reason for not taking costly action to reduce these acid emissions. Under a precautionary approach, the shifting of the onus of proof would have put pressure on the British to demonstrate that their emissions were *not* a primary cause of the acidification of the Scandinavian lakes (Deville and Harding 1997).

The precautionary principle goes some way to shifting the onus of proof in EDM from those who *claim* that environmental harm may occur from some human activity to those whose actions may cause change. Those causing the impact need to provide a convincing argument that their actions will not have serious or irreversible impacts on the environment which exceed long term benefits (Deville and Harding 1997).

The precautionary principle is relevant to environmental professionals and other environmental decision-makers at levels ranging from strategic policy to day-to-day operations. It first appeared in international agreements relating to the environment and has moved from there into domestic legislation and policy in a number of countries, including Australia. Hence professionals working in fields with links to environmental management are likely to be required to consider whether application of the principle is necessary and what responses constitute appropriate application. For example, for scientists the principle is likely to mean an increasing focus on scientific uncertainty; that is, how much can science tell us about the likely impacts of an activity on the environment, but importantly also, *what can it not tell us*, and whether, how and over what timeframe may the uncertainty be reduced? Engineers will be challenged to build precautionary measures into their development plans. These measures are likely to include process (for example, post-development monitoring and Environmental Management Systems) as well as structural measures. Economists may be required to do cost-benefit assessments of various precautionary measures. Lawyers will be required to advise on the legal interpretation of situations that may require application, or interpretation, of the precautionary principle (see Fisher 2007; Fisher et al 2006; Harding and Fisher 1999; O'Riordan et al 2001; Peel 2005).

9.10.1 Applying the precautionary principle

Applying the precautionary principle has been controversial due primarily to the open-ended nature of the definitions and, as with sustainability (see Chapter 2), we can identify both strong and weak applications. In applying the precautionary principle, a useful starting point is to provide a set of questions or filters which provide a structured framework for decision-making. Frameworks for such consideration have been provided by Deville and Harding (1997), the European Commission (see Fisher and Harding 2006), and Myers and Raffensperger (2006). Deville and Harding (1997) use a step-wise approach based on the key terms in common definitions of the principle: *scientific uncertainty*; *serious* or *irreversible threats*; *appropriate measures*, in terms of the issue under decision.

Is there scientific uncertainty about the possibility of environmental damage?

First, it is important to note that the precautionary principle applies to those situations where there is *scientific* uncertainty about cause and effect relationships and about the environmental outcomes of an activity. Such uncertainty may derive from a number of sources as discussed in Sections 9.5.2, 9.8 and Box 9.2. Hence *judgment* must be applied to decide the extent and nature of the uncertainty, and the potential to reduce uncertainty to a situation where we are confident about the impacts of our actions. If we have such confidence, the precautionary principle is, by definition, no longer relevant (rather, the decision is about *preventing* damage we know will result from these actions). However, even for such cases it is important to proceed in an anticipatory manner since the possibility of ignorance or indeterminacies regarding impacts cannot be ruled out (see 9.2).

Is there threat of serious or irreversible environmental damage?

Determining this involves social as well as scientific considerations (see Box 9.7) since people's perceptions (see 9.7.1) and values are involved (see also Chapter 3). There are some matters that all or most would agree on – for example that extinction of the koala would be an irreversible and serious matter, or the long-term contamination of prime agricultural land by radioactivity or hazardous chemicals would also be considered a serious matter, as would widespread global instability from anthropogenic climate change. Other matters may not find such ready consensus. For example, consider a proposal for land subdivision for new urban settlement which will involve the removal of a natural bushland community[21] which is widespread in the area and is home to the Brush-tailed Possum. Some will no doubt consider that since the community and this particular species are common, then loss over this relatively small area is not serious. Others will consider *any* reduction in the range of natural bushland and this species to be a serious matter.

Box 9.7: Judging serious or irreversible threats to the environment

Judging the seriousness of environmental damage depends on a number of factors

For example, if a dam is constructed for the generation of electricity, the seriousness of potential threats depends on:

---

21   In this instance, 'community' is used in the sense of ecology to refer to a naturally occurring group of organisms living together in a specified area (*Oxford English Dictionary Online*).

- the different values placed on the existing river and surrounding ecosystem by the general public, scientists and downstream irrigators (eg what is the degree of acceptable change?);

- the boundaries for defining and assessing the ecosystem and the possible threat (for example, what is relevant to the assessment?);

- the completeness of knowledge about the area (eg are there endangered species?);

- the care taken in construction, the scale of the dam and the ecological effects of the dam (size, spatial scale and complexity of environmental impacts).

Judging the reversibility of environmental damage is also a subjective matter:

- there may be scientific disagreement about the ability of the ecosystem to regenerate after construction, or the time needed for this regeneration;

- there may be different assumptions about the resources available or needed to restore the area.

Source: Deville and Harding 1997, p 25.

Despite the likely range of views as to what constitutes serious and irreversible environmental damage, it is possible to identify *types* of threats that most people would see as serious or irreversible. These include (Deville and Harding 1997):

- loss of biodiversity;

- damage to ecological processes;

- contamination of soils, water bodies and food chains;

- introduction of exotic organisms to ecosystems (such as species which do not naturally occur in the area, or new genetically modified organisms);

- release of new chemicals (new human-made chemicals which are not found in nature).

What measures should be put in place to prevent the possible environmental degradation?

Once it has been decided that the existence of scientific uncertainty coupled with the potential for serious or irreversible environmental damage warrants application of the precautionary principle, it is necessary to decide *what precautionary measures should be put in place*.

These could range from:

- refusing that the development or activity go ahead or continue;

- postponing the development or activity until more is understood about its impacts;

- requiring actions designed to prevent the impact in case it is serious. For example, re-quiring that pollution traps are installed alongside a road adjoining a national park in case there is a spill from vehicles carrying hazardous chemicals;

- requiring constant monitoring for impacts on the environment, and agreement that an activity which it is suspected may cause harm will be stopped immediately there is any indication of environmental degradation;

- putting in place compensatory mechanisms in case environmental harm occurs from an activity. For example, mining in an area may cause irreversible loss of biodiversity. To compensate for this possibility, the mining company may be required to set aside, and fund the management of, another area of similar habitat.

Precautionary measures may be both *direct*, as in these examples, or *indirect*, such as the introduction of administrative procedures, policies and legislation which make for a more precautionary approach in decision-making in that precautionary decisions are made at a higher (or earlier) level of decision-making about a potential threat (Deville and Harding 1997).

9.10.2 Who should participate in decisions on applying the precautionary principle?

It is clear from the discussion above that decisions involving the application of the precautionary principle, whilst *informed by science*, essentially involve *social questions* and decisions. These include: Are strong or weak precautionary measures required? Which specific measures are most appropriate? (see Deville and Harding 1997).

Once the information that is available from science is in the decision-making forum, scientific and technology experts are no better placed to participate in decision-making than are other experts or members of the community. Indeed, there may be considerable advantage in ensuring broad participation in such decisions. We all may bear the consequences of detrimental impacts, and hence we all have an important stake in the decision. In addition, by putting decision-making on issues involving uncertainty (and hence socially-based choices) partly into the court of the community, professionals and institutions do not have to bear full responsibility for outcomes (Harding and Fisher 1993; see also Chapter 5).

With regard to community participation in decisions on precautionary measures, there has been discussion on the value of moving upstream to a level of decision-making (see 9.10.1) that precedes the development of technologies. For example, with regard to nanotechnology, considering 'any potential social and ethical issues *before* significant research and development decisions are made and become locked in' (Rogers–Hayden and Pidgeon 2007, p 346) may be beneficial given its immense power to manipulate materials at the atomic level, and the uncertainty of outcomes associated with this. Although some nanotechnology products are already developed, major use of this technology is believed to lie in the next 10–50 years, so there is time for such an approach. Clearly, this is potentially a far stronger application of the precautionary principle than waiting until specific products are developed using nanotechnology before assessment takes place. However, much work and trial is required to determine methods for deliberation (Rogers-Hayden and Pidgeon 2007).

9.11 Conclusions

The need to formally incorporate procedures for acknowledgment and treatment of uncertainty into EDM has been increasingly recognised over the past few years as one important means for preventing environmental degradation.

This started with the inclusion within EIA of risk identification and analysis, primarily involving effects of industrial or technological activities on humans, infrastructure and the environment. More recently requirement for *ecological* risk assessment, involving much greater levels of uncertainty, has been included in legislation covering certain circumstances. As well, there has been a move towards formal requirement to use environmental risk assessment in setting strategic priorities for governments (Norton et al 1996) and regional natural resource management bodies (see Box 2.9). The private sector has similarly adopted risk assessment procedures for planning, minimising environmental impact and costly mistakes, and for maintaining or enhancing reputation. Accompanying these changes has been considerable reflection on the nature of uncertainty, the various forms it may take, and the need to more carefully and transparently acknowledge uncertainty in EDM.

Associated with this trend, guidance on how to *respond* in cases of scientific uncertainty where environmental impacts *may* be serious or irreversible, has been provided by the institutionalisation of the precautionary principle in legislation and policy around the world. While application of the precautionary principle has been contentious and much discussed, it has also been argued that '[I]n forcing public decision makers to think carefully about the scientific uncertainties involved in health and environmental decision making, the precautionary principle is perhaps one of the most significant principles of the contemporary era' (Fisher et al 2006, p 11).

A further important trend has been the increasing involvement of the social sciences in understanding factors involved in effective risk management. This has primarily concerned issues surrounding the participation of lay community members in decisions on risk, influenced by increasing recognition of the importance of community inputs (see Chapter 7). Such inputs are important to extend the knowledge, views and values brought to risk assessment, and also because those people that bear the risks identified by technical risk experts should have a say about the level and nature of risk they deem acceptable or intolerable. Linked to this latter point is the recognition that people perceive risks differently and that this is an important contributor to acceptability. Of course, public participation is dependent on effective risk communication involving two-way processes (rather than simply experts informing the community). Aside from community participation issues, the social sciences have also explored the influences of the broader policy frameworks and institutions of societies on risk management. These too are fraught with uncertainties and risks, and are an area of much debate within the social sciences (eg see Fisher 2007).

We have seen through this chapter the growing importance of the concepts of scientific uncertainty and risk in the way, at least Western, societies operate. If Beck (1992) is correct in his view that we now live in a 'risk society', where the distribution of risk has come to be a dominating concern of governance, then continuing collaboration between social and natural scientists in further developing understanding of risk management is vital. However, this is not a trivial task as the social sciences have to date shown that this integration of science and society in risk management is indeed complex and that we still have much to learn about effective processes.

10

Progressing Environmental Decision-making for Sustainability

10.1 Introduction

The chapters in this book have explored the complexities of environmental decision- making (EDM) within a sustainability framework. We have seen how EDM involves a diversity of actors as well as a host of institutions and how it requires consideration of multiple values and knowledges. Over the past 40–50 years communities have demanded greater and more effective responses to environmental problems and as a result, environmental considerations are now institutionalised into law, political platforms, policies and business plans. The questions we briefly explore in this chapter are: What effect (if any) is this having on reducing environmental pressures and impacts? And, what is required to develop EDM so that it will facilitate progress towards sustainability? We begin by considering the progress we are making towards sustainability.

10.2 Assessing progress towards sustainability

We saw in Chapter 1 that the term 'environment, refers to our surroundings. Narrow interpretations of environment refer to our biophysical surroundings, while broader inter-pretations also include the social, economic, political, and cultural contexts within which we operate. Therefore, measuring progress towards desired environmental outcomes may involve use of a range of indicators covering each of these areas.

Given this broad interpretation of 'environment', it is relevant to consider how measuring progress towards *sustainability* might differ from measuring progress towards a *broad set of environmental parameters*. We saw in Chapter 2 that sustainability has some special characteristics and involves the achievement of economic and social development whilst maintaining the long-term integrity of ecological systems. That is, to measure progress towards sustainability, we are concerned with *integrated* outcomes across at least the biophysical, social and economic aspects of the environment[1] with the interests of future generations an important criterion. This provides a very different challenge to measuring the specific performance of *each of* a broad range of *environmental* outcomes.

With this distinction in mind, let us consider, briefly, some aspects of our progress towards environmental goals and towards sustainability.

As the various chapters throughout the book have shown, there has been considerable activity in addressing environmental problems over at least the past 40 years. For a range of environmental parameters we have seen improvements, but often these have been replaced by new environmental impacts, and/or these gains may have been overwhelmed by growth in population and levels of consumption (see Foran and Gurran 2008; Hamilton 2003). Consider for example, the changing priorities and approaches to managing air pollution in Sydney over the past 60 years. During the 1950s the major recognised air pollution in the city was due to particulates from industry, domestic sources and power plants, visible as haze and measured through deposition on surfaces (Gilpin 1978). Measured deposition declined from the mid-1950s as devices to trap particulates were incorporated into emissions stacks (Gilpin 1978). However, over the decade from the mid-1960s to the mid-1970s, as motor vehicle numbers increased and the city grew, photochemical smog[2] developed as a new concern in Sydney, with motor vehicle emissions and the action of sunlight on these, an important contributing factor (Gilpin 1980). This in turn was addressed through legislated incorporation of catalytic converters into cars manufactured after 1986,[3] to reduce emission of compounds that lead to the production of photochemical smog. Over time as car numbers have increased it has been necessary to tighten emission standards and introduce further technical and/or social (reduce car travel, use public transport) solutions. However, despite these continuing actions, the Audit Office of New South Wales (2005) concluded that increased use of private cars made it unlikely that goals for photochemical pollutants would be met for Sydney. Particulate pollution remains an issue, but now fine particles (PM2.5[4] or less) which can penetrate very deeply into the airways of the lungs, are recognised as a major health hazard. Diesel vehicle emissions are an important source of these fine particles (Audit Office of New South Wales 2005). Emphasis has also recently moved to threats from indoor pollutants such as nitrogen dioxide from unflued gas heaters and volatile emissions such as formaldehyde from building materials, fixtures and fittings (DEC 2006a).

Since the early 1990s, 'sustainability' has increasingly formed the context for addressing environmental problems. However, the broad indicators we have available suggest that progress towards sustainability is slow. For example, we saw in Chapter 1 how broad

---

1   Note that a fourth dimension – governance – may also be included (see 2.5).

2   Photochemical smog is produced by the action of sunlight on nitrogen oxides and hydrocarbons to produce ozone (O_3) as a major component.

3   <www.epa.qld.gov.au/environmental_management/air/caring_for_our_air/?format=print> (accessed 25 April 2009).

4   PM2.5 refers to particles with a diameter up to 2.5μm.

ecological footprint measurements indicate that globally we are exceeding the regenerative capacity of the planet and thus we are essentially living off natural capital. This situation is far from sustainable. We also saw that trends in population growth and the need for developing countries to have more ecological space for development mean that our global ecological footprint is likely to increase over time; that is, the trend towards *un*sustainability will continue. As well, we saw detailed reports of ecosystem decay from a range of global assessments (eg MEA 2005a; UNEP 2007; WWF 2008).

For Australia, as discussed in Chapter 1, State of the Environment reports (SoERs) for different levels of government show particular concerns regarding water management and adaptation to drought, biodiversity loss, land degradation and potentially serious impacts from climate change (see 1.3). However, in terms of understanding the state of our environments and the success or otherwise of our actions to protect the environment, a major concern in Australia is the paucity of institutionalised long-term monitoring programs that will deliver robust trend information about the state of our natural systems. Over a number of years, many groups, including independent committees advising on SoERs, have drawn attention to this lack of important data (see Harding and Traynor 2003 for brief review up to 2002; see also 8.9). More recently, the independent group preparing the 2006 national SoER stated that although this was the third report since 1996 'it is still impossible to give a clear national picture of the state of Australia's environment because of the lack of accurate, nationally consistent, environmental data' (Beeton et al 2006).[5] Significantly, 'more than half the 100+ indicators for the national State of the Environment Report have poor data or no data' (Lindenmayer et al 2008b, p 228). The OECD in its 2007 performance review of Australia's environmental management noted the lack of consistent sets of environmental data from reports across the country and between different time periods, resulting in a lack of trend data (OECD 2007a, p 231). And the Wentworth Group of Concerned Scientists (see Box 5.10) has argued the need for a set of 'National Environmental Accounts of Australia',[6] based on the premise that the 'lack of an environmental accounting framework is one of the great failures of public policy of our generation and is at the core of our environmental problems' (Cosier 2009, p 1). Without long-term data sets, how can we assess the effectiveness and efficiency of policy initiatives and management actions? (Lindenmayer et al 2008b).

As these comments from independent groups indicate, progress on monitoring long-term trends of Australia's state of the environment has been inadequate. This has far less to do with inherent difficulties in the monitoring process itself, and much more to do with the lack of government commitment to institutionalise regular monitoring programs (Dovers 2008; Lindenmayer et al 2008b). In contrast to monitoring changes in the state of the environment, deciding how to monitor progress towards *sustainability* provides a greater conceptual challenge. As we have seen, sustainability is not just about environmental management, rather it involves simultaneously addressing environmental, social and economic parameters, with an emphasis on not only the present but outcomes for future generations. Hence, one approach might be to develop indicators relating to each of these pillars of sustainability, and there have been many attempts to develop such indicators (see 8.9; Bell and Morse 2008; Harding and Traynor 2003). However, this leaves the difficult issue of integrating the very different types of indicators and deciding how to deal with situations of poor performance in one or more aspects and success in others (Boarini et al 2006), as well as taking a long-term view.

---

5   Quote from <www.environment.gov.au/soe/2006/publications/report/key-findings.html> (accessed 8 April 2009).

6   <www.wentworthgroup.org/category/blueprints/> (accessed 12 April 2009).

As outlined in Box 8.9 there are now a number of indices[7] developed as attempts to represent progress towards sustainability. Consider as one example those associated with the concept of well-being. 'Well-being' is not a precise term, but generally agreed to include concepts of prosperity, health and happiness (Boarini et al 2006). To measure these concepts requires a mix of monetary measures with non-monetary measures relating to social and environmental parameters and the quality of governance and institutions (Boarini et al 2006). While the concept of measuring well-being is appealing there is still much work to be done in this field. For example, there is no standard set of indicators for measuring well-being, but rather, different groups adopt their own mix of measures (see for example ACT Government 2007; and the 'Gross International Happiness project'[8]).

One interesting attempt to integrate the socio-economic and ecological aspects of sustainability is the 'Happy Planet Index' (HPI) developed by the New Economics Foundation (NEF) in Britain. The HPI shows the 'ecological efficiency with which human well-being is delivered around the world'.[9] That is, it involves measures of life satisfaction, life expectancy, and the ecological footprint (EF) used to produce this well-being. Similar scores can be achieved through different combinations of these measures. For example, Australia scores poorly in the HPI largely because of its high EF, rather than because we have low life expectancy and/or are considered an 'unhappy' nation. The NEF suggests that the HPI is useful in highlighting unsustainable areas to be addressed, since much can be achieved through addressing the components shown to produce low scores. For the NEF, sustainability is about 'providing long-term well-being for all without exceeding the limits of equitable resource consumption'.[10]

But there are further layers of complexity in attempting to measure progress towards sustainability. For example, we explored in Chapter 2 (2.10) whether sustainability should be regarded as a 'journey' or a 'destination'. Depending on which definition is adopted, the parameters to measure sustainability are likely to be very different. At another level Bell and Morse (2008, p xvii) suggest that sustainability may be 'immeasurable', since 'so much of life is immeasurable' and 'we end up measuring things that can be measured and not things that should be measured'. As well, sustainability is a value-laden concept (see Chapter 2), so *whose* values will be used in deciding on progress towards sustainability, and how can this be decided? Clearly public participation (see Chapter 7) must play an important role in bringing values more explicitly into the process of determining what is important to measure, and how to evaluate the results. One method, most suitable for local communities or for organisations, is to envision a sustainable future (see 2.9.1) and then define indicators (see 8.9) linked to targets for achieving this future state, and monitor trends in these indicators.

Despite all this activity, it seems however, that we are still a long way from having an agreed means for deciding how best to judge progress towards sustainability. Nevertheless there are situations where broad agreement can be reached that our current situation is *un*sustainable (for example, pollution causing human deaths; loss of critical ecosystem services; gross disparities between people in access to basic needs such as food, water and shelter) and these should be addressed as a matter of urgency.

---

7   An index is a composite measure that integrates a number of indicators. Indices is the plural of index (see Box 8.9).

8   <www.grossinternationalhappiness.org/index.html> (accessed 25 April 2009).

9   <www.happyplanetindex.org/about.htm> (accessed 19 April 2009).

10 <www.happyplanetindex.org/reveal2.htm> (accessed 19 April 2009).

Progress towards sustainability may be examined at a wide range of levels of governance and for different sectors. Brief comments have been given above on the global and national scales (using EFs and a combined EF and well-being index) and on some environmental components of sustainability for Australia. It is beyond the scope of this chapter to explore other sectors and scales, but a brief consideration of the corporate sector is important given its potential to influence sustainability outcomes.

The adoption of sustainability practices by business has been both patchy and evolutionary. A series of six phases has been identified in the response of business to the sustainability challenge (Benn et al 2006). These are shown in Table 10.1 and may be seen as three waves along a spectrum of change towards sustainability (Kemp et al 2004). At one end of the spectrum are companies that reject environmental reforms and take a business as usual approach. Further along the spectrum are businesses that have taken some steps towards accommodating environmental matters into their production and management practices, under the rationale of compliance or efficiency. At the most progressive extreme (to the right of Table 10.1) are businesses that could be considered environmental leaders in their fields. In this group are companies that have reformed their business so that their environmental performance provides them with a competitive edge. In most cases these reforms extend well beyond technological fixes; often they entail a complete reformulation of business practices.

In relation to the phases in Table 10.1 it is likely that most organisations in Australia currently fall into the second wave (Phases 3 and 4) of corporate sustainability. Some businesses, such as Fuji-Xerox with its Eco Manufacturing Plant in Sydney, have moved to Phase 5 (Benn et al 2006). Interface, the much cited international carpet company, is another example of Phase 5 corporate sustainability (see Doppelt 2003; Hargroves and Smith 2005).

It is important to note that Table 10.1 is not suggesting that all organisations will move through each of these steps. Rather, organisations may leap-frog phases or move backwards, that is move away from previous sustainability practices (Benn et al 2006).

As discussed above, measuring progress towards sustainability is difficult. For the corporate sector, the Global Reporting Initiative (GRI)[11] has played an important role in facilitating use of common principles for businesses attempting to adopt a sustainability agenda, and disclose progress against it. The GRI's Sustainability Reporting Guidelines[12] provide: a framework for reporting (developed through dialogue with a range of interested actors from business, investors, civil society); guidelines and principles for report content and for setting of boundaries; and, indicators covering economic, environmental and social (labour practices, human rights, society, product responsibility) matters. While the problem of integration across environmental, social and economic parameters is not solved by the GRI approach, the set of possible indicators is comprehensive, and importantly, each organisation is required to consider its key impacts on sustainability outcomes, and to determine critical areas for reporting. The common GRI framework has been widely adopted, provides a credible disclosure format, and enables comparison across organisations.[13]

In sum, much has been done to address environmental problems over many years now, and more recently this has been within the broader context of sustainability. So how can we explain why progress has been relatively slow? Below we suggest that there is no one single

---

11   See also 5.3 and 8.10.

12   Available at <www.globalreporting.org/Home> (accessed 12 April 2009).

13   <www.ethics.org.au/about-us/ethics-services/responsible-business-practice/gri-in-australia.html> (accessed 28 April 2009).

Table 10.1 Phases in the development of corporate sustainability

1st wave Business as usual Opposition, apathy and ignorance		2nd wave Alert to external forces Attention to potential savings		3rd wave Change oriented Focus on sustainability	
Phase 1 Rejection	**Phase 2** Non-responsiveness	**Phase 3** Compliance	**Phase 4** Efficiency	**Phase 5** Strategic proactivity	**Phase 6** The sustaining corporation
• environment a free good for exploitation – impacts ignored. • employees exploited. • active opposition to constraints on activities. • community claims dismissed as illegitimate.	• environment impacts taken for granted. • human resource strategies absent or focus on compliant workforce. • ignorant or not aware rather than opposing an ethic beyond financial gain.	• focus on reducing risk of sanctions for failing to meet minimum standards as an employer or producer. • primarily reactive to legal requirements but some pro-activity regarding public image.	• focus on efficiency gains and avoidable costs for both human resources and environmental practices. • value of waste products for sale as resource. • start of recognising value of sustainability practices.	• sustainability key part of business strategy for competitive advantage. • proactive environment strategies – product and process redesign. • focus on achieving leading business practice, aims to be employer of choice. • corporate citizenship to build stakeholder support.	• sustainability strongly internalised in company ethos. • promotes sustainability values and practices in industry and society generally. • key goal to pursue equity and human welfare and potential, inside and outside the firm.

Table modified from Benn et al (2006); Dunphy et al (2007); Kemp et al (2004).

reason preventing progress but rather a mix of challenges relating to knowledge, politics, institutional arrangements and governance more broadly.

10.3 Major challenges in achieving sustainability

As we discussed in Chapter 2, sustainability issues carry a number of characteristics that make them particularly difficult to govern. They often pose problems with high levels of complexity and uncertainty, as well as broad-scale and irreversible impacts (Dovers 2005a). The so-called 'wicked' nature of many sustainability issues (see 2.2) also means that their boundaries are unclear and their underlying causes interconnected, dynamic and systemic. While many of these attributes also apply to other contemporary public policy issues, sustainability issues have the additional challenge of taking seriously the needs of future generations. Moreover, it is becoming increasingly evident that to achieve sustainability we need to fundamentally re-think many of the existing structures and systems of the way we live – our consumption, production and governance systems (Meadowcroft 2005; Voß et al 2006). For example, the way markets work and how they value environmental goods, the way we design our urban spaces, and the nature of purchasing and consumption. Perhaps one of the most difficult aspects of addressing sustainability issues is that the ultimate destination is often vague and/or contestable (Voß et al 2007). Defining goals for sustainability requires negotiating and reconciling competing social goals, values and interests (see Chapters 2 and 3). And this, as we have seen throughout the book, is what makes EDM so political. Ultimately the ambivalence that goes with the terrain of sustainability requires that we often have to muddle through and proceed adaptively, adjusting our destination as we proceed (Verweij and Thompson 2006; Voß et al 2007; Walker and Shove 2007).

It is not just that sustainability issues are inherently difficult to resolve in and of themselves, but they also pose significant challenges to the way decisions are conventionally made, particularly with respect to our systems of knowledge and politics, as well as our institutional arrangements.

10.3.1 Knowledge challenges

One significant challenge inhibiting our progress towards sustainability has been uncertain and incomplete knowledge (Grunwald 2007). As we saw in Chapter 6, conventional practices and institutions of science are not well-suited to the complex, interdisciplinary and dynamic nature of socio-ecological interactions. Much of the scientific production of knowledge is reductionist and thus does not deal well with the multiplicity of interacting factors shaping sustainability, and their dynamics (Voß et al 2007). Moreover, conventional scientific practices do not typically encourage the kind of interdisciplinary and transdisciplinary thinking that sustainability demands. Consider, for example, how the practices of observation and reproducibility apply to sustainability issues (Grunwald 2007):

- empirical observation is necessary but over long time frames;
- cause and effect relationships are important to understand but these are difficult to formulate given the multi-dimensional and dynamic nature of socio-ecological interactions;

- guidance on potential impacts is important but this requires extrapolating into the future regarding the assumptions and practices of how society might interact with its environment.

Ideally sustainability issues are informed by multiple sources of knowledge, including specialist expertise and extended forms of knowledge such as local and Indigenous knowledge (see Chapter 6; Brown 2008). In practice, however, decision-makers and professionals often struggle not only to source different forms of knowledge, but to integrate them (with acceptance) into EDM. Typically expert forms of knowledge receive far more attention because they are perceived to be more authoritative, rational and objective. In contrast local and Indigenous knowledge tends to be considered less informative or reliable. There are also challenges related to the commensurability of different sources of knowledge for sustainability. For example, when different kinds of knowledge point to different aspects of sustainability they can be difficult to integrate and at times contradictory. As Grunwald (2007, p 253) argues, when:

> [T]here is no means of integrating the diverging results into a quantitative balance and then deciding which contribution is dominant, the assessment exercise will be left up to careful and qualitative consideration as well as to complex processes of weighing arguments and defining priorities.

In other words, the production and use of knowledge about, and for, sustainability is itself a contested process shaped by social and political forces.

10.3.2 Political and institutional challenges

Our progress towards sustainability has also been hampered by a number of political and institutional barriers. Some of these relate to the nature of sustainability itself as a politically contestable concept – a point we touched on above. But there are also challenges that relate to the inadequacies of contemporary political systems to facilitate the kind of reflexive and adaptive governance that sustainability requires (Voß et al 2006).

A number of these political barriers relate to the failings of our political institutions to foster long-term and integrative thinking. For example, in Chapter 4 we discussed the impacts of short-term election cycles, and the ramifications of political boundaries that do not respect ecological systems. In the Australian context, our federal structure has also constrained more coordinated approaches to sustainability, and has often been used as a means to shift responsibilities between jurisdictions, or to postpone decisions (see Case Study A). In some cases relevant parties may be unwilling to commit to an integrated approach, particularly when there is a historical legacy of institutional antagonism, as has been the case with interstate conflict on water management in the Murray-Darling Basin (see Box 4.3).

In addition to political boundaries, progress towards sustainability can also be hampered by barriers that exist within and between institutions. For example, it is not uncommon for administrative units within the one agency or organisation working on related aspects of an environmental issue to be operating as isolated silos. As we saw in Chapter 4, the same phenomenon can also occur between institutions either because of a historical legacy, or because it serves a political purpose (see also 3.11.1). For example, for years Australian drought policy has been predominately under the management of different agricultural departments, and administratively separated from agencies that deal with water, environment and climate issues (Botterill and Fisher 2003).

Different actors also use political structures to promote their particular agendas. As we saw in Chapter 5, some actors are better resourced to influence decision-makers than others. This is particularly the case for those representing business interests, not only because of their financial power, but because they are often trying to protect the status quo, and their vested interests therein (see Case Study A). Policy inertia is often the product of powerful actors who resist the necessary changes that sustainability demands (eg Pearse 2007).

Power can also affect progress towards sustainability in more subtle ways. As we saw in Chapter 3, particular sets of values can dominate and shape the way societies perceive and respond to issues. Recall how the power of particular discourses (or set of ideas) on a phenomenon (such as climate change or acid rain) can influence the way institutions and actors frame, discuss and ultimately act on a sustainability problem or issue. In some contexts, particular discourses might dominate, for example, industrialism or resource exploitation, and this can impede alternative ways of understanding and pursuing sustainability (Dryzek 2005).

There are also particular kinds of political practices that affect our capacity to progress towards sustainability. Too often the conduct of politics requires reducing issues and their solutions to simplistic frames of black or white. This is exacerbated in adversarial political cultures like Australia's, where many issues are divided into two opposing party positions (Papadakis and Grant 2003). The simplification of complex issues is also fuelled by the lobbying and public relations efforts of pressure groups and policy entrepreneurs, where the craft is to promote succinct decisive messages (Eckersley 2003). For environmental issues this invariably means that science is used as a battle ground, while the uncertainties and complexities lurk undisclosed in the background (see Case Studies B and C).

Decision-makers also seek to make a visible difference during their political term, by focusing their policy efforts on visible well-defined actions to well-structured or contained problems (Althaus et al 2007). Sustainability problems thus tend to be addressed in bite-sized policy programs, with funding directed at those that are likely to have short-term and visible results. This tendency means that decision-makers usually have limited capacity or desire to acknowledge the uncertainty of issues, and invest in long-term planning programs.

Sustainability challenges another significant feature of political practice: its attachment to the notion of rational planning. This is the idea that societies can be rationally steered in a particular direction, where there is a clear goal, full knowledge about the effects of different courses of action, and the power to control the path of development (Voß et al 2007).[14] Planning of this sort is often characterised as 'top-down' or 'command and control' where the decision-maker knows exactly how to proceed and their task is to go forth and implement. But as discussed above, defining clear goals for sustainability is near impossible given the inherent uncertainty and complexity of many environmental issues, and the multiplicity of actors involved with different values and ideas about what constitutes sustainability. Moreover, since sustainability is an integrative concept it requires the cooperation and coordination of many different actors and institutions (Meadowcroft 1999). Such an undertaking means that the path towards sustainability cannot be steered by one single power, but rather it requires the cooperation of multiple actors (Voß et al 2007). The shift from top-down approaches towards more collaborative approaches to EDM is not easy (eg Wallington et al 2008). Most fundamentally it requires acknowledging that power

---

14   For an overview of rational planning, see Camhis (1979).

is distributed widely, and that solutions require joint problem solving and coordinated approaches (Meadowcroft 2007).

Ideally decision-makers adapt and update their policy positions in line with the changing values of the constituents they represent. But for sustainability issues this can be difficult. In some cases decision-makers fail to listen and act on the environmental preferences of their communities (see Case Studies B and C). In other cases, decision-makers might wish to promote sustainable outcomes by informing the community and promoting behavioural change, but are politically constrained from doing so. For example, an ambitious decision-maker might consider introducing a tax on cars entering the central business district of a large city to reduce traffic congestion and pollution (as they have done in London), but it might be considered politically infeasible due to the opposition from urban motorists who might hold crucial voting power.

Perhaps the most significant institutional barrier facing sustainability is that it requires transforming existing systems and patterns of production and consumption. As we saw in Chapter 2, sustainable development ideally involves balancing our economic needs with our ecological and social needs. Depending on our values, this balancing act can take us in many different directions. One popular proposal of the 1980s and 1990s was the idea of Ecological Modernisation (EM), which we introduced in Chapter 3. EM views environmental goals as mutually supportive with the goals of economic growth, and industrial capitalism more broadly (see Anderson and Massa 2000). In a practical sense, EM suggests that focussing and acting on the environment can be good for business. For example, by conserving materials, energy and water, industry can save dollars as well as promote their greener goods. Towards the end of the 1990s, commentators disillusioned with the capacity of EM to forge long-term change, proposed that sustainability requires dematerialising our economies (eg Hawken et al 1999; von Weizsäcker et al 1997). That is, we need to decouple environmental impacts from economic growth (see Chapter 2). While there are now countless frameworks and tools available to help with this task (see Chapter 8), none is able to address the underlying challenge that dematerialisation poses: to fundamentally change our patterns and systems of production and consumption, and to transform major socio-economic sectors including energy, transport, agriculture, manufacturing and construction (see Elzen et al 2004; Princen et al 2002). Facilitating these kinds of fundamental transitions will involve not only technological innovation but systems thinking, creativity, leadership, social change, and inevitably, a great deal of politics (Geels et al 2004; Hendriks and Grin 2007; Shove and Walker 2007).

10.4 Promoting change towards sustainability

We have seen above some of the major challenges in making progress towards sustainability. But what institutional, behavioural and system changes are needed to promote sustainability?

Researchers and commentators have suggested a wide range of changes. We can discuss but a few of the major suggestions here (see also: Blewitt 2008; Brown 2008; Doppelt 2003; Dovers 2001, 2005a, 2008; Dovers and Wild River 2003; Dryzek 2005; Dunphy et al 2007; Carter 2007; Goldie et al 2005; Lindenmayer et al 2008a; Lowe 2009; Ross and Dovers 2008; Yencken and Wilkinson 2000). However, it is important to note that there is no magic bullet in attempting to move towards sustainability; we need to advance on a number of fronts. And, we need to be sure that we do so in a manner that ensures that these actions complement one another in a timely fashion. For example, awareness and understanding of the need for change by the public may be an important pre-requisite for acceptance of changes in institutional arrangements and economic drivers that governments may choose to use. Education is an obvious vehicle for increasing awareness of issues, problems and remedies, but is much easier to achieve through formal educational channels to school and tertiary students than for the public at large. For the latter group, leaders and champions have played an important role in alerting the public to environmental problems and in gaining public engagement with the need for change. We will start by considering the role of leadership.

10.4.1 Leadership and champions

Environmental leadership has been defined as (Egri and Herman 2000, p 572):

> [T]he ability to influence individuals and mobilize organizations to realise a vision of long-term ecological sustainability. Guided by ecocentric values and assumptions, environmental leaders seek to change economic and social systems that they perceive as currently and potentially threatening the health of the biophysical environment.

There are many examples of leadership playing a vital role in changing the way individuals, organisations and societies address human-environment relationships and view possible future paths for society (see Blewitt 2008). For example, the role played by Rachel Carson in the early 1960s in drawing attention to the dangers of persistent pesticides in ecosystems, and the link between industrial activities and impacts on human and ecological health (see 1.4). Also Al Gore, who published *Earth in the Balance* in 1992, a book that made the *New York Times* best seller list, and in 2006 released his Academy Award winning documentary, *An Inconvenient Truth*, alerting to the dangers of climate change. These two leaders came from very different backgrounds. Carson was a marine biologist with exceptional skills for popular written communication. Gore was a United States Senator in 1992 and from 1993–2001 was the Vice-President. Gore also showed exceptional skills in delivering his message, but no doubt the spread of that message was facilitated by his high profile within United States politics. From Australia, scientist and environmentalist Tim Flannery has also displayed writing skills that enabled his highly acclaimed book on climate change, *The Weather Makers* (Flannery 2005), to influence a vast worldwide readership. These examples involve mass audiences reached by superior written and/or verbal messages *about* the environment with the aim of promoting action *for* the environment (see 6.2; also see 5.8 on the role of individuals in EDM).

There are also other ways that leadership may be demonstrated. For example, it may involve promoting on-the-ground activities. Australian Ian Kiernan was motivated by his dismay at seeing the polluted state of the world's oceans as he sailed in the solo round the world yacht race in 1997, to involve people in cleaning up their environments, and he founded the very successful Clean Up Australia,[15] in 1990. The idea of a mass clean up has been taken up by UNEP and Clean Up the World, launched in 1993, now involves around 35 million people from 120 countries.[16] Other leaders have specifically targeted the involvement of young people. For example, in relation to care of Australian waterways, leadership

---

15 <http://cleanup.org.au/au/> (accessed 21 April 2009).
16 <http://activities.cleanuptheworld.org/> (accessed 21 April 2009).

in engaging young people has been acknowledged through awards to Aaron Wood,[17] and to Sue and Col Lennox of OzGreen.[18] These leaders have sought to reach people by putting them *in* the environment with the aim of turning observation into action *for* the environment (see 6.2).

Young people themselves have demonstrated leadership on environmental issues, through attempting to influence behaviour change as well as lobbying governments on climate change.[19]

The examples above are primarily about leaders alerting members of the public to environmental issues and encouraging attitude and behaviour changes. But leadership may also be aimed at reforming the formal institutions and practices of government. For example, by lobbying (see 5.4) and persuading governments to change institutional arrangements, decision-making processes and economic drivers, to modes that will better facilitate sustainability outcomes. At another level it has been suggested that sustainability may not need charismatic leaders (Blewitt 2008, pp 226–227):

> [B]ut people who simply do, who guide, who advise, who nurture, who innovate and who embrace the natural world. So just as sustainable development may be conceived as a dialogue of values encompassing a myriad of perspectives and worldviews, approaches to leadership for sustainability may be equally diverse and multifaceted . . . In other words, it may all depend on circumstances, issues, philosophies, knowledge, values and feelings.

Much attention has also been directed to the role of leadership in bringing about organisational change towards sustainability. For business organisations, leadership in this field has become synonymous with the name Ray Anderson, the CEO of carpet manufacturer, Interface, who rapidly brought about innovative change in his firm (see 5.3). There are now many examples of different leadership approaches for organisations and a distinction has been made between transformational leaders such as Ray Anderson who 'through a series of motivating, inspirational, pragmatic, learning and empowering actions . . . altered the nature and purpose of his company and his employees' (Blewitt 2008, pp 228–229), and transactional leaders who seek change through management actions designed to provide incentives and disincentives to encourage employees to meet organisational goals (Egri and Herman 2000). There is now a developed and fast growing literature (for example: Doppelt 2003; Dunphy et al 2007; Egri and Herman 2000; Holliday et al 2002) on environmental and sustainability leadership in organisations that emphasises the importance of:

- the personal characteristics of leaders including integrity;

- the role of shared values;

- creating trust;

- generating passion;

- communication skills;

---

17   <www.wtcc.sa.gov.au/site/page.cfm?u=1340&c=10582> (accessed 21 April 2009).

18   <www.ozgreen.org.au/> (accessed 21 April 2009).

19   For example, the Australian Youth Climate Coalition (AYCC), <www.aycc.org.au/?page_id=350> (accessed 28 April 2009).

- ability to articulate corporate purpose and vision;

- capacity mobilisation and building;

- encouraging questioning by staff members and listening; and

- sensitivity to people's needs.

Importantly, leadership within organisations will be most successful in bringing about desired change for sustainability if it can mobilise governance systems that encourage dialogue and full involvement of all internal staff as well as external stakeholders (Doppelt 2003). Leadership need not only come from the higher management levels. Rather, employees need to feel valued and meaningfully involved in the change process and should feel empowered to take a leadership role (Doppelt 2003). As well, leadership for businesses has come from a range of organisations operating at the global level such as the World Business Council for Sustainable Development, and others that may facilitate progress towards sustainability through developing and promoting principles, standards and reporting mechanisms (for example, the GRI; see 5.3 and 10.2). In the context of local government, Brown (2008, p 143) provides examples of collective organisational change starting with a single committed individual forming the nucleus of an advocacy group within their council. Such individuals came from all levels of their organisation and ranged in age from 22 to 65 years.

There is no doubt that individual leaders can play a significant role in awakening interest and understanding regarding environmental and sustainability issues for the public at large and within organisations (see also discussion on policy entrepreneurs in 5.9). But leadership can take many forms and can have effect at a range of levels within societies. For example, governments are well-placed to play a strong leadership role, though many may argue that in relation to environmental issues, governments are often dragged into, rather than leading, action. It would of course be a brave government that took strong action on environmental issues unless it felt there was sufficient electoral support.

10.4.2 Adaptation and resilience

Given our increasing recognition of the complexity, uncertainty, open-ended nature, and hence 'fluidity'[20] of many environmental problems and sustainability issues, there has been growing interest in developing new approaches that can cope with such fluid situations (Voß et al 2007).

Any such approaches need to be set in a systems context. That is, we need to appreciate that environmental and sustainability issues typically involve inter-connections and interdependencies among many interacting components and processes. Of course there are numerous types of systems, each posing very different kinds of challenges for EDM. Many from engineering and technical backgrounds will be used to dealing with human-made systems, for example chemical processing systems located within a factory. Such systems are relatively straightforward because they comprise human-made components that are typically well-understood, and well-defined because the system can be clearly bounded by the factory walls (at least in terms of its internal workings[21]). When we enter the natural

---

20 In the sense that it is impossible to pin down many of these issues since contexts continually change and so may the views of relevant actors.

21 Of course this alters if we are interested in emissions of the plant into surrounding environments, and also if we include human factors associated with the operation of the plant (see 9.1).

world, systems become much more complex. For a start, as outlined in 9.1, there will be considerable uncertainty not only in understanding all the components of the ecosystem in question but also the biophysical processes linking these components, and links to, and influences from, a range of other adjacent (or even far removed, but linked through water flow or air flow) ecosystems. Even broader complexity comes from global biophysical influences such as climate change and stratospheric ozone layer depletion. But the natural world is set in the context of the social world adding further complexity and also uncertainty. This social context involves human values, interests and often conflicting views. Understandably, setting boundaries for matters to include in decision-making will involve judgment and inevitable subjectivity.

Confronted in EDM with these system characteristics we are forced to adopt new approaches that are flexible, anticipatory (and precautionary), adaptive, and able to deal with conflicting views of multiple actors.

High levels of uncertainty mean that we need to approach environmental problems cautiously. Decisions should give due regard to the precautionary principle (see 2.7 and 9.10). We should also review the effects and contexts of our decisions regularly to see whether they remain valid, or whether either our knowledge regarding the issue has changed, or biophysical or social contexts have changed. Regular review provides the opportunity to adapt to changed contexts, or indeed to modify decisions which prove ineffective in addressing an issue. Such adaptive management, or learning by doing, as discussed in 2.9.4, has increasingly become the framework for EDM. In an uncertain world, adaptive management throughout the full policy cycle (see 1.7) is a necessary prerequisite for sustainability. This is recognised by use of the term 'adaptive sustainability', as a concept of sustainability that places the 'requirement for the preservation of system resilience at the core of sustainability policy' (Brinsmead and Hooker 2005, p 73). In other words, policy for sustainability serves to preserve or enhance 'the adaptability, plus relevant resilience, of both the ecological and economic systems' (Brinsmead and Hooker 2005, p 143). We discussed resilience and adaptability in 2.9.2 and saw that resilience refers to systems that are capable of absorbing shocks (disturbances) yet still retain their basic functions, while adaptability refers to the capacity of actors in a system to manage its resilience.

Given the nature of sustainability issues as outlined especially in Chapter 2, but also throughout this book, it is not surprising that 'adaptive sustainability' policy is increasingly seen as the way forward. This approach is being adopted in many different spheres of activity including management of natural resources, and for industrial, economic and social systems (for example, see discussion in Cork 2009). One interesting recent application is the attempt to examine an adaptive energy policy for Queensland that can meet the challenges of uncertainty across technological, societal, ecological and economic dimensions (Brinsmead and Hooker 2008). Importantly, an exercise of this nature must involve examining such issues in the context of linked social and ecological systems and making connections across scales, whether these be spatial, organisational, institutional or in terms of governance (Walker and Salt 2006). However, despite this adoption of resilience in addressing sustainability, the development of adaptive sustainability policy is still in its formative stages (Brinsmead and Hooker 2005).

Linked to adaptability, and hence to adaptive sustainability, is the ability to learn. In one sense adaptation is all about learning, but this can take many forms. These include increasing our ability to analyse adaptive problems, and learning to keep our options open while we discover what a problem really is about, and the possible responses to it (Brinsmead and Hooker 2005). One form of learning that has attracted attention in complex natural resource situations involving multiple and possibly interdependent stakeholders and other actors, is 'social learning' (Ison et al 2007). Social learning is about collective learning and the making of collective decisions (see Brown 2008; Ch 4; Box 2.7; 3.11.2.1) and involves the 'co-creation of knowledge to understand issues and practices' (Blackmore 2007, p 516). It may be seen as an 'alternative policy instrument that draws on creative and adaptive processes among multiple users around environmental problems (or messes) leading to concerted action' (Blackmore 2007, p 519). Such a process facilitates negotiation over expectations in shared management of a natural resource. Social learning is more about 'construction' than 'instruction' (Blackmore 2007, p 519) and in that sense is very different to traditional, more technocratic EDM processes that rely on 'fixed forms of knowledge' applied to a problem. Instead, a social learning approach views knowledge as something 'constructed' through dialogue on an issue (Ison et al 2007, p 501).

10.4.3 Complementary and appropriate policy instruments

As we briefly discussed in Chapter 8, there are many things that governments can do to promote behavioural change for sustainability. For example, governments can (Howlett and Ramesh 2003):

- create laws and regulate to prohibit particular kinds of behaviour;

- develop incentives and disincentives, for example through taxes and subsides;

- build capacity by providing information and education;

- facilitate learning and joint problem solving through collaborative arrangements.

Striking the balance between the issue at hand and the appropriate policy instrument is difficult. Often there are multiple forces driving behaviour and these cannot be solved with one policy instrument alone. Also significant is that the underlying assumptions of particular policy instruments need to be recognised, and an assessment made as to whether the policy tool matches the issue at hand (Schneider and Ingram 1990). For example, an agency might embark on an eduction campaign to reduce energy usage under the assumption that consumers will use less energy provided they have access to the right knowledge. However, it may be that price incentives or disincentives are more powerful drivers of change.

In some cases, governments might avoid particular kinds of policy instruments because they are difficult to implement or politically unpopular. For example, taxes are far more politically controversial than subsidies. Other tools such as regulation require not only political will and resources, but they also need to overcome any potential opposition. This is particularly the case for strong forms of government regulation – so called command-and-control approaches – which can be resisted fiercely by business and industry groups (see Case Study A). Their preference is for more 'light-handed' forms of regulation such as voluntary agreements where affected groups have considerable flexibility in how they choose to achieve a particular environmental standard or targets (see Jordan et al 2003).

In recent years, economic incentives have also gained more currency in environmental policy, particularly in the form of market-based mechanisms, eco-taxes, subsidies and grants (Jordan et al 2003). Essentially these instruments seek to change behaviour by internalising the costs of environmental degradation or ecological services. In Australia this move has been particularly spurred on by various microeconomic reforms, and the idea that markets can play an important role in environmental protection (Papadakis and Grant 2003). However, as mentioned in Chapter 5 while some economic instruments might generate incentives for consumers and businesses to change their practices, they can obscure broader structural or historical reasons influencing behaviour. For example, in the area of water management, the way people use water is not only shaped by price factors (see Ison et al 2007), but by also by habits and social meanings of water for example, its association with cleanliness and comfort (Shove 2003).

While getting the choice and mix of policy instruments right is crucial for addressing specific environmental issues, pursuing sustainability requires much more. In the first instance, consideration needs to be given to processes and institutions that are capable of comprehending different problems, informing policy choice and delivering integrated solutions (Dovers 2008; Ross and Dovers 2008). An essential part of this is acknowledging that society cannot achieve sustainability through government intervention alone. As argued throughout this book, sustainability involves multiple actors and values, and thus the capacity of one actor alone, such as the government, to shift all necessary behaviours is extremely limited and unrealistic (Meadowcrowft 2007; Webb 2005). Instead, contemporary governance for sustainability requires that governments work in partnership with other actors to develop approaches that are 'robust, responsive, efficient and flexible' (Webb 2005, p 243).

10.4.4 Open and deliberative forms of governance

As we have stressed throughout the book, our capacity to achieve sustainability rests increasingly on collaborative efforts that involve government, business, NGOs and the broader public. From a governance perspective this requires opening-up decision-making procedures to different actors, alternative perspectives and new forms of knowledge (see Chapters 6 and 7). As Vigar and Healey (2002 p 529) argue, 'rather than search solely for scientifically robust policy solutions, a premium should be placed on designing processes that can build trust and understanding as policy evolves over time'.

In Chapter 7, we identified a range of reasons why more participatory forms of governing make sense for achieving sustainability. For example, participation can help to inject new forms of knowledge into a debate and thereby increase problem solving capacity and creative thinking (see Box 6.7); it can also promote legitimacy; and generate joint ownership to common problems. Above we also highlighted that sustainability problems typically involve situations where power is highly dispersed, and thus by their very nature they necessitate cooperative responses.

However, perhaps the most significant contribution that more open and deliberative forms of governance can bring to sustainability is that they enable relevant actors to reason together about shared goals and strategies. In other words it fosters social learning. Through deliberation actors are encouraged to (re)consider different values and preferences associated with an issue, and work towards collective outcomes (Baber and Bartlett 2005; Lafferty and Meadowcroft 1996).

To encourage the benefits that open and deliberative forms of governance can bring to sustainability, Vigar and Healey (2002) put forward the following principles:

- Articulation – the purpose and intent of governance needs to be clear.

- Framing – the governance approach needs to frame issues and procedures in such a way that it can communicate effectively and transparently to relevant actors.

- Coordination – is necessary to ensure that inter-related policies can connect across relevant organisations and boundaries.

- Legitimation – the process needs to be viewed as legitimate in the eyes of those affected, especially key stakeholder groups.

- Mobilising – to ensure that the governance efforts result in action, there need to be actors, networks and leaders to facilitate change (see 10.4.1 above).

10.4.5 Promotion of long-term policies and reflexivity

Sustainability also requires institutions and processes that facilitate long-term planning. Too often decisions are made on an ad-hoc basis, for example in response to current political pressures, or an immediate ecological crisis. But as discussed above, sustainability requires fundamental changes that can involve timeframes of 20–50 years and beyond. Moreover, during this period the goal posts of sustainability will be constantly changing (see 2.10). As Meadowcroft explains (2007, p 299): 'Sustainable development is not a spontaneous social product: it requires goal-directed intervention by governments and other actors'.

While long-term guidance is important for sustainability, as discussed above it also requires approaches that accommodate adaptability and are sensitive to context specific problems (see 10.4.2 above). Thus the kind of planning envisaged for sustainability is not of the 'rational planning' mode (as discussed above) but it needs to accommodate uncertainties, unknowns and changing preferences (Meadowcroft 1999). In other words approaches are needed that *steer* the creation of options and the exploration of alternative pathways, rather than those that determine in advance specific plans for implementation (Voß et al, forthcoming).

The types of steering or governance that promote such conditions are those that emphasise flexibility, learning and transformation (Voß et al 2007). One such approach is adaptive management, which emphases learning as discussed above.[22] Another approach is 'reflexive governance', which we introduced in Chapter 2. Reflexive governance refers to an iterative process of institutional transformation in which interdependent actors and institutions are encouraged to fundamentally reconsider roles and practices (Grin 2006). More practically reflexive governance involves a political process of creating spaces where different actors can come together to reassess existing institutions and practices in view of sustainability, and to develop step-wise strategies for their transformation (Hendriks and Grin 2007; Voß et al 2006).

More reflexive forms of governing for sustainability have begun to emerge recently, particularly in Northern Europe. For example, in the Netherlands long-term reforms for environmental policy are now approached under the agenda of 'transition management' (TMgt) (Hendriks 2008; Smith and Kern 2009) – a reflexive governance framework we introduced in Chapter 2. TMgt rests on the premise that sustainability requires the transformation of socio-technological systems such as those that provide energy, housing, transport, health and agriculture. These broad-scale systems pose a number of persistent problems for societies and their sustainability. What TMgt seeks to do is promote fundamental innovations in the structures and practices associated with these socio-technological systems (Loorbach and Rotmans, 2006). For example, rather than tackling energy supply issues simply through

---

22   For a discussion on a range of approaches for steering towards sustainability, see Voß et al (2007).

developing alternative technologies, TMgt aims to facilitate broad-scale changes in the entire system of energy provision and use, including technologies and their associated infrastructures, institutions, structures, administration and practices (Rotmans and Loorbach 2008).

So how do transitions come about and what ensures that they will necessarily lead to sustainability? At the heart of TMgt is a governance approach in which government works in partnership with innovators, entrepreneurs and stakeholders to develop broad sustainability goals or visions (Kemp and Loorbach 2006). These are then used to develop multiple 'transition pathways' (or possible routes) and typically would use backcasting (see 2.9.1) and include interim goals. Innovative experiments are then conducted to explore the feasibility of different transition pathways (Loorbach 2007). The entire TMgt process is adaptive, involving learning by doing, and emphasises the importance of interactions among stakeholders (as in adaptive co-management – see 2.9.4). Government then uses policies and strategies to stimulate and generally create appropriate conditions to facilitate the chosen transition paths. Given the numerous interacting systems involved, and lack of government control over a number of these (for example culture change), transitions cannot be controlled, but rather, may be steered, with the role of government best described as interactive rather than directive (Kemp and Loorbach 2006; Loorbach and Rotmans 2006; Meadowcroft 2005).

Emerging studies on the practice of transition management suggest that the framework needs to pay more attention to the political and democratic implications of large scale socio-technological change (Hendriks 2008; Meadowcroft 2005; Shove and Walker 2007). However as a framework for accommodating the kind of modulated and flexible planning that sustainability requires, TMgt shows considerable promise (Voß et al, forthcoming).

In addition to frameworks for steering change, long-term planning for sustainability also requires independent but accountable institutions for informing and assessing environmental decisions, and technology more broadly. On this issue, Dovers (2001, p 1) suggests that in Australia we need:

- A National Commission or Council for ESD to promote discussion and cooperative action between the three levels of government, the private sector and community groups;

- A Commissioner for ESD or Offices for ESD to ensure implementation of ESD policies in government agencies;

- An Australian Institute for ESD to generate new ideas, inform cooperative policy development, develop standards, prepare manuals and run training courses.[23]

10.5 Final reflections

Examples throughout this book show that the world is confronting intertwined ecological, social and economic stresses and impacts on a scale not previously encountered – anthropogenic climate change, loss of ecosystem services, population increase, poverty, terrorism and the financial crisis that began in the latter half of 2008. The reality is that underlying causes of problems such as these may brew for many years before a threshold or tipping point is reached and rapid change occurs. Once this occurs it may be very difficult or impossible to reverse the change (Cork et al 2007). And, the interconnected global society that we

---

23   See also 2.4.7 regarding the recommendations from an Inquiry into a Sustainability Charter carried out by a federal House of Representatives Standing Committee on Environment and Heritage.

now inhabit means that changes can move rapidly around the world – consider the speed with which the financial crisis impacted world wide in 2008. While such rapid changes may appear as environmental or social problems, typically the underlying causes will be a complex combination of factors across environmental, social, political and economic domains.

Growing realisation of the increasing likelihood of rapid changes in natural and socio-technological systems (see Cork et al 2007 for examples), has led to a focus on how we in Australia, and the global community, can best address and prepare for such events. An overarching response that is receiving much attention, is that given inevitable uncertainty regarding the future, our governance and management systems need to be adaptive, resilient and in some cases fundamentally reconsidered, as outlined throughout this book.

Achieving such changes will not be easy. For a start, we live in a very unequal world (see 1.3) and both the principles of sustainability and any hope for long-term world peace suggest that we need to ensure the poor of the world have a greater share of the world's ecological space. But we already live in a world where population size and continuing growth, coupled with increasing consumption of materials and energy, are the basic drivers underpinning the degradation of the Earth's ecosystems. Our societies rely on economic growth but increasingly it has been growth based on rising throughput of materials and energy and, in most developed nations, high levels of consumption of material goods – the throw away society. How can we turn this around and maintain a prosperous and just world with high employment rates? Many have argued that a switch to an economy emphasising services rather than a 'throw away' economy is part of the answer (see 2.9.2 and von Weizsäcker et al 1997). This might make sense in an ideal world, however, our governance systems are typically well entrenched and enmeshed with many vested interests that will resist change. It is clear that if change is to retain democratic ideals it will need to be both a bottom-up and top-down process (Hendriks 2008). In turn, this requires an active and involved community that will push for change. In this regard we have seen that there has been much recent attention to means for democratic deliberation and dialogue.

Perhaps our best hope for change may come from crisis, for it is often suggested that 'from crisis comes opportunity'. The Great Depression of the 1930s has been described as 'one of the most fertile periods in US history for social innovation' with a number of vital institutions, such as Social Security, being established (Phills and Nee, 2009, p 4). The current financial crisis could provide the opportunity for Australia to create needed jobs in areas such as renewable energy and environmental remediation that will help address both unemployment and environmental degradation (ACF and ACTU 2008). It can also provide the opportunity to make changes in our institutions and systems of governance for decision-making that can better meet sustainability challenges. The key question is – will we have the courage to make these changes?

Exploring Principal Themes Through Three Case Studies of Environmental Decision-making

This section provides three case studies to illustrate the main themes discussed in Chapters 1 to 10. While we have explored many of the themes through short boxed examples in each chapter, the case studies enable a deeper exploration by working through the story of an issue and analysing decision-making with regard to the principal themes. For example, the role of various actors, the influence of differing institutional arrangements, the influence of contrasting value positions, and so on.

None of the case studies illustrates every theme discussed in the book. But we have chosen them to complement one another so that combined they cover most of the themes. However, there is overlap and many themes are illustrated in each of the cases.

Table CS.1 provides a matrix with selected themes from each chapter on the vertical axis and the three case studies on the horizontal axis. It provides a structure for readers to do their own analysis of the case studies and a useful focus for discussion among readers on the themes explored in the book and how they relate to these case studies and to other current or past issues. Although the matrix is set up for 'tick the box' answers it will be clear to you that in most cases an elaboration of your answer beyond a mere 'tick' is warranted, and that this provides the basis for some spirited debate!

The structure of the case studies

Each case study outlines the story of a particular environmental issue. The introduction and the second section set the scene by providing important background information – What is the issue about? What are the key contexts – place, time, institutional settings? Who are the key actors and what are their roles? The third section outlines the nature of the debate or controversy. The fourth section (analysis) identifies the themes discussed in the book that are illustrated by the case study, and explores how those themes are revealed and played out in the controversy.

Each of the cases is likely to continue in some form into the future. Case Study B (Gunns Pulp Mill in Tasmania) is still very much a live issue at the time of writing and will be interesting to follow though to its completion. Case Study A (Container Deposit Legislation) although completed in terms of the New South Wales inquiry, is a matter that is set to re-emerge at the national level. Will it be in the form of nationally agreed container deposit legislation? Or, might extended producer responsibility policies be a means of dealing with this issue? What other possibilities are there? Case Study C (Toowoomba Water Recycling) is a matter of high national relevance at present as Australia is suffering water shortages in both urban and rural areas. It is likely this debate will emerge in many different settings across the nation into the future. Working through cases in the manner illustrated here is useful for developing analytical skills to better understand environmental decision-making. Our discussion of the three case studies presented in this book is but one view. What other interpretations can you suggest?

Table CS.1 Matching the case studies with selected main themes from Chapters 1 to 10

Suggested ranking for filling in the matrix
✓✓ = theme is strongly illustrated in this case study
 ✓ = theme is illustrated
 ? = possible illustration of theme depending on your interpretation of the issue

Did the case studies reveal . . .?	Case Study		
	A Container Deposit Legislation	B Gunns Pulp Mill	C Toowoomba Water Recycling
Chapter 1: EDM in a Complex World			
Rising social awareness of environmental issues			
Changing approaches to EDM (eg as illustrated in Table 1.2)			
The diversity of environmental professionals and wide range of roles they serve			
Chapter 2: Sustainable Development and Sustainability			
The application (and/or opportunity for application) of principles of sustainability (voluntary or formally required)			
Multiple/conflicting interpretations regarding application of ecologically sustainable development principles by stakeholders			
The tensions in applying sustainability as an integrating concept (ie trying to balance the TBL/QBL)			
Chapter 3: Values and Value Systems			
Influence of ethics, ideologies, paradigms, discourses on societal and individual value positions			
Influence of different values and perceptions on different stages of EDM especially: issue identification; problem framing; scoping of policy responses; and means (ie processes) for achieving goals			
The importance of early and fair hearing of views in order to understand the range of views and values regarding a project and to provide opportunity to accommodate these in project design and outcomes			
The ways governments deal with competing values			

Did the case studies reveal . . .?	Case Study		
	A Container Deposit Legislation	B Gunns Pulp Mill	C Toowoomba Water Recycling
Environmental disputes argued as disputes over 'facts' but in reality are disputes over values			
Chapter 4: Institutions			
The role and significance of political institutions in EDM			
Effects of the division of powers (three tiers of government) for EDM and governance – including intergovernmental conflict, buck passing and 'laboratory federalism'			
Use of integrative structures/processes to overcome division of power problems (eg ministerial councils)			
Influence of electoral systems on representation of environmental interests in parliament			
Influence of government agencies and advisory bodies on environmental outcomes			
Influence of political systems, ideologies, institutions on sustainability and environmental policy-making			
The role of global institutions and structures in EDM			
Chapter 5: Actors Outside Government			
Diversity of actors involved in EDM			
The multiplicity of roles actors play in EDM			
The ways actors engage in EDM and the associated opportunities and risks (eg cooption, funding, public credibility)			
Messy and networked nature of environmental governance involving actors from the state, civil society and the market			
Different forms of relationships between actors			
Varying influence actors have on EDM depending on their resources, position, power, expertise, reputation, organisational capacity, nature of the issue and so on			
The kinds of ethical issues and dilemmas that professionals working on environmental issues face			
Chapter 6: Multiple Knowledges			
The limitations of conventional ('normal') scientific and technical approaches in dealing with complex environmental decisions			
Opportunity for, and/or examples of, inclusion of non-expert knowledge in the decision-making process – type of knowledge?			
Examples of integration across expert disciplines and/or between expert and 'extended' knowledges – challenges/ problems associated with integration			

Did the case studies reveal . . .?	Case Study		
	A Container Deposit Legislation	B Gunns Pulp Mill	C Toowoomba Water Recycling
Examples of conflict between different knowledges			
Chapter 7: Public Participation			
Drivers for pubic participation (eg formal requirements for public participation or community 'right to know', moral reasons, advocacy reasons and so on)			
The role of the environmental professional and decision-maker in designing and facilitating public participation			
Varieties of public participation processes used in the case study			
The diversity of reasons why actors choose to engage (or not) in participatory processes for EDM			
The consequences of no/ inappropriate/ poorly executed participation processes			
Chapter 8: Tools for EDM			
The use of various analytical tools to manipulate and process data to inform and assist EDM			
The use of various behavioural tools to deliver policy outcomes			
Influence of subjective judgments, assumptions or bias in the selection and application of tools			
Limitations with tools (eg problems with setting boundaries, models, monetary valuation, impact assessment)			
The social and political influence on the use of decision-making tools			
Chapter 9: Uncertainty, Risk and the Precautionary Principle			
The inherent uncertainty in information for EDM			
Acknowledging, distinguishing between, and attempting to deal with, risk, uncertainty, ignorance and indeterminacy in EDM			
Setting of 'boundaries' for risk assessment			
Scope for subjectivity in hazard and risk identification			
Subjective judgments inherent in risk perception and risk management			
Problems in deciding/negotiating 'acceptable' risk			
The ramifications of not effectively communicating risk to the public and the role of trust			
Examples of application of the precautionary principle, or situations where it should/could have been applied			

Did the case studies reveal . . .?	Case Study		
	A Container Deposit Legislation	B Gunns Pulp Mill	C Toowoomba Water Recycling
Chapter 10: Progressing EDM for Sustainability			
Actual or potential challenges in implementing actions towards sustainability (eg from uncertain and incomplete knowledge; difficulty in valuation of environmental resources; different values in interpreting sustainability; political/institutional factors)			
Demonstrated stage of corporate sustainability (compare to Table 10.1)			
The role of leaders and champions in promoting change towards sustainability			
Evidence for open and deliberative forms of governance			
Evidence for long-term planning and reflexivity and adaptive management approaches			

Case Study A

Container Deposit Legislation[1]

A.1 Introduction

Most beverage containers produced in Australia carry a label meaningless to all but South Australians. It states: '10c refund at collection depots when sold in S.A.' Perhaps you have wondered why these containers are only considered to be of value in South Australia? In this case study we show how, behind this small label, there is a history of environmental conflict fuelled by competing pressure groups. Our exploration centres on the political events that surrounded a legislative inquiry in New South Wales into the costs and benefits of introducing a deposit-refund recycling policy, known as Container Deposit Legislation (CDL).

CDL is a policy instrument (see Chapter 8) for increasing the recycling rates of particular products, and it was once primarily used to reduce litter. CDL places a mandatory deposit on certain (usually beverage) containers to encourage consumers to return them for reuse, recycling or disposal. However, the potential impact of CDL on reducing litter and increasing recycling rates is highly contested. Critics argue that CDL only addresses a small fraction of the waste stream.[2] Recyclable drink cans and bottles made from aluminium, glass, plastic and steel account for around 10 per cent of the waste stream (CoA 2008, p 93), and they make up about a third of the litter stream (CUA 2006; KAB 2008; *The Age* 2008). Furthermore, the potential impact of CDL in New South Wales on recycling and litter rates is complicated because the State currently offers extensive kerbside recycling services (predominantly for household waste). The vexing question for decision-makers is thus: what additional benefits would CDL bring to the citizens and environment of New South Wales, and how well would it work alongside existing services?

In broad terms CDL belongs to a suite of policy approaches that embrace the concept of Extended Producer Responsibility (EPR). As mentioned in Chapter 2, EPR involves producers taking responsibility for all stages of a product's life from its production and use, to its post-consumer stage.[3] Ideally, producers consider the material and energy used in the product's design, its manufacturing, how it is consumed and its life after use. Along a spectrum of options for encouraging EPR, CDL represents a highly regulated approach where producers must comply with set mandatory deposits, and typically they are required

---

1   The author of this case study has drawn significantly from her primary research into this case, which is detailed in Hendriks (2002, 2004).

2   For an overview of the arguments put forward by critics of CDL, see White (2001).

3   From <www.oecd.org/document/19/0,3343,en_2649_34281_35158227_1_1_1_1,00.html> (accessed 25 November 2008).

to contribute additional funds to manage the collection system. In most States in Australia (where CDL is absent) local governments and their ratepayers bear most of the costs of litter collection and container recycling. Proponents of CDL argue that if introduced, CDL would shift these costs onto those responsible for the pollution – the producers and consumers of beverage containers.

Though applied widely throughout Europe, CDL has been the subject of controversy in Australia for almost 40 years. The debate is highly polarised with environmental groups and local governments in favour of CDL and the packaging and beverage industry vehemently opposed to it. Both sides of the debate lean heavily on environmental arguments as well as self-funded research to justify their position. For example, industry supports the idea of waste minimisation and argues that this is best achieved through voluntary agreements rather than through any form of mandatory regulation. Industry strongly supports the National Packaging Covenant (NPC), which is the main policy instrument in Australia for managing the environmental impacts of consumer packaging.[4] The NPC is based on a co-regulatory arrangement between government and key stakeholders in the packaging supply chain. It involves broad reduction targets, and provides industry with considerable flexibility regarding how it achieves these.

In contrast, environmental groups and local government contend that voluntary schemes are not working and that stricter forms of regulation are required to encourage industry to take responsibility for the materials embedded in the goods they produce. These groups are highly critical of the NPC arguing that it lacks specific targets and that to-date it has failed to effectively reduce packaging waste in Australia (see CoA 2008, pp 92–93).

Both groups in the CDL debate appear to share similar values on waste minimisation (the ends), but have different strategies (interests) in how to reach this goal (the means) (see Chapter 3). The preferred strategy of different groups depends largely on how the waste problem is framed. For example, is waste management viewed as part of a broader environmental challenge to reduce material consumption (the view of environmental groups), or is it seen as predominantly a public and domestic household problem that demands better education and recycling services (industry's view)?

In 1999 the New South Wales Minister for the Environment sought to rise above the fervent politics surrounding CDL and commissioned an independent assessment of CDL (hereafter referred to as 'the review'). Under the direction of Professor Stuart White at the Institute for Sustainable Futures (University of Technology, Sydney), the review team set out to examine the economic and environmental costs and benefits of CDL, as well as its potential social impacts. The latter dimension involved extensive social research into community preferences, including several participatory processes such as a citizens' jury. As we learned in Chapter 7, citizens' juries are participatory processes aimed at collecting policy advice from a panel of lay citizens. The CDL citizens' jury represented the first state-wide participatory process of its kind in New South Wales (see Hendriks 2002).

In this case study we trace the political events that unfolded during the CDL review. In particular, we explore the kinds of tensions that can arise when formal policy inquiries operate in highly charged political settings. We begin our discussion with some necessary background on the CDL debate including a brief overview of the key pressure groups and their polarised views on CDL. Next we examine some of the central themes emerging from this case, which include (i) the challenges of transcending polarised debates; (ii) the tactics and power of pressure groups in and around public inquiries; (iii) the politics of citizen engagement; and (iv) the challenges of governing environmental issues in a federal system.

---

4   See <www.packagingcovenant.org.au> (accessed 20 April 2009).

A.2 Setting the Scene

A.2.1 CDL and waste management

CDL first emerged in Australia in the early 1970s as a litter control measure. The legislation was enacted in South Australia in 1976 as a means to enforce voluntary deposit-refund systems for beer, soft drink and milk bottles, which had been in place since the 1950s. Over the years the use of CDL as a policy tool has expanded from litter control to waste management. In the late 1980s and early 1990s there was increasing pressure on State and local governments to reduce the volume of waste going to landfill. In response waste minimisation policies were developed to encourage recycling, and more ambitiously to reduce waste and reuse items where possible. Many local governments began to provide kerbside recycling services to collect paper, cardboard, bottles and later plastic containers.

While the Australian community has broadly embraced recycling practices (ABS 2006), the volume of waste, and hence the costs of its collection, continues to rise. This has put pressure on governments (particularly at the local level) to explore ways to increase recycling rates while keeping collection costs down. More problematic, is that while recycling may divert a proportion of this growing waste away from landfill, it tends to have limited impact on the overall flow of materials and energy in the economy (see Chapter 8). So greater attention is now being focussed on ways to encourage producers and their consumers to take more responsibility for the waste they generate, for example, through EPR initiatives.

In this context interest in CDL has grown considerably since the late 1990s across Australia and internationally. This has been fuelled in part by several studies indicating that where CDL is in place it results in high recovery rates of containers (see Productivity Commission 2006, p 210). Research from the South Australian experience has been particularly revealing; independent studies indicate that CDL has had a significant impact on recycling rates, particularly for products consumed away from home (see CoA 2008; White 2001). In South Australia, CDL has managed to achieve a recovery rate of about 70 per cent of containers (that are subject to deposit requirements) as compared to the national recovery (estimated to be around about 40 per cent) (CoA 2008, p 111). The South Australian Government has been so convinced of the effectiveness of CDL that in 2003 it expanded its system to capture a greater number of items from the waste stream including products containing: flavoured, non-carbonated waters, pure fruit juices and flavoured milks (SA EPA 2003). CDL also enjoys significant popular support both in South Australia and nationally, with polls typically indicating over 80 per cent support (see Carson et al 2002; CoA 2008, p 110).

Box A.1: How does the CDL system operate in South Australia?

In South Australia consumers pay a small deposit (10c) on beverage products which they can redeem when they return the container to designated recycling depots or retailers. Consumers who dispose of containers lose their deposit, but this can be redeemed by anyone willing to collect the container and take it to a depot.

The South Australian deposit system is effectively funded by beverage manufactures, who pay contractors ('super-collectors') handling fees to collect and recover containers. These handling fees are incorporated into the price of the product and passed onto the consumer. When consumers return their containers, the depot sorts them by material (plastic, glass and so on) and then sends them back to the relevant super-collectors. In return the super-collectors pay the depot a handling fee.

According to the South Australian Government (SA EPA 2004), the 'system guarantees that consumers are refunded and depots receive a handling fee. It also ensures that the respon-sibilities of both producers and consumers are maintained, from production to the collection of empty containers for recycling, reuse, or disposal for energy recovery'.

Source: Productivity Commission 2006, p 239; SA EPA 2004.

South Australia's success with CDL (both as a litter and recycling policy instrument) has sparked considerable interest in other jurisdictions across Australia over the past 30 years. As the only State in Australia where CDL operates, policy-makers around the nation have been interested to learn how the system functions, and how its recycling rates compare to those elsewhere. As we discuss towards the end of the chapter, there have been numerous inquiries into CDL around Australia since the late 1990s. Despite these investigations and strong public support for the introduction of CDL, no other State or Territory has enforced a similar mandatory deposit-refund system. In the analysis we explore some of the reasons why CDL is largely absent in Australia (beyond South Australia). We turn now to consider the specific policy experiences in New South Wales.

A.2.2 The New South Wales inquiry into CDL

In contrast to South Australia, the New South Wales Government has continuously rejected proposals for CDL and has preferred to take a more voluntary approach to regulating packaging waste. In its first piece of waste management legislation, the *Waste Management and Minimisation Act 1995* (NSW), particular industry sectors were required to produce and adhere to their own Waste Reduction Plans and targets. It was, however, written into the legislation that upon its review (five years later in 2000), the New South Wales Government would consider policy instruments, such as CDL, if industry had failed to meet it waste reduction targets. In other words, CDL was inserted into the legislation as a regulatory safety net.

When the 1995 Waste Act came up for review in 2000, the performance of industry's voluntary approach was not convincing. Some sectors, particularly the dairy industry, were in breach of meeting their targets and some such as the beer and soft drink industry had failed by some six months to report on their waste levels (White 2001). The New South Wales Government was under increasing pressure from local government and the minor political parties to demonstrate that it was at least considering CDL in order to fulfil the requirement of the 1995 Waste Act. It therefore instigated a formal review of the Act to be undertaken by the agency regulating waste issues, the New South Wales Environment Protection Authority (NSW EPA). However, since the NSW EPA had opposed CDL in the past and showed an on-going preference for voluntary policies, the review was commissioned externally.

In 1999, the New South Wales Minister for the Environment at the time, Bob Debus, com-missioned Professor Stuart White to conduct an independent inquiry into CDL. White's task was to assess the environmental, economic and social costs and benefits of CDL to the community and industry of New South Wales (White 2001). His assessment would be the first in Australia to draw on new local data on the environmental costs and benefits of recycling (Fullerton 2003). The review also involved extensive social research including: interviews with key pressure groups; a call for public submissions; a two-stage opinion poll; and a citizens' jury. Of particular interest was whether CDL should be introduced in New South Wales, the willingness of citizens to pay for CDL and the appropriateness of various deposit systems (such as returning containers to manufacturers via retailers, designated collection depots, reverse vending machines, part of an existing waste or recycling collection system).

The review team was particularly interested in eliciting community views on CDL especially with respect to cost, access and equity. Inclusive and deliberative forms of public participation were chosen in order to tease out any differences between the preferences of citizens and consumers. This dimension of the review's social research was considered significant because citizens in New South Wales currently bear some of the costs associated with kerbside recycling systems (through their rates), and as consumers they would bear some of the costs of a CDL system if introduced. Existing opinion poll data on recycling and CDL provided little insight into whether citizens' preferences differed from consumers' preferences. On an issue such as CDL the two cannot always be assumed to be equal. An individual may hold contradictory preferences depending on whether they have on their consumer or citizen hat (Achterberg 1996) – as discussed in 5.8. For example, as a consumer I might not want to bear the extra cost of a CDL system, but as a citizen I might support its overall benefits to the community in encouraging less litter and more recycling (see Carson et al 2003).

We now move on to explore the different actors involved in waste debates in New South Wales, and their relative position on CDL.

A.2.3 Actors and their roles

A host of actors were involved and affected by the CDL review including:

- **The New South Wales State Government**, which established an independent inquiry into CDL and then later expanded this into a broader inquiry into EPR.

- **Local government**, which manages waste and recycling services for residents.

- **The beverage, container and packaging industry**, which would be required to fund the management of a container deposit system if introduced.

- **Recycling industry**, especially those collecting glass bottles and plastic beverage containers.

- **Shops and supermarkets**, which would possibly need to provide collection facilities (if CDL were introduced) where consumers could redeem their container deposits.

- **Consumers of beverage products**, which may incur higher prices if a CDL system were introduced. These costs would be to fund the collection system, and are in addition to the actual deposit amount (such as 5c, 10c etc) that consumers would be eligible to redeem.

- **Consultants and researchers**, who work on waste management policy and develop and disseminate knowledge.

- **Pressure groups** representing the interests of the environment, packaging, anti-litter campaigns, the beverage and retail industry, the food and grocery sector, and the waste industry. Many of these groups had been part of the State Waste Advisory Committee (SWAC) – a consultative body established in the mid-1990s to advise the NSW EPA on waste issues.

Figure A.1 Key actors in the CDL debate

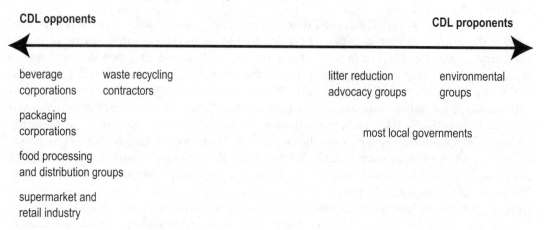

CDL opponents

CDL proponents

beverage corporations

waste recycling contractors

litter reduction advocacy groups

environmental groups

packaging corporations

most local governments

food processing and distribution groups

supermarket and retail industry

To appreciate the arguments of the key actors in this case study, it is useful to consider their positions within the polarised CDL debate. As shown in Figure A.1, relevant actors (mostly represented through pressure groups) are numerous at the extremes, but scarce in between.

Opponents of CDL are mostly from the private sector and include: beverage manufacturers (eg Coca-Cola Amatil, Cadbury Schweppes and the brewery groups Fosters and Lion Nathan Australia), the packaging industry, food processing and distribution groups as well as retail associations. Most CDL opponents campaign against CDL under large umbrella lobby groups, such as the Beverage Industry Environment Council (BIEC), which merged in 2006 with the Australian Food and Grocery Council.[5] Apart from BIEC, key industry groups campaigning against CDL include: the Packaging Council of Australia, the Australian Soft Drink Association, the Australian Retailers Association, and the Waste Contractors and Recyclers Association.

Opponent organisations argue that CDL is an inefficient and costly means to reduce litter and increase recycling rates. They also claim that CDL would involve large operational costs for industry and result in increased prices and inconvenience for consumers. Also in the CDL opponent camp are those in the business of collecting waste since they have a vested interest in maintaining waste volumes and kerbside recycling operations. Waste contractors, for example, argue that CDL would undermine existing recycling systems by removing valuable recyclables from the system.[6]

All these claims are countered by proponent groups, which include environmental and local government organisations. They argue that CDL would reduce litter and increase recycling rates as well as provide jobs and funds for low-income earners and charities (especially through additional collection of containers at large events). One of their key arguments is that CDL should be combined with kerbside systems to subsidise the rising costs of kerbside recycling, which is largely supported by local councils and their ratepayers (see CoA 2008). Local government associations have been instrumental in generating interest in CDL across Australia.

---

5   Since 2006, BIEC has been absorbed into the Australian Food and Grocery Council under its Product Stewardship Forum. See <www.afgc.org.au/index.cfm?id=447> (accessed 15 April 2009).

6   For an overview of the arguments put forward by CDL opponents, see CoA (2008) and White (2001, Vol III).

Without a doubt, CDL opponents are the strongest players in the waste debate. As we will show later in the analysis, industry groups have used their economic might to manoeuvre successive governments in Australia away from CDL (Carson et al 2002; Fullerton 2003).

A.3 The controversy

Of particular interest in this case study is the hostility displayed by certain pressure groups towards the CDL review, particularly its novel processes for seeking citizen input. In anticipation of resistance from various pressure groups to the CDL review's social research, the review team sought to involve them in the preparatory stages. For example, they invited representatives from all the major CDL pressure groups to participate in a Stakeholder Reference Group (SRG). The SRG group met on four occasions over a two-month period in the lead up to the citizens' jury. To the surprise of the organisers the first meeting was greeted with enthusiasm and cooperation. But the veneer of cordiality soon transformed into scepticism and resistance. By the fourth meeting the communication between parties had degenerated into a combat zone. Instead of focussing on the preparation of materials for the citizens' jury, the SRG turned into a combative session between the CDL opponents and proponents. In particular, industry groups began to challenge the entire purpose of the jury and attacked the independence and competence of both the organisers and the external advisory committee (set up to ensure rigour in the social research).[7]

Despite the fact that several procedural alterations were made to address concerns raised by pressure groups, behind the scenes some actors continued to question the purpose of the social research. For example, some industry groups claimed that the process was not only biased but pointless given that their market surveys provide an adequate assessment of public opinion. They also took to lobbying various ministers and eventually the Premier of New South Wales (at the time Bob Carr). On 21 December 2001 it is alleged that a delegation of industry heads from Woolworths, Coca-Cola, Schweppes Cottees, the Packaging Council of Australia and BIEC met with the Premier, and the Director-General of the Cabinet Office, Mr Roger Wilkins to discuss CDL. At this meeting the Premier is said to have 'emphatically ruled out CDL as an option for NSW' (Packaging Council of Australia 2001). According to another industry source, the Plastics and Chemicals Industries Association (PACIA 2000): 'The Premier directed the Cabinet Office to write to the Minister for the Environment immediately, indicating that overment [sic] policy was opposition to Container Deposit Legislation, on the grounds that it threatened successful kerbside systems and that the Inquiry should close'.

These alleged events raised serious questions about the government's intentions for the CDL review and its support from Cabinet. The rumours of the Premier's decision on CDL were certainly of no comfort to the review team, especially the organisers of the citizens' jury.[8] Why ask citizens to deliberate on a policy question for which the Premier had predetermined the outcome?

Much to the surprise of CDL opponents, the review and its social research continued with the Minister for Environment supporting the process, its independence and credibility of the

---

7   The comments made here are based on the author's observations of the four SRG meetings, which were held at the Institute for Sustainable Futures, University of Technology, Sydney between November 2000 and January 2001.

8   The author has been unable to officially corroborate whether or not the Premier ruled out CDL prior to the completion of the review.

organisers. It took another month before industry groups realised that the review was not going to go away. The strategic behaviour of the commercial pressure groups culminated a week before the jury, when they announced their withdrawal from the process. This move had the potential to jeopardise the entire citizens' jury, for without their involvement, the citizens' panel could only be exposed to one-half of the story and the process would then be open to criticisms of bias.

Remarkably, even after these events, the jury went ahead. In the end 11 randomly selected citizens came to Sydney to deliberate for two and a half days on the benefits and costs of CDL for New South Wales.[9] Typically in a citizens' jury process, the panel of citizens hears from and questions a range of actors and experts associated with the issue under deliberation (see 7.6.2). However, the absence of all the pressure groups in this case resulted in modifications to the jury design. Various perspectives of the debate were presented by government officials and academics rather than by representatives of pressure groups. The deliberations were affected by these amendments to the extent that citizens were frustrated at not being able to directly interact with interest groups during question time. In the end the citizens' recommendations reflected much of what industry had predicted and feared. Within the framework of a number of recommendations, they 'unanimously agreed to the implementation of CDL in NSW' (Citizens' Panel 2001, p 3). However, contrary to industry's concern that the panel would view them simply as the evil private sector, the citizens took many of the concerns of industry on board in their final recommendations.[10] Due to its controversial nature, the citizens' jury was assessed by an independent evaluator, who concluded that the process was open and rigorous, and successful in accessing the informed views of a diverse group of citizens (McKay 2001).

The turbulent times did not settle after the completion of the social research. Not long after the citizens' jury, the New South Wales Ministry for the Environment requested that the (CDL) review be expanded to consider other policy instruments that could foster EPR. As this decision was made relatively late in the review process, it made it unlikely that the CDL report would be finished in time to feed into the broader Waste Act Review as originally intended. Though the Ministry had received drafts of the CDL report as early as April 2001, it maintained for the next 10 months that the review was not yet complete. Whether intentional or not, the delayed release of the results from the CDL component of White's review restricted discussion on CDL during parliamentary debates on the proposed new waste legislation. This was not without criticism from members of the New South Wales Parliament, including the Greens MP, Ian Cohen (2001, p 16007):

> Why has the report not been released in time to feed into this process of legislative review? It would be a timely development if that report were tabled as part of this debate. It is several months since the Institute for Sustainable Futures provided its first draft of the inquiry to the Minister. Why is it necessary for an independent review to be sent back time and again to be rewritten? Was it just an exercise to buy time?

On 8 October 2001, four months *before* the government publicly released the review findings, the New South Wales Parliament enacted the new *Waste Avoidance and Resource Recovery Act*

---

9   For more detail on the citizens' jury, see White (2001, Vol III) and Carson et al (2002, 2003).

10 For example, amongst a number of qualifiers the panel emphasised: easy access to redemption venues (depot-collection centres), shared price increases between industry and consumers, industry involvement in the system design, and that CDL be introduced in combination with kerbside recycling (Citizens' Panel 2001).

2001. The Act abolished a number of institutions and replaced the industry Waste Reduction Plans with new arrangements and strategies including some voluntary forms of EPR. The new regulatory system was not well-received by CDL proponents and waste minimisation advocates. Local government representatives argued that it was just more of the same, with industry taking the voluntary road and consumers and ratepayers continuing to bear most of the responsibility for recycling (Woods 2002). So scathing was the Greens MP, Ian Cohen, that during parliamentary debates he suggested that the proposed Bill be renamed the 'Issues Avoidance and Waste Maximisation Bill' (Cohen 2001, p 16009).

The government finally released the entire EPR-CDL review report in February 2002. As anticipated, it sparked further controversy and unwanted debate for the Carr Government. The review concluded that CDL would be of net financial, environmental and social benefit to New South Wales. The financial and environmental benefits are largely related to reduced environmental cost of recycling containers using a combined CDL and kerbside recycling system, as opposed to producing new one-way containers from virgin materials, which are disposed of in landfills (White 2001). The social research demonstrated that there is strong community support for CDL provided that issues of equity and access are taken into consideration (Carson et al 2002; White 2001). An international study released around the same time also supported White's conclusions: that deposit-refund systems are one of the most effective means for achieving high container recovery rates (RW Beck 2002).

Contrary to the review recommendations, the New South Wales Minister for the Environment, Bob Debus, did not support CDL as an immediate option for New South Wales on two grounds. First, he claimed (Debus 2002, p 1) 'with the passing of the *Waste Avoidance and Resource Recovery Act* last year [2001], the Government now has a framework that provides for effective industry waste reduction'. This comment suggests that the CDL review was never intended to feed into the broader review of the 1995 Waste Act. Secondly, despite South Australia's demonstrated experience, he argued that due to cross-border issues, CDL cannot be pursued by a single State. The concern here was that consumers located in border regions would shift their purchases to other States to avoid the additional costs of their drinks. Using this rationale the Minister stated (Debus 2002, p 1): '[t]o help develop a national approach we will refer the report to the relevant federal, state and territory ministerial councils'.

To date CDL remains a deferred matter – awaiting intergovernmental consideration at the federal level. Another ironic twist in this tale is that while the CDL review appears to have had little direct impact on waste policy in New South Wales, its findings have sparked much interest from other State governments – a theme we explore in the analysis.

A.4 Analysis: what does the case study reveal?

The CDL case study illustrates a number of themes central to environmental decision-making. On a broad level it speaks to the enormous challenges that waste management poses to governments, communities and businesses. Indeed the central tenet of waste minimisation – that we should not just recycle but strive to reuse and reduce – is a message that cuts across well-established patterns of material consumption and reward systems at the heart of contemporary societies. Often our successes are gauged by what we consume (for example, what car we drive, the size of our house and so on), and we are rewarded through material goods (for example, the provision of corporate cars, or luxury items) (Hamilton and Denniss

2005). Clearly no one policy instrument like CDL is able to adequately address the broader structures and practices underlying our accumulating waste problem.

On another level the CDL case highlights the difficulties associated with assessing the costs and benefits of a particular proposal (here CDL). As we saw in Chapter 8 (see 8.5), Cost-Benefit Analysis (CBA) is a controversial assessment tool because it can produce different results depending on where the boundaries of the study are set, how impacts are valued, and who is said to benefit and pay. For many years assessments of CDL suggested that the costs of such a system for New South Wales would outweigh any benefits (such as increased recovery rates). However, the CDL review reached the opposite verdict primarily because it incorporated environmental and social costs and benefits into the analysis, particularly in relation to recycling. This component of the analysis was controversial, with many critics questioning the monetary values attributed to CDL's environmental benefits (eg Access Economics Pty Ltd, 2002).

The CDL case study also raises a number of significant governance issues. It demonstrates the ongoing politics that surround certain environmental policies, and the difficulties of promoting sustainability outcomes when there are competing agendas. Our analysis below focuses on these governance themes, particularly the influence and activities of pressure groups (Chapter 5). We also examine how citizen engagement can become highly politicised and consider the challenges of governing environmental change when there are conflicting values (Chapter 3), multiple jurisdictions (Chapter 4), and competing knowledge claims (Chapter 6).

A.4.1 The challenges of transcending a polarised debate

The ongoing polarised debates on CDL led the New South Wales Government to commission an independent inquiry – the hope being that it would be able rise above the politics and provide a 'sound and rational' assessment of the pros and cons of CDL for the State. While laudable, these goals were not realised. In the end the review and its social research incited further politics on CDL to the point where the lobbying efforts of industry allegedly led the Premier of New South Wales to go above his Environment Minster and promise that CDL would never be introduced. Why was it so difficult for the review to transcend the politics and polarisation of CDL?

There is no doubt that the goals of the CDL review including its social research were not well-served by the contentious nature of CDL. For almost 40 years there has been a continuous tug-of-war between competing groups. The issue remains polarised, positions are deeply entrenched, actors are highly choreographed and the arguments are well-rehearsed. The different pressure groups in the debate are also well coordinated, especially those from industry.

The debate has been continuously re-ignited over time as different groups seek to introduce new facts on CDL and its potential impact on New South Wales. Exchanges between opposing parties have largely involved firing-off report after report, each documenting the results of a study commissioned to support their agenda (eg BIEC 1997; Packaging Council of Australia 1989). This combative exchange of data can be likened to a battlefield; as soon as one side releases an independent study with all the 'facts', it is met by counter-report from the opposing side, and so on. In this process of data production different groups find material and results to support their value position. For example, they conduct opinion polls with leading questions or they make unsubstantiated claims about international experiences. There are also competing values and ideas from different groups about what the public thinks about CDL, and how they would behave in a deposit-refund system (see CoA 2008; White 2001)

This tug-of-war between the polarised groups seemed to intensify after the CDL review. For example, when the findings of the review were released (as part of the broader EPR report), the conclusion that CDL was of net benefit to New South Wales was quickly dismissed by industry. The CDL review had after all produced the results they had feared: it defied many conclusions drawn from their own studies – which is somewhat ironic given that the controversial environmental costing component of the report drew heavily on an industry-sponsored study (Nolan ITU and Sinclair Knight Merz 2001). Consistent with their previous actions, industry groups were quick to discredit the CDL review. BIEC on behalf of the packaging industry commissioned a critical assessment of the CDL review findings and process (Access Economics Pty Ltd 2002). The critique concluded that the CDL review was a 'selective', 'partial' and 'non-transparent assessment of the issues', which did not adequately address the terms and reference. It also found faults in the citizens' jury, claiming it was 'not representative', 'not balanced', and its recommendations 'impractical and/or uncosted' (Access Economics Pty Ltd 2002, pp 11–14). In a counter-response, White defended the review findings and its methodology (White 2002). With regards to the social research, he reminded industry representatives that they had approved the relevant survey questions during the SRG meetings. As for the claims of bias, White remarked that (2002, pp 6–7): 'it is regrettable that industry representatives saw fit to withdraw and therefore not expose themselves to the views of their "consumers"'.

The capacity to transcend polarised positions was also made difficult in this case study by the strong personalities involved in the debate. Most actors working on CDL have some sort of professional or personal attachment to the issue that makes letting go difficult. Some representatives have participated in the debate for many years as professional lobbyists, whose primary goal is to achieve their client's desired outcome. Other actors perform as zealots with long-standing personal attachments to achieving a particular outcome. Based on the author's observations at the CDL stakeholder meetings for the social research, the most influential personalities in the debate were those who had both a professional and ideological commitment to achieving a particular outcome.

A.4.2 The tactics and the relative power of pressure groups

The polarisation of the debate facilitated the creation of two distinct camps of CDL campaigners (opponents and proponents), each employing different tactics to influence the debate. As we saw in Chapter 5, there are many ways that pressure groups can influence environmental decisions. The CDL case illustrates some of the more strategic tactics that groups can employ to push their agenda. These include strategies to influence outcomes from both the *inside* (such as participating in committees, or commissioning research to produce 'facts' that support their position) and from the *outside* (such as lobbying ministers, and discrediting the independence and integrity of the process). Some actors also work *within* the system by forming alliances and coalitions with like-minded groups. For example, local government worked in close collaboration with environmental groups to counter the political force of the beverage and packaging industry. We also see strong evidence of networking, information sharing, strategising and even cartel activity (coordinated lobbying efforts).

In employing these strategies, the CDL case illustrates how some groups are more successful at gaining the attention of decision-makers than others. As mentioned earlier in the case, the groups opposed to CDL such as the packaging and beverage industry have been far more successful at promoting their demands than proponents. According to Carson et al (2002) these industry groups have exercised power by employing resources such as status, economic strength, solidarity and knowledge (see Smith 1997, pp 21–22). For example, for 15 years (between 1978–1993) the New South Wales Government entered into a deal with the packaging industry that CDL would not be introduced in return for industry's full sponsorship of the (then) State Pollution Control Commission's anti-litter campaign, *Do the Right Thing* (Cook 1993). Collectively, industry has financed independent studies to support their arguments that CDL would be disastrous for the job market and consumers.[11] Financial pressure is also exerted in the form of donations to major political parties in New South Wales and Australia. For example, in the financial year of 2000–2001, the Australian Electoral Commission reports that Coca-Cola Amatil Ltd made a contribution of $200,000 to the Australian Labor Party (ALP) National Secretariat. Similar donations have also been made by waste management companies, breweries and packaging corporations to the New South Wales ALP and ALP National Secretariat (see AEC 2002).[12] New South Wales is not alone in its receipt of funds from groups opposing CDL. After the Northern Territory Government backed down from supporting a CDL system in 2002, it is alleged to have received a contribution of $500,000 from the beverage industry pressure group, BIEC (Fullerton 2003). According to some sources, similar cartel activities and lobbying tactics have been employed elsewhere in Australia and internationally by the beverage and packaging industry to obstruct the introduction of CDL (see Boomerang Alliance 2006).

Groups campaigning in favour of CDL have struggled to mobilise their interests. Early campaigns in New South Wales were led by a small number of environmental activists, who later formed the Waste Crisis Network. Waste policies such as CDL suffer from a number of collective action problems so typical of many urban (or 'brown') environmental issues because they fail to attract community interest and momentum. As discussed in Chapter 5, environmental issues such as waste lack the capacity to generate public interest in the same way that green conservation issues can. Divided opinion amongst some environmental and community organisations on waste policies such as CDL and plastic bag levies has also hindered collective action. For example, the high profile community based organisation, Clean Up Australia, for many years has rejected CDL, though this position has been reversed in recent years (see CUA 2008).

It appears that as the CDL debate expanded from litter control into waste and resource management, it has attracted more supporters. Over the past 20 years the CDL proponent camp in Australia has grown from a small environmental campaign into a concerted effort backed by the majority of local governments around the State (see White 2001). During this time groups supporting CDL have generated their own powerful resources. Like industry groups they have sponsored studies and opinion surveys, and actively lobbied government. Since the early 2000s, proponent groups have adopted more sophisticated strategies such as forming coalitions and running media campaigns. For example, since the review, lobbying efforts have been forged by the Boomerang Alliance, which represents a national coalition of major environmental groups committed to eliminating packaging waste and promoting the adoption of EPR across Australia.[13]

---

11   See for example, BIEC (1997), and Packaging Council of Australia (1989).

12   For a discussion on the donations made by the beverage, packaging and waste industry to the New South Wales ALP and the ALP National Secretariat, see Slack-Smith (2002).

13   See <www.bringitback.org.au/boomerang> (accessed 20 April 2009).

A.4.3 The politics of citizen engagement

The CDL case also illustrates what can happen when long fought environmental battles between opposing pressure groups are opened up to broader community engagement. As we saw in Chapter 7, there are many reasons why decision-makers might want to engage the public in environmental decisions, for example, to explore new ideas, to gauge public opinion and to bolster political support. In this case the review team was primarily interested in determining the preferences of informed everyday people, and so chose participatory processes (such as a citizens' jury) aimed at inclusive and deliberative engagement. However, what this case demonstrates is the strong opposition that innovative forms of citizen engagement can face from powerful pressure groups (Hendriks 2002).

The idea of expanding public participation beyond stakeholders to everyday citizens was foreign to most of the pressure groups associated with the CDL issue for two key reasons. First, such actors were far more accustomed to lobbying and adversarial politics, than collaborating with their opponents and the community (see Hendriks 2002). Prior to the review most key interest groups associated with the CDL issue had formal access to the New South Wales Government via the State Waste Advisory Committee (SWAC), a consultative arrangement established as part of the 1995 Waste Act. SWAC brought together the polarised stakeholders associated with waste issues across the State including representatives from the beverage and packaging industry; environmental groups; local government and consumer groups. With competing agendas and no independent facilitator, it is no surprise that its members were highly dissatisfied with SWAC's procedures and progress (see Appendix in Hendriks et al 2001). One thing SWAC did achieve was that it acquainted its members, as well as the New South Wales Government, with the positions of key players in the debate, and the games they play. By the time the CDL review arrived in late 2000, SWAC members were at loggerheads. It was into this participatory context that the CDL review and its social research were introduced. Pressure groups particularly resisted the citizens' jury because it challenged existing roles and power relationships between pressure groups and decision-makers.

The second key reason why CDL pressure groups resisted the CDL social research related to the validity of the citizen input. Some interested representatives considered ordinary citizens to be inappropriate participants of the CDL debate because they lacked expert knowledge, association with waste issues, or experience with a CDL system.[14] This was particularly the perspective of representatives from industry groups who remained sceptical about extending policy discussions to the broader public. Decisions, they argued, should ultimately be up to government to determine in consultation with experts and 'appropriate' groups. In other words, lay citizens were largely considered a liability since their preferences were characterised as: invalid and unreliable; malleable, and corrupt.

The overall policy impact of the citizens' jury remains questionable. The citizens' recommendations unfortunately do not appear to have been well-integrated or implemented into the policy framework. According to proponents of CDL, the citizens' policy suggestions were buried in the aftermath of the broader EPR-CDL review.[15] It is no accident, they say, that the panel's recommendations were hidden in the third volume of the larger EPR-CDL review report. Others have remarked that the citizens' report has no political leverage

---

14 These comments are based on the author's observations of the four SRG meetings, which were held at the Institute for Sustainable Futures, University of Technology, Sydney between November 2000 and January 2001, as well interviews with relevant CDL pressure groups.

15 These remarks are based on interviews with several CDL proponents.

because industry groups continue to criticise the jury process and its organisers (for an overview of these arguments, see Hendriks 2002).

When a participatory process is at risk of being undermined or discredited by strategic actors, conveners can safeguard the process and its outcomes by demonstrating their credibility, independence and impartiality (Hendriks 2004). They might also want to ensure that the procedure is transparent and rigorous, for example, by establishing an external advisory committee. Ideally the membership of this committee should be a mix of representatives from pressure group and process thinkers, such as public participation practitioners. Mixed membership can encourage cross-fertilisation between content and process thinkers, and often the very presence of people from outside the policy network can have a civilising effect on strategic actors (see Renouf 1999). Independent facilitators or a well-respected chair can also be effective in ensuring that the advisory committee does not slide into a bargaining process. Conveners of participatory processes can also safeguard the process by increasing the public visibility of the process, for example, by involving high profile figures and encouraging media coverage.

A.4.4 The challenge of governing waste in a federal system

Waste management in Australia faces some of the inherent problems governing environmental issues in our federal system, as discussed in Chapter 4. Fragmentation between different levels of government is an ongoing challenge. For example, at present local government collects household items for waste disposal and recycling. State governments are constitutionally responsible for waste policy and therefore design policy and set targets, and the Federal Government plays a role in ensuring national coordination on waste management issues. As described above, the New South Wales Government used this policy fragmentation to their political advantage by deferring its decision on CDL to the Commonwealth level. In doing so CDL was effectively pushed politically into the national arena, where it remains (at the time of writing) under intergovernmental consideration. As discussed in Chapter 3, the deferral of controversial policy decisions, such as whether or not to introduce CDL, can be an effective political tool for dealing with value conflicts.

While the CDL review may have had little direct impact on waste policy in New South Wales, its findings have sparked much interest from other jurisdictions in Australia including the Northern Territory, Western Australia and Queensland (see Fullerton 2006; Productivity Commission 2006, p 246). One of the benefits of a federal system, as we noted in Chapter 4, is that States can copy and borrow policy initiatives from each other. This kind of policy transfer has been evident in recent developments on the regulation of packaging waste in other jurisdictions across Australia. For example, in 2006 Western Australia began looking seriously into CDL when the Western Australian Minister for the Environment formed a stakeholder advisory committee to advise on the suitability of a Container Deposit System for the State. In its report to the minster the committee concluded that container deposits would create significant increases in recycling beyond current levels for Western Australia, particularly for beverages consumed away from home (SAG 2007). The Western Australian Government has signalled its intention to introduce CDL (see Productivity Commission 2006, p 246), and is playing a leading role in investigating the viability of a national CDL scheme (WA DEC 2008).

CDL has also been under consideration in national debates on regulating packaging waste. In 2006, an assessment by the Productivity Commission concluded that CDL would be an inappropriate scheme for national consideration (Productivity Commission 2006, p 246):

Deposit-refund schemes are typically costly and would only be justified for products that have a very high cost of illegal disposal. Container deposit legislation is unlikely to be the most cost-effective mechanism for achieving its objectives of recovering resources and reducing litter. Kerbside recycling is a less costly option for recovering resources, while general anti-litter programs are likely to be a more cost-effective way of pursuing overall litter reduction.

However, debates on waste management resurfaced again with a change in the Federal Government in late 2007. In March 2008, the Senate requested an Inquiry into the Management of Australia's Waste Streams which included consideration of a national Drink Container Recycling Bill 2008 (CoA 2008). As part of its 18 recommendations, the Senate inquiry called on the ministerial council dealing with environmental matters (the Environment Protection and Heritage Council or EPHC[16]) to 'consider initiatives, including container deposit schemes, to improve away-from-home recycling' (p xi) and recommended 'that they work towards a national container deposit system' and that it 'consider the South Australian model and the Drink Container Recycling Bill 2008' (p xiii). In other words a decision on the CDL has been pushed aside again – this time onto the EPHC. Nevertheless the Senate is very clear in its views on CDL, as the following wording demonstrates (CoA 2008, p 9): '[T]he committee strongly recommends the EPHC consider a national container deposit system as part of its ongoing deliberations'. Given all these developments, the politics of CDL is set to continue on many fronts – particularly at the Commonwealth level as the EPHC enacts the Senate inquiry's recommendations.

A.5 Conclusion

The CDL case is rich in insights into the process and politics of environmental decision-making. Most notably the case reveals the kinds of challenges encountered when attempting to comprehensively analyse the environmental and social impacts of a particular policy instrument. Those working on waste policy at the time had hoped that the CDL review and its citizens' jury would inject independent insights into the debate. But those with an interest in maintaining the status quo held a different view. From its inception the review was plagued with power games and politics. The long history of pressure group contestation meant that the politics of CDL was inescapable – it shaped the way the actors engaged in the review and responded to its findings. Cynical readers may conclude that at the end of the day it is politics that counts, since the New South Wales Government chose to reject the conclusions of the CDL review, despite strong evidence of the environmental and social benefits of CDL. Yet the research emerging from the review does appear to have sparked interest in other Australian jurisdictions on the need to regulate packaging waste in such a way that responsibility is extended to producers and consumers.

There are also some institutional insights emerging from this case. In particular we observe a common tactic of political referral where controversial decisions involving the responsibility of multiple jurisdictions are pushed aside to different levels of government (in this case towards the Commonwealth). While local governments are generally in favour of CDL, they lack the constitutional power to enact and enforce such legislation. States on the

---

16   The Environment Protection and Heritage Council (EPHC) was established in June 2001 by Australian Governments (via COAG) to address broad national policy issues relating to environmental protection, particularly air, water, and waste matters. See <www.ephc.gov.au> (accessed 20 April 2009).

other hand have the power, but are caught between strong pressures from environmental and industry groups. CDL also represents a publicly popular policy instrument, and thus State governments across Australia have been reluctant to rule it out completely. At the same time they have faced considerable political pressure from powerful industry groups. The upshot of this tug-of-war has been to defer a decision on CDL to the Commonwealth Government – where (at the time of writing, January 2009) the issue remains unresolved.

The CDL case also illustrates the resistance and politics that participatory processes can generate. Here, public participation was instigated in a charged political setting as a means to move the debate beyond its polarised state. Yet some pressure groups greatly struggled with the notion of expanding the CDL debate to include everyday people. They held onto common concerns about the capacity of citizens to understand complex issues, and the validity of their knowledge and policy input (see Chapter 6). Industry groups were particularly fearful of citizen involvement because they were concerned that the citizens would simply recommend CDL on the basis of popular feel-good arguments. Some pressure groups may go to great lengths to resist citizen engagement. As seen in the CDL case, industry groups sought to undermine the citizens' jury process by lobbying in and around the process, pushing for procedural changes, and trying to discredit the organisers and the citizens' recommendations. The ultimate strategy is to walk away. Since no group in a liberal society can be forced to cooperate and stay at the table, veto remains a powerful weapon against attempts to facilitate dialogue with the community.

References

ABS, 2006, 4602.0 – Environmental Issues: People's Views and Practices, The Australian Bureau of Statistics, Canberra.

Access Economics Pty Ltd, 2002, Critical Assessment of the Independent Review of Container Deposit Legislation in New South Wales, Report commissioned by Beverage Industry Environment Council on behalf of the Packaging Industry Sector, Canberra.

Achterberg, W, 1996, 'Sustainability and associative democracy' in Lafferty, WL and Meadowcroft, J (eds), Democracy and the Environment: Problems and Prospects, Edward Elgar Publishing Limited, Cheltenham, UK, pp 157–174.

AEC, 2002, Analysis of Annual Returns, Australian Electoral Commission, <http://search.aec.gov.au/annualreturns/> (accessed 19 February 2002).

BIEC, 1997, Domestic Waste Management in Sydney: Costs and Efficiencies, Beverage Industry Environment Council, Sydney.

Boomerang Alliance, 2006, 'Revealed: Beverage Industry Secret Anti Container Deposit Plan in WA', <http://boomerangalliance.org/000_files/Media_release_on_Project_jet2.pdf> (accessed 26 November 2008).

Carson, L, White, S, Hendriks, C and Palmer, J, 2002, 'Community consultation in environmental policy making', The Drawing Board: An Australian Review of Public Affairs, 3 (1): 1–13.

Carson, L, White, S, Hendriks, C and Palmer, J, 2003, 'Combining a televote and citizens' jury in a legislative review' in Font, J (ed), Public Participation and Local Governance, Institut de Ciéncies Polítiques i Socials, Barcelona, pp 168–181.

Citizens' Panel, 2001, Citizens' Recommendations: Citizens' Forum on Container Deposit Legislation for New South Wales, Institute for Sustainable Futures, The University of Technology, Sydney.

CoA (Commonwealth of Australia). 2008, Management of Australia's Waste Streams (Including Consideration of the Drink Container Recycling Bill 2008), Senate Standing Committee on Environment, Communications and the Arts, Commonwealth of Australia Canberra.

Cohen I, 2001, 'Hansard: Waste Avoidance and Resource Recovery Bill Second Reading', New South Wales Legislative Council, Sydney, 29 June 2001.

Cook, D, 1993, 'Bottle Refunds on Way', *Sydney Morning Herald*, 18 February 1993, p 4.

CUA (Clean Up Australia), 2006, *Rubbish Report*, <http://www.cleanup.org.au/rubbishreport06/> (accessed 25 November 2008).

CUA (Clean Up Australia), 2008, *Submission to the Inquiry into Australia's Waste Management Stream Drink Containing Recycling Bill 2008*, <http://cleanup.org.au/PDF/au/cua-cdl-submission-2008.pdf> (accessed 25 November 2008).

Debus, B, 2002, 'Press release: Waste management report released', Sydney, NSW NSW Minister for Environment, 28 February 2002.

Fullerton, T, 2003, 'The waste club', *Transcript from Four Corners*, Australian Broadcasting Corporation, aired 8 September 2003, <http://www.abc.net.au/4corners/content/2003/transcripts/s941450.htm> (accessed 21 January 2009).

Hamilton, C and Denniss, R, 2005, *Affluenza: When Too Much Is Never Enough*, Allen & Unwin, Crows Nest.

Hendriks, CM, Carson, L and White, S, 2001, *Improved Processes for Public Participation in Policy Development on Urban Sustainability Issues. A Case Study on Waste Policy in NSW. Unpublished Report to the NSW Environmental Protection Authority*, Institute for Sustainable Futures, The University of Technology, Sydney.

Hendriks, CM, 2002, 'Institutions of deliberative democratic processes and interest groups: roles, tensions and incentives', *Australian Journal of Public Administration*, 61 (1): 64–75.

Hendriks, CM, 2004, *Public Deliberation and Interest Organisations: a study of responses to lay citizen engagement in public policy*, Unpublished PhD Thesis, The Australian National University, Canberra.

Hendriks, CM, 2006, 'When the forum meets interest politics: strategic uses of public deliberation', *Politics and Society*, 34 (4): 1–32.

KAB, (Keep Australia Beautiful), 2008, *National Litter Index 2007–2008*, <www.kab.org.au/_dbase_upl/NLI%20Report%200708.doc#_Toc205011206> (accessed 25 November 2008).

McKay, E, 2001, *Independent Evaluation of the Citizens' Forum on Container Deposit Legislation*, PJ Dawson Associates, Canberra.

Nolan ITU and Sinclair Knight Merz, 2001, *Independent Assessment of Kerbside Recycling in Australia*, prepared for National Packaging Covenant Council.

PACIA, 2000, 'Stop Press – latest developments on CDL in NSW', *Plastics and Chemicals Industry Association Member News*, December 2000.

Packaging Council of Australia, 1989, 'The environmental and economic impacts of compulsory deposit legislation', *Envirofacts*, vol 2, no 1.

Packaging Council of Australia, 2001, 'CDL-NSW: Carr Rules It Out', *Packaging Exposé*, 01/2001, 10 January.

Productivity Commission, 2006, *Waste Management*, Canberra.

Renouf, C, 1999, 'Rebirthing democracy: The experience of the first Australian consensus conference', *Consuming Interest*, 79: 16–19.

RW Beck, 2002, *Understanding Beverage Container Recycling: A Value Chain Assessment Prepared for the Multi-Stakeholder Recovery Project*, Report prepared by RW Beck with contributions from Franklin Associates Ltd, Tellus Institute, Boisson and Associates, Sound Resource Management for Businesses and Environmentalists Allied for Recycling.

SA EPA, 2003, *Waste to Resources*, Environment Protection Authority South Australia, <www.environment.sa.gov.au/epa/waste.html#cdl> (accessed 24 October 2003).

SA EPA, 2004, 'Container Deposit Legislation (CDL) – a South Australian Environmental Success Story', *EPA 074/04–March 2004*, South Australian Government, <www.epa.sa.gov.au/pdfs/info_cdl.pdf> (accessed 27 March 2009).

SAG, 2007, *Stakeholder Advisory Group Investigation into Best Practice Container Deposit Systems for Western Australia*. Final Report for the Minister for the Environment Western Australia, Stakeholder Advisory Group on Best Practice Container Deposit Systems for Western Australia, Perth, <www.zerowastewa.com.au/documents/sag_cds_report.pdf> (accessed 21 January 2009).

Slack-Smith, D, 2002, *Lay Citizens in the Democratic Waste Stream: Deliberative Democracy Recycled*, Unpublished Honours Dissertation Thesis, The University of Sydney.

Smith, R, 1997, 'Power' in Smith, R (ed), *Politics in Australia*, 3rd edn, Allen & Unwin, St Leonards, pp 17–34.

The Age, 2008, 'Less Rubbish on Clean up Australia Day', *The Age*, <http://news.theage.com.au/national/less-rubbish-on-clean-up-australia-day-20080302-1w74.html> (accessed 26 November 2008).

WA DEC, 2008, 'WA to head investigation into national container scheme', *Press Release*, WA Department of Environment and Conservation, Perth, <www.dec.wa.gov.au/news/minister-for-the-environment/wa-to-head-investigation-into-national-container-scheme.html> (accessed 20 January 2009).

White, S, 2001, *Independent Review of Container Deposit Legislation in New South Wales – Final Report – Volumes I, II, III*, Report prepared for Bob Debus, NSW Minister for Environment, Institute for Sustainable Futures, The University of Technology, Sydney.

White, S, 2002, *Response to Access Economics' Critical Assessment of the Independent Review of Container Deposit Legislation in New South Wales*, Institute for Sustainable Futures, The University of Technology, Sydney.

Woods, P, 2002, 'CDL: the NSW experience', paper presented to *Funding the Future Waste Conference*, Mackay, 4–5 July 2002.

Case Study B

Gunns Pulp Mill

B.1 Introduction

Today, I am proud to inform the Parliament that the Government has set in train the process that may see one of our dreams realised – a modern, world-scale pulp and paper industry that will maximise Tasmania's returns for its sustainable management of its forests, that will indeed reward Tasmania for the way it has cared for its forests . . . A pulp mill that meets the world's toughest emission standards, and that's what we'll have, will enable us to maintain a land, sea and air environment we can call pristine.

Lennon 2004[1]

This case study examines the controversy surrounding a proposal for the largest pulp mill in Australia to be built in the Tamar Valley, situated in the north of Tasmania, by Gunns Limited (Gunns). The above announcement by Tasmania's Labor Premier ignited an intense debate about the mill's economic benefits, impacts on Tasmania's forests and pollution effects on the productive and scenic Tamar Valley, which continues at the time of writing (April 2009).

Tasmania is not new to environmental conflict. Over the last five decades this beautiful island State has played host to many major environmental debates that have polarised the community and created bitter conflict amongst those holding opposing views and values about resource development and conservation. Ultimately, underlying these conflicts has been the question of determining the most appropriate economic future for Tasmania – should it be based on preserving Tasmania's natural assets that support local tourism and agricultural industries, or exploiting the environment through large-scale industrial projects? In the past, Tasmanian Governments have tended to favour the latter. Examples include hydro-industrialisation schemes such as the flooding of Lake Pedder which occurred in the early 1970s, the proposal for damming parts of the Franklin River in the 1970s and early 1980s and the proposal of the Wesley Vale pulp mill in the late 1980s. Strong public opposition and organised campaigning meant that neither of the latter two proposals went ahead, despite support from the Tasmanian Government.

Another long-standing issue on the development vs conservation battlefront is the 'forest war' between conservationists, government and the forestry industry. Much of Tasmania's

---

1   Extracts from Paul Lennon's (Tasmanian Labor Premier 2004–2008) ministerial statement to the Tasmanian Parliament on 26 October 2004.

tourism industry is based on the world-recognised pristine green image of Tasmania's native forests and particularly the magnificent old growth forests. Environmentalists view the logging of these high-conservation value forests as irreversible damage to their unique ecosystems, while the lure of economic prospects and employment opportunities has ensured government support for the Tasmanian forestry industry.[2]

The many attempts to resolve forestry conflicts have included a variety of institutional responses. Most notable are the National Forest Policy Statement (1992) and the resulting Regional Forest Agreements (RFAs) in 1999. These were decisive steps towards the twin goals of conservation and ecologically sustainable management of Australia's native forests, while providing security for the logging industry (Ajani 2007; Brueckner 2007; Lane 2003). However, the success of RFAs in reducing conflict has been limited (Lane 2003; Slee 2001) and the battles rage on.

It is not surprising, then, that the proposal by Gunns, Australia's largest timber and wood-chipping company, to build Australia's largest and allegedly the 'world's greenest pulp mill', in the Tamar Valley, was greeted with suspicion, criticism and hostility by many.

The planning and environmental approval process for the pulp mill commenced in 2004. Paul Lennon, the Labor Premier of Tasmania at the time, welcomed the mill as an opportunity for economic development, especially as it would produce wood pulp – a much higher-value export product than the currently produced and exported woodchips. He publicly argued that most Tasmanians would also welcome an environmentally and economically sustainable pulp mill development (ABC Tasmania 2003).

It seems the Premier grossly misjudged the sentiment of the Tasmanian community. The intensity of public reaction and opposition to the mill was akin to that of the campaign against the Franklin Dam. Controversy started over the mill's environmental impacts, in particular air and water emissions, and conflicting information about its benefits to the local economy. As the story unravelled, issues such as the consumption of natural resources by the mill, including large amounts of wood and water, emerged. Also claims of 'dodgy deals' between politicians and Gunns to fast-track the mill's approval process became apparent. Public concern over these issues led to plummeting approval ratings for the Premier, and eventually contributed to his resignation in May 2008. Concerns over the development of the pulp mill were not confined to Tasmania but shared by national and even international organisations.

Despite receiving bipartisan support from the Tasmanian and Federal Governments and Opposition as well as necessary planning approvals, the future of the pulp mill was not secured. In May 2008 Gunns' major financiers, the ANZ Bank, decided not to fund the $2 billion pulp mill project. The media portrayed this withdrawal of finances as a significant setback for Gunns (Figure B.1), although the company stood firmly behind their mill project. Gunns CEO, John Gay, confirmed their intentions at the company's Annual General Meeting in October 2008 by stating, '"[t]his company will continue the process as long as it takes to build the pulp mill in Tasmania"' (cited in Darby 2008).

This case study examines the decision-making processes concerning the pulp mill and offers insights into:

- the complexities related to the socio-political nature of sustainability problems;

---

2   The Tasmanian forestry industry is worth $1.3 billion dollars annually to the Tasmanian economy (FFIC 2008) and in 2005–2006, employed 6300 workers – approximately 3 per cent of Tasmania's employed labour force (Schirmer 2008).

Figure B.1 Headlines in Australian newspapers May to August 2008

Gunns may be out of ammo on Tasmanian pulp mill

Pulp mill dead, say opponents

Mill may be pulp fiction

Timber industry reels from finance withdrawal for pulp mill

- the difficulties associated with the interpretation of sustainability and the application of sustainability principles;

- the contested and value-laden nature of facts and knowledge and subsequent influence on problem framing;

- the influence of assumptions and subjectivity on the use of tools such as environmental impact assessment (EIA), modelling and cost-benefit analysis (CBA);

- the role of a diverse range of actors and the strategies they use to influence environmental decision-making (EDM);

- the influence of political pressure and corporate power.

To appreciate the full complexity of this case, that involves a multitude of actors, many problem frames and political and social agendas, we first need to explore the mill proposal and its context.

B.2 Setting the scene

B.2.1 The pulp mill proposal

Tamar Valley, also known as the valley of senses, is the oldest wine-growing region in Tasmania. The 58 kilometre long tidal estuary – the Tamar River – meanders through this picturesque valley renowned for its gorges, waterfalls, rainforests, wetlands, and nearby seal and penguin colonies. Although historically, mining and forestry have been the dominant industries in this part of Tasmania, it now has well-developed farming and fishing industries and a successful tourism industry built on fine food and cool climate wines.

The site for Australia's largest pulp mill development, proposed by Gunns Limited, is on the shores of the Tamar River, north of Launceston. The proposed project includes the pulp mill and associated structures including a wharf, landfill, water supply pipeline from Trevallyn Dam near Launceston, and a pipeline to transfer effluent from the mill to an ocean outfall in Bass Strait (Gunns Limited 2006a).

The pulp mill is planned to use woodchips from a variety of sources, including plantation and native eucalypts, to produce between 820,000 to 1.1 million air-dried tonnes (ADt) of pulp for the domestic and international markets in the Asia Pacific region (Gunns Limited 2006b). The production of pulp,[3] which is used to produce paper, would shift 'the State's production and export profiles away from raw commodity exports and simple manufacturing to more sophisticated value-added products' (Gunns Limited 2006b, p 3–103) and could potentially enhance Tasmania's economy through export dollars and increased job creation. According to one estimate provided by the project's General Manager, the mill would provide a 'tremendous boost to the Tasmanian economy' by creating 4000 direct jobs and 4000 indirect jobs during the construction phase, 1500 direct and indirect jobs during its operation and would boost the State's GDP by 2 per cent (Doogue 2005).

The pulp mill project required approval from the Tasmanian Government in accordance with the State's planning system and the Federal Government under the *Environment Protection and Biodiversity Conservation Act 1999* (Cth) (EPBC Act) (see 4.4.2). Due to the scale of this major development and its potential impacts on Tasmania's economy, in November 2004 the pulp mill proposal was declared a project of state significance (POSS) by the Tasmanian Government. This meant that the project would undergo an Integrated Impact Assessment (IIA) process and an Integrated Impact Statement (IIS) would be prepared by the proponent to determine the mill's economic, social and environmental effects.[4] The project was also deemed to have the potential to impact on three matters of national environmental significance, namely threatened species and ecological communities, migratory species and Commonwealth marine areas. As discussed in Chapter 8, the impact assessment process is intended to help decision-makers determine if the project should be given the green light and if so, under what conditions.

After a long and controversial assessment process, which began in 2004, both the Tasmanian and Federal Governments granted approvals in 2007. The Federal Government did, however, impose a number of conditions[5] including the submission and approval of an Environmental Impact Management Plan (EIMP) before commencing the mill's construction and operation.

B.2.2 The actors

In an era of global environmental governance a Tasmanian pulp mill project captured the attention and interest of an unprecedented cast of local, national and international actors. Such was the strength of opposing points of view and value positions that it led to a fierce debate between the protagonists and antagonists of the mill. Before we move on to highlight the many controversial aspects of this case study, we briefly introduce the main actors of this environmental conflict and identify their roles, positions and views in relation to the project. How these actors used their power and relationships to influence decision-making and outcomes is explored further below in the analysis (see B.4).

Gunns Limited – As the proponent of the pulp mill, Gunns, the oldest and biggest forestry company in Australia is at the centre of this controversy. It owns and manages approximately 200,000 hectares of plantations in Tasmania and operates sawmills, timber processing centres and veneer factories (Gunns Limited 2008). It is also Tasmania's only woodchipping company, and exports this product to the Asian market, mainly Japan, for pulp and paper production. In addition to its timber interests, Gunns also runs a managed

---

3   Described simply, the pulping process involves cooking woodchips to separate cellulose fibre which is then washed, bleached, dried and baled ready for sale (Gunns 2006a).

4   <www.rpdc.tas.gov.au/poss/generalinfo> (accessed 11 April 2009).

5   <www.gunnspulpmill.com.au/permits/epbc.php> (accessed 11 April 2009).

investment business, as well as Tasmanian based merchandising, construction and wine businesses, with their winery located in the Tamar Valley. The company employs about 1700 people and in the 2008 financial year reported an annual revenue of $862 million – an increase of 26 per cent from the previous year (Gunns Limited 2006c, 2008).

The proposed $2 billion pulp mill development in the Tamar Valley was part of a business expansion strategy for Gunns. This investment was justified by the need to process wood-chips into higher-value pulp before exporting, especially since the demand for this product for the production of paper was expected to grow in future. This downstream value-adding would improve financial returns to Gunns, its shareholders and contribute significantly to Tasmania's economic activity and employment (Gunns Limited 2006c).

Other business and industry – Other important actors upon which the success of this proposal hinged were Forestry Tasmania and the ANZ Bank. Forestry Tasmania is a gov-ernment-owned enterprise responsible for managing 1.5 million hectares of state forest land which contains 39 per cent of Tasmania's forests (Forestry Tasmania undated). A contract signed between Forestry Tasmania and Gunns ensured long-term supply of wood for the mill. Under this agreement, Forestry Tasmania would supply Gunns with 1.5 million cubic metres of plantation and native forest timber a year for 20 years (ABC News 2008a).

The ANZ Bank has had Gunns as their client since 1995 and was the potential key finan-cier for the mill, but made a decision to withdraw from funding the project in May 2008 (ABC News 2008b).

The fishing, farming, wine and tourism industries in the Tamar Valley also had a stake in this project, especially since the potential impacts of the mill (discussed below in B.3) could have an adverse effect on local environmental conditions and their businesses. The Tasmanian Fishing Industry Council was particularly concerned about the potential impacts of the mill's effluent on Bass Strait's marine ecosystem (TFIC 2007).

Political parties and politicians – Many politicians from all sides and levels of politics had their say about this project. The key figures responsible for the decision of approv-ing or rejecting the project based on the IIA were the Tasmanian (Labor) Premier, Paul Lennon (2004–2008) and the Federal (Coalition) Environment Minister, Malcolm Turnbull (2006–2007).

Premier Lennon was a strong protagonist of the pulp mill, mainly because of the future promise of economic growth and development it signified for Tasmania. Lennon was adam-ant that '"Tasmanians can have the best of both worlds, a pulp mill that is good for our economy and safe for our environment"' (cited in Ogilvie 2008).

Both Malcolm Turnbull, and later Peter Garrett, who was appointed the Federal Minister for the Environment, Arts and Heritage after Labor won government in 2007, have con-sistently shown their support for the pulp mill as long as strict environmental conditions imposed by the Commonwealth are met by the proponent.

The Federal and Tasmanian Greens have been key critics. Their Federal leader, Senator Bob Brown, has long been an active opponent of development that threatens Tasmania's pristine environment and its forests. In 1983 he led the blockade of the Franklin River Dam works and served a 19-day jail term for this offence (Negus 2003). Dr Brown and other Green MPs, including the leader of the Greens in the Tasmanian Parliament, Senator Peg Putt,[6] and Federal Deputy leader, Senator Christine Milne, have been vocal in both their criticisms of the mill's approval process and concerns about the severity of its environmental impacts.

---

6   Peg Putt announced her retirement from the parliament and politics in July 2008.

Senator Milne previously led a successful campaign against the Wesley Vale pulp mill in the late 1980s.

Government agencies – The Resource Planning and Development Commission (RPDC) is an independent statutory body that oversees Tasmania's planning system. It was responsible for assessing Gunns' IIS for the mill project and making recommendations to the Tasmanian Government on whether the project should proceed, and if so, under what conditions. The RPDC set up a Pulp Mill Assessment Panel (the Assessment Panel) for the purposes of this assessment.

In addition, Premier Lennon established the Pulp Mill Task Force (the Task Force) within the Department of Economic Development and Tourism with a view to keeping the community informed throughout the process and coordinating the involvement of relevant government agencies (Gordon undated).

Pressure groups – Many traditional and non-traditional groups became active during the conflict, including:

- Sectoral groups (for example, Construction Forestry Mining and Energy Union (CFMEU); Tasmanian Chamber of Commerce and Industry (TCCI)) which strongly supported construction of the mill based on the economic advantages it would bring to Tasmania;

- Environmental NGOs (The Wilderness Society (TWS); National Toxics Network (NTN)) and community-based groups (Tasmanians Against the Pulp Mill)) which campaigned against the mill because of concerns about environmental impacts and the approval process;

- Religious organisations, such as the Legana Christian Church, which were concerned that basic Christian values of honesty and due diligence should be upheld during the approval process (Gale 2008);

- International NGO, BankTrack,[7] which closely tracked the EDM process and supported the campaign against the mill; and

- Australian internet-based advocacy group GetUp![8] (see Chapter 7), which mobilised the community to influence financial institutions not to support the mill.

Experts and Professionals – Experts engaged by the proponent to prepare the IIS for the proposed mill were matched by counter-experts such as individuals and pressure groups, who made submissions to the Government highlighting many inaccuracies and weaknesses of the IIS. The Tasmanian chapter of the Australian Medical Association (AMA) is one such group that publicised the adverse health impacts of air pollution from the mill (AMA Tasmania 2006; Flanagan 2007).

Both Tasmanian and Federal Governments had their own experts to assess the IIS before approval was granted. The Tasmanian Government appointed international consultants Sweco Pic and ITS Global to assess the IIS against environmental emissions guidelines and social and economic benefits of the mill respectively.[9] The Commonwealth Scientific and Industrial Research Organisation (CSIRO) also conducted reviews of air and water qual-

---

7   <www.banktrack.org/show/pages/about_banktrack> (accessed 5 April 2009).

8   <www.getup.org.au/> (accessed 3 May 2009).

9   <www.justice.tas.gov.au/justice/pulpmillassessment> (accessed 3 April 2009).

ity aspects for the Tasmanian and Federal Governments, respectively. Most notable of the Federal Government experts is Dr Jim Peacock, Australia's Chief Scientist (2006–2008) and his expert panel of scientists whose brief was to assess 'scientific aspects' of the mill, that concerned matters of Commonwealth jurisdiction, that is, threatened species and ecological communities, migratory species and Commonwealth marine areas.

Individuals – An intriguing aspect of this case study is the unlikely individual campaigners it attracted. Businessman Geoffrey Cousins, who was once an adviser to Liberal Prime Minister John Howard, fought the battle against the pulp mill, not in Tasmania, but in Malcolm Turnbull's marginal seat of Wentworth in Sydney, because he was not satisfied with the Commonwealth's environmental assessment of the mill's impacts.

Other longstanding celebrity environmental activists who campaigned against the construction of this pulp mill include author and film-maker Richard Flanagan and horticulturist and television personality, Peter Cundall. Gunns brought in their own celebrity garden guru, Don Burke, to help garner support for the pulp mill (Denholm 2008).

Media – The involvement and interest of a large and diverse variety of media (newspaper, television, radio), both traditional and new (see Chapter 5), is evident from the media references used to write this case study. The media were used by journalists and other actors to inform the public about the various aspects of the mill proposal and as a platform through which opposing views were put forward. For example, controlled media releases by the proponent[10] focused on the benefits of the mill and countering negative messages delivered by mill opponents.

B.3 The controversy

Issues surrounding and contributing to the Gunns pulp mill controversy are multi-faceted and complex. On one level, the controversy is about the mill's process technology, use of chemicals and associated air and water pollution, leading to the simple framing of the problem as that of 'technology and pollution'. However as the debate gained momentum, a number of broader issues emerged including its economic and social costs and benefits, risks and uncertainties of impacts, effects on Tasmanian native forests, political accountability and influence, and corporate power and responsibility.

B.3.1 Pollution impacts and environmental concerns

The proposed mill plans to use the Kraft process[11] for producing pulp from woodchips. The environmental impacts of water and air emissions from 'boilers, incinerators, effluent treatment processes, chemical manufacturing operations, waste dumps and an ocean outfall for waste liquids' (Bell undated, p 3) were a major cause for concern for the many actors involved in this issue. The Chief Scientist's report found that 'the construction and operation of the proposed mill posed some residual risks and uncertainties for the three areas under commonwealth jurisdiction' (Australian Government DEWHA 2007, p 2). Despite

---

10   <www.gunnspulpmill.com.au/mediareleases.html> (accessed 4 April 2009).

11   In the Kraft pulping process, an aqueous solution of caustic sodium hydroxide and sodium sulphide is used to extract lignin from the wood fibre source in large chemical digesters. Lignin is a natural component of plants, together with cellulose and hemicellulose, but it is undesirable in pulp and paper, leading to yellowing and rapid degradation (Scandia National Laboratories 2006).

these concerns, Gunns and the Tasmanian Government continued to provide assurances to the public about the modern technology used by the mill to achieve tough environmental standards. For example, the Premier claimed that 'Tasmanians can be reassured that this mill will be world-class with leading-edge technology. As well, it will be subject to a very stringent environmental regulation regime' (Lennon 2007).

These promises of a 'clean, green, world-class and high-tech' pulp mill did not help allay the fears of many in the community who considered the environmental impacts to be significant and the information presented in the IIS prepared by Gunns to be inadequate, superficial and misleading. The media caught onto this and were reporting on the 'fictional' and 'illusionary' aspects of this proposal (Wright 2007).

Public scepticism about the sincerity of claims made by the Tasmanian Government and Gunns took seed when Gunns changed their original intentions of investigating a total chlorine free (TCF) process for bleaching pulp to one that uses chlorine dioxide as a primary bleaching agent (Buckman 2008). Concern over the use of chlorine compounds is linked with the release of toxic, carcinogenic substances such as dioxins and furans into receiving waters and the surrounding atmosphere. Following is a summary of environmental issues which were raised by many individuals and pressure groups that made submissions to the Tasmanian and Federal Governments during the assessment process.

Water pollution – The release of 64 million litres per day of effluent containing persistent organic pollutants (POPs) such as dioxins and furans to Bass Strait could lead to adverse impacts on the marine environment and human health due to bioaccumulation in the food chain (see 1.4). The public was well aware of these issues because of the previous case of high dioxin levels (above WHO standards) found in fish in Sydney Harbour in 2006. Health concerns about the high level of dioxins had led to the blood testing of commercial fishermen and their families and prompted the New South Wales Government to impose a temporary ban on commercial fishing in Sydney Harbour (ABC News 2006; *The Australian* 2006). However, Gunns claimed that the effluent going into Bass Strait 'will be cleaner than the water flowing beside the mill in the Tamar River' (Frame 2009).

The hydrodynamic modelling conducted by the proponent's consultants to assess effluent dispersion in Bass Strait was identified as misleading (Godfrey undated). Issues with modelling were also identified in the Chief Scientist's report which found that aspects of the biological and hydrodynamic assessment were inadequate and would have to be addressed in the EIMP (Australian Government DEWHA 2007). An error in the original reporting of the concentration of dioxins was later corrected and showed 45 times more dioxin concentration in the effluent than originally calculated (SMH 2006). This further exacerbated doubts about the accuracy of the information being provided to the public.

Atmospheric pollution – Particulate emissions from the mill's 130 metre high stack and its wood-fired power plant would cause nuisance odours and have adverse impacts on the health of the surrounding communities (Buckman 2008). It was argued that particulates would become trapped in the Tamar Valley and on wet and cold days this pollution would reach Launceston (The Greens Tasmania 2006a) and cause additional air quality problems in one of the Australia's worst air quality areas during winter months. In their position statement to the RPDC the Tasmanian branch of the AMA stated that the release of small particles, sulphur dioxide and other chlorinated, sulphur and nitrogen compounds from the mill could cause odour problems and had the potential of increasing morbidity and mortality (AMA Tasmania 2006).

The impact of the mill on anthropogenic climate change was also considered to be significant. A report by the Green Institute estimated carbon dioxide emissions to be at least 10.2 Mt CO_2 per annum which is equivalent to 2 per cent of Australia's total emissions in 2005 (Blakers 2007). This estimate includes emissions from the processing of pulp, log waste and other vegetation on the logging site (Blakers 2007). Other sources of CO_2 emissions include the wood-fired power plant, log harvesting and transport activities.

Impact on native forests – The pulp mill would use 4 million tonnes per year of wood-chips as feedstock. Views and assertions about the exact quantity and source of woodchips differed. On the one hand, Gunns claimed that no old growth forests, as defined by the RFA, would be used. In the initial stages a mixture of re-growth native forests, pine and eucalypt plantations would be used and within five years of mill operation 80 per cent of the woodchips would be sourced from plantations (Gunns undated). On the other hand, many conservationists and green groups argued that 80 per cent of the woodchips in the initial stages of the operation would come from native forests (Buckman 2008) and as the life of the mill extended beyond current RFAs there were no guarantees to ensure that logging would not be intensified and old growth forests cleared for woodchips. There were also concerns that consumption of such large quantities of wood could potentially have irreversible impacts on native forests, their ecosystems and threatened wildlife such as the Wedge-tailed Eagle and the Tasmanian Devil (The Greens 2006a).

Criticism was directed at both the RPDC's guidelines for the mill's impact assessment and terms of reference for the Federal Government's assessment as these did not include consideration of environmental impacts on the use of native forest for 'meeting the proposed mill's appetite for woodchips' (The Greens 2006a, p 29). The Wilderness Society (TWS) even initiated legal action in the Federal Court to challenge the Federal Government's decision-making process and its limited scope, especially the decision not to assess impacts of the mill on Tasmanian forests. TWS eventually lost this case, but were successful in delaying Minister Turnbull's conditional approval of the mill (Buckman 2008; TWS 2007).

Consumption and use of water – The proposed mill would use 26 billion litres of water annually (half of Canberra's yearly water consumption) mainly from Trevallyn Dam (near Launceston), and only a small percentage of water would be recycled (The Greens Tasmania 2006b). At a time of severe drought and water shortages throughout Australia, this was a concern shared by the whole community, including householders and Tasmanian farmers.

B.3.2 Economic and social issues

The calculation and distribution of costs and benefits of the pulp mill were a major point of contention. Questions were raised about who would get the benefits and who would pay, and what assumptions had been made for selecting and costing various parameters. Gunns was seen as the major beneficiary – while the environment, the public and other industries would be paying for Gunns' profits through negative impacts they would bear.

Based on Gunns' economic analysis, it was reported that over the long-term the mill would inject an extra $6.7 billion into the Australian economy and create about 1500 direct and indirect jobs during the period of its operation (Lennon 2007). The validity of these numbers was contradicted by many experts, largely because Gunns' economic analysis did not take into consideration 'externalities' such as the costs of pollution impacts on human health, the fishing, wine and tourism industries (The Greens 2006b). A cost-benefit analysis (CBA) prepared by a Tasmanian Business Roundtable for Sustainable Industries (LEC 2007) found that after including government subsidies and 'externalities', the mill could drain $3.3 billion from business and government (Brown 2007). Other reports considered the mill to be a high-risk venture based on the amount of resources it would consume and the stiff competition pulp from the mill would face from low-cost overseas pulp producers (ABC News 2008c). Findings of these reports were, however, refuted by the proponent and the forestry industry.

Another particular community concern was the Tasmanian Government's commitment to use taxpayers' money to fund a $60 million water supply pipeline to the mill from Trevallyn Dam. These economic issues raised questions about the costs incurred by the Tasmanian community, State and Federal Governments and the environment to provide profits for a corporation (The Greens 2006b).

B.3.3 Environmental assessment and approval process

The Tasmanian Premier had promised a transparent and detailed approval and assessment process: '[t]his will be a thorough approval process, a painstaking process. No stone will be left unturned. No voice will go unheard' (Lennon 2004).

In reality, the process did not meet the expectations of many in the community and led GetUp!'s spokesperson to state: '"[t]he entire process of approval has been fraught with undue kowtowing to Gunns' demands. After all, it was Gunns who demanded the state approval process be fast-tracked in the first place," Mr Coper said.' (cited in *The Age* 2008). This view was supported by many others. Figure B.2 represents some of the key events that led to mistrust and criticism of the government's handling of the assessment and approval process.

There were two particularly controversial aspects of the process. First, there were claims by opponents of the mill that the process involved unwarranted support for the mill from both State and Federal Governments and collusion between the Tasmanian Government and Gunns. As identified above (B.2.2), the Task Force and the Assessment Panel, were set up by the Tasmanian Government to undertake various aspects of the assessment and approval process. According to Bob Gordon, Managing Director of Forestry Australia and Executive Director of the Task Force:

> The Task Force undertook a massive education program, which included a traveling bus, to explain how pulp mill technology had changed, to familiarise people with the terminology that would be used during public debate and to quash myths perpetrated by those opposed to forestry projects.

> (Gordon undated)

However, the Task Force was viewed by many as being 'government's propaganda cheer leading squad' (BankTrack 2008) promoting the mill on their website,[12] through newsletters and bus tours (Gale 2008).

In 2007, the mill was given conditional go-ahead for construction, subject to 48 conditions placed by the Federal Government. Since then, both the State and Federal Governments have continued to grant extensions to Gunns on various matters. For example, the Federal Government gave Gunns a three-month extension in September 2008 for submission of the mill's EIMP, and then a 26-month extension in January 2009 to allow Gunns to provide

---

12   This website had been removed at the time of writing the case study.

Figure B.2 Pulp mill assessment and approval process – timeline of key events

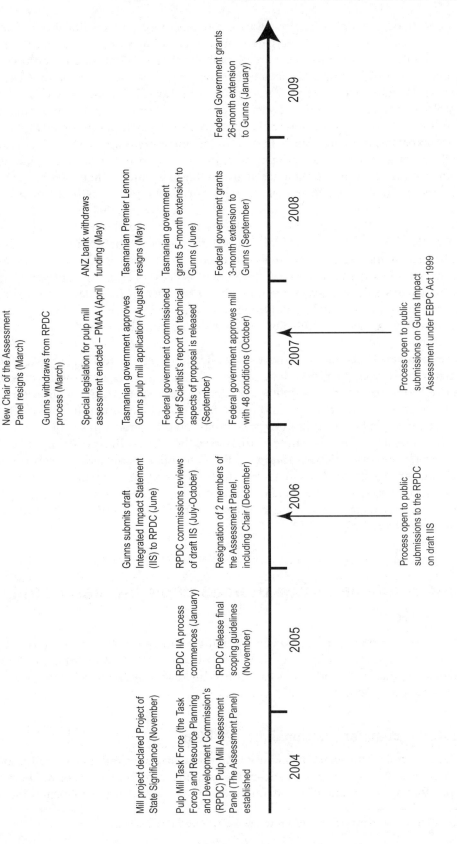

2004

Mill project declared Project of State Significance (November)

Pulp Mill Task Force (the Task Force) and Resource Planning and Development Commission's (RPDC) Pulp Mill Assessment Panel (The Assessment Panel) established

2005

RPDC IIA process commences (January)

RPDC release final scoping guidelines (November)

2006

Gunns submits draft Integrated Impact Statement (IIS) to RPDC (June)

RPDC commissions reviews of draft IIS (July–October)

Resignation of 2 members of the Assessment Panel, including Chair (December)

Process open to public submissions to the RPDC on draft IIS

2007

New Chair of the Assessment Panel resigns (March)

Gunns withdraws from RPDC process (March)

Special legislation for pulp mill assessment enacted – PMAA (April)

Tasmanian government approves Gunns pulp mill application (August)

Federal government commissioned Chief Scientist's report on technical aspects of proposal is released (September)

Federal government approves mill with 48 conditions (October)

Process open to public submissions on Gunns Impact Assessment under EBPC Act 1999

2008

ANZ bank withdraws funding (May)

Tasmanian Premier Lennon resigns (May)

Tasmanian government grants 5-month extension to Gunns (June)

Federal government grants 3-month extension to Gunns (September)

2009

Federal Government grants 26-month extension to Gunns (January)

further hydrodynamic modelling studies on the environmental effects of the mill's effluent before final approval is granted. This announcement cast doubts about the future of the mill. While some saw this as the 'death of the mill' (Arup 2009), others accused the Federal Government of granting favours to big business. The Greens Senator, Christine Milne, stated that 'the government is "bending over backwards" to facilitate Gunns' (The Greens 2008) and some pulp mill opponents were considering legal action against the Federal Government as this extension could contravene the EBPC Act (Arup 2009; Darby 2009).

A second related controversial aspect of the process was that some claimed it was fraught with political interference and corporate manipulation. There were considerable tensions between the RPDC's Assessment Panel and the Task Force. Three members, including two Chairs, of the Assessment Panel resigned during the period of assessment. These resignations came amid claims of political interference by the Task Force, which had exerted influence over the independence of the Assessment Panel, and the pressuring of public servants by Premier Lennon to fast-track the assessment and approval process (Putt 2007). The Chair of the Assessment Panel was cited as saying the RPDC would be compromised in the eyes of the public and the assessment process seen to be contaminated unless the activities of the Task Force were reined in (ABC News 2005). Such was the resonance of these claims that the RPDC distanced itself from the Task Force stating 'Government agencies, including the Pulp Mill Task Force, have no connection with the Commission or its assessment process'.[13]

In March 2007, Gunns withdrew its application from the RPDC, arguing that the assessment process was taking too long (Lang 2007). Under pressure from Gunns, the Premier moved to introduce the *Pulp Mill Assessment Act 2007* (PMAA), legislation for a special assessment process, which would allow the State Government to engage consultants to assess and report on the mill's environmental and economic impacts (Buckman 2008). After a short debate in the Tasmanian Parliament, the PMAA Bill passed both the Lower and Upper Houses of Parliament, allowing the Tasmanian Government to abandon the RPDC process, engage consultants to assess Gunns' IIS and hence expedite the approval process. This move was openly condemned by many actors. In particular, the Greens were reported to have said that it was 'an abandonment of due process and a capitulation of corporate bullying' (Ward 2007).

B.4 Analysis: What themes does the case study reveal?

It is evident from the discussion above that the intricate nature of this controversy set the scene for a complicated and conflict ridden EDM process. Many of the themes discussed in this book can be found in this case study, however our analysis below focuses on four of the more prominent themes.

B.4.1 A complex sustainability problem

The pulp mill controversy has many ingredients of a 'wicked' sustainability problem (see Chapter 2). Contentious issues such as the pollution impacts associated with the mill's operation are situated within a complex and multifaceted socio-political context where the

---

13   <www.rpdc.tas.gov.au/poss/pulp> (accessed 11 April 2009).

views and opinions of a diverse range of actors clashed as they disputed the many risks and uncertainties, and gains and losses associated with environmental, social and economic impacts of the mill. This study reveals the many challenges faced by those involved in decision-making on complex sustainability problems. Here we focus on the difficulties associated with the interpretation and implementation of sustainability.

Principles of ecologically sustainable development (ESD) are embedded in Australian institutional frameworks through policy and legislation. There are several examples of this in the case study including: the Commonwealth legislation (EBPC Act), the National Forest Policy Statement (1992), the Regional Forest Agreements (RFAs), as well as Tasmania's Resource Management and Planning System.[14] In addition, based on Gunns' commitment to sustainability the proposed mill was to utilise the best global technology and be the world's greenest pulp mill (Gunns Ltd 2008, p 12):

> Gunns has a strong and ongoing commitment to sustainability principles in its forest management and resource procurement activities. Gunns is setting new benchmarks through continuous improvement in environmental management with ongoing certification to ISO 14001 and the Australian Forestry Standard (AFS).

However, the contested interpretation of sustainability and its application caused much debate and raised many questions about the sustainability of this development.

Intergenerational and intragenerational equity – Responsibility to future generations is a special feature of sustainability (Chapter 2). The long-term impacts of the mill's operation on Tasmania's forest ecosystem through logging of native forests, loss of biodiversity and the consequences for climate change mean that the negative impacts of this development are likely to be passed on to future generations. Concerns about the effects of air and water pollution on the health of surrounding communities and the economic impacts on smaller businesses such as farming, fishing and wineries raise questions about intragenerational equity and environmental justice. *Would all parties equally bear the consequences of the development?*

Integrating the social, economic and ecological pillars of sustainability – Sustainability requires the integration of economic, social and environmental factors (see Chapter 2). Claims about the inadequacy of the economic analyses which failed to consider the cost of all social and ecological consequences on all stakeholders were rife during the debate (see B.4.3 for more details). The economic report prepared by the proponent's consultants ignored the risks to human and environmental health and did not internalise costs associated with the impacts on all parties (Edwards 2006; LEC 2007; Pullinger undated). *Was the decision to proceed with the mill based on an integrated approach to sustainability?*

Governance and public participation – Addressing complex sustainability problems requires collaborative governance and deliberative approaches to decision-making that incorporate broad public participation and include a wide set of knowledges (see Chapters 2, 3, 6 and 7). The RPDC process was open to the public and although opportunities for participation were mainly limited to written submissions, hundreds were received and 'the RPDC were able to review the claims and counter claims of proponents and opponents alike' (Gale 2008, p 268). However, after the enactment of the *Pulp Mill Assessment Act 2007*, flow of information was controlled by the Government and the process was closed to all but Gunns, the Government and their consultants (Gale 2008). As the issue progressed, opportunities

---

14   <www.rpdc.tas.gov.au/planning/rmps> (accessed 14 June 2009).

for public participation were curtailed further. According to Buckman (2008, p 143), '[a]fter Gunns' withdrawal from the RPDC, the federal government set up a new low-key assessment whereby the public could send comments to the company which would pass them on, along with its responses, to Canberra'. The Federal Government was also accused of protecting the commercial interests of Gunns as they refused Senator Milne's Freedom of Information request to publicly release a report by CSIRO that identified weaknesses in the hydrodynamic modelling conducted by Gunns (Milne 2008).

There were also claims that the Chair of the RPDC's Assessment Panel was inappropriately pressured by Premier Lennon 'to dump public hearings' in order to fast-track the assessment process (Flanagan 2007, p 25). These apparent attempts to exclude the public from participating in the EDM process led to the use of 'insisted' spaces (Chapter 7) such as public protests, targeted lobbying and media campaigns (see B.4.3) by those wanting to be involved in the EDM process. *Did the EDM process achieve transparent and inclusive governance?*

Uncertainty, risk and precaution – Uncertainty is an inherent feature of complex problems and needs to be appropriately managed using anticipatory approaches during EDM (see Chapter 9). Conditional approval to the mill was granted despite the many uncertainties and risks associated with its impacts. Many pointed out that the $2 billion development had the potential to cause irreversible loss of high-value biodiversity, contribute to global climate change and deplete water resources at a time of drought. Further, not considering fluctuations in global pulp prices during the economic analysis made it a high-risk business venture that exposed 'the Tasmanian public to the risk of on-going and significant "bailing out" subsidies' (Edwards 2006, p 1). *Was an anticipatory and precautionary approach used when assessing the risks associated with mill impacts?*

Box B.1: Is the pulp mill a sustainable development?

Whether we consider the mill to be a sustainable development or not depends on our views on the need for the mill and our interpretation of sustainability. Some opponents of the mill might not see the need for this mill. They might respond in the negative to the questions posed above and not consider it to be a sustainable development based on assertions that the mill:

- brings short-term benefits to the proponent, forestry industry and government at the expense of long-term damages to the environment and the broader community;

- does not achieve a balance between the pillars of sustainability, is biased towards the economic pillar, and is based on a weak sustainability position which allows substitutability between ecological, social and economic capital in order to maintain the constant capital requirement for sustainability;

- was not approved through a process of good environmental governance as public participation opportunities were limited and exclusive to selected parties; and

- is an environmentally and economically risky development.

Others, such as the proponent, CFMEU and TCCI, who support the development and see the need for it mainly as an economic stimulus, believe that it is sustainable as it:

- sources wood from sustainably managed forests, prevents shipping of woodchips to be processed in less environmentally friendly mills in Asia, while improving Tasmania's local economy (Frame[15] 2009);

- uses best available technology, best environmental management, focuses on occupational health and safety, and on balance, has a social benefit for the region (CFMEU undated);

- adopts the concept of sustainable development in the assessment of TBL (triple bottom line) impacts associated with the mill (TCCI 2006).

B.4.2 Values, facts and disputed knowledge

Many complexities of sustainability problems, highlighted above, stem from the contestation of value positions held by actors involved in the EDM process. These value differences influence the way we identify and frame issues and develop solutions (see Chapter 3). On one level the pulp mill dispute can be viewed as a clash between anthropocentric and ecocentric value positions. The proponent, Government and the forestry industry can be seen as anthropocentric economic rationalists who view the pulp mill as a means of providing economic prosperity for Tasmanians and a way of promoting their vested interests and world views, while the environmentalists and green groups can be seen as ecocentrics who consider the mill to be a threat to the health of the Tasmanian community, their environment and its ecosystem. This is not surprising given the history of the 'forest wars' and other environmental disputes in Tasmania (Lake Pedder and Franklin Dam), which ultimately have been about determining, sustaining and securing a vision for the economic, social and ecological future of Tasmania.

However, simply putting people in two boxes does not capture the diversity of actors involved in this case. In reality, as noted above (B.2.2) and further discussed below (B.4.4) the multitude of proponents and opponents came with a variety of views, interests and alliances which developed and evolved as the case progressed.

Consider, for example, the changing views of the Tasmanian Government, which had been an avid supporter of the development based on its economic benefits under the leadership of Premier Lennon. Later, under the new leadership of Premier David Bartlett, the Tasmanian Treasurer conceded that the economy of Tasmania was growing without the mill and it was 'not the be all and end all' (ABC News 2008d). Premier Bartlett also ruled out public funding of the $60 million water pipeline for the mill (ABC News 2008e).

Much of the conflict in this debate arose from the questioning of 'facts' and 'expert scientific knowledge' generated by the parties engaged in the pulp mill EDM process. All parties pushed their value positions under the veil of scientific expertise and objectivity. Gunns engaged many expert consultants to prepare the various aspects of the IIS such as environmental, social and economic impact assessments. Claims made in the IIS were contradicted by a barrage of counter-claims by many professionals, pressure groups and individuals (also see B.4.4), mainly through written submissions to the RPDC during 2006. These counter-claims were further refuted by supporters of the mill and 'independent' expert witnesses engaged by the proponent to undertake additional reviews of their studies. For example:

---

15   Calton Frame was the corporate and sustainability manager for Gunns Limited at the time of writing this case study.

- the professional body, AMA (Tasmanian branch) stated that the air pollution predictions made by the IIS were 'highly unreliable' as they were based on models that did not meet acceptable criteria and had failed to consider the adverse health effects of smaller particles (AMA Tasmania 2006, p 2). In contrast, Gunns' expert witness found that atmospheric emissions would have insignificant or negligible impact (Gunns undated);

- the pressure group, NTN was concerned about misleading claims made by Gunns about the state of the art nature of the technology proposed for the pulp mill. Based on the analysis of NTN, low effluent or closed-loop TCF technology was 'clearly a safer and more precautionary choice' as this eliminated the production of dioxins, furans and other toxic organochlorine compounds (Lloyd-Smith undated, p 4). However, in their submission to the RPDC, the CFMEU claimed that these assertions by NTN were incorrect and only created sensationalism and misinformation in the community (CFMEU undated).

This dispute over 'facts' and 'knowledge' reveals the subjective nature of 'science'. In the case of the pulp mill, some of this subjectivity arose from the narrow scoping guidelines for the IIA and the narrow terms of reference for the assessments by independent consultants (Sweco Pic and ITS Global) appointed by the Tasmanian Government, and the Commonwealth's Chief Scientist. This severely limited the ability of the environmental assessment to take into account major impacts of the proposed mill. For example, Sweco Pic's assessment of mill emissions against the RPDC's guidelines did not consider 'questions related to transportation, wood supply, tourism and agriculture' (Gale 2008, p 272; see also B.3.1). As discussed in Chapter 6, political and scientific processes are intertwined, and governments may set the study scope with a view to influencing an outcome they favour. This certainly rang true with some concerned groups, such as the NTN: 'This is not an environmental impact assessment but appears to be a political process designed to deliver a pre-determined outcome – which is the approval of the Gunns Limited's Bell Bay Pulp Mill' (Bell 2007, p 1).

B.4.3 The use of EDM tools

As discussed in Chapter 8, tools for EDM are used within a socio-political context and their application and outcomes are influenced by assumptions and choices. The influence of 'narrow boundary definition' for environmental impact assessment (highlighted above) is an example. Below we draw attention to some other subjective aspects of the tools used during the mill's assessment process.

Both Gunns and the Tasmanian Government had invested large sums of money and time (see Figure B.2) in the preparation and assessment of the IIS. It was reported that by July 2006 the company had spent $11 million and was expected to spend another $40 million before completion of the approval process (Gale 2008). However, despite the time and money spent, various shortcomings of the IIS and the Government's assessments were pointed out:

Independence of consultants – Scepticism about the independence of consultants who may gain from the approval and construction of the Gunns pulp mill cast doubts on the credibility of the Tasmanian Government's assessment of the Gunns IIS. According to one critic (Lang 2007):

This is precisely the problem – SWECO PIC is not independent from the pulp industry. If SWECO PIC decides that the project can go ahead, several of its past (and potential future) clients stand to win lucrative contracts supplying equipment and services to the pulp mill.

Issues of bias – The Social Impact Assessment (SIA) was subject to criticisms of bias. The summary of the community profile identifies high unemployment, an aging population and low levels of qualifications as key issues and opportunities (GHD 2006 cited in SourceWatch 2006). According to an opponent group (SourceWatch 2006), the SIA is tailored to deliver a particular view that supports the need for the mill. It gives 'the impression that this community will need the proposed development to rejuvenate the community, providing it with new work opportunities, an influx of young workers & higher levels of education & training'.

Modelling was used as a tool to predict the impacts of the mill's air and water emissions and for conducting economic analyses. As discussed in Chapter 8, the outputs from models can be limited due to uncertainties resulting from assumptions made about modelling parameters. These choices are inevitably influenced by the inherent biases of individuals and institutions conducting and interpreting the modelling. CSIRO's review of the air quality aspects of the mill identified some major omissions. For example, Total Reduced Sulphides (TRS) released from the mill had the potential to significantly affect air quality, but background concentrations and fugitive TRS emissions were not included in the modelling conducted by Gunns' consultants (Hibberd and Manins 2006).

The Chief Scientist's expert panel highlighted a number of weaknesses in the hydrodynamic and water quality modelling undertaken by the proponent including inadequate calibration and short run times (Australian Government DEWHA 2007) which introduced uncertainty about proposed water quality objectives being met at all times. Preliminary hydrodynamic modelling conducted by CSIRO, reported State permit conditions would be breached on 'an almost daily basis' (Herzfeld 2007, p 36). The 'inadequacies' of modelling and resulting risks were also identified in public submissions and media releases by pressure groups and individuals (for example, Sandery 2006).

The large difference between the results of the CBA commissioned by Gunns ($6.7 billion benefits) and the Tasmanian Business Roundtable ($3.3 billion costs) can be attributed to the assumptions made and methodology used while conducting economic analyses. The CBA conducted by Gunns was criticised for addressing only benefits while the costs associated with the mill were ignored (Edwards 2006). Another flaw noted in the 'benefits-only' (Biggs undated) Gunns' CBA was the failure to undertake a sensitivity analysis, and hence sensitivity to key parameters such as fluctuations in the price of pulp and discount rate was ignored (Edwards 2006; Gale 2008).

It would seem that the Gunns' CBA was conducted to emphasise the potential *benefits* (advantages) associated with the mill proposal, while down-playing the possible *costs* (disadvantages) in order to make the proposal look more attractive. Of course, similar inferences can be drawn about other parties who conducted CBA relating to the Gunns proposal! This bias towards a particular outcome and the failure to consider a full range of scenarios when using tools to assess the various impacts of the mill further reduced public confidence in the assessment process (see Chapter 8; Gale 2008).

B.4.4 **The influence of politics and actors**

The discussion thus far has identified the views, values and roles played by the broad range of government, non-government, business, professional, media and community actors *involved in* and *affected by* the pulp mill controversy. As highlighted in Chapter 5, to fully appreciate the power and vulnerabilities of these actors requires a deeper look at some of the *direct* and *indirect* ways such actors seek to influence the EDM process and its outcomes.

Political institutions and the public service – Both the Tasmanian and Federal Governments had environmental responsibilities in relation to the pulp mill. As seen in Chapter 4, this division of power can sometimes cause intergovernmental conflicts. However in this case, both levels of government were aligned in their assessment of the mill proposal. The tensions arose from the conflicts *within* State government – between politicians and public servants. Premier Lennon, who openly supported the mill proposal, was frustrated by the delays caused by the RPDC's scrutiny of the IIS which included requests for supplementary information from Gunns and their dissatisfaction with the inadequacies of the IIS. Two chairs of the RPDC's assessment panel resigned alleging political pressure and interference from Lennon and the Task Force, as discussed in B2.3.3 (Buckman 2008; Gale 2008). These incidents also highlight the ethical dilemmas professionals may face as public servants (see 5.10).

Corporate power and influence – Gunns wielded its corporate power in various ways in order to influence the outcome of the EDM process. Their influence on the Tasmanian Government was underpinned by the promise of economic growth brought by the mill. Gunns' withdrawal from the RPDC's assessment process can be seen as a tactic to pressure the Tasmanian Government into taking action to hasten the process. Gale (2008, p 265) suggests that one other explanation for doing so was the fear that the RPDC's recommendations would be 'heavily qualified, costly to implement, and commercially unacceptable'. This move was successful to the extent that it prompted the Tasmanian Government to enact the *Pulp Mill Assessment Act 2007* that allowed fast-tracking without the scrutiny of the RPDC.

Prior to the mill proposal, Gunns was actively demonstrating its corporate might when it came to environmental matters. In 2004, the company sued 20 activists and organisations for damage caused to the company by their activities including disruption of logging and woodchip operations, campaigns against shareholders, investors and banks (Carrick 2005; Chapter 5). Some have labelled the 'Gunns 20' case a 'SLAPP' (Strategic Lawsuit Against Public Participation) because it effectively sought to silence a group of actors for speaking out against logging (see 5.10). One interpretation of this case is that it was a pre-emptive strike to warn activists and to demonstrate Gunns' corporate power just before the proposal of the Tamar Valley pulp mill was put forward (Ethical Corporation undated).

Formation of alliances – The CFMEU, Gunns and the Tasmanian Government formed an 'iron-triangle' alliance in support of the mill. Also part of this alliance was the State Opposition, the Tasmanian Chamber of Commerce and the Forest Industry Association of Tasmania (Gale 2007, 2008). The strength of such an alliance is demonstrated by the fact that a previous alliance such as this, between the forestry unions, the Labor Tasmanian Government and the Liberal Federal Government, contributed to the ALP's loss in the 2004 federal election (Gale 2005).

Advocacy campaigns and influence on public opinion – The seemingly open support by the Tasmanian Government for Gunns helped to mobilise many traditional and non-traditional actors who used a variety of strategies to campaign against the mill (see B.2.2). One substantial outcome of their combined efforts was a public demonstration in Hobart one week before the 2007 federal election. This 'anti-mill' rally was attended by an estimated 15,000 people and was aimed at influencing the future government and mill financiers (TWS undated).

Traditional environmental campaigners such as the Tasmanian Greens, The Wilderness Society (TWS) and community pressure groups such as Tasmanians Against the Pulp Mill, mainly used media releases, submissions and advertising to get the attention of the public and decision-makers. Here we focus on some of the non-traditional actors and their strategies.

GetUp![16] and BankTrack exerted influence on the ANZ Bank to withdraw funding for the mill. For example, GetUp!, used the internet to mobilise their members, who included ANZ customers, shareholders or staff to write to the CEO of ANZ requesting that Gunns' credit line be cut. According to GetUp!'s website, 15,000 letters were sent in less than 20 hours.[17]

The involvement of businessman Geoffrey Cousins demonstrates the impact of policy entrepreneurs (see 5.9) who have the political and strategic know-how to run an effective campaign. In Mr Cousins' case he also had somewhat of a celebrity status as well as significant economic capacity. His strategy was to target the federal electoral seat of Wentworth (in eastern Sydney), which at the time was represented by the Coalition's Environment Minister Malcolm Turnbull. Cousins ran a full page advertisement against Turnbull before the 2007 federal election in the local newspaper – the *Wentworth Courier*. The advertisement read: 'Is Malcolm Turnbull the minister for the environment or the minister against the environment?' (Grattan and Topsfield 2007) and was signed by more than 100 Australian celebrities and business people including tennis champion John Newcombe, actors Bryan Brown and Rachel Ward (ABC News 2007). The timing of the campaign, just before the 2007 federal election was critical to its success as it was an opportunity to bring the pulp mill onto the national political agenda. Although Mr Turnbull won the seat of Wentworth, an opinion poll just prior to the election found that 98 per cent of the people polled were opposed to the mill (Jones 2007). It seems Mr Cousins strategy may have contributed to this 'anti-mill' community sentiment.

Corporate social responsibility – Although the ANZ Bank did not give specific reasons for withdrawing their funding support for the proposed mill, there are some plausible explanations, including demonstrating corporate social responsibility, commitment to sustainability and mounting public pressure against the mill. This explanation is supported by the ANZ Bank's commitment to social and environmental responsibility through the adoption of the Equator Principles[18] (see Chapter 5) and their new Forests Policy[19] (released in 2008). This decision by the ANZ Bank was applauded by many groups including BankTrack, TWS and GetUp!

---

16 On 30th April 2009, a three-quarter page advertisement was run in London's Financial Times urging European banks not to finance Gunns' pulp mill. This advertisement was run by TWS and financed through donations to GetUp! (ABC Local Radio 2009).

17 <www.getup.org.au/campaign/NoPulpMill&id=269> (accessed 6 April 2009).

18 <www.anz.com.au/about-us/corporate-responsibility/customers/responsible-business-lending/equator-principles/> (accessed 5 April 2009).

19 <www.anz.com.au/about-us/corporate-responsibility/customers/responsible-business-lending/policies-guidelines/> (accessed 5 April 2009).

B.5 Conclusion

The Gunns case study illustrates the complexities of addressing sustainability issues and the politically fraught nature of EDM. Despite Lennon's declaration that 'the legacy of Wesley Vale was a lesson in how not to realise a pulpmill' (Lennon 2004), stories of the two mills are uncannily similar. Wesley Vale was also plagued by pollution and technology concerns, had unwavering support from a Tasmanian Labor Premier, who passed special legislation to facilitate the approval process, and was given the go ahead by both State and Federal Governments (Buckman 2008). It seems that past lessons are easily forgotten by some, especially when strong world views and political agendas collide. Others, such as anti-mill campaigners, had learnt valuable lessons from past environmental conflicts in Tasmania. In both cases, well-organised public campaigns were pivotal in influencing key actors and their decisions. This resulted in the withdrawal of Gunns' main financier in 2008, and the withdrawal of one of the joint-venture proponents of Wesley Vale in 1989.

At the time of writing this case study (April 2009), the future of the Gunns pulp mill was still uncertain as finance for the mill had not been secured by Gunns. Although the global financial crisis of 2008–2009 is making it difficult for Gunns to raise credit for the mill, rising unemployment and a flagging economy could also convince governments to fund such large infrastructure projects that stimulate economic growth. It remains to be seen whether this pulp mill is 'the wrong mill, in the wrong place at the wrong time' (Biggs undated) and if it will ever be built. The socio-political and financial landscape at the time will determine these decisions.

References

ABC Local Radio, 2009, 'Anti pulp mill ad targets European banks', AM, 30 April, <www.abc.net.au/am/content/2008/s2556680.htm> (accessed 3 May 2009).

ABC News, 2005, 'Pulp mill taskforce responds to RPDC concerns', 27 June, <www.abc.net.au/news/newsitems/200506/s1401327.htm> (accessed 11 October 2008).

ABC News, 2006, 'Sydney Harbour commercial fishing halted', 24 January, <www.abc.net.au/news/newsitem/200601/s1553938.html> (accessed 4 April 2009)

ABC News, 2007, 'Stars sign on anti-Turnbull campaign', 28 August, <www.abc.net.au/news/stories/2007/08/28/2017143.htm> (accessed 3 April 2009).

ABC News, 2008a, 'Forestry Tasmania signs most significant deal ever', 26 February, <www.abc.net.au/news/stories/2008/02/26/2173347.htm> (accessed 11 April 2009).

ABC News, 2008b, 'ANZ pulls out of Gunns deal', 29 May, <www.abc.net.au/news/stories/2008/05/29/2259677.htm> (accessed 3 April 2009).

ABC News, 2008c, 'Report questions pulp mill benefits', 29 January, <www.abc.net.au/news/stories/2008/01/29/2148424.htm> (accessed 12 December 2008).

ABC News 2008d, 'Pulp mill not "be all and end all"', 23 June, <www.abc.net.au/news/stories/2008/06/23/2282703.htm> (accessed 10 October 2008).

ABC News, 2008e, 'Bartlett rules out public funds for pulp mill pipeline', 28 May, <www.abc.net.au/news/stories/2008/05/28/2258622.htm> (accessed 11 April 2009).

ABC Tasmania, 2003 'Tas Govt would welcome pulp mill proposal: Lennon', 18 June, <www.abc.net.au/tasmania/news/200306/s882154.htm> (accessed 6 June 2008).

Arup, T, 2009, 'Finance doubts for mill', The Age, 6 January, <www.theage.com.au/environment/finance-doubts-for-mill-20090105-7ail.html> (accessed 11 April 2009).

Ajani, J, 2007, The Forest Wars, Melbourne University Press, Carlton, Victoria.

AMA (Australian Medical Association) Tasmania, 2006, 'Position statement – Proposed Tamar Valley pulp mill', <www.amatas.com.au/index.php?item=file&target=ama_position_statement_pulp_mill> (accessed 11 April 2009).

Australian Government DEWHA (Department of Environment, Water, Heritage and the Arts), 2007, Advice of Australia's Chief Scientist: Chief Scientist's report on the scientific aspects of the Department of Environment and Water Resources recommendation report, relevant supporting documentation and public comments on the Gunns Limited pulp mill proposal (EBPC2007/3385) Tasmania, <www.environment.gov.au/epbc/notices/assessments/2007/3385/decision.html> (accessed 5 November 2008).

BankTrack, 2008, 'Dodgy deals – Gunns pulp mill proposal in Tasmania Australia', <www.banktrack.org/?id=74&show=167&visitor=> (accessed 20 June 2008).

Bell, L, undated, 'Submission to the RPDC on the proposed Gunns pulp mill proposal at Bell Bay', <www.justice.tas.gov.au/__data/assets/pdf_file/0011/69923/510_National_Toxics_Network.pdf> (accessed 11October 2008).

Bell, L, 2007, 'Pollution, risks, and non-compliance: NTN analysis of the SWECO PIC report on Gunns' pulp mill', <www.ntn.org.au/ntndocs/ntn_pulp_mill_analysis.pdf> (accessed 5 April 2009).

Biggs, J, undated, 'Gunns proposed pulp [sic] Tamar pulp mill and climate change', <www.garnaut review.org.au/CA25734E0016A131/pages/submissions#general> (accessed 28 April 2009).

Blakers, M, 2007, 'Gunns proposed pulpmill: greenhouse gas emissions', <www.greeninstitute.com.au/images/uploads/Gunns_pulpmill_-_greenhouse_emissions.pdf> (accessed 4 April 2009).

Brown, B, 2007, 'Pulp mill will cost clean, green jobs', *The Australian*, 13 September, <www.theaustralian.news.com.au/story/0,25197,22408099-5013480,00.html> (accessed 25 September 2008).

Brueckner, M, 2007, 'The Western Australian regional forest agreement: economic rationalism and normalisation of political closure', *Australian Journal of Public Administration*, 66 (2): 148–158.

Buckman, G, 2008, *Tasmania's Wilderness Battles: A History*, Allen and Unwin, Crows Nest NSW.

Carrick, D, 2005, 'The Gunns 20 litigation', *The Law Report*, ABC Radio National, 25 January, <www.abc.net.au/rn/talks/8.30/lawrpt/stories/s1287516.htm> (accessed 10 October 2008).

CFMEU (Construction Forestry Mining and Energy Union), undated, 'Submission of the Construction, Forestry, Mining & Energy Union to the Resource Planning & Development Commission on Gunns integrated impact statement for the proposed Bell Bay pulp mill', <www.justice.tas.gov.au/__data/assets/pdf_file/0006/69855/470_Construction,_Forestry,_Mining__and__Energy_Union_-_CFMEU.pdf> (accessed 11 April 2009).

Darby, A, 2008 'Pulp mill will be built: Gunns', *Sydney Morning Herald*, 31 October, <www.smh.com.au/cgi-bin/common/popupPrintArticle.pl?path=/articles/2008/10/30/1224956238450.html> (accessed 11 April 2009).

Darby, A, 2009, 'Garrett gives Gunns more time', *The Age*, 6 January, <www.theage.com.au/environment/garrett-gives-gunns-more-time-20090105-7aim.html> (accessed 11 April 2009).

Denholm, M, 2008, 'Garden guru Don Burke to help sell pulp mill', *The Australian*, 9 October, <www.theaustralian.news.com.au/story/0,25197,24468303-5006788,00.html> (accessed 11 April 2009).

Doogue, G, 2005, 'Clean green pulp mill or the son of Wesley Vale?' *Saturday Extra with Geraldine Doogue*, Radio National, 12 March, <www.abc.net.au/rn/talks/saturday/stories/s1321825.htm> (accessed 6 October 2008).

Edwards, N, 2006, 'Too much risk for reward – An analysis of the pulp mill returns to the people of Tasmania', Submission to the RPDC, <www.rpdc.tas.gov.au/__data/assets/pdf_file/0004/69214/114_Naomi_Edwards.pdf> (accessed 4 April 2009).

Ethical Corporation, undated, 'Further legal action for Australian logging company', <www.ethicalcorp.com/content.asp?ContentID=3644> (accessed 10 April 2009).

FFIC (Forest and Forest Industry Council of Tasmania), 2008, *The New Forest Industry*, <www.ffic.com.au/index.php?option=com_content&view=article&id=142&Itemid=151> (accessed 28 March 2009).

Flanagan, R, 2007, 'Gunns out of control: The tragedy of Tasmania's forests', *The Monthly*, May 2007, pp 20–30.

Forestry Tasmania, undated, 'About us', <www.forestrytas.com.au/about-us> (accessed 10 December 2009).

Frame, C, 2009, 'Forget emotion, what will the pulp mill achieve?', *The Age*, 12 January, <www.theage.com.au/opinion/forget-emotion-what-will-the-pulp-mill-achieve-20090111-7ecn.html?page=-1> (accessed 10 April 2009).

Gale, F, 2007, 'Good environmental governance and the Tamar Valley pulp mill: A comparative analysis of the RPDC and PMAA processes', Public lecture, <www.pulpmillfiction.org/docs/env_gov.pdf > (accessed 11 April 2009).

Gale, F, 2008, 'Tasmania's Tamar Valley pulp mill: a comparison of planning processes using a good environmental governance framework', *Australian Journal of Public Administration*, 67 (3): 261–282.

Gale, R, 2005, 'Old-growth logging: does it matter if environmental protection costs jobs?', *International Journal of Environment, Workplace and Employment*, 1 (2): 203–220.

GHD, 2006, 'Gunns Limited Bell Bay pulp mill IIS social impact assessment', <www.gunnspulpmill.com.au/iis/default.php> (accessed 10 April 2009).

Godfrey, S, undated, 'Inadequacies in the hydrodynamic modelling performed for Gunns pulp mill IIS', <www.environment.gov.au/epbc/notices/assessments/2007/3385/pubs/att-b7-3.pdf> (accessed 21 April 2009)

Gordon, B, undated, 'Sustainable value adding: the Tasmanian pulp mill project', <www.afg.asn.au/resources/pdfs/Conference2006-AbstractC5.1.pdf> (accessed 9 September 2008).

Grattan, M and Topsfield, J, 2007, 'Big names sign up for fight against pulp mill', *The Age*, 28 August, <www.theage.com.au/news/national/the-world-versus-malcolm-turnbull/2007/08/27/1188067032705.html> (accessed 21 April 2009).

Gunns Limited, 2006a, 'Bell Bay pulp mill draft integrated impact statement: Volume 1b', <www.gunnspulpmill.com.au/iis/default.php> (accessed 7 October 2008).

Gunns Limited, 2006b, 'Bell Bay pulp mill draft integrated impact statement: Volume 1a', <www.gunnspulpmill.com.au/iis/default.php> (accessed 7 October 2008).

Gunns Limited, 2006c, 'Gunns Limited Bell Bay pulp mill project: impact assessment for assessment under the Environment Protection Biodiversity Conservation Act 1999', <www.gunnspulpmill.com.au/epbc/default.php> (accessed 11 April 2009).

Gunns Limited, 2008, 'Annual Report 2008', <www.gunns.com.au/news/annual-reports/> (accessed 11 April 2009).

Gunns, undated, 'Bell Bay Pulp Mill – Environmental, economic and social update', <www.gunnspulpmill.com.au/> (accessed 10 April 2009).

Herzfeld, M, 2007, 'Preliminary hydrodynamic modelling of the Bell Bay outfall', Briefing document for the Independent Expert Group, CSIRO.

Hibberd, MF and Manins, PC, 2006, 'Review of air quality aspects of Gunns Ltd Bell Bay pulp mill draft Integrated Impact Statement', prepared for Resource Planning and Development Commission Tasmania, <www.justice.tas.gov.au/__data/assets/pdf_file/0017/70703/CSIRO_ReviewOfGunnsDraftIIS_Final4Oct.pdf> (accessed 15 April 2009).

Jones, T, 2007, 'Cousins weighs in on pulp mill debate', *Lateline*, ABC, 4 October, <www.abc.net.au/lateline/content/2007/s2051380.htm> (accessed 11 April 2009).

Lane, MB, 2003, 'Decentralization and privatization of environmental governance? Forest conflict and bioregional assessment in Australia', *Journal of Rural Studies*, 19 (3): 283–294.

Lang, C, 2007, 'Banks, pulp and people – A primer on upcoming international pulp mill projects', Urgeworld, Germany, <www.pulpmillwatch.org/media/pdf/BPP_A_FIN_2.pdf> (accessed 11 April 2009).

LEC (Launceston Environment Centre), 2007, 'Sustainable development in Tasmania: is the proposed mill sustainable?' Tasmanian Round Table for Sustainable Industries Project, <www.lec.org.au/roundtable.html> (accessed 11 April 2009).

Lennon, P, 2004, 'Ministerial Statement – Pulp and paper industry establishment process', 26 October, <www.parliament.tas.gov.au/HansardHouse/isysquery/a08a2755-219b-4025-9b34-8346d5d8c4ce/1/doc/> (accessed 22 April 2009).

Lennon, P, 2007, 'Why a pulp mill is good for us', *The Mercury*, 6 September, <www.news.com.au/mercury/story/0,22884,22371932-3462,00.html> (accessed 5 June 2008).

Lloyd-Smith, M, undated, <www.oztoxics.org/ntn/pulp%20mill%20brief.pdf> (accessed 4 April 2009).

Milne, C, 2008, 'Garrett must release critical CSIRO pulp mill report: stop protecting Gunns', Media Release, 21 August < christine-milne.greensmps.org.au/content/media-release/garrett-must-release-critical-csiro-pulp-mill-report-stop-protecting-gunns> (accessed 15 April 2009).

Negus, G, 2003, 'Senator Bob Brown', *George Negus Tonight*, ABC TV, 7 May, <www.abc.net.au/dimensions/dimensions_people/Transcripts/s849441.htm> (accessed 5/11/2008).

Ogilvie, F, 2008, 'Experts warn Gunns pulp mill may hurt Tas economy', ABC News, 21 September, <www.abc.net.au/news/stories/2007/09/21/2040325.htm> (accessed 11 October 2008).

Pullinger, P, undated, 'Submission to the Executive Director RPDC on draft IIS for proposed Pulp Mill', <www.justice.tas.gov.au/__data/assets/pdf_file/0006/69864/479_Dr_Phill_Pullinger.pdf> (accessed 11 April 2009).

Putt, P, 2007, 'Premier outlines his attempt to influence RPDC pulp mill assessment', 13 March, <www.tas.greens.org.au/News/view_MR.php?ActionID=2176-21k> (accessed 11 April 2009).

Sandery, P, 2006, 'Submission to RPDC: Hydrodynamic modelling studies which form part of the IIS for the proposed pulp mill development by Gunns Ltd at Bell Bay in the Tamar Estuary, Tasmania', <www.rpdc.tas.gov.au/home/rpdc_search_page?mode=results&current_result_page=1&results_per_page...sandery-13k> (accessed 11 April 2009).

Scandia National Laboratories, 2006, 'Kraft pulping process' <www.ca.sandia.gov/crf/viewArticle.php?cid=000016> (accessed 3 November 2008).

Schirmer, J, 2008, 'Forestry, jobs and spending: forest industry employment and expenditure in Tasmania, 2005–06', CRC Forestry Limited, Tasmania, <www.crcforestry.com.au/publications/downloads/forest-industry-survey-report_download.pdf> (accessed 28 March 2009).

Slee, B, 2001, 'Resolving production-environment conflicts: the case of regional forest agreement process in Australia', *Forest Policy and Economics*, 3 (1–2): 17–30.

SMH (*Sydney Morning Herald*), 2006, 'Pulpmill admits gross dioxin error', 20 September, <www.smh.com.au/news/national/pulp-mill-admits-gross-dioxin-error/2006/09/19/1158431711270.html> (accessed 3 April 2009).

SourceWatch, 2006, 'Evaluation of social impact assessment of Gunns Ltd Bell Bay Pulp', Mill', <www.sourcewatch.org/index.php?title=Evaluation_of_the_Social_Impact_Assessment_of_the_Gunns_Ltd_Bell_Bay_Pulp_Mill> (accessed 20 June 2008).

TCCI (Tasmanian Chamber of Commerce and Industry), 2006, 'Submission to the Executive Commissioner Resource Planning and Development Commission', <www.justice.tas.gov.au/__data/assets/pdf_file/0003/69510/266_Tasmanian_Chamber_of_Commerce__and__Industry_Ltd.pdf> (accessed 11 April 2009).

TFIC (Tasmanian Fishing Industry Council), 2007, 'Submission to the Department of Environment and Water Resources', <www.tfic.com.au/domino/tfic/tficweb.nsf/vwTitle/Pulp%20Mill> (accessed 11 April 2009).

The Age, 2008, 'Anger as Garrett extends Gunns deadline', 8 September, <www.theage.com.au/national/anger-as-garrett-extends-gunns-deadline-20080908-4c3w.html> (accessed 26 April 2009).

The Australian, 2006, 'Sydney fishos have high dioxins', July 20, <www.ausfish.com.au/vforum/showthread.php?t=53761> (accessed 4 April 2009).

The Greens, 2006a, 'Don't pulp our future'. A joint submission to the Resource Planning and Development Commission on Gunns' pulp mill proposal draft Integrated Impact Statement, Volume 1, <www.justice.tas.gov.au/__data/assets/pdf_file/0007/69622/301_The_Greens_Tasmania_Volume_1.pdf> (accessed 11 April 2009).

The Greens, 2006b, 'Don't pulp our future'. A joint submission to the Resource Planning and Development Commission on Gunns' pulp mill proposal draft Integrated Impact Statement, Volume 2, <http://tas.greens.org.au/publications/submissions/2006Sep25-SUBMISSION-PULP_MILL_DRAFT_IIS-VOLUME_2-web.pdf> (accessed 11 April 2009).

The Greens, 2008, 'Garret throws another lifeline to Gunns pulp mill', 8 September, <http://greens.org.au/media/2008/09/08/2629> (accessed 3 May 2009).

The Greens Tasmania, 2006a, 'Pulp mill haze: air pollution concerns grow', The Tasmanian pulp mill news. Campaign newsletter from the Tasmanian Greens State Parliamentarians, 18 September 2006, <http://tas.greens.org.au/publications/other/TAS_PULP_MILL_NEWS-EDITION_03-web.pdf > (accessed 11 April 2009).

The Greens Tasmania, 2006b, 'A very thirsty dinosaur of a mill', The Tasmanian pulp mill news. Campaign newsletter from the Tasmanian Greens State Parliamentarians, 18 September 2006, <http://tas.greens.org.au/publications/other/TAS_PULP_MILL_NEWS-EDITION_03-web.pdf> (accessed 11 April 2009).

TWS (The Wilderness Society), 2007, 'Court victory for the Wilderness Society', Media release, 31 May, <www.wilderness.org.au/articles/court_vic/?searchterm=%20federal%20court%20case> (accessed 10 April 2009).

TWS (The Wilderness Society), undated, 'Thousands march to halt the mill', <www.wilderness.org.au/articles/nov07_hobart_rally/?searchterm=None> (accessed 11 April 2009).

Ward, A, 2007, 'Pulp mill', *Stateline Tasmania*, 16 March, <www.abc.net.au/stateline/tas/content/2006/s1873879.htm> (accessed 9 June 2008).

Wright, T, 2007, 'Pulp friction – and illusion', *The Age*, October 6, <www.theage.com.au/news/in-depth/pulp-friction-151-and-illusion/2007/10/05/1191091367468.html> (accessed 11 April 2009).

Case Study C

Toowoomba Water Recycling

C.1 Introduction

Would you drink recycled sewage? More than 60,000 voters in Toowoomba, an inland town in South-East (SE) Queensland, were the first in Australia to seriously consider this rather provocative question. In 2005, Toowoomba City Council[1] (TCC) presented their community with a proposal for recycling the town's sewage and using it to replenish their fast-dwindling potable[2] water supply. A charged community debate on the risks and advantages of this water management option followed and led to a public referendum[3] to decide the future of this proposal. This local controversy became national news as other drought-affected Australian cities, such as Goulburn (New South Wales) and Bendigo (Victoria), anticipating similar debates, eagerly awaited the outcomes of the referendum. On 29 July 2006, the community of Toowoomba said a resounding 'No' (62 per cent) to introducing recycled sewage[4] into their drinking water supply, despite the town's water storage being at a low 23 per cent and lower than average rainfalls predicted for the future.

This case study analyses the story behind Toowoomba's water crisis and the events that unfolded during the recycled sewage debate to provide some explanation for why a thirsty town in a parched country voted 'No' to what some consider an obvious solution to their water problems.

Australia is the driest continent (after Antarctica) on Earth but, surprisingly the third highest per capita water consumer in the world (Radcliffe 2004). Impacts of high water consumption and a drought since the mid-1990s have resulted in depleted water supplies for urban and regional consumers, agriculture and the environment. Many cities and towns have gone through cycles of various levels of water restrictions and other options to address the impacts of drought and many have devised longer-term sustainable water management strategies. These include the use of rainwater tanks, stormwater reuse and desalination. In particular, Australians have been debating the costs and benefits of using recycled sewage

---

1   Toowoomba City Council was merged with seven other surrounding councils in March 2008. <www.toowoombarc.qld.gov.au> (accessed 1 May 2009).

2   Water suitable for drinking and culinary purposes on the basis of health and aesthetic considerations (CHOICE 2008).

3   Although media and other reports refer to the voting process on the recycled water issue as a referendum, according to the definitions provided by the Australian Electoral Commission it was technically a plebiscite (see <www.aec.gov.au/footer/Glossary_N_Z.htm> (accessed 1 May 2009)).

4   'Recycled sewage' is also referred to as 'recycled water' or 'reclaimed water'.

as part of their potable water supply. Many countries in the world treat sewage to high-quality drinking water standards and use it to supplement their potable water supplies. Examples of large-scale recycled water projects include Orange County in California where recycled sewage is injected into groundwater aquifers and Singapore's NEWater project where recycled sewage is mixed with water from reservoirs. Australian communities, however, have resisted this option for addressing water shortages. To date, recycled sewage in Australia has mainly been limited to non-potable uses such as industrial, irrigational and agricultural. When compared to recycling, desalination has been the preferable policy choice for expanding potable water supply, especially for coastal cities, primarily because it is the only non rain-dependent source of water (AWA 2007). For example, a desalination plant in Sydney was approved despite cost-benefit analysis (CBA) supporting the recycling option (Hurlimann 2007).

The public's acceptability of other options over recycling is often attributed to public views and perceptions about exposure to health risks from drinking recycled sewage and the 'yuk' factor associated with the 'psychological barriers' related to the source of such water, namely, raw sewage (Po et al 2004). Nevertheless, with a continuing drought and its severity predicted to increase in most of southern and eastern Australia,[5] communities and governments in these regions including SE Queensland, may have to reconsider their options.

Since Toowoomba's community rejected recycled sewage for drinking water purposes, the discussion on how best to tackle Toowoomba's and SE Queensland's continuing water woes has taken many interesting twists and turns. Although the focus of this case study will remain on Toowoomba, we will discuss the broader context and the story thereafter in the conclusion of this case study.

The story of water recycling in Toowoomba exposes a number of themes central to this book and offers insights into the following:

- The importance of values and perceptions, rather than technical risk assessments, in determining the level of risk acceptable to the public.

- The significance of public trust in authority and science in determining the outcome of issues that potentially impact on human health.

- The consequences of not involving the public in meaningful and interactive participation during the environmental decision-making (EDM) process.

- The power and influence of the media in framing a problem and steering environmental debate.

- The challenge of governing environmental resources over multiple levels of government.

---

5   Australian Government Department of Climate Change, <www.climatechange.gov.au/impacts/water.html> (accessed 13 April 2009).

C.2 Setting the scene

C.2.1 Toowoomba and the water crisis

The town of Toowoomba in SE Queensland has a population of 97,530 and is the largest inland regional city in Australia, excluding Canberra (TCC 2007). Toowoomba has a range of urban and semi-urban settlements and is the main activity centre for surrounding regions. Well-known for its parks, gardens, spring flower festivals and garden contests, Toowoomba has earned the title of 'the garden city'. Tourism booms during spring, attracting up to 25,000 visitors to the carnival of flowers (Australia Network 2007).

In 2005 the garden city was projected on to the national stage, not because of its spring flower carnival but Toowoomba City Council's (TCC) Water Futures Project – a plan to use recycled sewage to provide 25 per cent of its rapidly declining drinking water supply. This radical ground-breaking decision by the local council was a long-term strategy to cope with future demands and was driven by many factors including:

C.2.1.1 Decreasing water supply, predicted high population growth and continuing drought

Toowoomba's water supply comes mainly from its three dams (Cooby, Preserverance and Cressbrook) while about 15 per cent is sourced from groundwater bores. A long period of lower than average rainfall reduced the capacity of the water supply dams to 29.5 per cent by mid-August 2005 (*The Chronicle* 2005). This increased the city's reliance on groundwater, which was quickly exceeding safe water yields (Spearritt 2008) and threatened the long-term sustainability of groundwater aquifers. Moreover, the availability of freshwater in the future is constrained by the long drought and predicted unreliability of rainfall patterns associated with the impacts of climate change.

Toowoomba is located within SE Queensland which is the fastest growing region in Australia[6] and its population is predicted to increase from 97,530 in 2006 to 115,000 in 2026 (TCC 2007). Accommodating a fast-growing population within the context of drought and a diminishing water supply are significant challenges for Toowoomba.

C.2.1.2 Demand management measures[7] not sufficient

About 70 per cent of Toowoomba's potable water is used by residential customers while commercial, government and industrial customers use the remaining 30 per cent (TCC 2005). Toowoomba City Council (TCC), residents and businesses implemented many measures to reduce their water usage and slow down the depletion of water in their dams. TCC's demand management program 'Let's slow the flow' was supported by many behavioural tools such as education, advertising, rebates for water efficient fittings and appliances and severe water restrictions (see Chapter 8). These measures helped progressively reduce average water consumption from 418 litres/person/day (l/p/d) in 2001–2002 (TCC 2003)

---

6   <www.dip.qld.gov.au/seq> (accessed 28 January 2009).

7   Demand management measures are designed to reduce consumption of water and hence the demand on potable water supply. These include water restrictions, installation of water efficient fixtures such as low-flow shower heads, dual flush toilets and reduction of leaks.

to 210 l/p/d in 2005 by which time level 4[8] water restrictions were in force. This was much lower than SE Queensland's regional average of 300 l/p/d (TCC 2005). In September 2006 level 5[9] water restrictions were introduced in Toowoomba and were still in force at the time of writing this case study (April 2009). As a result, residential water consumption was down to 134 l/p/d by January 2009.[10] Even with these stringent water restrictions, the combined capacity of the three dams supplying Toowoomba was down to 9.7 per cent on 9 April 2009.[11] It is notable that during the same period, similar high-level water restrictions were also in force in most other areas of SE Queensland and residential water consumption was reduced to 162 l/p/d.[12]

C.2.1.3 Impacts on tourism and economy

Toowoomba's residents consider the town's parks and gardens to be of high quality and one of the reasons for the livability of the city and for its future economic growth and development potential.[13] Much of Toowoomba's tourism industry is also built around its reputation as the garden city. A diminishing water supply and restrictions on water usage were having a negative impact on not only the garden city's reputation, but also the nursery and garden industry. Lorraine Schiller, nursery and garden industry branch president and retail nursery owner, reported that sales had dropped dramatically and she had lost 40 per cent of her business by 2006 (ABC News Online 2006).

C.2.2 Toowoomba's Water Futures Project

The Water Futures Project was developed by TCC as a cost-effective, reliable and sustainable response to Toowoomba's dire water situation and its implications as discussed above. It was based on an integrated water management approach that considered efficient use and reuse of all available water (rainwater, stormwater, sewage) to reduce sole reliance on rainwater that fell on the catchment of Toowoomba's three dams. The Mayor of Toowoomba identified many sustainable aspects of the project including taking responsibility for future generations and fostering a culture that valued water as a precious resource rather than dumping it after one use (Thorley 2006).

The project's publicised benefits also included drought protection, maintaining Toowoomba's enviable lifestyle reputation and generating regional development and economic growth through the sustainable supply of recycled sewage to residences and businesses (TCC 2006a). A range of other potential water supply options were considered by TCC but rejected on various grounds. Examples include (TCC 2006a):

---

8   Level 4 restrictions prohibit all garden watering except with a bucket at specified times and all car washing except windows and mirrors.

9   Level 5 restrictions prohibit all outside watering using town water, topping up of pools and washing cars.

10   <www.toowoombarc.qld.gov.au/index.php?option=com_content&view=category&layout=blog&id=184&Itemid=166> (accessed 28 April 2009).

11   <www.toowoombarc.qld.gov.au/index.php?option=com_content&view=article&id=386:water-for-our-region&catid=30:water&Itemid=52> (accessed 13 April 2009).

12   <www.qwc.qld.gov.au/tiki-read_article.php?articleId=308> (accessed 28 April 2009).

13   Background Analysis Report-1 Toowoomba CBD Masterplan – Preliminary Scope of Works <www.toowoomba.qld.gov.au/index.php?option=com_docman&task=cat_view&gid=179&Itemid=107> (accessed 13 April 2009).

- Constructing a pipeline from other dams in SE Queensland, such as Wivenhoe Dam (about 40 kilometres from Toowoomba) to Toowoomba. Wivenhoe Dam supplies water to Brisbane and adjacent local authorities.[14] This was not considered feasible due to high costs ($115 million) and the unlikelihood of getting Queensland Government's approval for water allocation.

- Construction of a new dam (Emu Creek) in the Wivenhoe Dam catchment. This option was costly ($145 million), required long time frames and was rejected by the Queensland Government.

- Rainwater tanks on every property in Toowoomba. Not all homes were suitable for rainwater tank installation and the high cost ($175 million) was prohibitive.

It is notable that Toowoomba is an inland town about 110 kilometres from the nearest coastline and desalination was not a viable option.

The Water Futures Project included a number of measures such as compulsory rainwater tanks for new buildings and deep bores to access groundwater from the Great Artesian Basin. But by far, the major and most expensive ($68 million) aspect of this project was an 'indirect potable reuse'[15] system that would purify 5 billion litres of sewage every year to supplement Cooby Dam. The proposed sewage recycling process incorporated a multi-barrier approach and many treatment stages (ultrafiltration, reverse osmosis, UV disinfection, advanced oxidation) that the council claimed would produce high quality water – purer than was currently available and even suitable for kidney dialysis. The purified water would then be mixed with the surface water in Cooby Dam and further treatment provided at the existing Mount Kynoch drinking water treatment plant before being supplied to the community. In addition, a risk management and quality assurance system would be implemented to ensure drinking water quality (TCC 2006a).

C.2.3 The actors

The announcement of the Water Futures Project triggered a debate between those for and against the proposal. Later, the announcement of the referendum to decide whether or not recycled sewage would be added to Cooby Dam deepened this divide and split the community of Toowoomba into two camps – those arguing for a 'Yes' vote and those campaigning for the 'No' vote. What started as a local issue quickly became a matter that engaged water experts and politicians beyond Toowoomba – each having a strong view on this issue. Both local and national media also latched on to this debate and played a key role in reporting the views of both sides. Below, we identify the key actors and discuss their roles and positions with respect to the Water Futures Project and the use of recycled sewage for potable purposes.

C.2.3.1 The 'Yes' campaigners

Government and institutions: Toowoomba City Council's Mayor Di Thorley proposed and vigorously campaigned for the Water Futures Project. She considered the project to be a

---

14   <www.seqwater.com.au/content/standard.asp?name=WivenhoeDam> (accessed 19 April 2009).

15   Indirect potable reuse refers to a system where recycled water is mixed with surface water or ground water before being reused, whereas direct potable reuse refers to a system where recycled water is distributed directly from a wastewater treatment plant to a water distribution system (Po et al 2004).

unique opportunity for Toowoomba to lead Australia in responsible and sustainable water conservation (Thorley 2006). Six out of nine Toowoomba councillors were also in favour of recycled water and supported their Mayor's position on the sustainability, economic feasibility and safety aspects of the project (TCC 2006b). The project was to be funded equally by the three levels of government, federal, state and local, each contributing about $23 million. Queensland's Labor Premier Peter Beattie pledged his commitment to help fund 'the implementation of this innovative project' (TCC 2006c). As most of Queensland, particularly SE Queensland, was experiencing severe water shortages, the State Government was considering wider-scale use of recycled sewage for potable purposes and the success of Water Futures was crucial for the adoption and acceptability of recycled sewage elsewhere.

TCC had made a submission to the Federal Government for funding support through the National Water Commission's (NWC) Water Smart Australia Program. The Coalition Federal Government was of the view that the residents of Toowoomba should decide whether or not recycled sewage is introduced into their drinking water supply.[16] Their Parliamentary Secretary for Water, Malcolm Turnbull publicly supported the recycled water option (Millar 2006) but only agreed to provide funding if Toowoomba held a referendum and a majority of the community voted in favour of the proposal.

Business: The horticulture industry in Toowoomba was particularly suffering from the water shortages through loss of business and having to invest in new gardening techniques and drought tolerant plants (Australia Network 2007). The Nursery and Garden Industry Queensland urged residents to vote 'Yes' arguing that the project was the only rational and sensible plan for drought-proofing Toowoomba and supporting the town's green image, and its growing tourism industry into the future (TCC 2006d).

Experts and professionals: A number of experts and professional bodies who had long been researching and promoting the benefits of recycled sewage supported the Project including water industry associations (for example, the Australian Water Association), research organisations (for example, Cooperative Research Centre (CRC) for Water Quality and Treatment, Commonwealth Scientific and Industrial Research Organisation (CSIRO)) and individual water experts (such as Dr Greg Leslie who had previously worked on large-scale international recycled water projects). The Toowoomba project was an opportunity for these actors to provide facts and figures to the community to reassure and convince them of the merits of advanced water treatment technologies and safety aspects of using recycled sewage as drinking water.

C.2.3.2 The 'No' campaigners

Pressure groups and individuals: The most prominent community group running the 'No' campaign was CADS – Citizens Against Drinking Sewage. CADS was influential in the abandonment of previous water recycling plans for Maroochy Shire in Queensland (Stenekes et al 2001 in Hurlimann 2007, p 17). In Toowoomba, CADS was led by a local business operator and former President of the Chamber of Commerce, Rosemary Morley. Toowoomba's former mayor, millionaire and prominent property developer, Clive Berghofer was also a powerful 'No' campaigner (Roberts 2007). Another strong advocate for the 'No' case was Snow Manners, who became an elected member of council after winning a local by-election

---

16   <www.malcolmturnbull.com.au/Pages/Article.aspx?ID=405> (accessed 30 May 2008).

in 2006.[17] Their campaign concentrated on harmful human health impacts associated with drinking contaminated recycled water as well as damage to the city's image and future growth potential, such as a decline in property values, linked to people's negative perceptions about recycled water (Berghofer 2006).

Local councillors: Toowoomba councillors were split in their views, with three actively supporting the 'No' case. According to these councillors, the people of Toowoomba had been misled about the options available to Toowoomba. In their view other better solutions needed to be considered and this could only occur if a majority of the electorate voted 'No' (Berghofer 2006).

C.2.3.3 The media

The media reported extensively on Toowoomba's Water Futures Project. Both the supporters and opponents of the Project also used a range of media as their battleground. For example, television and radio interviews, news programs (*The 7.30 Report* and *Stateline* on ABC TV), letters to the editor and advertising space were used by each side to present their case to the public. The level of activity and interest this issue generated is evident from the following observation by a journalist:

> Every working day, from July 2005 to the poll 12 months later, I breathed water. As a fairly ignorant cadet newspaper journalist in regional Queensland I took on the job of reporting the biggest issue likely to hit the conservative Bible heartland before the second coming. I spoke in megalitres and membranes, talked with scientists, engineers, farmers and politicians about every facet of the liquid.

> (Donaghey undated)

C.3 The controversy

Potable water in Australia is traditionally sourced from dams and groundwater. With the development of integrated water management approaches, water authorities have been supplementing these sources with treated stormwater and recycled sewage for non-potable water uses. Communities in Australia have quite easily accepted this use of recycled water for non-potable purposes. Examples include Rouse Hill in Sydney, where treated sewage is brought into homes in a separate third[18] pipe and used for non-drinking purposes such as toilet flushing, and Port Macquarie in the mid-north coast of New South Wales where recycled sewage is used for irrigating sporting grounds and flushing toilets in some businesses and in commercial car washing facilities. But despite the availability of technology for treating sewage to a quality higher than that supplied from dams and groundwater and wide acceptance of water recycling as a concept for water management, Australian communities have been reluctant to use recycled water for potable water purposes (Po et al 2004).

Given this unsuccessful history, it was indeed a brave move on the part of TCC and their Mayor, Di Thorley, to put forward the Water Futures Project as the option for addressing Toowoomba's water crisis. For the Mayor, this decision was a matter of political will and

---

17 <www.toowoomba.qld.gov.au/index.php?option=com_content&task=view&id=264&Itemid=381> (accessed 26 April 2009).

18 The first and second pipes bring in potable water and take away sewage.

courage, '[i]f you spend less time worrying about whether you are going to be re-elected and more time thinking with your heart about what you need to do for your community it is a lot easier to make decisions' (cited in Frew 2005a).

What followed was a vigorous debate on the merits or otherwise of this project. Much of the controversy was about the public health risks associated with drinking recycled sewage. As indicated above, the Federal Government preferred the community of Toowoomba to decide the fate of Water Futures and hence their portion of funding for the Project was conditional on TCC holding a local referendum. This view was based on their belief that because the campaign against recycling had gained momentum it was not possible to determine community support without a referendum (O'Malley 2006). During the months prior to the referendum there was a flurry of campaigning activity from both the proponents and opponents of the Project. Both the 'Yes' and the 'No' campaigners used different strategies to inform the public about the 'truth' of matters related to the use of recycled sewage as a potable water source.

The proponents of Water Futures tried to dispel the perceived risks and the fear campaign of the opponents by providing the community with scientific information to argue that highly treated recycled water using advanced water technology was safe. Examples of various existing communities, overseas and in Australia, that use recycled water for potable purposes were cited as proof that there were few, if any, risks involved. These include Orange County California and Singapore where sewage treated to a high-quality is mixed with drinking water supplies, and others (London in the United Kingdom, and Windsor and Richmond in New South Wales) where sewage is treated to a lower quality and discharged into rivers which are used as water sources further downstream from the discharge points (Frew 2005b). One month before the referendum, the Australian Water Association ran a public forum on water recycling where engineers, microbiologists and environmentalists were offering advice to Toowoomba residents on their future water management options. This forum was attended by 250 residents who questioned the experts 'about their independence from the council, perceived conflicts of interest, and whether water treatment technology could protect people from contaminants that might still be unknown' (Frew 2006).

From the perspective of the 'Yes' campaigners, winning this debate was simply a matter of public education. It was assumed that once the community could separate the facts from the myths they would be able to make an informed decision. To this end the TCC established a website with detailed information about the project, distributed booklets and pamphlets, and encouraged residents to host 'kitchen table conversations' about Water Futures. They also created a community advisory panel to help residents understand the project (TCC 2006a).

The 'No' campaigners were concerned about Toowoomba residents being made guinea pigs and lab rats for Australia's first trial of drinking recycled sewage and the associated long-term human health risks. They claimed that the Project posed a range of health risks from cancer to 'gender bending' due to the presence of chemicals such as drugs and hormones that may not be removed by the wastewater treatment processes. Clive Berghofer, a property developer and prominent resident of Toowoomba, was particularly concerned about the reputation of his town and the resulting implications for future growth and development. Certain media stories had already nicknamed the town 'Poowoomba' (Millar 2006) and according to Mr Berghofer, '[n]o one will want to come and live here, people are already making jokes, thinking we are drinking the stuff now' (cited in Mitchell 2006). A range of methods, including the internet, petitions, advertisements, and public meetings, were used by those opposing TCC's Water Futures Project (Frew 2006). For example, Clive Berghofer authorised the publication of advertisements highlighting many reasons why the public should be sceptical and fearful of the recycled water option. Although accused of running a fear campaign by many, the 'No' campaigners provided strong arguments against some of the claims made by the proponents, including:

- Refuting misleading information put out by TCC and other 'Yes' campaigners on examples of recycled water projects similar to that proposed for Toowoomba. They asserted that no community in the world deliberately used sewage as a source for drinking water and hence long-term risks were not really known. These were backed up by detailed information about these projects, for example, 99 per cent of Singapore's NEWater was used for industrial purposes and only 1 per cent, as opposed to 25 per cent proposed for Toowoomba, was added to the drinking water supplies (Berghofer 2006).

- Reassessing alternatives already considered and dismissed by TCC (C.2.1). Many of these options including rainwater tanks for every building in Toowoomba, piping water from Wivenhoe Dam and the construction of a new dam were reconsidered by the 'No' campaigners and assessed to be viable in their judgment (Berghofer 2006).

Although the main thrust of the debate revolved around human health risk and perceived impacts, other related issues that fuelled the arguments included:

- Lack of public involvement before the announcement of Water Futures. Although TCC organised and ran a massive education campaign in the wake of the referendum decision, there is no evidence of the community being consulted during the planning stages of the project.

- Distrust in government and scientists to provide correct information to the community.

As mentioned in the introduction, the community of Toowoomba went to referendum on the question of '[d]o you support the addition of purified recycled water to Toowoomba's water supply' (Spearritt 2008, p 26) with almost 62 per cent voting 'No' to this question (Langford 2006). Since Toowoomba's rejection of Water Futures a lot of water has gone under the bridge. By October 2008, Toowoomba's water supply was down to less than 10 per cent and deep bores were being drilled into the Great Artesian Basin to access much-needed water for the town (Saggin 2008). In response to this urgent situation, the Queensland Government stepped in with plans and funds to construct a pipeline to pump water from Wivenhoe Dam near Brisbane, an option that TCC earlier rejected based on high costs and the difficulty of getting State Government approval. In an attempt to drought-proof the SE Queensland region, the State Government is also planning on recycling sewage from Brisbane for replenishing Wivenhoe Dam which will then be connected to the region by a water grid (Parnell 2008; Queensland Water Commission 2008). If this plan goes ahead, the Toowoomba community will end up with what they discarded in the referendum – recycled sewage for drinking water purposes. The irony of this situation was not lost on Di Morley from the CADS, '[a]s a community we have said no to drinking recycled water but apparently the voice of the people counts for nothing', she said. 'Is recycled water from the Brisbane sewers different to that of Toowoomba?' (cited in Morley 2008). We will return to the broader water management strategy for SE Queensland at the end of this case study.

C.4 Analysis: What themes does this case study reveal?

The Toowoomba controversy reveals that the issues surrounding recycled sewage are emotive and expose 'people's fears of governments, of science, of what someone else might put in their mouth' (Parnell 2008a). Below we will explore some key factors that influenced the EDM process surrounding the Toowoomba Water Futures Project.

C.4.1 Risk perception and public acceptance

Public acceptance is considered to be the most significant factor for the successful implementation of recycling projects and although people can see the logic of recycling wastewater, they still remain reluctant to use it for potable purposes (Po et al 2004). This definitely rings true for Toowoomba as at the heart of the debate was the public's unwillingness to accept recycled sewage for drinking water purposes, despite acceptance that Toowoomba had a serious water problem. Public acceptability levels are sensitive to various factors such as perceptions of risk, the disgust or 'yuk' factor, specific use of recycled water, the sources of water to be recycled, the issue of choice, socio-demographic factors and attitudes towards the environment (Po et al 2004).

Some of the debate can be attributed to the considerable disparity between technical conceptualisation of risk and public perception of risk (Chapter 9). Water experts such as Greg Leslie emphasised that there was more chance of getting struck by lightening or winning the lottery than of becoming ill by drinking recycled sewage of drinking water quality (Frew 2005b). Others such as Heather Chapman from the CRC for Water Quality and Treatment stressed the high-tech and safe nature of modern water treatment processes and was quoted as saying, '[t]he treatment processes are very, very efficient . . . Nothing is completely risk free, but the risk of these things is so tiny compared with the risks that we are exposed to daily, like getting in the car' (cited in Clausen 2006). However, these technical and scientific claims did not appear to dispel the public perceptions of health risks, such as fertility problems and cancers, from the effects of chemicals in recycled water.

According to sociologists the apparent disparity between technical risk classification and public perception of risk is related to a number of social, political and cultural factors (Chapter 9). First, let us consider Beck's notion of the 'risk society' (see 9.4) where modern communities are facing an increasing number of unknown and unintended consequences from industrial processes and technology. Beck also suggests that the public is sceptical of solutions that rely heavily on scientific and expert knowledge (Marks et al 2008). This may provide some reasons for public fear and unacceptability in the case of Toowoomba since the 'Yes' case was greatly reliant on claims made by experts about the low-risk nature of modern recycling technology. However, this expert advice failed to convince a majority of Toowoomba voters who remained concerned about the unknown long-term effects of an untested technology and critical of those propagating these views.

An alternative explanation of negative public perceptions of drinking recycled water is related to the 'yuk' factor and based on 'strongly held cultural constructions' about the purity and cleanliness of various types of water such as recycled sewage, stormwater, seawater and rainwater (Marks et al 2008, p 94). This was recognised by some experts, '[t]he issue isn't about producing safe recycled water at a risk level that's low enough that it doesn't constitute a serious risk. The issue is the public perception of drinking s—t, says

Dr John Radcliffe, commissioner of the National Water Commission' (cited in *Readers Digest* undated).

Strongly embedded cultural values and beliefs have a significant influence on public acceptability of water sources and their uses such as drinking, garden irrigation, toilet flushing, car washing (Marks et al 2008). For example, in a survey conducted by Flinders University, the public considered desalinated seawater to be a much cleaner source than recycled water derived from sewage and were much more willing to use it without hesitation for household purposes as compared to recycled sewage – 51 per cent versus 22 per cent (Marks et al 2008). Similarly, a reuse study in Australia by Hamilton and Greenfield (1991) suggests that recycled sewage is perceived as *'filthy* and *unclean'* (emphasis in original reference) and hence rejected for potable reuse (Po et al 2004, p 10). It seems that TCC were aware of these perceptions as all of their campaign material couches recycled sewage as 'purified water'! The 'unclean' origins of Toowoomba's 'purified water', though, were not lost on the 'No' campaigners.

Experts and decision-makers have traditionally tried to overcome these negative perceptions through a commonly held assumption that if members of the public were better educated and informed about specialist information on risk they would accept changes more readily (Stenekes et al 2006). This leads to expert-driven one-way communication approaches which fail to recognise the validity of perceptions and the importance of taking these seriously. As highlighted in Chapters 9 and 7, and in C.4.2 below, two-way risk communication, and more broadly public participation, such that experts and affected publics can discuss and negotiate perceived and calculated risks on an equal footing, can facilitate decision-making on complex and controversial environmental issues.

C.4.2 Trust and public participation

Studies on the lack of social acceptance of recycled water show that public perception is largely based on trust in the authorities and scientific knowledge. Early and meaningful public engagement is crucial to developing trust and maintaining long-term public support for recycling projects (Po et al 2004, 2005). It could be argued that the methods used by both TCC and the Federal Government to engage with the public were inappropriate.

In order to address the extreme water shortage problem and secure a long-term sustainable water supply for Toowoomba, TCC made an emergency decision to implement the recycled drinking water proposal without any public engagement. Once this decision was announced, TCC embarked on an education campaign which mainly relied on a one-way flow of information to persuade the public through social marketing and public relations exercises. For example, factual information was provided to the community through scientific panels, more than 160 public forums, advertising and taste-testing to bust the myths about the risks associated with drinking recycled water (ABC Online 2006). Many water experts also helped TCC to try to convince the community about the benefits and safety aspects of the proposal. Unfortunately these social marketing methods did not take into account the complex socio-political and cultural context of the recycled water problem and it is now widely accepted that such strategies do not work (Po et al 2005). As discussed in Chapter 7, the information end of the public participation spectrum (Table 7.1) leaves little room for interaction and dialogue between the public, experts and decision-makers. Such top-down, DAD (decide-announce-defend) approaches are also not successful for introducing change in essential services which are taken-for-granted (ABC Radio National 2007) such as water supply. In the end the fact that TCC imposed a decision on the community with minimal opportunities for public engagement meant that it struggled to develop trust and support from the public for the Water Futures Project.

Theoretically the public participation approach imposed on the Toowoomba community by the Federal Government is situated at the opposite end of the participatory spectrum to information provision (see Table 7.1). In essence the referendum handed over the democratic power of decision-making to the voters. Yet as mentioned in Chapter 7, referenda provide limited opportunity for the community to engage in *collective* reasoning about an issue; instead the issue is reduced to a 'Yes' or 'No' vote. As a consequence, the Water Futures referendum simply fuelled any already existing adversarial conflict, and further encouraged project proponents and opponents to convince the public (voters) to support their position.

The methods of public engagement used by the decision-makers in this case study relied heavily on the deficit model of community knowledge which assumes that knowledge held by experts must be given to the ignorant public and 'public involvement is seen as the acceptance or rejection of narrowly defined technological propositions and perceptions of risk by participants' (Petts and Brooks 2006; Stenekes et al 2006, p 121; also see 6.4.3). However, as discussed in Chapters 6 and 7, complex and controversial issues such as recycled sewage for potable use, where uncertainty and stakes are high, do not lend themselves to yes/no approaches to public input (such as a referendum) but demand procedures that facilitate informed and interactive discussion. More deliberative approaches are required that provide space where participants can express their concerns, questions and frustrations and work towards consensus-building rather than continued conflict (ABC Radio National 2007). Such an approach was taken for a proposed indirect potable reuse project in Goulburn, in New South Wales, which faced extreme water shortages around the same time as Toowoomba. The Goulburn-Mulwaree Council commenced their community engagement process by putting all options on the table so that their water management strategy could be developed through a genuine dialogue with the community (ABC Radio National 2007; Mehreen Faruqi[19]).

Some other factors that may have influenced the public's lack of trust in government, experts and decision-making (see Chapter 9) include past experiences of mishandled issues that impact on human health and the provision of conflicting and misleading information from the many 'Yes' and 'No' campaigners. The Chairman of the NWC convincingly stated that 'the science and health issues are "unambiguously manageable" and there is no scientific question about the health and safety of drinking recycled water' (Mitchell 2006). Supporting this view was Dr Greg Leslie who vouched for the safety of the water and said he would have no problems with his five-year-old drinking the water from the type of plant Toowoomba was proposing (Frew 2005b). For those who remember the BSE case (see 9.1) in the United Kingdom this may be reminiscent of the Agriculture Minister who made a great show of feeding his four-year-old daughter a beef burger in the midst of the scare![20] An issue closer to home was the Sydney water scare in 1998 when Sydney's water supply was contaminated by pathogens – *Cryptosporidium* and *Giardia*, which can cause illness in humans. Public trust in the government and their institutions was tested when a series of blunders in the handling of this outbreak were revealed. These ranged from 'condoning long-term decline in the catchment through to dubious pathogen monitoring arrangements', secret contracts between water authorities and the operators of the water treatment plant,

---

19   The author, Mehreen Faruqi, was part of the consultant's team engaged by Goulburn-Mulwaree Council to undertake the community engagement process for their water management strategy.

20   <http://news.bbc.co.uk/1/hi/uk/369625.stm> (accessed 18 April 2009).

as well as information that Sydney Water and the New South Wales Government knew of the presence of high levels of these contaminants in Sydney's water sources since 1992, but attempts to warn the public were quelled by the Heath Department (Frew 2005a; Healy 2001, p 126).

The 'No' campaigners had little trust in the assurances provided by experts and scientists and continued to air their concerns about the risks associated with drinking recycled water (Frew 2005a). Rosemary Thorley, the coordinator for CADS, was quoted as saying, 'We have examples where experts have told us thalidomide was safe, teflon was a recent one and the asbestos debate. We all thought those things were safe and went along that road and we're paying enormous prices now' (ABC Online 2006). They were also critical of TCC and the water experts for providing information which was misleading and irrelevant to Toowoomba's local situation, such as examples of other recycled water projects that had very little basis of comparison with Toowoomba (C.3).

To make matters more complicated, some experts who advocated a more cautious approach injected further uncertainty into the debate. For example, the Water Services Association's executive director raised questions about the risk and safety aspects, and emphasised the need to be 'reasonably prudent and cautious – maybe there are some things in the water we can't detect now' (cited in Clausen 2006).

With regards to the Toowoomba case it could be suggested that this proposal was unacceptable to the public and no amount or type of participation could have altered the outcome. However, in such a situation, early engagement with the public can provide an opportunity to help reveal public views, clarify conflicting information and discuss any alternatives.

C.4.3 The role of media

As we discussed in Chapter 5, the way the media selects and portrays issues to the public is shaped by multiple forces including audience demand. Currently, drought and water management are issues that have a captive media audience as most Australians have personally experienced some impacts of the drought such as water restrictions. A recent analysis of media coverage of water in Australia reported that between 1 January and 30 April 2007 there were 'more than 80,000 media news reports, feature articles, columns, letters to the editor and radio and TV program segments discussing water' (Media Monitors 2007, p 5). The tendency for media to focus on conflictual issues of environmental debates (see Chapter 5) is also evident from this report as the vast majority of discussion in the media comprises contradictory claims and counter-claims by the many actors who weighed-in on this issue 'with very little objective information and education for the public to make informed decisions' (Media Monitor 2007, p 5). This pattern of media reporting can be found during Toowoomba's sewage recycling controversy. The referendum provided the event around which much of the public debate was conducted through vigorous and combative media campaigns. This created confusion amongst the public and further fuelled the debate. Both parties framed each other's tactics as fear campaigns. Supporters of the recycled sewage option were accused of scaring the public by portraying this as the *only* alternative, while the fear campaign of the opponents was blamed for including much misinformation. The win of the 'No' vote is attributed by many to biased media reporting through the bombardment of 'misinformation and irrational argument, fueling the so-called "yuk" factor' by opponents of TCC's proposal (van Vuuren 2007). Such reporting which includes emotionally-charged headlines to conjure up negative images of 'drinking sewage' is hindering the adoption of recycling (Media Monitors 2007). Examples from Toowoomba include 'Poowoomba' and 'From toilet to tap'. This apparent bias can be explained by the tendency for the media to cast an issue in terms that resonate with existing social and cultural values (van Vuuren 2007, 2008). This explanation is consistent with the view that 'deeply embedded cultural understandings' of sewage as unclean and polluted is linked to public unwillingness to accept recycled sewage as drinking water (Marks et al 2008, p 92; C.4.1).

C.4.4 Challenges of governing water across multiple levels

In Australia, responsibility for the governance of various aspects of the environment is shared amongst Federal, State and local governments. This division of power can create both advantages and disadvantages for EDM (see Chapter 4). In the case of water management, the Federal Government's National Water Commission set up in 2004 is the 'lead agency for driving national water reform under the National Water Initiative – Australia's blueprint for how water will be managed into the future'.[21] In Queensland, State Government has the responsibility for overall water allocation, planning and management strategies while most local governments manage the service provision aspects of sewerage, water supply and stormwater systems. Local governments, though, have limited financial or decision-making power over environmental matters as they are reliant on funding from State and Federal Governments, especially for large infrastructure projects, and constrained by their policy and legislative frameworks. The complexities of federalism influenced the Toowoomba debate in a number of ways which created difficulties for the supporters of sewage recycling.

First, many water management options for Toowoomba were constrained because of the Queensland Government's policies and the SE Queensland Water Strategy.[22] These included some options considered by TCC and also put forward by the 'No' campaign, such as constructing a new dam. The catchment for the suggested dam (Emu Creek) was outside Toowoomba's jurisdictional boundaries and would reduce water flows to Wivenhoe Dam. According to TCC it would take 12–15 years to obtain State Government's approval for water allocation and it was unlikely that approval would be granted. Further, the estimated cost of building the dam, $145 million, was restrictive (TCC 2006a).

Secondly, TCC was reliant on funding from both Federal and State Governments to realise their Water Futures Project. As discussed earlier, Queensland Premier Peter Beattie expressed his commitment to fund the implementation of the project but Federal Government's funding support was conditional on Toowoomba City Council holding a referendum and gaining majority support from voters. The Federal Government's decision can be construed to be politically motivated for a number of reasons:

- Drought and water were predicted to be major issues for the 2007 federal election (Media Monitors 2007) with many communities facing a crisis and debating the pros and cons of recycled water. Although Malcolm Turnbull welcomed Peter Beattie's support for the project, being only one year away from the election, the Federal Government was not willing to take the risk of unequivocally supporting a water management option which was not acceptable to the majority of the electorate. This 'no-decision' position was ridiculed by the Federal Labor Opposition at that time as a 'failure of national leadership' and 'a politically convenient decision' which delayed Toowoomba's Water

---

21 <www.nwc.gov.au/www/html/7-home-page.asp> (accessed 19 April 2009).

22 <www.qwc.qld.gov.au/SEQWS> (accessed 16 April 2009).

Futures Project despite support from TCC, the Queensland Government and the NWC (Albanese 2006).

- Tensions can arise between the Federal and State levels of government due to different political parties in power. In this case, the Australian Federal Coalition Government may have been seeking to make a show of their power over the Queensland State Labor Government.

C.5 Postscript

The decisive referendum in Toowoomba did not signal the end of the recycled water debate, rather the beginning of a much wider discussion on the future use of recycled sewage for the whole SE Queensland region. As the water situation in SE Queensland continued to deteriorate the recycled sewage option was put back on the table, along with proposals for more dams[23] and desalination plants. However, this time Premier Beattie pledged to hold a plebiscite across Queensland to determine support for this recycling option. He also promised that adding recycled water to drinking water supply would be implemented only as a last resort – an Armageddon situation (Spearritt 2008; *The Australian* 2008). However, 'Armageddon' came swiftly. In January 2007, as dam levels across SE Queensland continued to fall, the Premier was left with no choice but to abandon the plebiscite and make a crisis decision to recycle sewage and pump it into Wivenhoe Dam. From here, a water grid[24] would supply water to 2.6 million consumers in SE Queensland, including Toowoomba residents (Roberts 2008a). The Coalition Prime Minister at the time, John Howard, supported the Queensland Premier's plan and urged other States to follow Queensland's example (ABC TV 2007).

Unlike Toowoomba's wastewater which originates mainly from residences, the wastewater being considered for recycling for SE Queensland contained industrial and hospital wastewater. This amplified the public's fear about risks associated with ingesting chemicals, viruses and other contaminants. While the Queensland Government insisted on the safety of recycled water, many actors including some of Toowoomba's 'No' campaigers, such as councillor Snow Manners were campaigning against this plan in Brisbane. More than 400,000 copies of a 20-page booklet entitled 'Think before you drink – Is sewage a source of drinking water?' were produced by Councillor Manners and distributed to Brisbane residents in 2007 (Meade 2007). Amongst other concerns, the booklet alerted the public to the risks associated with dangerous drugs and toxic chemicals potentially present in recycled sewage and proclaimed the inability of scientific authorities to test for these (Manners and Dowson undated). Quotes from scientists and experts were used to support the case against introducing recycled sewage into potable water supply, though some of the experts quoted in the publication later asserted that they has been misrepresented (Roberts 2007).

In September 2007, Peter Beattie resigned from the Queensland Parliament and his Deputy and Minister for Infrastructure Anna Bligh took over. Premier Bligh forged ahead with Beattie's plans for recycling sewage for drinking water purposes in order to

---

23 The proposed Traveston Dam on the Mary River was particularly contentious and strongly opposed by the local community.

24 This water grid was part of the Western Corridor Recycled Project which comprised a number of advanced water treatment plants and network of pipelines to supply industry and residents with purified recycled water (<www.westerncorridor.com.au/home.aspx?docId=1> (accessed 1 May 2009)).

drought-proof the region. However, by the end of 2008 wet weather had set in and dam levels rose from below 22 per cent to above 45 per cent. Criticism and controversy on the Queensland Government's water management strategy reached new heights after this respite from the drought (see Fraser 2008; Parnell 2008a, 2008b; Roberts 2008a, 2008b). Responding to the changed conditions, public opinion and upcoming State elections, Premier Bligh decided to take an 'emergency-use only' stance and set a trigger point for adding recycled water to Wivenhoe Dam as well as delaying the construction of Traveston Dam (Fraser 2008). Recycled water would now be added to potable water supply only when dam levels fall below 40 per cent capacity (Parnell 2008b). At the time of writing this case study, construction on the pipeline from Wivenhoe Dam to Toowoomba had commenced, the Western Corridor Recycled Water Project was complete and Traveston Dam was back on the agenda.

Toowoomba's, and more broadly Queensland's, story of water management illustrates many themes presented in previous chapters. Some, but not all of the themes exposed by this case study have been analysed in C.4. Hence we conclude this case study with some questions which facilitate further analysis of complex environmental issues and decision-making processes discussed in this book, especially those related to politics and governance.

- What lessons does this case study provide for engaging communities in finding solutions to conflictual, controversial and emotive issues?

- Why was the government in a situation where choices became limited and emergency decisions had to be made?

- Are governments justified in making rational and top-down decisions at times of crisis? Why?

- What role and power does the public have in steering governments towards making certain decisions?

References

ABC News Online, 2006, 'Water crisis threatens nurseries', 23 June, <www.abc.net.au/news/australia/qld/toowoomba/200606/s1670256.htm> (accessed 19 April 2009).

ABC Online, 2006, 'Water vote bigger than Toowoomba's woes', *Water*, 28 July, <www.abc.net.au/water/stories/s1699774.htm> (accessed 1 May 2009).

ABC Radio National, 2007, 'Science and the public's perception of water recycling', *Ockham's Razor*, 20 May, <www.abc.net.au/rn/ockhamsrazor/stories/2007/1925957.htm> (accessed 29 April 2009).

ABC TV, 2007, 'Recycled water inevitable in NSW, says PM', *The 7.30 Report*, 29 January, <www.abc.net.au/7.30/content/2007/s1835830.htm> (accessed 1 May 2009).

Albanese, A, 2006, 'Turnbull washes his hands of Toowoomba water recycling decision', Media Statement, 24 March, <parlinfo.aph.gov.au/parlInfo/search/display/display.w3p;adv=;db=;group=;holdingType=;id=;orderBy=;page=;query=SubjectId_Phrase%3A885%20SearchCategory_Phrase%3A%22media%22%20Dataset_Phrase%3A%22pressrel%22;querytype=;rec=2;resCount=> (accessed 19 April 2009).

Australia Network, 2007, Toowoomba Flowers, *Nexus*, 23 April, <http://australianetwork.com/nexus/stories/s1807955.htm> (accessed 29 January 2009).

AWA (Australian Water Association), 2007, *Water in Australia. Facts & Figures, Myths & Ideas*, Australian Water Association, Sydney.

Berghofer, C, 2006, 'Toowoomba decides: Water poll', Advertisement authorised by Clive Berghofer, July 2006, <www.valscan.com.au/webpaper.pdf > (accessed 22 January 2009).

CHOICE, 2008, 'Recycled drinking water: Myths and facts', *CHOICE*, March 2008, pp 12–16.

Clausen, L, 2006, 'Not a drop to drink', *Time*, 29 May, <www.time.com/time/magazine/article/0,9171,1198943,00.html> (accessed October 2006).

Donaghey, K, undated, 'Fear and loathing in the garden city', <www.magazine.walkleys.com/the_news/stories/fear_and_loathing_in_the_garden_city__20070816106/> (accessed 29 January 2009).

Fraser, A, 2008, 'Weather politics trumps policies', *The Australian*, 26 November, p 4.

Frew, W, 2005a, 'Sewage to star in water', *Sydney Morning Herald*, 15 July, <www.smh.com.au/news/national/sewage-to-star-in-water-plan/2005/07/14/1120934364087.html> (accessed 28 April 2009).

Frew, W, 2005b, 'The yuk factor', *Sydney Morning Herald*, 5 September, <www.smh.com.au/news/national/the-yuk-factor/2005/09/04/1125772411914.html> (accessed 28 April 2009).

Frew, W, 2006, 'Recycling splits a thirsty city', *Sydney Morning Herald*, 26 June, <www.smh.com.au/news/national/recycling-splits-a-thirsty-city/2006/06/25/1151174072057.html#> (accessed 19 April 2009).

Hamilton, GR and Greenfield, PF, 1991, 'Potable reuse of treated wastewater', Proceedings of the Australian Water and Wastewater Association 14th Federal Convention, Perth, 17–22 March, Volume 1, pp 497–506.

Healy, S, 2001, 'Privileging process over "fact": the Sydney water scare as "organised irresponsibility"', *Science and Public Policy*, 28 (2): 123–129.

Hurlimann, A, 2007, 'Time for a water "re-vision"', *Australasian Journal of Environmental Management*, 14 (1): 14–21.

Langford, R, 2006, 'Toowoomba says no', *The Courier Mail*, 29 July, <www.news.com.au/couriermail/story/0,23739,19955581–5005340,00.html> (accessed 20 January 2009).

Manners, S and Dowson, J, undated, *Think before you agree to drink*, <www.valscan.com.au/tbyatd.pdf> (accessed 29 April 2009).

Marks, J, Martin, B and Zadoroznyj, M, 2008, 'How Australians order acceptance of recycled water: national baseline data', *Journal of Sociology*, 44 (1): 83–99.

Meade, K, 2007, 'Water campaign hits below the belt', *The Australian*, 21 March, <www.theaustralian.news.com.au/story/0.25197.21419019-2702.00.html> (accessed 12 May 2009).

Media Monitors, 2007, 'Water in Australia – A drought of action: A flood of politics, vested interests and nimbyism', Research Report, CARMA Asia Pacific, Strawberry Hills, NSW, <www.mediamonitors.com.au/documents/Carma_Research_Report.pdf> (accessed 28 April 2009).

Millar, L, 2006, 'Poowoomba: "Turnbull supports treated sewage"', *AM ABC Radio National*, 29 July, <www.abc.net.au/am/content/2006/s1700353.htm> (accessed 11 November 2008).

Mitchell, S, 2006, 'The race to drink waste', *The Australian*, 2 March, Document AUSTLN0020060301e2320002u, <http://global.factiva.com.viviena.library.unsw.edu.au/ha/default.aspx> (accessed 30 April 2009).

Morley, P, 2008, 'Water on Toowoomba's election agenda', *The Courier Mail*, 28 January, <www.news.com.au/couriermail/story/0,23739,23122712-3102,00.html> (accessed 28 April 2008).

O'Malley, B, 2006, 'Crunch time for water recycling – Poll may be line in sand', *The Courier Mail*, 22 July, Document COUMAI0020060721e27m00022, <http://global.factiva.com.viviena.library.unsw.edu.au/ha/default.aspx> (accessed 29 April 2009).

Parnell, S, 2008a, 'Water uproar forces Bligh to change course', *The Weekend Australian*, 29–30 November, p 29.

Parnell, S, 2008b, 'Backdowns shake Bligh's leadership', *The Australian*, 27 November, p 5.

Petts, J and Brooks, C, 2006, 'Expert conceptualisations of the role of lay knowledge in environmental decision-making: challenges for deliberative democracy', *Environment and Planning A*, 38 (6): 1045–1059.

Po, M, Kaercher, J and Nancarrow, BE, 2004, 'Literature review of factors influencing public perceptions of water reuse', Australian Water Conservation and Reuse Research Program, CSIRO Land and Water.

Po, M, Nancarrow, BE, Leviston, Z, Porter, NB and others, 2005, 'Predicting community behaviour in relation to wastewater reuse: What drives decisions to accept or reject?', Water for a Healthy Country National Research Flagship, CSIRO Land and Water, Perth.

Queensland Water Commission, 2008, 'South East Queensland water strategy – March 2008', <www.qwc.qld.gov.au/SEQWS+document> (accessed 29 April 2009).

Radcliffe, JC, 2004, *Water Recycling in Australia*, Australian Academy of Technological Sciences and Engineering, Parkville, Victoria.

Readers Digest, undated, 'Drinking recycled water: The debate', <www.readersdigest.com.au/life/drinking-recycled-sewage-water-the-debate/article91459.html> (accessed 28 April 2009).

Roberts, G, 2007, 'Words twisted in anti-recycling propaganda', *The Australian*, 21 May.

Roberts, G, 2008a, 'Water boss denies conflicting roles', *The Australian*, 2 December, p 4.

Roberts, G, 2008b, 'U-turn on recycled industrial waste', *The Australian*, 6 November, p 7.

Saggin, G, 2008, 'Toowoomba taps into Great Artesian Basin', *ABC News*, 17 October, <www.abc.net.au/news/stories/2008/10/17/2393984.htm> (accessed 29 April 2009).

Spearritt, P, 2008, 'The water crisis in Southeast Queensland: How desalination turned the region into carbon emission heaven' in Troy, P, (ed), *Troubled Waters: Confronting the Water Crisis in Australian Cities*, ANU E-Press, pp 19–36.

Stenekes, N, Schaefer, AI and Ashbolt, NJ, 2001, 'Community involvement in water recycling – issues and needs' in Schafer, AI, Sherman, P and Waite, TD, (eds), *Proceedings from the Recent Advances in Water Recycling Technologies Workshop*, pp 113–124. Workshop held 26 November 2001, Brisbane, Centre for Water and Waste Technology, The University of New South Wales, Sydney, and the Environmental Protection Authority, Brisbane.

Stenekes, N, Colebatch, HK, Waite, TD and Ashbolt, NJ, 2006, 'Risk and governance in water recycling: Public acceptance revisited', *Science, Technology and Human Values*, 31 (2): 107–134.

TCC (Toowoomba City Council), 2003, 'Toowoomba City Council State of the Environment Report 2001', <www.toowoomba.qld.gov.au/index.php?option=com_docman&task=cat_view&gid=257&Itemid=107> (accessed 28 April 2009).

TCC (Toowoomba City Council), 2005, 'Water Futures – Toowoomba: Taking care of Toowoomba's future', Briefing paper, 1 July 2005, <www.toowoombawater.com.au/index.php?option=com_docman&task=doc_view&gid=32&Itemid=23> (accessed 28 April 2009).

TCC (Toowoomba City Council), 2006a, 'Water Futures Toowoomba: Securing a safe and sustainable water supply for our future', <www.toowoombawater.com.au/index.php?option=com_docman&task=cat_view&gid=34&Itemid=23> (accessed 28 April 2009).

TCC (Toowoomba City Council), 2006b, 'Why we're voting YES', <www.toowoombawater.com.au/index.php?option=com_content&task=view&id=165&Itemid=1> (accessed 13 April 2009).

TCC (Toowoomba City Council), 2006c, '"Yes" case education campaign to be fully funded', <www.toowoombawater.com.au/index.php?option=com_content&task=view&id=220&Itemid=52> (accessed 19 April 2009).

TCC (Toowoomba City Council), 2006d, 'Nursery & garden industry Queensland show their support', <www.toowoombawater.com.au/index.php?option=com_content&task=view&id=170&Item=52> (accessed 13 April 2009).

TCC, 2007, 'Our Toowoomba towards 2050: A vision for the future – a plan to guide us', <http://towards.toowoomba2050.com.au/content/view/3/4/> (accessed 26 April 2009).

The Australian, 2008, 'Far from Armageddon', 5 November, <www.theaustralian.news.com.au/story/0,25197,24603327-16382,00.html> (accessed 1 May 2009).

The Chronicle, 2005, 'New concern arises over city dam levels', 18 August, <www.thechronicle.com.au/story/2005/08/18/apn-new-concern-arises-over-city-da> (accessed 29 April 2009).

Thorley, D, 2006, 'Online opinion', 27 February, <www.usyd.edu.au/envsci/students/notes/air/toowoomba_awt.pdf> (accessed 19 April 2009).

van Vuuren, K, 2007, 'The role of press in reporting the water crisis', Public seminar, Centre of Critical and Cultural Studies, The University of Queensland, 9 October 2007, <www.cccs.uq.edu.au/index.html?page=58028&pid=16094> (accessed 28 April 2009).

van Vuuren, K, 2008, 'The impact of local independent newspapers in south east Queensland', *eJournalist* 8, (1): 54–73, <http://ejournalist.com.au/v8n1/Vuuren.pdf>(accessed 28 April 2009).

Reference List for Chapters 1–10

ABC (Australian Broadcasting Corporation), 2006a, 'Chant of the Scrub Turkey', television program, <www.abc.net.au/programsales/s1704731.htm> (accessed 29 March 2009).

ABC (Australian Broadcasting Corporation), 2006b, 'Interview – Dr Graeme Pearman', *Four Corners Program: Green House Mafia*, 13 February, <www.abc.net.au/4corners/content/2006/s1566857.htm> (accessed 26 February 2009).

ABC (Australian Broadcasting Corporation), Radio, 2008, 'Kirby: bring cameras into court', *AM Program*, 14 November, <www.abc.net.au/am/content/2008/s2419403.htm> (accessed 24 February 2009).

ABRCC (Australian Business Roundtable on Climate Change), 2006, *The Business Case for Early Action*, <www.businessroundtable.com.au/pdf/F078-RT-WS.pdf> (accessed 15 March 2009).

ACF (Australian Conservation Foundation), 1997, *ACF Membership Details*, obtained from Louise Sverns, Membership Coordinator for the ACF, Fitzroy, Victoria.

ACF (Australian Conservation Foundation), 2007, *ACF Annual Report 2006–7*, The Australian Conservation Foundation, <www.acfonline.org.au/uploads/res/1362_ACF_Annual_Report_2007_06.pdf> (accessed 18 February 2009).

ACF & ACTU, 2008, *Green Gold Rush: How Ambitious Environmental Policy Can Make Australia a Leader in the Global Race for Green Jobs*, Australian Conservation Foundation (ACF) and Australian Council of Trade Unions (ACTU), <www.acfonline.org.au/uploads/res/Green_Gold_Rush_final.pdf> (accessed 2 April 2009).

ACF, CHOICE and ACOSS, undated, *Energy and Equity: Preparing Households for Climate Change*, <www.acoss.org.au/upload/publications/papers/4204__EnergyEquity%20low%20res.pdf> (accessed 3 December 2008).

ACT Government, 2007, *Community Well-being Indicators. A Discussion Paper Prepared for the ACT Community Inclusion Board*, Social Policy and Implementation Branch, Policy Division, Chief Minister's Department, ACT Government, <www.cmd.act.gov.au/__data/assets/pdf_file/0014/1625/Community_well-being_indicators.pdf> (accessed 17 April 2009).

Adams, G and Hine, M, 1999, 'Local environmental policy making in Australia' in Walker, KJ and Crowley, K, (eds), *Australian Environmental Policy 2 : Studies in Decline + Devolution*, UNSW Press, Sydney, pp 186–203.

ADB (Asian Development Bank), 1990, *Environmental Risk Assessment: Dealing with Uncertainty in Environmental Impact Assessment*, Environment Paper No 7, Office of the Environment, Asian Development Bank.

AG DEH AGO (Australian Government, Department of Environment and Heritage, Australian Greenhouse Office), 2006, *Climate Change Scenarios for Initial Assessment of Risk in Accordance with Risk Management Guidance*, CSIRO, <www.climatechange.gov.au/impacts/publications/pubs/risk-scenarios.pdf> (accessed 31 March 2009).

AGO (Australian Greenhouse Office), 2006, *Topic 2: The IPCC Climate Change Scenarios*, Department of the Environment and Heritage, <www.climatechange.gov.au/science/hottopics/pubs/topic2. pdf > (accessed 6 March 2008).

Agterbosch, S, Meertens, RM and Vermeulen, JV, 2009, 'The relative importance of social and institutional conditions in the planning of wind power projects', *Renewable and Sustainable Energy Reviews*, 13 (2): 393–405.

Agyeman, J, Bullard, RD and Evans, R, 2003, 'Joined-up thinking: bringing together sustainability, environmental justice and equity' in Agyeman, J, Bullard, RD and Evans, B, (eds), *Just Sustainabilities. Development in an Unequal World*, Earthscan Publications, London, pp 1–16.

Albury, R, 1983, *The Politics of Objectivity*, Deakin University Press, Victoria.

Alexandra, J, 2007, 'Mobilising community science in Australia', Paper to the 3rd National Waterwatch Conference, November 2007, Canberra. <www.waterwatch.org.au/publications/2007conference/ pubs/alexandra.pdf> (accessed 25 August 2008).

Alford, J, 2002, 'Defining the client in the public sector: a social-exchange perspective', *Public Administration Review*, 62 (3): 337–346.

ALGA, 2008, *About ALGA*, <www.alga.asn.au/about/> (accessed 2 October 2008).

Allan, S, Adam, B and Carter, C, 2000, 'Introduction: the media politics of environmental risk' in Allan, S, Adam, B and Carter, C, (eds), *Environmental Risks and the Media*, Routledge, London, pp 1–26.

Allison, HE and Hobbs, RJ, 2006, *Science and Policy in Natural Resource Management. Understanding System Complexity*, Cambridge University Press, Cambridge.

Alsever, J, undated, 'What is crowdsourcing?', *BNET Briefing*, <www.bnet.com/2403-1324123-52961. html> (accessed 22 January 2009).

Althaus, C, Bridgman, P and Davis, G, 2007, *The Australian Policy Handbook*, 4th edn, Allen & Unwin, Crows Nest, NSW.

America*Speaks*, 2008, *Dialogue With the City*, <www.americaspeaks.org/index.cfm?fuseaction=page.v iewpage&pageid=586&parentID=686&grandparentID=473> (accessed 8 January 2008).

Anderson, MS and Massa, I, 2000, 'Ecological modernization – origins, dilemmas and future directions', *Journal of Environmental Policy and Planning* 2 (4): 337–345.

Annandale, D, Morrison-Saunders, A and Duxbury, L, 2004, 'Regional sustainability initiatives: the growth of green jobs in Australia', *Local Environment*, 9 (1): 81–87.

Ansell, C and Gash, A, 2008, 'Collaborative governance in theory and practice', *Journal of Public Administration Research and Theory*, 18 (4): 543–571.

ANZECC (Australian and New Zealand Environment and Conservation Council) State of the Environment Reporting Task Force, 2000, *Core Environmental Indicators for Reporting on the State of the Environment*, Environment Australia, Canberra, <www.environment.gov.au/soe/publications/ indicators/pubs/core-indicators.pdf> (accessed 16 March 2009).

Appelbaum, D and Lawton, S, 1990, *Ethics and the Professions*, Prentice Hall, Englewood Cliffs, NJ.

Armitage, D, Berkes, F and Doubleday, N, 2007a, 'Introduction: moving beyond co-management' in Armitage, D, Berkes, F and Doubleday, N, (eds), *Adaptive Co-Management: Collaboration, Learning, and Multi-Level Governance*, UBC Press, Vancouver, pp 1–15.

Armitage, D, Berkes, F and Doubleday, N, (eds), 2007b, *Adaptive Co-Management: Collaboration, Learning, and Multi-Level Governance*, UBC Press, Vancouver.

Arnstein, SR, 1969, 'A ladder of citizen participation', *Journal of the American Institute of Planners*, 35 (4): 216–224.

ASEC (Australian State of the Environment Committee), 2001, *Australia State of the Environment 2001: Independent Report to the Commonwealth Minister for the Environment and Heritage*, CSIRO Publishing, Collingwood.

Audit Office of New South Wales, 2005, *New South Wales Auditor-General's Report. Performance Audit. Managing Air Quality: Department of Environment and Conservation*, The Audit Office of New South Wales, Sydney.

Aulich, C and Nutley, S, 2001, 'The public sector' in Aulich, C, Halligan, J and Nutley, S, (eds), *Australian Handbook of Public Sector Management*, Allen & Unwin, Sydney, pp 1–10.

Aumônier, S and Collins, M, 2005, *Lifecycle Assessment of Disposable and Reusable Nappies in the UK*, Environmental Agency, Bristol, <www.nappyinformationservice.co.uk/news.htm> (accessed 14 March 2009).

Aumônier, S, Collins, M and Garrett, P, 2008, *An Updated Lifecycle Assessment Study for Disposable and Reusable Nappies*, Environmental Agency, Bristol, <www.randd.defra.gov.uk/Document. aspx?Document=WR0705_7589_FRP.pdf> (accessed 14 March 2009).

Australian Bureau of Meteorology, 2004, *Annual Report 2003–2004*, <www.bom.gov.au/inside/eiab/ reports/ar03-04/Meteorological_and_Related_Data_and_Products/> (accessed 25 August 2008).

Australian Government DEH (Department of Environment and Heritage), 2006, *Australian State of the Environment 2006 At a Glance*, <www.environment.gov.au/soe/2006/publications/summary/ index.html> (accessed 27 February 2009).

Australian Government, 2008, 'Caring for our country', <www.nrm.gov.au/funding/future. html#delivery> (accessed 10 June 2008).

Baber, WF and Bartlett, RV, 2005, *Deliberative Environmental Politics*, MIT Press, Cambridge, MA.

Bäckstrand, K, 2003, 'Civic science for sustainability: reframing the role of experts, policy-makers and citizens in environmental governance', *Global Environmental Politics*, 3 (4): 24–41.

Bala, JS, 2008, 'Measuring stakeholder value', KPMG Philippines website, <www.kpmg.com.ph/ cornerbfas20080819.asp> (accessed 17 March 2009).

Bang, H, 2003, 'A new ruler meeting a new citizen: culture governance and everyday making' in Bang, H, (ed), *Governance as Social and Political Communication*, Manchester University Press, Manchester, pp 241–267.

Barbour, I, 1980, *Technology, Environment and Human Values*, Praeger, New York.

Barnes, M, Newman, J and Sullivan, H, 2007, *Power, Participation and Political Renewal: Case Studies in Public Participation*, The Policy Press, Bristol.

Barnes, M, Newman, J, Knops, A and Sullivan, H, 2003, 'Constituting "the public" in public participation', *Public Administration*, 81 (2): 379–399.

Bates, G, 2002, *Environmental Law in Australia*, 5th edn, Butterworths, Sydney.

Bates, G, 2003, 'Legal perspectives' in Dovers, S and Wild River, S, (eds), *Managing Australia's Environment*, The Federation Press, Sydney, pp 255–301.

Bates, G, 2006, *Environmental Law in Australia*, 6th edn, LexisNexis Butterworths, Sydney.

Baumann, H and Cowell, SJ, 1999, 'An evaluative framework for conceptual and analytical approaches used in environmental management', *Greener Management International*, 26 (Summer): 109–122.

BCA, (Business Council of Australia), 2007, *Strategic Framework for Emissions Reduction* <www.bca. com.au/DisplayFile.aspx?FileID=117> (accessed 7 January 2009).

Beck, U, 1992, *Risk Society. Towards a New Modernity*, (translated by M Ritter), Sage Publications, London.

Beck, U, 1994, 'The reinvention of politics: towards a theory of reflexive modernization' in Beck, U, Giddens, A and Lash, S, (eds), *Reflexive Modernization. Politics, Tradition and Aesthetics in the Modern Social Order*, Polity Press, Cambridge, pp 1–55.

Beder, S, 1989, *Toxic Fish and Sewer Surfing*, Allen & Unwin, Sydney.

Beder, S, 1990a, 'Environmental Impact Statements: the ethical dilemma for engineers', *National Engineering Conference*, Institute of Engineers Australia, Canberra, 1990, 1–8.

Beder, S, 1990b, 'Environmental Impact Statements: The Ethical Dilemma for Engineers' in Beder, S, (ed), *Environmental Impact Statements: Selected Readings*, Environmental Education Project, Sydney University, pp 45–48.

Beder, S, 1992, 'Activism versus negotiation: strategies for the environment movement' in Harding, R, (ed), *Ecopolitics V: Proceedings*, Centre for Liberal and General Studies, The University of New South Wales, pp 55–61.

Beder, S, 1995, 'Engineers, ethics and sustainable development' in Chiara, MLD, Doets, K, Mundici, D and van Benthem, J, (eds), *Structures and Norms in Science*, Volume Two of the Tenth International Congress of Logic, Methodology and Philosophy of Science, <http://books.google.com.au/books?hl=en&lr=&id=oCkmraDmUUIC&oi=fnd&pg=PA127&dq=%22Beder%22+%22Engineers,+Ethics,+and+Sustainable+Development%22+&ots=UYww4hAqPf&sig=K_0PyUG7w-hy48gPwW1JGgWvSSEg> (accessed 19 March 2009).

Beder, S, 1996, *The Nature of Sustainable Development*, 2nd edn, Scribe Publications, Carlton North, Victoria.

Beder, S, 2002, *Global Spin: The Corporate Assault on Environmentalism*, Revised edn, Green Books, Vermont.

Beder, S, 2004, 'Moulding and manipulating the news' in White, R, (ed), *Controversies in Environmental Sociology*, Cambridge University Press, Cambridge, pp 204–220.

Beder, S, 2006, *Environmental Principles and Policies. An Interdisciplinary Approach*, UNSW Press, Sydney.

Beer, T and Ziolkowski, F, 1996, 'Environmental risk assessment: an Australian perspective' in Norton, TW, Beer, T and Dovers, SR, (eds), *Risk and Uncertainty in Environmental Management*, Proceedings of the 1995 Australian Academy of Science Fenner Conference on the Environment, Centre for Resource and Environmental Studies, Australian National University, Canberra, pp 3–13.

Beeton, RJS, Buckley, KI, Jones, GJ, Morgan, D and others, (Australian State of the Environment Committee), 2006, *Australia State of the Environment 2006. Independent Report to the Australian Government Minister for the Environment and Heritage*, <www.environment.gov.au/soe/2006/publications/report/index.html> (accessed 28 February 2009).

Bell, JNB and Shaw, G, 2005, 'Ecological lessons from the Chernobyl accident', *Environment International*, 31 (6): 771–777.

Bell, S, 2002, 'Institutionalism' in Summers, J, Woodward, D and Parkin, A, (eds), *Government, Politics, Power and Policy in Australia*, 7th edn, Pearson Education, Frenchs Forest, pp 363–380.

Bell, S and Morse, S, 2008, *Sustainability Indicators. Measuring the Immeasurable?*, 2nd edn, Earthscan Publications, London.

Benhabib, S, 1996, 'Toward a deliberative model of democratic legitimacy' in Benhabib, S, (ed), *Democracy and Difference: Contesting Boundaries of the Political*, Princeton University Press, Princeton, New Jersey, pp 67–94.

Benn, S, Dunphy, D and Griffiths, A, 2006, 'Enabling change for corporate sustainability: an integrated perspective', *Australian Journal of Environmental Management*, 13 (3): 156–165.

Berglund, C and Matti, S, 2006, 'Citizen and consumer: the dual role of individuals in environmental policy', *Environmental Politics*, 15 (4): 550–571.

Berkes, F, 2007, 'Adaptive co-management and complexity: exploring the many faces of co-management' in Armitage, D, Berkes, F and Doubleday, N, (eds), *Adaptive Co-Management: Collaboration, Learning, and Multi-Level Governance*, UBC Press, Vancouver, pp 19–37.

Berlin, I, 1997, *The Proper Study of Mankind: An Anthology of Essays*, Hardy, H and Hausheer, R, (eds), Chatto & Windus, London.

Bhaskar, V and Glyn, A, 1995, 'Introduction' in Bhaskar, V and Glyn, A, (eds), *The North The South and the Environment. Ecological Constraints and the Global Economy*, Earthscan Publications, London and United Nations University Press, Tokyo, pp 1–8.

Bickerstaff, K, 2004, 'Risk perception: socio-cultural perspectives on the public experience of air pollution', *Environment International*, 30 (6): 827–840.

Bingham, LB, Nabatchi, T and O'Leary, R, 2005, 'The new governance: practices and processes for stakeholder and citizen participation in the work of government', *Public Administration Review*, 65 (5): 547–558.

Birds Australia, undated, <www.birdsaustralia.com.au/> (accessed 25 August 2008).

Björklund, AE, 2002, 'Survey of approaches to improve reliability in LCA', *International Journal of LCA*, 7 (2): 64–72.

Black, J, 2008, 'Knowledge bases for prioritised investment in the environment: impact on the design and implementation of Western Australia's salinity investment framework', paper presented to *Twelfth Annual Conference of the International Research Society for Public Management (IRSPM)*, 26–28 March, Brisbane, <www.irspm2008.bus.qut.edu.au/papers/documents/pdf/Black%20-%20 Priority%20Setting%20and%20Dryland%20Salinity%20-%20IRSPM%20-%202008.pdf> (accessed 17 March 2009).

Blackmore, C, 2007, 'What kinds of knowledge, knowing and learning are required for addressing resource dilemmas? A theoretical overview', *Environmental Science & Policy*, 10 (6): 512–525.

Blewitt, J, 2008, *Understanding Sustainable Development*, Earthscan Publications, London.

Blowers, A, 1997, 'Environmental policy: ecological modernization or the risk society?', *Urban Studies*, 34 (5–6): 845–871.

Blutstein, H, 2003, 'Note from the field. A forgotten pioneer of sustainability', *Journal of Cleaner Production*, 11 (3): 339–341.

Boarini, R, Johansson, Å and d'Ercole, MM, 2006, 'Alternative measures of well-being', *OECD Statistics Brief*, No 11, May 2006, <www.oecd.org/dataoecd/26/61/36967254.pdf> (accessed 17 April 2009).

Bodnar, A, Castorina, R, Desai, M, Duramad, P and others, 2004, 'Lessons learned from "The Skeptical Environmentalist": an environmental health perspective', *International Journal of Hygiene and Environmental Health*, 207 (1): 57–67.

Boguski, TK, Hunt, RG, Chlakis, JM and Franklin WE, 1996, 'LCA methodology' in Curran, MA, (ed), *Environmental Life Cycle Assessment*, McGraw-Hill, New York, pp 2.1–2.37.

Boiral, O, 2002, 'Tacit knowledge and environmental management', *Long Range Planning*, 35 (3): 291–317.

Bolton, G, 1981, *Spoils and Spoilers: Australians Make Their Environment 1788–1980*, George Allen & Unwin, Sydney.

Botterill, LC and Fisher, M, (eds), 2003, *Australia: Beyond Drought: People, Policy and Perspectives*, CSIRO Publishing, Canberra.

Boutin, P, 2006, 'Crowdsourcing: consumers as creators', *BusinessWeek*, 13 July, <www.businessweek.com/innovate/content/jul2006/id20060713_755844.htm> (accessed 22 January 2009).

Bovaird, T, 2007, 'Beyond engagement and participation: user and community coproduction of public services', *Public Administration Review*, 67 (5): 846–860.

Bovens, M, 't Hart, P and Kuipers, S, 2006, 'The politics of policy evaluation' in Moran, M, Rein, M and Goodin, RE, (eds), *The Oxford Handbook of Public Policy*, Oxford University Press., Oxford, pp 319–335.

Box, WJ, 2002, 'Sustainability is IT', *Pollution Engineering*, 34 (1): 13–17.

Boyden, S and Dovers, S, 1997, 'Humans in the biosphere' in Diesendorf, M and Hamilton, C, (eds), *Human Ecology, Human Economy*, Allen & Unwin, St Leonards, Australia, pp 3–34.

Braat, LC and van Lierop, WJF, (eds), 1987, *Economic-Ecological Modeling*, Elsevier Science Publishers, Amsterdam.

Brenton, T, 1994, *The Greening of Machiavelli. The Evolution of International Environmental Politics*, Earthscan Publications, London.

Breusch, J, 2008, 'Split on clean coal cash', *The Australian Financial Review*, 15 April, p 8.

Brinsmead, T and Hooker, C, 2005, *Sustainabilities: A Systematic Framework and Comparative Analysis*, Cooperative Research Centre for Coal in Sustainable Development, Research Report 53, <www.newcastle.edu.au/centre/casrg/assessingsustainabilitydimensionsandimpacts.html> (accessed 27 April 2009).

Brinsmead, T and Hooker, C, 2008, *An Adaptive Energy Policy for Queensland*, Cooperative Research Centre for Coal in Sustainable Development, Research Report 92, <www.newcastle.edu.au/centre/casrg/assessingsustainabilitydimensionsandimpacts.html> (accessed 27 April 2009).

Brodnig, G and Mayer-Schönberger, V, 2000, 'Bridging the gap: the role of spatial information technologies in the integration of traditional environmental knowledge and Western science', *The Electronic Journal on Information Systems in Developing Countries*, 1 (1): 1–15.

Brown, AJ, 2008a, 'Ain't broke, but it needs fixing', *The Weekend Australian*, 26–27 July, p 29.

Brown, AJ, (ed), 2008b, *Whistle Blowing in the Australian Public Sector*, ANU E Press, Canberra.

Brown, AJ and Head, B, 2005, 'Institutional capacity and choice in Australia's integrity systems', *Australian Journal of Public Administration*, 64 (2): 84–95.

Brown, VA, 1997, 'Our core business is the future. Working towards Local Agenda 21' in Brown, VA, (ed), *Managing for Local Sustainability. Policy, Problem-Solving, Practice and Place*, Commonwealth of Australia, Canberra, pp 3–17.

Brown, VA, 2005a, 'Leadership in the local government sector: working from inside out' in Hargroves, K and Smith, MH, (eds), *The Natural Advantage of Nations. Business Opportunities, Innovation and Governance in the 21st Century*, Earthscan Publications, London, pp 289–298.

Brown, VA, 2005b, 'Knowing. Linking the knowledge cultures of sustainability and health' in Brown, VA, Grootjans, J, Ritchie, J, Townsend, M and others, (eds), *Sustainability and Health. Supporting Global Ecological Integrity in Public Health*, Earthscan Publications, London, pp 131–161.

Brown, VA, 2008, *Leonardo's Vision. A Guide to Collective Thinking and Action*, Sense Publishers, Rotterdam/Taipei.

Brush, SB, 1996, 'Whose knowledge, whose genes, whose rights?' in Brush, SB and Stabinsky, D, (eds), *Valuing Local Knowledge: Indigenous People and Intellectual Property Rights*, Island Press, Washington DC, pp 1–21.

Buckingham-Hatfield, S and Percy, S, (eds), 1999, *Constructing Local Environmental Agenda: People, Places + Participation*, Routledge, London.

Bulkeley, H, 2000, 'Discourse coalitions and the Australian climate change policy network', *Environment and Planning C: Government and Policy*, 18 (6): 727–748.

Burgman, M, 2005, *Risk and Decisions for Conservation and Environmental Management*, Cambridge University Press, Cambridge.

Buss, DM, Craik, KH and Dake, KM, 1986, 'Contemporary worldviews and perception of the technological system' in Covello, VT, Menkes, J and Mumpower, J, (eds), *Risk Evaluation and Management*, Plenum Press, New York, pp 93–130.

Byrne, J, Martinez, C and Glover, L, 2002, 'A brief on environmental justice' in Byrne, J, Martinez, C and Glover, L, (eds), *Environmental Justice. Discourses in International Political Economy, Energy and Environmental Policy*, Vol 8, Transaction Publishers, New Brunswick, USA, pp 3–17.

Cadbury, D, 1997, *The Feminization of Nature. Our Future at Risk*, Hamish Hamilton, London.

CAER (Centre for Australian Ethical Research), in collaboration with Deni Greene Consulting Services, 2005, The State of Sustainability Reporting in Australia 2005, Australian Government, <www.envi ronment.gov.au/settlements/industry/corporate/reporting/survey.html> (accessed 6 May 2008).

Camhis, M, 1979, *Planning Theory and Philosophy*, Tavistock Publications, London.

Campbell, A, 2006, *The Australian Natural Resource Management Knowledge System*, Land & Water Australia, Canberra, <http://products.lwa.gov.au/files/PR061081.pdf> (accessed 4 May 2009).

Carson, L, 2000, 'Democracy? Come back in four years . . .', *Northern Rivers Echo*, 22 June, p 9.

Carson, L, 2008, 'Creating democratic surplus through citizens' assemblies', *Journal of Public Deliberation*, 4 (1): Article 5, <http://services.bepress.com/jpd/vol4/iss1/art5> (accessed 3 November 2008).

Carson, L and Gelber, K, 2001, *Ideas for Community Consultation – a Discussion on Principles and Procedures for Making Consultation Work*, A report prepared for the NSW Department of Urban Affairs and Planning, Sydney.

Carson, L and Hartz-Karp, J, 2005, 'Adapting and combining deliberative designs: juries, polls and forums' in Gastil, J and Levine, P, (eds), *The Deliberative Democracy Handbook: Strategies for Effective Civic Engagement in the 21st Century*, Jossey-Bass, San Francisco, pp 120–138.

Carson, L and Martin, B, 1999, *Random Selection in Politics*, Praeger Publishers, Westport.

Carson, L and Martin, B, 2002, 'Random selection of citizens for technological decision making', *Science and Public Policy*, 29 (2): 105–113.

Carson, L, White, S, Hendriks, C and Palmer, J, 2002, 'Community consultation in environmental policy making', *The Drawing Board: An Australian Review of Public Affairs*, 3 (1): 1–13.

Carson, R, 1962, *Silent Spring*, Penguin Books, Middlesex, England (1965 publication).

Carter, N, 2007, *The Politics of the Environment. Ideas, Activism, Policy*, 2nd edn, Cambridge University Press, Cambridge.

Carver, S, Evans, A, Kingston, R and Turton, I, 2001, 'Public participation, GIS, and cyberdemocracy: evaluating on-line spatial decision support systems', *Environment and Planning B: Planning and Design*, 28 (6): 907–921.

Castells, M, 2004, *The Power of Identity*, 2nd edn, Blackwell, Oxford.

Chalmers, AF, 1982, *What is This Thing called Science? An Assessment of the Nature and Status of Science and its Methods*, 2nd edn, University of Queensland Press, St Lucia, Queensland.

Chappells, H and Shove, E, 2005, 'Debating the future of comfort: environmental sustainability, energy consumption and the indoor environment', *Building Research and Information*, 33 (1): 32–40.

Chapple, S, 2001, 'The EPBC Act: one year later', *Environmental Planning and Law Journal*, 18 (6): 523–539.

Chee, YE, 2004, 'An ecological perspective on the valuation of ecosystem services', *Biological Conservation*, 120 (4): 549–565.

Cheng, AS and Fiero, JD, 2005, 'Collaborative learning and the public's stewardship of its forests', in Gastil, J and Levine, P, (eds), *The Deliberative Democracy Handbook. Strategies for Effective Civic Engagement in the 21st Century*, Jossey-Bass (Wiley), San Francisco, pp 164–173.

CHOICE (Magazine of the Australian Consumers' Association), 1993, 'Nappies: the real dirt', *CHOICE*, 34 (11): 6.

Christoff, P, 1998, 'Degreening government in the garden state: environment policy under the Kennett Government, 1992–1997', *Environmental Planning and Law Journal*, 15 (1): 10–32.

Christoff, P, 2003, 'EPAs – Orphan agencies of environmental protection' in Dovers, S and Wild River, S, (eds), *Managing Australia's Environment*, The Federation Press, Sydney, pp 302–317.

Christoff, P, 2005, 'Policy autism or double-edged dismissiveness? Australia's climate change policy under the Howard Government', *Global Change, Peace and Security*, 17 (1): 29–44.

Christoff, P, 2006, 'Ecological modernization, ecological modernities', *Environmental Politics*, 5 (3): 476–500.

Clark, F and Illman, DL, 2001, 'Dimensions of civic science. Introductory essay', *Science Communication*, 23 (1): 5–27.

Clark, WC, 2007, 'Sustainability science: a room of its own', *Proceedings of the National Academy of Sciences (USA)*, 104 (6): 1737–1738.

Clark, WC and Dickson, NM, 2003, 'Sustainability science: the emerging research program', *Proceedings of the National Academy of Sciences (USA)*, 100 (14): 8059–8061.

Clarke, T, 2007, 'The materiality of sustainability. Corporate social and environmental responsibility as instruments of strategic change?' in Benn, S and Dunphy, D, (eds), *Corporate Governance and Sustainability. Challenges for Theory and Practice*, Routledge, London, pp 219–251.

CoA (Commonwealth of Australia), 1992a, *National Strategy for Ecologically Sustainable Development*, Australian Government Publishing Service, Canberra.

CoA (Commonwealth of Australia), 1992b, *Compendium of Ecologically Sustainable Development Recommendations*, Australian Government Publishing Service, Canberra.

CoA (Commonwealth of Australia), 1992c, 'Intergovernmental Agreement on the Environment', <www.environment.gov.au/esd/national/igae/> (accessed 29 March 2008).

CoA (Commonwealth of Australia), 2003a, *Employment in the Environment: Methods, Measurements and Messages*, House of Representatives Standing Committee on Environment and Heritage, Commonwealth of Australia, Canberra.

CoA (Commonwealth of Australia), 2003b, *Government Response to the Productivity Commission Inquiry into the Implementation of Ecologically Sustainable Development by Commonwealth Departments and Agencies*, Productivity Commission, Commonwealth of Australia, Canberra, <www.pc.gov.au/projects/inquiry/esd?SQ_DESIGN_NAME=printer_friendly> (accessed 20 March 2009).

CoA (Commonwealth of Australia), 2004, *Ways to Improve Community Engagement. Working with Indigenous Knowledge in Natural Resource Management*, <www.environment.gov.au/indigenous/publications/pubs/community.pdf> (accessed 15 January 2009).

CoA (Commonwealth of Australia), 2007a, *Sustainability for Survival: Creating a Climate for Change. Inquiry into a Sustainability Charter*, House of Representatives Standing Committee on Environment and Heritage, Canberra, <www.aph.gov.au/house/committee/environ/charter/report.htm> (accessed 29 March 2008).

CoA (Commonwealth of Australia), 2007b, *A National Plan for Water Security*, Department of Prime Minister and Cabinet, Commonwealth of Australia, Canberra.

CoA (Commonwealth of Australia), 2008, *Carbon Pollution Reduction Scheme, Australia's Low Pollution Future*, Department of Climate Change, Commonwealth of Australia, Canberra.

COAG, 2007, *Commonwealth-State Ministerial Councils: A Compendium* <www.coag.gov.au/ministerial_councils/index.cfm> (accessed 2 October 2008).

Colborn, T, Dumanoski, D and Myers JP, 1996, *Our Stolen Future. Are We Threatening Our Fertility, Intelligence and Survival? – A Scientific Detective Story*, Little, Brown and Company, Boston.

Cole, HSD, Freeman, C, Jahoda, M and Pavitt, KLR, (eds), 1973, *Thinking About the Future. A Critique of the Limits to Growth*, Chatto & Windus for Sussex University Press, London.

Colebatch, HK, (ed), 2006, *Beyond the Policy Cycle: The Policy Process in Australia*, Allen & Unwin, Crows Nest.

Common, MS, 1995, *Sustainability and Policy: Limits to Economics*, Cambridge University Press, Cambridge.

Common, MS, 1997, 'Roles of ecology in ecological economics and sustainable development' in Klomp, N and Lunt, I, (eds), *Frontiers in Ecology*, Elsevier Science Limited, Oxford, UK, pp 323–334.

Commoner, B, 1971, *The Closing Circle. Nature, Man, and Technology*, Alfred A Knopf, New York.

Connell, D, 2007, *Water Politics in the Murray-Darling Basin*, The Federation Press, Sydney.

Connell, D and Colebatch, HK, 2006, 'Creating a focus for policy: the evolution of the Murray-Darling Basin' in Colebatch, HK, (ed), *Beyond the Policy Cycle: The Policy Process in Australia*, Allen & Unwin, Crows Nest, pp 91–111.

Connelly, S and Richardson, T, 2005, 'Value-driven SEA: time for an environmental justice perspective?', *Environmental Impact Assessment Review*, 25 (4): 391–409.

Connick, S and Innes, JE, 2003, 'Outcomes of collaborative water policy making: applying complexity thinking to evaluation', *Journal of Environmental Planning and Management*, 46 (2): 177–197.

Convention on Biological Diversity, 1992, <www.cbd.int/tk/material.shtml> (accessed 30 July 2008).

Cook, I, 2004, *Government and Democracy in Australia*, Oxford University Press, South Melbourne.

Cook, I, Walsh, M and Harwood, J, 2009, *Government and Democracy in Australia*, 2nd edn, Oxford University Press, South Melbourne.

Cooper, T, Bryer, TA and Meek, JW, 2006, 'Citizen-centered collaborative public management', *Public Administration Review*, 66 (Special Issue): 76–88.

Cork, S, (ed), 2009, *Brighter Prospects: Enhancing the Resilience of Australia*, Australia 21, <www.australia21.org.au/pdf/A21%20Brighter%20Prospects%20Report.pdf> (accessed 27 April 2009).

Cork, S, Eckersley, R and Walker, B, 2007, *Rapid and Surprising Change in Australia's Future. Anticipating and Preparing for Future Challenges and Opportunities on the Way to a Sustainable Australia*, Australia 21, <www.australia21.org.au/pdf/Tipping2007.pdf> (accessed 28 April 2009).

Cosier, P, 2009, 'Accounting for nature', Paper to the Fenner Conference on the Environment, Environmental Decision Making, 10–12 March, 2009, Canberra, <www.landscapelogic.org.au/Fenner/Cosier.doc> (accessed 12 April 2009).

Costanza, R, Daly, HE and Bartholomew, JA, 1991, 'Goals, agenda, and policy recommendations for ecological economics' in Costanza, R, (ed), *Ecological Economics. The Science and Management of Sustainability*, Columbia University Press, New York, pp 1–20.

Costar, B, 2006, 'The electoral system' in Parkin, A, Summers, J and Woodward, D, (eds), *Government, Politics, Power and Policy in Australia*, 8th edn, Pearson Education Australia, Frenchs Forest, pp 187–205.

Cotgrove, S, 1982, *Catastrophe or Cornucopia: The Environment, Politics and the Future*, John Wiley and Sons, Chichester, UK.

Covello, V and Sandman, PM, 2001, 'Risk communication: evolution and revolution' in Wolbarst, A, (ed), *Solutions to an Environment in Peril*, Johns Hopkins University Press, Baltimore, pp 164–178.

Coventry, H, 2001, 'Human resource management' in Aulich, C, Halligan, J and Nutley, S, (eds), *Australian Handbook of Public Sector Management*, Allen & Unwin, Crows Nest, pp 74–85.

Craig, D and Davis, M, 2005, 'Ethical relationships for biodiversity research and benefit-sharing with Indigenous peoples', *Macquarie Journal of International and Comparative Environmental Law*, 2 (2): 31–74.

Craig, D, Ehrlich, K, Ross, H and Lane, M, 1996, *Indigenous Participation in EIA*, Report prepared for the Commonwealth Environmental Protection Agency, Australia, May 1996.

Crone, HD, 1986, *Chemicals and Society. A Guide to the New Chemical Age*, Cambridge University Press, Cambridge.

Crosby, N, 1995, 'Citizens juries: one solution for difficult environmental problems' in Renn, O, Webler, T and Wiedemann, P, (eds), *Fairness and Competence in Citizen Participation*, Kluwer, Dordrecht, pp 157–174.

Crosby, N, 1999, 'Using citizens' juries: a process for environmental decision making' in Sexton, K, Marcus, AA, Easter, KW and Burkhardt, TD, (eds), *Making Better Environmental Decisions*, Island Press, Washington DC, pp 401–417.

Crosby, N, Kelly, JM and Schaefer, P, 1986, 'Citizens panels: a new approach to citizens participation', *Public Administration Review*, 46 (2): 170–178.

Crosby, N and Nethercut, D, 2005, 'Citizens juries: creating a trustworthy voice of the people' in Gastil, J and Levine, P, (eds), *The Deliberative Democracy Handbook: Strategies for Effective Civic Engagement in the Twenty-First Century*, Jossey-Bass, San Francisco, pp 111–119.

Crowley, K, 2001, 'Effective environmental federalism? Australia's Natural Heritage Trust', *Journal of Environmental Policy & Planning*, 3 (4): 255–272.

Crowley, K, 2004, 'Environmental policy and politics in Australia' in Fenna, A, (ed), *Australian Public Policy*, Pearson Education Australia, Frenchs Forest, pp 388–419.

Crutzen, PJ, 2002, 'Geology of mankind: the Anthropocene', *Nature*, 415 (3 January): 23.

CSIRO, 2008, *Water Availability in the Murray-Darling Basin. Summary of a Report to the Australian Government from the CSIRO Murray-Darling Basin Sustainable Yields Project*, CSIRO Australia, <www.csiro.au/files/files/pna0.pdf> (accessed 8 April 2009).

Cullen, P, 1998, 'The role of science and scientists in environmental conflicts', *Australian Journal of Environmental Management – Fenner Conference Supplementary Edition*, November: 55–59.

Cutter, SL, 1993, *Living with Risk. The Geography of Technological Hazards*, Edward Arnold, London.

D'Cruz, D, 2003, 'NGOs: chasing the corporate dollar', *Review*, 55 (3): 27–28.

Dale, P and McLaughlin, JD, 1988, *Land Information Management: An Introduction with Special Reference to Cadastral Problems in Developing Countries*, Oxford University Press, Oxford.

Dale, VH and English, MR, (eds), 1998, *Tools to Aid Environmental Decision-Making*, Springer, New York.

Daniels, PL and Moore, S, 2002, 'Approaches for quantifying the metabolism of physical economies Part 1: methodological overview', *Journal of Industrial Ecology*, 5 (4): 69–93.

Daniels, SE and Walker, GB, 1996, 'Collaborative learning: improving public deliberation in ecosystem-based management', *Environmental Impact Assessment Review*, 16 (2): 71–102.

Darby, A, 2006, 'Gunns, greenies and the law', *The Age*, 29 August, <www.theage.com.au/news/in-depth/gunns-greenies-and-the-law/2006/08/29/1156617279358.html> (accessed 30 April 2009).

Davies, A, 2006, 'Appeal on green ruling likely', *Sydney Morning Herald*, 29 November, <www.smh.com.au/news/national/appeal-on-green-ruling-likely/2006/11/28/1164476204759.html> (accessed 30 November 2008).

Davies, HTO, Nutley, SM and Smith, PC, (eds), 2000, *What Works? Evidence-Based Policy and Practice in Public Services*, The Policy Press, Bristol.

Davis, A, 2003, 'Whither mass media and power?', *Media Culture and Society*, 25 (5): 669–690.

Davison, G, 2005, 'Rural sustainability in historical perspective' in Cocklin, C and Dibden, J, (eds), *Sustainability and Change in Rural Australia*, UNSW Press, Sydney, pp 38–55.

Dawson, JI and Darst, RG, 2006, 'Meeting the challenge of permanent nuclear waste disposal in an expanding Europe: transparency, trust and democracy', *Environmental Politics*, 15 (4): 610–627.

DEC (Department of Environment and Conservation), 2006a, *New South Wales State of the Environment 2006*, DEC Sydney.

DEC (Department of Environment and Conservation), 2006b, *Who Cares About the Environment in 2006? A Survey of NSW People's Environmental Knowledge, Attitudes and Behaviours*, DEC, Sydney <www.environment.nsw.gov.au/community/whocares2006.htm> (accessed 24 February 2009).

DECC (Department of Environment and Climate Change), 2007a, *NSW Waste Avoidance and Recovery Strategy 2007*, DECC NSW, <www.environment.nsw.gov.au/resources/warr/07242_WARRoverview07.pdf> (accessed 10 January 2009).

DECC (Department of Environment and Climate Change), 2007b, *NSW Extended Producer Responsibility Priority Statement 2007*, DECC NSW, <www.environment.nsw.gov.au/resources/warr/2007592prioritystatement.pdf> (accessed 10 January 2009).

DEHAA (Department of Environment Heritage and Aboriginal Affairs), Government of South Australia, 1999, *Environmental Performance Measures. Signposts to the Future*, State of the Environment Reporting in South Australia, Position Paper for Public Comment.

Denniss, R, 2009, 'Left and right agree on carbon tax', *The Australian*, 18 February, <www.theaustralian.news.com.au/story/0,25197,25070069-7583,00.html> (accessed 20 February 2009).

DeSimone, LD and Popoff, F, with the World Business Council for Sustainable Development, 2000, *Eco-efficiency. The Business Link to Sustainable Development*, The MIT Press, Cambridge, Massachusetts.

DeSombre, ER, 2005, *The Global Environment and World Politics*, Continuum, London.

Deville, A and Harding, R, 1997, *Applying the Precautionary Principle*, The Federation Press, Sydney.

Devine-Wright, P, 2005, 'Beyond NIMBYism: towards an integrated framework for understanding public perceptions of wind energy', *Wind Energy*, 8 (2): 125–139.

Dey, C and Lenzen, M, 1996, 'Do we really care about climate change?', *Search*, 27 (9): 277.

Diamond, J, 2005, *Collapse. How Societies Choose to Fail or Succeed*, Viking (Penguin), New York.

Diesendorf, M, 1997, 'Principles of ecological sustainability' in Diesendorf, M and Hamilton, C, (eds), *Human Ecology, Human Economy. Ideas for an Ecologically Sustainable Future*, Allen & Unwin, St Leonards, Australia, pp 64–97.

Diesendorf, M, 2004, 'Comparison of employment potential of the coal and wind power industries', *International Journal of Environment, Workplace and Employment*, 1 (1): 82–90.

Diesendorf, M and Hamilton, C, 1997a, 'The ecologically sustainable development process in Australia' in Diesendorf, M and Hamilton, C, (eds), *Human Ecology, Human Economy. Ideas for an Ecologically Sustainable Future*, Allen & Unwin, St Leonards, Australia, pp 285–301.

Diesendorf, M and Hamilton, C, 1997b, 'Introduction' in Diesendorf, M and Hamilton, C, (eds), *Human Ecology, Human Economy*, Allen & Unwin, St Leonards, Australia, pp xvii-xxi.

Dietz, T, Ostrom, E and Stern, PC, 2003, 'The struggle to govern the commons', *Science*, 302 (5652): 1907–1912.

DLG (Department of Local Government), 2006, *Planning a Sustainable Future: A Department of*

Local Government Options Paper on Integrated Planning and Reporting for NSW Local Government, <www.dlg.nsw.gov.au/Files/Information/Integrated%20Planning.pdf> (accessed 26 February 2009).

Dobson, A, 2000, *Green Political Thought*, 3rd edn, Routledge, London.

Dobson, A and Eckersley, R, (eds), 2006a, *Political Theory and the Ecological Challenge*, Cambridge University Press, Cambridge.

Dobson, A and Eckersley, R, 2006b, 'Introduction' in Dobson, A and Eckersley, R, (eds), *Political Theory and the Ecological Challenge*, Cambridge University Press, Cambridge, pp 1-4.

Doppelt, B, 2003, *Leading Change toward Sustainability. A Change-Management Guide for Business, Government and Civil Society*, Greenleaf Publishing, Sheffield, UK.

Dore, J, Woodhill, J, Andrews, K and Keating, C, 2003, 'Sustainable regional development: lessons from Australian efforts' in Dovers, S and Wild River, S, (eds), *Managing Australia's Environment*, The Federation Press, Sydney, pp 154-180.

Douglas-Scott, S, 1996, 'Environmental rights in the European Union: participatory democracy or democratic deficit' in Boyle, A and Anderson, M, (eds), *Human Rights Approaches to Environmental Protection*, Oxford University Press, Oxford, pp 109-129.

Dovers, S, 1997, 'Sustainability: demands on policy', *Journal of Public Policy*, 16 (3): 303-318.

Dovers, S, 2001, 'Institutions for sustainability', *TELA: Environment, economy and society*, Issue 7, <http://een.anu.edu.au/download_files/een0101.pdf> (accessed 15 December 2008).

Dovers, S, 2003a, 'Processes and institutions for resource and environmental management: why and how to analyse?' in Dovers, S and Wild River, S, (eds), *Managing Australia's Environment*, The Federation Press, Sydney, pp 3-12.

Dovers, S, 2003b, 'Discrete, consultative policy processes: lessons from the National Conservation Strategy for Australia and National Strategy for Ecologically Sustainable Development' in Dovers, S and Wild River, S, (eds), *Managing Australia's Environment*, The Federation Press, Sydney, pp 133-153.

Dovers, S, 2005a, *Environment and Sustainability Policy: Creation, Implementation, Evaluation*, The Federation Press, Sydney.

Dovers, S, 2005b, 'Clarifying the imperative of integration research for sustainable environmental management', *Journal of Research Practice*, 1 (2): Article M2 <http://jrp.icaap.org/index.php/jrp/article/view/11/30> (accessed 11 January 2009).

Dovers, S, 2008, 'Policy and institutional reforms' in Lindenmayer, D, Dovers, S, Olson, MH and Morton, S, (eds), *Ten Commitments: Reshaping the Lucky Country's Environment*, CSIRO Publishing, Collingwood, pp 215-223.

Dovers, S and Gullett, W, 1999, 'Policy choice for sustainability: marketization, law and institutions' in Bosselmann, K and Richardson, BJ, (eds), *Environmental Justice and Market Mechanisms*, Kluwer Law International, London, pp 110-128.

Dovers, S and Handmer, JW, 1995, 'Ignorance, the precautionary principle, and sustainability', *Ambio*, 24 (2): 92-97.

Dovers, S and Wild River, S, (eds), 2003, *Managing Australia's Environment*, The Federation Press, Sydney.

Downes, D, 1996, 'Neo-corporatism and environmental policy', *Australian Journal of Political Science*, 31 (2): 175-190.

Downs, A, 1972, 'Up and down with ecology – the "issue-attention cycle"', *Public Interest*, 28 (1): 38-50.

Doyle, T, 2000, *Green Power. The Environment Movement in Australia*, UNSW Press, Sydney.

Doyle, T and Kellow, A, 1995, *Environmental Politics and Policy Making in Australia*, Macmillan, South Melbourne.

Doyle, T and McEachern, D, 2008, *Environment and Politics*, 3rd edn, Routledge, London.

Dresner, S, 2008, *The Principles of Sustainability*, 2nd edn, Earthscan Publications, London.

Dryzek, JS, 1990, *Discursive Democracy: Politics, Policy, and Political Science*, Cambridge University Press, Cambridge.

Dryzek, JS, 2000a, 'Discursive democracy vs liberal constitutionalism' in Saward, M, (ed), *Democratic Innovation: Deliberation, Representation and Association*, Routledge, London, pp 78–89.

Dryzek, JS, 2000b, *Deliberative Democracy and Beyond: Liberals, Critics, Contestations*, Oxford University Press, Oxford.

Dryzek, JS, 2005, *The Politics of the Earth. Environmental Discourses*, 2nd edn, Oxford University Press, Oxford.

Dryzek, JS, Downes, D, Hunold, C, Schlosberg, D and others, 2003, *Green States and Social Movements. Environmentalism in the United States, United Kingdom, Germany & Norway*, Oxford University Press, Oxford.

Duffy, B, 1996, *Working the System: A Guide for Citizens, Consumers and Communities*, Public Interest Advocacy Centre (Pluto Press), Sydney.

Dunphy, D, Griffiths, A and Benn, S, 2007, *Organizational Change for Corporate Sustainability: A Guide for Leaders and Change Agents of the Future*, 2nd edn, Routledge, London.

Dutfield, G, 2004, *Intellectual Property, Biogenetic Resources and Traditional Knowledge*, Earthscan Publications, London.

Dye, T, 1972, *Understanding Public Policy*, 5th edn, Prentice Hall, New Jersey.

Earle, TC and Siegrist, M, 2008, 'On the relation between trust and fairness in environmental risk management', *Risk Analysis*, 28 (5): 1395–1413.

East, J and Wood, M, 1998, 'LANDCARE GIS: Evaluating land management programs in Australia', *Environmental Monitoring and Assessment*, 50 (3): 201–216.

Eckersley, R, 2003, 'Politics and policy' in Dovers, S and Wild River, S, (eds), *Managing Australia's Environment*, The Federation Press, Sydney, pp 485–500.

Eckersley, R, 2005, 'Ecocentric discourses: problems and future prospects for nature advocacy' in Dryzek, JS and Schlosberg, D, (eds), *Debating the Earth. The Environmental Politics Reader*, 2nd edn, Oxford University Press, Oxford, pp 364–381.

Economou, NM, 1993, 'Accordism and the environment: the resource assessment commission and national environmental policy-making', *Australian Journal of Political Science*, 28 (3): 399–412.

Economy, E and Lieberthal, K, 2007, 'Scorched Earth. Will environmental risks in China overwhelm its opportunities?', *Harvard Business Review*, June 2007: 88–96.

Eden, S, 1998, 'Environmental issues: knowledge, uncertainty and the environment', *Progress in Human Geography*, 22 (3): 425–432.

EDO (Environmental Defender's Office NSW), 1992, *Environment and the Law*, CCH Australia Ltd, North Ryde.

EDO (Environmental Defender's Office NSW), 2006, 'Submission on the environmental assessment for the proposed Sydney desalination plant', <www.edo.org.au/edonsw/site/science_advices.php> (accessed 8 March 2009).

EDO (Environmental Defender's Office NSW), 2009, 'Gunns' legal action against The Wilderness Society settled', *EDO NSW Weekly Bulletin*, 18 March, No 602.

Egri, CP and Herman, S, 2000, 'Leadership in the North American environmental sector: values, leadership styles, and contexts of environmental leaders and their organizations', *Academy of Management Journal*, 43 (4): 571–604.

Ehrlich, PR, 1968, *The Population Bomb*, Ballantine Books, New York.

Ehrlich, P and Ehrlich, A, 1972, *Population, Resources, Environment: Issues in Human Ecology*, 2nd edn, WH Freeman and Company, New York.

Einsiedel, E, 2007, 'Editorial: Of publics and science', *Public Understanding of Science*, 16 (1): 5–6.

Einsiedel, EF, Jelsøe, E and Breck, T, 2001, 'Publics at the technology table: the Australian, Canadian and Danish consensus conferences on food biotechnology', *Public Understanding of Science*, 10 (1): 83–98.

Ekvall, T, 1999, 'Key methodological issues for life cycle inventory analysis of paper recycling', *Journal of Cleaner Production*, 7 (4): 281–294.

Ekvall, T and Finnveden, G, 2001, 'Allocation in ISO14041 – a critical review', *Journal of Cleaner Production*, 9 (3): 197–208.

Elkington, J, 1998, *Cannibals with Forks. The Triple Bottom Line of 21st Century Business*, New Society Publishers, Gabriola Island, BC, Canada.

Elliot, R 1995, 'Introduction' in Elliot, R, (ed), *Environmental Ethics*, Oxford University Press, Oxford, pp 1–20.

Elzen, B, Geels, FW and Green, K, (eds), 2004, *Systems Innovation and the Transition to Sustainability: Theory, Evidence and Policy*, Edward Elgar, Cheltenham, UK.

English, MR, Dale, VH, Van Riper-Geibig, C and Ramsey, WH, 1999, 'Overview' in Dale, VH and English, MR, (eds), *Tools to Aid Environmental Decision-Making*, Springer, New York, pp 1–31.

ESRC (Economic and Social Research Council, Global Environmental Change Programme), 2001, *Environmental Justice. Rights and Means to a Healthy Environment for All*, Special Briefing No 7, University of Sussex, UK.

eWater CRC, 2007, 'Catchment modelling toolkit', <www.toolkit.net.au/cgi-bin/WebObjects/toolkit.woa/wa/productDetails?productID=1000000> (accessed 2 December 2008).

Ewing, S, 2003, 'Catchment management arrangements ' in Dovers, S and Wild River, S, (eds), *Managing Australia's Environment*, The Federation Press, Sydney, pp 393–412.

Factor 10 Club, 1995, *Carnoules Declaration*, Factor 10 Club, Friedrich Schmidt-Bleek, Wuppertal Institute, Germany.

Falk, J, Hampton, G, Hodgkinson, A, Parker, K and others, 1993, *Social Equity and the Urban Environment. Report to the Commonwealth Environment Protection Agency*, Australian Government Publishing Service, Canberra.

Farrelly, E, 2006, 'Victories for the environment turn up the heat', *Sydney Morning Herald*, 6 December, <www.smh.com.au/news/opinion/victories-for-the-environment-turn-up-heat/2006/12/05/1165080944851.html> (accessed 19 April 2006), p 1.

Farrow, S and Toman, M, 1998, *Using Environmental Benefit-Cost Analysis to Improve Government Performance*, Discussion Paper 99–11, December 1998, Resources For the Future, Washington.

Fenna, A, 2004, *Australian Public Policy*, 2nd edn, Pearson Education Australia, Frenchs Forest.

Fiksel, J, 2006, 'Sustainability and resilience: toward a systems approach', *Sustainability: Science, Practice, & Policy*, 2 (2): 14–21.

Fischer, F, 1990, *Technocracy and the Politics of Expertise*, Sage Publications, Newbury Park, California.

Fischer, F, 2000, *Citizens, Experts, and the Environment. The Politics of Local Knowledge*, Duke University Press, Durham.

Fischer, TB, 2003, 'Strategic environmental assessment in post-modern times', *Environmental Impact Assessment Review*, 23 (2): 155–170.

Fischer, TB and Seaton, K, 2002, 'Strategic environmental assessment: Effective planning instrument or lost concept?', *Planning, Practice and Research*, 17 (1): 31–34.

Fisher, E, 2007, *Risk Regulation and Administrative Constitutionalism*, Hart Publishing, Oxford.

Fisher, E and Harding, R, 2006, 'The precautionary principle and administrative constitutionalism: the development of frameworks for applying the precautionary principle' in Fisher, E, Jones, J and Schomberg, R von, (eds), *Implementing the Precautionary Principle. Perspectives and Prospects*, Edward Elgar, Cheltenham, UK, pp 113–136.

Fisher, E, Jones, J and Schomberg, R von, (eds), 2006, *Implementing the Precautionary Principle. Perspectives and Prospects*, Edward Elgar, Cheltenham, UK.

Fisher, E, Jones, J and Schomberg, R von, 2006, 'Implementing the precautionary principle: perspectives and prospects' in Fisher, E, Jones, J and Schomberg, R von, (eds), 2006, *Implementing the Precautionary Principle. Perspectives and Prospects*, Edward Elgar, Cheltenham, UK, pp 1–16.

Flannery, T, 2005, *The Weather Makers. The History and Future Impact of Climate Change*, Text Publishing, Melbourne.

Flannery, T, 2008, 'Now or never. A sustainable future for Australia?', *Quarterly Essay*, Issue 31, Black Inc, Melbourne, pp 1–66.

Fletcher, TD and Taylor, AC, 2007, 'Estimating lifecycle costs of structural measures that improve urban water quality', *Australian Journal of Water Resources*, 11 (1): 79–92.

Fletcher, W, Chubb, C, McCrea, J, Caputi, N and others, 2005, Western Rock Lobster Fishery, ESD Report Series No. 4, Department of Fisheries, Western Australia, <www.fish.wa.gov.au/docs/esd/esd004/esd0004.pdf> (accessed 6 March 2009).

Font, J, 2003, 'Local participation in Spain: beyond associative democracy' in Font, J, (ed), *Public Participation and Local Governance*, Institut de Ciències Polítiques i Socials, Barcelona, pp 125–145.

Foran, B and Gurran, N, 2008, 'Population' in Lindenmayer, D, Dovers, S, Olson, MH and Morton, S, (eds), *Ten Commitments: Reshaping the Lucky Country's Environment*, CSIRO Publishing, Collingwood, pp 169–177.

Foran, B, Lenzen, M and Dey, C, 2004, 'Using input-output analysis to develop "Triple Bottom Line accounts" for the Australian economy' in Ortega, E and Ulgiati, S, (eds), Proceedings of IV Biennial International Workshop 'Advancing Energy Studies', Unicamp, Campinas, SP, Brazil, June 2004, pp 373–388, <www.unicamp.br/fea/ortega/energy/B.Foran.pdf> (accessed 17 March 2009).

Forrester, J and Cinderby, S, 2005, 'Geographic information systems for participation' in Leach, M, Scoones, I and Wynne, B, (eds), *Science and Citizens. Globalization & the Challenge of Engagement (Claiming Citizenship: Rights, Participation & Accountability)*, Zed Books, London, pp 232–236.

Franklin, NE, 1992, 'Initiative and referendum: participatory democracy or rolling back the state?' in Munro-Clark, M, (ed), *Citizen Participation in Government*, Hale and Iremonger, Sydney, pp 55–69.

Fung, A, 2003, 'Survey article: recipes for public spheres: eight institutional design choices and their consequences', *Journal of Political Philosophy*, 11 (3): 338–367.

Fung, A, 2006, 'Varieties of participation in complex governance', *Public Administration Review*, 66 (Supplement, November 2006): 66–75.

Fung, A and Wright, EO, (eds), 2003, *Deepening Democracy: Institutional Innovation in Empowered Participatory Governance*, Verso, London.

Funtowicz, SO, Martinez-Alier, J, Munda, G and Ravetz JR, 1999, 'Information tools for environmental policy under conditions of complexity', *Environmental Issues Series*, No 9, European Environment Agency, Luxembourg.

Funtowicz, SO and Ravetz, JR, 1991, 'A new scientific methodology for global environmental issues' in Costanza, R, (ed), *Ecological Economics: The Science and Management of Sustainability*, Columbia University Press, New York, pp 137–152.

Furby, L, Slovic, P, Fischhoff, B and Gregory, R, 1995, 'Public perceptions of electric power transmission lines' in O'Riordan, T, (ed), *Readings in Environmental Psychology. Perceiving Environmental Risks*, Academic Press, London, pp 139–163.

Garnaut, R, 2008, *The Garnaut Climate Change Review. Final Report*, Cambridge University Press, Cambridge.

Gastil, J and Keith, WM, 2005, 'A nation that (sometimes) likes to talk: a brief history of public deliberation in the United States' in Gastil, J and Levine, P, (eds), *The Deliberative Democracy Handbook: Strategies for Effective Civic Engagement in the Twenty-First Century*, Jossey-Bass, San Francisco, pp 3–19.

Gastil, J and Levine, P, (eds), 2005, *The Deliberative Democracy Handbook: Strategies for Effective Civic Engagement in the Twenty-First Century*, Jossey-Bass, San Francisco.

Geels, FW, Elzen, B and Green, K, 2004, 'General introduction: systems innovation and transitions to sustainability' in Elzen, B, Geels, FW and Green, K, (eds), *Systems Innovation and the Transition to Sustainability: Theory, Evidence and Policy*, Edward Elgar, Cheltenham, pp 1–16.

Giddens, A, 1999, 'Risk and responsibility', *The Modern Law Review*, 62 (1): 1–10.

Gilpin, A, 1978, *Air Pollution*, 2nd edn, University of Queensland Press, St Lucia, Queensland.

Gilpin, A, 1980, *The Australian Environment. 12 Controversial Issues*, Sun Books, Melbourne.

Gilpin, A, 1995, *Environmental Impact Assessment (EIA): Cutting Edge for the Twenty first Century*, Cambridge University Press, Cambridge.

Glasson, J, 1995, 'Environmental Impact Assessment: The next steps?' *Built Environment*, 20 (4): 277–279.

Glasson, J, Therivel, R and Chadwick, A, 1994, *Introduction to Environmental Impact Assessment*, UCL Press, London.

Glicken, J, 2000, 'Getting stakeholder participation "right": a discussion of participatory processes and possible pitfalls', *Environmental Science & Policy*, 3 (6): 305–310.

Glover, D, 2006, 'Ideas with currency', *The Weekend Australian*, 13–14 May.

Goldie, J, Douglas, B and Furnass, B, (eds), 2005, *In Search of Sustainability*, CSIRO Publishing, Collingwood, Victoria.

Gończ, E, Skirke, U, Kleizen, H and Barer, M, 2007, 'Increasing the rate of sustainable change: a call for a redefinition of the concept and the model for its implementation', *Journal of Cleaner Production*, 15 (6): 525–537.

Goodin, RE and Dryzek, J, 2006, 'Deliberative impacts: the macro-political uptake of mini-publics', *Politics and Society*, 34 (2): 219–244.

Goodman, JC, 2005, 'What is a think tank?', National Center for Policy Analysis, <www.ncpa.org/pub/special/20051220-sp.html> (accessed 20 February 2009).

Gore, A, 1992, *Earth in the Balance: Ecology and the Human Spirit*, Houghton Mifflin, Boston.

Gough, J and Hooper, G, 2003, 'Communicating about risk issues', <www.europe.canterbury.ac.nz/conferences/tech2004/tpp/Gough%20and%20Hooper_paper.pdf> (accessed 8 March 2009).

Grafton, RQ and Robin, L, 2005a, 'Towards an understanding of the environment' in Grafton, RQ, Robin, L and Wasson, RJ, (eds), *Understanding the Environment. Bridging the Disciplinary Divides*, UNSW Press, Sydney, pp 1–7.

Grafton, RQ and Robin, L, 2005b, 'Bridging the divides' in Grafton, RQ, Robin, L and Wasson, RJ, (eds), *Understanding the Environment. Bridging the Disciplinary Divides*, UNSW Press, Sydney, pp 184–201.

Greene, D and Ryan, C, 1996, 'Life cycle assessment: Uses, benefits and difficulties' in *Tracking Progress: Linking Environment and Economy Through Indicators and Accounting Systems Conference Papers*, 1996 Australian Academy of Science Fenner Conference on the Environment, Institute of Environmental Studies, The University of New South Wales, Sydney, 30 September to 3 October 1996.

Greenpeace, 2007, *Greenpeace Asia Pacific Annual Review 07*, <www.greenpeace.org/australia/resources/reports/financial/annual-review-2007> (accessed 2 December 2008).

Greenpeace International, 2009, 'About Greenpeace', <www.greenpeace.org/australia/resources/faqs/about-greenpeace#abt_gp_q11> (accessed 18 February 2009).

Grenier, L, 1998, *Working With Indigenous Knowledge. A Guide for Researchers*, International Development Research Centre, <www.idrc.ca/en/ev-28703-201-1-DO_TOPIC.html> (accessed 29 July 2008).

Grey, G, 2006, 'Health policy' in Parkin, A, Summers, J and Woodward, D, (eds), *Government, Politics, Power and Policy in Australia*, 8th edn, Pearson Education Australia, Frenchs Forest, pp 497–522.

GRI (Global Reporting Initiative), 2006, *Sustainability Reporting Guidelines*, <www.globalreporting.org/NR/rdonlyres/A1FB5501-B0DE-4B69-A90027DD8A4C2839/0/G3_GuidelinesENG.pdf> (accessed 6 May 2008).

Griffiths, E, 2000, 'Integrating SoERs and management plans – myth or reality?', *State of the Environment Conference 2000: working towards sustainable communities*, 3–5 May 2000, Novotel Opal Cove Resort, Coffs Harbour, NSW, <www.isf.uts.edu.au/publications/griffiths2000integratingsoers.pdf > (accessed 19 March 2009).

Grin, J, 2006, 'Reflexive modernization as a governance issue – or designing and shaping re-structuration' in Voß, J-P, Bauknecht, D and Kemp, R, (eds), *Reflexive Governance for Sustainable Development*, Edward Elgar, Cheltenham, pp 57–81.

Groot, RS de, Wilson, MA and Boumans, RMJ, 2002, 'A typology for the classification, description and valuation of ecosystem functions, goods and services', *Ecological Economics*, 41 (3): 393–408.

Gross, C, 2007, 'Community perspectives of wind energy in Australia: the application of a justice and community fairness framework to increase social acceptance', *Energy Policy*, 35 (5): 2727–2736.

Grübler, A, Nakicenovic, N, Alcamo, J, Davis, G and others, 2004, 'Emissions scenarios: a final response', *Energy and Environment*, 15(1): 11–24.

Grundahl, J, 1995, 'Consensus conferences at the Danish Board of Technology' in Joss, S and Durant, J, (eds), *Public Participation in Science: The Role of Consensus Conferences in Europe*, Science Museum, London, pp 31–40.

Grunwald, A, 2007, 'Working towards sustainable development in the face of uncertainty and incomplete knowledge', *Journal of Environmental Policy & Planning*, 9 (3): 245–262.

Gumley, W, 2005, 'Under the microscope: biodiversity protection in Australia', *Law Institute Journal*, 79 (7): 58–61.

Gunningham, N and Cornwall, A, 1994, 'Legislating the right to know', *Environment Planning and Law Journal*, 11 (4): 274–288.

Gunningham, N, Kagan, RA and Thorton, D, 2003, *Shades of Green: Business, Regulation and Environment*, Stanford University Press, Stanford.

Gutmann, A and Thompson, D, 1996, *Democracy and Disagreement*, The Belknap Press, Cambridge, Massachusetts.

Hacking, T and Guthrie, P, 2008, 'A framework for clarifying the meaning of triple bottom-line, integrated, and sustainability assessment', *Environmental Impact Assessment Review*, 28 (2–3): 73–89.

Hajer, M, 1993, 'Discourse coalitions and the institutionalization of practice: The case of acid rain in Britain' in Fischer, F and Forester, J, (eds), *The Argumentative Turn in Policy Analysis and Planning*, Duke University Press, Durham, North Carolina, pp 43–76.

Hajer, M, 2005a, 'Coalitions, practices, and meaning in environmental politics: from acid rain to BSE' in Howarth, D and Torfing, J, (eds), *Discourse Theory in European Politics*, Palgrave Macmillan, London, pp 297–315.

Hajer, M, 2005b, 'Rebuilding ground zero. The politics of performance', *Planning Theory and Practice*, 6 (4): 445–464.

Hamilton, C, 1997, 'Foundations of ecological economics' in Diesendorf, M and Hamilton, C, (eds), *Human Ecology, Human Economy*, Allen & Unwin, St Leonards, Australia, pp 35–63.

Hamilton, C, 2001, *Running from the Storm: The Development of Climate Change Policy in Australia*, UNSW Press, Sydney.

Hamilton, C, 2003, *Growth Fetish*, Allen & Unwin, Crows Nest, New South Wales.

Hamilton, C, 2007, *Scorcher: The Dirty Politics of Climate Change*, Black Inc. Agenda, Melbourne.

Hamilton, C and Maddison, S, (eds), 2007, *Silencing Dissent: How the Australian Government Is Controlling Public Opinion and Stifling Debate*, Allen & Unwin, Crows Nest.

Hamilton, JT, 2006, 'Environmental equity and the siting of hazardous waste facilities in OECD countries' in Serret, Y and Johnstone, N, (eds), *The Distributional Effects of Environmental Policy*, OECD and Edward Elgar, Cheltenham UK, pp 227–285.

Hammer, C, 2008, 'Swipe at WWF over coal alliance', *The Age*, 17 April, <www.theage.com.au/news/national/swipe-at-wwf-over-coal-alliance/2008/04/16/1208025283455.html> (accessed 15 October 2008).

Hanley, N, 1992, 'Are there environmental limits to cost benefit analysis?', *Environmental and Resource Economics*, 2 (1): 33–59.

Hardin, G, 1968, 'The tragedy of the commons', *Science* 162 (3859): 1243–1248.

Harding, R, 1996, *Sustainability: Principles to Practice. Outcomes*, Fenner Conference on the Environment 1994, Department of the Environment, Sport and Territories, Canberra.

Harding, R and Fisher, E, (eds), 1999, *Perspectives on the Precautionary Principle*, The Federation Press, Sydney.

Harding, R and Traynor, D, 2003, 'Informing ESD: State of the environment reporting' in Dovers, S and Wild River, S, (eds), *Managing Australia's Environment*, The Federation Press, Sydney, pp 181–226.

Hargrove, EC, 1989, *Foundations of Environmental Ethics*, Prentice Hall, New Jersey.

Hargroves, K and Smith, MH, (eds), 2005, *The Natural Advantage of Nations. Business Opportunities, Innovation and Governance in the 21st Century*, Earthscan Publications, London.

Harremoës, P, Gee, D, MacGarvin, M, Stirling, A and others, (eds), 2002, *The Precautionary Principle in the 20th Century. Late Lessons from Early Warnings*, Earthscan Publications, London.

Harris, G, 2007, *Seeking Sustainability in an Age of Complexity*, Cambridge University Press, Cambridge.

Harris, S and Throsby, D, 1998, 'The ESD process: background, implementation and aftermath' in Hamilton, C and Throsby, D, (eds), *The ESD Process. Evaluating a Policy Experiment*, Papers from a Workshop organised jointly by the Academy of the Social Sciences in Australia and the Graduate Program in Public Policy, ANU, Canberra, 28–29 October 1997, pp 1–19.

Hart, P't and Vromen, A, 2008, 'A new era for think tanks in public policy? International trends, Australian realities', *The Australian Journal of Public Administration*, 67 (2): 135–148.

Hartley, N and Wood, C, 2005, 'Public participation in Environmental Impact Assessment: implementing the Aarhus Convention', *Environmental Impact Assessment Review*, 25 (4): 319–340.

Harvey, N, 1998, *Environmental Impact Assessment: Procedures, Practice, and Prospects in Australia*, Oxford University Press, Australia.

Hatfield-Dodds, S, 2006, 'The catchment care principle: A new equity principle for environmental policy, with advantages for efficiency and adaptive governance', *Ecological Economics*, 56 (3): 373–385.

Hatfield-Dodds, S, Turner, G, Schandl, H and Doss, T, 2008, Growing the Green Collar Economy: Skills and Labour Challenges in Reducing Our Greenhouse Emissions and National Environmental Footprint, Report to the Dusseldorp Skills Forum, June 2008. CSIRO Sustainable Ecosystems, Canberra.

Hawken, P, Lovins, AB and Lovins, LH, 1999, *Natural Capitalism. The Next Industrial Revolution*, Earthscan Publications, London.

Hay, P, 2002, *Main Currents in Western Environmental Thought*, UNSW Press, Sydney.

Head, B, 2007, 'Community engagement – participation on whose terms?', *Australian Journal of Political Science*, 42 (3): 441–454.

Henderson, C and O'Loughlin, L, 1996, 'The energy roundtable farce', *Chain Reaction*, 76 (December): 7.

Hendriks, CM, 2002, 'Institutions of deliberative democratic processes and interest groups: roles, tensions and incentives', *Australian Journal of Public Administration*, 61 (1): 64–75.

Hendriks, CM, 2005a, 'Participatory storylines and their impact on deliberative forums', *Policy Sciences*, 38 (4): 1–20.

Hendriks, CM, 2005b, 'Consensus conferences and planning cells: lay citizen deliberations' in Gastil, J and Levine, P, (eds), *The Deliberative Democracy Handbook: Strategies for Effective Civic Engagement in the 21st Century*, Jossey-Bass, San Francisco, pp 80–110.

Hendriks, CM, 2006, 'When the forum meets interest politics: strategic uses of public deliberation', *Politics and Society*, 34 (4): 1–32.

Hendriks, CM, 2008, 'On inclusion and network governance: the democratic disconnect of Dutch energy transitions ', *Public Administration*, 86 (4): 1009–1031.

Hendriks, CM and Carson, L, 2008, 'Can the market help the forum? Negotiating the commercialization of deliberative democracy', *Policy Sciences*, 41 (4): 293–313.

Hendriks, CM and Grin, J, 2007, 'Contextualizing reflexive governance: the politics of Dutch transitions to sustainability', *Journal of Environmental Policy & Planning*, 9 (3): 333–350.

Hendriks, CM, Dryzek, JS and Hunold, C, 2007, 'Turning up the heat: partisanship in deliberative innovation', *Political Studies*, 55 (2): 362–383.

Hennessy, K, Lucas, C, Nicholls, N, Bathols, J and others, 2005, *Climate Change Impacts on Fire-weather in South-east Australia*, CSIRO, <www.cmar.csiro.au/e-print/open/hennessykj_2005b:pdf> (accessed 31 March 2009).

Henry, D, 2006, 'Landcare: reconciling agriculture and conservation', paper presented to *International Landcare Conference*, 9 October, Melbourne, <www.acfonline.org.au/articles/news.asp?news_id=967> (accessed 19 February 2009).

Heywood, A, 1997, *Politics*, Macmillan, Basingstoke, UK.

Hillary, R, 1998, 'Environmental auditing: concepts, methods and developments', *International Journal of Auditing*, 2 (1): 71–85.

Hindmarsh, R and Matthews, C, 2008, 'Deliberative speak at the turbine face: community engagement, wind farms and renewable energy transitions in Australia', *Journal of Environmental Policy and Planning*, 10 (3): 217–232.

Hobson, K, 2002, 'Competing discourses of sustainable consumption: does the "rationalisation of lifestyles" make sense?', *Environmental Politics*, 11 (2): 95–120.

Holland, I, 2002a, 'Consultation, constraints and norms: the case of nuclear waste', *Australian Journal of Public Administration*, 61 (1): 76–86.

Holland, I, 2002b, 'Waste not want not? Australia and the politics of high-level nuclear waste', *Australian Journal of Political Science*, 37 (2): 283–301.

Holliday Jr, CO, Schmidheiny, S and Watts, P, 2002, *Walking the Talk. The Business Case for Sustainable Development*, Greenleaf Publishing, Sheffield, UK.

Holling, CS, 2001, 'Understanding the complexity of economic, ecological, and social systems', *Ecosystems*, 4 (5): 390–405.

Hope, J, 2008, *Biobazaar: The Open Source Revolution and Biotechnology*, Harvard University Press, Boston.

Hortensius, D and Barthel, M, 1997, 'Beyond 14001. An Introduction to the ISO 14000 series' in Sheldon, C, (ed), *ISO 14001 and Beyond. Environmental Management Systems in the Real World*, Greenleaf Publishing, Sheffield, England, pp 19–44.

Horton, D, 2004, 'Local environmentalism and the Internet', *Environmental Politics*, 13 (4): 734–753.

Howe, J, 2008, *Crowdsourcing. Why the Power of the Crowd is Driving the Future of Business*, Crown Business (Random House), New York.

Howes, M, 2001, 'What's your poison? The Australian National Pollutant Inventory versus the US Toxics Release Inventory', *Australian Journal of Political Science*, 36 (3): 529–552.

Howes, M, 2005, *Politics and the Environment: Risk and the Role of Government and Industry*, Allen & Unwin, Crows Nest, NSW.

Howlett, M and Ramesh, M, 2003, *Studying Public Policy: Policy Cycles and Policy Subsystems*, 2nd edn, Oxford University Press, Toronto.

Huggies Nappies, 2008, 'Huggies nappies and the environment', <www.huggies.com.au/OurProducts/TheEnvironment.asp> (accessed 14 March 2009).

Hunn, E, 1993, 'What is traditional ecological knowledge? in Williams, NM and Baines, G, (eds), *Traditional Ecological Knowledge. Wisdom for Sustainable Development*, Centre for Resource and Environmental Studies, Australian National University, Canberra, pp 13–15.

Hunt, S, Frewer, LJ and Shepherd, R, 1999, 'Public trust in sources of information about radiation risks in the UK', *Journal of Risk Research*, 2 (2): 167–180.

Hutchins, B and Lester, L, 2006, 'Environmental protest and tap-dancing with the media in the information age', *Media Culture and Society*, 28 (3): 433–451.

IAP2, 2005, 'The Brisbane Declaration', International Association for Public Participation, <www.iap2.org.au/resources/cid/24/parent/0/t/resources> (accessed 6 Jan 2009).

IAP2, 2007a, *IAP2 Spectrum of Public Participation*, International Association for Public Participation

(IAP2) <http://iap2.org/associations/4748/files/IAP2%20Spectrum_vertical.pdf> (accessed 6 January 2009).

IAP2, 2007b, *IAP2 Core Values of Public Participation*, International Association for Public Participation (IAP2), <www.iap2.org/associations/4748/files/CoreValues.pdf> (accessed 25 March 2009).

IISD (International Institute for Sustainable Development), 2007, GEO Resource Book – A Training Manual on Integrated Environmental Assessment and Training: Modules Overview, United Nations Environment Programme. <www.iisd.org/pdf/2007/geo_resource.pdf > (accessed 28 August 2008).

IPCC (Intergovernmental Panel on Climate Change), 2007, *Climate Change 2007: Synthesis Report. Summary for Policymakers*, <www.ipcc.ch/> (accessed 28 February 2009).

Irvin, RA and Stansbury, J, 2004, 'Citizen participation in decision making: is it worth the effort?', *Public Administration Review*, 64 (1): 55–65.

Irwin, A, 1995, *Citizen Science. A Study of People, Expertise and Sustainable Development*, Routledge, London.

Irwin, A, 2001, 'Constructing the scientific citizen: science and democracy in the biosciences', *Public Understanding of Science*, 10 (1): 1–18.

Irwin, F and Ranganathan, J, 2007, *Restoring Nature's Capital. An Action Agenda to Sustain Ecosystem Services*, World Resources Institute, Washington DC.

ISO (International Organization for Standardization), 2006, Environmental Management – Life Cycle Assessment – Principles and Framework, 14040:2006, (2nd edn).

Ison, R, Röling, N and Watson, D, 2007, 'Challenges to science and society in the sustainable management and use of water: investigating the role of social learning', *Environmental Science & Policy*, 10 (6): 499–511.

IUCN, UNEP and WWF, 1980, *World Conservation Strategy. Living Resource Conservation for Sustainable Development*, International Union for the Conservation of Nature and Natural Resources.

Ivanova, G, 2005, 'Queenslander consumers' willingness to pay for electricity from renewable energy sources' Ecological Economics in Action, ANZSEE 2005 biennial Conference 11–13 December Massey University Palmerston North, New Zealand, <www.anzsee.org/decconferpapers.asp> (accessed 19 February 2009).

Jacques, PJ, Dunlap, RE and Freeman, M, 2008, 'The organisation of denial: conservative think tanks and environmental scepticism', *Environmental Politics*, 17 (3): 349–385.

Jaeger, CC, Renn, O, Rosa, EA and Webler, T, 2001, *Risk, Uncertainty, and Rational Action*, Earthscan Publications, London.

Jakeman, AJ and Letcher, RA, 2003, 'Integrated assessment and modelling: features, principles and examples of catchment management', *Environmental Modelling and Software*, 18 (6): 491–501.

James, S and Lahti, T, 2004, *The Natural Step for Communities: How Cities and Towns Can Change to Sustainable Practices*, New Society Publishers, Gabriola Island, BC.

Jamieson, D, 1998, 'Sustainability and beyond', *Ecological Economics*, 24 (2–3): 183–192.

Jamieson, D, 2007, 'Justice: the heart of environmentalism' in Sandler, R and Pezzullo, PC, (eds), *Environmental Justice and Environmentalism. The Social Challenge to the Environmental Movement*, The MIT Press, Cambridge, Massachusetts, pp 85–101.

Jamison, A, 2001, *The Making of Green Knowledge. Environmental Politics and Cultural Transformation*, Cambridge University Press, Cambridge.

Janesch, D, 1997, *The Politics of Australia*, 2nd edn, Macmillan Education Australia, Melbourne.

Janssen, R, 2001, 'On the use of multi-criteria analysis in environmental impact assessment in the Netherlands', *Journal of Multi-Criteria Decision Analysis*, 10 (2): 101–109.

Jantsch, E, 1972, 'Towards interdisciplinarity and transdisciplinarity in education and innovation' in Apostel, L, Berger, G and Michaud, G, (eds), *Interdisciplinarity: Problems of Teaching and Research in Universities*, Center for Educational Research and Innovation of OECD, pp 97–121.

Jarvie, W, 2008, 'Working differently to make a difference in Indigenous communities', *Public Administration Today*, 14 (Jan/Mar): 5–13.

Jasanoff, S, 1997, 'Civilisation and madness: the great BSE scare of 1996', *Public Understanding of Science*, 6 (3): 221–232.

Jay, S, Jones, C, Slinn, P and Wood, C, 2007, 'Environmental impact assessment: retrospect and prospect', *Environmental Impact Assessment Review*, 27 (4): 287–300.

Jensen-Lee, C, 2001, 'The future of environmental issues on the mainstream political agenda', *Australian Journal of Social Issues*, 36 (2): 139–151.

Jobert, A, Laborgne, P and Mimler, S, 2007, 'Local acceptance of wind energy: factors of success identified in French and German case studies', *Energy Policy*, 35 (5): 2751–2760.

Johnson, BB, 1999, 'Exploring dimensionality in the origins of hazard-related trust', *Journal of Risk Research*, 2 (4): 325–354.

Johnson, M, 1992, 'Research on traditional environmental knowledge: its development and its role' in Johnson, M, (ed), *Lore: Capturing Traditional Environmental Knowledge*, Dene Cultural Institute and International Development Research Centre, Ottawa, pp 3–22.

Johnston, S, Gostelow, P, Jones, E and Fourikis, R, 1999, *Engineering and Society: An Australian Perspective*, 2nd edn, Addison Wesley, South Melbourne.

Jordan, A, 2008, 'The governance of sustainable development: taking stock and looking forwards', *Environment and Planning C: Government and Policy*, 26 (1): 17–33.

Jordan, A, Wurzel, RKW and Zito, AR, 2003, '"New" instruments of environmental governance: patterns and pathways of change' in Jordan, A, Wurzel, RKW and Zito, AR, (eds), *'New' Instruments of Environmental Governance? National Experiences and Prospects*, Frank Cass, London, pp 3–24.

Jørgensen, T, 1995, 'Consensus conferences in the health case sector' in Joss, S and Durant, J, (eds), *Public Participation in Science: The Role of Consensus Conferences in Europe*, Science Museum, London, pp 17–29.

Joss, S, 2000, *Die Konsensuskonferenz in Theorie und Anwendung*, Leitfaden Bürgerbeteiligung, Akademie für Technikfolgenabschätzung, Stuttgart.

Joss, S and Bellucci, S, 2002, *Participatory Technology Assessment: European Perspectives*, Centre for the Study of Democracy, London.

Joubert, AR, Leiman, A, de Klerk, HM, Katua, S and others, 1997, 'Fynbos (fine bush) vegetation and the supply of water: a comparison of multi-criteria decision analysis and cost-benefit analysis', *Ecological Economics*, 22 (2): 123–140.

Kajikawa, Y, 2008, 'Research core and framework of sustainability science', *Sustainability Science*, 3 (2): 215–239.

Kao-Cushing K, 2000, 'Why environmental management system standards matter', *Pacific Institute Report*, Fall, pp 6–10, <www.pacinst.org/publications/newsletter/fall_2000_newsletter.pdf> (accessed 29 September 2008).

Kasemir, B, Jaeger, CC and Jäger, J, 2003a, 'Citizen participation in sustainability assessments' in Kasemir, B, Jäger, J, Jaeger, CC and Gardner, MT, (eds), *Public Participation in Sustainability Science. A Handbook*, Cambridge University Press, Cambridge, pp 3–36.

Kasemir, B, Jäger, J, Jaeger, CC and Gardner, MT, (eds), 2003b, *Public Participation in Sustainability Science: A Handbook*, Cambridge University Press, Cambridge.

Kashefi, E and Mort, M, 2004, 'Grounded citizens' juries: a tool for health activism?', *Health Expectations*, 7 (4): 290–302.

Kates, RW, Clark, WC, Corell, R, Hall, JM and others, 2001, 'Sustainability science', *Science*, 292 (5517): 641–642.

Kellow, A, 1996, 'Thinking globally and acting federally: intergovernmental relations and environmental protection in Australia' in Holland, KM, Morton, FL and Galligan, B (eds), *Federalism and the Environment*, Greenwood Press, Westport, pp 135–156.

Kellow, A, 2007, *Science and Public Policy: The Virtuous Corruption of Virtual Environmental Science*, Edward Elgar Publishing Limited, UK.

Kellow, A, 2008, 'All in a good cause: framing science for public policy', Brisbane Club Lecture Series, Institute of Public Affairs, 1 May 2008, <www.ipa.org.au/library/publication/1210830063_document_aynsley_kellow_brisbane_club_speech.pdf> (accessed 20 March 2009).

Kemp, R and Loorbach, D, 2006, 'Transition management: a reflexive governance approach' in Voß, J-P, Bauknecht, D and Kemp, R, (eds), *Reflexive Governance for Sustainable Development*, Edward Elgar, Cheltenham, pp 103–130.

Kemp, V, Stark, A and Tantram, J, 2004, *To Whose Profit? (II): Evolution – Building Sustainable Corporate Strategy*, WWF-UK, <http://assets.wwf.org.br/downloads/to_whose_profit___evolution___completa.pdf> (accessed 30 December 2008).

Ker, P and Arup, T, 2009, 'Record low inflows to the Murray', *The Age*, 8 April, <www.theage.com.au/national/record-low-inflows-to-the-murray-20090407-9zor.html?page=-1> (accessed 8 April 2009).

Kerr, M, 2007, 'Kurnell desalination plant, private members statement', Parliament of NSW, Legislative Assembly, 31 May 2007, <www.parliament.nsw.gov.au/prod/parlment/hansart.nsf/V3Key/LA20070531040> (accessed 30 November 2008).

Khan, U, (ed), 1999, *Participation Beyond the Ballot Box: European Case Studies in State-Citizen Political Dialogue*, UCL Press, London.

Kickert, WJM, Klijn, E-H and Koppenjan, JFM, (eds), 1997, *Managing Complex Networks: Strategies for the Public Sector*, Sage, London.

Kim, KG, 1994, 'Learning from other cultures' in Cosgrove, L, Evans, DG and Yencken, D, (eds), *Restoring the Land*, Melbourne University Press, Melbourne, p 59–75.

Kingdon, JW, 2003, *Agendas, Alternatives, and Public Policies*, 2nd edn, Harper Collins, New York.

Kinnaird, M, 1990, 'The environmental impact statement: Its uses and abuses', paper to the *1990 National Engineering Conference*, Canberra, April 1990.

Kjær, AM, 2004, *Governance*, Polity, Cambridge.

Klauer, B, 2000, 'Ecosystem prices: activity analysis applied to ecosystems', *Ecological Economics*, 33 (3): 473–486.

Klinke, A, Dreyer, M, Renn, O, Stirling, A and others, 2006, 'Precautionary risk regulation in European governance', *Journal of Risk Research*, 9 (4): 373–392.

Knudtson, P and Suzuki, D, 1992, *Wisdom of the Elders*, Allen & Unwin, St Leonards, NSW.

Kolk, A, 2004, 'A decade of sustainability reporting: Developments and significance', *International Journal of Environment and Sustainable Development*, 3 (1): 51–64.

Komiyama, H and Takeuchi, K, 2006, 'Sustainability science: building a new discipline', *Sustainability Science*, 1 (1): 1–6.

Kooiman, J, (ed), 1993, *Modern Governance: New Government-Society Interactions*, Sage, London.

Koppenjan, J and Klijn, E-H, 2004, *Managing Uncertainties in Networks – a Network Approach to Problem Solving and Decision Making*, Routledge, London.

Korfmacher, KS, 2001, 'The politics of participation in watershed modeling', *Environmental Management*, 27 (2): 161–176.

Kørnøv, L and Thissen, WAH, 2000, 'Rationality in decision- and policy-making: implications for strategic environmental assessment', *Impact Assessment and Project Appraisal*, 18 (3): 191–200.

Kotchen, MJ and Reiling, SD, 2000 'Environmental attitudes, motivations, and contingent valuation of nonuse values: a case study involving endangered species', *Ecological Economics* 32 (1): 93–107.

KPMG, 2005, *KPMG International Survey of Corporate Responsibility Reporting*, KPMG International, Amsterdam, <www.kpmg.nl/Docs/Corporate_Site/Publicaties/International_Survey_Corporate_Responsibility_2005.pdf> (accessed 6 May 2008).

Kraft, ME and Clary, BB, 1991, 'Citizen participation and the Nimby syndrome: public response to radioactive waste disposal', *Western Political Quarterly*, 44 (2): 299–328.

Kuhn, T, 1962, *The Structure of Scientific Revolutions*, University of Chicago Press, Chicago.

Kuiper, G, 2001, 'Connecting science and policy? A case study of the use of "Australia: State of the Environment 1996"' in *Detecting Environmental Change, Science and Society Conference*, 17–20 July 2001, London, UK.

Lach, D, Rayner, S and Ingram, H, 2005, 'Taming the waters: strategies to domesticate the wicked problems of water resource management', *International Journal of Water*, 3 (1): 1–17.

Lafferty, WM and Meadowcroft, J, (eds), 1996, *Democracy and the Environment: Problems and Prospects*, Edward Elgar Publishing Limited, Cheltenham, UK.

Laffin, M, 1997, 'Public policy-making' in Smith, R, (ed), *Politics in Australia*, 3rd edn, Allen & Unwin, Crows Nest, pp 51–66.

Lane, M, 2006, *Critical Issues in Regional Natural Resource Management*, Paper prepared for the 2006 Australian State of the Environment Committee, Department of the Environment and Heritage, Canberra, <www.environment.gov.au/soe/2006/publications/integrative/nrm-issues/pubs/nrm-issues.pdf> (accessed 19 March 2009).

Lane, MB, 1999, 'Regional Forest Agreements: resolving resource conflicts or managing resource politics?', *Australian Geographical Studies*, 37 (2): 142–157.

Langdon, S, 2007, 'The nappy changers: breaking down the impact of a billion nappies', *ScienceAlert Australia and New Zealand*, <www.sciencealert.com.au/features/20071706-16008.html> (accessed 15 February 2009).

Laplante, D, 1993, *Model Code of Ethics: Final Approved Version*, World Federation of Engineering Organisations (WFEO).

Lash, S and Wynne, B, 1992, 'Introduction' in Beck, U, *Risk Society. Towards a New Modernity*, (translated by M Ritter), Sage Publications, London, pp 1–8.

Leach, WD, Pelkey, NW and Sabatier, PA, 2002, 'Stakeholder partnerships as collaborative policymaking: evaluation criteria applied to watershed management in California and Washington', *Journal of Policy Analysis and Management*, 21 (4): 645–670.

Lee, KN, 1999, 'Appraising adaptive management', *Conservation Ecology*, 3 (2): 3 [online] <www.consecol.org/vol3/iss2/art3/> (accessed 28 March 2009).

Leopold, A, 1949, *A Sand County Almanac*, Oxford University Press, New York.

Liberatore, A, 1995, 'The social construction of environmental problems' in Glasbergen, P and Blowers, A, (eds), *Environmental Policy in an International Context*, Arnold, London, pp 59–83.

Lichtenberg, J, 1996, 'What are codes of ethics for?' in Coady, M and Bloch, S, (eds), *Codes of Ethics and the Professions*, Melbourne University Press, Melbourne, pp 13–27.

Lidskog, R and Sundqvist, G, 2004, 'On the right track? Technology, geology and society in Swedish nuclear waste management', *Journal of Risk Research*, 7 (2): 251–268.

Lidskog, R and Sundqvist, G, 2005, 'Siting conflicts – democratic perspectives and political implications', *Journal of Risk Research*, 8 (3): 187–206.

Lifset, R, 1991, 'Greener than thou wars – raising the ante for life cycle analyses', *Biocycle*, 32 (April 1991): 76–77.

Lindblom, CE, 1959, 'The science of muddling through', *Public Administration Review*, 19 (2): 79–88.

Lindblom, CE, 1977, *Politics and Markets: The World's Political Economic Systems*, Basic Books, New York.

Lindenmayer, D, Dovers, S, Olson, MH and Morton, S, (eds), 2008a, *Ten Commitments: Reshaping the Lucky Country's Environment*, CSIRO Publishing, Collingwood.

Lindenmayer, D, Dovers, S, Olson, MH and Morton, S, 2008b, 'Synthesis and overview' in Lindenmayer D, Dovers, S, Olson, MH and Morton, S, (eds), *Ten Commitments: Reshaping the Lucky Country's Environment*, CSIRO Publishing, Collingwood, pp 227–231.

Linder, C, 1994, 'Agenda 21' in Dodds, F, (ed), *The Way Forward: Beyond Agenda 21*, Earthscan Publications, London, pp 3–14.

Livesey, SM, 2001, 'Eco-identity as discursive struggle: Royal Dutch/Shell, Brent Spar, and Nigeria', *Journal of Business Communication*, 38 (1): 58–91.

Lockwood, M, 2005, 'Integration of natural area values: conceptual foundations and methodological approaches', *Australasian Journal of Environmental Management*, 12 (Supplementary issue): 8–19.

Lohrey, A, 2002, 'Ground swell – the rise of the Greens', *Quarterly Essay*, 8: 1–86.

Lomborg, B, 2001, *The Skeptical Environmentalist. Measuring the Real State of the World*, Cambridge University Press, Cambridge.

Loorbach, D, 2007, *Transition Management. New Mode of Governance for Sustainable Development*, International Books, Utrecht.

Loorbach, D and Rotmans, J, 2006, 'Managing transitions for sustainable development' in Olsthoorn, X and Wieczorek, A, (eds), *Understanding Industrial Transformation Views from Different Disciplines*, Springer, Dordrecht, pp 187–206.

Lovell, DW, McAllister, I, Maley, W and Kukathas, C, 1998, *The Australian Political System*, 2nd edn, Addison Wesley Longman Australia, Melbourne.

Lovett, A, 2000, 'GIS and environmental management' in O'Riordan, T, (ed), *Environmental Science for Environmental Management*, 2nd edn, Pearson Education Limited, UK, pp 267–286.

Lovins, AB, 1977, *Soft Energy Paths. Toward a Durable Peace*, Penguin Books, Middlesex, England.

Lovins, AB, Lovins, LH and Hawken, P, 2000, 'A road map for natural capitalism' in Harvard Business School, (eds), *Harvard Business Review on Business and the Environment*, Harvard Business School Press, Boston, pp 1–34.

Lowe I, 2003, 'Science, research and policy' in Dovers, S and Wild River, S, (eds), *Managing Australia's Environment*, The Federation Press, Sydney, pp 472–484.

Lowe, I, 2004, 'The research community' in Maddison, S and Hamilton, C, (eds), *Silencing Dissent: Non-Government Organisations and Australian Democracy*, Allen & Unwin, Crows Nest, pp 60–77.

Lowe, I, 2009, *A Big Fix: Radical Solutions for Australia's Environmental Crisis*, Revised edn, Black Inc, Melbourne.

Lowrance, WW, 1976, *Of Acceptable Risk. Science and the Determination of Safety*, William Kaufmann Inc, Los Altos, California.

Lubit, R, 2001, 'Tacit knowledge and knowledge management: the keys to sustainable competitive advantage', *Organizational Dynamics*, 29 (4): 164–178.

Lukensmeyer, CJ, Goldman, J and Brigham, S, 2005, 'A town meeting for the twenty-first century' in Gastil, J and Levine, P, (eds), *The Deliberative Democracy Handbook: Strategies for Effective Civic Engagement in the 21st Century*, Jossey-Bass, San Francisco, pp 154–163.

Lunney, D, (ed), 1992, *Zoology in Court*, Royal Zoological Society of New South Wales, Mosman, NSW.

Lunney, D, Dickman, C and Burgin, S, (eds), 2002, *A Clash of Paradigms. Community and Research-based Conservation*, Royal Zoological Society of New South Wales, Mosman, NSW.

LWA (Land & Water Australia), 2006, *Improving the NRM Knowledge System for Regions*, Land & Water Australia, Canberra.

Lynch, G and Galligan, B, 1996, 'Environmental policymaking in Australia: The role of the courts' in Holland, KM, Morton, FL and Galligan, B, (eds), *Federalism and the Environment: Environmental Policymaking in Australia, Canada and the United States*, Greenwood Press, Connecticut, pp 205–223.

Lynn, FM, Busenberg, G, Cohen, N and Chess, C, 2000, 'Chemical industry's community advisory panels: what has been their impact?', *Environmental Science and Technology*, 34 (10): 1881–1886.

Lyytimäki, J, 2004, 'Producing multidisciplinary state of the environment reports: two tales from Finland', *The Journal of Transdiciplinary Environmental Studies*, 3 (2): 1–10.

Maasen, S, Lengwiler, M and Guggenheim, M, 2006, 'Practices of transdisciplinary research: close encounters of science and society', *Science and Public Policy*, 33 (6): 394–398.

MacGill, I and Betz, R, 2008, *A Lost Opportunity for Leadership*, Newmatilda.com, <http://newmatilda.com/2008/07/21/lost-opportunity-leadership> (accessed 17 February 2009).

Macgillivray, A and Zadek, S, 1995, *Accounting for Change – Indicators for Sustainable Development*, New Economics Foundation, London.

MacIntosh, A, 2006, *Environmental Protection and Biodiversity Conservation Act: An Ongoing Failure*, The Australia Institute, Canberra, <www.tai.org.au/file.php?file=WP91.pdf> (accessed 30 March 2009).

MacIntosh, A and Wilkinson, D, 2005, *Environmental Protection and Biodiversity Conversation Act: A Five Year Assessment*, Discussion Paper No 81, The Australia Institute, Canberra.

Maddox, J, 1972, *The Doomsday Syndrome*, Macmillan, London.

Mander, S, 2008, 'The role of discourse coalitions in planning for renewable energy: a case study of wind-energy deployment', *Environment and Planning C: Government and Policy*, 26 (3): 583–600.

Mansbridge, J, 2000, 'What does a representative do? Descriptive representation in communicative settings of distrust, uncrystallized interests, and historically denigrated status' in Kymlicka, W and Norman, W, (eds), *Citizenship in Diverse Societies*, Oxford University Press, Oxford, pp 99–123.

Marañón, E, Castrillón, L, Fernández, Y and Fernández, E, 2006, 'Anaerobic treatment of sludge from a nitrification–denitrification landfill leachate plant', *Waste Management*, 26 (8): 869–874.

March, JG and Olsen, JP, 1989, *Rediscovering Institutions: The Organizational Basis of Politics*, Free Press, New York.

March, JG and Simon, HA, 1958, *Organisations*, Wiley, New York.

Marks, J, Martin, B and Zadoroznyj, M, 2008, 'How Australians order acceptance of recycled water. National baseline data', *Journal of Sociology*, 44 (1): 83–99.

Marocco, J, 2008, 'Climate change and the limits of knowledge' in Vitek, B and Jackson, W, (eds), *The Virtues of Ignorance. Complexity, Sustainability, and the Limits of Knowledge*, The University Press of Kentucky, Lexington, Kentucky, pp 307–322.

Marsh, I, 2002, 'Interest groups' in Summers, J, Woodward, D and Parkin, A, (eds), *Government, Politics, Power and Policy in Australia*, 7th edn, Pearson Education Australia, Frenchs Forest, pp 345–361.

Marsh, I and Stone, D, 2004, 'Australian think tanks' in Denham, A and Stone, D, (eds), *Think Tank Traditions: Policy Research and the Politics of Ideas*, Manchester University Press, Manchester, pp 247–263.

Marshall, P, *Nature's Web. An Exploration of Ecological Thinking*, Simon & Schuster, London.

Martens, P, 2006, 'Sustainability: science or fiction?', *Sustainability: Science, Practice & Policy*, 2 (1): 36–41.

Martin, B, 1979, *The Bias of Science*, Society for Social Responsibility in Science (ACT), Canberra.

Martin, B, 1992, 'Intellectual suppression: why environmental scientists are afraid to speak out', *Habitat Australia*, 20 (3): 11.

Maruyama, Y, Nishikido, M and Iida, T, 2007, 'The rise of community wind power in Japan: enhanced acceptance through social innovation', *Energy Policy*, 35 (5): 2761–2769.

Matthews, T and Warhurst, J, 1993, 'Australia: interest groups in the shadow of strong political parties' in Thomas, CS, (ed), *First World Interest Groups*, Greenwood Press, Westport, CT, pp 81–95.

Matthews, T, 1993, 'Australian interest groups' in Richardson, JJ, (ed), *Pressure Groups*, Oxford University Press, Oxford, pp 230–244.

Matthews, T, 1997, 'Interest groups' in Smith, R, (ed), *Politics in Australia*, 3rd edn, Allen & Unwin, St Leonards, pp 269–290.

Max-Neef, MA, 2005, 'Commentary. Foundations of transdisciplinarity', *Ecological Economics*, 53 (1): 5–16.

McDonald, J, 2007, 'Politics, process and principle: mutual supportiveness or irreconcilable differences in the trade-environment linkage', *University of New South Wales Law Journal*, 30 (2): 524–547.

McDonald, M, 2005, 'Fair weather friend? Ethics and Australia's approach to global climate change', *Australian Journal of Politics and History*, 51 (2): 216–234.

McEachern, D, 1993, 'Environmental policy in Australia 1981–1991: a form of corporatism?', *Australian Journal of Public Administration*, 52 (2): 173–186.

McGrath, C, 2005, 'Key concepts of the Environment Protection and Biodiversity Conservation Act 1999 (Cth)', *Environmental and Planning Law Journal*, 22 (1): 20–39.

McLaren, D, 2003, 'Environmental space, equity and the ecological debt' in Agyeman, J, Bullard, RD and Evans, B, (eds), *Just Sustainabilities. Development in an Unequal World*, Earthscan Publications, London, pp 19–37.

MEA (Millennium Ecosystem Assessment), 2005a, *Ecosystems and Human Well-being: Synthesis*, Island Press, Washington DC, <www.millenniumassessment.org/en/index.aspx> (accessed 19 November 2008).

MEA (Millennium Ecosystem Assessment), 2005b, *Ecosystems and Human Well-Being: Current State and Trends. Findings of the Condition and Trends Working Group*, Island Press, Washington DC, Chapter 28, <www.millenniumassessment.org/documents/document.297.aspx.pdf> (accessed 15 April 2009).

MEA (Millenium Ecosystem Assessment), 2005c, *Living Beyond Our Means: Natural Assets and Human Well-Being*, Statement from the MA Board, <www.millenniumassessment.org/en/BoardStatement.aspx> (accessed 27 March 2009).

Meadowcroft, J, 1999. 'Planning for sustainable development: what can we learn from the critics?' in Kenny, M and Meadowcroft, J, (eds), *Planning Sustainability*, Routledge, London, pp 12–38.

Meadowcroft, J, 2005, 'Environmental political economy, technological transitions and the State', *New Political Economy*, 10 (4): 479–498.

Meadowcroft, J, 2007, 'Who is in charge here? Governance for sustainable development in a complex world', *Journal of Environmental Policy & Planning*, 9 (3–4): 299–314.

Meadows, DH, Meadows, DL, Randers, J and Behrens III, WW, 1972, *The Limits to Growth*, Universe Books, New York.

Meadows, DH, Meadows, DL and Randers, J, 1992, *Beyond the Limits. Global Collapse or a Sustainable Future*, Earthscan Publications, London.

Meeth, LR, 1978, 'Interdisciplinary studies: a matter of definition', *Change*, 10 (Report on Teaching 6): p 10.

Merchant, C, 1989, *Ecological Revolutions. Nature, Gender, and Science in New England*, The University of North Carolina Press, Chapel Hill, USA.

Merkhofer, MW, 1998, 'Assessment, refinement, and narrowing of options' in Dale, VH and English, MR, (eds), *Tools to Aid Environmental Decision-Making*, Springer, New York, pp 231–284.

Meyer, M, 2007, 'Increasing the frame: interdisciplinarity, transdisciplinarity and representativity', *Interdisciplinary Science Reviews*, 32 (3): 203–212.

Michaud, K, Carlisle, JE and Smith, ERAN, 2008, 'Nimbyism vs environmentalism in attitudes toward energy development', *Environmental Politics*, 17 (1): 20–39.

Miller, S, 2001, 'Public understanding of science at the crossroads', *Public Understanding of Science*, 10 (1): 115–120.

Mitcham, C, 1995, 'The concept of sustainable development: its origins and ambivalence', *Technology in Society*, 17 (3): 311–326.

Mitchell, RK, Agle, BR and Wood, DJ, 1997, 'Toward a theory of stakeholder identification and salience: defining the principle of who and what really counts', *The Academy of Management Review*, 22 (4): 853–886.

Mont, OK, 2002, 'Clarifying the concept of product-service system', *Journal of Cleaner Production*, 10 (3): 237–245.

Morrison-Saunders, A and Therivel, R, 2006, 'Sustainability integration and assessment', *Journal of Environmental Assessment Policy and Management*, 8 (3): 281–298.

Morrison-Saunders, A, Arts, J, Baker, J and Caldwell, P, 2001, 'EIA follow-up: roles and stakes in environmental impact assessment follow-up', *Impact Assessment and Project Appraisal*, 19 (4): 289–296.

Morrow, D and Rondinelli, D, 2002, 'Adopting corporate environmental management systems: Motivations and results of ISO14001 and EMAS certification', *European Management Journal*, 20 (2): 159–171.

Munda, G, 1996, 'Cost-benefit analysis in integrated environmental assessment: some methodological issues', *Ecological Economics*, 19 (2): 157–168.

Myers, NJ and Raffensperger, C, (eds), 2006, *Precautionary Tools for Reshaping Environmental Policy*, The MIT Press, Cambridge, Massachusetts.

Nancarrow, BE and Syme, GJ, 2001, *River Murray Environmental Flows and Water Quality Project: Stakeholder Profiling Study*, A Report to the Murray-Darling Basin Commission, CSIRO Land and Water Consultancy Report, Published by the Murray-Darling Basin Commission, Canberra.

Nash, R, 1990, *The Rights of Nature. A History of Environmental Ethics*, Primavera Press, Leichhardt, NSW.

Nason, D, 2007, 'Murdoch spells out news response to climate threat', *The Australian*, 10 May, p 3.

Nawrocka, D and Parker, T, 2009, 'Finding the connection: environmental management systems and performance', *Journal of Cleaner Production*, 17 (6): 601–607.

NCC (Nature Conservation Council), 2008, *What Is the Nature Conservation Council?*, Nature Conservation Council of NSW, <http://nccnsw.org.au/index.php?option=com_content&task=view&id=15&Itemid=123> (accessed 17 September 2008).

Nedovic-Budic, Z and Pinto, JK, 2000, 'Understanding interorganizational GIS activities: a conceptual framework', *Environment and Planning B: Planning and Design*, 27 (3): 455–474.

Ness, B, Urbel-Piirsalu, E, Anderberg, S and Olsson, L, 2007, 'Categorising tools for sustainability assessment', *Ecological Economics*, 60 (3): 498–508.

Netherwood, AL, 1998, 'Environmental management systems' in Welford, RJ, (ed), *Corporate Environmental Management: Systems and Strategies*, 2nd edn, Earthscan Publications, London, pp 37–60.

Neumayer, E, 2003, *Weak versus Strong Sustainability, Exploring the Limits of Two Opposing Paradigms*, 2nd edn, Edward Elgar, Cheltenham, UK.

New York State, undated, Department of Civil Service/Governor's Office of Employee Relations Work Force and Succession Planning – *Tools & Resources*, <www.cs.state.ny.us/successionplanning/workgroups/knowledgemanagement/terminology.html> (accessed 25 August 2008).

Newman, DM, 2006, *Sociology: Exploring the Architecture of Everyday Life*, Pine Forge, Thousand Oaks.

Newman, L, 2005, 'Uncertainty, innovation, and dynamic sustainable development', *Sustainability: Science, Practice, and Policy*, 1 (2): 25–31.

Niemeyer, S, 2004, 'Deliberation in the wilderness: displacing symbolic politics', *Environmental Politics*, 13 (2): 347–372.

Nix, M and Hill, C, 2001, 'Rapid accurate GIS updates with improved links to survey systems', *5th Global Spatial Data Infrastructure Conference*, 23 May 2001, Cartegena, Columbia, <www.gsdidocs.org/docs2001/GSDI-5_papers/Martin%20Nix-paper.doc> (accessed 24 February 2009).

Norton, TW, Beer, T and Dovers, SR, (eds), 1996, *Risk and Uncertainty in Environmental Management*, Proceedings of the 1995 Australian Academy of Science Fenner Conference on the Environment, Centre for Resource and Environmental Studies, Australian National University.

NRC US (National Research Council (US), Committee on improving risk analysis approaches used by the USEPA), 2008, *Science and Decisions: Advancing Risk Assessment*, The National Academies Press, Washington DC. Also available at <http://books.nap.edu/> (accessed 5 March 2009).

NSROC, 2008, *Northern Sydney Regional Organisation of Councils: State of the Environment Report 2007/2008*, <www.hornsby.nsw.gov.au/uploads/documents/NSROCSoE2007finallowres.pdf> (accessed 25 February 2009).

O'Reilly, T, 2005, 'What is Web 2.0. Design patterns and business models for the next generation of software', <http://www.oreilly.com/web2/archive/what-is-web-20.html> (accessed 15 June 2009).

O'Riordan, T, 1981, *Environmentalism*, 2nd edn, Pion Ltd, London.

O'Riordan, T, 1991a, 'The new environmentalism and sustainable development', *Science of the Total Environment*, 108 (1/2): 5–15.

O'Riordan, T, 1991b, 'Towards a vernacular science for environmental change' in Roberts, LE and Weale, A, (eds), *Innovation and Environmental Risk*, Belhaven Press, London, pp 149–162.

O'Riordan, T, 2000, 'Environmental science on the move' in O'Riordan, T, (ed), *Environmental Science for Environmental Management*, 2nd edn, Prentice Hall, UK, pp 1–27.

O'Riordan, T, Cameron, J and Jordan, A, (eds), 2001, *Reinterpreting the Precautionary Principle*, Cameron May, London.

O'Riordan, T and Rayner, S, 1991, 'Risk management for global environmental change', *Global Environmental Change*, 1 (2): 91–108.

OECD, 2000, *Engaging Citizens*, OECD, Paris.

OECD, 2001, *Citizens as Partners: Information, Consultation and Public Participation*, OECD, Paris.

OECD, 2007a, *OECD Environmental Performance Reviews – Australia*, OCED, Paris, <www.oecd.org/document/36/0,3343,en_33873108_33873229_39355364_1_1_1_1,00.html> (accessed 12 April 2009).

OECD, 2007b, *Open Government: Fostering Dialogue with Civil Society*, OECD, Paris.

OECD, undated, 'Extended Producer Responsibility', <www.oecd.org/document/19/0,3343,en_2649_201185_35158227_1_1_1_1,00.html> (accessed 19 February 2008).

Oxford English Dictionary Online, <http://dictionary.oed.com/>

PA (Philanthropy Australia), 2008, <www.philanthropy.org.au> (accessed 23 September 2008).

Page, B, 1997, 'Cabinet' in Smith, R, (ed), *Politics in Australia*, 3rd edn, Allen & Unwin, St Leonards, pp 124–139.

Painter, M, 1997, 'Elections' in Smith, R, (ed), *Politics in Australia*, 3rd edn, Allen & Unwin, St Leonards, pp 175–193.

Pakulski, J and Tranter, B, 2004, 'Environmentalism and social differentiation: a paper in memory of Steve Crook', *Journal of Sociology*, 40 (3): 221–235.

Papadakis, E, 1996, *Environmental Politics and Institutional Change*, Cambridge University Press, Cambridge.

Papadakis, E, 2002, 'Global environmental diplomacy: Australia's stances on global warming', *Australian Journal of International Affairs*, 56 (2): 265–277.

Papadakis, E and Grant, R, 2003, 'The politics of "light-handed regulation": "New" environmental policy instruments in Australia' in Jordan, A, Wurzel, RKW and Zito, AR, (eds), *'New' Instruments of Environmental Governance? National Experiences and Prospects*, Frank Cass, London, pp 27–50.

Parker, P, Letcher, R, Jakeman, A, Beck, MB and others, 2002, 'Progress in integrated assessment and modeling', *Environmental Modelling and Software*, 17: 209–217.

Parkin, A and Summers, J, 2002, 'The constitutional framework' in Summers, J, Woodward, D and Parkin, A, (eds), *Government, Politics, Power and Policy in Australia*, 7th edn, Pearson Education, Frenchs Forest, pp 3–21.

Parkin, A, Summers, J and Woodward, D (eds), 2006, *Government, Politics, Power and Policy in Australia*, 8th edn, Pearson Education, Frenchs Forest.

Parkinson, J, 2001, 'Deliberative democracy and referendums' in Dowding, KM, Huges, J and Margetts, H, (eds), *Challenges to Democracy: Ideas, Involvement and Institutions*, Palgrave, London, pp 131–152.

Parkinson, J, 2003, 'Legitimacy problems in deliberative democracy', *Political Studies*, 51 (1): 180–196.

Parkinson, J, 2004, 'Why deliberate? The encounter between deliberation and new public managers', *Public Administration*, 82 (2): 377–395.

Parkinson, J, 2006, *Deliberating in the Real World: Problems of Legitimacy in Democracy*, Oxford University Press, Oxford.

Pearce, D, Markandya, A and Barbier, EB, 1989, *Blueprint for a Green Economy*, Earthscan Publications, London.

Pearce, DW and Turner, RK, 1990, *Economics of Natural Resources and the Environment*, Harvester Wheatsheaf, New York.

Pearce, DW, Turner, RK, Dubourg, R and Atkinson, G, 1993, 'The conditions for sustainable development' in Pearce, D, (ed), *Blueprint 3. Measuring Sustainable Development*, CSERGE and Earthscan Publications, London, pp 15–27.

Pearse, G, 2007, *High and Dry: John Howard, Climate Change, and the Selling of Australia's Future*, Viking, Penguin Group (Australia), Camberwell, Victoria.

Pearse, G, 2008, 'Comment', *The Monthly*, 36 (July), <www.themonthly.com.au/tm/node/1080> (accessed 10 July 2009).

Peel, J, 2005, *The Precautionary Principle in Practice. Environmental Decision-Making and Scientific Uncertainty*, The Federation Press, Sydney.

Pepper, D, 1996, *Modern Environmentalism: An Introduction*, Routledge, London.

Peters, E and Slovic, P, 1996, 'The role and worldviews as orienting dispositions in the perception and acceptance of nuclear power', *Journal of Applied Social Psychology*, 26 (16): 1427–1453.

Peterson, MN, Peterson, MJ and Peterson, TR, 2007, 'Moving toward sustainability: integrating social practice and material process' in Sandler, R and Pezzullo, PC, (eds), *Environmental Justice and Environmentalism. The Social Challenge to the Environmental Movement*, The MIT Press, Cambridge, Massachusetts, pp 189–221.

Petts, J, 1999, *Handbook of Environmental Impact Assessment, Volume 1, Environmental Impact Assessment: Processes, Methods and Potential*, Blackwell Science, Oxford.

Petts, J and Brooks, C, 2006, 'Expert conceptualisations of the role of lay knowledge in environmental decisionmaking: challenges for deliberative democracy', *Environment and Planning A*, 38 (6): 1045–1059.

Phills Jr, JA and Nee, E, 2009, 'From crisis comes opportunity', *Stanford Social Innovation Review*, 7 (1): 4.

Pickerell, J, 2003, *Cyberprotest: Environmental Activism Online*, Manchester University Press, Manchester.

Pimbert, MP and Wakeford, T, 2002, *Prajateerpu: A Citizen Jury/Scenario Workshop on Food and Farming Futures for Andhra Pradesh, India*, International Institute for Environment and Development (IIED), London and Institute of Development Studies (IDS), Sussex.

Pincock, S, 2008, Food bowl to dustbowl? ABC Science, 14 August 2008, <www.abc.net.au/science/articles/2008/08/14/2335296.htm> (accessed 8 April 2009).

Pintér, L, Hardi, P and Bartelmus, P, 2005, *Sustainable Development Indicators – proposals for a way forward*, prepared for the United Nations Division for Sustainable Development (UN-DSD).

Pintér, L, Zahedi, K, Cressman, DR, 2000, *Capacity Building for Integrated Environmental Assessment and Reporting: Training Manual*, 2nd edn, IISD, UNEP, <www.iisd.org/publications/pub.aspx?id=310> (accessed 27 August 2008).

Plummer, R and Fitzgibbon, J, 2004, 'Co-management of natural resources: a proposed framework', *Environmental Management*, 33 (6): 876–885.

PMSEIC (Prime Minister's Science, Engineering and Innovation Council), 2002, *Sustaining our Natural Systems and Biodiversity*, Eighth Meeting 31 May 2002, <www.dest.gov.au/NR/rdonlyres/EE0F827A-94BB-4E0C-80F5-A058293F190C/2014/Sustaining_our_Natural_Systems_and_Biodiversity_Wo.pdf> (accessed 27 December 2008).

Pockley, P, 1999, 'The gene game', *Australasian Science*, 20 (9): 24–26.

Pohl, C, 2005, 'Transdisciplinary collaboration in environmental research', *Futures*, 37 (10): 1159–1178.

Pohl, C and Hirsch Hadorn, G, 2007, *Principles for Designing Transdisciplinary Research. Proposed by the Swiss Academies of Arts and Sciences*, Translated by Zimmermann, AB, Oekom Verlag, Munich. Summary available at: <www.transdisciplinarity.ch/documents/knowledgeforms_principles.pdf> (accessed 1 May 2009).

Pollack, HN, 2003, *Uncertain Science . . . Uncertain World*, Cambridge University Press, Cambridge.

Pope, J, Annandale, D and Morrison-Saunders, A, 2004, 'Conceptualising sustainability assessment', *Environmental Impact Assessment Review*, 24 (6): 595–616.

Pregernig, M, 2006, 'Transdisciplinarity viewed from afar: science-policy assessments as forums for the creation of transdisciplinary knowledge', *Science and Public Policy*, 33 (6): 445–455.

PRI (Principles for Responsible Investment), 2008, *Press Release: Principles for Responsible Investment: Signatories Double in One Year; 'Institutional Investors Taking Implementation to the Next Level'*, <www.unpri.org/files/PRI_press_release5.pdf> (accessed 18 February 2009).

Princen, T, Maniates, M and Conca, K, (eds), 2002, *Confronting Consumption*, MIT Press, Cambridge, Massachusetts.

Pring, GW and Canan, P, 1996, *SLAPPs: Getting Sued for Speaking Out*, Temple University Press, Philadelphia.

Putnam, RD, 1993, *Making Democracy Work: Civic Traditions in Modern Italy*, Princeton University Press, Princeton, N.J.

Rae, I and Brown, P, 2009, 'Managing the intractable: communicative structures for management of hexachlorobenzene and other scheduled wastes', *Journal of Environmental Management*, 90 (4): 1583–1592.

Ramsay, R and Rowe, G, 1995, *Environmental Law and Policy in Australia: Text and Materials*, Butterworths, Sydney.

Rann, M, 2009, 'Constitutional challenge on water trading', *Ministerial Statement, 5 March 2009*, Government of South Australia, Adelaide.

Rapport, DJ, 2007, 'Sustainability science: an ecohealth perspective', *Sustainability Science*, 2 (1): 77–84.

Ravetz, J, 1999, 'What is post-normal science', *Futures*, 31 (7): 647–653.

Ravetz, J, 2006, 'Post-normal science and the complexity of transitions towards sustainability', *Ecological Complexity*, 3 (4): 275–284.

Rawls, J, 1972, *A Theory of Justice*, Clarendon Press, Oxford.

Reddel, T and Woolcock, G, 2003, 'From consultation to participatory governance? A critical review of citizen engagement strategies in Queensland', *Australian Journal of Public Administration*, 63 (3): 75–87.

Reiche, D and Bechberger, M, 2004, 'Policy differences in the promotion of renewable energies in the EU Member States', *Energy Policy*, 32 (7): 834–849.

Renn, O, Webler, T and Wiedemann, P, (eds), 1995, *Fairness and Competence in Citizen Participation*, Kluwer, Dordrecht.

Rennings, K and Wiggering, H, 1997, 'Steps towards indicators of sustainable development: Linking economic and ecological concepts', *Ecological Economics*, 20 (1): 25–36.

Renouf, C, 1999, 'Rebirthing democracy: the experience of the first Australian consensus conference', *Consuming Interest*, 79: 16–19.

Resilience Alliance, undated, <www.resalliance.org> (accessed 18 November 2008).

Richardson, JJ, (ed), 1993, *Pressure Groups*, Oxford University Press, Oxford.

Riele, H te, Elburg, M van and Kemna, R, 2001, *Dematerialisation. Less Clear Than it Seems*, Report for the Dutch Ministry of VROM (Environment), <www.vhk.nl/downloads_2001a.htm> (accessed 9 February 2008).

Rio Declaration, 1992, <www.un.org/documents/ga/conf151/aconf15126-1annex1.htm> (accessed 26 March 2008).

Rittel, HWJ and Webber, MM, 1973, 'Dilemmas in a general theory of planning', *Policy Sciences*, 4 (2): 155–169.

Roberts, JT, 2007, 'Globalizing environmental justice' in Sandler, R and Pezzullo, PC, (eds), *Environmental Justice and Environmentalism. The Social Challenge to the Environmental Movement*, The MIT Press, Cambridge, Massachusetts, pp 285–307.

Robertson, D and Kellow, A, (eds), 2001, *Globalization and the Environment: Risk Assessment and the WTO*, Edward Elgar, Cheltenham, UK.

Robins, L and Dovers, S, 2007, 'NRM regions in Australia: the "haves" and the "have nots"', *Geographical Research*, 45 (3): 273–290.

Robinson, J, 2003, 'Future subjunctive: backcasting as social learning', *Futures*, 35 (8): 839–856.

Robinson, J, 2004, 'Squaring the circle? Some thoughts on the idea of sustainable development', *Ecological Economics*, 48 (4): 369–384.

Robinson, J and Tansey, J, 2006, 'Co-production, emergent properties and strong interactive social research: the Georgia Basin Futures Project', *Science and Public Policy*, 33 (2): 151–160.

Rodgers, E, 2008, 'Rudd unveils $100m clean coal plan', <www.abc.net.au/news/stories/2008/09/19/2369071.htm> (accessed 17 February 2009).

Rogers, PP, Jalal, KF and Boyd, JA, 2008, *An Introduction to Sustainable Development*, Earthscan Publications, London.

Rogers-Hayden, T and Pidgeon, N, 2007, 'Moving engagement "upstream"? Nanotechnologies and the Royal Society and Royal Academy of Engineering's inquiry', *Public Understanding of Science*, 16 (3): 345–364.

Rolston III, H, 1987, 'Can the East help the West to value nature?', *Philosophy East and West*, 37 (2): 172–190.

Rondinelli, DA and Vastag, GA, 1996, 'International environmental management standards and corporate policies: an integrative framework', *California Management Review*, 39 (1), 106–122.

Rootes, C, 1999, 'Acting globally, thinking locally? Prospects for a global environmental movement', *Environmental Politics*, 8 (1): 290–310.

Ross, A and Dovers, S, 2008, 'Making the harder yards: environmental policy integration in Australia', *Australian Journal of Public Administration*, 67 (3): 245–260.

Rotmans, J, Kemp, R and van Asselt, M, 2001, 'More evolution than revolution: transition management in public policy', *Foresight*, 3 (1): 15–31.

Rotmans, J, Kemp, R, van Asselt, M, Geels, FW, and others, 2000, 'Transitions and transition management: the case of an emission-poor energy supply' (in Dutch), ICIS (International Centre for Integrative Studies), Maastricht, The Netherlands.

Rotmans, J and Loorbach, D, 2008, 'Transition management: reflexive governance of societal complexity through searching, learning and experimenting' in Van den Bergh, JCJM and Bruinsma, FR, (eds), *Managing the Transition to Renewable Energy*, Edward Elgar, Cheltenham, pp 15–46.

Royal Society, 1992, *Risk: Analysis, Perception and Management*, Report of a Royal Society Study Group, The Royal Society, London.

Ryan, C, 2005, 'Integrated approaches to sustainable consumption and cleaner production' in Hargroves, K and Smith, MH, (eds), *The Natural Advantage of Nations. Business Opportunities, Innovation and Governance in the 21st Century*, Earthscan Publications, London, pp 407–429.

Rydin, Y, 2003, *Conflict, Consensus, and Rationality in Environmental Planning: An Institutional Discourse Approach*, Oxford University Press, Oxford.

Rydin, Y and Pennington, M, 2001, 'Discourses of the prisoners' dilemma: the role of the local press in environmental policy', *Environmental Politics*, 10 (3): 48–71.

SA EPA, 2003, *Waste to Resources*, Environment Protection Authority South Australia, <www.environment.sa.gov.au/epa/waste.html#cdl> (accessed 24 October 2003).

SA (Standards Australia), 2005, *Knowledge Management – a guide*, Australian Standard 5037–2005, Standards Australia, Sydney.

SA/SNZ (Standards Australia and Standards New Zealand), 2004a, *Environmental Management Systems – Requirements with guidance for use*: AS/NZS 14001:2004.

SA/SNZ (Standards Australia/Standards New Zealand), 2004b, *Risk Management*, 3rd edn, Australia/New Zealand Standard 4360:2004.

SA/SNZ (Standards Australia/Standards New Zealand), 2006, *Environmental Risk Management – Principles and Process*, 3rd edn, Handbook HB 203:2006.

Sadler B, 1996, Environmental Assessment in a Changing World: Evaluating Practice to Improve Performance: Final Report of the International Study of the Effectiveness of Environmental Assessment, prepared for the Canadian Environmental Assessment Agency and International

Association for Impact Assessment, Canada, <www.unece.org/env/eia/documents/StudyEffectivenessEA.pdf> (accessed 8 March 2009).

Sagoff, M, 1998, 'Aggregation and deliberation in valuing environmental public goods: a look beyond contingent pricing', *Ecological Economics*, 24 (2–3): 213–230.

Sagoff, M, 2008, *The Economy of the Earth: Philosophy, Law, and the Environment*, 2nd edn, Cambridge University Press, Cambridge.

Sandman, P, 1992, 'Hazard and outrage: reducing community outrage. Risk communication in controversy', Seminar presented to the CRC for Waste Management and Pollution Control, Sydney, 16 December 1992.

Sandman, P, 2007, 'Understanding the risk: what frightens rarely kills', *Nieman Reports*, 61 (1): 59–66.

Sant, B, 1992, *Understanding Environmental Economics*, Longman, Cheshire.

Saulwick, I, 2004, 'How wind power is dividing rural Victoria', *The Age*, 12 July, <www.theage.com.au/articles/2004/07/11/1089484241274.html> (accessed 25 January 2009).

Saunders, C, 1996, 'The constitutional divisions of powers with respect to the environment in Australia' in Holland, KM, Morton, FL and Galligan, B, (eds), *Federalism and the Environment: Environmental Policymaking in Australia, Canada and the United States*, Greenwood Press, Connecticut, pp 55–76.

Sauter, R and Watson, J, 2007, 'Strategies for the deployment of micro-generation: implications for social acceptance', *Energy Policy*, 35 (5): 2770–2779.

Sawer, M, 2001, 'Governing for the mainstream: implications for community representation', *Australian Journal of Public Administration*, 61 (1): 39–49.

Scanlon, J and Dyson, M, 2001, 'Will practice hinder principle? Implementing the EPBC Act', *Environmental and Planning Law Journal*, 18 (1): 14–22.

Schaltegger, S, Burritt, R and Petersen, H, 2003, *An Introduction to Corporate Environmental Management. Striving for Sustainability*, Greenleaf Publishing, Sheffield.

Schlosberg, D, 2004, 'Reconceiving environmental justice: global movements and political theories', *Environmental Politics*, 13 (3): 517–540.

Schmidheiny, S, with the Business Council for Sustainable Development, 1992, *Changing Course. A Global Business Perspective on Development and the Environment*, The MIT Press, Cambridge, MA.

Schneider, A and Ingram, H, 1990, 'Behavioral assumptions of policy tools', *The Journal of Politics*, 52 (2): 510–529.

Schneider, AL and Ingram, H, 1997, *Policy Design for Democracy*, University of Kansas, Kansas.

Schneider, SH, 1997, 'Integrated assessment of modeling of global climate change: transparent rational tool for policy making or opaque screen hiding value-laden assumptions?', *Environmental Modeling and Assessment*, 2 (4): 229–249.

Scrase, JI and Sheate, WR, 2002, 'Integration and integrated approaches to assessment: what do they mean for the environment?' *Journal of Environmental Policy and Planning*, 4 (4): 275–294.

Seargeant, J and Stelle, J, 1998, *Consulting the Public: Guidelines and Good Practice*, Policy Studies Institute, London.

SECIT and ALC, (Senate Environment Communications, Information Technology and the Arts Legislation Committee), 1999, *Environmental Protection and Biodiversity Conservation Bill 1998 and Environmental Reform (Consequential Provisions) Bill 1998*, Parliament of Australia, Canberra.

Serret, Y and Johnstone, N, 2006, *The Distributional Effects of Environmental Policy*, OECD and Edward Elgar, Cheltenham, UK.

Shabecoff, P and Shabecoff, A, 2008, *Poisoned Profits. The Toxic Assault on Our Children*, Random House, New York.

Sheate, WR, 1996, *Environmental Impact Assessment: Law and Policy – Making an Impact II*, Cameron May Ltd, London.

Sheate, WR, Dagg, S, Richardson J, Aschemann R and others, 2001, *SEA and Integration of the Environment into Strategic Decision-Making, Volume 3 (Case Studies)*, Final Report to the European

Commission,<http://ec.europa.eu/environment/eia/sea-support.htm> (accessed 4 September 2008).

Shepherd, A and Ortolano, L, 1996, 'Strategic environmental assessment for sustainable urban development', *Environmental Impact Assessment Review*, 16 (4–6): 321–335.

Shove, E, 2003, *Comfort, Cleanliness + Convenience: The Social Organisation of Normality*, Berg, Oxford.

Shove, E and Walker, G, 2007, 'CAUTION! Transitions ahead: politics, practice, and sustainable transition management', *Environment and Planning A*, 39 (4): 763–770.

Siebenhüner, B and Barth, V, 2005, 'The role of computer modelling in participatory integrated assessments', *Environmental Impact Assessment Review*, 25 (4): 367–389.

Simon, HA, 1979, 'Rational decision making in business organizations', *The American Economic Review*, 69 (4): 493–513.

Singer, P, 1975, *Animal Liberation: A New Ethics for our Treatment of Animals*, Random House, New York.

Singleton, G, Aitkin, D, Jinks, B and Warhurst, J, 1996, *Australian Political Institutions*, 5th edn, Pearson Longman, Frenchs Forest.

Skocpol, T, 1999, 'Associations without members', *The American Prospect*, 45 (July-August): 66–73.

Slovic, P, 1993, 'Perceived risk, trust, and democracy', *Risk Analysis*, 13 (6): 675–682.

Slovic, P, 1999, 'Trust, emotion, sex, politics, and science: surveying the risk-assessment battlefield', *Risk Analysis*, 19 (4): 689–701.

Smallacombe, S, Davis, M and Quiggin, R, 2007, *Scoping Project on Aboriginal Traditional Knowledge*, Desert Knowledge Cooperative Research Centre Report Number 22, Alice Springs.

Smil, V, 1989, 'Our changing environment', *Current Affairs Bulletin*, 66 (6): 4–10.

Smil, V, 1993, *Global Ecology. Environmental Change and Social Flexibility*, Routledge, London.

Smith, A and Kern, F, 2009, 'The transitions storyline in Dutch environmental policy', *Environmental Politics*, 18 (1): 78–98.

Smith, G, 2001, 'Taking deliberation seriously: institutional design and green politics', *Environmental Politics*, 10 (3): 72–93.

Smith, G, 2003, *Deliberative Democracy and the Environment*, Routledge, London.

Smith, R, 1997, 'News media' in Smith, R, (ed), *Politics in Australia*, 3rd edn, Allen & Unwin, St Leonards, pp 332–353.

Smithson, M, 1989, *Ignorance and Uncertainty: Emerging Paradigms*, Springer-Verlag, New York.

Smithson, M, 1991, 'The changing nature of ignorance' in Handmer, J, Dutton, B, Guerin, B and Smithson, M, (eds), *New Perspectives on Uncertainty and Risk*, Centre for Resource and Environmental Studies, Australian National University, Canberra and Australian Counter Disaster College, Natural Disasters Organisation, Mt Macedon, Victoria, pp 5–38.

Smyth, RB, 1990, 'EIA on EIA: Experience=a need for improvement' in *An Independent Review of Environmental Impact Assessment in NSW: How it can be Improved?*, Proceedings of a Seminar and Workshop, Environment Institute of Australia and Australian Association of Consulting Planners, 1990, The University of New South Wales, 29 August 1990.

Soderbaum, P, 2000, *Ecological Economics: A Political Economics Approach to Environment and Development*, Earthscan Publications, London.

Spangenberg, JH, 2005, 'Will the information society be sustainable? Towards criteria and indicators for a sustainable knowledge society', *International Journal of Innovation and Sustainable Development*, 1 (1/2): 85–102.

Spash, CL, 1997, 'Ethics and environmental attitudes with implications for economic valuation', *Journal of Environmental Management*, 50 (4): 403–416.

Spash, CL, 2000, 'Ecosystems, contingent valuation and ethics: the case of wetland re-creation', *Ecological Economics*, 34 (2): 195–215.

SRA USA (Society for Risk Analysis (USA)), undated, 'Glossary', <www.sra.org/resources_glossaryp-r.php> (accessed 5 March 2009).

Stanford Encyclopedia of Philosophy, 2004, 'Thomas Kuhn', <http://plato.stanford.edu/entries/thomas-kuhn/#6.3> (accessed 20 March 2009).

Star, SL and Griesemer, JR, 1989, 'Institutional ecology, "translations" and boundary objects: amateurs and professionals in Berkeley's Museum of Vertebrate Zoology, 1907–39', *Social Studies of Science*, 19 (3): 387–420.

Starkey R, 1998, 'The standardization of Environmental Management Systems: ISO 14001, ISO 14004 and EMAS' in Welford, R, (ed), *Corporate Environmental Management 1. Systems and Strategies*, 2nd edn, Earthscan Publications, London, pp 61–89.

Steffen, W, 2008, 'The future of Australia's environment in the Anthropocene' in Lindenmayer, D, Dovers, S, Olson, MH and Morton, S, (eds), *Ten Commitments: Reshaping the Lucky Country's Environment*, CSIRO Publishing Collingwood, pp 143–147.

Steffen, W, Crutzen, PJ and McNeill, JR, 2007, 'The Anthropocene: are humans now overwhelming the great forces of nature?', *Ambio*, 36 (8): 614–621.

Steger, U, (ed), 2006, *Inside the Mind of the Stakeholder: The Hype Behind Stakeholder Pressure*, Palgrave Macmillan, Houndmills.

Stern, Sir Nicholas, 2006, *Stern Review: The Economics of Climate Change*, HM Treasury UK, <www.hm-treasury.gov.uk/stern_review_report.htm> (accessed 30 April 2009).

Stewart, A, 1993, 'Environmental risk assessment: the divergent methodologies of economists, lawyers and scientists', *Environmental and Planning Law Journal*, 10 (1): 10–18.

Stewart, J, 2009 (in press), *Public Policy Values*, Palgrave, Basingstoke.

Stewart, J and Ayres, R, 2001, 'The public policy process' in Aulich, C, Halligan, J and Nutley, S, (eds), *Australian Handbook of Public Sector Management*, Allen & Unwin, Sydney, pp 20–35.

Stewart, J and Hendriks, CM, 2008, 'Discovering the environment' in Aulich, C and Wettenhall, R, (eds), *Howard's Fourth Government*, UNSW Press, Sydney, pp 206–226.

Stewart, J and Jones, G, 2003, *Renegotiating the Environment*, The Federation Press, Sydney.

Stewart, J, 2006, 'Value conflict and policy change', *Review of Policy Research*, 23 (1): 183–195.

Stirling, A, 2007, 'Talking point. Risk, precaution and science: towards a more constructive policy debate', *EMBO reports*, 8 (4): 309–315.

Stock, JT, 2006, 'The greens, democrats, minor parties, and independents' in Parkin, A, Summers, J and Woodward, D, (eds), *Government, Politics, Power and Policy in Australia*, 8th edn, Pearson Education Australia, Frenchs Forest, pp 258–279.

Stone, D, 2002, *Policy Paradox: The Art of Political Decision Making*, Revised edn, WW Norton & Co, New York.

Stone, D, 2007, 'Recycling bins, garbage cans, or think tanks? Three myths regarding policy analysis institutes', *Public Administration*, 85 (2): 259–278.

Strolovitch, DZ, 2006, 'Do interest groups represent the disadvantaged? Advocacy at the intersections of race, class, and gender', *Journal of Politics*, 68 (4): 894–910.

Summers, J, 2006, 'The federal system' in Parkin, A, Summers, J and Woodward, D, (eds), *Government, Politics, Power and Policy in Australia*, 8th edn, Pearson Education, Frenchs Forest, pp 135–159.

Susskind, L and Cruikshank, J, 1987, *Breaking the Impasse: Consensual Approaches to Resolving Public Disputes*, Basic Books, New York.

SustainAbility and UNEP (United Nations Environment Programme), 2002, *Trust Us: The Global Reporters 2002 Survey of Corporate Sustainability Reporting*, <www.sustainability.com/researchandadvocacy/reports_article.asp?id=131> (accessed 25 February 2009).

Suter II, GW, 2006, *Ecological Risk Assessment*, 2nd edn, CRC Press, Florida, USA.

Suzuki, D, 1995, 'Blinded by our minds', in *Science for the Earth. Can Science Make the World a Better Place?*, Wakeford, T and Walters, M, (eds), John Wiley & Sons, Chichester, UK, pp 3–17.

Sylvan, R and Bennett, D, 1994, *The Greening of Ethics*, White Horse Press/University of Arizona Press, Cambridge, UK and Tucson, USA.

Tadros, E and Robins, B, 2008, 'Wind farm vow to power desalination', *Sydney Morning Herald*, 14 May, <www.smh.com.au/articles/2008/05/13/1210444436869.html> (accessed 28 February 2009).

Taplin, R, 1992, 'Adversary procedures and expertise: The Terania Creek Inquiry' in Walker, KJ, (ed), *Australian Environmental Policy*, UNSW Press, Sydney, pp 156–182.

Taylor, DW, Sulaiman, M and Sheahan, M, 2001, 'Auditing of environmental management systems: a legitimacy theory perspective', *Managerial Auditing Journal*, 16 (7): 411–422.

TEC (Total Environment Centre), 2009, *Green Capital: Advancing Corporate Sustainability*, <www. greencapital.org.au> (accessed 18 February 2009).

Thacher, D and Rein, T, 2004, 'Managing value conflict in public policy', *Governance: An International Journal of Policy, Administration and Institutions*, 17 (4): 457–486.

The Australian, 2008, 'Federal government's climate adviser, Ross Garnaut savages climate change plan', *The Australian*, 19 December, <www.theaustralian.news.com.au/story/0,25197,24824505-12377,00. html> (accessed 18 February 2009).

The Blockaders, 1983, *The Franklin Blockades*, The Wilderness Society, Hobart.

The World Bank, undated, 'Indigenous knowledge for development results', <http://web.worldbank. org/WBSITE/EXTERNAL/COUNTRIES/AFRICAEXT/EXTINDKNOWLEDGE/0,,menuPK:825 562~pagePK:64168427~piPK:64168435~theSitePK:825547,00.html> (accessed 27 March 2009).

Therivel, R, Wilson, E, Thompson, S, Heanley, D and Pritchard, D, 1992, *Strategic Environmental Assessment*, Earthscan Publications, London.

Thomas, I, 1998, *Environmental Impact Assessment in Australia: Theory and Practice*, 2nd edn, The Federation Press, Sydney.

Thomas, I, 2005, *Environmental Management: Processes and Practices for Australia*, The Federation Press, Sydney.

Thomas, I, 2007, *Environmental Policy. Australian Practice in the Context of Theory*, The Federation Press, Sydney.

Thomas, IG and Elliott, M, 2005, *Environmental Impact Assessment in Australia*, 4th edn, The Federation Press, Sydney.

Thompson, D, (ed), 2002, *Tools for Environmental Management: A Practical Introduction and Guide*, New Society Publishers, Canada.

Thompson, E, 1997a, 'The Constitution' in Smith, R, (ed), *Politics in Australia*, 3rd edn, Allen & Unwin, St Leonards, pp 85–103.

Thompson, E, 1997b, 'The public service' in Smith, R, (ed), *Politics in Australia*, 3rd edn, Allen & Unwin, St Leonards, pp 140–155.

Tiffen, R, 2004, 'The news media and Australian politics' in Boreham, P, Stokes, G and Hall, R, (eds), *The Politics of Australian Society: Political Issues for a New Century*, Pearson Education Australia, Frenchs Forest, pp 201–219.

Tighe, PJ, 1992, 'Hydroindustrialisation and conservation policy in Tasmania' in Walker, KJ, (ed), *Australian Environmental Policy*, UNSW Press, Sydney, pp 124–155.

Tilbury, D and Cooke, K, 2005, *A National Review of Environmental Education and its Contribution to Sustainability in Australia: Frameworks for Sustainability*, Australian Government Department of Environment and Heritage and Australian Research Institute in Education for Sustainability (ARIES), Canberra.

Tillman, AM, 2000, 'Significance of decision-making for LCA methodology', *Environmental Impact Assessment Review*, 20 (1): 113–123.

Tillman, AM, Ekvall, T, Baumann, H and Rydberg, T, 1994, 'Choice of system boundaries in life cycle assessment', *Journal of Cleaner Production*, 2 (1): 21–29.

Tisdell, CA, 1991, *Economics of Conservation*, Elsevier, Amsterdam, Netherlands.

Toyne, P, 1994, *The Reluctant Nation: Environment, Law and Politics in Australia*, ABC Books, Sydney.

Tranter, B, 2004, 'The environment movement: where to from here?' in White, R, (ed), *Controversies in Environmental Sociology*, Cambridge University Press, Cambridge, pp 185–203.

Travis, J, 2008, 'Science by the masses', *Science*, 319 (5871): 1750–1752.

Tukker, A, 2000, 'Life cycle assessment as a tool in environmental impact assessment', *Environmental Impact Assessment Review*, 20 (4): 435–456.

Turner, G, 2008, *A Comparison of the Limits to Growth with Thirty Years of Reality*, Socio-Economics and the Environment in Discussion (SEED), CSIRO Working Paper Series 2008–09, <www.csiro.au/resources/SEEDPaper19.html> (accessed 10 April 2009).

Turner, K, 2007, 'Limits to CBA in UK and European environmental policy: retrospects and future prospects', *Environmental and Resource Economics*, 37 (1): 253–269, <www.ecologic.eu/soef/epos/download/turner_06.pdf > (accessed 13 March 2009).

UNCED (United Nations Conference on the Environment and Development), 1992, *Agenda 21*, <www.unep.org/Documents.Multilingual/Default.asp?DocumentID=52> (accessed 13 May 2009).

UNEP (United Nations Environment Programme), 2007, *Global Environment Outlook: Environment for Development (GEO-4)*, <www.unep.org/geo/geo4/media/> (accessed 11 April 2009).

UNEP (United Nations Environment Programme) undated, <www.unep.fr/pc/cp/understanding_cp/home.htm> (accessed 18 February 2008).

US EPA (United States Environmental Protection Agency), undated, 'Ozone layer depletion', <www.epa.gov/ozone/strathome.html> (accessed 31 March 2009).

Usher, PJ, 2000, 'Traditional ecological knowledge in environmental assessment and management', *Arctic*, 53 (2): 183–193.

van Brugge, R, Rotmans, J and Loorbach, D, 2005, 'The transition in Dutch water management', *Regional Environmental Change*, 5 (4):164–176.

van der Vorst, R, Grafe, A and Sheate, WR, 1999, 'A systematic framework for environmental decision-making', *Journal of Environmental Assessment Policy and Management*, 1 (1): 1–26.

van Kerkhoff, L and Lebel, L, 2006, 'Linking knowledge and action for sustainable development', *Annual Review of Environment and Resources*, 31: 445–477.

van Vuuren, K and Lester, L, 2008, 'Ecomedia: of angelic images and environmental values', *Media International Australia*, 127: 71–81.

Vanclay, F, 2004, 'The triple bottom line and impact assessment: how do TBL, EIA, SIA, SEA and EMS relate to each other', *Journal of Environmental Assessment and Policy Management*, 6 (3): 265–88.

Venkatachalam, L, 2007, 'Environmental economics and ecological economics: where can they converge?', *Ecological Economics*, 61 (2–3): 50–558.

Verweij, M and Thompson, M, (eds), 2006, *Clumsy Solutions for a Complex World. Governance, Politics and Plural Perceptions*, Palgrave Macmillan, Basingstoke, UK.

Victorian DSE (Department of Sustainability and Environment), 2009, 'Index of stream condition', *Our Water our Future*, <www.ourwater.vic.gov.au/monitoring/river-health/isc> (accessed 27 February 2009).

Victorian Women's Trust, 2007, *Our Water Mark. Australians Making a Difference in Water Reform*, Melbourne.

Viergever, M, 1999, 'Indigenous knowledge: an interpretation of views from indigenous peoples' in Semali, LM and Kincheloe, JL, (eds), *What is Indigenous Knowledge? Voices from the Academy*, Falmer Press, New York, pp 333–343.

Vigar, G and Healey, P, 2002, 'Environmentally respectful planning. Five key principles', *Journal of Environmental Planning and Management*, 45 (4): 517–532.

Vigon, BW and Jensen, A, 1995, 'Life cycle assessment: data quality and database practitioner survey', *Journal of Cleaner Production*, 3 (3): 135–141.

Vitek, B and Jackson, W, 2008, 'Introduction. Taking ignorance seriously' in Vitek, B and Jackson, W, (eds), *The Virtues of Ignorance. Complexity, Sustainability, and the Limits of Knowledge*, The University Press of Kentucky, Lexington, Kentucky, pp 1–17.

Voet, E van der, Oers, L and Nikolic, I, 2003, 'Dematerialisation: not just a matter of weight', CML

Report 160, Institute of Environmental Sciences (CML), Leiden University, The Netherlands, <www.leidenuniv.nl/cml/> (accessed 9 February 2008).

von Weizsäcker, E, Lovins, AB and Lovins, HL, 1997, *Factor 4. Doubling Wealth – Halving Resource Use*, Allen & Unwin, Sydney.

Voß, J-P, Bauknecht, D and Kemp, R, (eds), 2006, *Reflexive Governance for Sustainable Development*, Edward Elgar, Cheltenham.

Voß, J-P, Newig, J, Kastens, B, Monstadt, J and others, 2007, 'Steering for sustainable development: a typology of problems and strategies with respect to ambivalence, uncertainty and distributed power', *Journal of Environmental Policy & Planning*, 9 (3): 193–212.

Voß, J-P, Smith, A and Grin, J, forthcoming, 'Designing long-term policy: reflexivity and political robustness', *Policy Sciences*, Special Issue.

WA Government, 2003a, *Hope for the Future: The Western Australian State Sustainability Strategy*, Department of the Premier and Cabinet, Western Australia, Perth, <www.dec.wa.gov.au/our-environment/sustainability/state-sustainability-strategy.html> (accessed 20 December 2008).

WA Government, 2003b, *Consulting Citizens: Planning for Success*, Department of the Premier and Cabinet: Citizens and Civics Unit, Government of Western Australia, Perth.

WA Government, 2003c, *Dialogue with the City: Final Report of Proceedings*, Government of Western Australia, Perth, <www.dpi.wa.gov.au/mediaFiles/dialogue_finalproc.pdf> (accessed 23 March 2009).

WA Government, 2005, *Engaging with Indigenous Western Australians*, Department of the Premier and Cabinet: Citizens and Civics Unit, Government of Western Australia, Perth.

WA Government, 2006, *Working Together: Involving Community and Stakeholders in Decision-Making*, Department of the Premier and Cabinet: Citizens and Civics Unit, Government of Western Australia, Perth.

Wackernagel, M and Rees, W, 1996, *Our Ecological Footprint. Reducing Human Impact on the Earth*, New Society Publishers, Gabriola Island, Canada.

Wahlquist, Å, 2008, *Thirsty Country. Options for Australia*, Jacana Books, Allen & Unwin, Crows Nest, Australia.

Walker, B and Salt, D, 2006, *Resilience Thinking. Sustaining Ecosystems and People in a Changing World*, Island Press, Washington.

Walker, G, 2008, 'What are the barriers and incentives for community-owned means of energy production and use?', *Energy Policy*, 36 (12): 4401–4405.

Walker, G and Shove, E, 2007, 'Ambivalence, sustainability and the governance of socio-technical transitions', *Journal of Environmental Policy & Planning*, 9 (3): 213–225.

Walker, KJ, 1994, *The Political Economy of Environmental Policy: An Australian Introduction*, UNSW Press, Sydney.

Wallington, T, Lawrence, G and Loechel, B, 2008, 'Reflections on the legitimacy of regional environmental governance: lessons from Australia's experiment in natural resource management', *Journal of Environmental Policy & Planning*, 10 (1): 1–30.

Walsh, B, 2008, 'How many people does it take to make a new light bulb?', *Time*, 10 March 2008, <www.time.com/time/printout/0,8816,1721082,00.html> (accessed 9 July 2008).

Ward, I, 1995, 'Federal Government' in Henningham, J, (ed), *Institutions in Australian Society*, Oxford University Press, Melbourne, pp 13–32.

Ward, I, 2006, 'Media, power and politics' in Parkin, A, Summers, J and Woodward, D, (eds), *Government, Politics, Power and Policy in Australia*, 8th edn, Pearson Education Australia, Frenchs Forest, pp 363–379.

Warhurst, J, 2006, 'Interest Groups and Political Lobbying' in Parkin, A, Summers, J and Woodward, D, (eds), *Government, Politics, Power and Policy in Australia*, 8th edn, Pearson Australia, Frenchs Forest, pp 327–342.

Warmer Bulletin, 2005, 'Nappies: making the right choice', *Warmer Bulletin* 100, pp 32–35, Residua

Limited, <www.residua.com/Residua/Warmer_Bulletin_files/WB100.pdf> (accessed 14 March 2009).

Warren, CR, Lumsden, C, O'Dowd, S and Birnie, RV, 2005, '"Green on green": public perceptions of wind power in Scotland and Ireland', *Journal of Environmental Planning and Management*, 48 (6): 853–875.

Wawryk, A, 2004, 'Planning for wind energy: controversy over wind farms in coastal Victoria', *The Australasian Journal of Natural Resources Law and Policy*, 9 (1): 103–143.

WBI (World Bank Institute), 2002, 'Overview of use of benefit – cost and cost-effectiveness analysis for environmental management' in *Environmental Economics and Development Policy Course*, World Bank Institute, July 15–26, 2002, Washington, DC, <www.info.worldbank.org/etools/library/latestversion.asp?36508> (accessed 3 December 2008).

WCED (World Commission on Environment and Development), 1987, *Our Common Future*, Oxford University Press, Oxford.

Weale, A, 2001a, 'Can we democratize decisions on risk and the environment?', *Government and Opposition*, 36 (3): 355–378.

Weale, A, 2001b, 'Science advice, democratic responsiveness and public policy', *Science and Public Policy*, 28 (6): 413–421.

Webb, K, 2005, 'Sustainable governance in the twenty-first century: moving beyond instrument choice' in Eliadis, P, Hill, MM and Howlett, M, (eds), *Designing Government: From Instruments to Governance*, McGill-Queen's University Press, Montreal, pp 242–280.

Weber, S, 2004, *The Success of Open Source*, Harvard University Press, Boston.

Weir, M, 2003, 'Portman gets the go-ahead: shares up as EPA is overruled', *Western Australian*, 2 April.

Weiss, EB, 1990, 'In fairness to future generations', *Environment*, 32 (3): 7–11, 30–31.

Weller, P and Jaensch, D, (eds), 1980, *Responsible Government in Australia*, Drummond Publishing, Melbourne.

Wever, L, Dale, P and Chenoweth, A, 2008, *Professional Development for Environmental Practitioners in Australia Final Report*, Report prepared for The Environment Institute of Australia and New Zealand, <http://eianz.org/download.cfm?DownloadFile=7D9377C0-1372-403C-91EEE3B1C3DE3AAD> (accessed 24 February 2009).

WGCS (Wentworth Group of Concerned Scientists), 2002, *Blueprint for Living Continent*, Wentworth Group of Concerned Scientists, Sydney, <www.wentworthgroup.org/docs/blueprint_for_a_living_contintent.pdf> (accessed 25 February 2009).

WGCS (Wentworth Group of Concerned Scientists), 2003, *A New Model for Landscape Conservation in New South Wales. The Wentworth Group of Concerned Scientists Report to Premier Carr*, WWF Australia, Sydney, <www.wentworthgroup.org> (accessed 27 December 2008).

WGCS (Wentworth Group of Concerned Scientists), 2008, *Accounting for Nature. A Model for Building the National Environmental Accounts of Australia*, <www.wentworthgroup.org/docs/Accounting_For_Nature.pdf> (accessed 28 February 2009).

Wheeler, D and Elkington, J, 2001, 'The end of the corporate environment report? The advent of cybernetic sustainability reporting and communication', *Business Strategy and the Environment*, 10 (1): 1–14.

White, T, 1998, 'Get out of my lab, Lois! In search of the media game' in Hindmarsh, R, Lawrence, G and Norton, J, (eds), *Altered Genes*, Allen and Unwin, Sydney, pp 24–36.

Wild River, S, 2003, 'Local government' in Dovers, S and Wild River, S, (eds), *Managing Australia's Environment*, The Federation Press, Sydney, pp 338–362.

Williams, NM, 1998, *Intellectual Property and Aboriginal Environmental Knowledge*, Centre for Indigenous Natural and Cultural Resource Management, Discussion Paper No 1, Northern Territory University, Darwin.

Wilson, M, Schuh, C and Thompson, D, 2002, 'Environmental reporting' in Thompson, D, (ed), *Tools for Environmental Management: A Practical Introduction and Guide*, New Society Publishers, Canada, pp 209–230.

Wolsink, M, 2000, 'Wind power and the NIMBY-myth: institutional capacity and the limited significance of public support', *Renewable Energy*, 21 (1): 49–64.

Wolsink, M, 2007, 'Planning of renewables schemes: deliberative and fair decision-making on landscape issues instead of reproachful accusations of non-cooperation', *Energy Policy*, 35 (5): 2692–2704.

Wong, T, Fletcher, T, Duncan, H, Coleman, J and others, 2002. 'A model for urban stormwater improvement conceptualisation' in Strecker, E and Huber, W, (eds), *Global Solutions for Urban Drainage*, Proceedings of the Ninth International Conference on Urban Drainage, 8–13 September 2002, Portland, Oregon, USA, <www.iemss.org/iemss2002/proceedings/pdf/volume%20uno/358_wong.pdf> (accessed 2 December 2008).

Wood, C, 1995, *Environmental Impact Assessment: A Comparative Review*, 1st edn, Longman Group Limited, London.

Wood, C, 2003, *Environmental Impact Assessment: A Comparative Review*, 2nd edn, Pearson Education Limited, Essex.

Woodford, J and Millet, M, 1997, 'Australia in battle over Greenhouse', *Sydney Morning Herald*, 25 June, p 1.

Woodward, D, 2006, 'Political parties and the party system' in Parkin, A, Summers, J and Woodward, D, (eds), *Government, Politics, Power and Policy in Australia*, 8th edn, Pearson Education, Frenchs Forest, Chapter 9.

WRLDA (Western Rock Lobster Development Association), undated, <www.western-rock-lobster.com/> (accessed 6 March 2009).

Wüstenhagen, R, Wolsink, M and Burer, MJ, 2007, 'Social acceptance of renewable energy innovation: an introduction to the concept', *Energy Policy*, 35 (5): 2683–2691.

WWF (World Wide Fund for Nature), 2006, *Living Planet Report*, World Wide Fund for Nature, Gland, Switzerland, <www.footprintnetwork.org/newsletters/gfn_blast_0610.html> (accessed 12 April 2009).

WWF (World Wide Fund for Nature), 2008, *Living Planet Report*, World Wide Fund for Nature, Gland, Switzerland, <wwf.org.au/publications/livingplanetreport2008/> (accessed 6 April 2009).

Wynberg, R, 2004, 'Rhetoric, realism and benefit sharing: use of traditional knowledge of *Hoodia* species in the development of an appetite suppressant', *Journal of World Intellectual Property*, 7 (6): 851–876.

Wynne, B, 1989, 'Sheepfarming after Chernobyl: a case study in communicating scientific information', *Environment*, 31 (2): 10–15, 33–39.

Wynne, B, 1992, 'Uncertainty and environmental learning: reconceiving science and policy in the preventive paradigm', *Global Environmental Change*, 2 (2): 111–127.

Wynne, B, 1996a, 'Misunderstood misunderstanding: social identities and public uptake of science' in Irwin, A and Wynne, B, (eds), *Misunderstanding Science? The Public Reconstruction of Science and Technology*, Cambridge University Press, Cambridge, pp 19–46.

Wynne, B, 1996b, 'May sheep safely graze? A reflexive view of the expert-lay knowledge divide' in Lash, S, Szerszynski, B and Wynne, B, (eds), *Risk, Environment and Modernity: Towards a New Ecology*, Sage, London, pp 44–83.

Yencken, D and Wilkinson, D, 2000, *Resetting the Compass. Australia's Journey Towards Sustainability*, CSIRO Publishing, Collingwood, Victoria.

Young, IM, 2000, *Inclusion and Democracy*, Oxford University Press, Oxford.

Young, M, Shi, T and Crosthwaite, J, 2003, *Duty of Care: An Instrument for Increasing the Effectiveness of Catchment Management*, Department of Sustainability and Environment, Victoria.

Zhu, X, Healey, RG and Aspinall, RJ, 1998, 'A knowledge-based systems approach to design support systems for environmental management', *Environmental Management*, 22 (1): 35–48.

Zwart, I, 2003, 'A greener alternative? Deliberative democracy meets local government', *Environmental Politics*, 12 (2): 23–48.

Index